THE CRISIS OF ISLAMIC CIVILIZATION

THE CRISIS OF
ISLAMIC
CIVILIZATION

ALI A. ALLAWI

YALE UNIVERSITY PRESS

NEW HAVEN AND LONDON

For information about this and other Yale University Press publications, please contact:
U.S. Office: sales.press@yale.edu   www.yalebooks.com
Europe Office: sales @yaleup.co.uk   www.yaleup.co.uk

Set in Minion by IDSUK (DataConnection) Ltd.
Printed in the United States of America

Library of Congress Cataloging-in-Publication Data

Allawi, Ali A., 1947-
  The crisis of Islamic civilization / Ali A. Allawi.
    p. cm.
  Includes bibliographical references and index.
  ISBN 978-0-300-13931-0 (ci : alk. paper)
  1. Civilization, Islamic. 2. Islam--20th century. I. Title.

  DS36.85.A423 2009
  909'.09767082--dc22

2008047962

A catalogue record for this book is available from the British Library.

10 9 8 7 6 5 4 3 2 1

To SFH – who lit the way

To SHR – who lived the way

To the Folk of the Hyderkhana – who travelled the way

If you wish for a pearl
You must leave the desert
And wander by the sea;
And even if you never find
The gleaming pearl, at least
You won't have failed to reach the water*

*From Hakim Sanai: *Hadiqat al-Haqiqa* [The Walled Garden of Truth] (Octagon Press: London, 1974), translated from the Persian by D. L. Pendlebury. Hakim Sanai was an eleventh-century poet who lived in Ghazna, a town in what is now modern-day Afghanistan

Contents

Preface

The Iraq of the 1950s, in which I was raised, as well as the broader Arab and Islamic world of that time, were at a stage when the secular elements in society – the ruling political class and the cultural and intellectual elites – had moved far away from an overt identification with Islam. It then appeared to be only a matter of time before Islam would lose whatever hold it might still have had on the peoples and societies of the Muslim world. Even the term 'Muslim' was unusual for the period; Muslim countries identified themselves more in terms of national or ethnic status or ideological affinities.

Islam was not a noticeable factor in daily life. Religion was a mandatory course in school, it is true, but the life around us was clearly decoupling from Islam. Nobody taught us the rules of prayer or expected us to fast in Ramadan. We learnt the shorter verses of the Quran, but the holy book itself was kept on shelves or in drawers, mostly unread. The pilgrimage to Mecca was only for the old, atoning for the transgressions in their lives, in preparation for their inevitable end – more in the nature of an insurance policy than an act of piety. I don't recall ever coming across the word *jihad* in any contemporary context. The prevailing rhetoric was more to do with Arab destiny and anti-imperialism. A bit of religious fervour popped up during the Suez Crisis of 1956, when Cairo radio blared out martial songs calling for divine support against the Anglo–French–Israeli invasion, but that was about it. Women, not only in my own family but throughout the urban middle classes, wore only western clothes. They had long ceased to wear the *hijab*. The only connection to a pre-modern past that I had was my grandfather, who always wore the distinguishing – and dignified – dress of robes and turbans of an old-line merchant.

Apart from religious holidays, the public rituals of Islam were not widely observed. Friday congregational prayers were held, but certainly not with the same degree of participation or vigour that a person would notice nowadays. The formerly ubiquitous Sufi orders had lost most of their devotees, and what was left of them had become the object of faint ridicule by a knowing elite. I came across possibly one of the last of the wandering dervishes of the area – a *qalandar* – who showed up in front of our house in his patched frocks, carrying a ritual pike and a bowl. He was fed and sent on his way. Since, I have only ever seen one other such as him. The Shia rites of *Muharram* were celebrated, often wildly, but we were advised to stay well away from them. They were somewhat unbecoming for refined folk, who preferred to hold semi-literary soirées to remember the passion of the martyr Imam Hussein. Tears were ritually shed and after a short catharsis, normal conversation returned. Modernity was flooding in everywhere, and people seemed to want more of it. Cinemas and snack bars, cabarets and country clubs, freely flowing alcohol and mixed parties: Baghdad was turning into Babylon, its hedonistic predecessor of yore. And it was not much different, as memoirs of the times amply testify, in Casablanca, Cairo, Damascus, Istanbul, Tehran, Karachi and Jakarta. Secularism had the Muslim world by the throat. It may not have been in the very same form that I had experienced, but the result was the same. Islam was ignored, marginalized or rejected by the modernizing classes. It continued to provide some form of ethical scaffolding to people's lives, but even that became frayed as people moved into a modern and urban environment.

Neither did Islam's public position improve materially in the decade of the 1960s. This was the era of ascendant military dictatorships, nationalist ideologies and socialist and populist movements that dominated the landscape of the Islamic world. No one could foresee the comeuppance that these regimes would face in less than a decade and the public discrediting of their models for reform and modernization. The defeat by Israel of the combined Arab armies in the Six Day War was only one of the events that dramatically tipped the balance in favour of a resurgent Islam – a process which accelerated in the 1970s. Political Islam began to raise its head after years of lying in wait, being either ignored or persecuted. Another current also rose imperceptibly in those times: that of a re-spiritualized Islam that was breaking away from the hold of the traditional religious orders but remained in the shadows. It affected far fewer people and its presence and influence were scarcely felt in a world convulsed with dramatic political changes.

By the end of the 1970s the tide of militant Islamism seemed unstoppable and increasingly defined the idea of a resurgent Islam. The Iranian Revolution and its aftermath convulsed the planet. Political Islam erupted on the global stage in a huge social and political revolution and, whatever we may think of it, embodied the hopes and fears of millions of people around the world. A parallel revolution was also engulfing the world of Sunni Islam with the struggle against the Soviet invasion of Afghanistan and the rise of a radical *jihad*-inspired culture. The world in general and Muslims in particular were confronted with a host of questions and assertions about the role of Islam in society and politics. I daresay that every Muslim of that period was exercised, in one form or another – whether recoiling in alarm, being perplexed and anxious, or being an enthusiastic advocate – at the rise of political Islam and the increasingly assertive and controversial role of Islam in society.

For a long time, the two worlds of Islam which impacted on me – the outer world of political and social action and the inner world of spiritual and moral realization – seemed entirely at odds with each other. One was angry at its subordination, insistent on recognition and power, and challenging the status quo; the other was serene, introspective and immersed in the intangible. The fabric of the first was societies and nations; that of the second was the self and the individual. The rituals of worship in Islam were supposed to bridge these worlds, but they were bent to suit other demands. I began to recognize that the essential unity of Islam had been greatly diminished, if not quite yet destroyed. People could no longer move effortlessly between these two worlds.

Momentous crises affected the Islamic world in the past quarter century: the Iranian Revolution, the Iran–Iraq War, the invasion of Afghanistan, the siege of the Bosnian Muslims, the sectarian riots in India, the civil wars in the Sudan and Algeria, the Second Gulf War, the rise of the Taliban, the eruption of global terror linked to radical political Islam, and the invasion of Iraq and the sectarian carnage it unleashed. All these demanded engagement and action, no doubt, and they tilted the balance towards the political arena. As I became more involved in these crises in my writings, my speeches and then in direct political action, I found that only a few of the Muslims I encountered in the political arena could resonate with the spiritual or ethical aspects of Islam. In particular, Islamists behaved no differently from the rest, and often worse, as the prospects for power loomed for them in a number of countries, including Iraq. The Islam that I had experienced was increasingly devoid of any deeply ethical content and was at odds with my understanding of its own legacy. That is not to say that the preoccupation of the vast majority of Muslims with their outer condition was in any way reprehensible. But it was deficient, as it framed the crises Islam was facing mainly in terms of the political, social or jurisprudential aspects of the religion. The moral education of individual Muslims was an altogether different matter which did not fuse with the preoccupations of the leaders of the Muslim world, whether those in power or in opposition, in Muslim lands or in the growing diasporas in the West. Muslims may have been overwhelmed by the scale of the real or imagined disasters befalling them, but this should not have stopped them from holding up a mirror to themselves. What that mirror would have shown was a fading of their own civilizational drive and an increasingly obvious indifference to, and often abandonment of, the foundational ethical and spiritual bases of the faith.

I experienced this at first hand in the conflicts and wars that engulfed Muslims and the Muslim world in the past thirty years. The divisions within and between Muslims were breaking out into incredible paroxysms of violence. Sectarian, ethnic and racial hatreds continuously trumped the ideals of Islamic unity. The Iran–Iraq War and the internecine warfare which accompanied the withdrawal of the Soviets from Afghanistan were just such examples. It was in post-Saddam Iraq, however, that I could see how far into Islamic political and social life the crisis had seeped. The murderous violence unleashed by radical Wahhabi-inspired Islamists was accompanied by laborious jurisprudential 'justifications'. These were accepted by a large number of Muslims worldwide and they legitimated the indiscriminate slaughter of innocent civilians. The counter-terror which followed in the wake of these acts was mainly the doing of Shia militias and was largely arbitrary in its selection of victims. Hundreds of thousands of Iraqis were killed, millions were displaced or exiled, and the country descended into chaos and strife.

This ghastly work was done mainly by people who claimed to have an Islamic motivation for their deeds. Political Islamists of all stripes jettisoned their entire ideologies – for which many of their militants had given their lives – in indecent haste, as they scrambled for political advantage in the new order. Not once during my entire three-year stint in the Iraqi government did I witness a single episode of a formerly Islamist party, now in power, promoting or championing an Islamic cause it had earlier propounded in its manifestos. The ethical standards of the holders of public office fell to appallingly low and squalid levels. The obsessive drive for personal material gain at the public expense seized the minds of a great percentage of people in the political class and fed the extraordinary levels of corruption. It was a sad and dispiriting spectacle. Muslims by and large seemed to have cut themselves off from the wellsprings of Islamic ethics. I had actually guessed as much before I returned to Iraq, but it was in Iraq that I began to reflect on the matter systematically. The present book is the product of this effort. It is one person's attempt to understand the factors behind the decay of the spirit of Islam, and what the future holds if this process is not halted or reversed.

When my publishers first broached the idea that I might write a topical book on Islam, I was quite reluctant to do so. The bookshelves were already groaning with hastily written works on Islam. These were aimed mostly at satisfying a huge public demand for insights into, and explanations for, the phenomenal rise of violent political Islam and its impact on the modern world. After decades of indifference, when Islam was only of interest to academic specialists, diplomats, travellers and a few converts, Islam had burst again into western consciousness. Islam was presumed to be a mortally wounded civilization, one that was unable to adapt to modernity and could thus only be consigned to a fate of marginalization and ultimate disappearance. But an explosive revival of the faith had swept the Islamic world and was now spilling outside its borders. This unfamiliar manifestation of Islam became increasingly conjoined in the public mind with violence, revolution, instability and war. The association was further reinforced by the spectacular acts of mass murder and terror inflicted on New York and Washington on 9/11 and later in Madrid and London. These were mostly laid, consciously or not, at the feet of Islam.

It is not that I shied away from writing a book on political Islam because the field was already crowded with such works. Rather, in spite of its predominance in the calculations of policy-makers and in the public imagination, political Islam is only an aspect of the overall problem of Islam in the modern world. To my mind, political Islam is a manifestation of the ailment rather than the ailment itself. The fact that it has received the lion's share of attention does not automatically make its leaders and ideologues the arbiters of Islam itself. What concerned me was to discover the deeper roots of the crisis and, in particular, to find out whether Islam's apparent mismatch with the modern world is intrinsic to the religion itself or is due to some other factors – including the decay of its defining and vital forces.

I set out to write this book with the purpose of answering three basic questions. First, could one speak of a single Islamic civilization any longer, or had Islam broken down irretrievably into loosely connected cultural, national and ethnic units? Secondly, is a specifically Islamic civilization a recurrent or repeatable possibility, or has it been, as the critics and sceptics would argue, forever lost? Thirdly, under what conditions can Islam's civilizational presence return to the modern world? However, above all these concerns there is a fundamental issue, central to Islam and other world religions: can a modern society, with all its complexities, institutions and tensions, be built on the vision of the divine?

Islam forged a civilization which was unique and easily recognizable even as it crossed boundaries of race, tribe, language and geography. Its societies were infused by a spirit that gave a distinctive colouring to their institutions, politics, laws, arts and architecture, literature, science and scholarship. At its heart was an act of willing submission – the literal meaning of 'Islam' – to the divine reality from which all manifestations of its civilization ultimately derived. This ideal has remained intact ever since the inception of the religion, and in the final analysis it has been the bulwark which has so far stood against the dissolution of Islam into modernity. The transcendental ideal has remained constant across the different cultural traditions which make up the world of Islam. This has been frequently overlooked: the fact of Muslims' intrinsic diversity has overshadowed their unity. The book therefore addresses itself to the possibility of the survival and continuity of this ideal in the face of the monumental challenges that modernity and globalization have raised. In this sense, my book is not about the political, or even the religious, dimensions of Islam. It is more about whether Muslims can remain committed to the transcendent ideal and how this commitment would affect their conduct at the individual and social levels.

I have divided my narrative into four distinct but interconnected areas. In the Prologue I examine why the core of Islamic civilization is different from that of other civilizations, and in particular from the dominant and globalizing world order. The thread of the argument which runs throughout the book is that Islamic civilization, almost by definition, has to acknowledge the role of the transcendent (or the sacred, or the divine: call it what you will) in its make-up. If that element is absent, then Islam cannot be forced into the dynamics of modernity without its integrity being affected.

The first three chapters are a historical overview of the shocks to Islamic civilization provoked by its encounter with the expanding western powers and then with the forces of modernity. It spans roughly the period from the start of the nineteenth century to the 1970s. I am particularly interested in the reaction of those who recognized that there had been enormous changes in the world of Islam and who had struggled with their own responses in the context of an Islam which affirmed the significance of the transcendent. Many of the individuals I evoke here are not in the usual pantheon of figures associated with political Islam, but that does not diminish their importance. On the contrary, their reaction to the decline of Islamic life and culture may be far more pertinent to the issues we are facing now. The 1970s is also the period which saw the start of what I have called the counter-revolution of Islam – a tumultuous process which, at its base, is about recovering the vital energies of Islamic civilization. We are still living through this process, with no final resolution in sight.

In Chapters 4 and 5 I track the effect of the changes which have occurred over the past two centuries on the fundamental understanding of Islam and of its values. This process is necessarily more abstract, but I have tried to flesh out the narrative so as to make it more accessible for the general reader. I beg the reader's indulgence if the narrative becomes technical in places. However, this is essential to my argument. In these chapters I also examine the mechanisms by which Islam was gradually 'de-sacralized' and how this has affected entire aspects of how Muslims think and believe. I explore the efforts of a number of people who have attempted to stop secularist thought and knowledge from becoming the basic building-block of Muslims' education and to instil an ethics of virtue into the educational curriculum. I also deal with the all-important issue of the legitimacy and limit of change in Islam and with those who have challenged the prevailing boundaries. I have purposefully included figures who have tried to bring back the transcendent aspect of Islam to rectify the over-identification of Islam with its political or juridical side. Some of these figures are not that well known, but they provide a dramatic example of what could happen if prevailing orthodoxies are seriously challenged. The calls to reform Islam and the meaning of reformation in the context of established orthodoxies have been highly problematic.

Chapters 6 through to 10 deal with the outer effects of the erosion of the Islamic civilizational space on power, institutions, politics, values, economic life, and culture and society. These are the areas where the debate on the future of Islam has mainly taken place, but I have tried to introduce an ethical and spiritual dimension to the question of whether a uniquely Islamic order can ever be recreated again. The ascendant forces of the modern global order have made deep inroads into the outer world of Islam and, equally importantly, into the minds of Muslims. They may deny it and fight numerous rearguard actions, but this reality cannot be easily effaced – unless Muslims confront another harsh fact. Any civilization has an inner and outer aspect: an inner aspect of beliefs, ideas and values which inform the outer aspect of institutions, laws, government and culture. The inner dimensions of Islam no longer have the significance or power to affect the outer world in which most Muslims live.

This book is an amalgam of history, philosophy, theology, sociology, economics, politics – and a bit more. It is not an academic work, although I have tried to be scrupulous and consistent both in the narrative and in the use of sources. I am sure that a number of scholars and specialists will take issue with this or that argument or conclusion, but the book should be read as a continuous whole. At the same time, a number of people may think that my conclusions are overly stark, even pessimistic. I address my remarks here particularly to Muslims who are already struggling in a million ways to adjust their lives and values to the often harsh realities of the outside world. This book is not about Islam as a religion or as a code of outer conduct and transactions. I have no doubt that this Islam will continue into the indefinite future. This book is about Islamic *civilization* – a universe which is recognizably Islamic; draws its vitality and inspiration from the inner and outer aspects of Islam; and is the bridge connecting the two. It is this world that is in danger of disappearing.

The Axes of Islamic Civilization

Now on strangers does the world bestow its favours and esteem,
All we have been left with is a phantom world and a dream

Muhammad Iqbal, poet and philosopher, writing in his 1909 poem
of lament, 'Shikwa' ('The Complaint'), in *Shikwa and*
Jawab-i-Shikwa, transl. Khushwant Singh
(OUP/OXFORD INDIA PAPERBACKS: DELHI, 1981).

There is little doubt that the civilization of Islam is undergoing a monumental crisis. In one form or another, this crisis has been going on for well over two hundred years. It still has not worked itself out. Islam as a religion, as a method of worship for millions of believers, is most certainly alive and well. The vitality of the faith is palpable. So is what most people, especially in the West, understand to be Islam nowadays; namely the political and violent manifestations of radical Islam. These are ever present and have caused the rest of the world profound concern and anxiety. When Islam is seen only in terms of the ideology of political Islam, it is not in crisis, but rather one cause of crises. Both these aspects of Islam – religious observance and the political arena – seem to give the lie to the assertion that Islam is in retreat. But focusing on the religiosity of Muslims or on the rise of political Islam simply deflects or disguises the problem. The world which Islam had built over the centuries – its civilization in the broadest sense of the word – has been seriously undermined. How this came about and whether the damage inflicted on Islamic civilization is terminal or not is the subject of this book.

Forming a Civilization

All civilizations are balanced between the individual and the collective (or the group); and between this-worldliness and other-worldliness. Shifts between the relative importance of these cornerstones is what gives civilizations their distinctive colouring. Oriental despotisms were built on the glorification of the individual ruler, who was deified and raised above mere mortals. In the Roman Republic on the other hand, the virtues and ideals of society were embodied in group institutions such as the Senate. Roman civilization shifted when republican virtues turned to imperial grandeur and when the collective wisdom of the Senate was subsumed into the edicts and decrees of an individual emperor. In classical tyrannies, autocracies and despotisms, the will of the individual ruler becomes the determining and driving force of social action. In the totalitarian communist societies of the twentieth century the opposite was the case. Individual will was obliterated by the power of the collective manifested in a party or elite. This is the theory at least, but often the cult of the supreme leader is superimposed on the collectivist or corporatist ethos. Mao, Stalin and Hitler are just such examples. The modern West – particularly its English-speaking part – is defined by a decisive shift away from the collective and the sacred and towards the individual and the secular. In the self-image of the West, the individual is ennobled and given the power to determine the course of his or her personal development, together with that of society, through the idiom of rights and the practice of a democracy based on laws and rules. The main purpose of society becomes to provide the environment for individuals to develop their potential and, in the process, to enrich and advance society as a whole.

Other modern societies reject the notion that the individual should be the undivided focus of attention; they reverse the formula. The interests of the group – be it the party, the clan, the military or the nation – becomes paramount. Any number of states, including not a few democracies such as Japan and the Scandinavian countries, would tilt the balance towards the collective rather than the individual. Other countries explicitly seek to reconcile and balance the twin and often conflicting demands of individual and collective action through a calculus of shared interests. This is the basis of the progressive politics of the democratic left in western countries. But such attempts are often short-lived, as the exigencies of time and place impose the domination of one over the other. The demise of the communal spirit which has underpinned the post-war European welfare state and the social democracy it engendered is ample proof of this. Post-Soviet societies have violently oscillated between a rampant and often criminal individualism and a return to authoritarian hierarchies and structures.

Even religions have varied in the way they weigh the individual and the collective. Buddhism is essentially a solitary path to self-realization and fulfilment, while Judaism is eminently concerned with the collective trajectory, spiritual and worldly, of a particular people. At its heart, the Protestant reformation was about the possibility of the individual, through acts of personal piety and worship, to attain salvation specifically without the intercession of a hierarchical church. Most religions interpose a priestly class to act as interpreters and mediators between the individual and the object of worship. Depending on one's viewpoint, this learned class is either the curse of religions or its essence.

Critical disjunctions in human history occur when the individual paradigm is overturned or tilted in favour of the collective, or vice versa. These turnabouts are common in history. A new pattern of values becomes established and these continue to colour society until such time as another new set of circumstances forces a change. The precise moments or periods when these transformations take place are never clearly determined. Defeats in wars, famines and natural catastrophes, economic or financial collapses, generally result in the undermining of a prevailing system, while conquests, discoveries, and material abundance strengthen existing systems – at least in the short term. Such events can affect civilizations suddenly or in a long, cumulative process which creates incremental changes. But vestiges of replaced or overwhelmed civilizations may continue to exist and interact with the dominant order in ways which are not necessarily antagonistic, but which are invariably subordinate. More subtly, however, changes can operate at the individual level, and gradually, progressively, they generate internal forces which overcome the host system. For example, the small but coalescing groups of Christians within the Roman Empire gradually challenged the ethos of the Roman state. By the fourth century, Christianity had established its ascendancy over the old pagan order with the Emperor Constantine's conversion, an outcome which forever marked the destiny of the former territories of the empire.

The potential for tension between the individual and the collective is ever present in modern society. The former generally seeks to maximize his or her autonomy and freedom, while the latter seeks to establish its norms and rules and the power to enforce them. The tensions even inflect the ethical dimension. For example, while individuals pursue liberty, societies may seek social justice. One could conflict with, or even contradict, the other. An adversarial relationship almost inevitably ensues which is not always satisfactorily resolved at the political level, even in democracies. The post-war welfare-state balance, which allows for individual profit and self-interest but seeks to channel it to social ends through the redistributive power of the state, is a clumsy and often ineffectual compromise between the two elements.

The moral imperatives of earlier times – as manifested, say, in the nineteenth-century Christian socialist movement – which sought to focus on the obligation for charitable works and to help the needy through community-based or collective institutions, have faded. The philanthropists of the twenty-first century bear little resemblance to the great social reformers of the nineteenth and early twentieth centuries. It would be difficult to envisage today's billionaires spending their fortunes on founding experimental or utopian communities such as George Cadbury's Bournville village or Robert Owen's New Lanark. Society's concern for the weak and impoverished, briefly shining through a few decades after the Second World War, has been in serious retreat after the rise of neo-liberalism in the 1980s and thereafter. China appears well on the way to abandoning the collective principles of its formal allegiance to communism, while India – at least its 'progressive' middle classes – appears to be faintly embarrassed by the perceived archaism of the communal ethos of Mahatma Ghandi.

Paradoxes of the 1990s

The general drift of the western world in recent times has been towards some consensus on the primacy of individual over collective rights. This has been worked out in the unravelling of the post-war welfare state, as well as in the adoption by most of the world of the ideas of untrammelled individualism. Totalitarian anti-individual systems, such as the Nazi state and the Soviet empire, have been militarily defeated or have collapsed, leaving the field clear for the seemingly irresistible rise of a global civilization. The contours of this order are defined substantially by the West. The demarcation lines between the public and private domains have now become increasingly fuzzy. In fact, expanding the sphere of activity of the private sector has become almost synonymous with enhancing the rights of individuals as consumers. The functions of the state have been radically recast so that areas which were well within its exclusive remit, such as the provision of health and educational services, pensions, public transport, and even defence, became open to the private sector. Even states such as China, which are still officially communal in their ideology, have succumbed to the imperatives of the new order in their drive for economic growth. Witness the official indifference to the appalling conditions in many of China's factories and the armies of desperate unemployed which roam the Chinese countryside and haunt the margins of its exploding cities. Milton Friedman and Friedrich von Hayek became the icons of the times, rather than John Maynard Keynes or Karl Polanyi. The values of the European 'Enlightenment' have been dusted off and given a new lease of life by being conflated with 'universal' rights and values. The process has been accompanied by an aggressive insistence on the correctness and universal applicability of these values. Furthermore, it has become practically axiomatic that these rights and values are defined and achieved only within the context of liberal democracy, a market economy open to globalization and continuous technological progress.

Thus the sustaining vision of this period is one of mankind approaching the final resolution of the age-old conflicts between freedom and authority, between religious faith and secularism. The balance would tilt decisively in favour of freedom in all its manifestations: individual, social, religious and economic. This became commonplace in the 1990s, in the wake of the collapse of the Soviet bloc. But the march towards an 'end of history' and towards a benign symbiosis between the individual and the collective has been severely jolted by continuing (and possibly exacerbating) tensions between and within societies and individuals. The number of failed states has grown alarmingly, and many of the world's poorest countries have hovered on the brink of disaster – or even jumped into the abyss. Liberia, Sierra Leone, Rwanda, Burma, Iraq all mocked the easy assumptions and forecasts of the era. This was also the time when religious passions spilled over into the political arena. The wars caused by a disintegrating Yugoslavia as well as the Chechnya conflict had an overt ethno-religious dimension. Societies which followed the new prescriptions for economic success were faced with increasing internal economic inequalities and income disparities. In a 2007 report, the Asian Development Bank reported alarming rises in income inequalities in the decade leading to 2005, in fifteen of the twenty-one countries it had examined.[1] Income inequalities in the developed world, especially in Japan, the US and the UK, also rose markedly in this period. If anything, fragmentation and disorder ended up carrying the day, and demons that one thought would have been long buried or forgotten emerged to increase the sense of chaos and fear. What was seen as the dawn of a new golden age of tolerance and mutual respect turned out to be the harbinger of another cycle of fear and violence.

The celebration of individual freedoms and liberties has been short-lived. Collective anxieties – about other races, classes, ethnicities, sects, religions, and now entire civilizations – rather than communal solidarity, have replaced the euphoria that accompanied the fall of apartheid and the collapse of the Soviet system. Legitimate self-defence has given way to the doctrine of pre-emption and prevention. Individual rights to private property gave way to the imposition of market fundamentalism on downtrodden peoples and nations. The 1990s were full of this whiplash effect. By 2001, the decade that started with such promise had almost reversed itself entirely. At its heart, the tension was elemental, between fear and hope, control and freedom, hoarding and sharing, conquest and submission, and it was played out at the level of individuals, groups and even whole civilizations. Which set of elemental forces would predominate was to determine the course of events on the global stage. In the end, the baser forces have prevailed.

The Muslim world was not spared the paradoxes of the 1990s. Individual Muslim countries have with varying degrees of enthusiasm joined the globalization bandwagon, easily jettisoning their former allegiances in favour of the new verities, with all their promises and problems. Again, with a few exceptions, they succumbed to the military and political supremacy of the US on the world stage. But Islam, the invisible glue which binds Muslims into another set of loyalties and identities beyond the nation, has not yet acknowledged the inevitability of the new global civilization. It is Islam, rather than individual Muslim nations, that is seen to be at odds with the rest of the world.

The world perspective on Islam has been in many ways determined by the state of other societies, especially those of the West. During the long post-war boom which ended with the stagflation of the 1970s, western countries were formally indifferent to Islam, except perhaps as an ally in the cold war. Political Islam had not yet evolved into an intimidating external threat, and the army of Muslim migrants who flooded into Europe in the immediate post-war era to fill low-paying jobs silently accepted their social obscurity and exclusion. The boom times coincided with the rise of the welfare state in the western democracies. When the socially aware, communal or collective spirit was prevailing, the 'threat' from Islam was hardly ever mentioned, at least not in its present form. The traditional left in the West identified with the causes of anti-imperialism and alleviation of poverty in the developing countries and improvement in the lot of the migrant communities in their midst. In both cases, Islam, although mainly a passive bystander, was seen as a potential ally. There were a huge number of Muslims in the developing world, and they formed a significant percentage of the excluded migrants, especially in western Europe. The fear of Islam has followed the demise of social democracy in the West, and the decay of the socially centred movements in the developing world. The Reagan–Thatcher period in the 1980s coincided not only with the anxieties generated by the Iranian Revolution but also with the controversies surrounding Islam's apparent inability to accept western freedoms uncritically. This was best exemplified by the Rushdie affair, which poisoned intercommunity relations in the UK as well as in Europe.

The 1990s increasingly, and often fatuously, saw a connection between acts of terrorism and the religion of Islam, and also large-scale slaughter perpetrated mainly against Muslims: in Bosnia, Kosovo, Chechnya and Gujarat. 'Let Muslims understand', said a statement by the Hindu nationalist movement, the Rashtriya Sevayamsevak Sangh (RSS), 'that their real safety lies in the good will of the majority.'[2] This came not from some crank organization, but from a movement whose political arm, the Bharatiya Janata Party (BJP), led India's government for eight years after 1996. It was also the decade when the thesis of the 'clash of civilizations' became identified specifically with Islam and its inability to accommodate modernity. The thesis became a truth upheld, even fought for, by a huge swathe of groups, ranging from liberal columnists in western Europe to Serbian gunmen ethnically cleansing whole parts of Bosnia and mobs whipped up into a murderous frenzy by the right-wing Hindu extremists of the RSS in India. The growing tide of antipathy to Islam reached an apotheosis of sorts after the 9/11 attacks.

Blocking the Pathways of Islamic Civilization

History cannot be read, understood and interpreted according to a fixed set of rules and structures, but every epoch has its own patterns of explanation. In one epoch, the problem is couched in terms of individual rights, liberties and freedoms; in another, it is the duty of the individual to the collective; in yet another epoch, nations and their heroes are glorified and assigned almost mythic dimensions. But the temptation is always to consider the verities of a particular age to be universal and valid for all time and place. These renderings, which are frequently portentous and self-congratulatory, then come to define the political culture. They are often carried abroad by the triumphant civilization, and once there they inflict considerable damage and destruction on the host society and culture. Just think of the call of *La Mission civilitrice*, behind which imperialism hid its ugly face. In an essay extraordinarily entitled 'The Government of the Subject Races', Lord Cromer, the real ruler of Egypt in the years 1883 to 1907, wrote: 'We need not always enquire too closely what these people . . . themselves think is in their own interests. It is essential that each special issue should be decided mainly with reference to what, by the light of Western knowledge and experience . . . we conscientiously think is best for the subject race.'[3] Local 'modernizing' elites to whom power was frequently bequeathed by the departing imperial authorities were equally adept at tearing apart the fabric of traditional societies.

The entire edifice of latter-day Islamic societies has been subjected to this shock treatment at the hands of a host of would-be local reformers, determined to 'rescue' their societies from powerlessness, poverty and marginalization. They have drawn on a host of ideologies that promised an easy solution to the Muslims' dilemma, but these have nearly all failed. Another set of solutions are then trotted out, tried as palliatives for a diminishing time-span, and then abandoned as a lost cause. The procession of forgotten, discredited and discarded theories stretches as far as the eye can see. The uncritical adoption of whatever appears to be the prevalent mood in the West is an unfortunate feature of the make-up of the ruling elites in the Islamic world.

At the same time, no real attention has been given to the effects of impersonal forces on the world of Islam. These forces have gathered ever greater power since the collapse of the Soviet Union. They often eclipse the power of nations. Commodity, currency, capital and energy markets are not altogether under the control of nation–states, and their movements can have untold effects. Acting under the rubric of globalization, lightly regulated markets, unimpeded capital flows and financial liberalization, they have increasingly defined the substance of power. As the gap between what is perceived as the latent potential of the Islamic world and its reality of economic backwardness and political dependency becomes ever more obvious, the siren song of the ideologues of political Islam reaches more and more ears. Their image of a *pur et dur* Islam of old has proven very attractive, and not one to be easily forgotten.

The temptation, when times are dark, has always been to imagine a 'golden age', an Arcadia, or a City-on-the-Hill. All cultures and most religious traditions have it. John Bunyan's wonderfully constructed story, *The*

Pilgrim's Progress, can stand aside al-Farabi's vision of the 'Virtuous City', and both would appeal to the same desire for uplift, certainty, and a way out of an impossible present. They remain products of a nostalgic, even romantic, yearning and besides being works of literature or philosophy have little further practical consequence. But nostalgia can be a powerful force and, in time, can even be turned to quite dangerous ends. All 'fundamentalisms' are, in one way or another, an exercise in nostalgia. They claim to represent the essence, the kernel, the undivided truth of the idea or the religion, and they promise their adherents a pathway towards certainty and fulfilment. Once in power, all fundamentalists revert to type. Their claims that they can forge a new purpose for mankind and construct a system where the individual and society can grow and prosper invariably fail. A new tyranny arises as the early promise degenerates into a greedy monopoly on power or, worse, descends into chaos and a free-for-all.

All these factors have come together in the global preoccupation about Islam. Ever since the Iranian Revolution of 1979, Islam has been at the centre of the world's concerns. The fixation on Islam became even more pronounced after the attacks of 11 September 2001. The religion, the cultures, the civilization of Islam, Muslim nations and peoples, all became the subject of intensive exploration and probing by a huge array of analysts, from the most thoughtful to the most incendiary, from the most illustrious to the most obscure, from the most sympathetic to the most bigoted. Islam seemed to offer the perfect laboratory specimen for exploring what were essentially the concerns and preoccupations of others. The general tenor has been one of profound bias against Islam. The retort, on the part of those who supported the legacy of Islam, has been mainly defensive and apologetic. An important minority on both sides of the divide has been openly antagonistic. Every incident of terrorist violence has been magnified by some as a clear indicator of the malevolence that lies at the heart of Islam; every provocative newspaper headline has been pounced on as an example of the West's irredeemable hatred for Islam.

The crisis in Islamic civilization arises partly from the fact that it has been thwarted from demarcating its own pathways into contemporary life. The western mould of modernity has been superimposed on its world view, and Islam has been unable to relate to the modern world except through this awkward and often painfully alien framework. But Islam as a religion – or even as the remnant of a world civilization – has never surrendered wholly to the demands of a de-sacralized world of modernity. A rearguard action of resistance to the claims of secular modernity has waxed and waned over the past two centuries. Rulers over Muslims may behave atrociously, continuing the venerable traditions of misrule, violence and corruption that have plagued the Islamic world for most of its history. But the echoes of 'what could be' still reverberate among the multitude – and even among some of the elite.

The unease as to where Islamic civilization is heading, or is being pushed, provides the underpinnings for the stream of projects to 'reform' or 'revitalize' Islam. These have continued uninterrupted from the early nineteenth century to the present day. They have all relied on a reinventing of Islam by secularizing, liberalizing, historicizing or radicalizing Muslims' understanding of their religion. All these schemes have so far failed to stop the erosion of the vitality of Islamic civilization. One can only conclude, therefore, that individual and societal regeneration in Islam has either passed the point of no return or that its roots must be sought elsewhere than in the prescriptions of Islam's would-be reformers. What the reformers or critics of Islam failed to acknowledge is that the spiritual dimension of Islam has imbued the entirety of its civilization. Almost by definition, therefore, any starting point for revitalizing the world of Islam must begin with Muslims' connection with the transcendent reality which lies at the heart of the message of Islam. Regaining knowledge of the sacred is an essential requirement for this.

The Individual in Islam

Within this interpretation of the world view of Islam, the purpose of all knowledge must be to seek, find and affirm the divine basis of all right-thinking and right acting. The sharp dichotomy between the sacred and the profane – 'Render unto Caesar the things which are Caesar's, and unto God the things that are God's' – does not hold in Islam, if it despiritualizes the foundations of both individual and collective action. Rather than be separate, Islam requires that the two be reconciled. Otherwise, the teachings of Islam affirm, mankind would be denying the source of its vitality, and would be in a state of perpetual warfare with what ultimately sustains mankind's existence. Mankind's first order of duty must be to acknowledge, openly and freely, the basic principle which underpins its very existence. This has nothing to do with saving souls, redeeming sins or rejecting gross material existence. The Quranic text never ceases to admonish and remind mankind that its submission to the decrees of God must form the bedrock of any permanent, and permanently valid, ethic of being and action – a personal ethic as well as the basis for public organization. This is the starting point for all authoritative renderings of Islam, and it has survived the vicissitudes of time and place. It can brook no compromise. All authentic traditions of Islam carry this imprint, as they must.

It is in this sense that Islam departs from the mainstream of modern constructs of the individual and of the group. In classical Islamic doctrine, the problem of the nature of the individual as an autonomous entity endowed with free will simply does not arise outside the context of the individual's ultimate dependence on God. The Arabic word for 'individual' – *al-fard* – does not have the commonly understood implication of a purposeful being, imbued with the power of rational choice. Rather, the term carries the connotation of singularity, aloofness or solitariness. The power of choice and will granted to the individual is more to do with the fact of acquiring these from God, at the point of a specific action or decision – the so-called *iktisab* – rather than the powers themselves which are not innate to natural freedoms or rights. *Al-fard* is usually applied as one of the attributes of supreme being, in the sense of an inimitable uniqueness. It is usually grouped with others of God's attributes (such as in the formula *al-Wahid, al-Ahad, al-Fard, al-Samad*: The One in essence, state and being, and the everlasting), to establish the absolute transcendence of the divine essence. Man is simply unable to acquire any of these essential attributes. Therefore to claim the right and the possibility of autonomous action without reference to the source of these in God is an affront, and is discourteous to the terms of the relationship between the human being and God. The entire edifice of individual rights derived from the natural state of the individual or through a secular ethical or political theory is alien to the structure of Islamic reasoning. The individual has a reality, but this is contingent upon a greater reality.

None of the free-thinking schools in classical Islam – such as the *Mu'tazila* – could ever entertain the idea of breaking the God–Man relationship and the validity of revelation, in spite of their espousal of a rationalist philosophy. Man's ability to reason independently and to ascertain right from wrong – and therefore lay claim to autonomous action – is ultimately derived from the imperative that God acts justly and does so by empowering Man with the faculty of reason. One cannot eliminate God from the equation.

Latter-day thinkers such as the Franco-Algerian deconstructionist philosopher Muhammad Arkoun have raised the possibility of an alternative Islamic reasoning which could lead to an unravelling of dogmatic orthodoxies and the adoption by Muslims of what he calls 'the unthought-of and the unthinkable'. Presumably this would include accepting and adopting western notions of the individual, culture and rights. Even so, the bedrock of any Islamic sensibility must be the textual certainty of the Quran as the unaltered and unalterable word of God. Irrespective of how it is read or interpreted, the Quran necessarily introduces the divine into the actions and choices of human beings.

The God-Centred Community

At another level, the contemporary Arabic word for society (*al-Mujtama'a*) is a recent construct and was not used with the same sense in the pre-modern period. It is a composite word, invented to accommodate an understanding of the modern, western notion of society. In fact the Quranic term for 'community' – *Umma* – has often been used in juxtaposition with the term for 'society', implying (as it does) a community of believers. But here again, the term has nuances which go beyond the mere sense of 'grouping of people'. The Quran refers to the prophet Abraham as being an *Umma* in himself, in a clear allusion to the possibility of there being an identity between a community of believers and an individual, perfected person. In Islam, the individual generates from within the virtues of the community, and vice versa. So there is a continuum between the individual and the group, with little possibility of ethical atomization at the individual level or an oppressive conformity at the group level. The purpose of the righteous collective (and the individual) *Umma* is one which 'enjoins the Good and shuns the Unlawful'. This, of course, is the ideal. The reality is frequently perversely different, as when the moral police in Saudi Arabia and Iran go about their petty harassments under the banner of 'enjoining the good and shunning the unlawful'. Nevertheless, the ideal has not been erased from the consciousness of Muslims.

In the language of Islam, the simple affirmation *La Hawla wa La Quwatta illa Billah* ('there is no [independent] power or strength except from Allah') basically determines the parameters by which actions and decisions have to be measured. For Muslims, there is no escaping the consequence of such a declaration. It defines the individual immediately, governs his or her actions, and, equally critically, sets the boundaries and limits to the legitimate form and direction of such actions. Any collective of such individuals must follow along these very same principles. There can be no deviation from this affirmation and no let-up. This brings us to the notion of *Tawhid*, the spiritual mechanism by which individuals and society can function in an integral manner by referring all action to a higher principle.

A root principle in the world view of Islam is that no individual or social group, if it seeks harmony and justice, can assume the absolute power to determine its own ethical standards of conduct. The operative phrase here is the qualification regarding harmony and justice. There are any number of ethical models and norms of morality and moral conduct which do not seek their justification in anything but reason, utility, personal desire or natural rights. But Islam would venture that these cannot but be unstable. They lead to an incessant struggle between what is already established and alternatives seeking its overthrow and the establishment of a new ascendancy. An ethical system of dynamic stability and justice must derive its coordinates from outside itself. Life must derive from the 'life-giver' (*al-Hayy*); power, from the 'power-giver' (*al-Qadir*); and knowledge from the 'knowledge-giver' (*al-'Alim*). Only then can individuals and groups be guided and constrained by the only permanently legitimate form of authority.

It becomes clear now that the claim for absolute autonomy for man in the design of his moral universe is in itself an invalid and false claim within the framework of Islamic reasoning. However, Islam would reject the notion that human dignity is in any way diminished or compromised when one acknowledges the absolute as the source of authority; rather, this bestows dignity on humans and ennobles their actions: they are the actions of inspired beings, not of beings who move on the shifting sands of moral relativism. Certainty constrained by the permissible is the only way of correct action for individuals and societies. Once God's authority is established as the indispensable source for the ethical organization of human affairs, individuals and societies begin to follow a different trajectory for their development. It is clear of course that in only very brief instances in human history – if ever – has this imperative of total submission to an absolute moral arbiter directed individuals and societies. But this remains the ideal, even if it is flaunted in practice. This condition has nothing to do with a so-called theocratic, or even a religiously inspired, society. Such societies, more often than not, surrender power to a priestly class which uses an elaborate theology to justify the all-too-human basis of its order. But it has everything to do with a virtuous society in which individual action is built on a profoundly ethical foundation, derived from absolute moral archetypes.

This necessarily brings us to a problematic and frequently contentious issue, which has bedevilled Islamic history even in modern times: how can ethical designs and commands, which are anchored in Islam's affirmation of man's dependency on God, be reliably transmitted? How is one to determine truth and authenticity? God cannot be known directly. It is a feature of dependency that the dependant is always in a subordinate role. But there cannot be a value system determined by God if there is no reliable way of understanding its decrees and rules of conduct and action.

Islam postulates two essential ways of comprehending the divine plan. The first is based on reason. Man uses his intellectual resources to understand and then utilize God's decrees, so as to establish a moral order which will guide individuals and order societies. In many ways, though, a reason-based method cannot be valid at all times. In itself, it would be subject to varying interpretations determined by historical, social and cultural contexts. While there may be alternative readings of the divine text, there are nevertheless limits beyond which Islam will not acknowledge a purely reason-based outcome. First principles are immutable. Murder will always be murder; theft will always be theft. There is no room for relativism in the acceptance of first principles. Even schools within Islam that appear to acknowledge the validity of a reason-based argument in generating new understandings or interpretations of divine commands narrowly circumscribe the ambit in which such reasoning is allowed free play.

The second way of understanding the divine plan is through what has been called the revelatory experience, or prophecy. In this construct, God encompasses all of existence. The signs of God are disclosed to man in endless forms and manners, both measurable and immeasurable. It is essential therefore for man to have a reliable and true method of comprehending and interpreting the signs which emanate from this reality. The purpose of prophecy is to provide this indispensable medium for understanding the ways of God. In the Quran, God has chosen thousands of prophets to act as the bearers of this knowledge; some are known, such as Abraham, Moses, Jesus and Muhammad. Others are not. The Quran privileges some prophets over others, but they all fulfil the essential function of being reliable and trustworthy bearers of the truth to their own people and to mankind at large.

Most ethical systems which purport to rely on the sacred fall down at this point. The need for an intermediary to carry the signs and signals which allow the individual and society to relate to the absolute raises the thorny issue of what is a true, reliable and effective medium. In short, how does man know that the medium through which such an approach will be made is authentic? Ultimately, the purpose of all religions is to make intelligible the ways of God at the human level, but all religions have shown signs of deviation and atrophy; they become veils which actually hide the way to God.

Nevertheless, at the core of all great traditions of knowledge and wisdom is a frame for reaching a true cognition of the decrees of God. This frame relies on the existence of a perfected human being, who acts as a conduit for receiving and transmitting truthfully the message of being and of existence, and who realizes and confirms, in his or her person, the unfolding of the virtuous way. Such a person becomes the ideal model of behaviour and conduct, and is the standard by which actions, intentions and states are to be judged. The prophetic model establishes its authenticity in a variety of ways, but none more potent than when the model is accompanied by inspirations drawn from revelatory experiences. These form the basis of the textual record of the revelatory experience and confirm its authenticity. In this manner, the sayings and conduct of the Prophet Muhammad become the idealized form from which an ethically inspired life can be derived.

The last factor necessary to complete the framework of a God-based and timeless ethical system in Islam is the assertion that human virtues cannot exist in isolation from their roots in the attributes of God. Thus the panoply of human virtues – generosity, compassion, justice, clemency and so on – must trace their origin to the divine Oneness, where their essences are to be found. The meanings which infuse creation and all creative acts must relate to each other as well as to their origin. There are no human virtues as such. As one of Islam's greatest moralists, the Andalusian Ibn Hazm, wrote in the eleventh century,

> If you study the laws that regulate human nature and the development of different characters according to the mixture of elements rooted in their souls, you will surely become convinced that you have no merit from your own virtues, that they are only gifts from the Almighty . . . You should replace the pride that you take in your own virtues with acts of grace towards the one who gave them to you . . .[4]

Modernity and Islam

These basic principles of human and social organization have always been affirmed within the context of the world view of Islam. The interjection of the divine in the ordering of human relationships continues to waft over the world of Islam – even if it is no more than the use of the ubiquitous *inshallah* ('God's will') that accompanies any Muslim's discussion of the future. This notion has yet to be reduced to a figure of speech devoid of any positive statement about the world. Muslims, however, have been prone to assume that the virtuous community did indeed exist in the pristine world of early Islam, and to some extent human affairs have been seen in terms of the extent to which mankind has strayed from these founding principles. The contemporary Muslim world is, almost universally, contrasted unfavourably with the world of early Islam. This contributes to the prevailing sense of moral inadequacy that permeates Muslim societies whenever they are compared to the Medina of the Prophet and early caliphs.

Modern western society assumes a priori that this world view can and should change. The permissibility of change and the terms of such change become the battlefield between the traditional and the modern. The conflict between religious societies and avowedly secular ones has also been described in these terms, but this division is false. Overtly religious societies are not necessarily synonymous with traditional societies in their concern for the transcendent. Their claims are frequently based on the partial use of a historical narrative or on the selective and incomplete reliance on a holy text. More often than not, they degenerate into dogmatism and then tyranny, caricaturing in their action their own lofty principles.

Islamic society and individual moral conduct have moved away from reliance on the fundamentals of the revelatory experience and the example of the prophetic model. In a number of Muslim countries, a dogmatic scientism has driven the sense of the sacred away from private and public consciousness. Even in apparently traditional societies which have survived into the twenty-first century, including those which explicitly acknowledge the extra-human bases of morality and ethics, a similar condition prevails. The accretion of alienating religious dogma and the gradual distancing of the spiritual from the quotidian experience of Muslims have led to a similar moral alienation in those societies which claim continuity with, and allegiance to, a traditional moral order. They have all been infected with a modernity which does not recognize the sacred in practice, but such societies nevertheless maintain the fiction that they do. The petrodollar states of the Arab Middle East are a case in point. The result is not schizophrenia, but open hypocrisy between what people feign to believe and what they actually do believe.

The Islamic criticism of modern societies relates partly to the gradual erosion of the fundamental moral bases of individuals and societies and to their replacement by a relativism that allows for a crude utilitarianism and mindless consumerism. The manufacture of wants and desires, with little understanding of the true function of happiness – in particular, the absolute requirement that it should be shaped towards a meaningful end – has imprisoned the human self in its lowest common denominator. The self cannot break out of its self-made prison and is caught in a vicious cycle which condemns it to an incessant clamour for gratification. The function of the collective becomes one that seeks to assuage these desires, while at the same time developing the demand for newer desires. The engine – what the political philosopher Bertrand de Jouvenel termed 'the Minotaur' – crushes all in its path, and at the edge reduces human beings to machines of consumption.[5] A coarsening of the human condition prevails, even though it might be accompanied by a glittering materialism. Fear and anxiety, violence and aggression, are the obverse to the modern ethics of desires rooted in the material, as the individual and, more broadly, societies contemplate the possibility of losing the means by which their desires are to be gratified.

Islam's retort to this type of modernity does not, on the surface, appear to be much different from the arguments of all anti-modernists, including large swathes of the intelligentsia in the western world itself, as well as in other non-Muslim traditional societies. How does this reaction differ, one may well ask, from the moral conservatism of the Catholic church, the European New Right, the modern advocates of an ethics of virtues such as the philosopher Alasdair MacIntyre, or the neo-Confucianism of the proponents of 'Asian values'? The Russian writer and Nobel laureate, Alexander Solzhenitsyn, presaged many of these concerns in his celebrated 1978 commencement address at Harvard University, entitled 'A World Split Apart'.

The concerns of Islam are not too different, it is true, but Islam is, theoretically, the only force which can move beyond the polemical into the realm of the political, through its explicit connection with states and governments, and thus with power. It can therefore create the circumstances to propose and even go down an alternative route into modernity. There are dozens of nation–states which claim, one way or another, to be guided by Islam. These states could be active in defining other forms of modernity but there are few signs that anything like this has been taking place.

However, most if not all Muslim societies appear to have surrendered to the imperatives of the modern world, if not at the political level then at least at the economic and, increasingly, cultural levels. Within Muslim societies this process has gone furthest in the Arabic world, leading to a frightening bifurcation in the minds of people and engendering the extremes of garish opulence for the few and a destructive nihilism which affects a large number of disenchanted youth. There is no easy method to halt what appears to be an irreversible trend towards a permanent disjunction between the sacred and the profane.

The Rejection and Acceptance of the Unseen

Within the ambit of Islam's world view, modernity and its fragmented successors are all seen to be part of the spectrum which is anchored in a formal rejection of the unseen as the basis for any moral order. But the issue is not simply one of confrontation between the modern mind and a grab bag of revolutionary states, global terrorists and religious revivalists. The fact that mankind ignores, claims to refute, or ridicules the validity of moral absolutes, does not detract from their essential truth. Or at least that is what the traditions of Islam postulate. Whatever the outcome of a conscious rejection of this order, it does not affect the permanent existence of an alternative, more valid, order. In this regard, mankind receives its just rewards by failing to adhere to the principles of right living. Man's progress towards the ultimate good can only be advanced through a correct inter- action with the decrees of God. Felicity is an outcome determined by a correct interaction with these decrees.

The person who focuses on the unseen must also engage with the here and now. There have been centuries of human civilization whose axis has been other than the sacred. Notions of 'progress', 'modernity', 'scientific advance', carry different meanings for those who continue to maintain a sense of the sacred. If societies and civilizations are to reflect a renewed sense of the sacred, their values must be radically rethought in accordance with a new sense of priorities in the organization of human affairs. This, of course, would apply in particular to Muslim societies, which continue to claim a loyalty to, and inspiration from, the Quran and the example of the Prophet.

It is not that Islamic civilization or cultures have reflected an abiding concern with other-worldliness. This is manifestly untrue. The concern of their rulers and elites has not been much different in substance to the concerns pertaining in other civilizations. Power and control, conquest and aggrandisement, the history of Muslims is littered with tyrants and despots.

But the personal, and to some extent the social, spheres, have remained outside the ravages of the ruler's span of control. Islam's spiritual landscape has continued to be firmly based on a God-centred perspective of the cosmos, without serious disruption by either temporal or religious powers. Knowledge of the transcendent has informed the lives of the multitudes in spite of the general tolerance shown for libertines and free-thinkers in the history of Islam. The power of the mystical Sufi orders or *tariqas* and the spiritualized world of Imami Shi'ism ensured the centrality of the sacred in the private lives of people. Intra-religious wars within Islam were never as pronounced as they were in the history of the West. There is no Islamic equivalent to the Thirty Years War, at least in terms of its violence and duration, or to the long-drawn-out struggles of the Reformation and Counter-Reformation. The *Mihna*, a form of inquisition during the Abbasid period, were hardly occasions for mass slaughter, and where that did happen, as in Tamerlane's conquests of recalcitrant Muslim lands (Tamerlane himself was a Muslim), it was due to marauding armies rather than campaigns against schismatics or sectarians.

The closest thing, perhaps, to mass killings over a prolonged period were the successful campaigns in the sixteenth and seventeenth centuries to establish Shia Islam as the formal religion of Iran and the uprooting of the Fatimi Ismaili dynasty in twelfth-century Egypt by Saladin and his successors (which was accompanied by much less violence). Islam has had its share of terrorists and assassins – the latter are in fact a corruption of the dreaded 'hashashin', an Ismaili sub-sect active in the twelfth and thirteenth centuries, but these were well outside the core beliefs of Islam. The imposition of 'orthodoxies' of whatever variety was not generally accompanied by coercion and mass killings. The recourse to the burning stake or to the gibbet was not an acceptable option in the tussle between various religious schools, aided perhaps by the absence of any formal 'church' in Islam. (Rulers, of course, liberally used the executioner's sword when their powers were challenged.) Nevertheless, Islamic history does have its share of controversial executions of the unorthodox – such as the medieval mystics Husayn ibn Mansur Hallaj and 'Ayn ul-Qudat and, more recently and in the same vein, the Sudanese reformer Mahmoud Muhammad Taha.

Writers as diverse as the great medieval theologian al-Ghazzali (known as Algazel in the West) may have bemoaned the Muslim's loss of spiritual bearing, but they never despaired of their potential for reform or return to the 'true path'. Islam had its atheists – the *Dahriyuun* – as well as its doubters and sceptics, but none could break through the ramparts of belief (*iman*), inside which the vast majority of Muslims resided – and still do. Hope and salvation, both temporal and other-worldly, continued to be seen in the context of the spiritual architecture of Islam and not outside it. There was no Renaissance or Enlightenment in Islam, simply because its trajectory was different from that of the West. There was no need or requirement to dethrone its perspective on the created universe and on mankind, because it was seen and believed to be true and real. The cosmos was held by the 'breath of the all-merciful'; the revelatory experience of Prophet Muhammad was authentic and veracious; the textual base of the Quran was undoubtedly the word of God. *Homo Islamicus,* at least in the pre-modern period, was defined by the person's implicit trust in a divine order, mediated at the human level through prophethood. The ordering of daily lives was built on this bedrock of certainty; on belief in an invariant scale of right and wrong, in spite of the dishonesty of individuals, the injustices of society and the capriciousness of rulers. Not fatalism, but the sure knowledge that the inevitable divine justice would prevail. The individual who combined the sacred and the profane in his or her person may not have existed in an idealized form, but *homo Islamicus* was as close a copy of this as possible, at least in Islam's self-definition.

However, the world view of Islam began to be seriously eroded in the eighteenth and nineteenth centuries. This was not only because of the retreats of the Muslim empires of the period (Mughal, Persian and Ottoman) in the face of unrelenting pressures from the economically, militarily and technologically more advanced European powers, but, equally importantly, because of the inability of the religious, political and administrative classes to see the crisis affecting Islamic civilization in any way except as the loss of power or weakening of religious dogma. The divisions within the Islamic world quickly hardened, pitching traditionalists against modernists, secularists versus revivalists. The pattern repeated itself from Morocco in the west to Java in the east.

The idea of the nation–state, which arose particularly in the nineteenth century, challenged the Islamic political entity. Sultanate and caliphate were contested by political parties and by the modern military castes. *Imama* or rulership faced elected assemblies and notions of 'popular sovereignty'. Extended families were threatened by shifting economic foundations and women's rights. The power of the judges who ruled by Sharia had to concede to the new canons of secular civil and criminal law. The open marketplaces of bazaars, artisanship and traditional exchange patterns gave way to the corporation, interest-based finance and foreign investment. The list is almost endless and all-encompassing. A new world was perched uneasily on the partial ruins of the old. Muslims would not quite abandon the past, nor quite embrace the future. Their confidence crumbled as they reflected on what they had been and what had become of them. No wonder many thought that they had been abandoned by God.

As Iqbal wrote, in grief, while surveying this forlorn landscape:

All we had lived for was to battle; we bore the troubles that came,
And we laid down our lives for the glory of Your Name.
We never used our strength to conquer or extend domain,
Would we have played with our lives for nothing but worldly gain?
If our people had run after earth's goods and gold,
Need they have smashed idols, and not idols sold?[6]

Why on earth would anyone question and, heaven forbid, jettison this certain form of knowledge for a lesser and ephemeral vision? Why indeed? But this is what has undeniably happened.

CHAPTER 1

Tearing the Fabric

The rain cloud of adversity is spreading over their heads [Muslims].
Calamity is showing itself.
Inauspiciousness is hovering behind and in front. From left and right is coming
the cry; 'Who were you yesterday, and what have you become today! Just now
you were awake, and now you have gone to sleep!'

Prologue to the *Musaddas* of the Indian Muslim poet, Hali,

first published in 1879, on *The Ebb and Flow of Islam*

(TRANSLATED BY CHRISTOPHER SHACKLE AND JAVED MAJEED, OXFORD UNIVERSITY PRESS, DELHI, 1997), p. 103.

What marks the decline or end of civilization? It is clear that certain civilizations and cultures have irretrievably disappeared from the passage of human history. The Meso-American civilizations of the Maya are a case in point. They collapsed, leaving monuments to their former glory but little else besides.[1] Carthage was physically erased from existence by the punitive acts of a pitiless Rome – '*Carthago delenda est*', said Cato the Elder, and he meant it.[2] Most distinct civilizations, however, are either absorbed into more successful ones – frequently through conquest – or continue with their distinct patterns but in a greatly weakened or submissive state.

The Retreat of Islamic Civilization

The apparent decline of Islamic civilization has been grist for the historians' mill for over three hundred years, yet without any satisfactory and definitive conclusions as to its extent, causes, and prospects. The early versions of the decline of Islam connect it to the fall of Baghdad to the Mongols in the thirteenth century: a discredited thesis, but one which still colours the popular imagination. What it lacks in historical veracity it makes up with the sheer drama of the end of the Abbasid Caliphate. It also perpetrates the dangerously deceptive conflation of Islam with the Arabs, ignoring the continuing vitality of the post-Abbasid empires and states based in Iran, Central Asia, North India and, of course, the Ottoman world. A universal consensus has evolved, however, to the effect that Islamic civilization has been in decline since the seventeenth century and that the community of the 'World of Islam' – the huge hemispheric 'Islamicate' space[3] – has been under serious assault, both from within and without. The patterns of unity that marked this universe appear to have broken up, leaving powerful collective memories of what had been – imagined or otherwise.

Will the civilization of Islam ever be capable of regeneration in the form and extent of its past? Is this a dangerous nostalgia which could descend into an irascible sullenness – or, worse, into violence and terror? Islamic civilization has occupied a critical and commanding position in world history. However, the redefinition of the world according to the norms of modernity and the huge technological, cultural, military and economic power of the West, centred as it is around the United States, and increasingly also of East Asia, have consigned it to an essentially subordinate – and even meaningless – role. Islam, even on its own terms, appears to be at odds with the rest of the modern world. A once distinguished historian of Islamic civilization has ended up by treating the subject of his life-long studies as a form of tranquilizing drug, 'bringing comfort and peace of mind to countless millions', but little else besides – to relieve unrelenting poverty and underachievement.[4] At best, Islam is damned with faint praise which accentuates its marginalization and irrelevance.

This is not the only depiction of Islam. There are by now a large number of apologists who argue for Islam's compatibility with the modern world. They include Muslims and non-Muslims, scholars and laymen. Their musings are driven by a desire to make Islam fit into the shoe of modernity and into the world of universal human and democratic rights.

Both these attitudes can trace their lineage to similar debates, which have been raging ever since Islamic civilization moved from being the dangerous 'Other' to falling into the sphere of control of the European powers. There is a remarkable resonance between the spirited clashes of the nineteenth century among Islam's defenders and detractors and what is taking place now between proponents of the permanent ascendancy of the West as the engine of world history and those who believe in the potential of Islamic civilization to revitalize itself, regain its confidence and assert its vision on mankind. Now that Islam is once again the dangerous 'Other', the outcome of these debates can have momentous consequences.

These issues first broke into the public arena in the nineteenth century, as the European powers' hold on the Islamic world consolidated. European encroachments into Muslim territory had begun well before this period, but the protagonists were not primarily states but commercial companies with special, often monopoly, charters. Companies such as the English East India Company, founded in 1600, or the Dutch United East Indies Company (VOC), which was established in 1602, were also authorized to wage war and negotiate treaties. As these companies sought to dominate the trade in spices and other commodities and goods from territories ruled by Muslims, they encountered the first signs of popular resistance. In Java, a rebellion against the Dutch VOC company broke out in 1670, led by the charismatic Sufi Sheikh Yusuf al-Maqassari. Born into a noble family from the Celebes, he departed for Mecca when he was eighteen, to pursue his religious education. He was initiated into a number of Sufi orders and returned to become a teacher and spiritual guide (as well as son-in-law) to the Sultan of Banten in Java.[5] The rebellion was finally put down in 1683, whereupon Sheikh Yusuf at the age of sixty-eight was exiled to the Cape colony, which was also run by the Dutch East Indies Company. The few years that Sheikh Yusuf spent in the Cape colony before his death in 1699 left a lasting mark on the course of Islam in South Africa. His burial place in the Cape became a much visited shrine for the Muslims of South Africa.

But the age of the European commercial company brandishing a royal monopoly charter and acting as the vanguard of the penetration of Muslim lands did not last beyond the nineteenth century. It was now the turn of nation–states to dominate as imperial powers. The periphery of the Islamic world came under attack first. France launched its North African empire with the capture of Algiers in 1830, sparking a decades-long struggle against strong local resistance led by the towering figure of the Emir Abd el-Qadir. In 1858, following the savage repression of a widespread insurrection against British encroachments, Britain finally imposed its direct imperial authority over India, displacing centuries of Muslim control – even though mainly titular – over large parts of the sub-continent. The British government also abolished the East India Company, which had directly administered most of India. Britain added Egypt to its dominion over Islamic lands in 1882. By the end of the nineteenth century, entire swathes of Muslim territory fell under European control, leaving only a shrinking Ottoman Empire and the Qajar dynasty in Iran as much diminished states. By the end of the First World War, what remained of that rump became reduced even further, as the Ottoman Empire – for long the pride of Muslim power – was broken up into an array of successor states in the Arab Middle East and Turkey. Islamic civilization, which had nearly always been coeval with rule by Muslims over Muslims, had to contend with a drastically changed world order.

In earlier times, when Muslims came under the control of non-Muslim powers, the outcome was, more often than not, mass expulsions and an early form of 'ethnic cleansing'. The experience of Muslims in Spain after the fall of Granada in 1492 is a case in point.[6] The retreat of Ottoman power in the Balkans is another example where displacement and expulsion of long-settled Muslim populations was a concomitant of the establishment of nation–states in the former Balkan territories of the empire.[7] However, the crisis that affected the Muslim self-image as a result of the imperial invasions and intrusions of the nineteenth and twentieth centuries was of a qualitatively different nature. The incoming powers sought economic and political dominion and dispossessed and displaced large numbers of people in the process. But in only a few instances was there a concerted effort to replace the indigenous population through colonial settlements, or an ethnically or religiously motivated plan to denude the area of its Muslim population. That would come later. The projection of European imperial power in an almost effortless demonstration of its superiority in military, technical, material, organizational and governance matters challenged the core assumptions that underlay the world view of Islam. Nearly all contemporary Muslim observers of the unfolding drama of European conquest and expansion would bemoan the huge chasm which had opened between the capabilities of the two civilizations and the helplessness of Islam in front of the European juggernaut. As one would-be reformer wrote in 1879:

O, Sons of the East, don't you know that the power of the Westerners and their domination over you came about through their advance in learning and education, and your decline in these domains? . . . Are you satisfied after your past achievements . . . to remain in that wretched state into which you were plunged by ignorance and error?[8]

Missing the Danger Signals

The failure of Muslim rulers and societies to address the twin threats of growing European imperial power and the advent of modernity has exacerbated the Islamic crisis. At one level, this was prompted by the unwillingness of a long-dominant civilization, which had been confident of its superior worth, to engage with what it considered a lesser form. This is certainly the perspective of those who see Islam as engaged in a millennium-long struggle with other civilizations – in particular with Christendom – when, for most of the time, Islamic civilization was ascendant. The sense that Islamic civilization could learn anything of consequence from such cultures – until then considered marginal – was preposterous. The religion of Islam had been perfected, and Muslims, as long as they remained faithful to Islam's precepts, would ensure their victory in this world and the next.

At another level, this failure has more to do with the unprecedented rate at which the technical and scientific advances in the West developed after the seventeenth century; they created an almost unbridgeable 'technological gap' between the West and the Muslim empires of the pre-modern period. The adoption of the techniques of modern warfare and administrative organization by the Muslim empires of the era, mainly for defensive reasons, simply could not keep pace with the changes taking place in the West. It was almost inevitable that the confrontation, when it occurred, would be one-sided. Islamic civilization had perfected itself within its own realm and did not have the attributes necessary to confront a civilization organized along unfamiliar, and ultimately more dynamic, principles.

Of course, these arguments cannot be conclusive. Their starting point has mainly been an occidental framework leading to conclusions which are not shared by those whose conceptual basis is different. Another perspective is that of the West's overt proselytizers, be they religiously or racially inspired or simply intoxicated by the very success of western civilization. The much maligned orientalists of the nineteenth and twentieth century fit partly into this category, although it is not too clear how far they were motivated by their supposed role as imperialism's apologists and handmaidens. Muslim thinkers have understandably viewed the causes of their own decline from a different perspective, but they were certainly affected by the torrent of analyses of their civilization emanating from the metropolises of imperial power.

In all of these variants of the question 'What went wrong?', few have stood back to assess the failure of large parts of the Islamic world to recognize the danger signals. The initial threat came from the West as well as from the territorial expansion of the Tsarist state. It arrived imperceptibly and took Islam completely unawares. Islam did not face much of a menace from Hinduism, Confucianism or Buddhism. China had been inward-looking for centuries. Japan was an insular power and had effectively cut itself off until the arrival of Commodore Perry's flotilla of 'Black Ships' in 1853, in Tokyo Bay. The warships had been dispatched by President Fillmore as a show of force, with a demand that Japan open itself up to international trade. In most of India, Hinduism had been subordinate to the primacy of Muslim rule. Muslim travellers and diplomats in the West could not quite translate what they saw and experienced into an urgent clarion call to action. And, when the threat finally began to reach home – through military defeats, superior western technical and organizational skills, or seizure of markets by western manufactured goods – it was never recognized for what it was until it was almost too late.

For example, the gradual extension of the reach of the East India Company into large parts of India presaged the destruction of Muslim power in the sub-continent. But the campaigns of Tippu Sultan, the ruler of Mysore, were equally directed against recalcitrant Muslim princes and rulers who had made common cause with the company. In his final battle against the British in 1799, in the fourth Anglo-Mysore War, in which he was killed, Tippu Sultan had to face not only the troops of the company but an equally large force raised against him by the Muslim Nizam of Hyderabad. The flood of adventurers and land-grabbers into Algeria in the 1830s and 1840s did not galvanize all of Algeria's tribes into a common front in the face of the menace from foreign colonizers and settlers. Neither could these tribes relate the gathering threat to the inclusion of their territories into France's empire. There was little understanding of the dynamics of imperial powers, and the patterns by which their control and dominion were achieved were not fully understood by Muslims.

In other instances, the threats were simply ignored because recognizing them would have conflicted with one or more of the established centres of power. So the resistance of the Ottoman elite forces – the Janissaries – to wholesale reform and reorganization was partly due to their fears that their privileges and unique structures would be abolished. Similarly, the religious scholars – or *ulema* class – in nearly all the nineteenth-century Muslim empires refused to countenance the introduction of administrative, educational and legal reforms because that would have undermined their own status as guardians over law and education.

Muslim leaders of command and genius did appear on the scene but they were severely mismatched, especially when the European power would bring all of its material and organizational resources to bear. Frequently the leader of the time would be fighting several battles against his fellow Muslim rulers and putative allies as they would neither acknowledge nor accept his command, driven as they were by jealousies and fear of loss of power and status. Betrayals and double dealings by one's own people were the order of the day in the wars of Emir Abd el-Qadir against the French in Algeria (1832–47), or in those of Imam Shamil against the Russians in Chechnya and Daghestan (1834–59). This experience would be repeated whenever traditional leaders first rose to confront the intruders. In the case of Abd el-Qadir in particular, the necessary combination of religious authority and military prowess could have provided the prototype for the sort of leadership which was needed in order to secure for Islam the space for coming to terms with 'technification' and its profound implications, before European power became irresistible.[9]

The Resistance of Traditional Islam

The campaigns of Abd el-Qadir (frequently termed *jihad*) also provide tantalizing glimpses into the way particular Muslim societies could have slipped into the pathways of modernity on their own terms. Abd el-Qadir was not unaware of the material and technical advances of his adversaries. He confronted them regularly on the battlefield. In the state he ruled in Algeria he did try to introduce the elements of the new technical civilization, but always in a role subordinate to the Islamic nature of his government. His was the last generation of those who confronted these challenges from an Islamic framework that was not affected or distorted by a superimposed European imprint.

The overlay of modern western institutions and perspectives necessarily changed the state of mind of the next wave of Muslim leaders. This began roughly around the mid-nineteenth century. By that time, the effect of European ideas, institutions and power began to dominate the world of Islam. The prevalent world view of Islam, which Abd el-Qadir and his contemporaries held to be true, quickly turned into the 'traditional' view and, later, into the 'reactionary' view as they were rapidly supplanted by new frameworks. At its core, this view was based on the twin pillars of Sharia law governing outer life and the ethical foundations underpinning *tariqa* Sufism, foundations which provided for social solidarity. The latter were ubiquitous religious orders that existed throughout the world of Sunni Islam, with a rough counterpart provided by the popular piety associated with the veneration of the Imams in Shia Islam. There were other forms of popular organization that provided for social cohesion in the world of pre-modern Islam. In the setting of Islam's cities and towns, these included the craft and professional guilds associated with the *futtuwa* – or chivalric – movements. (In Ottoman Turkey, such guilds were known as *akhis*; in Iran, as the *javanmardi.*) These also had a profound ethical foundation and linked their adherents in a long chain leading back to the early spiritual masters of Islam.

The qualities that Abd el-Qadir exhibited during his near twenty-year struggle with the French – and, equally importantly, during his imprisonment in France and exile to Turkey and Syria – were a textbook case for the type of inspirational leadership that fitted into the heroic mould of Islamic history. In critical times, a leader would emerge who, by military, organizational or political genius, would overcome formidable odds, repel aggressors and re-establish justice and order. Saladin had been just such a leader – at least in the profane world. His valorous achievements against the crusaders had receded from popular memory and had languished for centuries, unrecognized, until they were resurrected in the nineteenth century and re-entered Muslims' imagination. In religious terms, it was the person of the Mahdi – the Redeemer – who played the role of the one who saved the Muslims from oppression and godlessness. The great revolt of the neo-Mahdi, Muhammad Ahmad, in the Sudan in 1881, against Anglo-Egyptian subjugation was just such a case of heroic leadership which combined the religious with the political and military element.

Abd el-Qadir combined several qualities in an epic struggle against the might of the French empire, a struggle which was ultimately doomed to failure. His extraordinary feats of chivalry became the stuff of legend and carried into his period of exile. His treatment of his enemies was invariably correct and marked by his meticulous observance of the Islamic rules of warfare. At one point, he released his French prisoners of war because his army did not have sufficient provisions for them. These were the very virtues that summed up the prototype of the inspired leader. They were undoubtedly rooted in a deep Islamic identity, through which events and personalities were filtered and assessed. Abd el-Qadir addressed the French not in the idiom of race or nation, but in that of the religion and the civilization it nurtured. 'How do you boast of the power of France without knowing the power of Islam? The past centuries are the best witnesses of the power of Islam and its victories over its enemies. And we – even though we may be weak as you claim – are strong by the grace of the One and Only God.'[10]

The response of Imam Shamil, a Sufi sheikh of the Naqshabandi order, as he was fighting the Russian incursions into the Caucasus in the same period would have been no different. There is some anecdotal evidence that Shamil may have met Abd el-Qadir in Mecca during the Hajj (the obligatory Muslim pilgrimage to Mecca) of 1825. These two Sufi adepts would later lead two of the most celebrated wars of Muslim resistance to European advances. Abd el-Qadir was immersed from his earliest youth into the Sufi *tariqa* of his father, Muhyi-el-Din, who was a sheikh of the Qadiri order and a follower of the great Andalusian medieval mystic, Ibn 'Arabi. The governments that Abd el-Qadir and Shamil established for brief interludes, before they were overwhelmed, were all Sharia-based. In the Caucasus, the period of Shamil's state is known as 'the time of Sharia'. There was no other model that they would, or could, have considered.

At the same time, Abd el-Qadir could sense the weaknesses of his society and was aware that the struggle might be unsustainable, not only because of the military imbalance but also because France embodied the desperate challenges of technological and organizational proficiency his world had not yet found means to cope with. The truces which he signed with the French and which punctuated the war were partly to do with his realization that the conflict could not, in the long run, work to the advantage of Muslims. Above all, time was needed – but it was not forthcoming. With his struggle being ended by a combination of extreme French brutality and serial betrayals by his allies, Abd el-Qadir opened another chapter, in many ways more remarkable, in his life. This phase saw the full flowering of his spiritual consciousness.[11] He understood that his outer *jihad* was lost because of the fatal weaknesses in his society and because of the absence of any tools in its armoury with which to confront the utterly new forces it was facing. In many ways, Abd el-Qadir was the last leader of the pre-modern Islamic era who sought to understand and address the challenges of the emergent world in terms of Islam's classical heritage. Until his surrender in 1847 to the Duc d'Aumale, Abd el-Qadir had spent his entire life without any serious exposure to Europeans or European ways, even though he had kept abreast of debates in the French Assembly in so far as they related to France's Algerian policies. After that, the Islamic response to imperial expansion and to modernity became inflected with the creeping modernization of Muslim societies. Even traditionalists – *malgré*

eux mêmes – were unable to frame a world view free from the new paradigms that were sweeping the globe.

Spirituality and Leadership in Islam

Abd el-Qadir's extraordinary spirituality has been virtually ignored in the
assessment of his significance as a leader. Nearly all biographies gloss over
the years of his exile in Turkey and Syria, when he appeared to have made
an accommodation with the French occupation of Algeria. Historians have
preferred to concentrate on his role as a military figure and, latterly, as a
nationalist hero. In fact it was not his careful observance of the outer rules
of Islamic conduct that was striking. This was the norm of nearly all
Muslim leaders of the period. Rather, it was his intense spiritual exercises,
which he conducted in private during his years of campaigning. A chronicler of Abd el-Qadir's wars was Léon Roche, a Frenchman who had feigned
to convert to Islam in order to join the emir's entourage. Roche, pretending
to be asleep, observed Abd el-Qadir at night during a siege of an Algerian
town in 1838. 'He was standing there three steps away from me. His two
arms were raised to the height of his head . . . He had come to an ecstatic
state. His aspirations towards heaven were such that he seemed no longer
to touch the earth.'[12] Abd el-Qadir's heightened self-awareness was central
to his persona. It continued in a more open and obvious manner in his
years of exile, especially as he settled into a more pronounced contemplative life in Ottoman Damascus. He was a noted commentator on Ibn 'Arabi
and wrote a magnificent spiritual work, the *Mawaqif*, on the milestones of
the spiritual seeker. In another extraordinary feat of chivalry and courage,
his mansion compound became a refuge for thousands of the Christians of
Damascus who were fleeing from the murderous onslaughts of the mob
during the Maronite and Druze wars in Mount Lebanon in 1860. Lanusse,
the acting French consul in Damascus at the time, credited him with saving
the lives of 11,000 Syrian Christians.[13]

   It would be impossible to separate Abd el-Qadir's conduct and achievements from his heightened spiritual awareness. This also explains the speed
with which he came to terms with French and, by inference, European
preponderance, and his subsequent reluctance to lend his name to anticolo-
nial agitation. His intense connection with the medieval master Ibn 'Arabi
went beyond his immersion in the latter's works. He visited his tomb in
Damascus during his earliest pilgrimage to Mecca, the Hajj, and in his exile
years Abd el-Qadir gave frequent instructions in the system of Ibn 'Arabi.

There is sufficient evidence to consider Abd el-Qadir to have been a follower of the Ibn 'Arabi school – the so-called Akbarian school of Sufism – even during his campaigns against the French. Before his death, Abd el-Qadir ordered that his body should be interred near the tomb of Ibn 'Arabi himself, and it was from there that his remains were returned to Algeria in 1966. The same Ibn 'Arabi would write in one of his masterful spiritual poems: 'My heart has become capable of all forms; for gazelles a meadow, for monks, a monastery.'[14] But at the same time he would not hesitate to admonish a ruler for not applying the precepts of the Sharia.

For Abd el-Qadir there was no contradiction between fighting the French for years, at immeasurable odds, and being prepared to walk away from this once it became obvious that it was no longer propitious to continue, but rather to acknowledge the changed circumstances. As he wrote to the French Provisional Government following the 1848 Revolution, protesting his imprisonment, which violated French oaths given at his surrender: 'I defended my country and my religion as long as I could . . . When I was conquered – when it was impossible for me any longer to doubt that God, for inscrutable reasons, had withdrawn his support from me – I decided to withdraw from the world.'[15]

The spiritual dimension of Islamic leadership was an essential component of the archetypal leader in pre-modern times. The systematic distancing of the requirements of spiritual attainment in the making of a leader became a trait of all later Muslim reformers and thinkers. In fact modernist Islam dismissed all claims for spiritual realization implicit in the Sufi orders. Later, this turned into outright hostility, opening the way for the elimination of the spiritual in determining the suitability of a ruler. This dichotomy between the wordly and the spiritual has always been a feature in Islamic history, and, more often than not, was settled in favour of worldly, cunning or duplicitous leadership. It goes back to the earliest days of Islam of the seventh century, when the archetypal worldliness of Mu'awiyya and his Umayyad descendants were pitted against the archetypal spirituality of the Household of the Prophet.

In practice, the exigencies of political power in Muslim lands have tended to ignore the imperatives of moral, let alone spiritualized, rule implicit in the world view of Islam itself. This trait has naturally accelerated in modern times, resulting in the astonishing argument made by modernists that it was the spiritual dimension of Islam, distorted by the Sufi orders, that led to the decay and decrepitude of Muslim countries and opened them to foreign exploitation and conquest. Spirituality became suspect and, with it, the possibility that leadership could arise from the inspired individual. This tendency was increased by the deterioration of the condition of the Sufi brotherhoods themselves. By the early twentieth century, colonial authorities had managed in many instances to undermine the traditional resistance to their power of the Sufi brotherhoods. The colonial governments encouraged the Sufi brotherhoods to concern themselves exclusively with spirituality, frequently by co-opting sheikhs of the orders who were willing to collaborate with, or at least tolerate, the presence of the colonial power. This neutralized the orders as a potential focus for dissent or resistance, and frequently put them on a collision course with the more radical, anti-colonial Islamic modernists of the times. For example, the anti-colonial Association of Muslim Scholars in Algeria was virulently opposed to the Sufi *tariqas* and saw them as an obstacle to raising the political consciousness of ordinary Algerians.[16]

Abandoning the Islamic World View

The mid-nineteenth century saw the Muslim world convulsed by the dramatic changes which jolted its consciousness. What united the disparate parts of the civilization of Islam at this point were the issues of foreign encroachments and Muslim weaknesses. To the new breed of Muslim thinkers and scholars, there was simply no room for the notion of the individual balancing between the demands of an inner ethic and an outer code of action. These were insufficient to address Muslim powerlessness in the face of unremitting imperial expansion. It was action, not contemplation, that was needed. What mattered was to refashion the understanding of Islam in ways which would ensure that Muslims had the wherewithal to confront the claims of the West to political, economic and military superiority. The sense of inadequacy in front of European civilization extended even to the moral sphere. Many exclaimed that it was now Europe that carried the virtues which Islam had claimed as its exclusive preserve.

A process was started which radically undermined the possibility of reaching a form of modernity that stayed within the framework of Islam. Critically, the gateway to modernity, and thus to re-empowerment, was seen as lying outside the civilization of Islam itself. In many ways, the need to justify the world view of Islam echoes the debates between the Muslims of the early centuries of Islamic civilization and the Hellenized and Christian populations who lived under Muslim rule and who doubted

Islam's superiority as a religion and as metaphysics. The great difference was that, in the earlier period, it was Islam that held temporal power and could determine the direction of its outcome. The situation was now reversed, with a confident and expansionist West relentlessly challenging the basic assumptions of a civilization which was clearly in retreat, at least in its territorial dimension.

Here the case of the successful modernization of Japan, which commenced in earnest only in 1868 after the Meiji Restoration, represents a serious counter-example and raises a dilemma concerning the apparent failure of modernization in the nineteenth-century Muslim world. In fact Egypt, which had became an autonomous political entity in 1821 under the rule of the Albanian Muhammad Ali, had embarked on an effort to modernize its state and society a full fifty years before Japan started its own process.[17] At the end of the century, Japan was well on the way to joining the advanced powers, while Egypt languished under British rule. In Japan, the emphasis was on strengthening the bonds of Japanese exclusiveness through education, through state Shintoism and through the traditional virtues of thrift, diligence and loyalty in order to construct a modern economy. These were the legacies of Japan's Tokugawa past, and they were not discarded or questioned in the Meiji reformers' plans. It is true that Japan's modernizing ethic involved an acceptance of certain western ways, especially in state administration and economic and technological management, but this acceptance was always discriminating, even eclectic. The alliance between a reforming bureaucracy and a nascent industrial and financial class did ultimately end in militarism, plutocracy and a catastrophic war, and the country had to be fundamentally recast in the post-war era, but this was by no means preordained.[18] In Egypt, the possibility of Islam providing a door to modernity was not only questioned; it was often rejected on principle. Worse, there was an attempt to shoehorn Islam into the constructs of modern science and rationality, the implicit assumption being that Islamic civilization was incapable of providing the foundations for its own scientific explorations and advance.

The illustrious Indian paedagogue and scholar Sir Syed Ahmad Khan had said as much. In an 1884 lecture on Islam, Sir Syed spoke of the need for a new rationality – a new theology which reinterpreted the sacred text of the Quran in the light of reason and science. This was the precursor to countless calls to re-read the texts of Islam in an allusive manner, from the angle of personal or social utility, democratic rights, socialism, feminism – or whatever the pressing issues of the time might have been.

In 1883, the noted French philologist Ernst Renan delivered a lecture entitled 'Islam and science', in which he asserted, *inter alia*, that the Arabs were hostile to science and philosophy and that whatever science had entered Islamic civilization came from non-Arab sources. A retort followed from the pan-Islamic agitator and ideologue, the Iranian-born Sayyid Jamaluddin 'al-Afghani'. He broadly agreed with Renan, but went several steps further towards a general denunciation of religious faith and of its incompatibility with the scientific spirit. Afghani wrote in his 'Response to Renan': 'A true believer must, in fact, turn from the path of studies that have as their object scientific proof ... What would be the benefit of seeking [scientific] proof when he believes he possesses it all?' Later in the article Afghani wrote, specifically as regards the Muslim religion: 'It is clear that wherever it became established, this religion tried to stifle the sciences ...'[19]

It is astounding that one of the greatest exponents of pan-Islamic revival, who had an unrivalled influence on his contemporaries, could hold his own civilization in such scorn. Afghani's thought influenced a great number of people and his speculations on Islam and science became received wisdom for the next century and set the pattern of subsequent views regarding the essential incompatibility between Islam and science.

The undermining of confidence in the ability of Islamic civilization to adapt to modernity extended over all aspects of life, propelled by the torrent of new thought flowing in from the West. The uncritical adoption of western ideas by leading reformers of the Muslim world, who had lost their connection with the universe of the spiritually balanced individual and community, contributed greatly to the collective loss of self-understanding which was felt in the entire Muslim world in the nineteenth century. One after another, the pillars of Islam's unique constructs were demolished, frequently without the proponents of an alternative being fully aware of the consequences of their acts.

One example is the financial and economic consequences arising from juridical opinions given by Muhammad Abduh, Afghani's foremost disciple and co-worker (until he broke with him). Abduh was an advocate of *ijtihad* – that is, the use of independent reasoning to reach juridical conclusions – and he extended its scope to cover areas that were not previously considered within its legitimate ambit. In this process, Abduh authorized, for instance, the establishment of interest-based banking in a 1903 *fatwa*. This legitimized the establishment of financial institutions of a western type, which set the pattern for economic development in Egypt and elsewhere in the Muslim world.[20] This simple move effectively put a stop to the possibility of developing any meaningful financial and exchange institutions which might have drawn on the tradition of Islamic economic and financial transactions, avoiding the religiously problematic issue of interest altogether.

Revivalists and the 'Golden Age of Islam'

Revivalist movements in Islam pre-dated the arrival of the Europeans. The eighteenth century saw the rise of a number of significant movements for reform and revival that sought to purify Islamic life and society. These coincided with the ebb of power that affected all the three main Muslim empires of the time. The leaders of these movements were mainly drawn from the ranks of the *ulemas* (religious scholars) and from the Sufis. The *ulemas* were appalled by the loosening of religious standards and the toleration of dubious, even pagan, practices that increasingly inflected popular Islam. This was especially evident in the multi-ethnic Mogul empire of India, with its large Hindu majority population, where an accommodating and syncretistic Islam was tolerated and even promoted by the court. The last of the powerful Mogul rulers, Aurangzeb, abandoned the policy of religious accommodation and sought to impose a strong Islamic identity on the empire. The Mogul state was greatly weakened by his death in 1707, and could no longer foster a powerful Islamic identity. The task of protecting the cause of Islam fell to the *ulemas.*

One of the first to rise to the task was Shah Waliullah Dahlawi (1703–62). Born in Uttar Pradesh in India, Shah Waliullah spent twelve years in Mecca and Medina advancing his religious knowledge and credentials. He was an advocate of a close reliance on the *Hadith* – the sayings of the Prophet Muhammad – as a guide to correct Islamic action and conduct. The emphasis on the authority of the *Hadith* is a common feature of Islamic reformers and revivalists, even into the present period. Shah Waliullah left over fifty major works in Arabic and Persian, including two, the *Sata'at* (*Shining Lights*) and the *Lamahat* (*Flashing Lights*), which are masterpieces of mystical philosophy. He was a tireless proselytizer for Islam and a champion of Islamic unity in India, and he sought an accommodation between the Shia and Sunnis. His son Shah Abdul Aziz was himself a noted scholar in the revivalist tradition. By that time India was slipping nearly entirely out of Muslim control, which prompted Shah Abdul Aziz famously to declare India to be *Dar-ul-Harb* ('The Abode of War'). India could no longer be considered a domain under Islamic law. Shah Abdul Aziz's 1803 *fatwa* was directed mainly against the British and called for a *jihad* against their presence.

In West Africa, the revivalist movements originated mainly from the Fulani people, with their deep Islamic attachments. Their spread into the Sahara brought them in contact with pagan and semi-Islamized tribes, which prompted one of the most famous *jihads* of the eighteenth and early nineteenth centuries, that of Usman dan Fodio (1754–1817). Usman never travelled to Mecca or Cairo for his religious education, drawing instead on the Sufi networks of the Sahara to which he belonged. Usman's preaching in the Hausaland – modern-day northern Nigeria – generated tensions with local rulers, which led to his call for a *jihad* in 1804. The wars were successful and Usman founded the Sultanate of Sokoto, which persisted until the British conquest of Nigeria at the end of the nineteenth century.[21]

The revivalist movements of the eighteenth and nineteenth centuries were also related to the rise of the Naqshabandiya Sufi movement, an order that sought to purify Sufism from practices and accretions that were unacceptable to the orthodox *ulema*.[22] A number of the leaders of the reform movements of the eighteenth and nineteenth centuries were themselves affiliated to the Naqshabandiya order, including Shah Waliullah himself. The anti-Dutch rebellions in Aceh (in northern Sumatra), throughout the nineteenth century, were also actively supported by the Naqshabandiya. A similar story unfolds in the Caucasus. Both major rebellions against the Russians, by Imam Mansur in 1785–91 and later by Imam Shamil, were led by Naqshabandiya sheikhs. In eastern Turkestan, Naqshabandiya sheikhs led uprisings against Manchu rule throughout the nineteenth century. Other Sufi orders of the period also sought to purify their doctrines and practices and bring them closer to orthodoxy. These orders would play a major part both in the revivalist movement and in the resistance to foreigners. The Sanusiya order founded by Muhammad Ali al-Sanusi (1787–1859) is a case in point. Al-Sanusi founded numerous lodges (*zawiyas*) in the Libyan Desert which acted both as a scaffolding for the nascent state and as the focus of resistance to French – and, later, Italian – advances into the Sahara.

Part of the message – and allure – of the revivalists consisted in their attempts to construct a 'golden age' of Islam, an age from which Muslims deviated, thereby condemning themselves to a secondary status. The many revivalist movements of the pre-modern period were ultimately eclipsed in their significance by the uncompromising and literalist monotheism associated with the Hanbali scholar[23] Muhammad ibn Abd el-Wahhab (1703–92) – the founder of the eponymous Wahhabi movement. Abd el-Wahhab had based his teachings partly on the rediscovery of the prolific writings and screeds of the medieval theologian Ibn Taymiyya, which purported to give substance to the notion of a golden age. The influence of the Wahhabis was limited to the wilds of the Nejd, until their aggressiveness pushed them out of their desert redoubts and into the Hejaz, the homeland of Mecca and Medina, and the fringes of Iraq. At that point the Ottoman authorities prevailed upon their then viceroy in Egypt, Muhammad Ali, to dispatch an expeditionary force into Arabia to destroy the Wahhabist state. The Wahhabis' 'capital', the village of Dari'yya, was razed to the ground in 1818 and its ruler, Abdullah ibn Saud, was hauled off to Istanbul, where he was put to death. This apparently ended the Wahhabist revival.

However, the themes associated with Wahhabism, especially its insistence that there was a 'pure' Islam relating to the early days of the Prophet and his immediate successors, became the stock in trade of the next wave of religious reformers of the nineteenth and twentieth centuries. Afghani, though a Shia by birth and thus an apostate in Wahhabi demonology, seemed to be the first to use the notion of a 'golden age' to whose values and conduct Muslims should return if they were to confront western advances. This idea was later built on by Abduh, who resurrected the phrase *al-salaf al-saleh* ('the righteous forefathers') to designate the idealized community of Islam. He included in it not only the companions of the Prophet and the early 'rightly guided caliphs', but also the carriers of the intellectual and religious legacy of Islam's middle period. This was an Islam where the rewards of scrupulous religious observance and obedience were political, intellectual and worldly success.

The *Salafiyya* movement, or Salafism grew out of Abduh's reformist circles. It called for a return to a 'fundamentalist' form of Islam before its purported corruption by centuries of lax Muslim rulers and superstitious customs and innovations. It evolved further with the writings of Abduh's disciple, Rashid Ridha (1863–1935), and his widely-read newspaper *al-Manar*. From its base in Cairo the paper reached the far corners of the Muslim world.

The *Salafiyya* movement owes its origins to an intellectual reaction to the plight of Muslims in the heyday of European ascendancy. It cannot seriously claim any continuity with the historical intellectual traditions of Islamic civilization. In this sense, fundamentalist Islam is an eminently modern phenomenon. Later in the twentieth century it converged with a Wahhabism which was re-empowered after the fall of the Arabian Peninsula to the forces of Ibn Saud in 1925. Both currents, Wahhabism and

Salafism, joined forces to redefine the practices, beliefs and norms of Islam for a great number of people.

By the end of the nineteenth century, the territorial, cultural and psychological unity of Islamic civilization had been torn apart. It was a unity based, in the final analysis, on the outcome of successive Muslims' interaction with the Quran and with the prophetic message in a geographical space which was continuous, or that at least allowed for continuous contact. Islam did not participate in the epochal changes that transformed western societies, and, when modernity finally came to its societies, it was frequently accompanied by a sense of degradation and failure. The notion of the autonomous individual dedicated to progress and freedom, and the idea of the mass, which interacts with history as class or nation, were utterly alien and too far removed from the legacy of Islam. Yet the elites of the Muslim world might have been able to connect with such notions, if only because they had the material wherewithal and the political or social desire to do so, and some were open advocates of an eventual – benign – melding of Islam with the West.

In his sojourns in Paris and London, Afghani was smitten with the freedoms and order of the West. 'In Europe I saw infidels who behaved as Muslims; in Muslim lands I saw Muslims who behaved as infidels,' he was reputed to have said. But the individual Muslim could not easily jettison his or her world view without a traumatic break with the past. How were they to acquire the virtues embodied in European civilization without seriously compromising or abandoning their own legacy? And what aspects of the West were they to acknowledge as the foundations of modernity? The Judaeo-Christian heritage? The literary traditions of France and England? Parliamentary democracy – or Prussian militarism? Renaissance art – or the philosophy of Kant? Many Muslims would in fact indiscriminately adopt the culture and customs of the West, seeing in them the prototypes of all that was vital and progressive. Entirely new arenas of art and culture appeared to beckon, from novel writing and playwriting to painting and the opera. But the ensuing hybrid culture would never amount to much. It was unable to establish its worth in modern terms by using contemporary aesthetic or critical standards. Islam's own heritage of high culture was being removed as the living and guiding tradition for the moral or creative Muslim, and it was replaced, sometimes by its own guardians, by something entirely alien: the imported culture of the West.

At the same time, the terms upon which modernity was introduced into Islamic societies were very different in form and intent from what was taking place in the West itself. It often arrived in garbled and barely recognizable form, mimicking rather than duplicating the original model. The comparison with Japan is, once again, very instructive. Tokyo University reached the heights of academic excellence, but not so Syed Ahmad Khan's Aligarh Muslim University, or the Egyptian University at Cairo, both of which were established along European lines and with the loftiest of intentions of bringing modern education to the elites.[24]

The disruption of continuity with the past was not something that the ordinary occidental needed to ponder or manage, even when historical change advanced at a rapid pace. After all, the locus of the great engine of transformation was firmly the West. The Muslim individual, increasingly disconnected from his past and not yet in the folds of the atomized crowd, had nowhere to turn for what was familiar and comprehensible. The divisions within Muslim societies became ever sharper as the nineteenth century came to a close. The work of Islam's modernizers was pushing religion increasingly into the private sphere, where it could never belong exclusively in any case. By trying to come to terms with European ascendancy, the reformers succeeded, perhaps unconsciously, in justifying an entirely different perspective on life. They used their own construct of Islam, one which was not contiguous with Islam's own past. They even purported to give it moral sanction. As the living edifice of the civilization was gradually being dismantled, Islam retreated into a historical consciousness which retained a still powerful sense of identity. It would emerge later in the twentieth century, in forms that would be scarcely distinguishable.

CHAPTER 2

The Break with the Past

The new age is like lightning; inflammatory is every haystack
Neither wilderness nor garden is immune form its attack.
To this new flame old nations are like faggots on a pyre;
Followers of the last Messenger are consumed in its fire.
Even today if Abraham's faith could be made to glow;
Out of Nimrod's fire a garden of flowers would grow.

Muhammad Iqbal, *Jawab-i-Shikwa*, p. 85

The break from the past experienced in the largest part of the Muslim world led to profound consequences both at the individual and social levels. The challenge of western dominance was not to be met through affirmation of the precepts of traditional civilization, expected to create a gateway into modernity. The weight of apologetic and defensive literature, stressing Islam's rationality and its support for scientific inquiry, might indicate otherwise. But this was more of an implicit admission of the failures of Islamic civilization to provide an entry into the modern world – as understood in European terms – and therefore to provide the essential access to wealth and power in order to confront the expansion of European empires. From now on, the division of the world of Islam between 'reformers' and 'secularists and westernisers' became sealed. The former sought to maintain a pivotal role for Islam in society, while the latter pushed towards restricting Islam's influence to the private sphere, in a secularized and modernized society. From the mid-nineteenth century right to the present times, this division has not really shifted in structure and has dominated the intellectual landscape of Islamic societies. The proponents of traditional Islam, reduced as they were to defending an ever-shrinking private space, were left behind, abandoned to individual piety and family bonds, while the outer manifestations of traditional Islam were being systematically demolished. By the beginning of the twentieth century, within less than fifty years, the institutions of traditional Islamic society and polity had virtually disappeared, in content if not quite yet in form.

The Collapse of Confidence

Why did most of the leaders and elites of a great civilization so quickly reject the possibilities of adjustments to modernity which may have been inherent in their own world? The reality of physical conquest is, naturally, one explanation, but this did not affect the entire Muslim world at the same time and to the same extent. Nevertheless, the dismantling of the Mogul state in India, for example, even in its final decrepit form, eliminated in one stroke an entire administrative and judicial class that had been organized, for better or worse, under a traditional form. In Algeria, of course, the extent of physical conquest was more far-reaching, as it led to the absorption of the country into the system of metropolitan France. The seizure of the domains of Islam from their historical guardians and the loss of access to state power and patronage greatly contributed to the alienation and powerlessness of those still steeped in traditional ways. A premium was thus placed on those who could adjust to the ways and perspectives of the conqueror. Some of the former elites adapted quickly and became the foremost proponents of secularization, not as a way of restoring Muslim power as much as a necessary precondition to joining the comity of modern states and nations. Military defeat and physical occupation initially engender a state of introspection rather than one of resistance, especially where there is a massive disparity in power between the contestants and limited access to the tools of resistance. The prospects for removing the occupier appear remote and breed a sense of helplessness. The virtues and methods of the occupier become exaggerated, while the alternative, be it the traditional way or active resistance, appear to lead to marginalization, lack of potency or destruction.

European civilization dazzled a large number of visitors from what was then known as the orient. They could not but help compare and contrast what they witnessed to conditions in their own societies. The stream of visitors and sojourners – such as the Egyptian Rifa'a al-Tahtawi, who spent the years between 1826 and 1831 in Paris, or Syed Ahmad Khan, who spent a year in England in 1869/1870 – were profoundly influenced by their experiences. Another traveller, Mohammad as-Saffar, dispatched to France by the Sultan of Morocco in 1845–6, returned to write:

> So it went until all had passed, leaving our hearts consumed with fire from what we had seen of their overwhelming power and mastery, their preparations and good training, their putting everything in its proper place. In comparison with the weakness of Islam, the dissipation of its strength, and the disrupted condition of its people, how confident they are . . .

He went on to attribute the Europeans' strength not to 'their courage, bravery or religious zeal, but because of their marvellous organization, their uncanny mastery over affairs, and their strict adherence to the law'.[1]

The corpus of European thought and intellectual and cultural achievement, particularly in its (then contemporary) form, was another source of wonder for the apprehensive Muslims of the time. A great deal of the biases of the early orientalists, for example, their focus on the classical age of Islam, and in particular on the Baghdad of the Abbasids, was internalized by the reformers when examining weaknesses in their own societies. Islam was seen to have 'peaked' by the end of the twelfth century and had been in regress ever since. This encouraged an attitude which minimized or trivialized the achievements of Islamic civilization since that period, partly because what came after was no longer centred on an imaginary Arab heart. The post-Abbasid world of Islam was deemed unworthy of comparison to the high culture of the classical period. The race was afoot to find out the culprits behind the decline of Muslims and their power. This, in so many words, was the stereotypical response of the cultivated Muslim to the Europe of the nineteenth century. This bedazzlement often bred a sense of inferiority, in particular if the material and cultural gaps with Europe loomed so large as to appear fearsomely daunting. It was far easier to assume the superiority of European modernity over Islamic 'obscurantism' and effectively to abandon all possibility of revitalizing Islamic civilization. Many would eventually choose this route.

A New Industrial Age

The decline in self-confidence accelerated as Muslims lost the certainty that comes from adhering to the unique vision of the world which their civilization offered. The understanding of fundamentals of perception, such as the nature of the self and the physical world, the ordering of personal relationships, the meaning and legitimacy of authority, the organization of society, or even the basics of existence such as man's ordering of space and time, changed in essential ways. The Islamic world view was in most ways different from, and often antithetical to, that of modernity. No civilization had to undergo the rapidity and scope of change that the world of Islam experienced in its tumultuous and incomplete transition to the modern. The transition which the West experienced during the eighteenth and nineteenth centuries, from an agrarian order to the industrial age, was turbulent enough, but was nevertheless conducted within the framework of the civilization itself. Enclosures of agricultural common lands were not forced by a foreign power; the design and manufacture of machines were not imported from an alien world; the factory system and the regimented labour force were not transposed from elsewhere. The modern industrial age may have started in a small corner of north-western Europe and New England, but it was connected, in a fundamental sense, with the legacy of the broader civilization of the West, and could not probably have arisen, *in a similar form*, anywhere else. At the same time, it could not have taken shape outside the political and legal framework of the nation–state and the attendant structures and institutions which evolved alongside the industrial revolution. The change in perspective, in skills and in disciplines which were required of the average Europeans or Americans in order for them to adjust to the needs of the age of machines and mass markets, were jarring, but not completely alien. In Islam they were catastrophically new.

Islam was a civilization pre-eminently mercantile.[2] The establishment, access and control over trade routes formed a key feature of the economy of Islam. This was, at its base, an agrarian world, but it relied on its merchants and traders to move the surpluses and the products of a highly skilled urban crafts culture over a far-reaching area. The geographical space of Islam was by far the widest known to man before the advent of the empires of Europe. It stretched right across the Eurasian land mass and into Africa, forming a distinct religious and cultural community, even though it was divided into different political states. Within the constraints of pre-modern travel, geographic mobility was widespread. Merchants and traders sought markets; but the notion that economic life should be built around the demands of impersonal market forces was alien to Islam. The Islamic polity did not organize its affairs so that the factors of production – of land, labour and capital – were traded as commodities. Neither did it adapt its laws – the multivariate Sharia law – to accommodate the needs of organized capitalism and financial intermediation. Sharia law was, if anything, a set of contractual principles which covered some aspects of personal and social relations. Marriage, for example, had no sacramental status, and the stigma of illegitimacy did not attach to the offspring of legally contracted secondary partners. A great deal was left out of Sharia law, leaving a large range of activities to be governed according to the interests of the contracting parties.

At the same time, Sharia law paid little attention to either ascribed or acquired status, unlike in Europe. Aristocracy simply did not exist as an enduring class based on hereditary land ownership. There were large and often powerful landowners, but the *taluqdars* and *zamindars* of North India, or the Turko-Circassian pashas of Egypt, did not constitute a feudal aristocracy.[3] Time was not measured in the daily work norm of the industrial West, but by the times of prayer. You did not meet someone after lunch, but after the midday prayers. The craftsman's hours were not measured by the mechanical clock of the factory worker. The members of the craft guilds – the *asnaf* in Persia or *harrafiyun* in the Arabic-speaking world – ordered their day by a mixture of intricately skilled work and regular worship. Their workday started with spiritual exercises and callisthenics, and paeans to the spiritual knights of Islam.[4] (The Japanese and Koreans had similar traditional practices. But, rather than abandoning them, they modernized them. The work-day in some major Asian corporations still begins with a song or hymn to the glories of work and the corporation.) But the ingredients for producing a uniquely Islamic entry into modern times, building on the main aspects of Islam's historical legacy, escaped its leaders and elites as they grappled with the prospects of being overwhelmed by European power and technology.

Making Nations and Races

The fracturing of the Islamic world's unity led to a proliferation of successor ideologies, vying for, or redefining, people's loyalties and identities. Nearly all of them were derived from European ideas or institutions. Probably the most enduring of the modern transplants into Islam was the idea of the nation–state. Wherever colonial rule operated, the organization of the conquered territory followed the pattern of a European nation–state. The historical empires of Islam that survived into the twentieth century followed suit, even though in an incomplete form. The process, of course, was finalized after the First World War, when the Ottoman Empire was recast as a number of nation–states and the Iranian state reconstituted itself as the Pahlavi dynasty. The nation–state was an entirely alien concept in Islamic political theory and practice. Dynasties drawn from particular ethnic or linguistic groups were common in Islam, but the idea of a nation in the European sense was utterly remote from its legacy.

The classic nineteenth-century definition of the nation was the one proposed by Ernst Renan[5] in his tract *What is a Nation?* (*Qu'est-ce qu'une nation?*). Renan may appear now as an antiquated figure, part of the Victorian era parade of philologists, political and economic theorists and philosophers who dealt with grand themes and schemes. (He is now best known for his controversial work *The Life of Jesus*, in which he sought to reinterpret scriptures in the light of modern standards of critical historiography.) Renan sacralized the nation by giving it a soul – the precursor of the *élan vital* which was the stock in trade of all twentieth-century nationalisms, not least of the invented nationalism of states built out of the wreckage of the Ottoman Empire and the dissolution of the colonial system:

> A nation is a soul, a spiritual principle … A large aggregate of men, healthy in mind and warm of heart, creates the kind of moral conscience which we call a nation. So long as this moral consciousness gives proof of its strength by the sacrifices which demand the abdication of the individual to the advantage of the community, it is legitimate and has the right to exist.[6]

The community takes precedence over the individual and defines the worth of the system. This was the common refrain of the early nationalists of the post-Islamic order who sought to reorganize their societies on what they believed were the foundations of the successful western model.

Nationalist thought was almost by definition secular[7] and appealed to the intellectuals of the period, who had despaired of – or refused to contemplate – the reform of Islamic political institutions. Religion, to the nineteenth-century mind of Renan, was simply an extension of the human imagination and did not have an independent existence as such. The work of orientalists simply reinforced the process of building on the nation–state and on the ideology of nationalism, regarded as a successor to the ecumenical universe of Islamic civilization. Research on the languages of

Islam – on the ethnic history of Turks, Arabs, Persians and Malays, and on the literary legacies of these groups – was the foundation of oriental studies in western universities. The first generation of Muslims who had been influenced by western scholarship and scholars on Islam, nationalism, secularism, utilitarianism and other doctrines of the nineteenth century provided the first glimmerings of an ethnically based nationalism. Islamic political theory and practice had no place for the nation–state.[8]

The adoption of the nation–state as a replacement for the Islamic polity required the invention of new words and concepts. There was no word in any of the languages of Islam that would parallel the meanings of 'nation' and 'nationalism'. Such meanings had to be contrived from other words, which did not convey the same meaning.

At the same time, the territorial sense of 'nation' as something confined within a strict geo-political space, where a common ethnicity prevailed, had never took root in Islamic political culture. Once again, the idea had to be applied awkwardly, using terms which did not quite fit the European meaning. There were different words for the territorial space that Muslims inhabited, such as '*watan*', '*bilad*', '*ardh*', but none carried the distinct modern sense of the word 'nation'. Appropriating the word '*Umma*', the Quranic term for a community of believers, to denote the idea of a nation was effectively an attempt to de-sacralize a term which was commonly understood by Muslims, but obviously with a different meaning. The idea of an Arab nation, or Turkic nation, embraced peoples who lived across a huge geographic area and were divided along numerous political states. It became more difficult to reconcile the notion of loyalty to a homogeneous national or ethnic group with the principles of loyalty to the Islamic *Umma*, which transcended ethnicity and linguistic barriers.

Race was also substituted for religion, with even less conviction. Europeans were stressing the supposed 'genius' or uniqueness of particular racial groups, and this was absorbed by those who sought an alternative level of certainty and identity to the one provided by Islam. Turks, Arabs and Persians were all encouraged to reach back into their past in order to evolve a narrative of glory and destiny that could provide a basis for renewal in the world order which was supposedly replacing Islam. The Quranic treatment of race was represented purely in terms of a group's adherence to the covenant with God. Wherever one group was singled out for preference, it was invariably in terms of its fidelity to the spiritual and ethical norms required of it. 'You were the best of mankind, enjoining what is good and eschewing the forbidden,' the Quran said. There is, of course, no denying that race was an element in the dynamics of Islamic civilization, as seen in the cultural wars of the *shu'ubiya*,[9] where the Arabs were pitted against the Persians; or in the latter part of the Ottoman Empire, where 'Arab' was a derogatory word, used by Turkish officialdom implying 'uncivilized' and 'uncouth'. The Arabs, in turn, would take inordinate pride in their language and in the fact that the Islamic message was in Arabic and was carried at first by Arabs. The ideologues of Arab nationalism frequently descended into a race-based exaltation of the Arab character, but their constructs were hardly original. Their drawings from nineteenth-century European thinkers were obvious.[10]

The systemization of archaeology in the nineteenth century also opened another avenue into the past for those seeking to refashion the loyalties of Muslims towards a non-Islamic, or even pre-Islamic, world. The uncovering of the histories of Babylon, Nineveh, the Pharaonic dynasties of Egypt, Persepolis, the Phoenicians – and even the Mediterranean as a cultural and civilizational unit – were all used in one form or another to relate to a remote past, with which Muslims, at least those of the Middle East, had little or no popular resonance. Nevertheless, these histories still featured prominently in the attempts to refashion identity, especially in the countries of the Levant and Egypt.[11]

Liberalism and extreme secularism represented another aspect of some of the systems that sought to replace the world defined by the precepts of Islam. The clearest case of this was in the drive of Mustafa Kemal to transform the newly established nation–state of Turkey along pronounced secular and westernizing lines, but the Turkish experiment was not duplicated in such sweeping and determined terms in other Muslim countries. Aspects of the Turkish reforms were tried in a number of Muslim countries, but their effects were muddled and shallow.

In Egypt, the political and cultural elite was not prepared or willing to jettison the entire legacy of Islam at one fell swoop, as the new leaders of Turkey had done. Nevertheless, Egyptian public policy was couched in secular terms. To some extent, the liberalism of the nineteenth century in Europe reconstituted itself on the banks of the Nile. Parliamentary institutions were patterned after Westminster, following the lead of Britain, the paramount power in Egypt during the first half of the twentieth century. The cultural pre-eminence of Egypt was unquestioned in the inter-war years, not only among Arabic-speaking peoples. The Cairo of the 1920s and 1930s was a ferment of literary and artistic experimentations which drew on modernity for their inspiration.

But, unlike in Turkey, these currents parted ways with, rather than rejected, the Islamic legacy. There was also considerable Islamic intellectual activity during this period. For example, the proselytizing for the Salafist strain in Islam emanated from Egypt, where Rashid Ridha's *al-Manar* newspaper was published, and Egypt featured one way or another in the projects to revive the caliphate and the various pan-Islamic ventures of the time.[12] However, it was the towering intellectual figure of Taha Hussein (1889–1973) in Egypt and the controversies he engendered that were characteristic of the period immediately following the end of the First World War. It was left to Taha Hussein and his supporters or detractors to confront the issue of a national identity and purpose by framing it along a significantly different basis to that of Islam. The effects of these conflicts resonated throughout the Muslim world.

Taha Hussein's childhood, memorably and movingly described in his autobiography, *Al-Ayam* (*The Days*),[13] was one of hardship and struggle, made even more difficult by blindness inflicted on him by an incompetent village barber who was treating him for a common eye infection. He rose through the traditional school system, which led him to the great religious institution of the al-Azhar University; then he moved on to the recently established Cairo University; he continued in France, where he received a doctorate from the Sorbonne. His writings were voluminous, comprising nearly sixty works, not all of them memorable. But he remained committed to the thesis of Egypt's essential 'westernness', which he elaborated upon in his work *Mustaqbal al-Thaqafa fi Misr* (*The Future of Culture in Egypt*).[14] In outline, his argument was that Islamic civilization was based on the willingness of early Muslims to borrow freely from the advanced world of the Persians and Byzantines and that Egypt should similarly borrow freely from the modern European world

At the same time, Egypt's integration into the West was, in important ways, a homecoming. Egypt, Taha Hussein contended, was always a part of the West rather than of the orient. Its geographical position, its Mediterranean culture, its Pharaonic, Ptolemaic, Roman and Byzantine past have all positioned the country firmly in the West. To this must be added the historical legacy which connected the Egyptians' mind with that of the ancient Greeks, turning Alexandria into a citadel of Greek philosophers. 'All of this,' he wrote, 'points out, in these modern times, that we should be connected with Europe by bonds that strengthen daily until we merge [into Europe] in meaning, form and reality. And we will not find this onerous, as the Egyptian mind is not different in its essence and nature from the European mind.'[15] In retrospect, the position of Taha Hussein might appear hopelessly disconnected from reality, but it had a profound effect on the country's elites, as it provided them with the intellectual justification to ape European ways and customs. This was the age when the ruling classes sent their children to British-style boarding schools, joined country clubs and held literary soirées, spoke at least two European languages, watched risqué films, attended the Cairo Opera, and read the first of the (proliferating) women's magazines.

Where Egypt led in those days, other countries followed, including the ruling groups of the Arab states of the Near East. The distancing from the world of Islam accelerated, a scant two decades after the collapse of the Ottoman Empire. The intellectual climate of the time, which continued at least into the 1960s, was anchored in an open acknowledgement of the superiority of modern civilization based on technology. This was exclusively identified with the West at first, and then, for a short period, with the Soviet bloc, as the perspectives associated with Taha Hussein's overt orientation towards the West became tempered partly by the anti-colonial struggle that was continuing in various parts of the Muslim world.

Dissenters of the Inter-War Years

In an age when secularism seemed to be entrenching itself irreversibly, there were hardly any non-traditional writers and scholars who explored the potential inherent in Islamic civilization to generate the changes needed for the new circumstances. Two who stand out above all others, in the age when Islam appeared to be receding from the public arena, were the poet of the sub-continent, Muhammad Iqbal, and the Kurd, Said Nursi of Turkey, known as Badiuzzaman ('the wonder of the age'). Both were deeply concerned with regaining the self-confidence of the Muslim in the face of huge threats affecting the integrity of Islamic civilization and the commitments of Muslims to the legacies of their past.

Muhammad Iqbal (1877–1938) is the great poet of modern Islam, whose prodigious talents and insights made him a remarkable force, not only in pre-partition India but in the wider Muslim world. He wrote in Urdu and Persian, although some of his important philosophical works were actually written in English. Born into a reasonably prosperous Muslim family in the Punjab in 1877, Iqbal studied at Lahore College, which was then directed by Thomas Arnold, a sympathetic writer and commentator on Islam. Later Iqbal attended Cambridge University and was awarded a doctorate by Munich University for his work on Persian metaphysics. He was greatly impressed by the dynamism of the West, contrasting it to the passivity that seemed to prevail in the Muslim world. But although his experiences in Europe were formative, he was not an uncritical absorber of the most fashionable trends in western philosophy. It has often been claimed that Iqbal was 'influenced' by the likes of Nietszche, Bergson and Whitehead, but this does not stand up to critical scrutiny. In many ways he was condescending to western philosophy, seeing it as inferior to the insights on the human condition emanating from Islam's own heritage. He wrote to Reynold Nicholson, the celebrated Cambridge scholar of Islam, that his ideas were rooted 'in the light of the Quran, and the Muslim Sufis and thinkers'.[16]

Iqbal's philosophy unfolded in his great poems written between 1909 and 1932 – 'Asrar-i-Khudi' (The Secrets of the Self)[17] and 'Javidnama' (The Book of Immortality), written in Persian, and 'Bal-e-Jabril' (The Wings of Gabriel), 'Shikwa' (The Complaint) and 'Jawab-i-Shikwa' (The Reply to the Complaint), written in Urdu – as well as in his philosophical prose work in English, *The Reconstruction of Religious Thought in Islam*. His writings in Persian were partly meant to reach a wider Islamic audience than that of the Muslims of India alone. Later his writings would be increasingly directed at Muslim Indians, as he joined others in crafting a political future for them.

Iqbal's poetry was a reflection of his own personal philosophy relating to the dynamic individual who seeks realization through a constantly ascending arc of action directed towards the infinite goodness that is God. While Sufism sought the immersion of the self in the divine oneness, Iqbal inverted the formula, whereby the destiny of the human being is to find fulfilment not in immersion, but in the realization of God's absolute uniqueness through the uniqueness of the individual. The divine attribute of Allah's uniqueness therefore becomes a template for the dynamic individual catalyzing all other attributes which are then manifested in such an individual. Thus creativity, innovation, wisdom and justice, which are subsidiary attributes of God's uniqueness, are manifested in ever greater degrees as the individual dynamically seeks to realize his or her individuality. The passage of time becomes a series of ever more expansive possibilities as the individual proceeds along the creative path. History comes to be connected to the actions of the dynamic individual and imbued with moral content, to the extent that it generates an enhancement of the godly virtues. Iqbal believed that it was Islam that provided both the moral and spiritual foundation for the dynamic individual. This dynamism must also be responsible, and bound by the outer constraints on individual action provided by the Sharia to ensure that the pathway to self-realization is not chaotic or socially destructive. Iqbal's vision is not that of an unbound Prometheus, but rather of a Prometheus who willingly constrains his actions within a set of overarching moral and spiritual imperatives. Therefore acknowledgement of change is fundamental not only to Iqbal's theory of the dynamic individual, but also to the meaning of human purpose. The corollary is that change becomes desirable and legitimate if it is initiated by the dynamic individual acting within the framework of Islam.

Iqbal saw Islamic history as the unfolding of actions of inspired individuals, starting from the first, the Prophet Muhammad, whom he linked to the Sufi notion of the 'perfect human', complete in his clear reflection of all the virtues of the Good.

The pencil of the Self limned a hundred to-days
In order to achieve the dawn of a single tomorrow
Its flames burned a hundred Abrahams
That the lamp of one Muhammad might be lighted.[18]

Ali, the fourth of the rightly-guided caliphs and the first imam of the Shia, also features prominently in Iqbal's pantheon of perfected beings who reach spiritual attainment by an irresistible drive for action.

The pith of Life is contained in action
The delight in creation is the law of Life
Arise and create a new world![19]

Iqbal was hardly a theologian, and his attempts to create a new world view based on his own, perhaps eclectic, understanding of the ultimate purposes of the Quranic message did not quite fit the classical systems of Islam. Nevertheless, it was probably the first modern attempt by a committed Muslim to rediscover the vitality of Islam in the light of the evolution of western philosophical thought and of the realities of the new, West-dominated world. As the prominent Islamic scholar Fazlur Rahman noted, his was the first personal effort to evolve a new system of thought that was consciously seeking to be authentic in Islamic terms – as authentic in its own way as, say, the medieval theology of al-Asha'ari, who laid down most of the main creedal doctrines of Sunni Islam.[20]

Iqbal's influence on his times, especially in providing the intellectual justification for establishing a state for Muslims in the sub-continent, has been subject to a great deal of controversy. There is, however, little doubt that his literary, metaphysical and political concerns framed the main problems of Muslims in an entirely new light in the modern period. How practical – or realizable – his philosophy of the dynamic individual could be was another matter. But Iqbal tried, and to a large extent succeeded, in giving his generation of Muslims, especially in the sub-continent, a huge boost of self-confidence. In his seminal address to the All-India Muslim League in 1930,[21] he laid out the basic principles of the Islam he believed in. 'Islam is itself Destiny and will not suffer a destiny!' – he proclaimed. He resisted the national or racial idea as a substitute for the loyalty of Muslims, and took direct issue with Renan's construct of a nation: 'The national idea is racializing the outlook of Muslims, and thus materially counteracting the humanizing work of Islam. And the growth of racial consciousness may mean the growth of standards different and even opposed to the standards of Islam.'

Iqbal was also dubious about the possibility – or desirability – of a Lutheran-style reformation in Islam that would lead to the separation of religion from the public arena. The prophetic experience in Islam necessarily implied the building of a social order.

It [the prophetic experience] is individual experience creative of a social order. Its immediate outcome is . . . a polity with implicit legal concepts whose significance cannot be belittled merely because their origin is revelational. The religious ideal of Islam, therefore, is organically related to the social order which it has created . . . The construction of a polity on national lines, if it means displacement of the Islamic principle of solidarity, is simply unthinkable to a Muslim.

In the same address, Iqbal raises the demand that Muslims of North-West India, roughly the area covered by today's Pakistan, should form a consolidated state of their own.

Iqbal created a spiritual universe which combined the apparently contradictory elements that preoccupied Muslim minds for more than a millennium: the issue of free will and that of predestination. The individual in Iqbal's world can only be a realized being if he or she strives for perfection through moral action. The individual thus has the possibility of absolute agency if that person fulfils the pattern of divine uniqueness through the dynamically active self. Iqbal's philosophy stands in marked contrast to the accusations of passivity which were attached to the Sufis of Islam's later period. The reality, however, is that Iqbal used the model of spiritual ascent through various stages of realization which is implicit in all the Sufi mystical orders, but he externalized the spiritual drive, from an inward to an outward journey. Iqbal's spiritual person is supremely active, but also always grounded in the ethical precepts of the religion of Islam. It is a public unfolding of spiritual realization through rightly guided action. Iqbal shifted the focus of his reconstruction of Islamic life squarely back to the individual, whom he treated as the main agent of change and growth.

Iqbal died in 1938, ten years before the founding of the state of Pakistan as a homeland for India's Muslims. His last Urdu poem, entitled 'Hazrat-i-Insan' ('The Human Being'), included the line:

This world is an invitation for the human being to look; for every secret is given an instinct to jump out of its closet
they are the tears of human blood that the Almighty has used for stirring storms in His oceans.

It ends thus:

If I am the end of all, then what lies beyond? Where lies the limit of my unending adventures?[22]

The connections between the Muslims of the Indian sub-continent and the Ottoman Caliphate were long-standing and deep. The *Khilafat* (caliphate) movement in India started as a call to safeguard this venerable institution from its possible abolition by the victorious allies in the First World War.[23] However, the movement was more to do with the political organization of India's Muslims, and it was an instrument supported by Ghandi for joint Muslim–Hindu action in the struggle against the British Raj. When the caliphate was finally abolished, this was effected by the radical secularists of the new Republic of Turkey led by Mustafa Kemal, and not by the British.

The Indian *Khilafat* movement was left high and dry, and its leaders retreated back into their strictly parochial concerns. They could neither reverse nor soften the absolute determination of Mustafa Kemal and his allies radically to overhaul the entire bases of Turkish society and culture and cast them in an entirely western mode. It was left to a dwindling band of Islamically minded figures, working under incredibly adverse conditions, to confront the might of a powerful centralizing state and the iron will of its leader, Mustafa Kemal. The most significant among these figures was Badiuzzaman Said Nursi. His life and work crystallized the dilemmas and challenges facing the piously minded as the structures of their world were being systematically dismantled. The course these Islamically minded people followed and the movements they founded played a central part in the survival of Islamic consciousness both in the individual and in the group, under the harsh rule of secular, even atheistic, regimes.

Said Nursi was born in the village of Nurs in eastern Anatolia, of Kurdish parentage, in 1877. He later divided his life into two periods: the 'Old Nursi' and the 'New Nursi', roughly paralleling the last years of the Ottoman Empire and the founding of the Republic of Turkey. In the 'Old Nursi' Said was a precocious, somewhat arrogant, young man, who delighted in debating with religious scholars. He moved to the capital Istanbul in 1907, partly to secure official support for his project for a university in eastern Anatolia. There his path crossed with the Young Turks, whose call for a constitutional government he initially supported. During the First World War he was made a regimental commander on the Turkish eastern front, was captured by the Russians, made a successful escape, and returned to a hero's welcome in Istanbul in June 1918 as the Ottoman Empire was facing final defeat. In 1920, while visiting the cemetery of the Companion of the Prophet Abu Ayub al-Ansari on the outskirts of Istanbul, Nursi had a significant spiritual experience, where he recognized that the old order had died, and his old self with it. The 'New Nursi' was born.[24]

Nursi's work with Islamic associations and groups, and his war hero status, provided him with several invitations to Ankara, where the Turkish Grand National Assembly had congregated to chart out the contours of the new republic. Nursi was dismayed by the overt secularism, irreligiousness and western orientation of the officers and officials who dominated the proceedings, and felt that Islam was being marginalized, and even targeted, in the new order. 'When I came to Ankara in 1338 [1923], the morale of the people of faith was extremely high as a result of the victory of the army of Islam over the Greeks. But I saw that an abominable current of atheism was treacherously attempting to subvert, poison, and destroy their morale,' he would write later.[25] He had several altercations with Mustafa Kemal, finally abandoning Ankara to the new political class.

Within a few years, Turkey was remade in the vision of its new leaders. The caliphate was abolished; Islam was disestablished; the Sufi orders were banned; the *ulema* class was disbanded; Islamic dress was forbidden; the alphabet changed from the old Arabic script to the Roman script; religious education was deliberately ignored; and Islamic law was replaced by European civil and criminal codes. The destruction of Islam's presence in Turkey seemed only a matter of time.

Nursi began his decades-long work to develop a vision of Islam and an understanding of the Quran that preserved the vitality of the faith for the community of Muslims in Turkey during its times of greatest adversity and danger. The Turkish state was actually at war with the Ottoman past, especially with its Islamic legacy, which flew in the face of the mantra of the new order: to be modern, secular, nationalist and European. The Kemalist state relentlessly hounded Nursi, who struggled in the face of exile, frequent arrests and imprisonment, and incessant harassments by the authorities. It was during this period that he compiled the greatest work of his life, which had the most profound influence on generations of Muslims: the *Risale-i Nur*, or *The Epistles of Light*.[26]

The *Risale* consists of a series of treatises on the Quran. They are not so much exegeses as flashes of insights, allegories and arguments, whose objective is to set out proof for the divine existence and unity. They are addressed to an audience which Nursi presupposes to have been infected with the virus of unbelief or scepticism, or to be enamoured with the promises of science and materialist basis of modernity. The work aims to fortify the reader in light of the positivist and materialist philosophies of the new order in Turkey, and by inference elsewhere in the Muslim world, to reaffirm the foundations of faith and Islam's ultimate veracity. Nursi was critical of the traditional Islamic schools, the *madrassas*, and their ossified approach to the teaching of religious doctrines. He knew that they would not be able to provide the necessary intellectual instruments for a reinvigorated Islam, especially under the siege conditions of republican Turkey. His *Risale* was just such an instrument. It would infuse the reader with a spirituality that would reach both the reader's reason and heart. He believed that the *Risale* would allow the reader to affirm his or her belief in Islam and respond to the barrage of irreligiosity emanating from the state and the new cultural and educational elite of the country. The *Risale* is not political, except by being subversively insistent on Islam at a time when the state had chosen to enforce a radical *laïcité*. It was this feature of Nursi's work, together with the fact that circles of followers were using his treatises to continue their engagement with Islam, that drove the authorities to arrest and imprison Nursi on numerous occasions until his death in 1960.

The *Risale* has no particular order or logical structure. It covers nearly the entire gamut of the doctrines and creeds of Islam, explained or refor- mulated according to Nursi's own unique method and style. There are considerable digressions into philosophy, classical Islamic mysticism, musings on the nature of science and on the Quranic message. Nursi uses the form of questions and answers as a didactic tool to provide proof for his readers for all the axiomatic assertions of Islam and of the Quran – including the miracle of the Quran itself, the ascension of the Prophet Muhammad and divine unity. The last section of the *Risale*, entitled 'The Thirty-Third Word', summarizes Nursi's belief that the entire cosmos and the individual point unerringly towards the existence of divine unity: 'I hope this thirty-third word ... may help an unbeliever to accept belief, and that it may strengthen the belief of one whose belief is weak.'

In many ways, the *Risale* was meant to be the foundation text for study circles whose cumulative experience with it would add to, and refine, Nursi's main arguments. Nursi emphatically denied that he was starting a new Sufi *tariqa*, which was one of the charges laid against him by the authorities. In fact he often stated that the time of the classical *tariqas* had ended. But his work is intensely didactic, and is structured so as to be read, discussed and acted upon. At the start of his exile Nursi had neither any personal resources nor a large body of followers. As the *Risale* took shape, it would be circulated among small groups of local people and then labo- riously transmitted through hand copies, in an early form of samizdat.[27] It was read by ever-growing numbers of people who connected with its message – couched in optimistic, constructive and positive tones – rather than with the author. Throughout this period, Nursi, while not being completely self-effacing, would encourage his students (for that is what he called his readers) to concentrate on the text, and not on its author. Inculcating belief in the truth of the Quran and Islam was more important to him than the creation of any political movement or party. He saw his work as one of infusing a new moral consciousness into, or re-moralizing, Muslims as they confronted the tide of aggressive secularism represented by the new Turkish state. They could then assist in creating an environ- ment where Islam and its ethic could gradually seep back into the public space through the actions of rightly guided people. Their duty was to sustain and nourish their belief, and not to confront the far superior force of a militantly secular government.

As their numbers increased, Nursi believed that Muslims' intensive exposure to the Quran and to Islam through his teachings would create a powerful
momentum and a force for change. It was a brilliant and inspired mechanism
for ensuring the spread of a message through a wide spectrum of small
groups – what might be called 'micro-structures' – which could coalesce into
a 'movement', but which had none of the hierarchical structures or charismatic leadership that guide such mass organizations, and no identifiable
political programme. The open structures of the movement were an essential
feature of the community that Nursi and his followers envisaged. They were
the most effective and durable methods to 're-moralize' individuals and
communities.

Nursi was not against the secular system *per se*, which he understood
to express the state's neutrality towards contending belief systems. He
was against a state which was actively and harmfully irreligious – against
secularism as a cult, or as a religion in its own right. Nursi's work set the
stage for the subsequent emergence of Islam as a social and political force
in Turkey, and tinged it with its characteristic moderation. The *Nur*
movement – the name given to the groups following the teachings of the
Risale – both grew and fractured after Nursi's death in 1960. But its legacy
included the rise of powerful civil society organizations such as the educational movement associated with Fethullah Gulen, a Nursi follower in
his youth. Parts of the *Nur* movement organized themselves for political
action, in spite of Nursi's warnings about the dangers of Islamic political
parties in an age when society was not yet reconstituted along moral lines.

The Resilience of Islamic Loyalties

In the two decades after the end of the Second World War, the retreat of
Islam further into the private domain seemed irreversible. The establishment of the state of Pakistan in 1947 as a homeland for India's Muslims
appeared to reverse the process. After all, here was a state whose entire
raison d'être was the Islamic identity of its people.

'You have demanded Pakistan on the ground of your being Muslims,
and on this ground alone,' said Muhammad Asad, the Austro-Jewish
convert formerly known as Leopold Weiss, in a radio broadcast on
Pakistan radio in September 1947.[28] The founding of Pakistan was greeted
by pan-Islamists everywhere as a huge victory heralding the impending
return of Islam to the public arena. In fact it was nothing of the sort.
Pakistan soon fell under the sway of the military–bureaucratic–feudal

classes, and Islamic political parties were left as spoilers and kept outside the political process. The Arab world, Iran, and South-East Asia were all under the control of leaders and parties who were either indifferent or hostile to the idea of broadening Islam's role in the public sphere. Even in Turkey, which had a mild relapse from its harsh policies of secularization under the decade-old premiership of Adnan Menderes,[29] the relaxation of the state's hostility towards Islam ended in tragedy. Menderes was executed after a 1960 coup launched by young army officers.

As the 1960s were drawing to a close, the disjunction between the verities of Islam and the world that modern Muslims were creating seemed to put an end to the idea of Islam as a vital world civilization. The developing chasm appeared unbridgeable. Traditional Islam seemed relegated to folk memory, even though few Muslim states would explicitly acknowledge their abandonment of Islam as an element of their identity. The past was buried – or at least that was what some of the Islamic world's most acute observers said. Enough doubt about Islam had been sown in the minds of people that an arch-secularist, Habib Bourguiba, the president of Tunisia, could have himself filmed in 1960, in the fasting month of Ramadan, with a glass of orange juice in his hand. A particularly bilious article denouncing Islam appeared in the Syrian military's magazine in 1969 – something which had previously been unthinkable. Islam belongs to the museums, the author wrote. And, even though the article was followed by disturbances and protest and the author (and editor) was jailed, this appeared, to all intents and purposes, to be a trial balloon. If the times were not propitious for burying a religion which was deemed anachronistic and irrelevant, then sooner rather than later such an opportunity would arise again.

Of course, matters did not quite turn out the way the apostles of progress and modernity had expected, and for this reason we have to ask how, in the space of less than a few years – roughly from the mid-1970s onwards – Islam would reappear as possibly the single most significant determinant of people's loyalties and identities throughout the Muslim world. The dormant, apparently fatally wounded civilization sprang to life in ways that no one had (or could have) foreseen. How could decades of secularism, military cliques and one-party ideological states, strident nationalist propaganda, ruling groups that fancied themselves to be modernizing educational systems modelled after the West, and increasing integration into world economies – how could all these factors fail to create an irresistible momentum, which would mark the death knell for Islam's world view?

The resilience of Islam, after nearly two centuries of unequal engagement with the West, escaped many. It was implicit that the juggernaut of technology and the West's preponderance in nearly every field of human endeavour would overwhelm the civilizational reality of Islam. 'Islam as an identifiable institutional tradition may not last indefinitely,' wrote Marshall Hodgson at the end of his magisterial work *The Venture of Islam*, published posthumously in 1974. The civilization would be 'secularized', and would survive as one of the creative sources of a culture where people had long ceased being Muslims. The historian Albert Hourani, who was more focused on the Arabs than on Islam *per se*, did not veer too far from the same conclusion. Islam could not outlast modernity and ultimately would sink in the face of the new loyalties springing up everywhere. There was no answer to the challenges of modern times except through the framework of the institutions and perspectives of the western world. It was in the West that modernity arose, and it was there that the implications of modernity on individuals and societies were being addressed.[30]

Islam suffered consecutive blows in many Muslim lands, in the long period which started after the First World War and culminated in the 1970s. The state was recast in any which form, without any popular sanction. The decision to expropriate agricultural land or to abolish religious foundations undermined the economic bases of Islamic institutions. Muslims were taught that they were now uniquely Arabs or Turks or Iranians and that they should attach greater or even exclusive loyalty to these ethnicities, because that was the way into joining the ranks of the rich and powerful. Their education would be managed so as to inculcate in them the new definitions of citizenship, progress, enlightenment – all derived from the prevailing ethos of the advanced countries.

However, the mechanisms for affecting individuals and managing their transformation so as to make them fit with the outer schema of things were both crude and ill-judged. The recovery of Islam in people's consciousness is only partly due to the failure of the systems which replaced the Islamic polity – and, later, colonial territories – to offer a modicum of continuity and meaning to their populations. More importantly, these systems never achieved the desired legitimacy in the minds of Muslims, so as to be able realistically to replace the older loyalties. Eighty years of the most intensive and determined drive to westernize and secularize Turkey could not erase the powerful hold that Islam still has on people's sensibilities. Egypt-as-Europe could not survive the Second World War, and it is now an affectation of a small section of the ruling class. Arab nationalism crashed with the defeats of the 1967 war. The Algerian socialist revolutionaries, heroes to the entire Third World after their victory in 1962, turned into a corrupt and brutal kleptocracy. The Iranian monarchy of the Pahlevis appropriated the legacy of ancient Persia to create a new ethos, only to see itself buried by the Islamic Revolution of 1979.

Of course, some of the changes that overcame the Islamic world during this period have stuck and are now acknowledged as both valid and meaningful. The nation–state is unlikely to be replaced as the primary political unit for Muslims in the short term. Neither will the heightened awareness of ethnic and linguistic differences between Muslims. But these changes will all have to contend with the primordial loyalty that individual Muslims have clearly demonstrated for Islam. The significance of this is clear. The re-evaluation of the premises of life that modernity has imposed on Muslims has not yet led to a complete cleavage from that sense of the sacred which the allegiance to the religion of Islam implies. The physical and spiritual realms that Muslims inhabit cannot be neatly separated, even though modern life seems to make it a precondition that the two are kept distinct. The return of Islam into people's consciousness, which has been dramatically demonstrated since the mid-1970s, should not have been a surprise. Islam never left people's minds. The return was not caused by the growth of political Islam or by the Islamists' coming to power in a number of countries. In many ways, political Islam is antithetical to the spiritualized individual. It is the individual who has kept open the possibility of reaching a new equilibrium in Muslim societies by refusing to acknowledge that spiritual impoverishment was a necessary by-product of material advancement – an equilibrium which did not stray too far from the spiritual dimensions of Islam.

The French essayist and novelist Julien Benda wrote a short tract in 1927, entitled *La Trahison des clercs* (*The Betrayal of the Intellectuals*), about the failure of Europe's intellectual elites to stem the growth of extreme nationalism and militarism in the inter-war years. He accused them of abandoning the ideals of their vocation and immersing themselves in proselytizing through theories of race, nation and class. An equivalent charge might easily be laid at the feet of the Muslim intellectual class. But the sources of western culture were at best superficially understood by this class. There was a constant tension between their adoption of the mode of thought and analysis of the occidental mind and the harsh realities of the political, cultural and economic dependence of their countries. The drift from Islam was often accompanied by a belated recognition of the merits of the civilization itself, especially when Islamic themes of justice and equality appeared more reasoned and more certain than their western counterparts. Islamic socialism, that strange hybrid which achieved a brief prominence in the 1950s and 1960s, was just such an attempt to merge a pre-eminently western notion of socialism with Islam's egalitarian drive. Even the great westerniser Taha Hussein would revise some of his theories as Europe descended into war, when he took a renewed interest in Islam's potential for human renewal and reform.[31]

The age when the verities of Islam faced their most concerted questioning lasted roughly from the end of the First World War to the mid-1970s. The Islamic world was coming under sustained assault from nearly all points of the compass. Islamic civilizational space had already been disrupted in the nineteenth century by colonial expansion and conquest, and the period after the First World War started with the dismantling of its last empire, the Ottoman state. In rapid order, the modern world encroached on the minds, hearts and perspectives of people. New ways of thinking forced themselves on the Muslim mind, eliciting a huge spectrum of responses, from total rejection, to bewilderment, to enthusiastic adoption. It was the likes of Iqbal and Said Nursi that strove to redefine the parameters of a response which, they believed, was grounded in an authentic understanding of Islam: the heroic model of Iqbal's inspired individual and the re-moralized community of Nursi. Both were emblematic of their time. Iqbal sought to regain the Muslim's self-confidence as he or she saw the power and grandeur of the past and compared it to the abject realities of the present state of dependency, foreign control and marginalization. Nursi confronted a different challenge: not so much the enemy without as the enemy within – the cumulative, subtle, and not so subtle, pressures to abandon religious faith and belief in Islam as either harmful or immaterial to societal advancement into the modern world.

The echoes of the crises of those times continue into the present era, but the landscape has changed significantly. The '-isms' of those times – socialism, communism, nationalism, statism – entered and exited the Islamic world, losing their ideological fervour but leaving some traces behind. The new pressures, however, would be equally relentless in the Islamic world.

CHAPTER 3

The Counter-Revolt of Islam

The poisonous culture of imperialism is penetrating to the depths of towns and villages throughout the Muslim world, displacing the culture of the Quran . . . Invoking Islam and pretending to be Muslims, they [the leaders of Muslim states] strive to annihilate Islam, and they abolish and obliterate the sacred commands of the Quran one after the other.

Ayatollah Khomeini in a message circulated to pilgrims in February, 1971

The sad dismemberment of Islam's last universal state, the Ottoman Empire, followed within fifty years by the dissolution of the European colonial empires, completed the transformation of Islam's political space into nation–states. Even though the mass at large continued to have a powerful affinity with Islam, it was the ruling and mainly secular elites that dominated the new nation–states and their political agendas. Islam was pushed, at least officially, well into the background. By the end of the 1950s, the world of Islam appeared to be well on its way towards entering the final stages of its transformation according to the norms of a modernizing and industrializing world. The issues were adaptation and adjustment. Muslims could choose, theoretically at least, their pathway into the modern world, but the choice was not one between Islam and the others. That argument had already been settled – or so it seemed. It was now more a matter of which claims would prevail: those of the western democracies, the Soviet bloc, or home-grown variants of radical nationalism and socialism. Traditional societies were everywhere in retreat.[1] Bluntly put, Islam was a relic of the past and would survive only as a private faith and a loose set of moral and ethical principles. 'Mosque-going' would follow church-going, and Islam would succumb to the laws of social, economic and cultural progress.

Islam's 'Irrelevance'

It was taken for granted that the Judaeo-Christian tradition framed the development of the West and its intellectual tradition, and that the modern world was an outcome of this legacy. But in the period leading up to the 1970s there was still doubt regarding the possibility of Islam accepting the essential changes to its character which modernity implied. The traditionalism that was seen to be embedded in Islam's social, religious and family structures was too deep and ancient to accommodate the demands of modernity. Islam therefore had to be bypassed. Islam was thus a phase, and not a platform for the evolution into the modern world of those loosely categorized as Muslims.[2] Of course, in the titanic struggle between the West and the Soviet bloc, the West sought to draw on the political support of Islam, which was by definition opposed to the atheistic aspects of communism. But this did not deflect from the ultimate fate of Islam as a separate pole of power and civilization in its own right. The 'clash of civilizations' would come later.

The post-colonial order bequeathed a series of nation–states in the Muslim world that belonged firmly to what was then called the Third World. A variety of militant secularists, radical nationalists, revolutionary socialists, military dictators and demagogues ruled most of the Muslim world. Islam became subsumed into this Third World, or, as Fernand Braudel wrote, rather cruelly but accurately, 'Islam relapsed into that inferno or purgatory of living humanity that we euphemistically call the Third World'.[3] The exceptions were the traditional Arab monarchies and the Pahlevi dynasty in Iran. The former had already been consigned to a fate of oblivion for its supposed backwardness and obscurantism. The Iranian Empire, though, fancied itself as a radical modernizer in the Meiji sense, while at the same time embodying the legacy of Iran's pre-Islamic past.

The relationship between Islam and the new radical and modernizing ethos was troubling. By the 1970s the myriad Muslim nation–states had become far stronger and more centralized. The more radical of them were determined to refashion their citizens' loyalties and identities at breakneck speed. They adopted post-war ideologies, mainly derived from the European left. These were invariably imposed on society at large by a dominant intellectual and political class, and were frequently applied coercively. Left behind was the moral glue which kept society functioning and the inherent heterogeneity – or, in fashionable parlance, pluralism – which was a feature of Islamic societies. The drive to impose a particularistic non-Islamic, or even un-Islamic, agenda on these new nation–states was breathless and sweeping. At first this affected only a small portion of society, primarily urban dwellers. Thus the imposition of state ownership on huge swathes of the economies of these countries, through nationalizations or expropriations, only affected foreign capitalists and the small indigenous business class. Inculcations of the new values of nation, race and class through the educational system could not amount to much in the short term, given that most people existed as rural dwellers, on the margins, and were mostly illiterate. But it was bound to have a cumulative effect as more people were drawn into the increasing number of modern schools.

The crucibles of wars and of economic, social and cultural struggles, extended over a long and continuous period of time, were an absolutely essential component of the evolution of modern western societies. These ingredients were simply not present in the Muslim world when it was subjected to the modernizing schemes of its new elites. The uneven and often shallow roots that these notions put down in Muslim societies coexisted uneasily with the patterns of the past. They were neither completely rejected nor absorbed constructively, leaving an awkward and barren blend of the two worlds as their legacy. This was a far cry from Islam's creative encounter with the Hellenistic and Persian worlds in the early stages of its expansion into a world civilization. At the same time, external threats and internal failures compounded the sense that the unprecedented changes through which Muslim societies were passing were not leading to the promised land of material abundance and to the regaining of Muslims' dignity and strength. The secularizing and modernizing experience of the early to mid-twentieth century turned out to be a prelude to something else. This period, when the transformation of the Islamic world was being confidently predicted, was simply an interregnum.

Of course, few people could have predicted the evolution of Islam from the 1970s onwards, the resilience of the Islamic world view and the turn to extreme radicalism. In the interregnum, especially during the period after decolonization, political Islam was hardly the force it would later become. Even states which were avowedly 'Islamic' – such as Pakistan, which was founded on the theory that the Muslims of India were an identifiable nation – were dominated by a secularized elite and by the military. The two largest Islamist political parties of the times, the Muslim Brotherhood in Egypt[4] and the Jama'at Islami in Pakistan,[5] did not seriously threaten the political order. They may have come close to it in Egypt, but the state's ferocious response after the attempt on the life of the Egyptian leader Gamal Abdel Nasser in 1954 effectively removed them for a long time as a serious challenge to the military-led regime. There were earlier social action groups which drew their inspiration, including their political ideology, from Islam and from the ideas of Salafist reformers, but their scope and organization were far more constrained. All these earlier groups were studiously non-political, in that they did not directly challenge the colonial authorities and were mainly concerned with warding off threats to the Islamic identity of their countrymen in the face of colonial deracination policies; and with a slackening or loss of religious practice and consciousness among them. However, both the Muslim Brotherhood and the Jama'at Islami were a new type of political organization. They evolved an ideology which was mainly premised on the revival of Sharia as the best and surest way to re-establish the primacy of Islam in state and society. The antidote to modernism, secularism and nationalism was the return of the Sharia as the fulcrum of a revitalized Islamic political world. A call for the explicit conjoining of Sharia and state became the foundation of the new idea of an 'Islamic state'. This was one of the key components of the worldwide phenomenon that made up the 'Islamic awakening', which has preoccupied the world for the better part of the last thirty years.

The Revolt of Islam

The revolt of Islam – which was in reality more of a counter-revolution against the cumulative effects of two centuries of retreat – had been gathering momentum during the entire period when Islam's prospects appeared most bleak. At first the revolt unfolded in small increments, but later in spectacular fashion. These increments took myriad forms: a dramatic popular revolution, reminiscent of the great revolutions of history; a successful *jihad*, which helped to bring down the Soviet superpower; the visible and vocal rejection, by a large number of Muslims, of the verities of secular modernity; the sudden reappearance of Islamic norms and constructs in the public life of Muslims and Islamic societies. Leaders of Muslim states were shocked by the power of this revitalized

Islam and by the threats it posed to the established ruling groups. Governments and societies in the West had to contend with it in their very midst. Communities which had hitherto remained invisible and were written off as hopelessly outside the *zeitgeist* sprang into life with a stunning (if often reactionary) vitality. This was especially true of the often angry second generation of Muslim immigrants to western Europe, who had not been or would not be assimilated. The international order was jolted by the need to accommodate or contain its geopolitical expression. But the Islam which emerged had been fundamentally affected by the experiences of the past decades.

The hesitant and defensive Islam, which marked the years when all the structures of the old Islamic order were being dismantled or challenged, appeared to have altered in unimaginable ways. The image of a Muslim world which was thrashing around in order to avoid the fate of irrelevance had become established in the West. But within a decade, the entire perspective would change.

The revolt of Islam which started in the 1970s was the first event that swept the entire Muslim world since the advent of the modern age. In less than a decade it put its mark on nearly every Muslim country, as well as on the ever-growing world of Muslims in the West. It was not concentrated in one area, neither did it revolve around a single ethnic or linguistic group. This was a matter of civilization rather than of nationality or culture. The issues that affected each particular component of global Muslim society might have been profoundly different, but they had a common unifying thread which was played out against a shared background. The accumulation of anguish at nearly two centuries of constant retreat and misrule by native elites who were disconnected, in fact and spirit, from Islam's legacy burst forth in a number of ways and and through a number of channels.

What appeared to be confusion of thought and a surfeit of reactions was in fact the natural response of an intricate system trying to adjust to severe external and internal jolts which threatened all aspects of its existence and survival. The revolt of Islam was partly the result of a new generation's emergence on to the political and social landscape. It looked afresh at modernity, western ideology and political notions, and re-read Islam's legacy and history. A re-invention of Islam, the better to manage the transition of its societies into a position of power and respect in the world, was taking place. But this was not, and could not be, a total make-over of the civilization, even though the revolutionaries of the time thought that it was.[6]

Islam's developing response was taking place in four distinct arenas: ideas; institutions; the social; and the political. In each of these areas, the prompting came from the continuing challenges of the modern world and at the same time from the internal conditions within Muslim lands themselves.

The defensive Islam of the interregnum could not offer a basis for counter-attack. The call for a return to the faith was an insufficient retort to the obvious seeping of vitality, power and authority from the world of Islam. Realization of the absence of the divine from modern western experience required a sea change in the perspectives of Muslims, if they were to come to terms with its consequences. The self-serving platitude that the West was 'materialist' while the East was 'spiritual' did not offer a programme either for material or spiritual advancement. At best, it might have encouraged an increased piety or a self-absorbed religiosity. At worst, it led to the vague thinking which sought to 'spiritualize' western institutions without understanding the wellsprings of these institutions and their anchoring in the specific historical experience of the West.

To some extent this was recognized by the reformers of the late nineteenth and early twentieth centuries. They, with only a limited exposure to, and understanding of, the West, sought to reinterpret the basis of Islamic knowledge and experience so as to come to terms with what they perceived to be the West's strengths: its rationality and science. But the Islamic thinkers and reformers of the interregnum were operating in an entirely different landscape. They had to contend with ruling classes who were committed not only to modernizing but often to westernizing their societies. These elites, unlike those of the nineteenth and early twentieth centuries, mainly rejected the possibility that Islam would provide a gateway into the modern world. Moreover, they adopted notions such as nationalism, both as a governing ideology and as an alternative to the Islamic loyalties of their people. Thus the Islamic thinkers of the period of the interregnum were doubly challenged. They had to confront both this internal reality, where Islam was often rejected as an organizing principle for society, and a purely external challenge, which emanated from the western and communist worlds.

A Vanishing Vitality

The interregnum thinkers were greatly affected by their direct encounter with colonialism and with Marxist determinism. The colonial experience crystallized the civilizational aspects of the triumph of the West. This triumph was seen in stark terms when the realities of conqueror and conquered were laid side by side and measured against each other. Islam, or at least its civilizational component, was found wanting. This was the position of the Algerian thinker, moral philosopher and educationalist Malek Bennabi (1905–73). He evolved a complex theory of the rise and fall of civilizations and set the West's dominance over Islam in terms of the Muslims' propensity to allow their minds to be colonized – his thesis of *colonisabilité*.[7] Probably more so than any other systematic Islamic thinker of the modern period, Bennabi brings the focus of civilizational regeneration squarely back to Man as an individual actor and agent. His concerns were, unusually, non-political; he was one of the few thinkers of the times whose constructs were not directly related to the seizure of political power or control of the state. He was the last of the pre-radical thinkers of his generation, being overtaken in influence by the rise of the ideologies of political Islam and its proponents. Apart from the originality of his thought, he stands out among his peers through his willingness to delve into individual conduct and perception as a precondition for successful societal and cultural regeneration.

According to Bennabi, all civilizations arise as a result of a religious principle which articulates the contours of the civilization. Religion organizes the vital forces of human beings and moves them from being dominated by their animal drives and survival instincts to a level where these are tamed under the spiritual domain of religion. In Islam, this phase corresponded to the prophetic period and its immediate aftermath. It culminated in what Bennabi called the 'age of the spirit'. As the civilization expands, it also increases in complexity and resources, opening the second stage of civilizational progress, the 'age of reason'. This phase weakens the original religious impulse, and society begins to lose its commitment to the moral precepts of its religious base, even as it extends itself materially and intellectually. Nature reasserts its control over the individual and society, gradually reducing the civilization's vitality and leading to its decay and retrogression. Societal bonds gradually unravel, ending the civilizational cycle. 'Intelligence is constantly the function of the spirit: when the latter no longer possesses its purity, the former no longer has all its depth,' Bennabi wrote.

Bennabi avers that there are two phases which mark the evolution of mankind: the pre-civilizational and post-civilizational. In the former, human beings have the *potential* for creating a civilization, such as the pre-Islamic Arabs; in the post-civilizational phase, human beings have lost the capacity for civilizational action. Muslims are now in a condition where their civilizational power is exhausted. They are entrapped in 'the deadly syllogism "We are Muslims, therefore we are perfect", which tends to sap all perfectibility in the individual by neutralizing in him all concern for attaining perfection,' he wrote.[8] Society breeds immobilized individuals who are mired in their mediocrity, inaction and pride. These form the new moral elite of post-civilizational Islamic man. Moral paralysis leads to intellectual paralysis. Thought petrifies 'in a world which no more reasons, since its reasoning has no longer a social object.'[9]

Bennabi traces back that period of the beginning of the Muslim decline to the collapse of the Almohad dynasty (*Almuwahidun* in Arabic) in North Africa and Spain in the eleventh century. That point in time marks an inflection in the evolution of Islamic society whereby the civilizational *élan* goes into reverse. Muslims begin to lose their creative vitality, partly because of their inordinate success. In some respects Bennabi's observation mirrors Gibbon's remarks on the decline of the Roman Empire: 'The decline of Rome was the natural and inevitable effect of immoderate greatness. Prosperity ripened the principle of decay; the cause of the destruction multiplied with the extent of conquest; and, as soon as time or accident had removed the artificial supports, the stupendous fabric yielded to the pressure of its own weight.'[10] Bennabi's thesis is not entirely cyclical, for it presupposes that effort would be needed to bring post-civilization man back to his pre-civilization potential. The imprint of the great fourteenth-century Muslim philosopher of history Ibn Khaldun is clearly here.

Whatever one thinks of Bennanbi's theory of the rise and fall of civilizations, it is his assessments as to what the conditions are for Islam's civilizational revitalization that are the more apt. He establishes a formula whereby civilizational action is composed of a triad of elements: the human factor; the resources at society's disposal; and the effects of time. The catalyzing agent of all three is the religious drive. Bennabi's theory applies to all civilizations and it presents the Judaeo-Christian tradition as the central element of the West's civilization. The combination of the necessary elements for civilizational action becomes inert when a civilization has lost its catalyzing energy. The loss of the religious drive in Muslim societies – specifically, the loss of moral precepts for societal and individual action – has driven Muslims societies to become entirely dependent on the products and processes of other civilizations' works. Dependence and impoverishment are the inevitable consequences.

The building of human relations in functioning societies follows a related pattern. The socialized individual – or person (*shakhs* in Arabic) – joins the universe of ideas and matter to form the components of society. Bennabi lays a great stress on the endurance of vital ideas as the main element in the revitalization of broken societies. He gives as an example the rise of Germany from the ashes of war when the element of matter (or resources) had been destroyed. However, ideas by themselves are insufficient for the survival of societies if human bonds have been weakened. The overwhelming of Muslim Andalusia by the less intellectually developed Spanish Catholics was due to the latter's greater advantage in social cohesion. In a most telling metaphor, Bennabi compares modern Islamic societies 'to a rider who has lost control over the stirrup and failed to recapture it'. Islamic civilization, he writes,

is blown off course by contradictory and conflicting ideas: on the one hand, the ideas which put it face to face with the problems of technological civilization without establishing real contacts with the roots of that civilization and, on the other, the ideas which link it to its original cultural universe without embracing the archetypes of this universe . . .'

A key element in Bennabi's construct is the idea of *colonisabilité*, or the propensity to accept uncritically the norms, values and precepts of dominant or conquering civilizations. He considers Islamic societies in their 'post-civilization' phase to be particularly vulnerable to this charge. Muslims would not have been so thoroughly imbued with western notions had they not already been prone to accept them. Civilizations that are overwhelmed have already been defeated before the direct encounter with the dominant powers ever takes place. Their vitality has been lost and they are easy prey. The dominant civilization need not actually embark on physical conquest to achieve its objectives. The colonized society and, more importantly, the colonized individual have succumbed to the norms of the conqueror, often with little or no resistance.

Bennabi was, of course, greatly influenced by the Algerian experience, but his thesis is presented as a universally valid construct. Nevertheless, Bennabi was not uniformly pessimistic about the future of Islamic civilization. The seeds of rebirth were scattered, but they often fell on ill-prepared ground. The efforts of the nineteenth-century reformers and modernizers have left little of consequence, but at least they kept open the possibilities for reversing the process. 'The reformist movement did not know how to transform the Muslim soul or to translate into reality the "social function" of the religion [but] it did succeed in breaking the static equilibrium of the [post-civilization Muslim] epoch,' he wrote.[11] The call to return to the pristine past of early Islam did not, however, lead to a return to the consciousness of the early Muslims, but to the theologies and disputations of medieval Islam. Bennabi also had profound observations to make on the culture of rights and demands which had displaced the sense of duty and obligations inherent in Islam. Even projects that may appear to entail a 'return' to Islamic life, such as the call to reinstate the Sharia, are couched as political demands, irrespective of whether the individual applies the conditions of Sharia to his or her own conduct. The Muslim world becomes denuded by grand schemes and projects which are then expressed as political demands, while the need is for a series of smaller, even personal, changes in perspective and behaviour which may collectively produce an environment more conducive to societal regeneration.

It is from this perspective that Bennabi presents his proposals for the recreation of the moral Islamic person through a broad cultural programme. He presents culture as a unifying force which allows entirely disparate people to share in a common response to matters that affect society at large. He recognized, of course, that the problems of Muslim societies are partly caused by the discontinuities which exist between the culture of the elites and that of the common man, discontinuities which, over time, have widened to the point where the two sets of people inhabit different worlds, often not even sharing a common language. Once again, his reference point is the North African countries which emerged out of the French colonial empires and their Francophone elites. But his arguments can easily extend to other parts of the Muslim world, where the issues of language and cultural expression have yet to be dealt with.

Bennabi's sensibilities never reached a wide audience in the Muslim world, mainly because his programme was not couched in political terms. His concern with the development of an aesthetic sensibility in the Muslim mind was lost on his contemporaries. His understanding of work was in terms of achievement, pride and excellence. But all this was disconnected from the desperate daily grind that most people had to struggle through – the stultifying routine of overstaffed bureaucracies, or the mad rush to accumulate wealth, legitimately or otherwise, wherever the opportunity afforded itself. To him, pride in craftsmanship, deep knowledge of the structures of the professions and of the workings of productive organizations, attention to detail and method, diligence and perseverance in application were the essential preconditions for the successful transplantation of modern economies into the Muslim world. But this ran counter to the mechanistic or credentials-obsessed understanding of work and status which permeated the post-colonial Muslim world. Bennabi's critique was exceptionally apt, but it had to fight for attention with an Islamic world which was more interested in projects for seizing, through political action, the commanding heights of power as a gateway to the civilization's revival.

The 'Religious Intellectual' and the 'Intellectual of Religion'

The growth of the phenomenon of the 'religious intellectuals' could also be traced to the period of the interregnum. These were individuals who combined an abiding interest in Islam as an ideology for change with varying degrees of exposure to the West. They stood in contrast to those whose training had been in the more traditional routes of the seminaries and colleges of Sunni and Shia Islam. Shiism would also feature prominently in the eruption of Islam on to the public arena in the 1970s. The relationship between the religious intellectuals and the *ulema* would not always be smooth. The traditional *ulema* saw religious intellectuals mainly as interlopers, while the frequently anti-establishment tone of the latter often descended into a campaign against the role and power of the *ulema*. This was especially true in Shia Islam, where there was a clear hierarchy of religious authority, culminating in the higher ranks of the *mujtahids* and grand ayatollahs. However, at the time when secular governments were in control in many countries across the Muslim world, rivalries were buried in the face of a common enemy. A few of the traditionally educated *ulema* would embrace the generally uncomfortable intermingling of western thought into the categories of Islam, while an even smaller number of the religiously minded intellectuals would carve out a privileged status for the traditional scholars in their vision of a revived and purified Islam. Later, when Islam would be a far more prevalent consideration in the public sphere, these latent conflicts would break out, often in a violent and even bloody *dénouement*.

Both these currents, however, developed a treatment of the issues that faced Islam in ways that were novel and appealing to the newly literate and urbanizing classes in the Muslim world. Unlike Bennabi, whose theory of civilizational cycles did not look for its origins or justification in doctrinal Islam, the new order of religious intellectuals sought to connect their expositions to the doctrinal creeds of Islam and to novel readings of formative events in Islamic history that could be used to illustrate or confirm their views. The radical *ulema*, on the other hand, re-read the corpus of Islamic doctrine in order to deduce from it principles which could be classified as 'modern' and which could therefore increase Islam's appeal to the secularized or secularizing classes.

In the world of the Shia, the figures of Ali Shari'ati (1933–77) in Iran and Ayatollah Baqir al-Sadr (1935–80) in Iraq represent the twin poles of the modern educated intellectual: Shari'ati blended Islam and radical western social and political theory into a new amalgam, whereas al-Sadr was the traditionally educated seminarian trying to come to terms with ideologies of the period and defuse their appeal within an Islamic frame-work. Shari'ati died in mysterious circumstances in London in 1977, a few months before the start of the cataclysm which would turn into the Iranian Revolution, while Ayatollah Baqir al-Sadr was murdered in 1980, a year after the triumph of the Iranian Revolution.

In the world of Sunni Islam, the most potent of the religious intellec-tuals was Sayyid Qutb (1906–66), held by many to be the inspiration behind the radicalization of political Islam and the birth of the *jihadi* culture. Qutb became the chief spokesman for the Muslim Brotherhood after its suppression in 1954, and continued as its main pamphleteer and ideologue until his execution in 1966.

Prior to the 1980s, when political Islam became divided along sectarian lines, there was a great deal of intermingling of Shia and Sunni modernist thought, with little of the sectarian tensions that would emerge later. There was a common enemy: the centralized, secularized state, whether it was militarily dominated, an absolute monarchy, or a dithering traditional order. The writings of Qutb and Abul A'ala Maududi (1903–79), of India and then Pakistan, were an important inspiration for the nascent Shia Islamist movement; as were those of Baqir al-Sadr and Shari'ati before the division of political Islam into its Shia and Sunni components.

All these thinkers were attempting to come to grips with the political dimensions of Muslims' relative powerlessness and with the deep sense of injustice that was festering behind the authoritarian surface of Muslim countries. Most of them did not really understand the dynamics of change in western societies, and by the time Islam supposedly caught up with one western system the world would have moved on to another set of concerns. A game of catching up is an enduring feature of Islam's encounter with the prevalent ethos of the western world. There is a dated-ness that is clearly apparent in much of the writing of this period.

Nevertheless, the views of these authors were held in high esteem by their audiences in the urban centres of the Muslim world, including young Muslims. They were on much surer grounds, though, when they dealt with the ailments of their own societies and when they drew on Islam's history and doctrines to buttress their arguments.

Ali Shari'ati, a graduate of the French university system, was deeply influenced by the writings of the anti-colonialist Franz Fanon, together with the works of the existentialist philosopher Jean-Paul Sartre and his former communist professor of sociology, Georges Gurvitch.[12] Returning to Iran in 1964, Shari'ati taught at various universities, but his principal platform was the Ershad *husseiniya* (meeting hall) in Tehran, where he lectured regularly to a packed audience on Islam, on modernism and on an unorthodox interpretation of Shia doctrines. Shari'ati's principal method was to use the pathos inherent in the Shia traditions of martyrdom and suffering and to relate them to the striving for justice and equality found among the disadvantaged in Iran and elsewhere. He related key events, episodes and heroes of Islam – especially Shia Islam – which resonated with the public at large, to modern ideological theories, mainly radical or utopian. Thus his book on the Prophet's companion, Abu Dharr al-Ghaffari, was to turn this ascetic and pious man into a paragon of utopian socialist action, who did not flinch from speaking the truth in the face of power. He used the pattern of the life of the Prophet's daughter, Fatima, as a way of introducing the idea that women's rights and empowerment were central concerns of true Islam.

Shari'ati also tried to link the reactionary aspects of clerical power in Iran to the idea that there were two distinct phases of Shiism (and, by inference, of Islam as a whole). The first was the true Islam, associated with the model of Ali, the Prophet's cousin and son-in-law and the first of the Imams of the Shia; and so-called Safavid Shiism, which Shari'ati related to the seizure of Shia Islam by the clerical classes in alliance with the Safavid dynasty. The latter introduced Shiism, forcibly, as the state religion of Iran in the sixteenth century. Shari'ati narrative suggested an ideal Islam of the early period and a deviant Islam, associated with abusive power and control by usurpers. In some ways, this narrative followed the Sunni Salafi call for a return to the ways of the early pioneers of Islam, as a precondition for 'purifying' it from its unacceptable accretions. But Shari'ati was far more influenced by Marxism than he let on, and this infused into his utopian Islam a clear inclination in favour of revolutionary struggle against the rich and powerful.

However, Shari'ati encroached on dangerous territory and his writings strayed too far from conventional Shia positions. There was an unmistakable residue of distaste for the Shia religious hierarchy, which he had implicitly held responsible for the decline of the vital spirit of Islam. Several of Iran's ayatollahs issued *fatwas* against him – but not, significantly, Ayatollah Khomeini; they accused him of un-Islamic writing and supported the authorities' actions against him and the closure of the Ershad meeting hall.[13] The hierarchy had closed ranks against an interloper, and, even though Shari'ati was posthumously rehabilitated after the Iranian revolution, he still remains a controversial figure in the world of reformist Shia Islam. In the final analysis, Shari'ati could not challenge the guardians of the faith, partly because he was unskilled and without the appropriate credentials in the doctrines of Shia Islam.

The other attempt at affirming the significance of Islam in a modern context came from the opposite end of the spectrum: that of the religious authority trying to refute the truth and the appeal of the ideologies of the time by subjecting them to a critical analysis, based on an Islamic argumentation. Such was the method of Ayatollah Baqir al-Sadr in Iraq, a precocious and original thinker whose education was undertaken entirely within the traditional seminary or *hawza*.[14] The rise of communist movements in Iraq was seen as a dangerous threat to the Shia masses, whose recent urbanization made them a prime target for intellectuals preaching the doctrines of liberation through class struggle. Al-Sadr's main focus was the educated youth, whose drift towards ideologies other than Islam he sought to reverse. His works, especially his critique of communism and capitalism in *Iqtisaduna* (*The Islamic Economy*) and *Falsafatuna* (*The Islamic Idea*), had a profound influence on the generation who came of age in the 1960s and 1970s. In these works al-Sadr deconstructed Marxism and capitalism and sought to demonstrate their inability to produce a just and equitable society, which only Islam could do. His analysis of liberal capitalism and communism was based on the sources available to him: mainly an inadequate set of indifferently translated works of the western classics of philosophy and political economy. The *hawza* in Iraq simply did not have the intellectual means to examine systematically the contents of western thought in all its variety and complexity. This shows through quite painfully in al-Sadr's work. But he did succeed – and brilliantly – in breathing new life into Islamic categories of thought and doctrine on important principles of political economy and moral philosophy.

Al-Sadr's treatment of property rights, economic relations and the nature of the just society, income and wealth distribution, the factors of production, and finance and interest, was unique up to a point. It constituted a towering achievement in bringing Islamic thought to bear on the understanding of the modern world. But, in as much as it was pioneering and fecund when seen in an Islamic context, it was insufficient as a critique of modern thought. The relative isolation of al-Sadr from the world's centres of intellectual activity and his dependence on translations and indirect assessments show through in his work. Al-Sadr was not hounded by the religious establishment, partly because of his lineage and impeccable seminary credentials. But the hierarchy did look askance at his works, seeing in them a drift from the traditional concerns of the grand ayatollahs. Even so, al-Sadr had enormous impact on the religiously minded youth and inspired a large number of people into religious activism and into Islamist politics. He was arrested and executed by the Baath authorities in 1980, a few months before the outbreak of the Iran–Iraq war.

The Spread of Islamism

The spread of these early Islamist ideas and doctrines was facilitated by the increasing literacy, but also by their authors' skilful use of both traditional institutions and the new universities for the diffusion of their version of political Islam. Maududi's party, Jama'at Islami, was frequently in conflict with the Pakistan authorities and was shut down from time to time. Maududi himself was put in jail several times. But Pakistan's censorship rules were generally lax, and its political persecutions were short-lived. Maududi's ideas could circulate freely and were not proscribed as such in Pakistan. The Jama'at Islami party was the main instrument for the propagation of Maududi's thought to Urdu speakers. His writings were translated into all the major languages of Islam, where they became a cornerstone of modern Islamist thought.[15] Their impact was especially significant among Arabic speakers.

The situation with the Muslim Brotherhood in Egypt was far more uncertain. Following the execution of Sayyid Qutb in 1966, a large number of the Brotherhood's stalwarts left Egypt for Saudi Arabia and North Africa, especially Algeria. In the case of Saudi Arabia, the policies of King Faisal were decidedly in favour of pan-Islamic causes. King Faisal himself was a pious, even ascetic, Muslim. But equally important factors behind Saudi Arabia's Islamic policies were the dangers from aggressive Arab nationalist doctrines and threats emanating from Nasser's Cairo. Nasser had dispatched an Egyptian military expeditionary force in support of the republican side in the Yemen civil war. The long-established monarchy had been over-thrown by a military coup in 1962. The Saudis viewed the presence of an Egyptian army in the Arabian peninsula as a direct threat to their stability and countered by increasing their support for Egyptian Islamic activists and for the writings of the main Sunni Islamic thinkers. The Muslim Brotherhood members who went to Saudi Arabia were especially active in the new universities and in the secondary schools, where a large number found jobs as teachers and instructors. In its modern form in Saudi Arabia, political Islam could be traced to the arrival there of a number of the Muslim Brotherhood's senior leaders in the 1960s and 1970s.[16]

The situation in North Africa was somewhat different. The 'Arabization' campaigns of the post-independence states of North Africa sought to rectify a dangerous imbalance caused by the Francophone educational policies of the former colonialist authorities. The campaign required the import of a large number of Arabic-speaking teachers from the eastern Arab lands. This was especially the case in Algeria, where the French had been most determined to reduce Arabic to a secondary status. Teachers were recruited into the educational systems of these countries from as far away as Iraq, but mainly from Egypt. A good percentage of the teachers brought in from Egypt was connected to the Muslim Brotherhood in one way or another. These teachers would provide an important platform for the propagation of Islamist ideas into the North African milieu in the period of the 1960s and 1970s.[17]

In the Shia world, the *hawza*, the traditional scholarly circles of learned ayatollahs, constituted the most important vehicle for the dissemination of Islamist ideas held by the politically oriented ayatollahs. In Iraq, the advent of the Baath Party to power in 1968 put an end to the open discussion of Islamist ideas in the *hawza*, and political Islamists of all stripes were aggressively targeted and frequently murdered. Ayatollah Khomeini, who was in exile in Iraq for most of the 1960s and 1970s, limited his political works to theoretical jurisprudential and theological discussions on the nature of Islamic government. In Iran, the situation was somewhat less repressive. Although the Shah had declared war on 'black' (that is, clerical) reaction as part of his White Revolution of modernization,[18] his secret police were more concerned with the threat emanating from the Marxist left. Politically oriented ayatollahs such as Taleqani and Mottahari were allowed some leeway for expressing their views, in between bouts of arrests. They were able to meet with a select group of their students or, more openly, in the Shia meeting halls, the *Husseiniyas*.

The period which preceded the global upsurge in Islam was also one which saw for the first time a serious attempt to modernize the interpretation of the Quran – the so-called science of *tafsir*. A re-reading of the foundational text of Islam in the light of contemporary conditions became essential for Islamists, mainly in order to provide Quranic sanction for their projects of social and political reform.[19] These *tafsirs* fell into a number of broad categories. The first was the reading of the Quran which emphasized Islam's role as a catalyst of social change; this was a form of 'liberation theology' best exemplified by the multi-volume work of Sayyid Qutb, which was written mainly in prison and entitled *Fi Dhilal al-Quran* (*In the Shade of the Quran*). This work was not in the line of the Salafist exegesis produced by Rashid Ridha's *al-Manar* newspaper in the earlier parts of the century, which revolved around the harmony between Islam, science and reason.[20] Qutb's exegesis was far more political in intent and was meant to seek Quranic sanction for fighting tyranny and to confirm Qutb's main contribution to Islamic political theory – namely the concept of the *jahili* society (literally, the ignorant or pagan society). This was essentially the diametrical opposite of Islamic society, one which every believer would be obliged to struggle against. Qutb extended the scope of the *jahili* society beyond its historical and religious understanding of pre-Islamic Arabia, to include not only western societies but also secular Arab and other nominally Muslim states. Qutb's radical re-reading of the Quranic text was profoundly significant for the burgeoning Islamist movement. It anchored its political certainties in the ineffable text of the Quran and gave it a legitimacy in the eyes of the wider Muslim public which the movement would not have enjoyed otherwise.

Another category of *tafsirs* included the rationalist interpretations or explanations of the Quran, such as the *The Message of the Quran*, possibly the most influential of the interpretations of the Quran in English.[21] This text was written by Muhammad Asad, whose interpretation of the Quran was greatly influenced by the rationalist (*Mu'tazila*) school in classical Islam and by the great classic *tafsir* associated with al-Zamakhshari. It was, nevertheless, an innovative attempt to convey a rationalist interpretation of the Quran in a more accessible and persuasive way to modern readers. Asad's work had royal patronage. In 1963, Prince Faisal (later king) of Saudi Arabia instructed the Saudi-linked Muslim World League to subscribe in advance to Asad's translation. However, even before its full publication in 1980, the translation and commentary fell foul of the *ulemas* of Saudi Arabia. In 1974, on the basis of a number of already translated sections of the Quran, Asad's efforts were denounced on the grounds that they were too metaphorical and modernist. The *ulema* banned the book's circulation in Saudi Arabia. It was left to Saudi Arabia's oil minister, Ahmad Zaki al-Yamani, to come to the rescue of Asad's crowning life achievement. Yamani, a personal friend and admirer of Asad, bought nearly 25,000 copies of Asad's translation and commentary, filling the gap that was left when the Muslim World League failed to meet its commitment to purchase these copies. Asad's translation and commentary had wide appeal among English-speaking Islamic activists, especially in Europe, South Asia and Malaysia.

The Re-Emergence of Islam

Ideas and textual re-readings, in and of themselves, do not produce epoch-making changes. The potential for revolt in the world of Islam against the traumatic changes of the past century and a half might have always been there, but it took a series of powerful changes to make this revolt explicit. The dethroning of prevailing ideologies and systems required an explicit manifestation of their failure before their wholesale abandonment by the people at large. Something of this kind happened with the catastrophic defeat of the combined Arab armies of Egypt, Syria and Jordan by Israel in the 1967 war. While the immediate outcome was a shrill insistence on the continuation of the struggle and a temporary upsurge in the appeal of revolutionary movements, the effect on the Muslim world was a thorough discrediting of the claims of nationalism and socialism as organizing principles of Muslim states and societies. The systems which prevailed in the defeated Arab states professed the very same nationalism and socialism that had been seen earlier as the gateway to modernizing and re-empowering the Arabs. Islam loomed as the only credible alternative. In one state after another, the 1970s saw the demise of radical socialist or nationalist governments. Egypt's Anwar Sadat drew on Islamic political movements as part of his campaign to eliminate the remnants of Nasserism; the populist Bhutto was hanged in Pakistan by a military dictator bent on Islamizing the country; while Turkey's descent into near civil war in the 1970s between the extreme left and right drove the army, the bastion of the secular establishment, to open the way for a guarded re-entry of Islam into the political sphere. However, what shifted the balance in the Muslim world towards an open association of the modern state with Islam was the Iranian revolution of 1979, which installed an avowedly Islamic republic as the model of government.

A rapidly expanding population, urbanization, increased literacy, growing income disparities between and within Muslim states, and an exploding oil price all played their part in setting the stage for the re-emergence of Islam on to the public arena. But it was a fundamentally different Islam from the one which had virtually disappeared in the post-Second World War era. The failure of transplanted western institutions and ideologies to set abiding roots in the Muslim world was clear, but the effects of decades of rapid fire change could not be easily dispelled.

For a brief moment after the success of the Iranian revolution a possible future beckoned, built around the experiences, nascent institutions and ideology of the revolution. In its early days, the Iranian Revolution transcended its exclusive association with Shiism. Not only Islamic activists of all stripes, but revolutionaries such as the PLO leader Yasser Arafat flocked to Tehran. The septuagenarian Ayatollah Khomeini became an iconic figure, with his ubiquitous visage replacing the radical heroes of bygone years. But the coalition that drove the shah out of the country fell apart as the Shia religious hiearchy asserted its control under the leadership of Ayatollah Khomeini. While in exile in Iraq, the Ayatollah had extended the principles for the rule of the jurisprudent in an Islamic government, which was a radical departure from Shia theology and Muslim political thought. The Iranians voted for a constitution that gave supreme power to the jurisprudent, Ayatollah Khomeini, and they created new institutions which solidified the power of the religious hierarchy over the state. The Council of Guardians, the Council of Legal Mediation, the status of *Rehber* or supreme religious authority were all drastic innovations in statecraft. There was no precedent for them, but, for a while, they appeared to be the structures of the type of government that Muslims were thought to yearn for.

However, Islam was not to be defined by the rulings of a *mujtahid* (Shia senior cleric), irrespective of his power and authority in his own land. The Iranian Revolution, which sought to present itself as an Islamic, and not a purely Shia revolution, was quickly typecast as in fact just that. After all, it derived its ultimate authority not from God but from the hidden Twelfth Imam of the Shia, through his authorized agents: the Shia circle of learned *mujtahids*. The Shia hierarchy, which had maintained some of its vigour although it was declining during the last years of the Pahlavi dynasty, had no counterpart in the Sunni world. The al-Azhar University of Cairo, the classical source of authority of Sunni Islam, had been emasculated by Nasser and could in no way provide the ideological or theological counterweight to the nascent world of revolutionary Shia Islam. It was left to the Saudi clerical establishment, built on the bedrock of Wahhabi thinking, to galvanize the Sunni world by way of a contribution to the revolt of Islam. The opportunity afforded itself shortly after the Iranian Revolution.

The Islamic centenary fell in November 1979, which coincided with the beginning of the fourteenth century in the Islamic calendar. On 20 November 1979, a large group of religious zealots, fired by a deep hatred for the Saudi royal family and for the evils perceived to beset Saudi society, seized control over Islam's most sacred site, the sanctuary and mosque of the Kaaba in Mecca.[22] They proclaimed the imminent coming of the Mahdi, the Redeemer, and they confronted the Saudi state with its gravest internal crisis for several decades. After several days of intense fighting, the rebels were overwhelmed and a large number of them executed. Most of the leaders of the rebellion had studied or had been trained under the aegis of the senior Wahhabi cleric Bin Baz. The Saudi authorities had to obtain a *fatwa* from Bin Baz before they could enter the mosque to confront the rebels. The formal recognition by the Saudi royal family of its dependence on the Wahhabi *ulema* class to fend off challenges to its legitimacy altered the balance of power inside Saudi Arabia in a fundamental sense.

In a quid pro quo for their support in ending the siege of the sacred mosque, the Wahhabi clerics were now empowered with near-total control over Saudi educational and social policy, and were provided with the means to carry the Wahhabist message worldwide. 'The royal family had to promise the clerics that it would reverse the slow modernization that had been occurring in the kingdom up until then. The royals fulfilled their promise. In the weeks after the siege ended, female newscasters were taken off television; the enforcement of the ban on alcohol became much more severe.'[23]

Within a matter of a few years, fuelled by the hundreds of millions of dollars that the Saudi treasury was giving them, the Wahhabi version of Islam began to be spread wherever Saudi money could reach. In a very short period of time, a marginal splinter group in Sunni Islam became its defining theology. The virulent hatred of the Shia which Wahhabi Islam harboured could now be used to put a stop to the conceit that the Iranian revolution was pan-Islamic and not irredeemably sectarian in character. At another level, the spread of Wahhabi and neo-Salafi thought became the main ideological drive behind the Afghan war of resistance against the Soviet occupation. *Jihad* could now be safely undertaken well away from Saudi Arabia, proving Wahhabism's commitment to one of the main pillars of Islam without threatening the stability and security of the Saudi royal family. 'The Saudis were all too happy to redirect the zeal of Juhayman's [the leader of the rebels] sympathizers toward a new enemy – the godless Russians.'[24]

There were signs of a resurgent Islam everywhere else in the Islamic world. In the 1980s Algeria, the bastion of revolutionary socialism, was swept with riots which set the stage for the emergence of the mass Islamist political party, the FIS (the Islamic Salvation Front). This party nearly achieved power when about to win the elections of 1992. But the army cancelled the elections, an event that sparked a decade-long civil war in which over 150,000 people lost their lives. Egypt was racked with an Islamist insurrection in the 1990s. The perennial problem of the Egyptian state – how to contain the power of the Muslim Brotherhood – became more acute as the Brotherhood was clearly the most popular political movement. This problem also migrated to Jordan, where the authorities had to manipulate the electoral results in order to deny power to the Brotherhood's offshoot. The newly independent Muslim states of the former Soviet Union were also confronted with the rise of Islam after decades of near extinction. Indonesia, Malaysia, Pakistan – all had to contend with societies which were more avowedly Islamic in customs and norms.

Most of the twentieth century now appears to have been a period during which Islam awaited the right set of conditions for its resurgence. But that resurgence did not bring forth the reality of a new order. Islam burst out of its confinement as an elemental, even inchoate, force, flying in every direction and trying to seek its balance. Nationalism and socialism may have been forced into retreat, but the modern world was not relinquishing its hold over large parts of the elites of Muslim societies. Neither was political Islam speaking in one voice: it had split into opposing Shia and Sunni camps, and these were feeding the fires of sectarianism in a far more virulent form than had ever been experienced before. At the same time, Islam's reappearance as a guiding principle in state and society obliged Muslims to confront a whole multitude of fundamental issues, which were covered up when the reins of power were in the hands of others. Civilization had to be recast in a landscape where the preceding century and a half had created new realities in self, society and the state. The footprints of modernity – and the bungled attempts to come to terms with it – were everywhere in Islamic society. The ethics and values of Muslims were undoubtedly affected by secularism and the consumer culture. The institutions of state and government were recast in forms which the rest of the world could understand and relate to. The economies and markets of Muslim countries were drawn into the global system of trade, investment and finance. The educational institutions were all based on western paedagogical models. The nuclear family and the modern workplace affected traditional ideas of gender and family. New problems of urban chaos, overpopulation and environmental degradation were added to the unremitting poverty and backwardness in which most Muslims lived.

The third age of Islam's fateful encounter with modernity had begun.

CHAPTER 4

Disenchanting the World

If Muslims really want an Islamic social order, then they must examine every aspect of modern life from the perspective of Islam and make necessary corrections . . . Then they should integrate the new knowledge into the corpus of the Islamic legacy by eliminating, amending, reinterpreting and adapting its components according to the world view of Islam.
Mahathir bin Muhammad, Prime Minister of Malaysia, speaking at the Third International Conference on Islamic Thought, Kuala Lumpur, May 1984

At the beginning of the 1970s, modern urban societies in most Islamic countries had become indistinguishable from their counterparts in other developing countries. Amongst the elites, the wealthy and most of the middle classes, the lifestyles and, increasingly, the mores of the West prevailed. By the end of the decade, however, everything had changed. The world watched the astounding spectacle of hundreds of thousands of men and women, including legions of *chador*-wearing women, joining in marches and demonstrations which called for the overthrow of a westernizing shah. Iran under the shah's autocratic rule was assumed to have joined the irresistible march to modernity. But re-Islamizing society was not simply a matter of changing one's dress, or of using Islamic inflections in one's speech. The Shia Islamic revolutionaries of Iran and the ascendant Salafis/Wahhabists of the Sunni world shared at least one thing in common. Political power had to be actively used in order to reverse, or at least halt, the spread of secular modernity. Islamizing society and its individuals became a matter of minds and hearts. Muslims had to be taught to think as Muslims before they could be expected to act as Muslims. The 1980s represented the age of the great cultural revolutions in the world of Islam.

Reworking States and Societies

The successful Iranian Revolution in 1979 handed power not only to the traditional clerical classes under the leadership of Ayatollah Khomeini, but also to a number of 'religious intellectuals' who, at least in the early days, were given the task of remaking Iran's cultural, mass-media and educational policies within a new Islamic framework. Iran's universities, which were seen as a hotbed of the revolution's erstwhile leftist and liberal allies, were all closed in 1980, in preparation for their re-opening under a new Islamic dispensation. The closure of the universities was preceded by a speech by Ayatollah Khomeini where he attacked the universities' previous secular bent. Khomeini spoke of 'the need for a fundamental revolution in all universities throughout the country' and called for 'a purging of the universities of professors affiliated to the West or the East . . . and turning universities into a healthy environment for the flourishing of sublime Islamic sciences'. He then added: 'We are not afraid of economic sanctions or military intervention. What we are afraid of is western universities and the training of our youth in the interests of West or East [the communist bloc].'[1] The Committee for the Islamization of Universities was formed with the task of supervising this process. In its early days the committee included individuals such as Abd el-Karim Soroush, who later went on to become a fierce critic of clerical rule and of the authoritarian direction of the Islamic Republic.[2] Hundreds of professors were purged in this cultural revolution, and liberal and leftist student organizations were all closed or forced to go uderground. The committee reported to a higher governmental body, the Cultural Revolution Headquarters, which supervised other initiatives for the Islamizing of society, including the formulation of acceptable dress codes for women, the expansion of the Islamic content of the media, and an increased use of Arabic and Quranic terms in the educational system.

In Saudi Arabia, the 1980s saw an increasingly conservative environment accompanying the defeat of the extreme Wahhabist insurgents who had occupied the Grand Mosque in Mecca. The authorities were determined to counter the widespread appeal of the insurgents' message regarding the profligacy of the ruling family and the supposed social laxity which followed in the wake of the explosive development of the Saudi economy in the

1970s. However, the emphasis in Saudi Arabia was on the enforcement of a rigid and doctrinal version of Islam, which emphasized conformity and extreme social conservatism rather than the search for a new Islamic vitality. The 1980s saw a rollback of whatever limited freedoms had been granted to women in earlier periods. For example, the need for females to be accompanied by a male relative as their guardian when they travelled abroad, a rule which had been overlooked in the past, once more became mandatory. This drastically reduced the number of females studying abroad on scholarships. Governmental support and funding for the religious police – the *mutaw'a* – greatly increased during this period. The remit of this body extended beyond the previously limited functions of ensuring that men attended the ritual public prayers; the religious police now acquired broad powers to monitor and control all aspects of public behaviour. The Saudi clerical class of the senior Wahhabi *ulema* was given a near-sacrosanct status, and the government would allow no serious opposition to their rulings. The religious content of the national curriculum was expanded even further, and theological studies in the Wahhabist tradition were encouraged in the universities. An army of graduates in religious studies flooded into a workforce which had no particular need for their skills, in an economic environment which was severely affected by the collapse in oil prices during most of the 1980s. Many of them were then encouraged by their clerical mentors, and even by the government, to find an outlet for their energies and ideals in the *jihad* of Afghanistan.

In Pakistan, Islamization was a central feature of the policies of the military dictator Zia ul-Haq, who had come to power in a coup in 1977. Shortly afterwords, Zia's predecessor (whom Zia had deposed), namely the former Prime Minister of Pakistan, Zulfiqar Ali Bhutto, a secular populist politician, was tried and hanged for murder in April 1979. Zia's Nizam-e Islam (Islamic Order), which he first promulgated in December 1978, represented a concerted effort to redefine Pakistan's judicial inheritance.[3] Pakistan, like India, used English common law as the basis for its legal system – a legacy from the days of the Raj. Through a series of ordinances which introduced the so-called *Hudud* laws, Pakistan's penal codes were now amended to bring them (purportedly) in conformity with the Sharia. This affected punishments for crimes all across the board, from theft and adultery to alcohol consumption. The law concerning evidence was altered in ways which affected women's rights. In addition, to curse the Companions of the Prophet or to show disrespect for the Prophet and his Household became criminal offences. Followers of the Ahmadi sect, a nineteenth-century offshoot of Islam, were declared non-Muslims. A Federal Shariat Court was established in 1981, with *ulema* as full-time judges. A number of Islamizing measures affected the banking system, for instance, the formal abolition of bank interest as a form of usury (*riba*), but this was circumvented by the banks' rebranding of 'interest' as 'profit', an obvious subterfuge.

But the process of Islamizing society by enforcing Sharia-based laws began to founder when *zakat*, the Islamic wealth tax, was introduced in a form which was not acceptable to the Shia Muslims of Pakistan. These represented about 20 per cent of the populaton. By politicizing the juridical differences between two main branches of Islam, the Zia Islamization reforms increased the tensions bewteen Shias and Sunnis. The reforms lacked a legtimizing consensus. The Shias and the Sunnis were not the only components of society which did not see eye-to-eye on all these refroms. Many in the professional middle classes, trained as they were in the secular system, would also not adjust to, or accept, the new Islamic order.

De-Sacralizing Islam

Throughout the 1980s, one Muslim country after another began to adopt Islamizing policies, partly in recognition of the rising significance of Islamic loyalties and partly because the resurgent Islamic political movements could be useful as allies to the ruling groups in domestic power struggles. The official support and encouragement of Islamizing policies created the impression that Muslim countries were embarking on a process of reconstructing themselves as consciously Islamic societies. However, the reality of decades of Islam's marginalization in public life and institutions, and the cumulative effect of modernity and secularism on the Muslim mind, could not be erased by top-down Islamizing policies, no matter how sweeping or draconian. An entirely different approach was needed, one that would aim at nothing less than recovering an Islamic perspective as the default position of the average Muslim, as well as of the elites and leaders of Islamic society. It was this desire that drove some of the best Muslim minds of the 1980s to align themselves to the Islamizing policies of receptive governments and to produce the intellectual underpinnings of the Islamization process.

However, the increasing political assertiveness of Muslims on the world stage was not matched by a renewed expression of Islam's civilizational vitality. Muslim societies of the 1980s were still sunk in a deep quandary, being simultaneously apologetic, defensive, sensitive and nostalgic about their legacy and its place in the world. Ever since the nineteenth century, the study of Islamic history and society had been dominated by western scholars and writers.[4] They created narratives and types of Islam that were accepted, often uncritically, by their Muslim students and audiences. Western analytic methods and systems in historiography, psychology, social and political science, and even theology, were brought to bear on key aspects of Islam and imposed their own standards and rules of interpretation on it.[5] Quietly, subtly, Muslims surrendered their own understanding of their civilization and their own world view to a jumble of precepts defined and elaborated upon by others. Islam increasingly came to be seen through the prism of western scholarship and modern concepts. Those who sought their own paths of knowledge and understanding of Islam fell on the meagre intellectual and educational resources of the Muslim world, mired, as most of them were, in a deadening scholasticism. Or they could join the ranks of the ever-growing political Islamist movements and take to the metaphorical barricades, intellectual or otherwise. The world of Islam, indeed the Islamist comprehension of the world, was being de-sacralized right in front of the eyes of Muslims, without their full recognition of what was happening, and often with their complicity.

By the time of Islam's counter-revolution, which started in the 1970s, the dismantling of the structures of the Islamic world view had been well under way for decades. This was particularly true in relation to language, the most fundamental building-block of Islamic expression and understanding. A succession of language reforms in the twentieth century in most Muslim countries had ended by decoupling the language of Islam from its principal spiritual mooring – that of understanding God's purpose. There were three aspects to this matter.

The first aspect was related to the loss of connotative meaning attached to key Arabic words which explained, guided or reflected Man's spiritual quest. The second aspect was related to the 'modernization' of the Arabic language, in reckless abandon of its purpose both as a tool for understanding the Islamic message and as the vehicle for the culture of Arabs and the civilization of Islam. The third aspect was related to the drastic overhaul of both the scriptural basis and the contents of non-Arabic languages through which Islamic life and civilization were expressed in the non-Arab areas of Islam.

This is what happened to the meaning of a number of key words which are part of the Arabic of the Quran. There were always two 'Arabic' languages: one was necessary to read and understand the Quran in order to uncover the mysteries of the dialogue between God and Man; and the other was the language and culture of Arabs and of the civilization associated with Islam when these were expressed through the medium of Arabic. Quranic Arabic, in the formulations of Islam, is a sacred language; and, although it is clearly the language of the Arabs of Quraish (the Prophet's tribe), it is also the medium through which the Quran was expressed. Preserving the integrity of Quranic Arabic is therefore vital in understanding the spiritual knowledge borne by the Quran.

The degradation of the language of the Arabs has been one of the most damaging acts of the Arab cultural modernists. In fact, modern Arabic could well be called neo-Arabic – its literary lions having repudiated its legacy nearly entirely. 'Its leaders are for the most part men who have drunk from other springs and look at the world with different eyes,' as the great Harvard scholar of Islam, Sir Hamilton Gibb, asserted.[6] The willingness of the literary elites to break with the extraordinary capacity of the language to express ideas and concepts with exactitude has turned Arabic into yet another vehicle for the secular mind. For generations of Muslims, the opposite was the case: the Arabic of the Quran was a source for accessing a spiritually charged universe.

But this fate should not have befallen Arabic – or even the other languages of Muslims, languages which have been 'Islamized' in order to absorb the world view of Islam all the better. The exactness of Arabic is in fact one of the properties used to derive meaning from the Quran, since knowledge of the language, of its root structures, grammar and the range of acceptable usage, is essential to understand the Quran properly. The 'modernization' of Arabic has created two languages: an arcane Quranic Arabic, understood only by lexicographers, seminary students and grammarians; and a vernacular Arabic through which popular and literary cultures are expressed. The unifying features of Arabic as both the sacred language of the Quran and the literary language of Arabs, deriving its vitality from its uniqueness as a gateway into the unseen, has been lost.[7]

The de-Islamization of the language can be exemplified through changes in the meaning of words such as *deen*, '*aql* and *ilm*. In the modern rendering of the word, *deen* simply means religion. In the Quranic Arabic, however, *deen* is the indebtedness of the created to the Creator which is to be discharged in life according to a particular prescription, the ways of Islam or the unsullied revealed religions. Another word, '*aql*, is now used synonymously with the words for 'human reason' or 'mind'. In the Quranic

Arabic, *'aql* designates the faculty of intellection which can discern the divine. The Quranic Arabic referred to fundamental truths, which are peculiar to Islam. Their new usages on the other hand allowed for entirely new constructs to prevail, often privileging the new meaning over the old.

For example, the term for 'secular' in Arabic masks the way in which the new representation of the word undermines a fundamental Quranic depiction of the world. *'Ilmaniyya* – the Arabic equivalent of 'secularism' – is a word derived from the root *ilm*, which, loosely translated, means knowledge and in modern usage designates specifically scientific or rational knowledge. *'Ilmaniyya* thus becomes the pursuit of scientific or rational knowledge in an uncompromising, positivist way. *Ilm* appears in the Quran on numerous occasions and relates to the form of knowledge that leads ultimately to God. It is what God imparted to Adam, allowing mankind to distinguish between the absolute and the relative. It is also one of the attributes of God: *al-'Aleem*, 'the All-Knowing'. In Islam, knowledge of the outer world was known specifically as knowledge of the 'depicted': *ilm ul-rusum*. It had its place, but people of taste and discernment would always seek out the permanent, lasting knowledge, the Quranic knowledge or *ilm*, and, within it, they would pursue the outer forms of knowledge as a secondary purpose.

The last nail in the undermining of the languages of Islam was the abandonment of the Arabic script. The most famous case, of course, was Mustafa Kemal's replacement of the Arabic script with the Latin alphabet in the notation of Turkish. The decision to reject the script and the language of the Ottomans, who had been the guardians of Islam for centuries, was a conscious choice made in favour of the international script of the West.[8] It brazenly signalled a total rejection of the past and a breathless desire to join the 'civilized' world. In late 1928, Turkey passed a law prohibiting the use of the Arabic script in the public arena. An entire culture had to evolve that was cut off from its past. This was soon followed by the translation of the Quran into Turkish, and its recitation was conducted in the vernacular – an affront to the piously minded. The abandonment of the Arabic script (which was undertaken as a symbol of liberation from a backward past) was partially justified through the argument that the Arabic script was unsuited to Turkish and could not properly convey new ideas and concepts emanating from the West.

The association of the Latin script with 'civilization' was, of course, a non-starter for European Jews, who consciously chose Hebrew and the Hebrew script as the national language of Israel. Hebrew and Arabic share a number of common characteristics and structures. It is curious that in Turkey the Arabic script was seen as a reactionary relic, whereas in Israel Hebrew was selected as the language (and script) of a country which placed itself consciously inside the western intellectual tradition. Other Muslim languages were also allowed to atrophy, especially by colonial administrators. The Jawi script, also based on Arabic, was widespread in the Malay-speaking world and its earliest use was traced to an inscription on a stone in the early fourteenth century. But both the British colonial powers in the Federated Malay States and the Dutch in the Indonesian Archipelago used the Latin alphabet for writing Malay, a practice which continued into the post-colonial era. (However, the Jawi script does have a limited use in official documents and continues to be taught in schools as a way of gaining access to reading the Quran in the original Arabic.)

Some have celebrated the break between Arabic and Islam. The novelist and Noble laureate V. S. Naipaul has made the assertion that Islam is the religion of the Arabs and was foisted on non-Arab peoples by force. The 'converted' people of Islam have lost their connection with their own identity and pre-Islamic past, and are therefore condemned to a limbo of worshipping in an alien language and of relating to sacred places in foreign lands. Naipaul was primarily concerned with the Muslims of India and Pakistan. The thrust of his argument was that the eradication of the connection with the sacred language of Islam would facilitate their reconciliation with their pre-Islamic legacy. 'It [Islam] has had a calamitous effect on converted peoples. To be converted you have to destroy your past, destroy your history. You have to stamp on it, you have to say "my ancestral culture does not exist, it doesn't matter".'[9]

The Battlefields of Islamic Knowledge

Language was one battlefield in de-Islamization. Knowledge was another way in which Muslims were alienated from their own legacies. The issue was not the juxtaposition of 'knowledge' against 'ignorance'. No sane person would dispute the fact that science and technology have generated immense benefits for mankind and have ameliorated the human condition. But the dissemination and utilization of knowledge does not take place in a vacuum. It is supported by a massive infrastructure of educational and research institutions, enterprises, media and public agencies, all the while woven together by beliefs and values that presuppose a certain purpose to the entire process.

The western university system, for example, evolved from its roots in the religious scholasticism of the colleges of Oxford, Cambridge and Paris into an entirely secular and humanist enterprise. (A little noted fact: the medieval inns of court of London and Paris, the precursors of the college system, were directly borrowed from the mosque–*madrassa* complexes of Islam through the crusaders of the Knights Templar.)[10] That process took several centuries, and even in the late nineteenth century the religious bias of a number of Europe's ancient universities was clear. In the end, the modern conception of the university was completely severed from its religious foundations and became the model for the formal process to acquire knowledge. God and religious knowledge (in the commonly understood sense) were relegated to divinity departments and to professional seminaries. Knowledge was decoupled from moral or religious purpose, except in the few cases where there was an overwhelming ethical implication to the acquisition of such knowledge. The development of the atom bomb, for example, did create considerable moral dilemmas for a number of the physicists who had worked on the programme, and, in a similar vein, the issue of genetic modification, or stem cell research, also raises issues concerning the purposes of the 'right' type of research. But these are exceptions, which serve indeed to highlight the absence of any non-materialistic scale of measuring the value of research and education.

The western system of knowledge acquisition is based on a constant challenge to the prevailing verities. Progress is measured by questioning and doubting – which overthrows established ideas and principles and replaces them with new ones. Truth becomes relative and conditional, subject to 'the present state of knowledge'. Islam does not refute the requirement to challenge orthodoxies which have ossified in an incorrect or blatantly false understanding of reality. However, it does subject human effort to the absolute imperative to observe and understand outer reality, so as to marvel more fully at the infinite manifestations of reality.

The purpose of knowledge is to demonstrate the truth of the Quranic verse: 'We will show them our Signs in the Horizons and in themselves until the Truth is manifested for them.' The Muslim world's religious institutions, where this kind of knowledge was supposed to be gained, have deteriorated disastrously in the pre-modern and modern periods. These institutions were not interested in God's signs. They had sunk into an archaic scholasticism which, at its best (for instance, in Iran's seminaries), could still produce some illuminated beings with deep philosophical insights on man's condition, but at its worst produced ignorant bigots and pedants.

Unfortunately, the problem with the type of knowledge that Muslims were acquiring was not recognized until several generations of graduates, schooled in the new-style academies, had come and gone. The traditional Islamic colleges were increasingly irrelevant to the ruling elites, who saw nothing in them except the regurgitation of useless knowledge. Their only purpose was to produce individuals who could minister to the religious and ritual requirements of society. The attempts to 'modernize' al-Azhar, which started in the late nineteenth century with Muhammad Abduh, were effectively abandoned as the youth of Egypt preferred to flock to the new secular universities, with their promise of instant access to modernity and culture.[11] The great Zaytuna mosque–*madrassa* complex in Tunis, which formed the heart of the teaching of Islam in the North African context, was emasculated by the French colonial authorities and was degraded by the post-colonial rulers of Tunisia.[12] The Shia centers of learning in Najaf and Qum fared a bit better until they were, in turn, targeted by radical, modernizing regimes.

By the end of the 1960s, the landscape of traditional Islamic learning was indeed bleak. The Islamic *madrassas* and universities were barely able to do their job of producing individuals competent at least in matters of doctrine and faith. Any pretence on the part of these graduates that they were the inheritors of Islam's legacy of profound respect for learning had been long abandoned. Individual scholars of immense intellectual power and curiosity continued to shine through, but they were constrained by the archaic and introverted life of institutions which had been reduced to mere shadows of their former significance. Islam's insistence on 'seeking knowledge even unto China' was not going to be headed by the anachronistic traditional Islamic colleges. Neither were the new universities interested in propagating the world view of Islam, since their models and standards were firmly anchored in the West.

Secularism's Trap

Into this unpromising environment there emerged the figure of Syed Naquib al-Attas, a philosopher and educationalist of genius and profound insight, the closest thing to a polymath that modern Islam had produced. Syed Muhammad Naquib al-Attas was born in 1931, in Java, into a family which traced its origins to the Arabs from the Hadhramut area of the Arabian Peninsula who had migrated to the East Indies. His appellation 'Syed' denotes direct descent from the lineage of the Prophet Muhammad through the Prophet's grandson, Hussein. His early instruction was in the Islamic sciences, Malay language, literature and culture.

After school, al-Attas joined the Malay Regiment, which at that time was commanded by British officers. He went on to Sandhurst, Britain's military academy, and was commissioned as an officer in 1955. However, al-Attas was drawn to the metaphysics of the Sufis, and his travels in North Africa and Spain, where he witnessed Islam's civilizational possibilities, left a deep impression on him. Resigning his commission, he continued with his philosophical studies. His thesis (completed in 1962) was a two-volume work on the mysticism of Hamza Fansuri, a sixteenth-century Sumatran Sufi. Al-Attas returned to Malaysia and held leading positions in the country's nascent university system. In 1987 he founded the post-graduate institute that would embody his teachings on the Islamization of knowledge: the International Institute of Islamic Thought and Civilization (ISTAC).[13]

Al-Attas created the concept of an Islamization of knowledge in 1978, in his work on Islam and secularism.[14] He formulates his philosophy around key Islamic concepts whose essential meanings and functions have been grievously eroded by the elemental drive in modern western civilization to eliminate the presence of the divine in the world. According to al-Attas, the decay of Islamic civilization is mainly due to the displacement (in Islam) of the original meaning of knowledge by its mirror reflection. Now this opposite of knowledge dominates the intellectual, political and social landscape of Islam. This *ersatz* knowledge dissolves Muslims' concern with the ethics of conduct and devalues the significance of the primordial contract between God and Man.[15]

Al-Attas talks about two types of knowing: the rational, which derives from experience, and the knowledge of God which lies at the heart of Islam. While the West uses knowledge to produce the good citizen ('second-order knowledge'), the pursuit of knowledge in Islam aims to produce the good human being ('first-order knowledge'). Knowledge of the first order leads to certainty and truth; knowledge of the second order leads to temporary truths and 'enmeshes [man] in the labyrinth of endless and purposeless seeking'. First-order knowledge allows people repose and constancy, while the second type of knowledge leads to continuous doubt 'and the possibility of perpetual wandering spurred on by intellectual deception and self-delusion'. There is no room in Islam for the myth of Sisyphus, perpetually rolling the stone up a hill, only to see it roll down again. Neither does al-Attas acknowledge the existence of tragedy and drama in the human condition. These are necessarily derived from the view of man that sees in him the inability ever to arrive at a condition of steadfastness and serenity. In Islam, these values are guaranteed for the person who acts out his or her part of the divine covenant.

According to al-Attas, secularism is the West's retort to the existence of a divinely ordered world. The Harvard theologian Harvey Cox defined secularism as 'the loosing of the world from religious and quasi-religious understandings of itself, the dispelling of all closed world views, [and] the breaking of all supernatural myths and sacred symbols'.[16] When this condition commences, it is almost impossible to reverse. Presumably the same dynamics would apply to Islamic societies who may, Canute-like, try to stop the march of history, but in the end will be overwhelmed by it. Secularism thus becomes a process which, although originating in the specifically western context of the conflict between church and state, assumes the dimensions of a universal force, under which all sacral systems are bound to perish. It is an inevitable stage in the unfolding of the evolution of humanity from infantility to maturity; it removes the props which religion provides for humankind and it forces the latter to fall on its own resources in ordering or confronting life's challenges.

In some ways this process cannot be denied. The entire inheritance of the Judaeo-Christian tradition seemed to end up in the secular state, which, in as much as the march of the West is equated with the triumph of the West, will ensure its own transference ultimately on to non-western societies. However, al-Attas rejected the idea of secularism as a stage in the development of Islamic societies. In fact he goes one step further, stating that all true religions would reject the idea that the divine should be banished from the public sphere. Christianity in the West is in fact an aberration of the original Eastern Church. It is an uncomfortable amalgam of Hellenstic – Roman traditions, fused with Judaic religious structures. Secularism is not embedded in the true biblical faith – at least not by recourse to the saying of 'Render unto Caesar what is Caesar's'. In fact Muslims do recognize the veracity of Christianity, but not necessarily in its western version. Thus the evolution of western societies do not reflect the evolution of Christianity as such – or at least of the Christianity which is acknowledged in the Quran as being an original and authentic faith.

But Islam cannot and should not follow in the path of the West and prostate itself to secularism, as this process is entirely related to the unique historical experience of the West. Historicity cannot be part of the reality of Islam. Islam is a revealed religion which has a set of necessary obligations to impose on all its adherents; these include knowledge of the self, and therefore of God. This is a key element in al-Attas's conception of the primary form of knowledge. Such knowledge does not 'evolve' or change. Islam's systems of values are non-temporal and cannot be deconsecrated or subjected to relativism. Neither should Islam be taken in by the arguments of the West's philosophers, scientists, economists, sociologists, psychologists and the like – who, by their very nature, deal in doubt, uncertainty, scepticism and conjecture. Their views are bound to change and, with them, today's preoccupations become tomorrow's memory. Al-Attas was writing this in the late 1970s, when the issue of religion and the public arena appeared to have been definitively settled. The Iranian Revolution had not happened, and the explosive eruption of religion back into the western imagination was a long way off.

In the past three decades, the issues of secularism and Islam have moved centre-stage as the world seeks to 'uncover' the religious basis of Islam's violent fringe. The thesis of previous times, that Islam will inevitably bow to the winds of secular change – a discussion which was carried mainly in polite terms in the West – has now been superseded by the urgency to find a solution to the supposed proneness of Islamic religious culture to extremes of violence. It is all very reminiscent of John Buchan's classic 1916 novel, *Greenmantle*, where the Foreign Office mandarin tells the hero: 'Islam is a fighting creed, and the mullah still stands in the pulpit with the Quran in one hand and a drawn sword in the other. Supposing there is some Ark of the Covenant which will madden the remotest Moslem peasant with dreams of Paradise? What then, my friend?' Nearly a century later, the same message is emanating, if not from Whitehall, then from the right-wing think-tanks in Washington and from bloggers on the world wide web.

The secular make-over of Islam has virtually become a national security issue for the US and increasingly for Europe, as both are anxious about the supposed dangers of a 'clash of civilizations' or the presence of large Muslim minorities in their midst. The word 'secular' itself, which had almost lost its significance and resonance in the western world, has been revived as capturing one of the defining characteristics of western civilization – indeed of all modern civilizations. Secularism has been elevated to a precondition for having the whole range of human and civil rights that western society is proud of. In particular, the freedom of expression and the rights of women have been made contingent on the existence of a secular culture and society. They cannot flower if society is overly concerned with the rights of religious believers.

Religion comes to be, then, reduced to a privately held belief system, which should in no way be afforded any special protection or privilege. If Islam as a total system of beliefs cannot be secularized, then the next best solution is to find a means by which Islam can be made to step aside from the public arena, while the state and, if possible, society are secularized. Finally, where secularism has established itself as a doctrine of the state and belongs in the self-description of the ruling groups, as in Turkey or Tunisia, Islam should not be allowed back into the political arena without iron-clad assurances that it would not repeal or dilute secularizing measures. Secularists – whether self-proclaimed or genuine – in Muslim lands and communities have received a new boost to their cause as they hitch themselves to this heightened western concern for the direction of Islamic societies.

Balancing Thoughts and Deeds

'Fatalism' had always been one of the characteristics of Islam, at least until quite recently. The ability of the poor peasant, or the urban worker, to put up with incredible hardships and privations was glibly attributed to the 'fatalistic' streak in Islam, which is supposed to derive from Islam's exclusive concern with ethereal knowledge. The image of the happy Egyptian peasant or of the Pakistani street sweeper, who accept their lot in life without protest or qualms, lingers in the mind as one of the side-effects of a belief in an unalterable predestination. But this is patent nonsense. Islam is founded on the knowledge of the unseen that is given through inspiration or acquired by God's permission. Islam insists that it is this hierarchy at whose apex is the knowledge emanating from God that should be understood and respected. Man therefore would not be cut off from the source of knowledge by focusing his effort on a secondary form of knowledge, which can turn to self-deification. The journey of each human being has a destiny, an end: from pre-existence to existence in time, then to death, then to another passage, namely into post-existence. The ordering of the world is related to this certainty and the presence of human beings in time and space must be balanced alongside it.

If secularism is understood as concern – but not over-concern – for the life of this world, then Islam recognizes its role in the balanced society, all the while affirming the reality and priority of a higher form of knowledge. Al-Attas makes a crucial distinction in this regard. Secularism, as commonly understood, is an exclusive concern for the 'here and now' and a denial of the validity of other world views in ordering the affairs of mankind. Islam does not demean contemplation or reflection on the wonders of nature, but it does claim that man should marvel, not at nature, but at the Signs of God which are manifested in nature. Thus denying the reality of the orders of nature is in some ways an affront to God, but man's discoveries of the mysteries of creation are only further means to perceive the unseen. Modern secularization is a form of war against God. Its end product is the diminishing of human beings by decoupling their lives from purpose and direction. Nature is robbed of its magic; values are de-consecrated and public life is de-sacralized.[17]

Metaphysical Sufism has influenced a number of important Islamic thinkers, including al-Attas. It has driven the reformulation of classical Islamic terms for a modern audience, but without the loss of an essential spirituality and without straying far from its commitment to an Islamic Sharia. It provides a formidable challenge both to Salafi Islam, with its concern for power and outer rules of conduct, and to 'liberal' Islam, with its focus on rights and freedoms, which has almost become a branch of the western intellectual tradition. Metaphysical Sufism is a masterful synthesis of philosophy and theology. The resultant body of knowledge, frequently called *hikma* or wisdom, provides for its adherents an appropriate access to understanding the ways of God. The starting point is a perfected model, from which mankind devolves rather than evolves.

The notion that human beings evolve from a lower to a higher state of knowledge, from a lower to a higher organism, simply does not arise in the framework of metaphysical Sufism. It is not that biological evolution (in the Darwinian sense) does not take place. Islam is not a literalist religion in this regard. It is rather that man aspires to a higher model of being, whose contours have been already determined. The process of this arc of ascent, as it were, passes through several fields, including a perfection of the qualities of moral worth. The moral elevation of mankind is unrelated to the biological process. Its template has already been set before eternity, and man is pre-programmed to seek this end state. The more human beings align themselves to this primordial condition, the more they will realize their essential humanity. This goes beyond the virtues that are specifically generated through a moral philosophy anchored in human reasoning. True Muslims must therefore cultivate, as a vital ingredient, a religious sensibility based on the Quran and on the prophetic example. This sensibility, which can discern limits, boundaries, and purposes of moral conduct, is acquired through a process which al-Attas calls *ta'adib*, the knowledge of appropriate moral action – a term derived from the root word *adab*, which can also mean 'courtesy'.

Thus *ta'adib* goes beyond the normally understood meaning of 'educating people'. The Muslim community cannot begin to approach the elements of essential knowledge if they have not been trained to exhibit the right 'courtesy' towards this knowledge. Each aspect of this courtesy must be appropriate. Thus *adab* to the self is to know the components of the self – from the animal, rational and inspired components to the serene self. *Adab* to family, to friends, to community, to society, to leaders, must also reflect the essential aspects of appropriateness, of intentions, of behaviour and of action. *Adab* to language and literature is to place words in their proper context and to set them in an order that produces intelligibility and creativity.

The malaise of Muslim society is the degradation of *adab*, understood in the terms of appropriate action in an appropriate setting. And this deplorable condition is directly attributable to the corruption or abandonment of authentic knowledge in favour of the secondary variety. 'Because of the intellectual anarchy that characterizes this situation, the common people become determiners of intellectual decisions and are raised to the level of authority on matters of knowledge. Authentic definitions become undone, and in their stead we are left with platitudes and vague slogans disguised as profound concepts,' wrote al-Attas in his *Prolegomena to the Metaphysics of Islam*.

The Idea of the Islamic University

In 1973, al-Attas addressed a letter to the Organisation of the Islamic Conference Secretariat in which he set out the basic outlines of his critique of the state of knowledge among Muslims and formulated the need to found an authentically Islamic educational philosophy that would remedy this condition. In his letter, al-Attas suggested the founding of a university which would be based on a conception of knowledge that was different from that of western universities. This new university would aim to produce 'the complete man, or the universal man . . . a Muslim scholar who is universal in his outlook and is authoritative in several branches of related knowledge'.[18] Later, al-Attas followed this up with a proposal for the formation of an Islamic university which he presented to the First World Conference on Islamic Education, held in Mecca in 1977. A decade later, al-Attas founded the International Institute of Islamic Thought and Civilization (ISTAC) in

Kuala Lumpur, to put his ideas into practice. The Institute was formally opened in 1993 and moved into a complex of buildings designed by al-Attas himself. The campus adhered to the classical symbols of Islamic art and architecture, from its orientation towards Mecca to the harmonious blending of its landscape and buildings with the natural environment.

The institute evolved as a postgraduate university with a unique approach to the teaching of Islamic thought, within the parameters of al-Attas's philosophy. Its curriculum was based on the division of knowledge into the categories of the permanent and the changing. ISTAC eschewed the traditional division of the academy into courses and departments, building the curriculum around broad themes of Islamic thought, Islamic science and Islamic civilization. It attracted a range of scholars and students and began to develop a worldwide reputation.

ISTAC's setting on the outer rim of the Islamic world initially also worked to its advantage, as the institute was sheltered from the over-politicization of higher education of the Middle East, as well as from bureaucracy and heavily-handed security. ISTAC used English as the main medium of instruction, without, of course, eliminating the necessary grounding in the Arabic language.[19] English was rapidly becoming an important language of expression for Islamic thinkers and intellectuals, and certainly it dominated in the academic and scholarly treatments of Islam.

However, the entire experience was cut short when al-Attas was summarily removed from his position of founder–director and forcibly made to retire in 2004. He and his institute became the victims of an ongoing war, within the world of higher education in Malaysia and the wider Muslim world, around the issue of the meaning of the Islamization of knowledge and of the functions and purposes of an Islamic university. Al-Attas also fell foul of the petty jealousies and envies which prevail whenever a new and potentially revolutionary idea begins to take root. ISTAC was subjected to a barrage of criticism when it began to lose its official support. Al-Attas was seen as both eclectic and elitist. The public could not relate to ISTAC's scholarly output, and al-Attas' attempts to engage the community through his weekly lectures floundered. Foremost among al-Attas' associates was Wan Muhammad Nur, an accomplished scholar in his own right and something of a Boswell to al-Attas; but neither he nor the others could make the Attasian system intelligible to the wider public. Al-Attas's work was frequently portrayed as impenetrable and obscure; it never caught the wider imagination. Al-Attas himself achieved near-iconic status in the rarefied academic world of metaphysical Sufism, with ISTAC receiving visiting scholars and dignitaries from all parts of the world. But his achievements proved insufficient when the decisive moment arrived. This occurred in 1998, when the Deputy Prime Minister of Malaysia, Anwar Ibrahim, lost out in a titanic power struggle with the Prime Minister, Dr Mahathir bin Muhammad. Anwar was subsequently tried and imprisoned. He had been a radical Islamist student in his younger days and a strong proponent of the idea of Islamizing knowledge. While serving as minister of culture and later education in the early 1980s, Anwar had advocated the founding of specifically Islamic universities and lobbied the Organisation of the Islamic Conference to sponsor the idea of Islamizing knowledge officially.

Anwar himself was an Islamic theoretician of sorts and had sponsored the founding of ISTAC. On his demise, the knives were out for al-Attas. He had no official champions left, and the widespread international calls for his reinstatement and the continuation of ISTAC's autonomous status fell on deaf ears. ISTAC was absorbed into the International Islamic University of Malaysia, a bastion of the alternative school of 'Islamizing knowledge' that was diametrically opposed to al-Attas' concern for the significance of primary knowledge and the nurturing of individuals who strive for moral clarity as a precondition for scholarly excellence.

The alternative school was far more influential and better funded than that of al-Attas's. It rose to prominence in the 1980s and was built around the person of Ismail Raji al-Faruqi, a Palestinian–American academic who had studied at al-Azhar and at a number of North American universities.[20] His effort was backed by the financial might of Saudi Arabia and led to the establishment of a number of 'Islamic universities' in several Muslim countries. The objectives were to Islamize specific disciplines, especially in the social sciences, to better serve the cause of Islam. An intricate and global network of intellectuals, academics, government officials and wealthy patrons was interwoven by a Saudi-backed, Virginia-based think-tank: The International Institute of Islamic Thought (IIIT), which was initially headed by al-Faruqi, became instrumental in organizing conferences and seminars around the world. Its aim was to push for the idea of Islamizing knowledge and to inaugurate universities which reflected an Islamist ideology tinged by Salafism. For a while, higher education policies in a number of important Muslim countries such as Pakistan and Malaysia were greatly influenced by the studies and position papers that IIIT developed. Leaders as disparate as Zia ul-Haq in Pakistan and Mahathir bin Mohammed in Malaysia embraced the Islamization of knowledge, primarily to bolster their Islamic credentials in increasingly conservative and religiously observant societies.

However, in spite of the huge resources devoted to the propagation of this version of the Islamization of knowledge, nothing of consequence emerged. It was far easier to discuss and argue about the theory of Islamizing disciplines than to address the practical issues of how to teach chemistry, for example, or how to structure a meaningful social science research project using Islamic value-markers.

The Islamization-of-knowledge project has sputtered on into recent times, with little of the former zeal and conviction. The Islamic universities which arose in the 1980s are far closer to the conventional models, while they maintain the fiction that they are somehow different. IIIT itself had a brush with the US authorities in the post 9/11 world. The Virginia offices of one of its offshoots were raided in 2002 because of its links with suspicious Islamic charities, which were alleged to have funnelled money to proscribed organizations.[21] Al-Faruqi, who is mostly associated in the public mind with the Islamization-of-knowledge thesis, met a tragic end. In 1986 he and his wife were found murdered by a man wielding a knife in their Pennsylvania home. The murders were never satisfactorily solved and the suspicion remains that the killings were politically motivated.

Al-Ghazzali and Modern Times

The work of Al-Attas and others on Islamizing knowledge echoes that of Islam's greatest scholarly figure, Abu Hamid al-Ghazzali, who died in 1111.[22] A great number of the reforming scholars and intellectuals of modern times had tried to emulate the effect of Ghazzali's magnum opus, *The Revivification of the Sciences of Religion* (or the *Ihya*, as it is popularly known), on the lives of Muslims and on the course of Islamic civilization. Ghazzali is one of the few figures outside metaphysical Sufism who have crossed the divide between the theological worlds of the Sunni and the Shia.[23] Encyclopaedic in scope, his work covers the entire gamut of religious life, from the basics of worship and transactions to the prophetic model, the encouragement of an ethics of conduct based on the virtues and, finally, a guarded acknowledgement of inspiration as a source of knowledge and the cultivation of an inner, even mystical, spirituality.

In earlier works, Ghazzali also attacked the use of rational Hellenistic philosophy as a yardstick by which to gauge the veracity of religious faith. The exchange between Ghazzali and his contemporary, the Andalusian jurist and philosopher Ibn Rushd (known in the West as Averroes), was 'settled', at least in the Sunni Islamic world, in favour of Ghazzali. This fact was presumed to have sealed the fate of philosophical inquiry in Sunni Islam until the modern era. Islam became immune to rationalist discourse – or so the claim ran. A version of this assertion is frequently made by critics of traditional Islam, from the neo-conservatives to Muslim liberals, and constant repetition has turned it into a supposedly defining feature of Islam, which sets it apart from the West. Modern Islamic civilization cannot be revived if there is no philosophical inquiry, and we have to blame Ghazzali for this unfortunate condition.

The 'failure' of Islamic civilization to produce modernity on its own is seemingly caused by Ghazzali's hold on subsequent Muslim life. The other current evolving in that period was the metaphysical Sufism associated with the person of Ibn 'Arabi, the possessor of one of the greatest mystical imaginations in history. Ibn 'Arabi's disciples carried this highly developed and aesthetic imagination into the eastern Islamic lands, helping to create a culture of 'high' Sufism which appealed not only to the Sunni world but, through fusion with the philosophy of Avicenna, into the Shia world. This elitist, even solitary, metaphysical Sufism stood apart from the intellectual currents of the times, but this did not stop it from being targeted as deviant and heretical by radical Salafis, conservatives and the clerical classes.

How Do Muslims Think?

The 1980s was the decade when consciously modern Islamic institutions and universities were being established, premised on the foundational principle of a unique Islamic knowledge. But in the same decade, in the western rim of the Islamic world, the Moroccan Muhammad 'Abid al-Jabiri was developing an entirely different perspective on the 'problem' of knowledge in Islam. Al-Jabiri, probably the most significant Muslim thinker of the age who wrote in the medium of Arabic, challenged the idea of a single form of Islamic knowledge. His most important contribution to Islamic thought is his three-volume work *Naqd al-'Aql al-'Arabi* (*The Critique of the Arabic Mind*), which, in spite of its title, deals mainly with the structure of Islamic knowledge.[24] Al-Jabiri argues that the formulation of the main outlines of Islamic knowledge did not happen during the prophetic period, in the seventh century or soon thereafter. Rather, it occurred as Islam settled over a vast empire and began to contend with developing systems of thought, which could explain and contextualize its world view.

In the early centuries of Islam, three distinct forms of Islamic knowledge evolved, each of them reflecting a particular way of interacting with the religion of Islam. The first was textually based (or *al-bayan*, as al-Jabiri termed it), and relied on the study of the foundational texts of Islam and the biography, sayings and actions of the Prophet Muhammad. It drew on the Quran and on prophetic narrations. These textual sources are authoritative by definition, so that no other form of knowledge can be used to alter decisions and rules derived from their proper textual analysis. The mechanisms by which such knowledge can be correctly drawn then become the appropriate fields of inquiry. In this sense, Islamic knowledge of the *al-bayan* form involves a meticulous concern for the Arabic language and grammar in order to find (or tease out) correct inferences and to trace the development of theology, jurisprudence and legal reasoning as the main components of Islamic knowledge.

According to al-Jabiri, this form of reasoning has reached an end. There are only so many formulations which can emerge from using these particular tools of inquiry, and they had all been reached a few centuries after the founding of Islam. All that can be usefully said on the matter has already been said. In this form of knowledge there is no room for natural or common law, unless such laws submit themselves to the superior truth inherent in the proper understanding and reading of the Quran and the prophetic traditions. This is the type of reasoning which prevails among the Salafists and Wahhabists of the modern era.

The second form of knowledge is one which al-Jabiri terms *al-irfan*, or mystical knowledge which derives from a spiritually inspired inner state or from persons whose inspired state is unquestioned. This form of knowledge includes all the esoteric branches of Islam – Sufism and Shiism, the philosophies of illumination and *hikma* ('wisdom' philosophy), and branches of Islamic cosmology such as astrology, alchemy and numerology. Al-Jabiri repeats the claim that this form of knowledge originates in eastern mystical traditions which preceded Islam. It creates a universe of symbols and allusions, of hidden and manifest meanings, of 'higher' and 'lower' forms of knowledge. By its very nature, mystical knowledge is not bound by any specific or invariant rules and can lead in an infinite number of directions. It feeds and informs the aesthetic and cultural sensibilities of Islam, but it has no (or only little) value in the management and ordering of worldly matters. Muslims who are prone to this type of thinking have basically 'retired their intellect', as al-Jabiri termed it.

The third form of knowledge relates to, or is derived from, observation and empirical evidence, or *al-burhan* (literally 'proof'). This knowledge is based on causality and thus allows for the evolution of a rationality anchored in natural laws. The weakness of Islam, according to al-Jabiri, is that, although *al-burhan* knowledge was potentially capable of evolution into an Islamic form of modern rationality, its development was truncated. First, it was invariably held to be of secondary value compared to the other two forms of knowledge. Its practitioners found themselves serving the other two types of knowledge and were inhibited when they contradicted the foundational texts of Islam. Secondly, and this is crucial to understanding al-Jabiri's hypothesis, 'rational' Islam was mainly an outcome of western Islam – that is, the Islam of Andalusia and the Maghreb. Figures such as Ibn Rushd, Ibn Khaldun and the theologian al-Shatibi were the main proponents of an empirical and utilitarian Islam. The dichotomous division into a western and an eastern Islam is central to al-Jabiri's system. The full development of the rationalizing potential of western Islam was blocked by the attacks on philosophy, on reason and on the uninspired human intellect carried by generations of scholars, Sufis and theologians. The western tradition died out, leaving Islamic knowledge to be defined by its foundational texts and by its esoteric and mystical dimension. Reason became a tool for the further enhancement of the other two kinds of knowledge rather than being allowed to develop a separate and independent existence.

The problem of Islamic thought, as al-Jabiri sees it, is that it is caught in a vicious circle. The systems of knowledge which evolved were sufficiently self-reliant not to incorporate any significant external influences. Once rationality was assigned to a secondary and supportive role, empirical knowledge was devalued, and whatever achievements could be attributed to it were later subsumed within the European experience. The Europeans succeeded in transcending the limiting features of religious knowledge and built their civilization of science and technology on the back of a systemic break with the past. Empirical knowledge based on observation, testing and measuring became the gauge for interpreting and exploiting the natural world. Meanwhile, Islamic thought continues to revolve in knowledge systems whose essential features have been fixed. The authority of the past becomes supreme and makes any departure from its authoritativeness appear suspect. Al-Jabiri has called for a new rationality in Islam, drawing its inspiration partly from the abortive western Islamic model, and engaging Islam in a new dialogue with critical reason, empirical evidence and utilitarian considerations.

Al-Jabiri's criticism of knowledge based simply on textual reasoning is valid, but, using his criterion for the final purpose of knowledge, he fails to see the potential in the 'retired intellect' of the mystical stream in Islam, which he contemptuously dismisses. He shares the common prejudices of both conservatives and modernists against the rejuvenating possibilities of a spiritualized Islam.

The various projects for rediscovering the source of true knowledge in Islam are an immense undertaking, certainly greater than the capacities of any one individual, institution, or even lifetime. But it is a tribute to the pioneers of this movement that they have shown the courage to plant the first seeds, even though most of them have fallen on thorny ground. In many ways, al-Attas's vision is the one which has met the challenges of time. Muslims have to go back to first principles and rediscover the innate capacity to acknowledge the Signs of God in themselves and in the far horizons – a capacity which the Quran calls *fitrah*, the original crack through which the divine light shines inside human beings. The premise – which is correct – is that this primary knowledge is the *sine qua non* for any subsequent development of a specifically Islamic civilization. Other systems of Islamizing knowledge refashion the outer world first – legally, politically, institutionally, methodologically – and leave the refashioning of the individual for later. In the final analysis, the Attasian vision of the Islamization of knowledge is a form of moral philosophy rooted in religious faith. It is focused on the recovery of the virtuous person as a precondition for the emergence of a moral order. It is also a philosophy of responsible freedom, as the 're-moralized' person conducts himself or herself freely within the parameters of appropriate action – or, in al-Attas's terms, with *adab*.

However, the attempts to refashion the Islamic perspective faltered, being unable to quite shake off their academic pedigree or to disentangle themselves from governments and their educational bureaucracies. In the Islamic world, modern secular education had become too ensconced to be seriously challenged by international conferences on Islamizing knowledge and by impassioned speeches by scholars indignant about the decay of Islamic civilization. At the same time, the many Muslim governments which took up the cause of Islamizing knowledge did not see it as anything more than a tool designed to enhance their power and authority. As in most other 'waves' of Islamic reform, the tide of the Islamization-of-knowledge project crested and then retreated, leaving very few traces of its potential for promoting vital change in Islamic civilization.

The decade of the 1980s thus ended not with the nurturing of Islam's creative forces but with establishing the primacy of political Islam and its agendas. The defeat of the Soviet expedition in Afghanistan provided an enormous boost to the cause of militant Islamist forces worldwide. This coincided with the retreat of radical Shia Islam as Iran emerged from the almost decades-long Iran–Iraq war. Iran was exhausted and its revolutionary drive was now contained, if not fully eliminated.

CHAPTER 5

The Reformations of Islam

When the West reconciled religion and freedom, it did so by making the individual the focus of society, and the price it has paid has been individualism run rampant, in the form of weak marriages, high rates of crime, and alienated personalities. When Islam kept religion at the expense of freedom, it did so by making the individual subordinate to society, and the price it has paid has been autocratic governments, religious intolerance, and little personal freedom.

James Q. Wilson 'The Reform Islam Needs', *City Journal*, vol 12, no 4, 2002.

The global concern with Islam's reformation began to emerge at the end of the 1980s. Almost on cue, Islam arose to take the place of the communist bloc in the demonology of the former cold war warriors. The decade of the 1990s was dominated by a growing sense of alarm in most of the world about the threat from politically radical Islam. The return of thousands of Arab fighters to their homelands from the Afghan war set the stage for violent challenges to the status quo in a number of Muslim countries. This was only slightly counter-balanced by concern for the plight of Muslims at the receiving end of the others' violence, especially in the Balkans. The West, in particular, began seeing Islam in a new light, partly as an energizer of forces which were bent on challenging western hegemony and the rules of the new, unipolar order. Samuel P. Huntington produced his important thesis on the 'clash of civilizations' in a 1992 essay, which was later expanded into a book.[1] Islam was clearly identified as the main protagonist of conflict and discord in the world. Two years earlier, in 1990, the historian Bernard Lewis wrote a very influential essay on the 'Roots of

Muslim rage'. It was subtitled 'Why so many Muslims deeply resent the West, and why their bitterness will not be easily mollified'.[2]

The 1990s also saw the rise of the neo-conservative movement in the US. Neo-conservatives held often deeply antipathetic views about an unreformed Islam which were reflected in the think-tanks and journals which represented their ideological line. Commentators such as Daniel Pipes became influential advocates of a secularized Islam and contributed to the climate of opinion which divided Islam into a moderate wing, which acknowledges the supremacy of western values, and a recalcitrant radical wing, which is bent on confronting and undermining the West. The idea that Muslims in the West could be some kind of fifth columnists for radical Islam gained currency in the 1990s. It coincided with the recognition that Islam had set deep roots inside western societies and that a large cohort of European-born Muslims was angry and in danger of becoming radicalized. 'Islamophobia' entered the lexicon. It was defined in 1997 by the British Runnymede Trust as the 'dread or hatred of Islam and therefore . . . the fear and dislike of all Muslims'.[3]

But it was after the 11 September 2001 attacks on New York and Washington that the calls to 'reform' Islam reached unprecedented and cacophonous levels. It was not only intellectuals and scholars that made these demands. They were joined by politicians, journalists, novelists, actors, media stars and all manner of self-proclaimed experts on Islam. Everyone sought to find the reasons behind the self-immolation of a few nihilists. Those who tried to limit the debate to the culpability of the perpetrators themselves were drowned out by the often explicit assertion that the entire heritage of Islam was at fault. It appeared as if the whole world had closed ranks and was pointing an accusing finger at Islam. The expressions of revulsion which were manifested towards the terrorists by a huge number of Muslims – including tens of thousands of candle-bearing Iranians, who expressed their solidarity with the victims and their families – made little impression in the overall mood of disgust, sourness and fear that gripped the world. Some academics and clergymen sought to refute the connection of the terrorists with Islam, but few paid attention to them.

The parade of apologetic Muslims who popped up on the post 9/11 airwaves, failed to dent the profound anti-Islamic sentiment that had taken hold.[4] Of course, as the aftershocks of the attacks subsided, more nuanced and reasoned analyses of Islam were formed. but the underlying thrust did not materially alter. Islam was in sore need of a reformation, and it would be cajoled, pressured, goaded and, if need be, forced into accommodating and acknowledging the values of the modern world. An entire industry emerged that purported to understand and explain the causes of Islam's 'retrogression', its inability to modernize and its supposed proneness to violence and intolerance.[5]

Reforming a Recalcitrant Religion

The calls to reform Islam in the post-9/11 world all had the same objectives: to remould the environment of Muslim countries and societies towards realizing a specific set of desirable outcomes in the future. What these outcomes were depended, of course, on who was prescribing the reform. In this sense, would-be reformers of Islam would include not only liberals but radicals and fundamentalists, and Muslims as well as non-Muslims who had appropriated for themselves the right to intervene in, or to direct, the affairs of Muslims. The idea was to encourage a gradual or abrupt break with those elements of Islam that were seen to be problematic in terms of the reformers' own goals. These goals included the enhancement of the internal security of the US or European countries, the secularization of Muslim societies, the spread of human and civil rights, or, from another perspective, the imposition of a theocracy and the return to an imaginary past. Apart from the breath-taking arrogance, and even stupidity, of these projects – for who has ever heard of reforming Buddhism, Hinduism or Confucianism, let alone Christianity, as a global objective? – it is clear that real damage could result if reformers were afforded the means to implement such designs.

In every age since the eruption of the West into the Islamic heartlands, an act which is best symbolized by the Napoleonic occupation of Egypt, Islam has had its share of philosophical 'fixes' for the Muslims' dilemma. In many ways the history of modern Islamic thought can be read as one continuous series of remedies to what was perceived as decline and impending doom. However, the vital factor that made the preoccupation with Islam more serious and ominous this time was the switch of the world's hyper-power from a policy of benign neglect, and (frequently) cynical indifference towards the travails of Muslims, to one of combating, literally, the forces of radical Islam on a global basis. The vast resources of the United States were brought to bear on the 'problem' of Islam and on the reformation of Islam.[6]

One of the more potent ideas for the reformation of Islam was in reality a repetition of the old nineteenth-century critique of Islam by the latter-day heirs of Renan and the likes of Sir William Muir, a Victorian author of a vituperative but influential biography of the Prophet Muhammad.[7] The backdrop had shifted away from Islam's compatibility with science and rationalism towards Islam's compatibility with the supposedly universal values embodied in modern democratic societies. The old criticisms remained, but they were overshadowed by newer and more immediate concerns. Islam was now being assessed in relation to concepts such as pluralism, universal human rights, democracy and freedom. The linear view of human progress and cultural evolution, drawn from the western experience, became the test-case for Islam's path towards its own reformation. A reductionist rendering of the Reformation in Europe became the model Islam should follow. Islam had to be challenged by disruptive, provocative and possibly subversive readings of its own dogmas and creeds. In the process, Islam would be refashioned so as to provide a welcome reception to the notions of the liberal democratic world.

The parallels with the Christian Reformation were fallacious. Reasoning by historical analogy was the vogue in the post-9/11 environment, but the inferences drawn were hopelessly inappropriate for Islam. The Reformation affected the Catholic Church in central and western Europe only. The unity of Christendom had been sundered with the division of the Roman Empire, and the eastern church had already had a physically separate and independent existence from the western church for nearly a millennium before the Reformation. The narrative of the Reformation in western Christianity, to which Islam was compared, had as its starting point the revolt of the individual against the authority of a hierarchical institution, whose presence and intercession with God was essential as a matter of dogma. The ground was prepared by humanist scholars such as Erasmus and by the opening of a reinterpretation of the scriptures based on his accurate translations.

The victory of science and natural philosophy over theology and dogma was another immensely significant outcome of the Reformation, as the linear narrative would have us believe. The Catholic church, at the height of the Thirty Years War, saw fit to subject Galileo to the Roman Inquisition for his heretical beliefs on the laws of motion, but religious faith was no match for empirical evidence in the understanding of the natural world. The story of the benefits of the Reformation continues into the political arena, where the religious dissenters of England, Germany and the Low Countries, moving across the Atlantic, plant in the New World the seeds for the separation of the state from an established church. In economics and business, the Calvinist doctrines relating to the interconnection between thrift, work and the salvation of the elect are held to be the causal factors in the advance of capitalism, and hence of modern business organizations.[8] The industrial revolution is thus only one step away from the Reformation. Who can doubt that the industrial revolution started in the Protestant strongholds of England and north-western Europe?

The Reformation becomes a pre-history of the Enlightenment, which finally succeeds in banishing religion from the public arena. A monolithic Latin Christianity is fragmented into a multifaceted faith with many churches; religious wars are replaced by religious toleration, which is only a transit station to secularism, and then to pluralism. Both the Reformation and the Enlightenment are necessary phases in the 'taming' of religious faith and in opening mankind to the possibilities of a post-religion order. Now – if only Islam could follow the same path – without, of course, the two hundred years of violence and devastation which the Reformation actually unleashed – then Islam would be shorn of its dogmatic certainties, which are antithetical to human advancement. It could then fit into the structures of the modern world.

This bare outline of the march of the West has been questioned and in many cases discredited by historians, but is still presented as incontrovertible evidence for Islam to undergo a similar rite of passage as western Christianity.[9] On closer inspection, however, the utility of the analogy falls apart; the parallels are absurd.

Islam does not have a church with a fossilized hierarchy at whose apex rests a supreme religious authority. Reforming such a church has no meaning in the Islamic context. Perhaps the Islamic revolution in Iran introduced the rule of a church-like hierarchy, but this was the result of an epochal and revolutionary event, and an inversion of the idea of a Protestant-type reformation. A religious hierarchy was imposed on the state when none had existed before, scarcely a reformation in the European sense. At the same time, the majority of Muslims were not living in countries governed under Sharia law, with the exception of a few self-consciously Islamic states such as Saudi Arabia and, lately, Iran. It was difficult therefore to posit the reformation of Islam specifically in terms of reforming the Sharia, if its provisions were no longer applicable outside the framework of family law or personal law.

The abandonment of Sharia law had been effected, by and large, during the colonial and immediately post-colonial era. So the effect of Islam, either on the formal structures of government or on its laws, has been minimal in most of the Islamic world. Among Muslim communities in

Europe or in countries where Muslims formed a large minority, Muslims were subjected to the law of the land. In India, the large Muslim population had recourse to Sharia rulings only in matters of personal or family law. The putative calls to reform Islam could not apply to Muslims states or to their legal systems, except in matters of personal law. Reforming Islamic personal law certainly did have implications for gender rights, but this was a special, limiting case. Islam was therefore not an obstacle for the reformation of state structures or for the introduction of new political doctrines. The 'conflict' between Islam and democracy could not arise in the context of Muslim countries whose entire political legacy was based on an authoritarianism which only used Islam to justify its rule. Outside of the few 'Islamic' states and traditional monarchies such as Morocco, Islam was not used to justify the legitimacy of the ruling groups, except through a formal and meaningless lip-service to Islam as the religion of the state in the constitutions of a number of Muslim countries. In addition, the number of Muslims living in actual or self-proclaimed democracies reached more than a third of the entire world's population of Muslims. The issue was not therefore, reforming an Islam already in power, but reforming an Islam which *could* come to power – a crucial difference.

The Islam that could come to power was a worrisome eventuality. The proposals for reforming Islam took on a precautionary, even pre-emptive character, especially when they emanated from those keen to avert a repetition of the Iranian Revolution, the spread of radical Wahhabism, or the *jihadi* culture of al-Qaeda and its offshoots. The ideology of the terrorists was assessed alongside Islamic orthodoxy, to see if the two were intertwined. What were the roots of terror and radicalization? The last time when Islam, as a religion and as a civilization, was subjected to such intense scrutiny was in the nineteenth and early twentieth centuries, when European imperialists were encountering widespread resistance.

The rise of totalitarian states and the cold war relegated Islam to being a minor concern, except where its political influence coincided with the national liberation movements of the period. However, as the dismantling of the colonial empires was a firm policy position of the US, it was unlikely that Islam, as an enabling ideology in the anti-colonial movement, would incur the wrath of the US. In fact, the usefulness of Islam as a counterweight to communism was also a feature in the cold war, although the CIA seems not to have financed Islamic movements directly or supported Islamic causes through front organizations such as the Congress for Cultural Freedom.[10] Nevertheless, Islam became a firm ally of the West during the final years of the cold war, when Afghan *mujahidin* movements, stiffened with Arab and central Asian volunteers, helped to bring the Soviet empire to an end. But the period that followed the collapse of the Soviet bloc put paid to this indifference, and the old prejudices and concerns rose up, being backed even by allies from within the Muslim world itself.

The Turn to Violence

In the search for culprits for Islam's turn to violence, most roads passed through Wahhabism and went back to the medieval theologian Ibn Taymiyya. But there was a short interlude between the 1980s and the mid-1990s when revolutionary Shia Islam was probed in order to reveal its potential for causing violence and instability. The argument was that Shiism is inherently revolutionary and disruptive, and this was the drive behind most of the insurrectionary movements in Islamic history. It is prone to being led – or misled – by its guardians, who, uniquely in the world of Islam, have a status which is equivalent to an official religious hierarchy. Shia rituals have the capacity to galvanize emotions to dangerously unstable levels. Their images of martyrdom and sacrifice can be exploited by unscrupulous leaders to mobilize millions of the faithful to acts of violence and self-sacrifice. The example of the hordes of Iranian youth willingly going to their certain deaths in the Iran–Iraq war, carrying plastic keys to the gates of Imam Hussein's shrine in Karbala, was frequently used to emphasize the irrational nature of the passions that motivated the Shia. Images of crowds beating their chests and hitting their heads with the flat of swords were powerful reminders that a religion of lament can quickly turn its energies from self-inflicted wounds to an outer enemy.

But shiism is also characterized by an introversion which denies the legitimacy of any state authority and stays well away from political entanglements.[11] This feature formed a counter-narrative to the revolutionary Shiism of Ayatollah Khomeini. Upon his death, the revolutionary and destabilizing zeal of Shiism seemed to decline, leaving only the Islamic Republic of Iran as the dangerous force to be reckoned with – and not Shiism per se. During the build-up to the invasion of Iraq, the public image of Shia Islam was also softened as the US sought allies among the Shia opposition in exile and developed a working relationship with the Grand Ayatollahs of Najaf. But the possibility that Shia Muslims would ever lead a world-wide pan-Islamic movement opposed to the West was a non-starter, given the distinct minority status of the Shia in Islam. This was an issue which was deliberately played upon by both conservative and radical Sunnis, to dispel the appeal of revolutionary Islam emanating from Shia Iran. It was unlikely, therefore, that the majority of Sunnis would look to Shiism for their revolutionary prompting. Burrowing into the arcane corners of Shia theology to find the roots of Islam's revolutionary potential against the West was soon abandoned.

However, nearly all the latter-day radical and terrorist Islamist groups claim a fealty to the ideas of Ibn Taymiyya. Ahmad Ibn Taymiyya was born in 1263, into a family of well-known scholars and jurists. His thought was directed towards the orthodox in the Sunni world and towards what he saw as the corruption of Islamic life through the spread of laws and customs that were outside of the ambit of the Sharia or the prophetic practice. His railings at *bida'a* (the introduction of reprehensible innovations into Islam) were partly aimed at the entrenchment of traditions not rooted in Islam in the thirteenth-century world of Damascus, which he inhabited. Syria at that time was under the rule of the Mamelukes, a Caucasian slave dynasty based in Egypt. Ibn Taymiyya believed that there was always a basis for a single valid Sharia ruling for any event or circumstance. It was the function of the jurists and *ulemas* of Islam to find this ruling. To this effect, he moved away from the traditional categories of using analogous reasoning or the consensus of scholars to limit the range of acceptable Sharia-based rulings. By rejecting both the principle of emulating prior scholars (*taqlid*) and the restrictions on open-ended interpretations of Islam based on independent reasoning (*ijtihad*), Ibn Taymiyya established the possibility of finding Sharia-based solutions for any set of problems and conditions, solutions that were free from the shackles of orthodox restrictions.

Ibn Taymiyya's own rulings (*fatwas*) were voluminous and dealt with every conceivable subject. His compendium continues to be a source of religious inspiration for every modern Wahhabi or Salafi Muslim. In some ways, his rejection of blind imitation may have appeared to be liberating and potentially constructive, but there was a sting to the tail. The spiritual life of Islam became entirely Sharia-defined. Everything that didn't meet the test of Ibn Taymiyya's singular Sharia-based ruling became a form of *bida'a*, and therefore reprehensible and to be shunned. His understanding of the Quranic text was entirely literalist, to the point of being anthromorphic. He would affirm that God literally had hands and a face. He detested shrines and the ceremonies associated with the birth or death of Sufi saints. His attitude to the Shia, in whatever form, was implacably hostile and aggressive. The Shia, of course, returned his hatred of them with their own unflattering epithets. His attitude to Sufism is riddled with contradictions and ambiguities, ranging from complete condemnation and accusations of polytheism to a grudging respect for a few of its leading saintly figures. His hatred for the medieval mystic Ibn 'Arabi was intense – a trait which has carried to his modern-day followers.

Ibn Taymiyya's effects on Islam have not been entirely constructive. His constant campaigns of vilification, directed as they were against all and sundry and mixed with the occasional profundity, led to his being severely reprimanded by the leading scholars of the time. Even his own students condemned him for his indiscriminate attacks on the pious and righteous and for his constant hurling of the accusation of *bida'a*.[12] For his rejection of key tenets of orthodox Sunni thought, Ibn Taymiyya was sent to prison by four judges representing the four schools of law in Sunni Islam.

Even though hundreds of thousands of Damascenes attended Ibn Taymiyya's funeral, his influence was quickly forgotten in the world of Islam and remained so until the advent of Ibn Abd el-Wahhab, the founder of the eponymous Wahhabi movement in eighteenth-century Arabia. Ibn Abd el-Wahhab relied on Ibn Taymiyya as the main source for his own *Kitab at-Tawhid* (*The Book of Unity*), the founding text of Wahhabism. However, the legacy of Salafism, which is a diluted version of Wahhabism, has been more pervasive in Muslim lands. Salafism, which was more 'contemporary' and less doctrinally primitive, has relied more extensively on the works of Ibn Taymiyya.

In Egypt, it was the arrival of the Tripolitan Muhammed Rashid Ridha in 1897 that gave Salafism its first pan-Islamic champion. Ridha's *al-Manar* newspaper was a mouthpiece for the ideas of Ibn Taymiyya, and his deep dislike for Sufism, together with his insistence on the *ijtihad* model of Ibn Taymiyya, coloured his modernism. *Al-Manar* had a huge impact and provided the principal intellectual prop for the spread of the Salafi movement to the far corners of the world – in fact, wherever the newspaper was read.

The Wahhabi/Salafi strain in Sunni Islam remained a minority position throughout most of the twentieth century. Nearly all state-sponsored religious establishments in the Sunni Muslim world were dominated by an innate conservatism and avoided any direct political action that challenged the status quo.[13] However, the rise in power of the Saudi state and the enormous growth of its financial resources paved the way for the widespread diffusion of its official Wahhabi doctrine. The centre of gravity of the Sunni world has thus shifted markedly in the past two decades towards the Wahhabi/Salafi interpretations, rooted as these are in the system of Ibn Taymiyya. The effect has been to radicalize Sunni Islam by weakening its connection with the classical schools of law. These were inherently moderate, restrained and subtle in their decisions, and allowed for considerable flexibility and leeway in their implementation. Invariant rulings, which held sway for all times and places, were the exception rather than the rule. The rise of the Wahhabi/Salafi system challenged these schools at a number of levels. Wahhabi/Salafi thought followed Ibn Taymiyya in rejecting allegiance to any of the four schools of law as a formal requirement for the believer. The result was a barrage of obligatory rulings which ignored the laborious and limiting process by which conclusions and decisions had been previously achieved.

The richness and variety of Islam was gradually stifled by tying the believer down through an incredible array of detailed regulations and rules. As the scholar Khaled Abou el Fadl wrote in his 2001 dissection of the new authoritarianism in Islam, *Speaking in God's Name*.[14]

Essentially, contemporary *ijtihad* efforts often were the product of an authoritarian process that yielded closed determinations, which effectively signalled the death of the same legal system that the *ijtihad* efforts hoped to reinvigorate. The usual process, if one can call it a process, of this code-like new *ijtihad* largely consisted of citing some anecdotal evidence or selective reports attributed to the Prophet, and then declaring the law of God to be such-or-such.

Given that the system is designed to produce uniquely 'appropriate' rulings, the end result is that Wahhabism/Salafism becomes a vehicle for a wide range of rulings which have canonical force. The death knell for Islamic law is sounding. All its vitality, originality and appositeness fades away, turning it into a massive manual with rulings often drawn from the shoddy scholarship of bigoted clerics and Islamic activists with little jurisprudential training.

Some of the rulings that have emanated from the official Wahhabi council for legal opinions in Saudi Arabia have been truly outlandish and are objects of ridicule. A good many of them relate specifically to women, their freedom to work and travel, and their permissible inner and outer garments.[15] Other rulings from Wahhabi clerics have been used by terrorists and *jihadis* to justify all manner of atrocities, including the 9/11 attacks. In a taped interview after the 9/11 attacks, Bin Laden is seen discussing them with a Saudi cleric who then gives the matter his blessing. *Fatwas* by radical Wahhabi clerics have justified mass murder against the Shia in Iraq, Pakistan and Afghanistan as well as a virulent hatred for the Sufi orders and for any manifestation of local Islam, and have provided the religious cover for a good part of the terrorism which has plagued the world.

Accommodation and Tolerance

Mutual tolerance between the varieties of Islamic faith and practice and accommodation of the non-Muslim populations who lived alongside Muslims formed an important element of Islamic civilization. Necessarily, the lead had to come from the majority religious group – the Sunni orthodoxy in most cases – which acknowledged the legitimacy and rights of the minority groups. The operative word in Islam is accommodation, not tolerance. Accommodation is a permanent arrangement which implies the creation of a recognized and legitimate space for other religious and doctrinal groups. Toleration on the other hand assumes the supremacy of one over the other but allows the other to exist on sufferance. The Sunni–Shia relationship throughout most of Islamic history was one of accommodation rather than toleration, in spite of important theological differences.[16] Apart from the historical and social circumstances that would have encouraged accommodation between the various sects of Islam, the charge of *kufr* (infidelity) in Islam is a very grave one, and all Islamic schools of law use extremely strict and narrow criteria in defining it. The purpose is to avoid any possibility of bloodshed and sedition, and of breaking the prized unity of the Muslim *umma*.

The great theologian al-Ghazali wrote the definitive treatise on the charge of *kufr*. In essence, any person who declares the statement of faith of Islam, 'There is no God but Allah, and Muhammad is His messenger', is *ipso facto* a Muslim.[17] Al-Ghazali states categorically that 'there should be no branding any person an Unbeliever over any secondary issue whatsoever as a matter of principle'. The Shia doctrine of the hidden imam might be objectionable, as it is according to al-Ghazali, but it is unconnected with the fundamentals of the faith. This narrows unbelief either to denying the unity of God or to denying that the Prophet Muhammad was truthful in delivering his message. This viewpoint was echoed by the Shia grand ayatollahs. A number of them throughout history would have harsh words to say about the companions of the Prophet, the Prophet's wife, Aisha, and the caliphs who preceded Ali. But, in spite of their hostility to these key figures in Islam, such ayatollahs would not cast any Sunni Muslim into the circle of *kufr*. Thus the leeway for accommodating diversity was very broad, and only a few extremist groups whose roots are in Islam are excluded from the community of Islam. These extremists – many of whom venerate Ali, the first imam of the Shia, to the point of deification – are excluded because they implicitly deny the unity of God in their belief in immanence (*hulul*) and in doctrines such as transubstantiation. In the evolution of Islamic civilization, some of these extremists, for instance, the Nusairis and the Druze of Greater Syria, were pushed out of the main urban areas of Islam into mountain redoubts until modern times.

The absence of a supreme ecclesiastic authority – even in Shia Islam, where the grand ayatollahs can and do disagree among themselves – makes it difficult to realize the establishment of a single orthodox dogma over all Muslims. The natural state of Islam is therefore diversity, and a broad range of sects and groups do co-exist within it. In fact, there is an oft-quoted narration from the Prophet which celebrates the diversity of opinion within the scholars of the faith. It is astounding, in modern Salafi eyes, for example, that the highest offices of the Abbasid Caliphate could ever be held by Shia. But the triumph of the Wahhabi/Salafi school has eroded the natural elasticity of the Islamic community. The Wahhabi/Salafi school could now claim that they had the right to determine who was within the faith. The closing of the Islamic mind, at least in this respect, is very much a modern phenomenon.

The global spread of Wahhabism/Salafism is directly attributable to the massive financial support which is provided for the Wahhabi *da'awa* (or mission) by the Saudi state, and lately by wealthy businessmen and merchants.[18] The role of Wahhabist propaganda in the radicalization of Muslim youth in the ghettoes of western Europe or in the villages and slums of South Asia has been well documented. The sum total of this relentless activity to force the world of Sunni Islam into the straightjacket of Wahhabi/Salafi thought has been the creation of the scaffolding of a new type of religious authority in Sunni Islam, one which may portend the establishment of a church-like institution which may come to dominate the world of Sunni Islam.

The eagerly anticipated Islamic 'Reformation' may very well end up as the diametrical opposite of what was expected: as a rigidifying of Islam managed by a uniquely intolerant and narrow-minded class of clerics, drawn from a backwater of Islamic civilization and willingly cut off from the magnificent panorama of Islam's intellectual tradition. This process has been growing exponentially over the past four decades. The bastions of traditional Sunni learning have been undermined by their adoption of Wahhabist/Salafist thought and by the latter's devaluation of the classical Islamic tradition.

The prevailing Wahhabi/Salafi ascendancy has had a profound effect on the world of Sunni Islam, contributing in no small measure to the narrowing of Muslims' religious and spiritual sensibilities. A dark cloud hovers over the world of observant Sunni Islam. The concern with the minutiae of religious life, the micro-regulation of daily activity, the smugness that accompanies dogmatic certainty, the joylessness of a fastidious religiosity, the lack of interest or curiosity either in the past or in the multivariate aspects of Islam, have all crept into the religious culture of observant Muslims. The celebrations, commemorations and acts of piety that gave Islam its dramatic sweep have been forced out. Local variants of traditional Muslim festivals – such as the veneration of the Prophet – are dismissed as *bida'a*; public expressions of spirituality are denied legitimacy. The culture of Islam is drained of vitality by a barren utilitarianism which shamelessly draws on the scientific and technical achievement of others and celebrates a crude materialism. It has no aesthetic sensibility and little or no literary creativity. When did this world last produce a single work of abiding scientific, intellectual or literary merit, and who are its great architects, calligraphers or poets?

But there are tell-tale signs that the Sunni world is beginning to resist the type of future that this implies. The grip that Wahhabist/Salafist thought was developing over Muslims suffered a serious setback after the 9/11 attacks. Muslims were driven – partly by the ferocious attacks on their faith which came from all quarters – to question the modern course of Islam. The need to re-examine entire aspects of Islam, including the rigid conservatism which was increasingly becoming its defining feature, was an important side-effect of the post-9/11 fallout on the worldwide community of Muslims.

Non-Arab Muslim countries which had sent hundreds of students to the Wahhabi academies of Saudi Arabia began to question the wisdom of this move. Countries such as Morocco, with its strong and historical commitment to the Maliki *madhab* (school of law), became suspicious of the Wahhabi doctrine which denied the need to abide by the rulings of a particular school of law. They were also suffering from the 'blowback' of returning Moroccans who had studied Islam at these schools and who had contributed to the radicalization of Moroccan Islam. Sufi orders began to proliferate anew, even inside the Wahhabi stronghold of Saudi Arabia. In 2005, thousands of mourners attended the funeral of a well-respected Sufi Sheikh in Mecca, Sayyid Muhammad Alawi.[19] He had been ostracized by the Wahhabi establishment and forbidden to hold classes in the Grand Mosque of Mecca. The terrible sectarian carnage in Iraq after the 2003 US invasion and its aftermath also gave pause to those who anathematized the Shia. Calls for inter-sectarian dialogue multiplied, leading to the 2005 Amman Message of leading scholars of Sunni and Shia Islam.

The Amman Message

A number of organizations had been created in the past to try to bring together the two great schools of Islam. The most notable attempt was in the 1940s, when the al-Azhar University sponsored a formal body designed to draw together the two schools.[20] However, with the increasing influence of anti-Shia Wahhabism on Sunni thought, this effort languished. The Amman Message of 2005 was initiated by the king of Jordan and aimed to make clear the legitimate schools of Islam, the conditions of declaring a person an apostate, and the authorities entitled to issue rulings on matters of Islamic law and jurisprudence. It came at a time of increased sectarian tensions throughout the Muslim world – tensions partly brought on by the Iraq crisis and by increasing fears about international terrorism's possible use of Islamic religious rulings in order to justify acts of violence and indiscriminate killings. Scholars from all the major Islamic schools of thought assembled in Amman. Crucially, the Saudi government encouraged the participation of its state-sponsored *ulema* organizations in the conference, and both Iran and Iraq sent high-level delegations from their Shia hierarchies to Amman. The result was an unequivocal call for Muslim unity; a condemnation of terrorism; and a forbidding of unsubstantiated *fatwas* issued by illegitimate groups who claimed religious authority.[21] The conference's recommendations and resolution were approved by all the participants, as well as by the Saudi government. The Saudi government had formally acknowledged that the Shia are in fact Muslims after all.[22]

The resolution affirmed the proximity to each other of the rulings of the religious schools of Islam and the fact that they all adhered to the essential 'pillars' of Islam. But, much to its credit, the resolution did not shrink from admitting that there were important theological differences between the sects. Finally it denounced the issuing of *fatwas* by unauthorized individuals, a decision clearly aimed at radical and terrorist groups.

Acknowledgement of the schools of Islamic jurisprudence (*Mathahib*) within Islam means adhering to a fundamental methodology in the issuance of *fatwas*: no one may issue a *fatwa* without the requisite qualifications of knowledge. No one may issue a *fatwa* without adhering to the methodology of the schools of Islamic jurisprudence. No one may claim to do unlimited *Ijtihad* and create a new opinion or issue unacceptable *fatwas* that take Muslims out of the principles and certainties of the *Shari'ah* and what has been established in respect of its schools of jurisprudence.[23]

This vigorous statement from the assembled dignitaries of Islam reaffirmed the authority of tradition. Its focus on the schools of Islam stressed the significance of centuries of learning in the formulation of Islamic rulings. Its signatories included, unsurprisingly, all the official religious institutions of the main Islamic countries, as well as important centres of learning and scholarship such as al-Azhar. Scholars associated with the Salafi strain of Islam also signed up – including Yusuf al-Qaradawi, a former stalwart of the Muslim Brotherhood, who now headed a state-sponsored religious council in Qatar. The Saudi state stood firmly behind the new efforts to improve sectarian harmony. These efforts reflected both the reformist tendencies of King Abdullah ibn Abd el-Aziz and genuine fears regarding the uncontrolled activities of the radical Wahhabi clerical class. Nevertheless, the statement carried only a few signatories from the Wahhabi establishment. The *raison d'état* that drove the Saudis and others to sign up for the declaration was not met by the Wahhabi establishment with an equal commitment to the new era of inter-sectarian harmony and brotherhood.

A follow-up conference to the Amman meeting of Sunni and Shia scholars was held soon thereafter in Mecca. But in February 2006, scarcely six months after the Mecca conference, one of Shia Islam's most sacred sites, the al-Askariya Shrine of the Two Imams in Sammarra, Iraq, was blown up by operatives of al-Qaeda in Iraq. This unleashed an orgy of violence, mainly directed at the Sunni population of Iraq. The ensuing mayhem reached near civil war levels, with thousands killed and hundreds of thousands internally displaced or fleeing to nearby countries.

The more radical Wahhabi clerics in Saudi Arabia applauded the destruction of the shrine, while the officially sanctioned groups mostly kept silent. Ibn Jibreen, a notoriously anti-Shia cleric, was widely believed to have encouraged his followers to spread an 'underground' *fatwa* calling for the destruction of all shrines, as shrines would encourage idolatry. Wahhabi practice in Saudi Arabia and Afghanistan is replete with incidents where historical sites, shrines and tombs have been desecrated or destroyed. A notable case which achieved international notoriety was the 2001 destruction of the giant Buddha statues in Bamyan province, Afghanistan, by the Taliban.[24] Ibn Jibreen himself posted *fatwas* relating to the Shia and the Sufis which were uniformly scathing and condemnatory. The wars within Islam were not going to disappear so quickly.

Reformers and Their Discontents

A good portion of these religious disputes was also to do with the acceptable limits up to, and conditions in, which change can be tolerated within Islam without destroying its essential features. The issue of what is incontrovertibly fixed in the religion of Islam and what is capable of change has existed throughout the whole history of Islam. Heresies, and even new religions such as the Bahai faith, grew when what was thought to be fixed was challenged and overthrown.[25] The need to limit the scope of change before it turned destructive to the core doctrines of Islam became of paramount importance.[26] The evolution of the four main schools of jurisprudence as a type of orthodoxy in Sunni Islam happened in response to the ever-present risk of schisms and divisions affecting the Islamic community. Shiism, itself doctrinally different in important ways from Sunni Islam, also evolved its own form of orthodoxy, albeit after a considerable length of time. In both cases, the impulse was to control what was permissible, to establish authoritative structures for the belief systems and practices of the faith, and to ward off the possibility of deviations and unacceptable innovations.

There are in reality only three aspects to the question of immutability in Islam: the first deals with the relationship between God and the individual; the second with the relationship between humans themselves; and the third with the relationship between the human being and his or her own self. All these aspects must come together as a whole, to establish what is unalterable. If the common denominators between the three are established, then these must, almost by definition, be considered the axioms of Islam. Thus an inner spirituality which does not express itself in creedal doctrines or in an institutional and legal framework is intrinsically deficient. Similarly, the insistence on a particular aspect of Sharia law which is not matched both by an inner ethic, and by a divine sanction becomes untenable in terms of its immutability. Within the framework of classical Islamic categories, these relationships are expressed as *Sharia* (the relationship between humans); *Tariqa* (the relationship between the individual and the self) and *Haqiqa* (the relationship between God and the human being).[27]

A major expounder on the problem of what is fixed and what is changeable in Islam – indeed in religion as a whole – is the contemporary Iranian philosopher Abd el-Karim Soroush. Born in 1945 and educated in Iran and at London University, Soroush was one of the stalwarts of the Iranian Revolution of 1979. For a while, as a member of the Cultural Revolution Committee, he was responsible for revamping the Iranian higher education system, the vetting of academics and the reconstitution of the curriculum. Later he fell out with the new clerical establishment and became a well-known dissident Islamic thinker, part of the uniquely Iranian class of religious intellectuals. Soroush has been under constant harassment and threats of attack by agents of the Iranian establishment, but he has stood his intellectual ground, inside Iran as well as in numerous appearances at various international conferences and academic institutions. Although his interests are wide-ranging and include the relationship of Islam with democracy, human and civil rights, gender issues and political pluralism, he is best known for his theory of the expansion and contraction of religious knowledge. Enthusiastic western commentators have called him 'the Islamic Luther', seeing in his work the possibility of Islam's supposedly long-delayed reformation.[28]

Soroush's principal contention is that there is a distinction between religion per se and religious knowledge.[29] Religion, he asserts, is divine, having been revealed by God, but human beings are left to realize the purposes and precepts of religion. They do so through religious knowledge, which is 'entirely human and subject to all the dictates of human knowledge'.[30] Soroush reformulates the old adage of the metaphysical Sufis that, while the *Haqiqa* (that is, reality or God) is absolute, the Sharia is relative, but Soroush does so within the terms of his own philosophy of religion. Thus Sharia becomes not a creed ordained by God, immutable and fixed, but rather one which allows for change and refinement within Man's own interpretations of religious knowledge. Religious beliefs, no matter how intensely held, represent no more than one's own understanding of religion. Religious knowledge forms part of any number of humanistic sciences and philosophies, and is no different in essence from, say, sociology or metaphysics. It has 'a collective and dynamic identity and that remains viable through the constant exchange, cooperation and competition of scholars'.[31] It may be full of errors or full of insights, but it will still be a human formulation – subject to contraction and expansion within a temporal framework.

So divine effulgence created a sacred space in which the explorations of religious knowledge can take place. It is not a secular construct, since the purpose of those who seek religious knowledge is to find the divine principle behind mankind's condition and endeavours. 'For the believers, religion quickens the blaze of the sublime quest, delivers from inner attachments, grants ascent above earthly concerns . . . and induces a sense of utter wonder so that one may hear the call of "God is the Truth" from every particle in the universe.'[32] Religious knowledge on the other hand is 'a sincere attempt to understand [the Prophetic] message through repeated consultation with the sacred text and the Tradition. Scholars of religion have no other status or service than this.'[33] They cannot appropriate for themselves the infallible or unerring status of prophets or imams.

Soroush's own theory has to be put in the context of the Iranian Revolution; of his disenchantment with its domination by the *ulema* and with the establishment of the quasi-infallible status of the *wilayat-al-faqih* (rule of the jurisprudent); and of his constant brush with the authorities on matters of doctrine, democracy, and human rights and freedoms. The theory undermines the intellectual and religious foundations of the Islamic Republic by denying the legitimacy that the *mujtahids* give themselves as the final arbiters of religious law and doctrine. If religious knowledge is changeable and dependent on knowledge from *outside* the religious context, then it certainly follows that the *ulemas* cannot make such astounding claims.

The entire body of the Sharia is then recast in this context, and the received body of doctrines and practices relating to Islam are regularly questioned. Modern notions of freedoms, rights and democracy are reconciled with religious knowledge rather than tested against some invariant standard of reference drawn from traditional theology or jurisprudence. Soroush's ideal is not a secular, not even a democratic, society but a religious community where the sense of the sacred hovers over humanity. Knowledge of the sacred, however, is derived from the collective human experience in all the sciences and disciplines. Soroush's reconstruction of Islamic knowledge opened the way for including all manner of constructs into the body of 'religious knowledge' as defined by him – from the culture of rights to the issues of secularism, freedom and democracy. Soroush does not quite acknowledge that western liberal values automatically become a part of the religious knowledge of our time, but he comes close to it. He is always careful to couch his analyses in general terms and categories, without specifically adopting the notion that liberal values are a necessary concomitant of contemporary religious knowledge. For example, he attempts to strike a balance in his treatment of the modern notion of human rights versus the traditional emphasis on human duties to God. Human rights are a central element of modern political conditions and must therefore be taken into account when developing a religiously sanctioned system of government.

A similar indirect case is made for democracy within a religious society. Soroush sees a religious society as being essentially moral and therefore acting as the moral conscience of a democratic order. Democracy functions best when its leaders are subjected – or subject themselves – to moral rather than legal sanction. There is a natural affinity between a democratic sensibility and a religious morality.

The Soroushian world view targets the Sharia foundations, that is, the relationship between human beings, of Islamic civilization. By denying immutability and, by inference, the validity of the systems which limit independent reasoning in religious decisions either to a privileged class of *ulema* or to a very narrowly circumscribed ambit of acceptable topics, the Sharia loses its innate conservatism. In fact the Sharia may well not be necessary for an Islamic society, at least in its traditional form. Secular law and the notions of liberal democracy can be a valid substitute as long as society as a whole retains its commitment to religious faith and uses a morality derived from religion in order to supervise and monitor those who exercise power. One assumes that Soroush's religious society would automatically confirm the relationship between God and the human individual through belief in the sacred and in its absolute transcendence.

In his later writings, Soroush has given more attention to the relationship between the human being and the self, with his increased interest in the mystics of Islam, and especially in the Sufi poets of Islam's middle centuries who wrote in the medium of Persian. The poet Jalaluddin Rumi looms large in his concerns, with the majestic sweep of his great poem the 'Mathnawi' and its intoxicating love of God. Once again, Sufism is brought as a form of traditional cover for a system which could be misinterpreted, as it veers dangerously away from the Islamic mainstream. But Soroush stays defiantly within the bounds of Islam and could in no way be considered a secular modernist of any kind. His ultimate purpose is to revive

Islam by broadening its concern with ideas and structures which are outside of its inherited legacy and by engaging with modern values and systems. If the traditional forms in which the Sharia and its guardians are cast have to be sacrificed, then so be it. It may even be a religious duty to dare to consider new forms in which God's purpose is to be manifested.

However, Soroush's theory is held together by the finest of threads, namely the assumption that God's purpose cannot be ascertained at all times absolutely in the same way, as the domain of the sacred is forever barred from humans, with very few exceptions: the prophets and those granted mystical insights. Nevertheless, the entire edifice of Islam is built on the indisputable existence of a sacred text and of the historical being who was Prophet Muhammad – to, and through, whom the text was revealed. The text itself cannot be relativistic, although it may assume the relativity of aspects of it which deal with worldly matters. Rules for approaching the understanding of the sacred text have to be established, otherwise the text will sit in a vacuum – an undiscovered gem. Soroush suggests that the standards used for reading the Quran should be based on the body of human knowledge outside the domain of the strictly religious. In this manner the rules of interpretation of the Quranic text will be shifting and necessarily inexact. But no body of knowledge can possibly exist without rules and axioms.

So an entire building-block of Islamic thought – the transmitted part – becomes essentially tentative and imprecise. It is difficult to see how Soroush's concept of religious knowledge would have any future in Islam. It will be simply overwhelmed by the profane world. Sorush's ideal society is more akin to the mildly moral consciousness which exists in social democracies, but his is expressed in religious and sacred, rather than in humanist, idioms. Perhaps this would be an improvement on life in a theocracy, but it is hardly the desired destination for a consciously Islamic civilization.

Testing the Limits of the Permissible

Soroush questioned the static nature of the Sharia itself, but he did not refashion the meaning of *ijtihad* (independent reasoning). He placed the entire Sharia within the orbit of his definition of 'religious knowledge', that is, a man-made construct which should be periodically re-examined in light of the state of knowledge and experience in other fields of human endeavour. He did not stray into the more serious problem of questioning the immutability of the Quran; he maintained throughout the incomparability of the text and its divine provenance. Neither did he question prophecy and the person of the Prophet Muhammad in the spiritual universe of the believing Muslim. But others who were less cautious did so.

One of these was the Sudanese reformist thinker and political activist Mahmoud Muhammad Taha, who paid for his transgressions with his life.[34] Taha was born around 1910 in the Sudan. He gravitated towards politics, founding, with others, the Republican Party, which was devoted to combating colonialism and the deep sectarianism within Sudanese society. He was imprisoned in the late 1940s, and while in jail he became a firm adept of Sufism, immersing himself in prayer, fasting and adopting various ascetic practices. Jail was for him, as for so many others, a form of *khalwa*: the obligatory retreat for those who set themselves on the Sufi path. He seemed to have been deeply influenced by the concepts of the 'perfect human' and of the 'unity of being', which are associated with the great medieval Sufi master Ibn 'Arabi and his successors.

In the mid-1980s, Taha fell foul of the military regime of Nimairi, which had started out as a revolutionary clique inflected with communist thought. After a series of abortive coups and challenges, Nimairi proclaimed his regime's allegiance to political Islam and introduced Sharia law in Sudan. Taha's many opponents inside the regime and among the Islamist movement pushed for his arrest and trial for apostasy. He had already been found guilty of apostasy by the *ulemas* of Sudan, who obtained two legal opinions on him from the al-Azhar University in Cairo and from the World Islamic League in Mecca. Taha was hanged on 18 January 1985 on the accusation of apostasy.

Taha was an extreme individualist. He is one of the few thinkers in modern Islam who build their system on the individual – what he called *fardiyya*. The purpose of human existence, for him, is to achieve absolute individual freedom within a society which exhibits total social justice. 'The individual man and woman is the ultimate end, and everything else is a means to this individual, including the whole of creation and the Quran,' he wrote. Taha's system can be best described as the application of the metaphysical Sufi doctrine of the unity of being to the conditions and circumstances of modern Muslim societies. Inasmuch as the purpose of revelation is to enable the individual to seek salvation by recognizing the signs of God in one's self and in the outer world, the individual's quest reaches its culmination as the veils between God and human beings are removed.

Taha recasts the devotional underpinnings of Islam, especially prayer, in terms of their historical setting and of the evolution of the individual's own spiritual reality and psychology. The more evolved a person is, the less he or she needs to be bound to the strict forms of the received acts of worship. There is the formal Islamic prayer, and there is the prayer of the individual who sees in each act of this sort a direct dialogue with God. There are the formal mechanisms for interpreting the Quran, and then there is the quest for the deeper, more subtle meanings which remove the barriers between the worshipped and the worshipper. Everything dissolves into the recognition that there is nothing in creation but God. Even prophecy becomes linked to the state of the individual's own elevated spirituality. To rely on the Prophet's sayings and conduct for one's own actions and beliefs is a sign of spiritual immaturity, which needs to be transcended as one moves along the spiritual path.

This radical view goes well beyond the attempt to recast the Sharia in light of modern conditions. Basically, Taha is saying that modern conditions afford the spiritual person a far greater range of options than past conditions. The spiritualized individual in Islam understands and appreciates prophecy, but he or she must situate it in an age where the possibilities of direct spiritual experience were far fewer than they are today. Prophecy becomes a non-essential item in religious awareness, at least for those who have progressed along the path of realizing God's purpose and of sensing that, in the end, God is all.

Taha was equally radical in his treatment of the Quran. He uses the division of the chapters of the Quran into the Meccan and Medinan phases, as a clear distinction between those chapters that can inspire the individual's quest for enlightenment – the Meccan verses – and those which deal with the more worldly matters of human relationships and social organization – the Medinan verses. The latter are clearly historical in nature and content and have no relevance to modern conditions. Nevertheless they are part of the totality of the Quran, which has both a temporal and a non-temporal aspect to it. The Meccan verses, on the other hand, are not situated in time. They are universally valid for the spiritual seeker and they are a powerful aid to the full realization of Man's spiritual potential. In the end, even the Quran will vanish in the direct encounter between the human being and God. Nothing, as the Quran says, will be left except the visage of God. This goes even beyond the bounds of ecstatic Sufism, which sought to find the inner, esoteric dimensions within the outer forms of Islamic worship and conduct.

Taha ends by denying the validity of the Medinan verses for modern conditions; essentially he rejects the Sharia as merely a historical legacy whose utility has been superseded. The legacy of Islam becomes nearly entirely ephemeral, with the exception of the supercharged spirituality of the Meccan verses. Taha abandons the Sharia leg entirely, leaving the plumbing of the individual's spiritual psychology and the Meccan verses of the Quran as the way to a revitalized Islamic civilization. This becomes his account of the 'second coming' of Islam.

The philosophical elegance of Soroush's theory of religious knowledge and the spiritualized individualism, even iconoclasm, of Taha are expressions of a profound unease, even fear, concerning the ability of Islamic societies to join the concert of materially and culturally more advanced societies. They open avenues for explorations and discussions, but they do not serve as platforms for further evolution or development. The orthodox establishment closes ranks and the innovators are marginalized, then practically ignored. Taha was executed and Soroush is hounded by the thugs of the reactionary clerics. There is, however, a common concern which seems to unite nearly all the would-be reformers of Islam – namely the issue of the Sharia, the outer rules and strictures of Islam. Nearly all seek to reform, modify or eliminate the Sharia, or, from another part of the spectrum entirely, to insist on its validity in its undiluted form. This focus on the Sharia distorts the essential unity of Islam, creating an unbalanced structure and proposals for change which are incomplete. Too much focus on the Sharia leaves spirituality in the shadows; too little Sharia-focus creates an unrecognizable and deficient Islam. As the moderate Sufis used to say: 'He who seeks spiritual awareness without constraining himself by the outer law is liable to heresy; he who seeks only the outer law without spiritual attainment opens the way for corruption.'

Towering above these concerns is the religious genius of Muhammad ibn Idris al-Shafi'i, an eighth-century jurist who framed the essential characteristics of Sunni Islam and whose influence, if only by example, extended to the Shia world. The formulation that Islam is the 'book and the way' of the Prophet (*Kitab wa Sunna*) is so rooted in Islamic consciousness that it would be impossible to consider Islam outside of this context. The edifice of the Sharia was built on the practice of the Prophet Muhammad, known through an authentic system of traditions attributable to the Prophet himself. The canons of prophetic traditions – such as those of Muslim or of Muhammad al-Bukhari – become foundational texts for Sunni Islam. Shafi'i allowed some leeway to the individual jurists mainly through reasoning and the consensus of scholars, but their scope was severely circumscribed. The corpus of the Prophet's sayings and actions become the essential yardstick by which God's purpose can be ascertained. Their permanence assumed an inviolate status, and ignoring or circumventing the Sharia became tantamount to belittling the prophetic experience.

Soroush and others would place the system of Shafi'i squarely in the category of acquired religious knowledge, but this system is so fundamental to the subsequent unfolding of Islamic thought and life that it is unlikely to be easily or painlessly superseded. Many writers have held it primarily responsible for the rigidity of the Islamic world view, but this is entirely false and unjustified. The bridge between the permanent, or absolute, sacred knowledge and the ephemeral has to be, in itself, sufficiently immune to tampering. It is not that the system of Shafi'i is sacred in the conventional sense, but it is a good and continuing guide to the knowledge of the sacred within Islam. For over a millennium, this and similar systems which purport to translate the absolute into the relative have proved resilient and flexible, and have met the needs of Muslims and Islamic society. There is little in them which is inherently reactionary or obscurantist. They also have overwhelming support from the mass of Muslims, to whom they are addressed in the first place. In Islam, changing the terms of the relationship between God and the human being without preserving the central role of prophecy and the person of the Prophet Muhammad is a futile effort. In the pre-eminently religious world view of Islam, a Sharia will always be necessary. The inherited forms of the Sharia may be amenable to change, but the displacement of the Sharia and a disenchanted world of Islam are an altogether different proposition.

The Future Understanding and Practice of Islam

An Islamic reformation can also produce totally unpredictable outcomes. The calls for *ijtihad* or independent reasoning, for example, are based on the assumption that a rational and humanist ethos will govern the reasoning process. But in fact *ijtihad* has not so much modernized the faith as led to the questioning of a flexible and accommodating orthodoxy by the radically reactionary ideology of religious fundamentalism. This ideology can drift towards violence and terror at one level, as in fact it has already done; it can also become the handmaiden of powerful princes and dynasties, as the alliance between reactionary Wahhabi clerics and the worldly Saudi royal family amply demonstrates. Both these elements were discernable in the Protestant Reformation, and similar trends are emerging within Islam.

The remaking of a civilization will not be a simple and short affair. Easy and simplistic predictions, which rely on historical analogy or on the inevitable surrender to the forces of technology and economic power, are bound to be wrong. The Reformation took nearly two centuries before the end of the wars of religion could be proclaimed. The crises within Islam have not yet reached a full-scale war between the sects, although they came dangerously close to that result in recent years in the Arab Middle East, as they did in Iraq during the 2005–7 civil strife and in Lebanon after the brief war between Israel and Hezbollah in the summer of 2006. The brew is dangerously unstable and it is being added to, on an almost daily basis, by outside meddling which is driven by ignorance, sheer bigotry and unwillingness to accept a world view which, no matter how confused, dazed and tattered at present, might nevertheless offer an alternative vision of life for a significant portion of mankind.

The cast of characters and ideas competing for attention and power in the world of Islam is as varied as that of the Reformation in Europe. It is unlikely that one set of ideas or doctrines will prevail, or that one state will emerge as the nucleus of a new world power or, in the nightmare of national security policy planners, as a super-Islamic state. It is too early to say which way the wind is blowing. There is still a host of issues and problems that have to be resolved, but one can isolate a number of them for special attention. These include the narrowing of Sunni thought, the prospects for Iran's unique form of religious government and the long-term effects of the West's intervention in Muslim affairs, which is partly motivated by the imperative to contain radical political Islam.

In this confused and turbulent landscape the prospects for traditional orthodoxies may appear uncertain, but their resilience should not be underestimated. It is likely therefore that the varieties of orthodoxies will continue to define the landscape of Islam. What type of orthodoxies will prevail? Will there be space for other forms of Islamic expression, small or large, marginal or significant? At the broadest level, the Sunni world will have to determine for itself whether the historical schools of Islam and their collective traditions continue to form the backbone of jurisprudential rulings during the long process of adjustment which is the revolt of Islam. The challenge from a vigorous and well-funded Wahhabi/Salafi movement is far from being contained, but at least the response to its radical and violent wing is no longer so supine. Particular schools of Sunni Islam, aided by the state, may re-assert their authority in countries with which they had been historically associated. This seems to be happening in Morocco, where the Maliki school of law is being re-emphasized as state policy; as well as in Malaysia, where the Shafi'i school of law has been intimately connected with the Islamization of the Malays.

We may see a greater identification of the varieties of Islam with the major specific ethnic and cultural groups of the historical civilization of Islam: the Arab world; the South Asian world; the Malay world; the African world; and the Turkic-speaking world – each of these containing between 200 and 400 million Muslims. A reinvigoration of Sufi orders and of less structured spiritual movements is already apparent, recreating the diversity and the spirit of inner directedness which has been the hallmark of pre-modern Islam. A specific 'diaspora' Islam may also emerge, dealing with the particular needs and requirements of Muslims, both immigrants and converts, in a western context. It is in this arena that the more pressing issues of identity, citizenship and religious loyalty, and integration and multiculturalism will have to be resolved – or left festering. English has already joined Arabic, Persian and Urdu, the classical languages of Islamic high culture, as a medium for expressing ideas in modern Islam. Its widespread use by western-educated Muslims is bound to have an effect on the evolution of Islamic culture and civilization. This is a powerful unknown, as English brings with it the possibility of articulating entirely new concepts.

The Shia world, also a block of nearly 200 million Muslims, is one that cuts across ethnic and cultural lines. Shiism will continue to be coloured by its status as the national religion of Iran and by the powerful role of Iranian ayatollahs. But it will have to contend with the possibility of a reinvigorated and independent hierarchy emerging from the upheaval in Iraq. A combination of a territorial Shia hierarchy, focused on a particular country but with grand ayatollahs hailing from different parts of the world (a phenomenon which seems to be emerging in Iraq), may co-exist with a 'national' Shia authority, as in Lebanon. These various outcomes for the Shia would have to deal with the centralized religious authority of the Iranian state under its supreme religious ruler. The course of Shiism in the world will most certainly be affected by the future of the Iranian theocratic regime and, to a lesser extent, by the revitalization of the seminaries and academies of Najaf. Whether they will ever match the sheer scale and scope of the state-sponsored institutions of Iran is a moot point.

The challenge of dissident Islamic groups to the ruling orthodoxies will always be there; it may even be exacerbated. The challenges may come from political groups, but they could also be mass movements associated with charismatic leaders or apocalyptic expectations. Mahdist movements, to which the Shia are particularly prone, are already proliferating. They may not overthrow the prevalent orthodoxies, but they will always be an irritant and a refrain.

The sum total of these changes, played out over decades, will determine the course of Islam in the twenty-first century. The reformation of Islam will be an incremental process of change and adjustment, punctuated by upheavals, crises and traumas that will feed back into the adjustment process.

In reality, these issues, although critical to the course of Islam, pale in significance in the face of the main question. Will Muslims continue to affirm the power of the unseen, as understood in the religion of Islam, in the ordering of their private and public lives and in their societies? The Reformation may have well started as a reaction against a worldly church and from the intense desire to find an individual pathway to God. In that sense, the Reformation had a profoundly spiritual aspect. But it could well be argued that the intervening centuries of instability and violence sealed the fate of a public religiosity. Divisions within Christendom became definitive; kings and emperors grew in influence as the state consolidated its power against ecclesiastical authority, and the personal and spiritual was left behind.

The belief, widely held in modern Europe, that religion is inherently divisive is certainly traceable to the travails of the Reformation. But, as a way station to secularism and modernity, the European wars of religion may have been a necessary precondition. Would Luther have embarked on his epoch-changing calls for reform if he could have foreseen the 'end of God' in the ordering of human affairs? In the final analysis, as Harvey Cox wrote in his brilliant 1964 book *The Secular City*, the entire thrust of modernity, urbanization and secularization is to force Christianity into finding 'a non-religious interpretation of biblical concepts'. He goes on to say: 'It will do no good to cling to our religious and metaphysical versions of Christianity in the hope that one day religion or metaphysics will once again be back.'[35] Quoting a prison letter from the German pastor Dietrich Bonhoeffer, who was murdered by the Nazis just before the end of the Second World War, Cox wrote: 'We are proceeding toward a time of no religion at all ... How do we speak of God without religion?'[36] In another prison letter, Bonhoeffer would write: 'The world that has come of age is more godless, and perhaps for that very reason nearer to God, than the world before its coming of age.'[37] If that is the final state of the Protestant Reformation, how can (or, more appropriately, how will) Muslims ever regard Islam in these or in similar terms?

It is very difficult to conceive of the withdrawal of Islam from the public sphere as an essential component of Islam's self-realization. A desacralized world is not fertile ground for the nurturing of a private faith and is far from the reality of Islam, both past and present. The privatization of Islam may be the ardent wish of both God-intoxicated individuals and secular modernizers, but it does not appeal to the broad sweep of Muslims, who still expect to see a public manifestation of Islam in their daily lives. It is this inherent difficulty in separating the public from the private aspect of Islam, and the individual Muslim from Muslim society, that makes the task of 'reforming' Islam so fraught with difficulty and unpredictability.

CHAPTER 6

Territory and Power

From the very outset, Muslim civilisation was built on foundations supplied by ideology alone. It has never had anything to do with the concepts of race or nation. ...Ours has always been an ideological civilization – with the Law of the Qur'an as its source and, more than that, as its only historical justification. To speak of the Muslim ummah *as something politically justified and culturally valuable ... and in the same breath to question the importance of Islamic Law as the form-giving element in our life is hypocritical or, alternatively, an outcome of ignorance.*

Muhammad Asad, writer and essayist, *This Law of Ours and Other Essays*

(DAR AL-ANDALUS: GIBRALTER, 1993), p. 29.

The famous 'clash of civilizations' thesis glossed over an issue of singular importance. Of all the great civilizations of the world, it was only Islam that had no state 'champions' who could act out their role on the global stage. The West was amply championed by the United States as well as by the countries of western Europe, directly or through the EU. The Hindu world was practically contiguous with the sub-continental state of India. Confucianism was coterminous with China. Even orthodoxy was championed by the new Russian state built on the debris of the former Soviet Union. Each of these states could embody and defend the principles of their civilizations and had the necessary resources, concentrated in a few powerful nation–states, to be able to do so. Only Islam lacked the essential 'core state' advocate, or empire, which might, singly or with a few allies, be able to defend its interests and values without reference to other powers.

It is ironic therefore that, whenever Islam was singled out as the main protagonist in the 'clash of civilizations', little notice was taken of the disproportionate power between Islamic states in their fragmented and disjointed nature and the large state actors of the other civilizations. The collective organizations of Muslim states were never a match, in terms of will, purpose or power, to the large state actors of other civilizations.

The Absence of Islamic Territorial Power

The destruction of the last Islamic empire put paid to the possibility of a large well-resourced state emerging as a replacement power for the Ottomans. Elsewhere when non-western civilizations came under foreign control, the post-colonial order still allowed the formation of super states. China regained its territorial unity, with the exception of Taiwan, after the victory of the communists in 1949. India, even after the division from which Pakistan and, later, Bangladesh emerged, kept most of its territory and the vast majority of the world's Hindus. But the successor states to the last Muslim empires were not reconfigured as large units. The chimerical drive to unity attempted by the Arabs in the 1950s and 1960s was never a real substitute, in Islamic terms, for the dissolved Ottoman Empire. The largest Arab state, Egypt, was far too poor and weak to be a serious champion for Islam and Muslim causes. Pakistan abandoned any claim to playing a role in this regard, preoccupied as it was with the threats of war or with actual wars with India. Iran, after its 1979 revolution, tried to carve a role for itself as the defender of Islam, but its Shia identity limited its appeal and influence on the wider stage. Islamic civilization was decoupled from large states and empires that could effectively embody or defend its message. Samuel P. Huntington called this condition 'consciousness without cohesion'.[1] Ever since, Islamic civilization has been in search of a paladin.

For a while, this condition was of minor significance. The world was defined by conflicts other than the supposed 'clash of civilizations'. During the cold war period, the absence of an Islamic core state was not material to the stand-off between the West and the Soviet bloc. The West and the Soviets sought allies from individual Muslim states and not from Islam as such. While the West in its propaganda chose to draw Islam into its orbit by emphasizing the godlessness of the communists, Muslim leaders who had allied themselves with the Soviets were focusing on the virtues of Islamic socialism and on its proximity to the egalitarian doctrines of communism and collectivism.[2] The collapse of the Soviet bloc and the ethnic wars of the 1990s, in which Muslims were disproportionately involved, raised the spectre of a worldwide pan-Islamic movement, bent on recreating a new Muslim empire. Public opinion in the western world was agitated by garbled notions of what the *Umma* of Islam actually meant. The pan-Islamic calls for *jihad* by Bin Laden were mixed up with the widespread concern that a radical Islamic super state – the bogeyman of an Islamic caliphate – could arise. This state would lay a prior claim on the world's Muslims, especially in the West.

The notion of an empire inspired by a world religion was not only alien but quite frightening, not only to westerners but also to the huge number of countries which abutted on the Islamic world. Part of the problem related to the vast geographic spread of Islam, which covered the middle belt of the Asian land mass, a good part of Africa and footholds inside Europe itself. A universal empire which might be territorially contiguous with the reach of Islam would be an incredible prospect. In fact no such empire could ever be stable except for very short periods of time; it would probably crumble as the peripheral parts pulled away. Although it's an unrealistic fantasy, the fear of such a state ever emerging has had a powerful hold on the imagination of people, both on its proponents and its detractors. Pan-Islamism was used to bolster the authority of the Ottoman Empire in its last decades and was in fact state policy under Sultan Abdul Hamid.[3] It never amounted to much, apart from the scattered and ineffectual involvement of the Ottoman Empire on behalf of beleaguered Muslims or Muslim causes outside its territorial control. It had a brief flurry of life in the 1920s, when it provided the ideological fervour behind the Indian *Khilafat* movement[4] and attracted a number of peripatetic intellectuals such as the Lebanese prince Shakib Arslan, who tried to promote the idea of Muslim political unity.[5] It emerged again, but in a totally different guise, in the 1990s, this time being allied to the rise of transnational Islamist movements. Some of these – for instance *Hizb-ul-Tahrir*, which had established itself as a formidable movement in central Asia – had an explicit pan-Islamist ideology and called for the establishment of a new Islamic caliphate.[6]

One of the side-effects of the 'clash of civilizations' theory – which was first advanced in 1991 by Bernard Lewis, the eminent historian of Islam – was to place Islam at odds with a coherent state structure through which other civilizations appeared to function. Islam was the perpetual 'outsider', whose political manifestation would be disruptive and destabilizing to the prevailing world order. On the one hand, the prospects of Islamic 'unity' would be dangerous if unity were to lead to the formation of large political entities which might be widely spread geographically or might dispose of considerable resources. On the other hand, it was assumed that Muslims were alienated from the very countries in which they lived because their consciousness as Muslims did not square with the demands of loyalty to the nation–state. This was an issue for Muslim diasporas in the West as well as for a disaffected, radicalized youth in a number of predominantly Muslim countries.

The terms of Islam's encounter with the world's power structures changed once again after the 9/11 attacks. The 'clash of civilizations' thesis, after its heyday in the 1990s, was replaced by the war on terror and the assertion of the US's singular status as the world's hyper-power: the so-called unipolar world theory. 'Either you are with us, or you are with the terrorists,' said George W. Bush.[7] For individual Muslim countries the choice was stark. Most, of course, succumbed to the threats or blandishments of the US and, recognizing their powerlessness in front of America, accepted whatever they were told they should do. In a celebrated altercation between Pakistan's intelligence director and Richard Armitage, the deputy secretary of state, following the 9/11 attacks, Pakistan was threatened with oblivion if it did not toe the line. Armitage was reported to have warned the intelligence director: 'Be prepared to be bombed. Be prepared to go back to the Stone Age.'[8]

Bullying Muslim states was easy enough. There was no Muslim state or states which singly or collectively rose to the status of a world class power and which could challenge the war on terror. The war against terror was really a war against Islam itself, reinforcing its 'outsider' status in the constellation of states and civilizations.[9] The residue of hostility, suspicion and fear of Islam had not disappeared from the western mind and it could easily be dredged up to stiffen the charge that Islam as a whole was the culprit.

One of the agendas of the war on terror, therefore, was the western-led drive to reform and reconstruct Islam, even though none of the Muslim states could pose any serious military threat to the US. Although Islam no longer had a territorial power base of any consequence, it still could rely on the loyalty of millions of Muslims to the idea of Islam and on their willingness to spring to its defence if it was threatened. The goal of the West's campaign was to adjust the Muslims' understanding of Islam so that it could fall into line with the global order dominated by the precepts of liberal democracies. But the US is no longer as omnipotent as it was in the decade after the fall of the Soviet bloc. The world order is still evolving. Now, no single power predominates; US power is in retreat, partly due to the overreach of the war on terror and also to the vast expenditures necessary to sustain its hyper-power status. The rise of non-western powers such as China, which do not share the West's preoccupation with reforming Islam, has removed the reformation of Islam as a global objective.

In this multi-polar world, Islam is once again the outsider. The larger nation–states of Islam such as Egypt, Turkey or Indonesia are not viewed as nodes of possible power in their own right, but as 'prizes' for actual or evolving power structures. In this changing world, the US has to face challenges from an expanding EU and a mercantilist China, each of which is determined to develop a network of allies and clients from the roster of countries which are doomed – or destined – to dependency. These countries are drawn irresistibly into the larger orbits, partly for economic development reasons and partly for security. The strategy therefore for Muslim states is to manoeuvre between these three power blocs – or to commit to one of them – and extract whatever advantage they can for themselves and their people. Thus Morocco would naturally fit into the expanding EU, given its trade links with Europe and the presence of a large number of its migrants there. At the same time, Morocco could become more integrated – or perhaps more dependent on the EU – as it becomes an important retirement destination for elderly Europeans attracted by its proximity, its lower costs and its abundant labour for personal service. Indonesia will fit into an expanding Chinese economic zone, with its diaspora Chinese population playing an important part in its economic development and drawing it nearer to China.

Power and Consciousness

This state of affairs is a bitter pill for many Muslims to swallow. The powerlessness of Islam in a world bestridden by large states, core states, hyper-powers and emerging giants is too obvious not to merit attention. Practically every configuration of the global power equation over the past century has been expressed in terms which take no account of Islam as a relevant political force – except, of course, when Islam is connected to a threat such as international terrorism or the unassimilablity of Muslim minorities. For a large percentage of Muslims, loyalty to Islam is not restricted to the religious sphere. Apart from the special case of Judaism, adherents of the other major religions do not equate their religious faith with a political community. In Islam, the loss of territorial empires has not been matched by the complete displacement of Muslims' loyalties in favour of the nation–state. Islamic political unity, no matter how chimerical or utopian, continues to exert a powerful political appeal.

This transnational but invisible bond which connects the world of Islam is in itself a type of virtual empire – an 'empire of consciousness'. It has no equivalent in the real political world. Were such a state (or such a grouping of states) to emerge, it would probably be resisted as dangerously destabilizing for the global order – as well as for smaller Muslim states who survive under the protective wing of larger powers. In fact the opposite ought to be the case. It is the absence of any formal and substantial Islamic political presence at the global level that contributes to instability and disorder. But the association of Islam with fanaticism and violence is deeply rooted in the psyche of westerners. Islam has also become a bogeyman to Hindu fundamentalists, who have succeeded in demonizing its presence in India in the minds of millions of that country's aspiring middle classes.[10] There is no doubt that the prevailing sentiment of hostility towards Islam and Muslims informs the calculations of the policy planners.

The world's power brokers have persisted in denying the legitimacy – or desirability – of a potential new force which could provide some coherence to the political expression of Islam as a civilization. The frantic drive to contain the aftershocks of the Iranian Islamic Revolution and the impact on other Muslim countries is a case in point. The western powers worked with the established Middle Eastern autocracies and dictatorships to stop the 'infection' from the revolution spreading. (It was much the same as European monarchical powers striving to snuff out the effects of the French Revolution.) Fragmentation and dependency is a more acceptable condition for Islamic states as far as the West is concerned. The last thing they want is the risks in dealing with a formidable new Muslim political power.

That the permanent disempowerment of Islam, by freezing it out from the international system, is somehow conducive to stability because of Islam's 'problematic' nature, or because of its inherent tendency to violence and disruption is, at best, questionable. This ostracizing increases rather than contains the sense of alienation which infects a large proportion of the youth in the Muslim world as well as the radical Muslim fringe in the West. This is further exacerbated by the widespread belief that most Muslim rulers are hopelessly compromised by their dependence on the West and are therefore unlikely to defend Islam and Muslim interests. They are seen either to be colluding with the reigning powers or to be too indifferent or powerless to influence the treatment of Islam and Muslims in the world. The cooperation of many Muslim countries with the legally questionable

US policy of the 'rendition' of terror suspects is a case in point.[11] The defence of the human and legal rights of the suspects is left to western lawyers and agencies. No Muslim government has directly challenged the US on this matter, even when its own citizens have been involved. How can this be anything other than weak or craven collaboration?

So far, the main concern has been to limit the growth of 'Islamic' states; that is, governments whose institutions and laws are derived from versions of Islamist ideologies. These are judged to be confrontational, radical and disruptive, if not to global order then at least to regional stability. The pan-Islamic pretensions of such states may push them to claim extra territorial rights, moral if not legal, to intervene on behalf of beleaguered Muslim minorities, or even in the internal affairs of other Muslim countries. The drive to contain Iran and the isolation of Sudan reflect one aspect of this. Neither of these states has even remotely the potential for growing into the missing Islamic actor on the world stage.

However, this is only one facet of the issue. In fact, the potential for forming 'Islamic' states in Muslim countries is determined primarily by local factors, such as the strength of the Islamist movement and the resilience and power of the governing order. And in spite of the formidable odds against them, Islamist groups, when they do succeed in achieving power, are soon bogged down in the minutiae of governing and remaining in power. They add very little as effective advocates for Muslims on the world stage, and cannot contend with global powers on a reasonably equal footing.

Global powers generally do not emerge as a result of a conscious design – although China after the Deng reforms of the 1980s was a planned venture into the global arena by a hitherto isolationist power. Global players evolve because of particular historical, social and economic circumstances which allow them to realize great power status and to project their power on to the world stage. The few existing Islamic states have been unable to coalesce into anything powerful on the global stage.

Power and Stability

The world system is not based on equity and fairness, but the absence of these factors is a major source of instability and extremism. So far, there has been no support for a concert of Muslim countries that assumes a more assertive position on the international stage. The most likely such organization, the Organisation of the Islamic Conference (OIC), has neither the mandate nor the desire to extend its reach beyond pious calls for Islamic solidarity and infrequent and toothless statements of condemnation for particularly objectionable acts targeting Muslims or Islam. Its origin as a Saudi-sponsored Islamic counterweight to Nasser's Arab nationalism has never quite left its trace. Nor are its members prepared to cede power and influence to it. If there is to be an Islamic global power, it will have to be found elsewhere other than in the feeble multilateral Islamic organizations that actually exist.

Not all Muslims would agree that to flourish Islamic civilization needs the protection of a powerful state. A Muslim state's open embrace of Islam and Islamic causes is not only anathema to secularists, but can also lead to dangerous foreign entanglements and reaction. For example, a public Arab, Turkish or Iranian espousal of the cause of Kashmiri Muslims will antagonize India, with which a number of these countries have vital relations. Nor was there much official protest from Muslim countries against the pogroms of Indian Muslims after the destruction of the Babri mosque in 1992. The treatment of Burma's Muslim minority, which accounts for nearly 10 per cent of the population, by the military-dominated government has been appalling. According to Human Rights Watch, Muslims have been barred from the army and from the government, and suffer from severe discriminatory policies.[12] But Indonesia and Malaysia, two countries where Muslims are the majority, both co-members (together with Burma) in the Association of Southeast Asian Nations (ASEAN) would jeopardize their relations with the Burmese government over this matter if they were to protest – and they aren't prepared to go down that road.

Cultural differences lie at the heart of the conflicts and struggles that underlie the 'clash of civilizations' thesis. Religion is, of course, only one aspect of civilization, but the religious inheritance is probably the most significant and salient characteristic of a civilization. Hence western civilization is underpinned by the Judaeo-Christian tradition, even as the major western powers are determinedly secular and liberal in their political culture. In a similar vein, China is the inheritor of the Confucian legacy, even though it is currently governed by a nominally atheistic communist state. Each civilizational group is assumed to have a number of key features and values which are then projected or protected by the core states of that group. In the last decade, the assertion of essential western values by the major European powers and by the US – values that are supposed to determine western civilization, what separates 'us from them' – has frequently been made in contradistinction to radical Islam. In such a context, the affirmation of what the West is about obliges its 'adversaries', or even peers, to define themselves along equivalent civilizational lines. Thus the 'Asian' values propounded by the East and South-East Asian, countries – loyalty to the family, hierarchy, order and social discipline – are compared and contrasted with western values, providing the Asian economic renaissance with a rootedness in the spiritual and religious traditions of Asia.

No Muslim state has proclaimed that its adherence to Islamic norms of conduct and behaviour has been the essential factor in its success in worldly matters. Thus, where Muslim countries have excelled (in relative terms), say in Malaysia, the cause is partly attributed to 'Asian', rather than to Islamic, values. Similarly, the success of Turkey in transforming its economy is attributed to the modernization of its corporate culture along modern capitalist lines rather than to a particularly Islamic quality of its economy or society. Dubai, the glittering emirate which sees itself as the embodiment of the wired and globalized city, compares itself, if it ever does so any more, to Singapore and Hong Kong, and not to some Islamic paradigm of success.

Many Muslims feel that the modern West 'excludes' Islam.[13] The exclusion takes a variety of forms and feeds on the collapse in self-confidence which Muslims have undergone over the past two centuries. It involves the conscious erasure in the western public mind of the interchange between western civilization and Islam, which intersected in many times and places: during the seven centuries of Muslim rule over Spain; during the Ottoman expansion into south-eastern Europe; and even during the crusader states' interactions with their Muslim environment. There are, of course, vague reminders that medieval Christian theologians and philosophers were influenced by Muslim thinkers such as Averroes; or that the Muslims were the repositories and transmitters of ancient medical knowledge. But the connection between that Islam and the modern-day version is never acknowledged. Mostly, the modern West, egged on by its cultural elites and the tabloid press, is horrified by any suggestion that Islam could contribute to the betterment of mankind or that it could have anything of note to say about the modern world and its path of development. What is so good about a backward faith which stones people, burns books, abuses women and launches unprovoked attacks which kill thousands of innocent office workers?

This is the core of the western refusal to countenance a role for Islam on the world stage – beyond the narrow recognition that there are a number of nation–states which happen to be Muslim and that perhaps a quarter of the world's population is Muslim. This blanket exclusion generates an equivalent response, at least from those Muslims who are exercised by what the rest of the world thinks of them: a fawning desire to be acknowledged as worthy of joining the club of civilized peoples and nations; or the angry rejection of those who had denied them 'respect'. The former impulse drives the desire of the plutocrats of the Muslim world towards distorted imitation, obscene consumption and opulence, and the absurd attempts to acquire cultural status by importing, wholesale, campuses of western universities or entire museums and their contents. The latter impulse drives the politics of resentment and envy, which at its edges feeds into nihilism and terrorism. Both have their roots in the desire for acknowledgement and respect.

Such attitudes are also related to the question of power – specifically, whether the kind of power that Islam wields has any relevance or significance to the modern world. The absence of a state champion on the global stage is ultimately related to the power that such a state can bring to bear. Behind all power there is the element of force: real force, which can be applied to real situations to achieve real ends.[14] Islam can only count in the world of global realpolitik if the power which emanates from it is capable of affecting outcomes to the advantage – or at least not to the detriment – of Muslims and Muslim countries. The world community – a euphemism for whichever state or group of states has the upper hand globally – has not been confronted so far with the need to accommodate the influence of Islam as expressed through a powerful state – notwithstanding the Iranian and, to a lesser extent, the Saudi claim to act on behalf of Islam. If anything, the revolutionary character of Islamic power as embodied by the Iranian state may never be recognized as a legitimate global expression of Islam. The Saudi claim to global Islamic authority is linked mainly to its power over oil and to the huge financial resources that this power can generate. (It also helps the Saudis' claim to privileged status that their country holds the site of Islam's two sacred cities, Mecca and Medina.) So far the Saudis, with only a partial and very limited exception related to the war of October 1973, have not used their control over the world's largest source of oil to influence western policies. In 1973, the Saudis under King Faisal, who was indeed motivated by pan-Islamic causes, embargoed the sale of oil to the US in retaliation for the US support of Israel. It is inconceivable that the Saudis will ever use this 'weapon' again in support of Arab or Islamic causes. They are too entangled with their strategic alliance with the US to consider such a course, and they are frankly fearful of the US response.

The Saudis have not shirked from using their oil power to assert their leadership claims *within* the Islamic world, but, all else being equal, it is highly improbable that Saudi Arabia can ever rise to the ranks of global power on its own. However, it may do so if it succeeds in dominating the world of Sunni Islam through the latter's adoption of the tenets and world view of Wahhabism. If that happens, then there will be a confluence between the interests of the Saudi state, representing some thirty million people, a small to medium power by any standard, and the world of Sunni Islam, some one billion strong. The rise of Saudi Arabia to global status can only take place if the hold of traditional or moderate Sunni Islam on the loyalties of the world's Muslims is reduced. This is an ongoing struggle and it is still unclear whether such an outcome is probable, but the immense wealth of the Saudi state and the impoverishment of most Muslim societies might tip the scale in that direction. Many Muslim states, such as Turkey, the Maliki countries of North Africa and Indonesia, will always hold out against Saudi Arabia's claims to undivided religious authority, but others, such as Egypt and Pakistan, may succumb to the Wahhabization of their Islam. These two nations may provide the critical mass for the rise of Saudi Arabia to global status as the representative of most of Sunni Islam. An unwritten contract might even be struck between Saudi Arabia and Iran, whereby each would recognize the other as a representative of the world's Sunni and Shia Muslims, respectively, in preparation for the rise of both these states to global power status. A further potential source of global power is represented by the enormous funds at the disposal of the small oil-exporting countries of the Gulf. But these countries are even more hesitant than Saudi Arabia about using their resources to establish a position on behalf of the world of Islam. They are too small, too vulnerable and too dependent on the military and security of the US ever to mount a serious challenge.

The kind of power that Islam may exert on the global scene is directly related to whether that power is connected to a state champion or whether it will be expressed in some other way. This is the authority which comes from the faith itself and from the fact that more than a billion Muslims adhere to it – and not to a powerful state actor which disposes of large military and economic resources. This type of power – moral authority – was the type that was contemptuously dismissed by Joseph Stalin. 'How many divisions does the Pope have?' he was quoted as saying. It is clear, though, that there is a basis and some reality to this form of intangible power. The demise of communism in eastern Europe can be linked credibly to the deep involvement of the Catholic church in the affairs of mass protest movements such as the Solidarity trade union of Poland. However, how far could this have succeeded without another, more formidable, alliance between the church and the Reagan administration, designed to undermine communism?[15] Could it be, then, that the power of belief can only be expressed if it is harnessed alongside state actors?

So a state actor is, at present, a precondition for admission to the world's upper reaches of power wielders. At the moment, Islam has no relevance in the actual division of the world into spheres of influence, control or contestation. Non-state forces in the global order – for instance, impersonal financial and commodity markets, concentrations of wealth in private hands, and even transnational criminality, have not reduced the significance or primacy of the state. It may very well be that the state falls under the increasing influence, if not control, of those who dispose of vast private assets, but the institutions of the modern state, especially its coercive force and its law-making functions, are still needed to project power. For the foreseeable future, therefore, state actors will continue to dominate the world stage.

Far from being a credible megapower, Islam is treated as a disruptive force, virtually synonymous with terrorism. The epithet 'Islamo-fascism', which is now loosely applied to the manifestations of terrorism, is in itself a loaded word, as it connects a repugnant ideology with an entire religion. The mobilization of world opinion against this form of terrorism has taken place at the expense of the image of the religion and civilization of Islam as a whole, notwithstanding the weak tokenistic assertions that terrorists only represent a fringe among Muslims. Islam cannot and should not be afforded a place in the global power system except, and only if necessary, in the form of single nation–state actors who happen to be Muslim.[16] This, of course, carries a fundamental paradox. No present Muslim state can claim to be a global power; and no Muslim power can claim to act on behalf of Muslims unless it clearly represents a majority of Muslims.

The fragmentation of Muslim states makes them secondary actors to the larger powers. During the cold war, a number of Muslim countries thought that, together with other non-Muslim developing countries, they could create a node of countervailing power in the form of the Non-Aligned Movement. This was totally ineffective in creating a third way between the West and the Soviet bloc. Neither was the movement particularly concerned with reflecting specifically Muslim causes or advancing the reach of Islamic civilization. The successors to the Non-Aligned Bloc – for instance, the idea of the 'South', the anti-globalization movement or the environmental movement – make an uneasy fit with Islam, even though a number of the causes espoused by these movements are held in common with Muslim countries and by a large number of individual Muslims. These movements operate at a 'second degree' of power, in the sense that they cannot themselves expect to control the global agenda. They can apply pressure and even be able to set part of the agenda, but they cannot be expected to define the world stage like the great powers or power blocs.[17] They are also, to some extent, single-issue movements, which can be expected to fade once their main concerns are absorbed into the mainstream of global power politics. Climate change and environmental awareness are clear examples of causes which have gone this way.

Global Power and Global Concerns

The division of the world into major power centres which are challenged, but not threatened, by an array of single-issue or 'dissident' movements such as environmentalism or anti-globalization is likely to persist into the future. This is another challenge for an emergent Muslim global power. So far it is unclear whether the pathway to global power and influence for medium-sized states, which is what most Muslim countries are, can be based on the championing of these global issues. There have been attempts, for example, to establish a development bank for the 'South', to bypass the Bretton Woods institutions such as the World Bank or International Monetary Fund (IMF).[18] The latter, together with the World Trade Organization, are hopelessly subservient to the interests of western powers. These projects may not actually succeed, however, if their funding continues to be dependent on capricious leaders or on the global capital markets and the investment institutions which underpin them. The latter are integrated into a world financial system which has, at its apex, the finance ministries and central banks of the major western powers. The room to manoeuvre is small indeed. Similarly, the idea of Islamic banking, regarded as a self-contained system for the financing of enterprises and individuals along Islamic lines, in spite of its promising beginning, has degraded into a subdivision of conventional financing. It is dependent on its survival on the goodwill of the international banks and global markets, and it cannot claim to form the basis for an alternative financing system.

No Muslim state has followed the recent lead of Venezuela or Bolivia in a reprise of third-world radicalism. The anti-globalization movement does not make much sense to large Muslim countries such as Indonesia, Egypt or Pakistan, which are trying to jump on to the globalization bandwagon as a doorway to a better economic lot for their citizens. Nor are medium-sized Muslim states likely to take the lead in the global environmental movement. Few of them are over-concerned about climate change and global warming, given that their electricity generation is dependent on dirty fuels such as coal and residual heavy oil.

The effort to redefine the world in order to accommodate Islam is also problematic. At the political level, the world is divided according to hierarchies of power and influence, at the top of which sit the US, the EU and – now – China and Russia. It is also divided according to civilizational categories which more or less group the world into 'core states' which represent specific civilizations, with the exception of Islam. These two categories often overlap, but also generate paradoxes. For example, the EU is a separate node of power to the US, but both are 'champions' of western civilization. The institutions attached to both categories of power do not recognize Islam as an autonomous category. For example, the UN system is based on strict adherence to the principle of national sovereignty, but it falls under the control of great state powers in matters of significance. The West has a specific security institution for its own needs and purposes: NATO. The Bretton Woods institutions – the World Bank and the IMF – divide the world along geographical, not civilizational, boundaries and are under the control of major financial powers, which for a very long time meant the US. EU institutions respond to a Eurocentric view of the world and relate to the policies of the major EU countries with regards to the rest of the world. Thus the EU pulls the former successor states of the Soviet Union with a Muslim majority – the so-called 'Stans' – into its orbit, even though it stretches the geographic limits of Europe to absurd boundaries: the borders of China! The European Bank for Reconstruction and Development has pushed the limit of its definition of 'Europe' to Tajikistan and Kyrgyzstan. A medium-sized Muslim country such as Turkey or Morocco is now faced with the prospect of joining a number of power groupings, none of which has a specifically Islamic make-up. The Euro-Med grouping of countries or the associate memberships of the EU are examples. This tends to make the possibility of forging an Islamic power grouping so much more difficult. It would have to provide a credible alternative or enhancement of organizations such as NATO, the EU, the World Bank system, and so on. These have the benefit of decades of operational history behind them; institutional depth; organizational scope; and powerful political backing.

There is, of course, another way in which Muslim states have strived for great power status, if only by association. Strategic alliances with the US have become the norm for a number of Arab countries of the Middle East. Some, for instance, the Saudi-American alliance, have been going on for decades. Others are more recent, but the common denominator for these alliances is a reliance on the protective security umbrella of the US. A thicket of relationships in the military, security and economy arenas follows, which makes it well nigh impossible for these countries even to contemplate any alternative to their strategic alliance with the US. These countries will never form the core of a concert of Islamic countries as long as their dependence on the US continues. In fact Arab countries have taken a back seat in the recent efforts to draw Islamic countries together, leaving the initiative to non-Arab Muslim countries.

An Islamic Financial Bloc

Muslim countries might have forged a power bloc unique to themselves in the financial arena. One of the most advanced Muslim countries in terms of its integration into the global economy and of its own internal economic diversification and openness to foreign investment is Malaysia. Under its formidable former Prime Minister, Mahathir bin Muhammad, Malaysia raised the possibility of reforming its economy in ways which might well have led to the establishment of an Islamic power bloc. Mahathir rejected the prescriptions of the international banking and financial community during the 1997 Asian crisis and adopted contrary policies to pull Malaysia out of its economic tailspin. His policies were notably effective. This emboldened him in his next dramatic move, which was a proposal to use a gold-based currency for intra-Islamic trade.

The significance of Mahathir's initiative and the panic-stricken response it engendered, especially from the technocracy of Malaysia and other Islamic countries, were directly related to the initiative's potential in creating an Islamic grouping outside the established international financial and banking system. Mahathir's proposal was coming not from some gold bug or monetary crank but from the highly respected prime minister of a leading Muslim country. In a speech to a group of Islamic bankers in Kuala Lumpur on 25 June 2001, Mahathir set out the case for an Islamic trading bloc with its unique gold currency. Mahathir called for the establishment of bilateral payment arrangements for trade between Islamic countries and for the establishment of a common currency in gold to act as a medium for these payments. This would encourage trade between Islamic countries and the development of a trading bloc between them. An Islamic economic community might evolve later on, but only after the gold dinar would have become established; not only trading blocs, but an entire financial community would revolve around it. 'Effectively the use of the Islamic [gold] dinar will create an Islamic trading bloc. Such a trading bloc will be a powerful voice in international trading regimes and in the shaping of the new financial architecture,' Mahathir said.[19]

Mahathir's proposals were for a gradual and guarded introduction of the gold dinar and elements of an Islamic trading bloc, so as to avoid any disruption to the existing system. He was particularly careful not to call for the replacement of the domestic currency of Malaysia or any other Muslim country with the gold dinar, but to limit its initial use only to inter-Islamic payments arrangements.[20] Part of Mahathir's reason for exploring the evolution of a trading and financial bloc outside the control of the multilateral institutions was the bitter experience of Asian countries with the IMF's prescriptions for economic stabilization during the financial crisis of 1997.[21]

The Mahathir proposals seemed very threatening to all those with a vested interest in the existing global financial and trading system. The hue and cry with which his proposals were met ranged from mocking and derogatory remarks, to quiet sabotage by central bankers and international finance officials. While Mahathir was at the apex of his power the Malaysian establishment continued to go through the motions of supporting his proposals, but this support withered away and died after his departure from office. The proposals were received with no more than polite interest in other Islamic countries with some economic clout, notably in the oil-producing countries of the Gulf, but they were never taken very seriously by the major economic actors of the Islamic world such as Saudi Arabia.

The whole episode could be written off as the quixotic pet scheme of an authoritarian figure whose time in power was coming to an end. Many people in fact did take this attitude and linked the proposals to Mahathir's other controversial comments, especially his attacks on hedge funds and speculators as the principal causes of the Asian financial crisis of 1997. However, on closer examination, the drama of the rise and fall of the gold dinar plan says a great deal about the weaknesses, dependency and lack of confidence of most countries of the Islamic world in asserting their power on the world stage. The first group which attacked the gold dinar idea was, of course, the technocracy of the Bretton Woods institutions and the

western central banks, which was wedded to the principle of the demone-
tization of gold and its removal from the international financial architecture. An entire body of similar experts in Islamic countries, who had been
trained in modern economic and financial theory in western academies or
who had worked in multilateral institutions or international banks, was
also solidly ranged against the gold dinar idea. They stood four-square
against it, partly because it went against the conventional wisdom of the
international financial community, and partly because of their inability to
conceive of any valid alternative to the existing economic and financial
order – and one that could better serve the interests of the Islamic world.

At another level, the timidity with which the Gulf countries engaged with
Mahathir's proposals was such that they betrayed their underlying fear of
possible reprisal action from the western powers for seriously backing and
adopting the gold dinar. The opportunity was missed to create a significant
trading and payments bloc which might ameliorate that instability of
financial markets which nearly sank the Asian economies in 1997. Huge
opportunity losses were incurred by Islamic countries as a result of not
accepting the idea of a gold-based payment system that would have been
uniquely favourable for advancing the scope of trade and finance between
them. In 2001, when Mahathir first made his proposals, the level of foreign
exchange holdings of the Islamic world (mainly in the oil-producing countries) was probably in the vicinity of $800 billion, held mainly in US dollars.
If even half of these had been switched to gold at that time over a two-year
period, the total value of these gold holdings, in today's prices, would have
reached nearly $2 trillion. This 'windfall' could have been partly applied to
alleviate the poverty and underdevelopment so obviously prevalent in a
huge portion of the Muslim world.

The gold dinar episode is only one of the many failed attempts of the
Muslim states to build effective collective organizations with some power
and relevance. The Islamic banking industry is another such example. It
started as a social solidarity movement in rural Egypt, with the founding
of the Mit Ghamr Islamic Savings Bank in 1963. It was immediately
successful and within less than four years it had over 250,000 depositors.
The bank basically established that Muslims would flock to interest-free
banking and lending if these were made available. Within a few years,
Islamic banks, most of which were by now being established on normal
commercial lines, had spread throughout the Muslim World. Islamic
banking started as a serious attempt to create financing mechanisms which
genuinely sought to avoid dealing in interest-based products. These could

have provided the sinews for drawing together the economies of the Muslim countries. However, they turned into gigantic banks and financial institutions which are now integrally connected to the conventional banking world.

Some pan-Islamic initiatives have succeeded within their own narrow ambits – in particular the cultural and economic institutions affiliated to the Organisation of the Islamic Conference such as the Islamic Development Bank – but they have never achieved critical mass to act as significant counterweights, or alternatives, to the multilateral organizations. Neither a top-down approach (such as state support for a common Islamic gold currency) nor a bottom-up approach (such as the essentially private sector-led Islamic banking industry) has metamorphosed into a global factor. The contrast stands out between these essentially Islamic initiatives and, say, the success of the euro as the common currency in most of the EU, or the remarkable growth of western private equity and hedge funds as arbiters of international investment flows. Even now, when the so-called sovereign wealth funds of (mainly) the Gulf oil-producing countries are looming ever larger in the calculations of global money and investment managers and regulators, the thrust has been to contain their influence within the existing global financial order. Their potential for being an anchor stone of a new Islamic investment system is deliberately curtailed.

A New Islamic Zone

The idea of pan-Islamic unity as the realistic final goal of Muslims' political action is as chimerical as a union of, say, the English-speaking world. While Muslims may have a common political culture and may share other affinities, there has been no real political unity among them. Western civilization expresses itself on the international scene through a variety of overlapping organizations and institutions. These may be separate and distinct, but they all partake in the defence and support of their civilization whenever there are perceived threats to western values or strategic interests. At one level they may compete, as for example when the US finds itself in competition with the EU for influence and control over resources. At another level, there are existential issues which demand a common position. As the French newspaper *Le Monde* headlined after the 9/11 attacks, '*Nous sommes tous Américains*' – 'We are all Americans'. The 'we' did not refer so much to the world as to the West in particular. Solidarity with the US rightly trumped all other considerations. In many ways,

Islamic civilization too has to be seen in these 'decentralized' terms. Individual Muslim countries have grouped themselves in associations – geographic, economic, environmental, national or cultural – but, unlike the West, they have not kept a close eye on the welfare of Islamic civilization as a whole. With a few honourable exceptions mainly from non-Arab Muslim countries, they have shirked from defending Islam's ultimate values whenever these were seen to be under threat.

Islam today lacks both core states and an effective group of Muslim states to act in unison on global issues. So far, non-state global forces such as transnational corporations or financial and commodity markets have not generated structures where their power can be separately manifested. When they are obliged to interact with governments and states, they have to seek support from formal state actors and connect with such states' own power networks. No oil company, for example, no matter how powerful financially, can achieve its global objectives without some form of association with, or support from, a government. These companies do influence the nature and leadership of governments, but they still have to respond to governments and states and work within their laws and regulations. Market forces, no matter how powerful, also do not operate in a vacuum. The framework of regulations and controls which are increasingly superimposed on supposedly free markets lends itself to guidance and manipulation by powerful states. The surveillance of the US Treasury on money flows around the world to intercept terrorist financing or to track sanctioned countries is just one example of the powerful hold that state actors can have on free markets. By denying or restricting access to the huge American market, the US can compel international banks to comply with US ground rules for the monitoring of international funds. The EU, by acquiescing to these rules, can then make them globally applicable. Markets lose their autonomous power and become subservient to the interests of state actors. It will be a long time before non-state players will have the necessary power to act autonomously on the global stage, without reference to states and governments.

Islam must somehow generate for itself, at least for the next few decades, a way in which its views and interests are recognized and respected on the global stage. Joining other world religions in matters of common interest is one obvious way. But there are only so many issues on which Islam can join hands with other world religions. Nevertheless, common positions were developed by the Catholic church and by a number of Islamic countries on gender issues, on sexuality and on the reproductive rights of women – at a number of UN conferences, notably the one in Beijing in 1995. Catholicism has a major advantage compared to other world religions, as the political manifestation of its church, the Vatican State, is internationally recognized as a state. The Catholic church therefore sits at these world conclaves on a par with the world's nation–states. Islamic sensibilities at the Beijing Conference could only be manifested through positions taken by Iran, Pakistan and Egypt. Nevertheless, the joint action between these two world religions changed the wording and the emphasis of the final statements of these conferences.

Islam is unlikely to be recognized as a world power like the Catholic church. The church achieved its status – or was reduced to it, on another reading – through the particular historical relationships between it and the European powers, especially Italy. No Islamic religious structure can ever evolve into a state in the same manner as the Catholic church's Vatican State – that is, as a universal institution, hierarchically managed and endowed with a territorial seat of power. This will come about if and only if one or more Islamic states become the undisputed representative(s) of a part of Islam. If a core state representing Islam is unlikely to come about, then another form of global power status must be pursued.

The celebrated medieval Muslim traveller Ibn Batutta could travel from his native Tangiers to the far reaches of Asia and experience a civilization which was held together by a common set of values and institutions. The vast land mass over which he roamed was peopled by different races speaking different languages and was governed by different rulers. But he could act as a judge in the far-away Maldives when he was called upon, because of his familiarity and expertise in a law which held sway over all of Islamdom's vast territory. The reality of a borderless world may create an improbable future for the world of Islam; but, if its civilization influence is to persist, then the implication is that Muslims' allegiances and identities may still be affected by this ideal. The realization of this ideal in a constructive and peaceful way is possible only if the nations and groups over which an Islamic loyalty continues to prevail reconstruct their societies to reflect this ideal better. They must avoid both a facile 'Islamization' process built on a narrow and bigoted definition of the Sharia and frequently coerced by force and intimidation, and the dilution of Islam's essence through periodic bouts of 'reformation', modernization and secularization.

CHAPTER 7

Where Next for the Islamic State?

The existence of several nations under the same State is a test, as well as the best security of its freedom. It is also one of the chief instruments of civilisation; and, as such, it is in the natural and providential order, and indicates a state of greater advancement than the national unity which is the ideal of modern liberalism.

Lord Acton, nineteenth-century British Historian:
Essay on 'Nationality', 1862

The countries which make up the Muslim world embrace a dizzying variety of governments and state structures – ranging from virtual western democracy to the outer reaches of ideological despotisms and theocratic rule. Nearly all these countries claim allegiance to, or at least respect for, Islam. Some states have enshrined Islam as the sole source of legitimacy and authority of the state; others have assigned Islam a privileged role in the law; while others affirm some religious or cultural affinity to it. With the exception of Turkey and a few central Asian republics, none of these countries has sought to distance the state from Islam. None of these countries has committed its people to a society based on non-religious principles.

At the same time, about a third of the world's Muslims live in countries which are organized along recognizably democratic lines, with proper legal assemblies, political parties, elections and an adherence to the principles of human and civil rights. With the demise of Saddam Hussein's tyranny in Iraq and the collapse of the Taliban in Afghanistan, no Muslim state appears to match the egregious levels of violence and despotism which were prevalent in the former Soviet empire, in China during the Mao years, or in Hitler's Europe. It is true that a number of Muslim countries have been given the epithet 'rogue state' – Sudan, Syria and Iran come to mind – but the world is not threatened directly by any Muslim state or power bent on domination or empire.

Nevertheless, there is growing anxiety about the possibility of some cataclysmic event erupting from the Muslim world – perhaps some violent and destabilizing global calamity born of the spectacular acts of terrorism undertaken in the name of Islam, of the appeal of *jihad*-inspired Islamism, of the brittleness and instability of some key Muslim states and of the patent dissatisfaction and disquiet of most Muslims about their condition. So there is real fear of the spread of 'Islamic states' or of the imposition – but never adoption – of Sharia law. Underlying all these concerns is the assumption that Islam is ultimately a totalizing ideology, intent on imposing its world view wherever possible. As such, Islam would have a dangerous propensity to disrupt the established order. For the West, its outer political manifestations need to be contained and the scope of Islam limited to religion only. The ideal would be to transform the practice of Islam into a personal faith, a matter between an individual and his or her religious sensibilities.

These fears are in no way alleviated by the counter-argument that Islam is a complete way of life, each part of which is integrally connected to the other, so that the spiritual must necessarily coalesce with the social and the public. The institutions which govern the Islamic world cannot draw their legitimacy from any source other than Islam, and the demand for a state which respects and reflects the pre-eminence of Islam is a natural concomitant to this principle.

Not every Muslim believes in the ideal of an Islamic state nor does every Muslim in fact agree that founding a state is necessary either for the protection of Islam as a religion or as a way of propagating the faith. The vision of an Islamic state has a long and complicated history, going right back to the existence of an ideal Muslim community built around the Prophet's city of Medina. It is connected to the nature of just rulership over Muslims, as well as to Quranic and Prophetic exhortations for the founding of a political community. Although the political spectrum accommodates almost ever shade of opinion, in practice very definite lines in the sand are being drawn.

The demand for an Islamic state is fundamental to the future of Islam and the appropriate government for Muslims. In Islamic history, the idea of Muslims living under non-Islamic rule or rule by non-Muslims was a rare and unhappy experience. The indubitable fact remains that Islam as a faith and a world civilization grew under the wings of states and empires which were ruled by Muslims and for Muslims. All the states of Islamic civilization, until very recently, could fairly claim to be 'Islamic'.

Indeed, there was enough in common to suggest a specifically Islamic form of political life. This political world was not derived from any specific theory or doctrine about the nature of Islamic government, but rather from the experience accumulated over centuries which laid out certain ground rules concerning power and political authority as well as the duties of the rulers and of the ruled. Running these states was a relatively loose, non-institutional affair, mainly concerned with generating revenue for the needs of the ruler; for the functioning of government; with administering the Sharia law; and with providing for defence of the territory or for military expansion and conquest. One way or another, personal rule was exercised in the form of kingship, itself based on some tribal or kinship formula, and this is key.

In fact the great fourteenth-century Muslim philosopher of history Ibn Khaldun postulated that kinship, or tribal solidarity, was the essence of Muslim rule and power.[1] A sultan – a profane title for 'one who wields power' – was a more common form of ruler than a caliph or imam – one whose authority also derives from a religious or spiritual foundation. But the rapidity with which the Muslim states retreated, and then collapsed, in the face of western power made it impossible to evolve these traditional Islamic forms of rule and government in the nineteenth and twentieth centuries. With only a few isolated exceptions, such as the dynasty in Oman, every other Muslim state had had to develop its institutions of rule and government within the demands of the (western) modern state: they are creations of an epoch in which the traditional forms of Islamic government had been well nigh obliterated.

Islam and Political Power

Many modern thinkers have argued that Islam lacks a tradition of political theorizing – at least in the western sense of the word. The popular belief is that western political thought evolved in a linear and progressive fashion, from the ancient Greeks right down to the fully formulated ideas underpinning liberal democracy and human rights which are now prevalent. Along the way, Christianity, which might have been provided a religion-based political framework, withdrew from the field. Christianity either was compelled to abandon any claim to temporal power – a fact commonly attributed to the victory of 'Enlightenment' ideas – or, in a minority perspective, it had never sought to impose its writ on the political world.

'The Church has therefore tended to recognise the business of governing human society as a human business, and the Christian as both a servant of God and a citizen of the secular order,' wrote Roger Scruton.[2] He went one step further by directly attributing 'Enlightenment' secular ideals to Christianity itself. 'The Enlightenment conception of the citizen, as joined in a free social contract with the neighbours under a tolerant and secular rule of law, derives directly from the Christian legacy,'[3] he wrote. By this token, the establishment of liberal democracy as a purely western creation happened both *because of* and *in spite of* Christianity!

Islam, of course, did not partake in the evolution of western thought towards this ideal end, and therefore, by the reckoning of its critics, could not have generated the same lofty principles that underpin western civilization. Nor did Islam create the frameworks which protect these principles or encourage the kind of allegiance to them that gives these ideas such legitimacy and potency. Having distinct public and private spheres is supposedly alien to Islam. The notion of the nation is unfamiliar to Islamic thought. With few exceptions, such as Ibn Khaldun, there are no influential political thinkers in the history of Islam whose works can provide intellectual and moral underpinnings for the political order.

Of course, what all these critics really mean is that Islam has not produced a political theory or practice that fits with the western liberal democratic tradition. While this may be literally true, the conclusion that Islam has not produced a logically consistent and relevant political theory is patently false.[4] It pretty much embodies the easy generalizations and intolerance to other world views that is characteristic of many proponents of the universal import of western values. Islamic civilization, in its heyday, also suffered from an excess of self-confidence bordering on hubris, which led it to dismiss the achievements of other civilizations. Historians have made a career of cataloguing the 'closing' of the Islamic mind, and some, such as Bernard Lewis, have constructed it into a decisive factor behind the decline of Islamic power.[5]

There was nothing inexorable about the refinement of liberal values and the establishment of a now widespread democratic and rights-based political culture. There were many non-liberal thinkers in the West, some of whom, such as Marx, became unwitting handmaidens to the rise of totalitarian dictatorships. The European right, in its fascist, Nazi or ultra-nationalist guise, can also draw on a rich western tradition of theorizing about race, ethnicity, nation and *Volk*. Imperialists could easily balance the most delicate sensibilities about domestic political rights with a total disregard for the rights of subject races. The anti-clerical and vigorously secular and liberal French Third Republic presided over some of the worse colonial indignities. The victory of democratic values was not foreordained, but it came partly by force of arms after the horrors of two world wars.

In Islam it is neither possible nor desirable to build an edifice of power and authority divorced from the revealed commandments of God. These decrees can be either explicit or derived through reflection, reason and inference. Power may be usurped and Muslims may stray from God's decrees, but, still, genuine political order has to rest on the subordination of human decisions to divine patterns. Law, and lawmaking, become therefore the fundamental and defining aspects of Islamic political culture. The Sharia, as the epitome of the divinely inspired social order, rules supreme. Or at least that was the theory. The practical realities of founding a state, ruling a far-flung empire, reconciling military and civil power, finding a way to treat non-Muslims and Muslim heterodoxies – and a huge array of other issues – have generated alternate political treatises. These were not based on theology, but rather dealt with the real and live issues of statecraft and of the transfer of power.

In certain ways, Islamic civilization developed out of the tensions between the sacred law and the exigencies of political life. Whenever rulers strayed too far from the divine ideal, the Sharia would be brought to bear to correct the imbalance. Jurists would fulminate against the godlessness of royal courts, the intrusion of alien practices or the irreligiousness of the public. *In extremis*, they would lend their support to insurrections against the established order or to movements of revival and reform. Whenever the Sharia stood in the way of the resolution of practical problems – say, in the transfer of power from one ruler to the next – new dispensations would have to be created, simply to allow for continuity in the community's life. This happened after the Mongol invasion, which destroyed the Abbasid Caliphate, Islam's most significant institution. Islamic leaders had to recognize the new, unwanted temporal authority and a means had to be developed to deal with its presence and to acknowledge its immense military power.

The Shia and the Sunni branches of Islam would agree that it is the duty of the state to reflect the divine commands through the Sharia.[6] They differ, though, on who has the authority and under what conditions people are able to exercise power. Whether one accepts the Shia case for charismatic leadership, the imam, or the Sunni version, the sultan and the caliph, the early Islamic state was built on personal rather than institutional rule. Such rule was legitimate only to the extent that the ruler obeyed and enforced the Sharia. As the empire consolidated, earlier models of kingship and power were introduced, drawn especially from the Persian imperial traditions of absolute monarchy.

Islam has not lacked utopian political thinking. The medieval philosopher al-Farabi's 'Virtuous City' is partly based on Plato's *Republic* and Plato's *Laws*.[7] Al-Farabi and others, such as Ibn Sina (Avicenna), attempted to bolster the Islamic polity by embracing the ancient Greeks. The idea was to integrate the non-religious into the Islamic world view. This type of ideal commonwealth, rooted in the universe of Islam but using Platonic archetypes, makes a more dramatic appearance in the latter part of the twentieth century.

The entire system of the Islamic Republic of Iran is a mixture between traditional Islamic political categories and specifically Shia notions; it also involves concepts and ideals drawn directly from Plato through al-Farabi and other Muslim philosophers. Nietzsche said that 'Christianity is Platonism for the people'. But Platonism, ironically, has been given an honoured home in Islamic Iran rather than in an expected western context. In fact Platonism has become a controversial issue in the West, being maligned as much as respected. Its detractors, for instance, Karl Popper, see it as the harbinger of tyrannies;[8] its proponents, such as the philosopher Leo Strauss, see the philosophy as introducing the ideals of virtuous conduct into political life. Nevertheless, the fact that there are Platonic concepts in Islamic political philosophy does not make Islam a 'western' religion, even though in many ways Islamic political thought draws on much the same wellsprings as western thought. Islam simply reached different conclusions and ends.

Islam has generated a number of vital political institutions and structures that are indeed unique to its civilization. The meaning of Islamic government and state is at the heart of the contemporary crisis. Shia Islam has manifested itself in the model of the Islamic Republic of Iran, but is this model ideal? There is still a great deal of resistance, within established Shia circles, to many elements of the Iranian state, particularly to its very 'Platonic' notion of the empowered jurist. Sunni Islam has to struggle with a much broader set of issues, mainly emanating from the total disappearance of the institution of the caliphate.

The Caliphate

The institution of the caliphate symbolizes the former world power of Islam. The yearning for its reinstatement has been a constant theme for radical Islamists, while the possibility of its regeneration has also created an opposite feeling – one of gnawing anxiety that, in spite of all the odds, the caliphate might re-emerge and assert itself as a vehicle for pan-Islamic unity. Its formal abolition in 1924 in Turkey, when the last Ottoman caliph, Abdul Majid, was sent off into exile, did not quite end the system as a political force. Congresses were held soon afterwards to explore the devolution of the title and position to a number of potential candidates from the roster of Muslim kings, but these ended in quarrels and disputes.[9] These claims quietly lapsed and the caliphate seemed destined to be forgotten as a relic of Islam's past, unsuited to modern times and conditions. But it has refused to go away.

The idea of the caliphate continues to exert a powerful pull on Muslims, and its restitution has been skilfully employed by Islamists of all hues as a shorthand for the emergence of a Muslim super-state able to bestride the world stage. Even non-radical Islamists are attracted to the ideal, seeing in it the assertion of a global Islamic identity that must be reckoned with, as well as a way out of the perceived powerlessness and marginalization of Muslims. Others point out the enormous difficulties of resurrecting an institution which had vanished for nearly a century and consider its rebirth to be a hopeless dream.

It is the politicization of the idea of the caliphate and its pivotal role in the ideology of radical Islamists that has brought a non-existent institution into the public domain. The deputy leader of al-Qaeda, Ayman al-Zawahiri, writing to Abu Musab al-Zarqawi, the then head of al-Qaeda's affiliate in Iraq in 2004, said: 'If our intended goal in this age is the establishment of a caliphate in the manner of the Prophet and if we expect to establish its state predominantly – according to how it appears to us – in the heart of the Islamic world, then your efforts and sacrifices – God permitting – are a large step directly towards that goal.'[10] The caliphate was appropriated by al-Qaeda as their end goal and, *ipso facto*, became an ideological tool in the war for Muslim minds.

For the West, then, the caliphate re-emerged as a deeply threatening possibility, and one that had to be countered by the world at all costs. Speaking just before the fifth anniversary of the 9/11 attacks, President George Bush conjured up the demon of the caliphate. 'They [radical Islamists of al-Qaeda] hope to establish a violent political utopia across the Middle East, which they call a "Caliphate" – where all would be ruled according to their hateful ideology . . . This caliphate would be a totalitarian Islamic empire encompassing all current and former Muslim lands, stretching from Europe to North Africa, the Middle East, and Southeast Asia.'[11] Extraordinary. The speech appeared to be straight out of John Buchan's First World War thrillers about a pan-Islamic plot to subvert the world.

All the old fears and anxieties have now reasserted themselves, and the idea of the caliphate has become part of the rhetoric of the war on terror and on the utopian visions of radical Islamists. There are only a few cases where a phantom institution could exert such a powerful pull on the public imagination. It would seem that there are indeed atavistic fears buried deep. Caliphate, *jihad*, fanaticism, crusaders, inquisitions – all blend into each other and become a phantasmagoria of fearsome proportions.

The modern ideal of the caliphate is primarily political. However, from the earliest days of Islam, the institution was infused with religious symbolism and duties. The word 'caliph' itself means 'deputy' or 'successor' and was used with reference both to God and to the Prophet, in the sense that the power of the caliph derives from his relationship to the Prophet and to its divinely inspired status. The caliphate as an office passed through a variety of stages before it was associated with supreme institutional power in the world empire of Islam. The early successors to the Prophet Muhammad are given a special status in Islamic history and are known as the 'rightly guided' caliphs. Not only were they responsible for leading the community of Muslims in spiritual matters, but they also had to contend, at short notice, with the administration of large territories and armies. The principle was established that Muslims are bound together by a common reverence for the Sharia and that the leadership of the community was obliged, by divine decree, to protect and implement the religious law. The caliphate became the symbol of the unique nature of the Muslim order, reflecting the supremacy of Sharia law and thus underlining the supremacy of divinely inspired decrees over all other human considerations. Ultimately, the function of the caliph is to uphold the rule of this law.

Whether Muslim practice ever achieved this ideal is another matter altogether. The Umayyad caliphs were seen as usurpers by a good part of the Muslim population and their reign was cut short, after eight decades, by the successful Abbasid revolution. A branch of the Umayyads re-established their rule in Andalusia and proclaimed a caliphate there in the tenth century. This lasted for less than a century. The Abbasid Caliphate itself moved from an absolute monarchy through various stages, until it had progressively to surrender power to a variety of kings and sultans who ruled in its name. They were the actual lords over the Islamic empire. The Abbasids also had to contend with a 'counter-caliph' who was a member of the Ismaili Fatimid dynasty in Egypt. The Mongol invasion ended the caliphate in Baghdad, and the institution effectively disappeared from the Muslim world until it was resurrected by the Ottoman sultans. As the Ottoman Empire came under increasing pressure from Russia and the western powers, the caliphal aspects of Ottoman rule became more pronounced, mainly as a rallying point for the Muslims of the empire. With the advent of Sultan Abdul Hamid, who came to power in 1876, Ottoman rule became ever more consciously Islamic and the institution of the caliphate became the Ottoman's defining feature for the Muslims of the empire.

There is no unified doctrine of the caliphate. Nevertheless, the existence of a caliphate has been integral to the idea of Islamic civilization. This identification with the caliphate does not seem to have entirely disappeared from the Muslim consciousness even though the last caliph departed eighty years ago. It is linked to the pristine age of the first caliphs of Islam; to the high culture and civilization of the Abbasid Caliphate; to the determined efforts of the Ottoman Caliphate to maintain and defend the last multinational Islamic state. But, above all, the calls for the return of the caliphate are related to the principle that the foremost duty of the ruler – or, in modern terms, of the state – in Islam has been to act as the essential safeguard for the Sharia. The establishment of Islamic government through a caliphate thus becomes a precondition for re-weaving the community of Muslims into the Quranic *Umma*, which orders its life according to the sacred law.

However, the reality is such that the caliphate, at least in its historical form, is unlikely to be resuscitated. The current division of the Muslim world into nation–states, republics and monarchies, democracies and autocracies, is too far advanced to assume that they could ever be regrouped within a single empire or super-state inspired by religion. The only Muslim state which has consciously tried to establish a unique form of Islamic government, with its institutions modelled on an idealized Islamic order, is Iran. The rule of the jurisprudent in Iran is partly based on the claim that that feature approximates the model of the government of Imam Ali, the fourth rightly guided caliph in Kufa in the seventh century. Elements of the Khomeini-inspired model of the just ruler can be found in some Sunni versions of the caliphate, so that it is not impossible to imagine an equivalent form of government in a Muslim country with a Sunni majority. So the caliphate may reappear, in the guise of individual rulers whose power and authority is partly based on their religious knowledge and on their functions as protectors of the Sharia.[12] Or it may devolve upon a group (or assembly) of Sharia scholars who would collectively assume the functions of a caliph.

The resurrection of the caliphate is inextricably bound up with the establishment of the Sharia inside a specifically Islamic state. Most Muslim countries continue to allude to the Sharia as a source of legislation, but this hardly privileges the Sharia as the guiding spirit behind the reordering of society. The idea of the Sharia continues to alarm large parts of the world, not least the elites of the Muslim world. But the opposite is also true. The rejection of the Sharia by nominal Muslims is equally shocking – perhaps more so – as it implies their decisive break with the community of Muslims. Respect for the Sharia as a principle lies at the heart of Muslim social cohesion.

Fear of the Sharia, on the part of westerners and some modern secular Muslims, is real. Lying behind their concern is a virtual terror that, if any concessions are made to the Sharia, the entire, laboriously constructed, edifice of modern secular states would crumble. But surely these fears are related to the way the Sharia is understood and implemented – not to the principles of the Sharia itself? The Sharia must be separated from the huge body of law which purports to cover every conceivable aspect of a Muslim's life and with which it has been associated in the past.

Advice and Consent

Personal rule has often been the norm in Islamic history. The ruler has an almost unlimited right to exercise power in executive and even legislative matters. The ruler's power and prerogatives have only been challenged in those areas where the Sharia has made explicit injunctions. The example of the rightly guided caliphs is instructive. They faced little institutional constraint on their exercise of power after their appointment as caliphs, whether by designation, selection or by public allegiance. This pattern of personal rule, where power is vested in an individual, the emir, has continued throughout Islamic history. It was seriously questioned and modified only towards the end of the nineteenth century and the beginning of the twentieth with the demands, in Ottoman Turkey and then in Qajar Iran, for checks on the power of the ruler – the check being implemented through constitutions and elected chambers. Unfortunately, as a result of this it has become commonplace to equate the uninterrupted rule of autocrats with a supposed Islamic sanction of autocracy, or even predilection for it. It is only a short step from autocratic government to arbitrary government – the bane of Muslims over the centuries. So a representative government emerges only in the context of the Islamic world's interaction with western notions of democracy. The possibility that Islamic civilization, under its own impetus, would produce its own version of checks and balances on rulers and its own system of rights and duties, compatible with its own legacy, is paid scant attention.

The deterministic reading of western political history which proposed the inevitable universal spread of liberal democracy was not only a fashionable conceit which accompanied the fall of communism. Many writers entirely discount the possibility of Islam 'maturing' into a political culture which values rather than debases the ideals of individual liberty and of responsible government. Autocratic government is equated with Islam, and this forces an inadequate and apologetic counter-response to the matter of Islam's compatibility with specific forms of western-inspired political doctrines or institutions. Few point out that the maturing of Islam's political culture into the modern period was thwarted by the violent disruption of Islam's civilization by European powers. The pre-modern systems of government, wherever they survived the colonial and post-colonial onslaught, had to adjust to new circumstances under tremendous pressure from the dominant western powers. Where such pressures materialized in an environment which had not been completely seized by the western powers, the results were mainly positive and pregnant with possibilities for improvement. The Iranian Constitutional Revolution of 1906–9 is a case in point. It provided a formal structure for the state through the drawing up of a constitution and it established a parliamentary government with recognizably democratic features.

The Iranian Constitutional Revolution of 1906–9 was as much influenced by changing Islamic political thought as it was by the wholesale and uncritical adoption of western notions of parliamentary rule. In one of the great Islamic political statements of modern times, a group of leading Iranian ayatollahs based in Najaf, in Iraq, writing in 1908, openly supported constitutional government.

The meaning of freedom in constitutional states is not absolute license, which would permit everyone to do what they like to the point of violating the lives, property and dignity of others. Such a thing has never existed and will never exist in any community of human beings, as it would result in nothing other than absolute disruption and general anarchy in the affairs of the people. On the contrary, the meaning of freedom is the liberty of the general public from arbitrary and unaccountable government by force, so that no powerful individual could use his power against the least powerful of the community and impose anything on him except that which is permitted by the law of the land, before which all the people – be they shah or beggar – would be equal. And freedom in this sense is a rational process and one of the pillars of the Islamic faith.[13]

Foreign intervention and meddling, and the First World War, put an end to the experiment and the country descended into chaos. But the memory of the event was seared into the Iranian political imagination, so that the massive demonstrations that preceded the Iranian Revolution of 1979 openly displayed their debt to the 1906 Iranian Constitutional Revolution.

These tender shoots of an indigenous and authentic Islamic response to the political challenges of the modern era were snuffed out, partly through the reassertion of autocratic rule, but mostly through the destruction of the Islamic political space in the period after the First World War. In colonized Islamic countries, the adoption of a limited form of western parliamentary rule set the pattern for the future evolution of institutions, doctrines and mind-sets which were drawn from the European experience. Rights and duties of the state and individual, political freedoms, the purposes of political action, were all cast in the new political language drawn from the West, and were enacted in an environment which had been moulded on the colonial and post-colonial experience. Under such circumstances, the evolution of institutions which might have been both modern and within the spirit of the Islamic legacy was impossible.

From this perspective, the criticisms levelled at Islam's ability to generate political structures and doctrines consistent with the present global world view are seriously deficient. Were Europe, say, to have fallen under the sway of a different civilization in the mid-eighteenth century and only to have recovered in the past few decades, no one would have expected it to have produced the entire gamut of liberal democratic institutions and practice in the short term. (The experience of eastern Europe after the fall of communism may indicate otherwise. Although democracies were established in eastern Europe relatively quickly, these countries had immense support from the European Union in the development of their democratic institutions. It is highly unlikely that those European countries with no democratic legacy could have duplicated these institutions and democratic practices without major external support.)

The typecasting of Islamic rule as entirely autocratic may be partly validated by history, but it is certainly not sanctioned either by the Quran or by the Prophet's sayings. The Islamic basis for representative government derives from a short but decisive Quranic verse, demanding that consultation should be the basis of any system of authority. 'Their [Muslims'] communal business is to be transacted in consultation among themselves.'[14] In many readings of this verse, the injunction insists that all political transactions must involve consultation across the entire community; in effect, across the entire adult population. Elections and legislative assemblies automatically follow this injunction in the modern context, as there are no specific rules describing how to go about the consultation. Restricting consultation to the worthy and notables of a community is an alternative way to interpret the verse, but this has now become a minority view.

Nearly all Muslim states with a formal democratic structure for their politics have based their institutions and laws on western models of representative government and the division of powers. Turkey, Pakistan, Indonesia, Iraq are all examples of political systems mainly derived from the principles of western-style parliamentary government, with political parties, raucous electioneering and liberal expenditures of money. They are 'Islamic' only to the extent that there is recourse to the people at large for selecting their representatives, but there are no efforts to evolve other characteristics which would validate them from an Islamic perspective. For example, it is assumed that candidates for public office would thrust themselves on the electorate and would use whatever legal means are available to achieve their electoral ends. This runs counter to the well-authenticated prophetic saying that one should not solicit an office of authority, but rather that others should offer it to the person.[15] The idea that the electorate should actively seek out worthy candidates for public office implies a great deal of involvement on the part of local groups, communities and neighbourhoods – what is now called civil society – in selecting the person with the right attributes. The normal practice is for candidates to be vetted by political parties and then 'sold' to the public in political campaigns; or a candidate with resources is able to buy his or her way into public office.

These constraints on political action may appear unworkable or utopian, but they all relate to the earlier idea of courtesy and appropriateness of action, which is central to Islam. Introducing this courtesy into public life is in marked contrast to the adversarial relationship that lies at the heart of modern politics. There is no reason why a re-creation of the public domain in Islam should not draw on more worthy examples of the public spirited figure of the western democratic tradition. Rather, Muslim reformers and liberals assume that politics should always be organized along whatever lines seem to prevail at the moment in the West. The degradation of political life in the democratic world is due in no small measure to the loss of the sense of public duty and the virtues that go along with it. The over-professionalization of politics, the power of the mass media over political outcomes, the corrupting role of money in the electoral process, the manipulation of public opinion, are all features of modern democracies. They are being replicated in Muslim countries which base their politics on democratic processes simply because they have accepted the premises of adversarial politics. Such features are in fact made worse by the proneness to demagoguery and crass populism, which feed on grievances and envy, as well as by the widespread prevalence of corrupt practices. They significantly denude the ideals of democracy and diminish, if not eliminate, the possibility of a new form of representative government, which may sit well within the spirit of Islam.

Sovereignty

The question of the sources of the sovereignty of the state in Islam has become a charged issue. It is now taken as axiomatic that nation–states are the only recognized political authorities in the world and that sovereignty resides not in kings and monarchs but with the people. 'We, the people . . .' is how the US constitution begins; and nearly all modern states, with the exception of some countries with a Muslim majority, explicitly attribute sovereignty to the people. The few non-Muslim states which are partly constructed on a religious identity have evaded the issue. Israel, for example, does not have a written constitution which would oblige it to define itself either in religious or in secular terms. Most Muslim states pay at least lip service to their loyalty to Islam, but that is entirely different from attributing sovereignty to God. Iran obviously is an exception, where constitutional arrangements are all premised on the flow of authority from a theocentric world view. Saudi Arabia has no constitution as such, and, when pressed, its leaders state that the: 'Quran is our constitution.' The historical experience of the Muslims with autocratic and arbitrary governments has clouded the issue of sovereignty. Most of them would assume that sovereignty is held by whoever holds power. Power confers legitimacy – or at least the others' acquiescence to its exercise – and thereby relegates the issue of sovereignty to the realm of speculative political philosophy.

However, the growth of Islamist movements and their success in establishing their power in places such as Iran and Sudan have reopened the question of the sovereignty of the state in Islam. All Islamic scholars – and even ordinary believing Muslims – will affirm that sovereignty, in the sense of ultimate dominion or power and authority, belongs to God. For the state, or even for mankind, to assert this role is an act of usurpation and gross impiety. Muslims also, by an act of volition, submit to this authority of God, so that the universal community of Muslims constitutes a state – in the sense of an order or a condition – where the laws of God reign supreme. The Islamic *Umma*, therefore, does not quite correspond to the modern state, since it combines territoriality with non-territoriality, transcendence with temporality. Nevertheless, Islamic government cannot be based on the actual rule of God. Imam Ali, the fourth of the rightly guided caliphs, confronted this issue when his authority was challenged by the Khawarij rebels with their slogan 'Governing belongs only to Allah'. His reply was that their statement may have been superficially correct, but the inference they drew from it was wrong.

> It is true that the verdict lies only with Allah, but these people say that the function of governance is only for Allah. The fact is that there is no escape from the ruler, good or bad. Through the ruler tax is collected, the enemy is fought, roadways are protected and the right of the weak is taken from the strong till the virtuous enjoys peace and is allowed protection from the oppression of the wicked.[16]

The agency of human beings under the governance of God is a necessity for any functioning political order. But this has not stopped either Islamists or, paradoxically, western critics of Islam to make the same allegation the Khawarij made. The Islamic injunction that governance belongs to God is equated, without qualification or reservation, to a rigid, unchanging theocracy, eliminating the imperative for a human interpretation of God's law. 'The Islamic state was in principle a theocracy – not in the western sense of a state ruled by Church and the clergy, since neither existed in the Islamic world, but in the more literal sense of a polity ruled by God,' writes the western scholar on Islam, Bernard Lewis.[17] This is taken as a given, and all subsequent analysis is predicated on this narrow assumption. Such a view leads to the assertion that an Islamic government, *ipso facto*, is ranged against all forms of democratic practice or human rights legislation, as these supposedly interfere with God's ultimate sovereignty as expressed through the revealed law. No account is taken of the numerous passages in the Quran which explicitly authorize human beings to act as God's representatives and agents on earth. Human beings acting as God's agents implies that they must have the ability and will to do so, and therefore to assume the burden of responsibility for their actions.

Islam and the Political Order

The nature of an Islamic political order, especially if it actually materializes in a number of countries, would be a matter of great concern to the world's other powers. The idea of the adversary – the 'enemy' – is never far from the surface in the world's political order, and the liberal democracies of the West are no different in this regard. In many ways, the prized tolerance of these societies has an obverse side in the form of an intolerance or disregard for other civilizations, which may not subscribe to the 'universal' nature of western values. The past two decades after the fall of the communist system provided clear indications of this fact. The replacement of the communists by the Islamists – even by Islam in its totality, though this is not explicitly stated – with Islam becoming *the* enemy, within and without, is an obvious example. Well before 9/11, Islam began to replace the Soviet bloc as the real threat that needed to be countered. It is not so much that western democracies need enemies to justify their continued existence; this is the preserve of dictatorships and tyrannies, which use the notion of an ever-threatening and looming enemy in order to stay in power. Rather, western liberal societies ascribe their success to the superiority of their values, processes and institutions, which were realized only after long and agonizing periods of struggle and war. Other civilizations may share in some of these values, but the values themselves will always remain uniquely western. The possibility that different civilizations may generate similar values and results is hardly acknowledged in practice. The western liberal model is taken as the yardstick and other systems are gauged by the degree to which they vary from it. For example, the convergence of communism and capitalism towards some form of common future was a recurrent theme in the 1960s and 1970s. That ended with the Soviet invasion of Afghanistan, which seemed to break the ground rules of convergence.

Détente was replaced with confrontation – between a West which was good and the evil empire of the Soviets.

The Bush rhetoric directed against radical Islam is in essence no different from the pattern of defining an external enemy and then mobilizing the country around the fear that that enemy would prevail. 'They hate what we see right here in this chamber – a democratically elected government. Their leaders are self-appointed. They hate our freedoms – our freedom of religion, our freedom of speech, our freedom to vote and assemble and disagree with each other,' said Bush in his speech to Congress after the 9/11 attacks.[18] Then he introduced the qualification that the enemy was not Islam, but a variant of Islam. However, this qualification needs to be placed in the context of a continuously evolving politico-military strategy to contain radical Islam. This strategy has so far involved the invasion and occupation of two Muslim countries; the expenditure of huge resources on countering Islamist thought; the support for ersatz democracies in Muslim countries; and direct intervention in the domestic affairs of scores of Muslim countries. It is hard to see how all this differs from the mobilization necessary to fight what the neo-conservative writer Norman Podhoretz has called the 'Fourth World War' – the war between western civilization and a supposedly Islamist barbarism.[19]

In Europe the process is somewhat different, in that radical Islam is not seen to be the enemy without so much as the enemy within, in the form of multitudes of immigrant Muslims bent on perpetrating their 'illiberal' values. In both cases, however, a process of crystallizing the notion of an enemy around Muslims and Islam is now well advanced. Europe's much prized multiculturalism is under serious assault for allowing Muslims a space to live out their lives according to their values.[20]

Population Movements and Migration

One gauge of a civilizations' attractiveness is the extent to which others are drawn into its zone. On this criterion, Islam has been an eminently successful civilization for most of its history. The huge populations of the territories which came under its control were not, in the main, converted to the faith by force. In certain areas, such as South-East Asia, the conversion of the population to Islam was largely prompted by the example of Muslim merchants who settled there rather than by military conquest.[21] Even in the nineteenth century, as Islamic power was visibly diminishing, the lands of Islam were still attractive to large numbers of people from outside its civilization, including many from southern Europe who were seeking their fame and fortune. But within a few decades of the twentieth century the situation became reversed. It was now the Muslims who were leaving the lands of Islam – at first in a trickle, but later by the millions – and making their way to the West.

As Islam spread out of its Arabian heartland, the newly conquered lands were not overwhelmed by the large-scale migrations of Arab tribes into their territories. By and large, the Arabs and their allies formed a small ruling elite, and the indigenous peoples of the conquered lands at first kept their religious affiliations. Islamic law guaranteed toleration for Christians and Jews as 'People of the Book'. It may have been a reluctant toleration, but it was toleration nonetheless. However, another factor played a part in the treatment of the non-Muslim conquered peoples: the poll and land taxes that these had to pay as non-Muslim subjects of the Muslim state. There was at first a strong disincentive on the part of the state to encourage the conversion of the conquered peoples to Islam, as this would entail a serious revenue loss. However, the passage of time ensured that the vast majority of the conquered peoples would convert to Islam. The phenomenon was encouraged by a variety of factors such as the conversion of the leaders of the indigenous elites; intermarriage; proselytizing by missionaries; and economic or social advantage.[22] The process was self-enforcing, especially as it took place in an environment of continuing political and military dominance by Muslims. A stability of the religious identity of the majority of the inhabitants was achieved, and newcomers such as the Turkic tribes from Central Asia or the Mongols were absorbed into the Muslim milieu.

Population movements within the Muslim world were a natural concomitant to environmental and resource pressures, changes in political boundaries, economic opportunity and conquests. But until very recently they took place inside the world of Islam and did not spill outside its frontiers. There were no Muslim migrants who followed the Europeans into the New World. Islamic law relating to migration and conversion developed therefore in conditions where Muslims were not only the dominant political class, but also the majority of the people.

The fact of the matter is that traditional Islamic jurisprudence does not allow for migration into a land where Islam is not the ascendant creed. Not all schools of jurisprudence have identical rulings on migration. The Maliki creed is probably the most insistent on the duty of Muslims to leave countries where Islam's preponderance has been lost. But nearly all the schools agree that Muslims are simply not authorized to sojourn in such territories, except under very narrow conditions of *da'awa* (calling people to Islam) or trade.[23] The early Muslims were allowed to leave for Abyssinia, but that was only because an Islamic polity had not yet been established. Later, this would lead to the now famous division of the world into *Dar-ul-Islam* and *Dar-ul-Harb* – the abode of Islam and the abode of struggle. *Dar-ul-Islam* was theoretically treated as one homeland. Whenever Muslim territory fell under the control of others, Muslims were not only encouraged but legally enjoined to leave the land. This happened for the first time when nearly 50,000 Muslims left Sicily after its conquest by the Normans in the eleventh century, fleeing to Egypt and North Africa.

The relentless push of the *Reconquista* over the centuries led to hundreds of thousands, possibly millions, leaving the territories re-conquered in Spain; again, they made mainly for North Africa. This was before the wholesale expulsions of Spain's Muslim population in the late sixteenth and early seventeenth centuries. The Muslims who stayed behind in these lands were derogatorily termed in Arabic, *mudejans* – literally a reference to domestic or tamed animals – a noun which later gave rise to the Spanish word *mudejer*. The same pattern of large-scale emigration, partly prompted by religious injunctions, occurred whenever Muslim territory changed rulers, and in such diverse places as the Balkans, the Caucasus and (more recently) the Indian sub-continent and Palestine. The Arab Middle East is full of people whose predecessors had come from Chechnya, Dagestan, Central Asia and, of course, Andalusia. A significant minority of Turkey's citizens originate in the former territories of the Ottoman Empire which were lost to Serbia, Greece, Roumania and Bulgaria.

However, as Muslim communities established themselves and grew in the West, the traditional laws on migration and sojourning in non-Islamic lands had to be reviewed. There was no point in emphasizing the impermissibility of migration for economic betterment when this had already occurred, and a new consensus among Islam's scholars had to be developed to address the real issue affecting Muslims' faith and practice in the West. Both the Sunni and Shia schools developed nearly identical rules governing the presence of Muslims in the West.[24] They were concerned above all to preserve the religious identity of the Muslims there, and built their rulings around the paramount issue of maintaining the integrity of Muslims' religiosity and their families. But the emphasis was on accommodating the fact of the Muslim's presence in the West rather than on justifying it or encouraging actual emigration from Islamic lands. The traditional rulings applied: it was better for Muslims not to leave the lands of Islam; and, if the observance of Islamic practices became problematic in one country – say, when Southern Yemen was formally a communist country – the Muslim's first duty was to leave that land for other Muslim countries.

A comprehensive set of Sharia rulings has evolved over the past two decades which clearly stipulate that the main criterion by which a Muslim can justify his or her presence in non-Muslim lands is the degree to which he or she can retain the faith. Any possibility that the Muslim's faith, or that of his or her family, might be diminished as a result of his or her presence in the West immediately nullifies the dispensation to live there. In this case, the persons concerned must, as a matter of religious duty, leave the West for a Muslim country. The only admitted exception is when the Muslim in question fears for his or her life, were he or she to return to a Muslim country. The rulings are silent as to whether a Muslim is allowed to leave a Muslim land without due cause. One is recommended to leave for a non-Muslim land if, and only if, this is in the cause of spreading the religion.

While these rulings allowed for the continuing presence of Muslims in the West, they raised another set of vexatious questions, mainly relating to the contradictions and difficulties of abiding by the Sharia in a country whose social, cultural and political mores are at odds with it. A host of issues arise in this way for the observant Muslim – from allowing children to watch certain types of television programmes to finding the right niche and time to perform one's obligatory prayers at the workplace. The prevalence of alcohol in social settings, the easy mixing of the sexes and the indifference of the public to modest dress for women are other examples of the daily pressures which the observant Muslim faces in a modern western setting.

All contemporary Muslim scholars emphasize the need to maintain the Islamic identity of Muslims abroad in preference to their racial or national identity. The growth of a primary Muslim identity amongst second-generation Muslims in the West is not only a result of the weakening of their parents' original ethnic or racial bonds, but an affirmation of a religious loyalty. This raises yet another set of critical issues regarding a Muslim's ultimate loyalty in a western setting: will loyalty to the nation–state or to particular national values and ideals trump the Muslim's sense of bonding with other Muslims worldwide?

These rulings have had another important effect on Muslim communities, especially in Europe. They have pushed them to create a plethora of Muslim organizations which cater to the religious, educational and cultural needs of the community. The most significant among such institutions has been the Muslim school. In only a few European countries has the state allowed for state-funded Muslim schools. The UK, for example, has only four such schools, catering for perhaps a thousand pupils. State funding for Muslims schools has been an extremely sensitive issue and generates much heated public debate between the advocates of a multicultural approach to education and those who see Muslim schools as a breeding ground for intolerance, gender inequality and a secluded lifestyle. In reality, the state in Europe is closely interwound with the church and religion in the provision of education. The Church of England, the Catholic church and the Jewish community all manage a large number of state-funded schools in the UK, and the practice has hardly generated any controversy, even from many ideological secularists. But there continues to be a strong unease about official support for Muslim schools, even when the few schools which do exist have an excellent academic record and have produced well rounded and well adjusted graduates. Many people still choose to see Muslim schools as nothing more than radical *madrassas*, bent on undermining western values and societies and planting the seeds of an alien culture in the midst of a post-modern and post-religious Europe.

The contemporary Sharia rulings on migration have removed the sharp historical distinctions between 'the abode of Islam' and 'the abode of struggle', and have created a third category: a conditional authorization to remain in non-Islamic lands. But they have not quite removed the lingering feeling among many Muslims in the West that the undoubted freedoms and material rewards which they enjoy do not compensate for their presence in an environment which is indifferent, if not hostile, to Islam. Unlike their forebears, these migrants have been very unsuccessful in attracting a large number of converts from the indigenous population and thereby creating a synthesis between Islam and its host environment. Islam in the West, with the exception of African–American Muslims, still consists overwhelmingly of migrants from Muslim lands and their offspring. If anything, the flow of 'converts' is more in the other direction: a large number of Muslims in the West have become effectively secularized and maintain only a symbolic connection with Islam. The Muslim communities in the West are thus maintained by natural growth and by the inflow of migrants rather than by the far more significant process of converting large numbers of the indigenous populations to Islam.

Often European or American converts to Islam, as well as second- and third-generation Muslims born in the West, are far more literal in their interpretations of the religion and are highly critical of their native societies and cultures. They tend to idealize the conditions of the Muslim world, where they believe that the practice of Islam is more pristine and less affected by modernization and by the 'moral turpitude' which is supposed to prevail in the West. A particularly poignant case can be drawn from the experience, in the early 1980s, of a party of reasonably affluent British Muslims, mainly converts, who sought to establish a Muslim's right to dwell anywhere in the Islamic world.[25] After surveying the Islamic world, they focused on the United Arab Emirates and headed for Abu Dhabi. The leader of the group arranged to meet the chief judge there – a venerable and erudite Islamic scholar – and presented him with the desire of these British Muslims to settle in the UAE in order to perfect their faith. Did not their religion enjoin them to leave the land of unbelief and move wherever Islam was in the ascendant? The chief judge, who was sympathetic to their cause, asked them to wait for a short period while he consulted with the authorities. A week later, he met the group again. With tears in his eyes, he told them that their request had been flatly denied. It had not been possible to accede to their request, he said – knowing full well that they were within their rights as Muslims to ask for full residence in that country. The group returned to Britain, rather sheepishly, after a few weeks. The country to which they had wanted to emigrate, the UAE, had turned them down, citing impossibly restrictive and discriminatory immigration policies. The whole notion of an Islamdom (*Dar-ul-Islam*) where a Muslim can travel and settle freely had been thrown out of the window.

Muslims in Western Europe

Muslims' deep reluctance to migrate outside of the lands of Islam until well into twentieth century was greatly affected by the colonial experience. The overthrow of Muslim rule, the exposure to the superior technical and material civilization of the West and the integration of insular economies with the European metropolises conspired to weaken the ingrained resistance to leaving the lands of Islam.

Religiously minded people escaping colonial domination still sought refuge in the Muslim world, but this was necessarily limited given the restricted opportunities for livelihood in countries such as Saudi Arabia and Egypt of the 1930s. Large-scale movements of Muslims outside the Muslim world into the West started in the post-First World War era. Significant numbers of North African male labourers moved to France in search of work. They were joined by demobilized soldiers from North Africa who remained in France after the end of hostilities. The process accelerated after the Second World War, with the retreat of the colonial empires and the critical labour shortages in western Europe. By the 1960s large numbers of North Africans had moved into France and Belgium; South Asians into the UK; Indonesians into Holland; and Turks and Kurds into Germany. They took on jobs which the indigenous people would not accept, at low-pay levels. Most came from rural areas and were often members of ethnic minorities or migrants from particular regional areas, for instance, the Berbers of Algeria, the Kurds of Turkey or the Kashmiris. These groups were disproportionately represented in the early migrant communities in Europe. They also concentrated in particular areas such as capital cities or traditional industrial centres, for instance, those for textile manufacturing, creating an impression of dense multitudes even though the overall population of Muslims in these European countries is relatively low. The stagflation of the 1970s, which affected the western world, put a stop to the easy migration policies of earlier times, and a raft of laws and regulations followed that severely restricted the flow of unskilled and semi-skilled migrants into western Europe. Henceforth, most legal migration involved family reunification. The 1980s saw another spate of migration into western Europe from Muslim lands, but this time it was driven mainly by asylum seekers, often with advanced educational qualifications and skills. These came from countries such as Lebanon, Iraq, Iran, Afghanistan, Somalia and Yugoslavia, which were torn by war and civil strife. The period from the 1990s to the present has been one of large-scale *illegal* migration from a variety of Muslim and non-Muslim countries. A large number of European countries, such as Spain, Italy and Greece – countries with little experience in migrants from other cultures and religions – began to be affected by the flow of Muslims into their territories. Officially, the population of Muslims in western Europe is about fourteen million, that is, less than 4 per cent of the total population of the EU. Unofficially, however, the figures quoted sometime exceed twenty million. The concentration of Muslims in the major cities of France, Germany, the UK, and now Italy and Spain, creates an altogether different impression about the numbers of Muslims in western Europe.[26]

The legal position of Islam inside western European countries depends on the status and nature of the relationship between state and religion in particular countries. In some countries, for instance, in France, the government has sponsored officially sanctioned organizations through which the state interacts with Islam on matters of religious practice such as the operation of mosques and preaching. In others, the state follows a policy of benign neglect, except where the activities of Muslims are seen to impinge on public order or security, or are seen to be in violation of laws on gender and sexual discrimination, freedom of expression or racism.[27]

Western European countries do not compile official data on their Muslim populations. Muslims are grouped under different data collection categories such as national or geographic origin, or race and ethnicity. However, through cross-referencing and targeted studies, a grim picture emerges about the socio-economic conditions, alienation, discrimination and marginalization of the Muslims of western Europe. In all the European countries, the unemployment figures for Muslims are on average far higher than for western Europeans: often twice or three times the levels of the equivalent population control group. For example, unemployment among Muslim females in the UK in 2005 reached 20 per cent, compared to about 7 per cent for women generally. In Belgium, in 2005 the unemployment rates for Turkish and Moroccan nationals (nearly all of them Muslims) were nearly 40 per cent, compared to 7 per cent for Belgian natives. Discrimination in employment practices is also rampant. In Germany, more than half of Turkish job applicants claimed that they suffered discrimination in one form or another. The prevalence of widespread discrimination in recruitment practices is confirmed by a host of studies and surveys. A British radio station, BBC Radio 5, conducted an experiment whereby fifty firms were approached by six fictitious individuals with similar qualifications but with different-sounding names, which suggested English, African and Muslim backgrounds. Only 9 per cent of those with a Muslim-sounding name were called for an interview, compared to 13 per cent for the African and 25 per cent for the English names. A similar test was conducted in France in 2004, where a person with a North African name had five times less chance of being accepted than a person with a French name. The paucity of Muslims in managerial slots in major public and private enterprises of western Europe is striking, as is the near absence of top executives with a Muslim background from major western corporations and public bodies.[28]

In western Europe Muslims score poorly in educational attainment. The lack of official statistics in Europe, with the exception of the UK, does not conceal a clear picture of Muslim underachievement. In the UK, Britons of Pakistani and Bangladeshi origin are at the bottom of educational league tables. Nearly a third of Muslims working in the UK have no educational qualifications; they are the lowest in the country. The same sad figures carry across other areas of social disadvantage such as housing, where Muslims suffer from high levels of homelessness, poor-quality housing, poor neighbourhoods and high levels of personal insecurity. Again, the prisoner population in western Europe is disproportionately Muslim. In Britain, Muslims account for 11 per cent of the prison population, compared to their 3 per cent share of the general population. In Holland, the respective figures are 20 per cent versus 5 per cent. In France the figures are even more shocking: 60 to 70 per cent of the prison population is Muslim, while Muslims make up perhaps 10 per cent of the population. While French government officials explain these discrepancies by pointing out the poverty of the Muslim population, Muslim community leaders in France blame decades of government policies which have helped to isolate Muslims in impoverished suburbs with inferior facilities, away from available jobs.[29]

The dire socio-economic conditions of most Muslims in western Europe dovetail into the widespread belief that Muslims and Islam will not be accepted as integral components of western societies. The term 'Islamophobia' was coined to express this attitude. Its general use has been to describe unacceptable behaviour towards or prejudicial views about Muslims. However, many liberals in the West have shied away from using the expression. The struggle against discrimination in Europe has been framed by these people only in terms of race or ethnicity. The various national and European laws which have emerged to redress the situation have been written with the intention of reversing racial discrimination. To acknowledge that an entire religion might be the target of discriminatory practices does not accord well with the conventional view that discrimination revolves around conditions a person has no choice about, such as the colour of their skin or their national origin. Moreover, Islam is now seen by many in the 'progressive' community in the West to be a religion which mistreats certain groups, for instance, women and homosexuals, and is riddled with anti-Semitism and political intolerance. These suspicions about Islam, which come from the Left, are matched by the prejudices of the Right, which equates Islam with terrorism and regards Muslims as subversive elements inside western societies. But the fact that anti-Islam prejudices are widely shared simply confirms the real and pernicious nature of Islamophobia in the West, especially in western Europe.

The Runnymede Trust, in its landmark 1997 study on Islamophobia, has set out eight characteristics of the phenomenon.[30] All of them – from the perception of Islam as a violent and barbaric religion to the acceptance of widespread anti-Muslim feelings and behaviour – are amply evident, but not quite yet recorded in official statistics. In opinion surveys, the attitudes towards Muslims of other western Europeans are mostly unfavourable. In Germany, for example, 80 per cent of respondents equated Islam with terror. In Spain, more than half of the respondents to a survey classified Islam as violent and over 80 per cent considered Muslims to be authoritarian. Half the Italians who completed a survey thought that Muslims 'have cruel and barbaric laws' and support international terrorism. Only in the UK did the majority of respondents have an overall friendly attitude to Islam.[31] The media feeds Islamophobic tendencies in western society and uses epithets, half-truths and downright lies which would normally subject them to a barrage of lawsuits from anti-racist or anti-Semitic groups.

Eurabia

The generally negative attitude to Islam in the West was exacerbated by the terrorist attacks of 11 September 2001 and by the bombings in Madrid and London which followed in their wake. Fear and uncertainty about the long-term implications of the presence of Muslims in the West feed into alarmist and even apocalyptic predictions about Europe's future and the future of western civilization itself. What had been the preoccupation of extreme right-wing writers and politicians in the previous decade has moved firmly into the mainstream, with highly respected figures such as the historian Niall Ferguson raising alarm bells about Europe's demographic 'bust' and about the process of reverse colonization led by the Muslims. These views have coalesced into the theory of 'Eurabia', whereby the expanding populations of Muslims in Europe will overwhelm their host societies or at best will force the fragmentation of European states into mutually hostile enclaves, where Muslims and Islamic law and customs will dominate. The theory is premised mainly upon the continuing low birth-rates of indigenous and ageing Europeans, on the decline of Christian observance and on Europe's indiscriminate culture of toleration. As Ferguson wrote in a *New York Times* op-ed on 4 April 2004, when he first saw the model of the minarets of Oxford's Centre for Islamic Studies, he thought of Gibbon's celebrated *Decline and Fall of the Roman Empire.*

The collapse of European civilization has been predicted before, not least by writers such as Oswald Spengler, whose 1918 book *The Decline of the West* had an enormous impact on the ideas and politics of the inter-war years. The Eurabian thesis plays on deeply felt European anxieties about the unassimilated Muslims in their midst. These anxieties have been fed by a barrage of books and reports emanating from neo-conservative writers and think-tanks from the US. They contrast martial Americans with effete and spineless Europeans, who allow their continent to be overrun by terrorists and by Islamic zealots. Riots in the north of England are seen as the opening salvoes of a war of *jihadis*; the high-crime suburbs of Paris are described as Muslim 'No-Go' zones; a cerebral lecture by the Archbishop of Canterbury on using aspects of Sharia law in Muslim personal relations becomes a capitulation to Islamist demands.

The discovery that a wide network of Islamist terrorists and *jihadis* had established itself in the capitals of Europe in the 1990s, especially in London, added further grist to the mill of the advocates of the Eurabian thesis. These networks were mainly responsible for the planning of the 9/11 attacks and the subsequent attacks in Madrid and London. It was now the turn of the more flexible and accommodating policies towards Muslims pursued by successive British governments to came under the withering scrutiny of neo-conservatives and other right-wing opinion leaders. The word 'Londonistan' was coined by the journalist Melanie Phillips to describe the ease with which Islamist radicals established themselves in the capital and the widespread network of Muslim organizations which sustained them.[32]

There is no doubt about the appeal of the idea of Eurabia, even if its fringes are populated by extremists with preposterous assertions about an Islamic conspiracy to subvert Europe. These claims are no different in substance from the absurd allegations found in the early twentieth-century forgery, *The Protocols of the Elders of Zion*, about a Zionist plot to dominate the world; nor is their depiction of Muslims any different from the xenophobic and racists fears which gripped western Europe when the pogroms in Russia had driven hundreds of thousands of impov-erished Jews westwards.[33] At the heart of Eurabia there is the idea of a demographic time-bomb – an inexorable process of population shift which will gradually overwhelm Europe. But the numbers underpinning this claim are themselves highly suspect. It is very difficult to see how Europe's current Muslim population of about fifteen to twenty million could ever grow to pose a serious threat to Europe's total population of nearly 450 million – even if Turkey, with its seventy million Muslims, were to be allowed into the EU as a full partner.

The shrillness and persistence of the Eurabian argument is having some effect on policy-makers in Europe. Citizenship tests which emphasize knowledge of western values have become mandatory in many European countries, and governments are moving towards recognizing 'official' Islamic bodies that would draw Muslims into the cultural mainstream. But advocates of the thesis still wring their hands about the future of Europe. Some, such as Ferguson, have already half-consigned Europe to a future of decay and decline. One outcome he suggests is 'a creeping Islamicization of a decadent Christendom'.[34] Another is a violent backlash against immigrants, particularly Muslims; this should lead to mass deportations of illegal immigrants; far more draconian border controls; and financial incentives for migrants to return to their native countries. However, the advocates of the Eurabian thesis would not be satisfied by these measures; they smack of too little and too late. Their arguments are veering close to the solutions adopted in seventeenth-century Spain when the country was dealing with its own Muslim 'problem' – that of the Moriscos. Although mass expulsions of Europe's Muslim population are highly improbable, the mass abandonment of Islam by Europe's Muslims may not be so, if that would be the price for integrating Europe's Muslims into the West.

Rediscovering or developing the political basis of a new Islamic civilization has to take place in this context. The question becomes whether there is wholesale acceptance of the West's definition of universal values and acknowledgement that Islam must move towards adopting them, or whether Islam should continue to seek the meaning of the universal – including that in political values and institutions – in its own legacy. For example, the advocates of 'Muslim Democracy', a movement akin to Christian democracy in Europe, are at the forefront of redefining the meaning of the political in Islam in western terms. Anwar Ibrahim, the former deputy prime minister of Malaysia, whose arrest on trumped up charges after the 1997 Asian crisis became an international *cause célèbre*, is a proponent of the connection between universal values (those of the West) and Muslim democracy. The AK Party in Turkey, which won a resounding re-election victory in 2007, is also seen as the model of a

Muslim democratic party: a pragmatic political movement which is, essentially, socially conservative, economically liberal, and indifferent to the calls for the introduction of the Sharia.

The political dimension of Islam is irrelevant to the governing programme of these parties, and Islamic values become subsumed under a general conservatism and right-of-centre politics. In essence, Muslim democracy is a pathway to a secular and ultimately western definition of the political rather than a re-expression of the political in Islam. It may prevail in the face of the nihilistic and destructive alternative of radical Islamism and in the face of more openly secular and westernising political currents in the Muslim world. As a phenomenon, it has garnered the support of western governments – even though the Turkish model of Muslim democracy owes its success to the particular conditions in Turkey and to the rise of the religiously observant and socially conservative Anatolian middle classes.[35] But Muslim democracy is unlikely to resolve the conundrum which Muslims face when they are dealing with the political: the need to evolve a privileged place for the sacred in the structuring of the Islamic political order.

In the past, the Sharia provided this essential link. It is conceivable that a re-thinking of the Sharia and of the legitimately political in Islam will provide the mechanism through which a new understanding of the meaning of the sacred in Islamic political life can be realized. To some extent, this strategy was attempted in Iran; but, even after nearly thirty years of Islamic revolution, the institutions of the state are far from being stable or their contours and powers clear. There has been a great deal of resistance to the main features of the Islamic Republic, especially to its crystallization around the person of the leader and to the growth of a clerical political class. This has come not only from secularists and western minded people, but also from important elements of the *ulema* hierarchy and from most religious intellectuals. Whether the Islamic Republic survives in its present form is a moot point, but it is certainly an experiment whose outcome will have profound effects on the Islamic world.

CHAPTER 8

Human Rights and Human Duties

Freedom is to act as one's real and true nature demands and so only the exercise of that choice which is of what is good can properly be called 'free choice'. A choice for the better is therefore an act of freedom ... Whereas a choice for the worse is not a choice as it is grounded in ignorance ... it is then also not an exercise in freedom because freedom means precisely being free of domination by the powers of the soul that incites to evil.

Syed Muhammad Naquib al-Attas, Malaysian philosopher
and educator: *Prolegomena to the Metaphysics of Islam*
(ISTAC: KUALA LUMPUR, 1995), p. 33

The tensions and crises that have punctuated the relationships between Islam and the West in the modern era are between two entirely unequal parties. In the past two decades, Islam has been in the dock of world opinion. It has been obliged to respond to a questioning, and even an indictment, of its values and principles. Islam has been challenged over its contribution to, or encouragement of, the instability, violence and mayhem caused by a few of its adherents. Muslims have been put on the defensive and feel besieged by accusations and obloquy from all quarters. Age-old charges which might not have been out of place in the nineteenth century, and which might even seem medieval, are hurled at Muslims and Islam; to them are added new accusations, specific to modern times. The onslaught is unremitting; no sooner is one issue resolved than another quickly emerges to replace it. There are wars going on everywhere: from the 'war for Muslim minds', to the 'war for the soul of Islam'; from the 'war on terror' to the wars in Iraq and Afghanistan. European parliamentarians discuss the finer aspects of Islamic jurisprudence and US presidents pontificate on the merits of the Islamic religion. Islam is the fodder for scare-mongering headlines of the gutter press, but it also preoccupies the more sedate and thoughtful of the world's media. Islam has become the foil for whatever set of precepts defines the modern mind. Whenever gender issues are discussed, Islam's treatment of women becomes the other, unacceptable, alternative. Whenever freedom of speech is seen to be threatened, it is Islam that is doing the threatening. Whenever freedom of worship is restricted, it is Islam that is condemned for its supposed intolerance of other religions and its degrading treatment of its minorities. The ancient Islamic term for 'protected minorities', *al-Dhimmis*, is now turned against Islam as proof of its in-built proclivity to discriminate.

You [the western public] don't understand or don't want to understand that if we don't oppose this, don't defend ourselves against this, don't fight, *Jihad* will win. And it will destroy the world that, good or bad, we've succeeded in building, changing, improving, and making a little more intelligent, i.e. less bigoted or even without bigotry. And with that it will destroy our culture, our art, our science, our morality, our values, and our pleasures . . .

wrote the Italian journalist Oriana Fallaci a few weeks after 11 September 2001.[1]

The animus against Islam could partly be explained by the hysteria that gripped the western public after the attacks of al-Qaeda on New York and Washington. This was further exacerbated by the 2004 bombings in Madrid and those of 2005 in London. All of this fed into the vastly disproportionate military and security response of the US and its allies to what was, after all, terrorist acts and not a declaration of war by a state, let alone by a civilization. But the grounds for the demonization of Islam had already been set in the past decade, and even earlier.

Islam and the Universal Declaration

The idea of Islam as the 'other' is, of course, not new. But it lay dormant for most of the twentieth century. Its reappearance with such virulence in recent times is quite shocking. What is notably different now is the extent to which it has seeped into popular culture and into the politics of the West.

The 'orientalism' of earlier times was a preoccupation of narrow elites; of administrator–scholars; of founders of new academic disciplines; of writers and artists with peculiar aesthetic sensibilities. It penetrated the popular mind through colonial wars and jingoism, but its duration as a factor in the public imagination was short. There were other, more pressing, dangers: internal economic collapse during the great depression, the threat from the totalitarian dictatorships of Europe, and finally the cold war. For most of the twentieth century, the defeated and prostrate Islamic world was hardly fit to challenge the West in any meaningful way. No one cared much, but Islam was still a vaguely felt threat or problem, even in the days immediately after the Second World War. As the world was convening to establish the institutions of the UN and to formulate the 1948 Universal Declaration of Human Rights (UDHR), the possibility of an Islamic 'exception' to the evolving doctrines on human rights was hardly an issue. The entire effort paid only lip service to the concerns and world views of other civilizations. No one, of course, was in any position to challenge the victorious Allies or to engage in any serious debate about what were essentially philosophical and religious issues. The cold war had not quite started, so, although the Soviets were prevaricating, they nonetheless went along with the final draft.

The commission set up to oversee the drafting of the Universal Declaration was chaired by Eleanor Roosevelt, but the special rapporteur (or coordinator) was Charles Malik of Lebanon. In fact he wrote the preamble of the Declaration of Human Rights and was responsible for several articles that strove to give the document a proper, universal import. The other members of the commission included a French legal expert, René Cassin, a Canadian UN administrator and legal scholar, John Humphrey, and P. C. Chang of China. Cassin, a noted scholar of Jewish origin, had lost members of his family in the Holocaust. Later, in 1968, he went on to win the Nobel Peace Prize. P. C. Chang represented the Republic of China, before the victory of the communists under Mao in 1949 sent the remaining members of its government into exile on the island of Taiwan. He received his doctorate in philosophy from Columbia University, and his own views were heavily influenced by Confucian thought.

But it was Malik who was the pivotal figure in the work of the commission. Malik, a philosopher and diplomat, had studied under Alfred North Whitehead at Harvard. His Lebanese origin made him, as it were, a surrogate for the absent Muslim voice in the commission, but that created an erroneous assumption. Malik was not only a committed Christian – what would be termed a fundamentalist today – but held views that were deeply antithetical to Islam. In later life, he became an ideological mentor of the Lebanese Forces, a right-wing Christian militia during the Lebanese Civil War of 1975–1990. He was responsible for statements such as: 'I believe that the Graeco-Roman–Judaeo-Christian tradition, with all its rich inner manifold and even contradictions, is the greatest and deepest and truest living historical fact in existence . . .'[2]

At the UN of that period, some of the motley states which represented 'Islam' – all of them impoverished, dependent and weak in the pre-oil era – abstained from the vote on the declaration. They neither appreciated its import nor were prepared to argue, or were capable of arguing for a different, more inclusive document. The Soviet bloc reacted mainly in terms of the declaration's emphasis on individual rather than social rights. In the end, Charles Malik, an indefatigable lobbyist and networker,[3] managed to neutralize the suspicions of the Soviets, partly by incorporating some of their concerns into the final draft. The Soviets also abstained from the final vote. The declaration was passed and became 'universal': the official global statement on human rights.

The point, however, is not to disparage the declaration, but rather to situate it in the context of its age. The document was drafted, to all intents and purposes, by a body dominated by western powers and with a spoiler's role for the Soviets. It became the foundation stone of the world's understanding of human rights. It has since achieved almost sacrosanct status, and is the leitmotif for all discussions on human rights. At the time, very few critics of the declaration saw it as the product of a specific civilizational or cultural world view. Superficially, the declaration appeared to be a natural outgrowth of the 'four freedoms' proclaimed by Roosevelt to form the basis of the post-war order: freedom of expression; freedom of worship; freedom from want; and freedom from fear. Nevertheless, none of the authors of the declaration would have explicitly associated it with a particularly 'western' concept of human rights. The epithet 'universal' which was attached to the declaration gave it finality and an elevated position from which it could preside as the world's conscience. Human rights were indeed universal and emancipatory. Those who fashioned this document nearly sixty years ago could not have anticipated that the worthy principles embodied in the declaration would become a tool to challenge Islam on its commitment to, or acceptance of, universal human rights. Islam was simply not on their radar screens.

Are human rights universal, or are they rooted in specific western experience? If they are indeed an outcome of Malik's concept of a

'Graeco-Roman–Judaeo-Christian' basis of western civilization, then their adoption by other civilizations, and specifically by Islam, affirms the 'victory' of western civilization in the modern world. These rights include the ideals of liberalism, democracy and secularism. If Islam were to adopt them *in toto*, the separate civilizational space Islam could claim for itself would end. If other civilizations reject these values as purely western formulations (and here again, Islam is the one seen to hold out), then the West has a new civilizing mission: namely to act out its historical role of representing the final state of human political order. Its values – including its definition of human rights – become the globe's values. Alternatively, if the values of the declaration are indeed universal, then their roots must be present in all civilizations. A new consensus on human rights has to develop from an inter-civilizational exchange, which would include all the world's religions and civilizations in order to generate a new Universal Declaration of Human Rights. But this is hardly on the cards. In fact, the proliferation in the western world of official agencies and non-governmental organizations devoted to the propagation and monitoring of human rights makes it clear that no one in the West is prepared to budge from the position that the declaration is globally applicable, if not yet enforceable.

Are human rights an essentially western construct? There is little doubt that the idea of human rights can be traced both to biblical sources and to the notion of a natural law which would be separate from divine revelation. The Bible talks about Man being created in the image of God, and St Paul's letters emphasize the equality of mankind in Christ. The natural law tradition goes back to the ancient Greeks, through the idea that human beings are endowed with inalienable rights which derive from an unwritten law or a higher principle. Then there is the Protestant Reformation, which asserted individual conscience as the foundation for an authentic faith. English common law and its concern with inheritable rights is another noted source for the ideal of human rights. The privileging of the individual over the collective is a common theme in these traditions of human rights, and it has underpinned the Universal Declaration. Its preamble is replete with words such as 'inalienable' and 'inherent'. The French Revolution's Declaration of the Rights of Man, the Magna Carta, writs of habeas corpus, Christian theology, the US Constitution and Bill of Rights – all these are sources for modern human rights. So in this sense human rights are indeed a product of the western tradition.

However, it was never inevitable that this particular aspect of the western tradition would prevail. What we have now is the development of one out of the many routes that western thought and practice on human rights could have taken before it settled on the present formulations. The appalling horrors of the Second World War, at least in the European theatre of war, were committed in the western sphere and influenced this development very much. Stopping their recurrence was an essential purpose of the Universal Declaration: 'Disregard and contempt for human rights have resulted in barbarous acts which have outraged the conscience of mankind,' it declaims. But this has not always been so. Medieval Christian theology celebrated what was hierarchical in nature and thus it fostered inequality within the order of things. The Protestant Reformation had deeply authoritarian features to it. Luther's spiritual equality with other Christian believers did not extend to non-Christians and did not challenge the political and social order. There is an entire tradition in western political and moral thought which decries individual human rights and fears them as undermining collective rights and the sense of community, and as being a source of alienation. The most powerful critique of the modern notion of human rights came from the most significant religious institution in the West: the Catholic church. It was not until the Second Vatican Council of 1965 that the church finally made its guarded peace with the modern human rights movement. Until that time, religious freedom was a mortal sin in Catholic theology, and freedom of expression was a license to disorder and chaos. The issue of 'reproductive rights' – an element in the panoply of human rights – continues to be hotly disputed by the Catholic church.

Modern human rights are situated in a post-traditional society, a society divorced from its roots in the ethics of religion or philosophy. Such rights are not so much a feature of western civilization as a natural concomitant of the development and progress of modern, technology-based and market-driven societies. Human rights are an aspect of the political debate and can be subject to variations and change. They are given a concrete reality by laws and institutions, none of which has any overarching ethical framework. Whatever stands in the way of the adoption of human rights as the hallmark of this post-modern society is considered irrelevant or, worse, an obstacle to be ignored or removed. Human rights become 'de-traditionalized'. The conditional recognition of human rights by the Catholic church, for example, is in practice irrelevant. The church's ethical arguments against abortions carry no weight in the political debate on reproductive rights. There are many countries with a Catholic majority which pay no heed to the Church's rulings in these matters, especially in

Europe. Islam, of course, is twice damned. Not only are its ethical arguments ignored entirely, but it is seen as a positively retrograde force in so far as it declines to participate in the post-modern order. This argument has been frequently employed by 'progressive' figures in Europe who denigrate Islam, associating it with a pre-modern world view which has no place in Europe. Their reasoning has gained currency as Europe wrestles with the implications of multiculturalism and its perceived failure in integrating Muslims into wider European society.

The Universal Declaration of Human Rights, in spite of misgivings about its provenance, was a praiseworthy project in many ways. It set standards which would later confront the world of Islam with a definition of universal rights, which might in turn conflict with Islam's own possible interpretations of human rights. Some of the articles of the declaration were loaded, and appeared to have been primed to elicit a negative response from Islam. Article 18 is a case in point.[4] It affirmed the freedom not only to choose one's faith but also to change it. It was introduced specifically by Charles Malik, who knew very well that an act of renunciation of Islam by a born or converted Muslim would have problematic consequences.

The declaration's effectiveness during the cold war was limited, in spite of the frequent appeal to its principles by organizations such as Helsinki Watch, which monitored the Soviet bloc's human rights record. It mainly stayed dormant throughout the cold war years, but sprang to life again in the 1980s as the Soviet Union began to lose its grip over its east European satellites.

In the intervening period, Muslim states had paid scant attention or respect to the idea of human rights, having being lulled into a false sense of security by the certainties of the cold war. From the Arab world's ubiquitous *Mukhabarat* to the shah's SAVAK, the secret police apparatuses which kept most Muslim leaders in power were deeply complicit in illegal killings, deportations, kidnappings and torture. Their human rights abuses went unnoticed in the confrontation between the Soviet bloc and the West.

It was only after the demise of the Soviet bloc that the Muslim countries began to notice the fact that they had unwittingly signed on to a document whose underlying principles they may not have fully shared. The declaration, and the phenomenal growth of the human rights movement in the 1990s, began to focus the spotlight on Muslim countries and their appalling human rights record. In 1990 Muslim leaders convened in Cairo and produced an alternative Islamic version of human rights. This became known as the Cairo Declaration on Human Rights. It was officially adopted in 2000 by all the countries of the Organisation of the Islamic Conference. The spirit of the Cairo Declaration is fundamentally different from that of the Universal Declaration. It firmly sets the Islamic understanding of human rights in terms of the Quran and of the Sharia. Human rights derive from the dignity conferred to Man by God's ascription of vice-regency to Man, and the Sharia is the fundamental basis for understanding and interpreting these rights.

Human Rights in Islam

Human rights and their universal application are rightly seen as a defining challenge to the principles of Islamic life and civilization. The issue is now highly politicized, especially with the rise of Islamophobia in Europe, the outcries over the imposition of the Sharia and the war on terror, which – wittingly or otherwise – has conflated the entities 'Islam' with 'violence' in the minds of millions of people. Human rights have become an either/or issue: either Islam accepts the universality of the rights embodied in the UN Declaration and subordinates its own ethical foundations to it, or it opts out and charts its own way of formalizing human rights in Islam. The collapse of the Soviet bloc and its half-hearted attempts to present economic and social rights as an alternative axis for a human rights doctrine gave a huge fillip to the universality of the concepts underpinning the 1948 UN Declaration. Nearly all the European states of the former Soviet empire signed on to the dominant West-inspired human rights movement.

Many people in the Islamic world see the human rights movement as the thin edge of the wedge: under the influence of human rights the building blocks of the Islamic world view would be gradually dissembled. This suspicion is behind the attempt to articulate an independent Islamic doctrine of human rights.[5] Although the authors of the Cairo Declaration may not have realized it at the time, the formulations used in the document were very much derived from modern preconceptions, garbed in the language of the Sharia. Rights in Islam had previously been formulated in terms of duties and obligations of people to each other: to those in authority over them, to those subordinate to them, and, above all, to God. Whatever rights human beings have are thus the outcome of individuals and societies fulfilling their duties and responsibilities to each other. There are a few rights which are explicitly recognized as such in the Quran – parental rights over children, for example – but most rights are in the nature of obligations. The rights of God over Man are met through acts of worship and devotion. The right to work exists because human beings have a duty to work and strive to improve their lot; the right to free expression exists because man has a duty to seek the truth and its fulfilment. Even in matters which are not on the surface contentious – such as the right to justice – the 'right' arises in consequence of the fact that others – the state, the judiciary, or those in power – have not fulfilled their duty to provide or dispense justice.

So rights are attached to a nexus of obligations, responsibilities and duties. This is the heart of Islam's perspective on rights. Unfortunately, this is barely discernable in the Cairo Declaration. Clearly, the notion that fulfilling duties and obligations is at the core of being human is deeply antithetical to the modern individualist sensibility. It smacks too much of authoritarian states and institutions, of inflexible and burdensome religious duties, of the shackling of the Promethean spirit of man by a chain of do's and don'ts. But if all these have created an inheritance which is now being rejected by the modern western imagination, as it seems to be, there is no compelling reason why Islam should follow the same trajectory. Where will the human rights movement ultimately stop, in its endeavour to remove all restrictions and curbs on the individual? The right to life may become diluted, in time, by utilitarian and 'ethical' calls for euthanasia. The destruction of the family as the fundamental building-block of all societies, or of the institution of marriage, is well under way.

One cannot and one should not expect that such proposals, which might be deemed 'desirable' in the context of the enlargement of individual human rights, are automatically adopted by cultures which do not subscribe to the same assumptions. The Cairo Declaration is severely deficient because its drafters did not convincingly address the need to define human rights in terms of Islam's own spiritual and metaphysical framework. As with so many other attempts to offer an Islamic gloss on global issues, the Cairo Declaration is simply not particularly rooted in the Islamic experience or in any deep understanding of the issues at stake. It is an inadequate response to a dominant paradigm and it suffers the same fate as other 'Islamic' responses to whatever challenges the modern world hurls at Muslims.

Nevertheless, no matter how one takes the issue of human and social rights and duties, the Islamic world has been woefully poor in meeting its own standards of human rights. What is more galling is that, while there are numerous governmental and non-governmental agencies in the western world that monitor human rights abuses, the Muslim world has no organization or group of any consequence that does the same. The human rights movement, which played a large part in galvanizing and supporting the east European revolutions of the 1980s, had based its moral and legal authority on the human rights conventions of the UN.[6] There are few groups whose function is to ensure that Muslim countries which have signed up the Cairo Declaration actually meet its stipulations. There are any number of human rights activists in the Muslim world who are connected with the global human rights movement and monitor human rights abuses in the context of the UN declarations and conventions. The abuses in the Muslim world are monitored and exposed by local chapters of international organizations such as Human Rights Watch or Amnesty International. However, the very few Muslim human rights groups that are built explicitly around ideals of an alternative Islamic human rights doctrine have been singularly ineffective in exposing abuses in Muslim lands.[7] Their credibility is often compromized by their connections to national governments and agencies. When real human rights abuses involving Muslim states are uncovered by western-oriented human rights activists or oganizations, they are often either ignored or denounced as examples of nefarious plotting by groups determined to undermine Islam. Case upon case is uncovered, ranging from the persecution of minorities such as the Ahmadis of Pakistan or the Baha'is of Iran to the stoning of purported adulteresses in Nigeria and the amputation of criminals' hands in the Sudan. The unrelenting pressures released on Muslim countries and on individual Muslims by the torrent of allegations of human rights abuses go a long way to explain Muslim sensitivities to the claims of the universal validity of human rights norms. But this in no way justifies the general indifference shown by Muslims to the actual abuses going on right under their noses.

These are legion, and are a real challenge to the significance of the Cairo Declaration; their sheer number makes them difficult to tackle. The Cairo Declaration decries genocide, but one of the OIC member countries, Saddam's Iraq, has only recently massacred its Kurdish population. Article 3 of the Cairo Declaration, which sets the principles of warfare, has been flagrantly ignored in most of the wars involving OIC member countries, for instance the Somali and Afghan civil wars and the war in the south of the Sudan. Articles dealing with torture and the inviolability of the individual are routinely ignored when Muslim states feel under threat. The indiscriminate slaughter of civilians by the state security apparatus of Algeria in the 1990s civil conflict is a case in point, as are the measures deployed by the Egyptian government to combat militant Islamism in the same period. Article 20 bans torture and arrest without due cause and process, but torture and abuse of prisoners are common practices in the authoritarian states of the OIC, which includes nearly all the Arab countries. Article 6 guarantees the dignity of womankind, only to see its stipulations flouted by innumerable cases where women have been treated in a degrading and cruel manner on account of local tribal or social customs. Article 7 guarantees the rights of children. Abused, abandoned and mistreated children – let alone the widespread use of child labour – are a common feature of Muslim countries such as Bangladesh, Egypt and Pakistan. Article 8 guarantees the right to justice. Muslim countries have probably some of the worst judicial systems, where corrupt judges, overloaded courts, cumbersome and unfathomable legal systems conspire to undermine one of Islamic civilization's key props: the delivery of fair and speedy justice by incorruptible judges with real authority. The list goes on. Nearly every aspect of the Cairo Declaration is discounted in practice; there is no effective mechanism, either governmental or that generated by civil society networks, to monitor and ensure compliance with its terms.

Critics of a specifically Islamic doctrine of human rights focus on the 'out' clause – namely the Sharia. Articles 24 and 25 of the Cairo Declaration specifically give the Sharia the overriding legal and moral authority to determine the definitions of the categories and of human rights. The implication is that the Sharia does not see eye-to-eye on human rights issues with the universal codes adopted by the UN and other international conventions. So it becomes impossible to achieve a universally acknowledged set of standards and rules for human rights to which all nations must adhere, and Islamic countries are afforded an opt-out from these agreements. But this, by itself, engenders a circular argument; it leads either to a cultural relativism whereby each civilization is entitled to its own standards of human rights, or to the imposition of a supposedly universal standard of human rights on all cultures. The main issue, as far as Muslims should be concerned, is the real status of human beings in the Islamic world and the problem of whether their rights, no matter how derived, are abused or ignored.

Whether the Sharia will always veer towards the same definition of human rights as the liberal democracies is an interesting issue. In the majority of instances it does, and Muslim countries should be held accountable for their human rights record under these specifically Islamic codes. Where they might not, there are still ample opportunities to discuss and probe the limits of the Sharia as it relates to the rights and duties of mankind. However, the debate over cultural relativism and the universality of human rights breeds a hostile defensiveness on the part of Muslims. They are asked to jettison a foundation of their world view in order to conform to a universal code to which they feel they have little to contribute. This drives many Muslim states towards proposing a review of the Universal Declaration.[8]

The defence of an Islamic norm for human rights is often hypocritical. The rhetoric of an Islamic basis for human rights frequently camouflages a cavalier disregard for the very Islamic values that the countries in question purport to promote. Muslims' confidence in their own capacity to address the issue of human rights would be immeasurably boosted if the human rights record of the Islamic world were to live up to Islam's own codes of practice. It is hopeless for Muslim countries to rail against a western conspiracy to undermine Islam by imposing western standards of human rights, if the human rights record in Muslim countries is dreadful. Muslims must denounce abuses, demand the abandonment of unacceptable conduct, and confront governments with their human rights record – framed, where possible, within the ethical norms of Islam. Governments will then find it more difficult to disguise their abusive behaviour by using cultural norms or traditional customs as their justification; they will be unable to reject criticism with a blanket condemnation of human rights codes as a western invention.

Freedom of Expression

A valid and effective Islamic version of human rights would not only serve the interests of Muslims, but might introduce a needed balance to the global human rights movement. The balance between freedom of expression and incitement, for example, is tilting dangerously towards license. If this is the general direction of unlimited freedom of speech, then an Islamic view, which places weight on responsibility and accountability for what one may say, might be a cure. This is, of course, one of the more contentious issues, and it has driven a wedge between liberals in the West and Islam. At heart, the dispute is about whether freedom of expression is absolute: a right which emanates from the dignity of being human and which should be restrained only in extreme conditions, for instance, war. This is certainly the position of the Universal Declaration of Human Rights and one can follow its subsequent unfolding in modern liberal societies of the West. When Muslims and Muslim states are judged by these standards, they are seen to be wanting. Their response is usually expressed in the language of authoritarianism – the state, or religion, must not be undermined by irresponsible statements and declarations – but hardly ever in terms of their adherence to Islam's own understanding of freedom of expression. A return to first principles would help here; the roots of freedom of expression in Islam must be discovered and elaborated upon in a systematic and consistent manner. Such a process would be connected to the contemporary definition of the phrase 'freedom of expression' and not to one derived from the limited (and possibly different) meaning it had in earlier times.

This *ijtihad* (independent reasoning to achieve valid juridical conclusions) must therefore be rigorous in scholarly terms as well as fully aware of the moral, political and even metaphysical meanings attached to this particular freedom in modern times. Too often the 'universal' definition is taken for granted, and then reformers seek to find the justification for it, a posteriori, in Islamic jurisprudence. The results are then hotly disputed among more traditional scholars, who reject them on the grounds of their being unacceptable innovations or pandering to western definitions. The alternative route is also fraught with problems. Traditional scholars draw on history, precedent and analogy to interpolate the meaning of freedom of expression, and produce rigid and narrow definitions which do not fit with the modern, broader significance of the concept.

The right of the human being to freedom of expression does not derive in Islam solely from the person's inherent dignity, which would entitle the man or woman to this right. There is also the matter of purpose. What is the purpose of the right to free expression if that right does not seek to find or to advance the cause of truth, Islam would ask? The Quran is replete with references to *Haqq* – the Truth – and in fact this is one of the attributes of God. This, the purposeful stance of the fully empowered being, is what stands at the heart of freedom of expression. Of course, democratic ideas of freedom of expression were also imbued with the notion of truth, but this aspect of the matter has been whittled away over the past few decades.

It is not that freedom of expression is absolute in liberal democracies. It is not. There are specific legal limits – for instance regarding the denial of the Holocaust (which is considered a crime) or on malicious slander – but most of these have been removed as the definition of freedom of expression has expanded. The scope of obscenity charges, for example, has been drastically restricted in the past decades. However, non-legal constraints on the freedom of expression continue to hold, being prompted mainly by what public opinion determines to be the limits of free expression. While in the past these limits may have owed a lot to religious or moral scruples, today they are more influenced by the media and 'opinion leaders' in society. Attacks on people on grounds of race and ethnicity are deemed unacceptable – and even criminalized in certain countries – but not attacks on grounds of religion. An individual is deemed to have chosen his or her religion, but not his or her ethnicity or race.

The attacks on Islam have come from a variety of sources, but many are in one way or another related to the issue of freedom of expression in Islam. The Rushdie Affair, for example, in the end came down to a clash between the advocates of unrestricted freedom of expression and Islamic notions of blasphemy. (Politically, of course, the Rushdie affair had far more to do with the disorientation and marginalization of recent migrants to the UK and with the intense, almost blind, hatred which certain members of the West's intellectual elites have for Islam.) The Rushdie Affair was only the progenitor to a rash of similar confrontations which took place, mainly in western Europe, between Muslims and the advocates of absolute free expression. The Danish cartoons controversy and the murder of the Dutch film-maker Theo van Gogh simply confirmed to the West the censorious and repressive features of Islam. Muslims, of course, saw it differently – as a calculated, gratuitous attack on the faith of a deeply disadvantaged and politically weak minority, and an attack designed to humiliate and incite.

There is probably little common ground between absolute freedom of expression and desirable limits of free expression in Islam. 'Political correctness' in the western world plays a decisive role in limiting the freedom of expression among the intelligentsia. It is partly borne out of guilt: guilt about the horrors of the Holocaust, which were mainly ignored or acquiesced to by a substantial number of people (including intellectuals) during the 1930s and in wartime Europe, and guilt about the undercurrent of racism which was part and parcel of colonial projects. The extent of the awareness and complicity of Europeans, both in western and in eastern Europe, in the decimation of their Jewish and gypsy co-citizens during the Second World War has only recently come to light. In most of the western world, Holocaust denial and overt racism have become criminalized, and anti-Semitism is no longer publicly tolerated in any form. But this sentiment does not quite apply to Islam. For example, a bill proposed by the British government in 2004, which intended to criminalize incitement to religious hatred and was mainly aimed at preventing Islamophobic behaviour, was watered down and finally dropped. It faced a chorus of protests from across the whole political spectrum, most of them couched in convoluted arguments about why freedom of speech should not be constrained by religious sensibilities. It was clear that the attempt to give Muslims in Britain some legal cover against violent acts or speech which targeted them as Muslims had no appeal, especially for opinion leaders, politicians and intellectuals.[9] Freedom of speech is in fact constrained in many instances in the West; but Muslims see the insistence on an absolute right to freedom of speech on the part of those who target them or their faith.

Islam not only respects but also demands freedom of expression. The Quranic injunction to 'enjoin the good and shun the evil' is impossible to act upon if human beings are not allowed to speak and act freely. But the concept of *hisbah*, which embodies this injunction, has been perverted over time. It is now associated with the notorious moral police of some Muslim countries who take it upon themselves to ensure that Muslims conform to the supposedly Sharia-ordained outer norms of conduct, such as ensuring that couples who appear together in public are related or legally married, or that women are wearing the appropriate articles of clothing. In an erudite and comprehensive work, *Freedom of Expression in Islam*, the Afghan scholar Muhammad Hashim Kamali sets out specific principles from which an entire doctrine of free speech can be derived.[10] These principles are derived from the fact that many actions which are deemed praiseworthy in Islam can only be undertaken if one has the ability to express oneself freely. These include the proffering of sincere advice (*Nasihah*); the need to consult (*Shura*); personal reasoning; the freedom to criticize; the freedom to express an opinion; the freedom of association; and the freedom of religion.

These rights are not absolute. They are constrained both morally and legally. The moral constraints on freedom of expression are found in all the great religions. They are built-in safeguards that prevent injustice, abuse and strife. Back-biting, slander, ridicule and exposing the weaknesses of others are all exhortations that carry no legal but only a moral compunction. The arts of comedy or satire might suffer if such compunctions are carried to extremes, but Islam would not specifically restrict them. Islamic literature is full of irreverent and satirical poets, who carica-tured rulers and the high and mighty. Some in fact carried their license into dangerous territory. The blind medieval poet Abu 'Aala al-Maari, for example, went so far as to denounce religion and all that was sacred in Islam. The Hajj was a pagan institution; religion, including Islam, was for knaves or fools. 'Do not suppose the statements of the prophets to be true; they are all fabrications. Men lived comfortably till they came and spoiled life. The sacred books are only such a set of idle tales as any age could have and indeed did actually produce,' he wrote. Elsewhere al-Maari declared:

Falsehood has corrupted all the world
That wrangling sects each other's gospel chide
But where not hate Man's natural element
Churches and mosques had risen side by side.[11]

He even challenged the literary merit of the Quran by claiming he could equal it in his poetry. (But, although he indeed produced a parody of the Quran, he did admit to its literary inferiority.) Al-Maari was not a hermit or a recluse so that his rank impieties and heresies would not have gone unnoticed. He lived to be eighty-four, and, according to the traveller and fellow poet Nasir-i Khusraw, who visited him at his home town, he was very rich, revered by the townsfolk, and had over two hundred students who came to attend his lectures on literature and poetry.[12]

What al-Maari and scores of other libertines and free-thinkers in Islam had done was to exercise their freedom of opinion, unrestrained by any moral compunction or special fealty to Islam. They were not punished – as their contemporaries in medieval Christianity would certainly have been – nor were they socially censored or ostracized. Personal unbelief and even mockery of the faith may have been reprehensible, but formed an insufficient basis to condemn and punish the violators. However, there are specific instances where the Sharia calls for legal restraint and in this sense it can be said to limit the freedom of expression. Some of these restraints, for instance, malicious slander or libel, would be recognizable in modern western societies. Others such as blasphemy are hold-overs of laws on the statute books in some western countries and are not enforced in the present time. Speech or action which encourages *fitnah* (sedition and conspiracy) against legally constituted authority is a punishable offence. It would be no different from sanctioning those who conspire to overturn or undermine the legal order in any democratic state.

The modern Muslim state has ignored the wide latitude given in Islam to the exercise of freedom of expression. But this is more to do with the structures of authoritarian states and governments than with Islam as such. Most of these governments attained power in ways which the Sharia would condemn: military *coup d'état* or assassinations and killings. Most of the world sees Muslims and Muslim rulers who flagrantly violate universal standards of human rights and freedoms, but does not pause to consider whether these violations are in any way allowed or tolerated by Islam. It is automatically assumed that because they are perpetrated by Muslims they must have the sanction of the religion in whose names these violations are often committed or justified. But those who denigrate Islam's commitment to freedom of expression appear to have a strong case in the very special and limited issue of the Islamic position on apostasy and blasphemy. This is typical of the clash between the values of a secular modernity and a religiously inspired world, one which has been relegated to the past in most liberal democracies. That blasphemy and apostasy can be considered to be crimes is astonishing to most secular-minded people. The idea itself smacks of heretics burnt at the stake and of massacres of innocents in religious wars – a past which is best transcended rather than relived.

However, the easy generalizations about Islam and its attitude to blasphemy and apostasy are not borne out either by history or by law. Although all the major classical Islamic schools of jurisprudence agree that the death sentence should be prescribed for both blasphemy and apostasy, there is a significant and growing body of dissenting opinion on this matter.[13] The dissenters base their argument, *inter alia*, on the explicit Quranic verse stating that there is no compunction in matters of religion. In the early community of Muslims, the acts of blasphemy and apostasy had clear political and religious implications. The nearest approximation to these provisions in modern times would be high treason. As the nascent community of Muslims became established, so did its confidence in its survival and growth. Islamic history presents only a few instances where people were tried and put to death specifically for these crimes. The scale of these incidents pales in comparison to that of the European wars of religion, where tens of thousands were put to death for their beliefs.[14] The rarity of these crimes in Islam may be put down either to fear of retributive justice or to the fact that the legal authorities preferred to overlook such crimes – probably because of a general unwillingness to acknowledge that they merited the death sentence, or that they threatened the integrity of Islamic society.

In modern times, the issue of blasphemy or apostasy hardly ever materializes in the Islamic world, and when it does it is often sensationalized by the western media and treated as a significant issue in Muslim society. It does not occur to Islam's critics that the vast majority of Muslims may not be particularly interested in changing their religion or in deriding its tenets and its Prophet. A basically theoretical concern about the 'barbarism' of Islam's apostasy and blasphemy laws has been transposed as a defining feature of the civilization. The resources and power of parts of the media in the West, and their deliberate targeting of Islam and Muslims, frequently overpower any attempt to provide a balanced perspective on the matter. Punishments for blasphemy and apostasy are lumped together with child brides, women in *burqas*, the stoning of adulterers, the flogging of wine-drinkers, and the execution of homosexuals, to generate a ghastly and frightening image of Islam. It may sell newspapers and bring audiences to TV channels, but it hardly serves the purpose of truth.

On Balance, Equality and Justice

The issues related to rights and values that are facing Islamic civilization are real enough, but they cannot be treated one-dimensionally. It is not enough to 'capitulate' to the incessant calls for the implementation of universal rights, neither is it possible to hide behind an all-too-human rendering of the Sharia and claim eternal validity for its rulings. The middle ground, if there is one, between an aggressive universalism and a defensive parochialism, is also an inadequate end result for what, after all, is a set of existential questions. These go to the heart of what Islam means and its relationship to the ideas of justice and equality. Whenever such issues are raised, the proper course is to return to first principles. For example, the landmark decisions of the US Supreme Court in the 1950s and 1960s on civil rights drew on basic principles (such as equal protection) in order to overturn two centuries of racist and discriminatory legislation.[15] Many of these former laws had been approved by the Supreme Court itself in earlier times. The continuation, in the statute books, of such a racist and discriminatory legislation threatened to poison the politics of the US, and even to destroy its foundations of democracy and the equality of its citizens under law. The crisis in Islamic civilization is broader. It is not restricted to one or two glaring aspects of abuse that need to be overturned or addressed. There is no single authority which could do the overturning; in fact there are numerous authorities, some of them self-appointed, which claim the right to interpret Islam. This process is incremental and may go on for decades before a new paradigm is established to which most Muslims would subscribe for most of the time.

There are numerous passages in the Quran which discuss the matter of the median way, the balance and scale of things. Balance is one of the defining features of Islam: balance between the individual and the collective; between the physical and spiritual; between the private and the public domain; between men and women; between rights and duties. Whether Muslims like it or not, the balance inside Islam has been ruptured and the civilization has lost its poise. Retreat into a self-enclosed space is not an option. An ever-changing world is too demanding and intrusive to allow this. The values of modern societies are a constant challenge and refrain to Islam, and their main demands have seeped into the public consciousness of Muslims. They have to determine whether the values in question are instrumental to the enhancement of justice and the possibility of living the good life. Muslims also have to determine whether these rights are derivable from the Islamic legacy itself, and at the cost of what modifications and changes.

Women's rights, for example, is an issue that will not be explained away by reference to the fact that Islam honoured women in the Arabia of the seventh century, that women's rights are enshrined in the Quran, or that women dominate the private space in Islamic life. All these facts are true, but they bear little relation to the real condition of women in Muslim societies and the raw deal they receive under the camouflage of the Sharia. Seeking a balance in the male–female relationships in Islam requires not only a re-examination of the roots of inequality but also a redefinition of the role of men according to the Quran and the Sharia. Balance is not a compromise between inequality and equality, but a separate state which strives for a harmonious, just and stable outcome. In the case of women's rights, not only the women are to observe modesty and courtesy in their outer behaviour and inner disposition; men are also obliged to do the same. But Muslim societies are mainly patriarchical, often reflecting historical tribal values which privilege males over females. These values have persisted into modern times, so that the Quranic standards of conduct demanded of men, especially in terms of fairness to women, are often ignored or flaunted in practice. Women's rights in Islam cannot be enhanced without a parallel insistence that men must also adhere to Quranic injunctions concerning their behaviour and conduct.

In the end, Muslims must themselves decide what human rights mean in Islam and whether these rights must be affirmed consciously rather than adopted under pressure or international scrutiny. However, the starting point must be whether Muslims actually want these rights for themselves, not only because they are sanctioned by jurisprudence but – and perhaps more importantly – because they promote justice. The concept of '*Adl* (justice) is specifically mentioned in many instances in the Quran. Justice in Islam is a universal moral truth, and the creation of a just order – political as well as religious – ought to be a primary focus of any Islamic rule or government. The fact is that Muslim states pay scant attention to Quranic justice and have not developed any body of human rights principles which are based on justice. But the establishment of a more just society may in fact be the way forward for an evolving Islamic doctrine of human rights. The inequality of women in society, for example, violates the concept of '*Adl* in many fundamental ways. '*Adl* can be used to reinterpret or challenge important rulings which have determined the Islamic position on these matters, creating a new Islamic 'architecture' of human rights. Regardless of whether these rights accord with the rules of international conventions, it is crucial that they occupy a prominent place in the political and moral lives of Muslim societies.

CHAPTER 9

Wealth and Poverty

Civilization and its well-being as well as business prosperity depend on productivity and people's efforts in all directions in their own interest and profit. When people no longer do business in order to make a living, and when they cease all gainful activity, the business of civilization slumps and everything decays.

Ibn Khaldun, fourteenth-century Muslim philosopher of history.

The contrast between Islam's self-image as a historical civilization of fabulous cities, material prosperity and technical sophistication and the bleak impoverishment and backwardness of its present economic realities could not have been starker. The arts of commerce and enterprise were honoured and celebrated in a religion founded by a Prophet who had been a merchant. They centred at first around the mercantile communities of Arabia. Long-distance trade, the commercial partnership, the mutual assurance against merchandise losses, even an original form of the bill of exchange, were all features of Islamic commerce and trade, well before their appearance in medieval Europe. The great historian of the Mediterranean, Fernand Braudel, emphatically attributes nearly all the major innovations of modern commercial life not to the medieval Italian city–states, but to the world of Islam. 'To admit the existence of these borrowings [from Islam] means turning one's back on traditional accounts of the history of the West as pioneering genius, spontaneous inventor, journeying alone along the road towards scientific and technical rationality.'[1]

The vigour of Islamic trade and the relative prestige of its merchants and artisan classes compared favourably with the general hostility of the medieval church to commercial life and disruptions to the hierarchical feudal order. Muslim rulers vied to attract communities of merchants and tradesmen to their metropolises. 'We extend this invitation to illustrious personages, great merchants desirous of profits, or small retailers,' stated a thirteenth-century notice to the merchants of the world by the governors of Egypt and Syria.[2] Great trading cities throughout the world of Islam, from Malacca to Surat, from Salonika to Marrakech, were testimonials to Islam's openness to commercial activity. Long-term sea voyages, huge caravans – one of them led by over '35,000' camels – a vigorous artisan culture built around craft guilds, all bespoke of an active economic life with many of the very same features that would later mark the rise of capitalist enterprise in the West. This whole magnificent panorama began to crumble precipitously within a few centuries of the modern era. European travellers seeking the fabled cities of Islam – Timbuktu, Samarkand, Golconda – found decrepit, filthy cities populated by an impoverished mass of abused people. By the time Napoleon had landed in Egypt in 1798, the Egyptians no longer had a use for the wheel.[3] They relied entirely on beasts of burden and animal transport.

Islam and Economic Decline

The relative decline in Muslim living standards has been unrelenting ever since 1798, and perhaps has accelerated in recent times, while hitherto laggard countries such as China and India have forged ahead in the economic race. What used to be reviled as the 'Hindu rate of growth' – a condition that appeared to afflict the centrally planned, overregulated and low-growth economy of post-independence India – now applies to Muslims. If the oil producing countries of the Muslim world are taken out of the equation, the decline would be even more pronounced. By some measure, Muslim countries generate only 6 per cent of the world's wealth, while accounting for nearly 22 per cent of its population.[4] However, to jump to the conclusion that somehow 'Islam' is responsible for this laggardness is patently absurd.[5] The geographic spread and variety of countries represented under the rubric 'Islamic country' is simply too broad to allow for a meaningful comparison with other control groups of countries. Muslim and non-Muslim countries in the same geographic zone do not show much variance in terms of their income per capita or of their levels of economic development. Thus Pakistan's GDP per capita is not too different from that of India; Malaysia's statistics in this regard are in fact better than Thailand's; Turkey outpaces any number of Balkan countries; even in

Africa, majority Muslim countries such as Senegal are as well off (or as badly off) as their non-Muslim neighbours. The issue is not whether Islam is a factor in the economic growth of countries. The evidence is clear that, in determining the performance of Muslim countries, one must look for other elements than the fact that they are Muslim. In fact Muslim countries perform better than non-Muslim countries of the same geographic zone in a wide array of other human development indices. For example, population growth in Indonesia, the largest Muslim country, at 2.6 births per woman is now well below that of the Philippines or India. Female infanticide – that is, selective abortions designed to dispose of female foetuses – is far more prevalent in the growth economies of China and India than in the supposedly misogynist world of Islam. Geography and the condition of neighbouring countries continue to be far better indicators of a country's economic performance than the religious affiliations of its people.[6]

But this has not stopped Islam's detractors from seeing its 'deadening' hand behind the poverty and backwardness of Muslim societies. The 'reasons' for poor performance include Islam's prohibitions on interest and the poor levels of economic participation of women in Muslim societies – which would supposedly be due to the built-in patriarchy of Muslim societies. Then a type of intellectual pincer determines the argument. On the one hand, Muslim societies are no different from other developing countries and should be subject to the same rules of social and economic analysis. There is no Muslim 'exceptionalism', and therefore no reason why one should seek an Islamic path to human improvement and felicity. On the other hand, there persists the argument that there is something peculiar to Islam that must be reformed or eliminated if Muslim societies are to progress. This argument in fact plays on the theories which make Islam – as an ideology – hostile to the underlying premises of a dynamic world market. Thus globalization and the possibility of nations emerging out of poverty are made subject to the adoption of an interconnected set of economic, commercial, financial and governmental policies which are firmly derived from the western experience.

Obviously, this is not the case for countries in East Asia and China which have openly flaunted these nostrums to achieve their own economic break-outs. Instead, such economic policy prescriptions are foisted on the remaining countries which, for a variety of reasons related to their endemic weaknesses and scarcity of resources, are obliged to listen and to act on this advice or face the (often unforgiving) consequences. In fact Islam does have the potential to generate an entirely different strategy for economic development and growth, and not one that necessarily stands in opposition to the prevailing paradigms. The academic Charles Tripp has called such an Islamic framework the 'moral economy', emphasizing Islam's concern with the ethical dimensions of economic and financial activity.[7] But the process of building the scaffolding for a new political economy has not even started. Some experiments which began with great promise – such as the idea of an Islamic finance – have been grotesquely distorted and turned into caricatures. Their creative potential has been destroyed through serial accommodations to the demands of international finance and the profit-maximizing owners and managers of the so-called Islamic banks.

Islam has never developed a separate theory of political or moral economy in the way that economic science and analysis have evolved in the western tradition. There are few thinkers in Islam who have ever discussed economic matters as a separate discipline. The western tradition of writing economics, from Adam Smith to Malthus, Ricardo, Mill and into modern times, simply has no equivalent in the realm of Islam. Islamic economics are embedded in the broader framework of the jurisprudence of transactions and in the scholasticism of the moral philosophers and theologians of Islam. None of the key concepts of economic thought – markets, the nature of value, productivity, utility, efficiency, growth, to name just a few – exists with the same definition, or even broad meaning. The Sharia did not leave much room for economics. Wherever the issues of prosperity of the community or welfare of the common person were discussed, this was part of the same tradition of exhortatory writings to the ruler about the value of a sound currency, about fairness in dealings and about the risks of punitive taxation. Otherwise it was assumed that people were ordained to conduct their business affairs and transactions within the bounds of the Sharia and its detailed norms concerning the permissible and the lawful in economic conduct and behaviour.

The moral underpinnings and purposes of economic and trade regulations in the traditional Islamic order were accompanied by a massive legacy of detailed rulings on the fundamentals of economic rights and duties, as well as on the nature and scope of business contracts and commercial dealings. This legacy extended to a detailed and sophisticated treatment of almost all aspects of economic activity, including the permissible role of the ruler as regulator and protector of the public interest, as enforcer of standards and measurements and as overseer of the public markets.[8] The nexus of the Islamic economic order did not operate in a legislative and regulatory vacuum but through a highly developed and effective system of laws, institutions and practices administered by judges and public officials. Nevertheless, the broad sweep of Islamic business and economic regulations could not prevent the decay of the economic life of Muslims or the gradual erosion of the Islamic commonweal; as in most other realms, the two were conflated. The decline in Muslim economic and technological power was coupled with the prevalence of the 'pre-modern' mind-set of Sharia law, so that reform (or, more often, disregard) of the Sharia became a precondition for the modernization of economies. An entire world of economic opportunities then becomes possible.

Modern economic and business institutions were imported wholesale, from the limited liability company to the interest-based unit which characterizes the world of modern banking and insurance. Foreign rules which allowed for these institutions to exist in Islam became the law of the land. Swiss commercial codes, British company acts, French banking ordinances all supplanted the Sharia, and an entirely new judicial system accompanied them which could interpret and render judgement according to the new commercial rules. With the new economic horizons came new risks, including borrowing at unsustainable rates and levels. The massive indebtedness of the Ottomans and Egypt to foreign bankers and creditors in the latter part of the nineteenth century culminated in spectacular bankruptcies, which handed the management of these countries' economic affairs to foreigners.[9] Capitalist enterprise in the Muslim world rapidly evolved during the colonial period and supplanted the traditional forms of trade and the merchants' organization. Craftsmen were displaced by modern industrial production; self-financing or collective financing was displaced by banking loans and credits; paper currency replaced bullion-backed money. In the process, the Sharia's ability to regulate economic life and transactions became a distant and irrelevant memory. In any case, the Sharia itself had long been disconnected from the administration of Muslim lands.

As Muslim countries emerged from foreign tutelage in the post-Second World War era, nearly all of them were poor and economically backward, but then so were many other countries which had no connection with Islam but which would later evolve into economic giants. Korea and Taiwan in the 1950s had lower per capita incomes than many Muslim countries of the Middle East. Colonial authorities often bequeathed good administration and infrastructure to newly independent majority Muslim states.[10] It was not Islam but appalling misrule, maladministration and injustices that dogged Muslim countries and pushed them to the lower rungs of development. The abysmal quality of government, the high levels of corruption and influence peddling, the abuse of public office, the capricious and arbitrary rulings of the authorities, unfair and unsustainable burdens of taxation – all these conspired to ensure the stagnation and impoverishment of Muslim countries. But the same judgement could also be applied to any number of non-Islamic countries of the developing world.

Globalization and the Islamic Economy

The increasing pace of globalization and the supposed connection of Islamic radicalism to impoverishment and backwardness in Muslim countries have reopened the debate on the future of the Islamic economy. The various 'consensuses' which have driven western economic policy prescriptions over the past two decades, ever since the fall of the Soviet bloc, have had their advocates in the Muslim countries. It has become almost an article of faith that the eradication of poverty, improvement in levels of income and the provision of employment opportunities are predicated on the integration of the Muslim world into the global economy. The 'universalization' of economic values, such as market values, is part of the same process pushing for the global prevalence of democratic politics and liberal freedoms. Once again, an idealized experience – for example the efficiency of unfettered markets – is shorn of its more uncomfortable manifestations and is then presented as a set of necessary policy reforms and initiatives essential to the achievement of prosperity. These very proposals are hardly uncontroversial, even in the West itself, but they assume a measure of finality as they achieve the status of conventional wisdom or 'best international practice'.

There is an obvious agenda behind proposed economic strategies. The notion of free markets, property rights, the rule of law, competition, limited state interference, good 'governance', have become integral to the idea of a dynamic economy. It is assumed, almost in the same breath, that no societies other than liberal democracies have been able to generate these necessary preconditions. This basically eliminates the possibility of similar initial conditions being generated in different forms in non-western societies. The anti-globalization rhetoric that has emerged to challenge the prevailing orthodoxy also suffers from the same ailment – namely the imperative to dominate the agenda and to set the alternative vision. Thus the critics of globalization turn to the evidence of growing inequality, unequal trade relations, financial market turbulence and panics, powerful but unaccountable transnational corporations and weakening and decrepit states in order to damn the march of the integrated global economy.

Islam is par excellence a civilization bound by its adherence to law – albeit Sharia law. The idea of the rule of law does not seem, however, to apply to the rule of the Sharia. None of the champions of the rule of law as an essential component of a successful economy would ever extend its definition to include Islamic law. Thus a society bound by Sharia law is not, on this reckoning, a society which respects the rule of law as understood in the West or by secularists of the Muslim world. Excluding Islamic law from the constellation of 'acceptable' laws automatically eliminates the possibility that Islamic countries can reconstruct their economic relations on the basis of Islamic law rather than on the conventional understanding of law. Islam's views on property rights, individual ownership, regulations of the marketplace and so on, become an irrelevance or, worse, a part of the conspiracy to revive 'medieval' laws and institutions. Similarly, the idea of the market is strictly derived from the almost sacred and wondrous market of the 'invisible' hand worshipped by the advocates of globalization. The underpinnings of functioning markets are automatically assumed to be limited to the experience of the western world. Only these markets are able to generate mutual trust, openness and transparency and a fair and level element of competition so as to ensure their own proper functioning. Enlightened self-interest manifested through individuals and corporations is assumed to lead to the desired social end of maximizing output and incomes. Market failures and manipulations, monopolistic practices and the periodic financial panic and bank runs which grip markets are aberrations which do not shake the confidence placed in the 'creed' of the market in any way.

The global financial crisis of 2008, for example, has involved massive state interventions to stablize the world financial system in an ongoing process that will ultimately cost the taxpayers hundred of billions, even trillions, of dollars. Commercial and investment banks, brokerage houses, mortgage providers, insurance companies, consumer credit firms, and all manner of other financial firms have fallen across the world like nine pins. The system has been nearly brought to its knees by irresponsible, deceptive and outrageously greedy practices of bankers and senior executives of financial companies. But apart from sanctimonious calls about the need for greater regulation and oversight, there has been little or no questioning of the underlying assumptions of the liberal market order. In fact, the opposite is true. Leaders of the major western economic powers, worried lest the crisis might give rise for calls for a rethink of the free market policies that have dominated the world since the fall of the Soviet empire, have reaffirmed their commitment to liberal capitalism. They have striven to nip in the bud any call for a serious reordering of the global monetary and financial systems. The Islamic world, true to form, sits mutely by as the crisis laps on its shores, and few have seen it as an opportunity to examine, let alone halt, the rush to duplicate the elements of a financial system that is prone to such extreme swings. The possibility that the financial crisis gripping the world could be used to advance the principles of a new economic and financial model for the Muslim world is therefore unlikely to materialize.

Well meaning Muslims have to contend with an uncomfortable reality when they are confronted with the system of modern economics, business and finance. Economic theory and policy is driven by western social science, and the rules and practices of modern business and finance derive entirely from the western system. This is why an Islamic critique of the system always appears to be hopelessly archaic or cranky. In this sense, the nascent 'discipline' that passes for Islamic economics has suffered from two incurable ailments. The first is that its original exponents were untutored in the ways of the modern world and approached the problem mainly through a jurisprudential or moral construct, with little regard for the changed circumstances of the world. The second is that they began to address these issues well after the supremacy of the western economic model became established. In no area has this been more serious than in that of *riba* – usury or interest.

The prohibition on usury is a core teaching of Islam, no matter how the matter is dressed up in terms of defining 'acceptable' versus 'usurious' interest rates. Finance (and finance capitalism) is a hugely problematic area in Islam, but this did not hinder the very rapid spread of these institutions in Muslim lands. Several *ulemas* gave enabling rulings to the establishment of interest-based organizations and opened the way for mainly foreign-controlled banks to emerge and dominate the economies of Muslim states. 'National' banks were established everywhere in Muslim lands, including the Ottoman Empire and the Qajar state in Iran: the Ottoman Bank and the Imperial Bank of Persia were established in the late nineteenth century. By the 1920s, local indigenous businessmen had already founded banks along conventional lines, sometimes with the tacit support of a few of the *ulema*. The Misr Bank group in Egypt and the Rafidain Bank in Iraq were founded with local capital in the 1920s and 1930s. After the Second World War, there was a rush to form banks in all the newly independent Muslim states such as Pakistan, Malaysia, and Indonesia, and this trend accelerated in the 1970s with the establishment of various 'national' banks in the Gulf countries. One should note that the vast majority of these later financial institutions were founded by local capitalists, sometimes with government support. They all participated enthusiastically in one of the great transgressions of Islam. Banking and the formation of banks became the most coveted enterprise in the Middle East throughout the various oil booms; even now, the youth in the Gulf countries, Saudi Arabia and in fact anywhere in the Muslim world, seeks out jobs within the banking sector for prestige, income and security.

Islamic Banking

The failure of Islamic economics and finance, in spite of the billions that have been poured into various Islamic financing institutions, especially Islamic banks, is symptomatic of the unwillingness to face the issue of the nature of legitimate transactions in the context of Islamic rulings, and of the yawning chasm between them and what passes for 'Islamic' these days. This is the core of the problem, and it is not easily resolvable except through a drastic overhaul of the institutions, structures, laws and policies antithetical to Islam. The Islamic banking movement is a good example of a process which became more and more distant from its original premise as the movement was obliged to 'compromise' with well entrenched interests and markets. The Islamic banking movement in its modern corporate form was started in the late 1970s, with the formation of Dar al-Mal Group by the Saudi Prince Mohammed al-Faisal. Its main purpose was to soak up the billions of dollars that the pious maintained in interest-free accounts in conventional banks. These pools of capital were so vast that in the period between 1975 and 1982 a large chunk of the profits of multinational banks, such as Citibank and the HSBC Group, came from their Saudi and Gulf operations. These banks drew huge funds from pious depositors at no cost to these banks in the periods when interest rates reached 20 per cent.

Islamic banking was conceived as an alternative, or as an operation parallel, to western finance, and from its early days its main concern was to establish its legitimacy in the West as a complementary financial vehicle – eccentric in style but nevertheless acceptable to the conventional banking world. Such a system could not conceivably evolve into a proponent of legitimate Islamic transactions and finance. There were (and there still are), sometimes at the most senior levels of these institutions, bankers who are cognisant of the dilemma but who are unable to break out of the box. Daily, the task of reforming these institutions becomes more and more remote. There are now a huge number of interlocking mechanisms which appear to have rendered the Islamic banking movement tame enough to be acceptable to the international interest-based financial system. It is now not uncommon to have Islamic banking 'windows' in the major conventional banks, or even entire Islamic banks, which are owned by the behemoths of global finance. In fact Islamic banking products are seen as major profit earners for the main international banking groups, whose interest in Islam and its moral economy is precisely nil. International Islamic banking conferences and symposia attract hundreds of participants from the major western institutions. The IMF and World Bank are frequent co-financiers with Islamic banks, and Islamic banking is now taught as a course in many western universities, including the bastion of global capitalist education, the Harvard Business School.

The whole tortuous mechanism of pricing products and services in Islamic banks is a prolonged exercise in artful delusion. Ultimately, and very simply, the pricing of Islamic banking products is directly linked to the prevailing market rate, in spite of convoluted explanations and manoeuvrings that appear to indicate otherwise. Technically, Islamic banking products are based on the sanctioned forms of Islamic financing such as profit participation, mark-up financing, venture capital and leasing, and so on. Transactions are then presented to a 'Sharia board' composed of Islamic scholars and worthies, who are then called upon to pass judgement on the permissibility of the deal. The entire system is self-serving and relies on acquiescent boards and elaborate artifices that appear to meet the outer forms of the Sharia, with no regard for its inner meaning and purpose. The Islamic finance system now includes so-called Islamic investment trusts, which invest in stock markets but avoid companies in the liquor or gambling businesses. Most of these are managed by western or westernized fund managers, completing the iron lock that the global bankers have on the funds of Muslims throughout the world.

The irony is that most of the depositors in Islamic banks are ordinary, pious people or institutions such as religious foundations or Hajj funds, and they believe that their funds are now handled by intermediaries who have no connection with the world of interest. Most depositors do not have a clue as to the true disposition of their money, leaving the utilization of these funds to the advantage of large corporate borrowers and wealthy individuals. At the same time there has been the usual spate of scandals, misappropriations and thefts, starting with gold and commodity frauds, and the impossibly poor loan portfolios at some of the larger Islamic banks. The gullibility of the pious depositor has also led to huge losses at pyramid institutions in Egypt and Syria which claim to be based on the Sharia. An attempt is now afoot to create a money market between Islamic banks, to redress their dependence on western money and capital markets. However, it is unlikely that this will insulate the economies of Muslim countries from the instability and buffeting of international markets.

The truth is that these are, at best, palliative measures which do not go to the heart of the problem: namely the incompatibility of most aspects of modern finance with the teachings of Islam. The genuine reformers within the Islamic banking world are now beginning to recognize that Islamic banking is an oxymoron, and that the entire Islamic banking movement is a deeply flawed affair, designed to disguise under an Islamic cover what is considered usurious activity. Most western institutions deal with Islamic banks from a perspective of advantage and deep cynicism. They scoff at the convoluted mechanisms designed to cover up the effects of using interest-based pricing rules, but they play along for their own ends. Those who work for Islamic banks often have absolutely no interest in maintaining this pretence and forthrightly admit that their banks are only peculiar forms of conventional banking institutions.

The Prospects for an Islamic Economic Order

There is no doubt that globalization, especially in relation to individual economic rights and freedoms, is antithetical to the fundamental features of an Islamic economic and social order. Liberal capitalism is predicated on the individual actor driven by self-interest or greed and constrained only by law. The entire scaffolding of the modern capitalist era presumes the individual to be an irreducible actor. The ideas of duty, charity, solidarity and self-sufficiency do not sit well with the premise that it is only through cultivating and channelling selfishness and greed that economic activity can be optimized. People tend to be acquisitive and predatory; the function of a well ordered economy is to direct these energies into a socially productive direction. But this natural disposition does not square well with the idea that humans can perfect – or at least aspire to perfect – their qualities and that a moral imperative should underlie human action. Islam does not deny human follies and greed, but these must always be tempered through a constant questioning of the purposes of human action. The creation of wealth should be a by-product of moral action, not the purpose of work.

The spread of globalization and the liberal economy, with its latest onslaught on the world view of Islam, has created another battleground for the loyalties of Muslims. The expansion of globalization is championed not only by the major western economic powers but also by the international financial institutions which frequently act as their proxies on the world stage. These have had a significant impact on the world of Muslims, and not only in negative ways. A great deal of effort had to go into undoing the decades of *dirigiste* economic management that denied the role of the individual in the economic life of societies. The centralized policies of state-ownership were frequently applauded by the very same institutions which would now turn against them. The Muslim world swung from state-controlled economies to a patchwork dismantling of the command economy, only to hand over huge swathes of the now privatized economies to cronies and protégées of the ruling cliques. Huge fortunes were made either from the abuse of licensing power – as in the rise of the ubiquitous mobile telephone billionaire – or through the knocked-down purchases of state assets and land by well connected individuals. Privatization, de-regulation, licensing of monopolies, all played their part in the shift of economic power from a poorly managed and frequently corrupt state sector to a better managed but predatory form of capitalism. The whole process was applauded by the international community as signalling the entry of the Islamic world into the new era of globalization and free markets. The basis for an Islamic economic order receded still further.

In reality, an Islamic economic order can only be renewed if certain fundamental reforms are undertaken. The axes of the modern economy are so distant from the moral economy of Islam that nothing short of a spectacular break would suffice to bring to life a new Islamic economic order. The main features of an Islamic economy have been in an eroded state for several centuries, so that most are merely religious vestiges of a long-forgotten past. By the time of the revolt of Islam in the 1970s, the elements of an Islamic economy were simply theoretical constructs, which may have featured in the education of seminarians but had no place in the modern economy. Only a few countries such as Saudi Arabia maintained a *zakat* (Islamic wealth tax) collection department as part of the public finance architecture of the state. The vast majority of Muslim countries had relegated the use of Islamic taxes to voluntary religious tithes, leaving public finance to the usual array of revenue-generating taxes and duties: on incomes, sales, customs, and so on. Agricultural taxes, which were essential to the functioning of the rural economy in Islam, also vanished, and were replaced by modern equivalents which had no echo in Islam's past.

The use of paper currency, issued by a central bank and 'backed' by foreign exchange reserves, also became widespread in the nineteenth century, gradually decoupling the classical forms of the Islamic unit of exchange – the gold-based dinar and the silver-based dirham – from its historical association with bullion.[11] The unit of exchange in the world of Islam, allowing for the fact that it had atrophied and been allowed to debase over the centuries, was definitively terminated with the rise of modern central banking. In the colonial and post-colonial period, many Muslim countries used the same or equivalent currencies as their European overlords. This explains the widespread use of the colonial French franc, or the British pound in the Sterling area – both of which tied the dependent economy to the metropolis and its needs.

Islamic finance is part and parcel of the world view of Islam. It is not just a tool. *Zakat*, for example, is not simply a revenue-generating wealth tax. It is mentioned on numerous occasions in the Quran, in the same breath as the offering of prayers. It is a fundamental aspect and a pillar of Islam, and an act of worship designed to bring human beings closer to God. Thus the offering of *zakat* is not simply the parting with a portion of one's wealth for the public good. While it is essential to the financial integrity of the Islamic state, it is also a process that will purify the person. The actual handing over of a proportion of one's annual wealth is designed to make the process of giving what one holds dear an essential aspect of worship. 'You will not gain righteousness unless you part with what you hold dear,' the Quran admonishes.[12] *Zakat* talks about property as a responsibility. Property is not decoupled from its social use; neither are property owners, or holders, able to ignore their roles as trustees over the property. The reintroduction of *zakat* as part of the recent make-over of some Muslim states keen to brandish their Islamic credentials has not been an altogether happy experience. This is partly due to the cynicism of the official classes and business elites, who see in the *zakat* movement a retrograde step against the modernization – or westernization – of their societies. Leftists rant at *zakat's* supposed regressive tendencies and at its bias against the rural economy; more business-minded groups see *zakat* as an instrument which blocks the flow between Islamic countries and the major world economies. They also claim that *zakat* impedes the flow of foreign investment, as international investors may not be able to deal with an unfamiliar tax regime capriciously applied.

Nevertheless, an Islamic economy cannot function without a central role for the instrument of *zakat*. In fact, even in the West, a wealth tax as an alternative to all the complex tax measures that encumber tax codes has been seriously mooted. For example, the Yale academics Bruce Ackerman and Ann Alstott in their seminal work *The Stakeholder Society* came down in favour of a 2 per cent wealth tax as the most efficient and fair way of resolving the growing inequalities in American society and of reuniting citizens in a new common bond.[13] Ackerman and Alstott would probably be shocked to find that the arguments they have used in support of a wealth tax, althrough couched in technical language, are remarkably similar to the Islamic case for *zakat*. The latter is calculated on a somewhat different basis for net wealth, but the level of 2.5 per cent of the net taxable wealth is practically the same as in *The Stakeholder Society*. Of course, no pious Muslim would relate the necessity for *zakat* to the efficacy of a new form of wealth tax. However, the acceptability of *zakat* as a primary element of a new, revenue-generating and redistributive, order might make sense if it is de-Islamized. It needs to be renamed and couched in the language of social science, carrying the imprimatur of academic respectability. It might even receive the ultimate accolade: acknowledgement by Washington-based multilateral institutions such as the World Bank and the IMF.

The average Muslim's commitment to the idea of *zakat* is muted; this is reflected by the loss of charitable giving, which lies at the heart of Islamic redistributive justice. The wealthy who live in Muslim lands are often unwilling to share their riches through charitable acts and through the endowment of foundations. The pages of the world's business newspapers are crammed with the faces of the new plutocracy of the Muslim world, mostly connected as it is, one way or another, to the explosion in oil wealth and the massive transfer of the world's savings to the oil producing countries. Most of this wealth continues to be concentrated in so-called sovereign wealth funds, but a great deal has cascaded down to various princes and potentates and to the cronies and fixers who feed in the public trough. These form the new Muslim super-wealthy class. A few are genuine businessmen who have made their fortunes by dint of hard work, entrepreneurship and the nurturing of markets, but most have achieved their wealth by the tried and true methods of being proximate to power.

The Muslim world's wealthy are notorious for their private indulgencies and excesses, and for their lack of any public spiritedness. There are no major research foundations, universities, hospitals or educational trusts funded by large charitable donations. The scale and scope of the philanthropic work of the modern West – especially the US – is inconceivable among the Muslim rich, even though their individual fortunes run into billions of dollars. Where charitable donations continue to have an impact is among the middle classes in Muslim countries with a poor to middling income. It is salutary to see the extent to which civil society groups in countries such as Pakistan are increasingly taking on the responsibility of providing essential services for the public, in the light of the decay, inefficiency and often near-collapse of governmental services in education, health care and disaster relief. The story is similar for Egypt and Morocco, where Islamic welfare organizations frequently connected to Islamist parties are providing services the provision of which the government seems to have abandoned.

This type of service-based charitable work is an essential element of the Islamic economy, weaving, as it were, religious obligations with a strong sense of social justice and moral responsibility. The pious foundations – the *Awqaf* – were the historical institutions which provided these services but they, too, have atrophied with the passage into modernity. The endowment of large public buildings and social institutions by the rich and powerful is no longer a practice in the Muslim world. The *Awqaf* have turned into bureaucratic and often venal organizations; they manage specific mosques and their attached properties, and are answerable to a government agency.[14] The old *Awqaf* institution was far more central to the life of Muslim society, because it grouped mosques with markets, hospitals, caravanserais, soup kitchens and schools – the living commercial and spiritual heart of Muslim cities. No wonder that one of the first acts of the 'modernizing' governments – whether colonial powers such as the French in Algeria or military–bureaucratic rulers such as in Turkey and Egypt – was to smash the independence of these pious foundations. How ironic that contemporary reformers want to promote 'civil society' institutions, when authentic Islamic models, honed over centuries of service, have been systematically undermined and destroyed.

The Problem of Interest

It would, of course, be impossible to reconstruct the basis of an Islamic economy without tackling the problem of interest. For centuries no scholar of any note would question the prohibition on usury, as it clearly was one of the absolutely reprehensible acts condemned in the Quran. However, the dam was breached when one of the early pioneers of Islamic 'modernism', Sheikh Muhammad Abduh of Egypt, authorized the payment of interest to savers in the Egyptian Post Office Bank. The argument he advanced – which has formed the basis for all subsequent justifications for decoupling 'permissible' from 'impermissible' interest – was that the Quranic prohibition on *riba* was limited to a specific form of usurious lending prevalent in pagan Arabia.[15] The practice in effect led to the multiplication of debt in the event of late payment, effectively enslaving the debtor to the creditor. Thus 'reasonable' interest, which is more of a charge for the use of money, is an acceptable practice if it does not lead to acts of injustice in the creditor–debtor relationship.

Of course, Abduh's *fatwa* on *riba*/interest did not single-handedly open up the Islamic economic system to conventional banking and finance, but it was a major breach in the ramparts of Islamic orthodoxy on a central aspect of what constitutes legitimate financial dealings in Islam. Over time, the practice of receiving and paying interest, a hitherto furtive exercise whose practitioners were socially ostracized, became commonly accepted in the Muslim world. The boundaries of the fixed and of the changeable in Islam were once again radically shifted in order to accommodate the exigencies of the times. Finance capital, and an ever-growing financial sector, which is the hallmark of modern economies, became established in a part of the world which could, conceivably, have developed alternative systems of financing production and investment and of securing people's savings. But capitulation to the world of modern finance was not complete. The fact remained that the utilitarian and historical justification for reconsidering the identity between *riba* and interest was not entirely convincing. The common person was suspicious of such self-serving arguments, and the attraction of interest-bearing deposits was still often outweighed by powerful religious scruples. The rise of the Islamic banking movement coincided with the political and social ferment in the Islamic world of the 1970s and was primarily driven by lingering public suspicion relating to interest-bearing accounts and the work of commercial banks. It is thus doubly incongruous, even disturbing, that after waiting for nearly a century for the production of financial practices and institutions that reflect the teachings of Islam, the Islamic banking movement, which was the outcome, was subverted for the purposes of finance capital.

Legal trickery is what allows Islamic banks to circumvent the appearance of charging interest and shows them to be merely a sub-category of conventional banking. A key contract of Islamic banks, the so-called mark-up financing, is no different from a medieval process condemned by the church, by which lenders can extract interest from borrowers through a set of interlocking, but apparently separate, financial transactions.[16] Islamic bankers meeting at their jamborees freely admit that the type of financing they are engaged in is no different in substance or intent from their previous work in conventional banks. At the same time, as the author and critic of Islamic finance Tarek el-Diwany wrote, 'small and medium sized Muslim-owned businesses are offered no Islamic finance facilities at all. When they do finally encounter a financing proposal from an Islamic bank, many of these businessmen quickly become cynical because the financing cost is fixed at the outset of the financing agreement.'[17] The academic Charles Tripp also maps out the distortion of the Islamic banking movement as it lurched away from its initial purpose. 'As the Islamic financial sector grew, mobilizing substantial sums of capital, many of the original intentions faded from view . . . The goal of reinforcing the bonds of community, and the ambition of restoring unity between people's material transactions and the spiritual dimension of their lives, gave way before the need for financial institutions to survive and thrive . . . in a global market dominated by long-established and highly competitive institutions which had historically shaped the rules of the market itself . . .'[18]

Poverty and the Economies of the Islamic World

The Islamic world combines the extremes of wealth and poverty. On the one hand there are the oil-producing countries of the Gulf, whose official overseas assets alone are estimated at nearly $2 trillion.[19] The bulk of these resources is kept in the form of investments in the financial instruments of the developed world, and in particular in US Treasury bills and bonds. The private sectors of these countries also dispose of enormous wealth. The lists of billionaires in the business magazines always include dozens of businessmen from the Arab Gulf countries. At the same time, Muslim countries such as Pakistan, Bangladesh and Indonesia are crowded with the poor – as more than half the population often survives on less than $2 per day. These contrasts between fabulous wealth and grinding poverty pose a serious dilemma for Muslims, which is only partly mitigated by the migration of the poor to the booming economies of the oil-producing countries.

The countries of the Muslim world are dispersed over a large geographic region: they spread over three continents, from Albania in Europe to Mozambique in southern Africa, Morocco in North Africa and Indonesia in the Far East. There are even significant Muslim concentrations in South America; in Guyana, Muslims account for nearly 15 per cent of the population. But, even though Muslim countries are well endowed with economic resources in different sectors and have the potential to develop as a vast trading region, they continue to lag behind the rest of the world. With a total population approaching 1.5 billion people, the fifty-seven-member countries of the OIC account for nearly 22 per cent of the world's population. But they generate only 6 per cent of the world's GDP and 9 per cent of its total exports.[20] On a purchasing-power parity basis, the per capita gross national income of the OIC countries in 2006 reached only $3,600 per annum, compared to $35,500 in the rich world (and an average of $5,600 in the rest of the developing world).[21]

The total output (GDP) of the fifty-seven OIC countries in 2007 approached $3.2 trillion, compared to a 2007 GDP figure of nearly $14 trillion for the US alone. The entire Islamic economy accounts for less than 23 per cent of the US economy. The output of the Muslim world is less than 10 per cent of that of the West, defined in economic terms as the US and the EU. If the economies of the OIC countries which export fuel are excluded from the tally, the total GDP of the non-oil OIC countries amounted to a paltry $1.9 trillion in 2007 – that is, less than 13 per cent of the US economy and less than 6 per cent of the economy of the West. The scale of the economic imbalance between the western world and the Muslim world is glaring.

Out of the world's fifty-five least developed countries, twenty-two are countries with a Muslim majority, whose economy relies mostly on the production and export of a few non-oil primary commodities. Excluding the special case of the oil-exporting countries, most Muslim countries are heavily indebted to outside creditors. The World Bank ranks thirty-three out of the OIC's fifty-seven countries as moderately to heavily indebted; and they include fifteen Muslim countries grouped under the Heavily Indebted Poor Countries (HIPIC) classification.[22] Inequality between Muslim countries is also heavily skewed. The average income per capita in fourteen of the OIC fuel-exporting countries is seven times higher than that in the other twenty-one least developed OIC countries. The richest Muslim country (the United Arab Emirates) has an astounding per capita income, 200 times that of the poorest country, Somalia. No such variations are remotely evident in the western world, where the income distribution between countries is far more even.

Only six Muslim countries are classified as high-income countries, all of them being oil and gas exporters, while twenty-six are low-income countries and twenty-five are middle-income countries.[23] The least developed OIC countries accounted for 27 per cent of the overall population of the

OIC but for less than 7 per cent of the OIC output. Out of the twenty-two least developed Muslim countries, only three (Yemen, Bangladesh and Afghanistan) are outside Africa. A second group of Muslim countries has been classified by the IMF as 'fuel exporting countries'. These are a mixed bag; at one level they include Qatar, with a population of less than a million and a per capita income of over $70,000 in 2007, and, at another level, Nigeria, with a population of 145 million and a per capita GDP of less than $1,000 in 2007. The largest economy in the OIC countries at present, with the ramp-up in oil prices, is Saudi Arabia, which has a GDP in excess of $400 billion. Turkey is the largest non-oil economy in the OIC, with a GDP figure also nearing $400 billion; it is followed by Indonesia (at about $375 billion) and Iran (at about $250 billion). The biggest non-oil exporter in the Muslim world is Malaysia, whose manufacturing sector is well integrated into the global supply chain for electronics and electrical goods.

The economic performance of the Muslim world is, in the final analysis, greatly dependent on the performance of a few of its larger economies, especially the oil-exporting giants of the Gulf region. But the wide income disparities within the Muslim world and the vastly different economic structures that separate the main economies such as that of Turkey and Saudi Arabia from the large number of very poor countries greatly restrict the possibilities of intra-Islamic economic cooperation. The fuel exporters are all linked to the vast network which comprises the global energy market, while exporters of manufactured goods such as Malaysia are part of a global supply chain which connects their output to the demands of the large consumer markets in the developed world. Most Muslim counties are still reliant upon the export of primary products and are at the mercy of price fluctuations in the global commodities markets. While sky-high oil prices are helping Muslim oil exporters, they are punishing the many countries in the Muslim world that are net energy importers. This is affecting a whole range of Muslim countries, from Bangladesh to the deeply impoverished Sahelian countries of Africa. The explosion in agricultural prices, especially for oil seeds and grains, also disproportionately affects the Muslim world, which is a net importer of food. It is only now that serious attention is being paid to increasing the scale of intra-Islamic cooperation in the production of foodstuffs.[24]

The private sector in the Muslim countries has also languished and lags behind others in the emerging markets. Very few companies in the Muslim world have the weight to compete seriously or to bring innovations into the global market. Of the twenty largest corporations in the Muslim world, seventeen are oil and gas companies, in most cases state-owned.[25] The largest private company in Islam is the Turkish Koc Group, a diversified holding company with revenues of about $35 billion for 2007 and comparatively small by international standards. In fact Turkish private sector companies dominate the roster of the largest Muslim groups, followed by Saudi, Emirati, Malaysian and Kuwaiti groups. Most of them grew on the back of closed markets and state sponsorship, although the degree of government support and protection for large private groups in the Muslim world has diminished in the past decade. With a few exceptions, Muslim private companies are not market leaders or innovators in the global economy and are not serious competitors with the large multinational corporations. The exceptions are in those areas where there has been a definite competitive advantage, for instance, in the energy sector or, in the case of Turkish companies, international construction. SABIC, a majority state-owned petrochemical business, has succeeded in expanding outside of Saudi Arabia on to the international scene and is now a global player of the first order. Another internationally successful enterprise is Emirates Airlines; and yet another is the telecommunications groups Orascom of Egypt and MTC-Zain of Kuwait. Sime Darby of Malaysia is an important competitor in the plantations sector. The increasing sophistication of a number of Gulf enterprises, sparked by the oil-driven economic growth in the Gulf region, also bodes well for the rise of the Muslim multinational company on the world stage; but these good signs are still the exception.[26]

However, a number of interesting developments are taking place that might augur a new age of intra-Muslim cooperation in the private arena. The vast oil surpluses filtering to the private sector of the Gulf countries are not all being invested in western capital or property markets, as has happened in previous oil booms. The growing corporate sectors in the Gulf countries are now directing an increasing part of their funds towards investments in nearby capital-starved Muslim countries, where they have some advantage over the multinational corporations.[27] These markets are frequently too small, or are seen to be too risky, for corporations based in the major capitalist countries. Thus the investment flows from the Gulf countries into markets such as Pakistan, Egypt, and Morocco have grown significantly, giving rise to regional enterprises with large market shares in the major Muslim countries. For example, the MTC-Zain group of Kuwait is now a major player in the telecommunications sector of a number of Asian and African countries; and UAE banks are active investors in the banking sector of Pakistan. The rise of large, well capitalized hedge funds and private equity groups based in the Gulf is also contributing to the flow of investment capital between Muslim countries. These funds and groups are targeting the energy, ports, cement and the hotel and real estate sectors in a number of middle-income Islamic countries.

It is possible that regional corporation will play a part in the limited reintegration of the major Islamic economies and will succeed where interminable conferences and governmental declarations of intent have failed. Muslim-owned enterprises are also creating a network of alliances through organizations such as the World Islamic Economic Forum and the Islamic Chambers of Commerce and Industry. They are still nascent networks that are no match for the more established World Economic Forum in Davos or the business alliances of global enterprises, but they are promising beginnings. These developments may draw the economies of Muslim countries together, especially those comprised within a new 'Greater Gulf Co-Prosperity Sphere', but they are entirely separate from the issue of the revival of the Islamic moral economy.

In essence, the growth of the regional multinational company, or even the expansion of Islamic banking into many Muslim markets, is not entirely synonymous with the revival of Islamic norms of economic conduct and the purposes of economic activity. These have been overshadowed by the wholesale adoption of modern capitalist standards for the management of economies. It is immaterial to the consumer in Pakistan whether his or her mobile phone comes through the courtesy of an Egyptian or a Norwegian company; neither does it make much difference if the rules of banking for a Muslim-owned bank are exactly the same as for one of the behemoths of international finance. It may provide some measure of pride that at least some of the major sectors of the Islamic economy are controlled by home-grown or Muslim-owned enterprises and that these are providing a quality service or a product of quality at fair prices, but the decay of the Islamic underpinnings of economic life still continue apace.

Modern corporations, wherever they may be, follow the same broad business objectives. In fact, from a strictly ethical perspective, western corporations may be far more advanced than their Muslim-owned counterparts. The ethics of business are now taught in major business schools throughout the western world, while corporate social responsibility is a growing issue for international companies. There are few, if any, major Muslim-owned corporations that follow the same rigorous standards of ethical conduct which prevail in a large number of multinational corporations. For example, the extensive deforestation in Indonesia and Malaysia is the work of indigenous corporations. Such a pattern of resource exploitation is unlikely to occur with a major multinational corporation that has to answer to governments, 'ethical' investors, non-governmental organizations and an irate public. Labour exploitation and the use of child labour are rampant in the private sectors of Muslim countries which export textiles, sports goods and footwear – for instance, Egypt, Pakistan, Indonesia and Bangladesh. No major western corporation involved in, say, footwear marketing could withstand the criticism and lawsuits arising from its employment of child labour or from its abuse of workers in its overseas factories.

Globalization will certainly threaten the possibilities of building an Islamic economy, not because Muslim countries will be excluded from the process, but because they can only be included within the terms of the globalization process itself. Thus apparently salutary developments, such as the growth of Muslim-owned corporations and increasing investment flows between Islamic countries, may strengthen economic cooperation and build the elements of a market economy in the Islamic world. But they will not by themselves create the bases for regenerating Islam's moral economy and the fundamentally different perspectives on economic and financial transactions that this would entail. Certain aspects of the globalization process are essential for recreating an Islamic economic space, for instance, the free flow of goods and capital between countries. However, Islam parts company with the globalization process if the means and purposes of economic activity stray far from the world view of Islam.

The failure of the Muslim world seriously to contemplate a radical departure from the conventional model of economic development has strengthened the hands of the advocates of globalization inside the Muslim world. The distancing of Islam from the ethical dimensions of economic life in the Muslim world will accelerate. There is no unique Islamic currency bloc; no special arrangements to expand and harmonize economic relations between Islamic countries; and no strong commercial organizations that could regenerate Islamic economic life at the business and trade levels. The massive opportunity to do so, which was created by the growth of Islamic banks, has been squandered as the Islamic banking movement surrendered to the expediencies of joining the international capital markets. The banks accepted a walk-on role in the international financial system rather than building the sinews of a new Islamic financial architecture. The sniggering and timid prevarications that accompanied Mahathir's bold call for an Islamic currency constitute another example of a lost opportunity to build the essential currency foundations of an Islamic economy. Another prospect to do so is presenting itself with the unprecedented accumulation of financial resources in the Arab oil-exporting countries. These can provide the wherewithal for a massive expansion of the range of activities and resources of the pan-Islamic institutions which do work (such as the Islamic Development Bank), perhaps creating a new set of economic institutions to pull the Islamic world together. Simply applying the criterion of *zakat*, or 2.5 per cent of the net financial wealth of these countries, to the sovereign wealth funds of the GCC oil-exporting countries would yield an *annual* figure of $75 billion in resource transfers to the poorer Muslim countries.[28] This would dwarf all the official aid flows presently flowing to these countries. Whether the political and business elites of the oil-exporting countries will seize this chance is another matter altogether.

CHAPTER 10

The Decline of Creativity

And they said, 'Come, let us build for ourselves a city, and a tower whose top will reach into heaven, and let us make for ourselves a name . . .'

Genesis 11: 4

But Pharaoh said, 'O Haman! Build me a lofty tower that haply I may attain to the right means – the means of approach to the heavens . . .'

Quran 40: 36/37

Islamic civilization was the preserver and then transmitter of the sciences and philosophies of the ancient Greeks to pre-Renaissance Europe. Many works of the ancient Greek philosophers and natural scientists were translated by scholars, often Arabic-speaking non-Muslims, and absorbed into Islamic civilization. It was in this Arabized and Islamized form that they were then translated in the early Middle Ages into the Latin of Christendom, mainly through the Muslim-dominated but cosmopolitan centres of learning in Spain such as Toledo and Cordoba. The Muslims themselves had independently developed an advanced understanding of the physical and life sciences; they were versed in widely different fields such as mathematics, astronomy, optics, and the entire spectrum of the medical arts and sciences. In mechanical engineering the Muslims developed technologies which were useful in agriculture (water mills and complex irrigation systems) as well as in warfare. In some of their ingenious mechanical contraptions, Muslim scientists prefigured the computer. The arts and architecture of Islam created styles and structures of their own, as well as an urban landscape which was intimately connected to the spiritual, religious and social requirements of Islam. The music of the Muslim world also reached heights of sophistication in modalities and was marked by refinement and intricate nuances. The music of the Arabs, of Persia and of Indian Islam was unique to each particular culture, but it shared common roots and often used similar instruments. The principles of Quranic recitation, the call to prayer and religious chants (*dhikr*) of the Sufi orders, provided a further element of bonding and unity throughout the Islamic world.

Why and how this creative drive, which is the essential feature of all vital civilizations, dried up in the Islamic world remains a vexed issue. In many areas and with very few exceptions, the cultural world of Islam has retreated to the point where there is no continuity whatsoever with the past achievements of the civilization. Islam has fractured and been replaced wholesale by cultural expressions of an inadequate modernity or by a sentimental pastiche and weak connection with the glories of the Islamic past (for instance, the frequent naming of hospitals after the great Ibn Sina – Avicenna – or the ubiquitous use of arches to denote a faintly 'Islamic' look to buildings).

The Roots of Islamic Creativity

No single person has been more responsible for enlightening the world as to the true wellsprings of Islamic culture and science than the Iranian-born scholar and philosopher Seyyed Hossein Nasr.[1] A deeply original and prolific writer, Nasr was born in Iran in 1933, into a family of well known scholars and physicians. He studied physics at MIT and obtained his PhD from Harvard in 1958, with a thesis which focused on the history of Islamic science. He returned to Iran, where he became a highly regarded scholar and pedagogue. He was the founder of the Imperial Iranian Academy of Philosophy and the head of the Iranian technological university, Aryamehr. After the Iranian Revolution of 1978–9, Nasr was obliged to leave Iran and joined the George Washington University, where he is now professor.

Nasr had become deeply influenced by the writings of the 'Traditionalists', a group of mainly European writers and scholars, some of whom had converted to Islam.[2] This circle drew its inspiration from the remarkable French thinker René Guénon.[3] Guénon lived out his late life in Cairo and took the name of Abd el-Wahid Yahya; he died there in 1952. The circle also included the Swiss metaphysician Frithjof Schuon, the art historian Titus Burckhardt and the museum curator and librarian Martin Lings (also known as Abu Bakr Seraj-ed-Dine). These were the leaders of the group who espoused the idea of a 'perennial philosophy' and sought to find the transcendent unity of all religions in their inner, esoteric dimension. According to the Traditionalists, the continuity with authentic religious traditions was the only means by which human beings could connect to the 'primordial' religion.

Each of the great religions of mankind, if practised genuinely and within its own spiritual and ritual framework, could be a valid pathway to the original primordial faith and thus to knowledge of God. Therefore a Christian, a Buddhist and a Muslim could equally connect to the essence of religion itself, if they took on the hues of the established, traditional pathways of their particular religion. In Christianity, it was the monastic, contemplative tradition, and the mystical experiences of figures such as Meister Eckhart and St Theresa of Avila that led to the inner essence of the religion. In Islam this path was Sufism, especially the metaphysical Sufism associated with the medieval master Ibn Arabi.[4] Nasr became a close confidant of Frithjof Schuon and for a long time was the most visible Muslim advocate of the perennial philosophy.[5]

In a series of writings of what he termed 'traditional Islam' (as opposed to modernist/liberal and fundamentalist Islam), Nasr firmly attributed the loss of the creative impulse in Islam to the inversion and then displacement of the traditional perspective which had underpinned the civilization of Islam.[6] Nasr explored a variety of issues which impinged on the contemporary Muslim world, from the ecological crisis to the atrophy of science, art and architecture in Muslim countries. He takes strong exception to the idea of Islamic modernists that science is value-free and thus its pursuit, within the norms of modern science and scientific experimentation, can only be for the general good of Islam. (Modernist Muslims as well as fundamentalists have always maintained that Islam encourages the pursuit of scientific knowledge.)

The problem with science for the sake of science is that it denies the indisputable historical fact that science in Islam was conducted within a frame of reference which was specifically Islamic – that is, that the pursuit of scientific goals was encouraged as part of the overall quest of Man to see and affirm the signs of God in nature. As Nasr wrote, 'Islamic science came into being from a wedding between the spirit that issued from the Quranic revelation and the existing sciences of various civilizations which Islam inherited and which it transmuted through the spiritual power into a new substance, at once different from and continuous with what had existed before'.[7] Technological developments in Islam, for example, instruments such as the astrolabe, had precise functions related to the times of prayer, the beginning and end of the fast of Ramadan and the direction of the *Qibla* (Mecca). Similarly, Islamic medicine was based on the assertion that the human body was a microcosmic reflection of the cosmos and that a balanced interrelationship between mind, body and spirit was essential to maintaining the health and vigour of a person. The idea of preventive medicine, the holistic approach to well being and the treatment of illnesses were integral to Islamic medicine. It was on the basis of this world view that the edifice of Islamic culture and civilization was built. Islam recognized above all that the domain of the infinite, of boundless knowledge and limitless growth, does not belong to human beings.

To a large extent, therefore, the observation that Islamic civilization did not 'progress' into a modern world order based on technology is immaterial. Its trajectory in pre-modern times did not entail the dramatic shifts which have made the industrial revolution possible in the West. Machine production in factories for a mass market, protected by laws that enshrined absolute private property rights, could not have evolved in an Islamic context. The artisan and craftsman culture which was the mainstay of the production of goods in the pre-modern Islamic economy was imbued with the Islamic world view, which combined work with the life of the spirit. In fact Nasr demonstrates conclusively that Islamic technology was indeed concerned with practical innovations such as wind and water mills, distillation processes and engines of war. 'The technology [that the Muslims] dealt with was one which utilized natural forces within the environment in question, making the maximum use of human skills and causing the minimum amount of disturbance within the natural environment.'[8] A number of the medieval Muslim treatises on machines and processes came remarkably close to anticipating their modern equivalents. But Nasr states unequivocally that Muslims did not venture into this terrain and never seriously considered utilizing such technological innovations in order to change their economic life and means of production. The break with the sacred could not take place within Islam. The impetus had to come from elsewhere.

Nevertheless, Islamic science and medicine continued to thrive within their own terms of reference, until the fateful encounter with the expansionist European powers. The collapse of innovation and creativity in the world of Islam was not the result of the fall of the Abbasid Empire in the thirteenth century, but a much more recent phenomenon. It is intimately connected to the abandonment of the underpinnings of the traditional

Islamic world view, in the past two centuries, by a succession of secular-minded and fundamentalist Muslims. The first jettisoned this world view as a matter of principle; the second accepted the fruits of western civiliza-tion with no understanding of their roots in the western experience. They simply 'Islamized' them. Purpose and meaning was lost.

Nasr's analysis of the predicament of modern Muslims has important prescriptive implications, particularly as the Muslim innovative capacity has degraded in a fundamental sense. The creative output of the twenty or thirty million Muslims of the Abbasid era dwarfs the output of the nearly one-and-a-half billion Muslims of the modern era. In science and tech-nology the statistics are truly daunting – and depressing. Using 2006 data, the Muslim countries of the OIC have 8.5 scientists and technicians per 1,000 population, compared to a world average of 40.7 and a developed-world figure of 139.3. The entire Muslim world contributed 1.17 per cent of the world's scientific literature, compared to 1.48 per cent from Spain alone. The OIC countries spend 0.3 per cent of their GDP on research and development, compared to the global average of 2.4 per cent. The listing goes on to include the paucity of published journal articles, university science faculty rankings and patents.[9]

Some scientists and educators have used the relative and absolute decline of Muslims' innovative capacities to call for a redoubling of the secularization efforts in Islamic societies and for a complete and final divorce between science and any religious bearings. Part of their argument is based on the false premise that Islam and the scientific method are in fundamental contradiction; this echoes the German sociologist Max Weber and his assertion that Islam lacks the ideational bases for proper scientific inquiry. The physicist Pervez Hoodbhoy, chair of the physics department at one of Pakistan's leading universities, has repeated the old chestnut that Islamic norms of worship – the five daily prayers, the fast of Ramadan – are antithetical to a proper work ethic and should be more 'balanced', whatever that means.[10] The fallacy of such arguments is readily apparent when one considers that abiding by these cornerstones of Islamic ritual in no way diminished the productive and innovative capabilities of Muslims in their golden age. A completely different view is held by apologists of Islam, who see all manner of scientific predictions embedded in the Quran. Maurice Bucaille is a case in point. A French doctor who ran a surgical clinic at the University of Paris, Bucaille produced a book in 1976 which purported to show that the Quran prophesied a number of discoveries such as the Big Bang.[11] Apart from advancing such dubious claims, which were based on readings of Quranic verses connected with cosmology, the book is a parody, both of science and the sacred functions of Quranic verses. Nevertheless, it has had an immense circulation and influence and is used as a polemical tool to convince people of the identity between Islam and modern science.

But neither the arguments of secular humanists such as Hoodbhoy nor those of the fundamentalists, who see the Quran as a science textbook, can resolve the conundrum that affects the capabilities of Islamic culture. The issue is whether Muslims can arrest and then reverse their relative cultural decline within the terms of reference of their own civilization – and not within the terms of reference of the imagined Islamic community of the fundamentalists, or within the norms of secular modernity. It is Nasr who has had by far the more insightful and telling response. The traditionalist critique of both fundamentalism and secularism can be extended to nearly all other areas of human endeavour where modern Muslims have fallen woefully short of their own civilization's standards – as well as of the norms of the contemporary world. From art and architecture to education, environment and the quality of daily life, the condition of Muslim societies – not excepting the odd hyper-wealthy oil producing fringe – is unenviable.

The Decay of Islam's Urban Civilization

The focus of Islamic civilization has always been the city – the *medina*, from which the Arabic word for civilization derives: *tamaddun*. Mecca itself, the Mother-of-Cities,[12] as the Quran calls it, was the launching platform for the message of the Prophet, and a nexus of the caravan trade of Arabia. Medina, to which the Prophet departed in the celebrated *hegira*, and which became the functioning capital of the first Islamic political entity, would always be the model Islamic city. It would inspire the founders of the myriad cities that sprang up in the wake of Islam's expansion and would figure significantly in the redesign of historical cities such as Damascus, Alexandria and, later, Istanbul, cities which fell under Muslim control.

The Islamic city has important features and characteristics which identify it as uniquely 'Islamic' in terms of its physical lay-out and the division of urban functions into specific categories. The position and scope of the religious, educational, legal, governmental and economic institutions, as well as that of public markets, gardens and amenities such as the ubiquitous public baths integrated all these into a recognizably and distinctly Islamic pattern. There is a remarkable unity in the 'feel' of Islamic cities, even when they are dispersed across different continents and cultures. From Kano to Cairo to Lahore, Islamic cities would resonate to the same distinctive rhythms of life. The location of the city may have been dictated by military or commercial considerations, but their inner lay-out and organizing principles were derived unequivocally from the religion of Islam. Life in the cities was a permanent reminder that the urban dweller was part of the community of Islam and that he or she was expected to abide by the norms of the civilization. Above all, the regular calls to prayer from the minarets, the congregational and Friday prayers, and the great festivals associated with the end of the fasting month, the Hajj and the celebration of the Prophet's birthday, gave all Islamic cities an overarching spiritual and religious dimension.

Nearly all official posts in the Islamic city were derived from the Sharia – from the position of governor to that of judge, and market regulator to the police (*Shurta*) – and the duties of these officers required a commensurate set of institutions with their own spatial requirements. There are clearly demarcated areas of the Islamic city, for example, where the legal and governmental institutions were assembled. The office of *Wali* or *'Amil* (governor), whose main duty was to maintain law and order, was close to that of the police and the administrative courts that handled routine complaints. The *Qadi* (judge) was responsible for the administration and provision of justice in personal and family law, and in commercial and other contract disputes. The *Muhtasib* was a unique office and institution in Islam. Although its main function was the supervision and regulation of public markets, it was also responsible for upholding the overall standards of public decency and conduct.[13]

This post would later be disparaged as representing the 'moral police' which restricted individual rights and freedoms. In reality, however, the *Muhtasib* was an essential element in the functioning of the Islamic city within the precepts of the Sharia. Rather than the caricature of the harsh enforcer of rigid moral codes, the *Muhtasib* is better seen as a type of all-purpose ombudsman and inspector with wide-ranging responsibilities, which were as diverse as ensuring the cleanliness of the water supply or enforcing professional standards on doctors and apothecaries. All these institutions ultimately derived their legitimacy from the Sharia and were organized to facilitate an urban life which revolved around the Sharia and its ethical rulings.

The unique educational institutions of Islam were also an important element in the organization of the Islamic city. The mosque was not only the focus of public worship but also the centre of wide-ranging educational and learning functions attached to it. In time, the main mosque complexes became prototypes of the public university. Prominent teachers and lecturers established *halaqas* ('circles') which attracted students from all corners of the Islamic world and beyond. The subjects of study were by no means restricted to the religious sciences; they involved the teaching of language, linguistics, and poetry. Strictly academic disciplines such as philosophy or the sciences were conducted in special academies. These were akin in many respects to Plato's Academy in Athens and to the schools that flourished in the Hellenic world and in the early Byzantine period. Primary education, where children acquired the three 'Rs as well as a knowledge of the Quran, was conducted in schools known as the *kuttab*. These were often attached to the mosque. The *madrassas* – which have now gained notoriety as a hotbed for the teaching and propagation of Islamic radicalism – were established as mainly state-run institutions, primarily to propagate the official version of Islam. They were often endowed with magnificent buildings in the main cities of Islam, with ample facilities for libraries and accommodation. (A famous *madrassa* in Baghdad, the Mustansiriyya, which was founded in the thirteenth century, is still in use today as part of the Mustansiriyya University.) Medical education was conducted in special institutions, the *bimaristan* (a name of Persian origin), which were a form of early hospitals. They doubled up as centres both for treating patients and for teaching medicine.[14]

The public markets of Islamic cities were frequently housed in specialized buildings or complexes which could extend over many kilometres, in labyrinthine passages. The grand bazaars of Istanbul, Isfahan, Aleppo and Damascus are extant and are examples of the scale of the goods markets of Islamic cities. These and many others continue to thrive even in modern times. The markets were complex institutions governed by their own internal regulatory bodies, and ultimately fell under the inspectorship of the *Muhtasib*. In larger cities, the markets included *khans*, central courts around which a number of shops were grouped. Markets were within walking distance of the main city mosques, and activity ceased during times of prayer.

Apart from high government officials, the military and the *ulema* classes, the population of the Islamic city was divided into guilds according to their craft or trade. These were further integrated into the Sufi orders through the *futtuwwa* (chivalric movements). They were anchored in the spiritual life of Islam and sought to connect themselves, through a chain of initiatory rites, to the Imam Ali and his close follower Salman al-Farisi. (Imam Ali is seen by nearly all Sufi orders and the guilds as the fount of spiritual wisdom and chivalric conduct.) In some of the larger cities of Islam, the guilds were also connected to the office of the supreme Sufi master, the doyen of the descendants of the Prophet Muhammad: the *Naqib al-Ashraf.* Craftsmen and artisans were thus intimately connected to the spiritual life of the community and saw their work in terms of fulfilling their duties and obligations to God. A detailed set of guidelines, rules and rituals governed the passage of the initiate from apprentice to artisan to master. At nearly every step of the way, the rituals were marked by specific Quranic recitations and spiritually charged utterances, invocations and exclamations. The head of the guild was known as the sheikh of the guild and although the office was frequently inherited it could only be so with the approval of guild members.[15]

The art historian Titus Burckhardt encapsulated the spirit of the guilds in an interview with one of the last descendants of an ancient line of craftsmen in the city of Fez – a comb maker. The man described his profession and his understanding of it.[16]

I myself acquired [the skill] only after many long years and even if I wanted to, I could not automatically pass it on to my son . . . This craft can be traced back from apprentice to master until one reaches our Lord Seth, the son of Adam. It was he who first taught it to men, and what a prophet brings must clearly have a purpose. I gradually came to understand that there is nothing fortuitous about this craft, that each movement and each procedure is the bearer of an element of wisdom. But not everyone can understand this. But even if one does not know this, it is still stupid and reprehensible to rob men of the inheritance of prophets, and to put them in front of a machine where, day in and day out, they must perform a meaningless task.[16]

Islam's urban vitality – especially in the Arab lands – had begun to deteriorate well before the advent of the European empires. Baghdad, the city of fabled fame, was a disease-ridden backwater with less than 100,000 people in the mid-seventeenth century. Cairo did not fare much better in the long period of Mameluke misrule, which ended with Napoleon's conquest of Egypt. The description of Muslim cities, with the exception of Istanbul and a few other Ottoman cities, by pre-modern European travellers was uniformly bleak and depressing. But what the European incursions did was to superimpose an entirely different ordering of the urban space, shattering or bypassing Islam's traditional urban structures and styles of building. In this way Islam's urban civilization suffered just as much as other main tenets and values of Islam. The make-over of the Islamic city was simply an extension of what was happening in the legal, social and economic spheres. In Morocco, the French established entirely new cities alongside the old. They drew away not only the governmental, administrative and judicial services, but also the mercantile and political elites.[17]

The same pattern was followed in other cities of the Muslim world which came under the control of foreign powers. The new areas had different names: the European quarter, the cantonment, the garden city, but they all served the same purpose. They created a new urban form, which had no connection with the Islamic past. The new cities and quarters were designed to house the foreigners and their local allies, dependants and imitators. It became a matter of social prestige to be associated with the modern ways of the new quarters, with their European conveniences and amenities. The old Islamic cities were abandoned to the working and artisan classes and to the remnants of the traditional classes. Within a few decades, the entire Islamic urban order had ended. The old Islamic city was now associated with all that was retrograde and served no better function than to act as the repository of the exploding population of the urban poor, fed as this was by massive flows of migrants from the rural areas. The old educational establishments were replaced by the modern universities. These were invariably sited in the new towns or quarters. The judicial functions of the *Qadi* were displaced by new legal systems, which came with the European powers; the guilds were decimated by competition from cheap foreign manufactures and modern domestic industries; public markets were supplanted by modern retailing. It is only in our day that a creeping gentrification is bringing back some vitality to the historical cities of Islam. But this has nothing to do with a revitalized Islam; it has more to do with French fashion designers ensconcing themselves in old merchants' houses, or with boutique hotels squatting in former Sufi lodges and catering for the super-wealthy.

Crowding, visual ugliness and squalor are the lot of most of the cities of Islam. The elites are well insulated from these unpleasantries through gates, high walls and a physically separate life in terms of work, leisure, shopping and education. But these very elites have invited the calamities on the Islamic city through their insistence on perpetrating whatever is fashionable in the West, irrespective of its appropriateness. The aesthetic sensibility of the modern minded Muslim has altered with the loss of its moorings in the traditional. The result is there for all to see: a hodgepodge of building styles; poor quality of construction; the loss of any order and purpose to town planning; constant assaults on the senses by discordant and jarring sights and sounds. The modern Islamic city simply groans under this weight. Populations explode while services collapse; the rich flee to their bastions while the poor endure and suffer the miseries of daily life. Cairo, Karachi, Dacca, Jakarta all have populations of over ten million, with miserably small budgets and rotting infrastructures and dwellings. Smaller cities such as Damascus and Rabat still send an echo of their former urban graces, but the relentless pressures on the integrity of the city are there. And everywhere the corruption and venality of public officials joins hands with the greed of developers and speculators to reduce whatever remains of the urban civilization of Islam.

But the degradation of Islam's historical cities is not entirely due to the westernized elites. The ravages wrought by the Wahhabis of Saudi Arabia on the fabric of the two holiest cities in Islam, Mecca and Medina, are well known. The extent of the damage wrought on these two cities has been exposed mainly due to the heroic efforts of the Jeddah-based architect and historian Sami Angawi,[18] who wrote about the wanton destruction of millennium-old buildings, in both Mecca and Medina, under the aegis of the Wahhabi clerical establishment. The clerics had ruled that historical sites such as the Prophet's birthplace could become virtual shrines and thus potentially objects of worship in themselves. In conclusion, they reasoned, it would be best if these buildings and sites were demolished, lest they give rise to idolatry. Their rulings have been generally welcomed by the political and commercial classes, who saw in the destruction of these buildings new opportunities for commercial profit from land speculation and development. According to Angawi and others, nearly 95 per cent of the historical buildings in the two holy cities have been demolished. Whenever a historical site which has any connection with the prophetic period is uncovered by archaeologists, the bulldozers move in to pull it down and pour concrete over the site. Other historical buildings (such as the Ottoman fortress which guarded Mecca) have been demolished in order to make way for high-rise buildings and shopping centres.[19]

The most egregious developments have been around the Grand Mosque of Mecca. Pilgrims are now regaled with buildings that dwarf the sanctuary. They are festooned with multimedia images of fast food chains and consumer product manufacturers. High-rise buildings proliferate, some of them offering time shares or retreats in order to be 'near God', as the advertisements put it. A privileged view and access to the sanctuary is promised; but this defeats the entire purpose of the Hajj, where the equality of human beings in the eyes of God is affirmed. Wealth and advantage become the norm rather than the simplicity of the pilgrim's lot. A huge shopping mall, the Abraj al Bait complex, complete with food courts and an indoor amusement park, sits right opposite the sanctuary. It is as if the courtyard of the basilica of St Peter's in the Vatican had been turned into a tawdry shopping strip. The night market of Mecca where pilgrims traded their wares is long gone, having being replaced by the world of global brands and air-conditioned malls. A similar destructive pattern has played itself out in Medina, where the demolition of historical tombs and burial sites of the family and companions of the Prophet has been going on apace since the founding of the modern Saudi state. For a while, the Prophet's burial site in the sacred mosque of Medina was also threatened by zealots of the Wahhabi sect, who considered veneration of the Prophet by the multitude of Muslims as bordering on the deadly sin of polytheism (*shirk*).

The lack of reverence for the past and for the Muslim sacred places is not restricted to Saudi Arabia. The old city of Cairo was visibly crumbling under decades of official neglect. Masterpieces of Mameluke and Fatimid buildings were left in ruins. They have only recently been the subject of official concern, after incessant prodding from concerned architectural historians and international organizations. In fact, it is through the efforts of the small but relatively wealthy Bohra and Ismaili communities that some of the masterpieces of Cairene architecture have been preserved. Sana'a, the capital of Yemen, with its astonishing architecture, also laboured under years of neglect, and throughout the Muslim world individual buildings and old quarters have been allowed to wither and decay until fairly recently. Shiite pilgrimage sites have generally fared better, but they are now faced with a different set of problems as the number of pilgrims and visitors increases exponentially. The temptation to follow the Saudi pattern of grandiose and expensive extensions and ornamentations to sacred buildings and sites, in an increasingly commercialized environment, is ever present.[20]

Islamic Dystopias

The medieval Islamic political philosopher al-Farabi described the type of regime that would be most conducive to the happiness and welfare of mankind. His vision, a good four centuries before Thomas More's *Utopia*, demanded that citizens should be virtuous by dint of their knowledge of the divine and of natural beings and, equally importantly, that they should act upon this inerrant knowledge. Other regimes are ignorant, wicked or erring: ignorant because they have no knowledge of the divine or of the natural order; wicked because they possess such knowledge but do not act upon it; or errant because their citizens have acquired false or corrupted knowledge. Al-Farabi's classification drew not only on Islamic themes of revelation and prophecy, but also on the Greek philosophers of antiquity, in particular Plato. He is therefore an ideal proponent of the balanced Islamic civic order, poised between reason and revelation, between the sacred and the profane. Deviations from the ideal occur whenever citizens pursue other goals, by choice or necessity. Impoverished societies necessarily seek to meet the bare essentials of life. Al-Farabi calls 'vile' regimes which seek wealth and prosperity for their own sake. 'Base' regimes are those that are hedonistic. Regimes of tyranny seek to impose their domination on others. And regimes of 'corporate associations' – the closest that al-Farabi came to modern-day democracy – are those where the citizens are free to do what they wish. In the absence of the perfected 'Virtuous City', al-Farabi is firmly in favour of the proto-democracy of the regime of corporate associations. Even though most of its citizens would be corrupted by luxury, such a city nevertheless allows for the development of the arts and sciences – and freedoms – necessary for the establishment of the virtuous regime.

The cities and societies of the modern Muslim world no longer revolve around the rhythms of Islamic life in any meaningful way; nor are they striving for an ideal form of civic and political organization, which could provide a vision and direction for their evolution. In fact, some have strayed so far from the mean that they are at risk of turning their worlds into nightmarish dystopias. Both extreme wealth and extreme poverty have played their part in distorting the vision of the ideal society, whether that of al-Farabi's 'Virtuous City' or the model of a just and equitable society reflected in the Prophet and his companions' Medina – or the ideal of a democratic and open civic order.

The extreme fundamentalist vision of an ideal Islamic order is frightening in its implications. Like a horror film, it has seized the world's imagination, particularly as glimpses of this bizarre order have been caught in the Taliban of Afghanistan. A contrived religious archaism can only have a deadening effect on Islamic life and society. The insistence on facial hair for men; the banning of music; the refusal to countenance education for girls; the degrading treatment of women; the disregard for non-Islamic archaeological patrimony; the easy executions, amputations and corporal punishment – are all caricatures of what ultra-conservative Islam has in store when it effects power. But a deliberate backwardness cannot survive for long, even if it succeeds in locking itself away from the world. There are many instances where Muslim rulers have chosen to insulate their societies from outside influences – pre-1970s Oman comes to mind – only to see the barriers swept away with a change of regime. Reactionary dystopias cannot last long in the modern era.

Nevertheless, the type of world which is being created in the aftermath of the collapse of the Soviet bloc and the unprecedented flow of funds into the oil-producing countries of the Gulf is even more insidious for the regeneration of Islamic civilization. Three factors are at work here, combining to produce a radically altered vision for the Muslim world – in spite of the present obsession with fundamentalism, which appears to be spreading everywhere. The collapse of the Soviet bloc gave a huge boost to the ruling oligarchies and sovereigns of the Muslim world. The rhetoric of democratization which followed in the wake of the collapse of the Soviet empire has been overwhelmed by the reality of the massive transfer of public resources to a new class of entrepreneurs and plutocrats. The members of this class are not only interlinked with the ruling political classes of Muslim countries, but are part of a network which binds them closely to the globalized world economy and to the centres of financial and economic power in the West.

Wherever in the Muslim world one turns, from North Africa to the Middle East or to Central and South-East Asia, the same patterns have emerged and are now solidified. The powerful industrial, financial and commercial groups have too much at stake in the status quo ever to consider how their wealth and power could be used to create a new basis for the growth of a specifically Islamic civilization. Their control over the media in particular – especially over the ever-present satellite channels – pushes for the westernization of young Muslims and for the transforma-tion of their culture into a purported global youth culture. The invasion of Muslim personal space in the name of cultural freedom and entertainment was not possible before the advent of these mainly unregulated channels.

A second factor is the rise of the Gulf on the world stage, a phenomenon entirely due to the massive financial surpluses which are accumulating in the region: the figures, in absolute or real terms, dwarf all other previous oil booms. The combined oil-exporting revenues of the Gulf Cooperation Council countries (GCC) in 2007 approached $400 billion. By 2020, the oil windfall to these countries could exceed $9 trillion.[21] These funds are unprecedented and have made the GCC countries a global financial powerhouse. But the utilization of these official resources to further the integration of the Muslim world or the underpinning of a new currency (or payments medium) is simply not on the cards. In fact the opposite is likely to happen: the finances of these countries will be even more inter-linked with the global financial order. The travesty of 'Islamic' banking has already been alluded to. It will simply not be possible to make these Islamic institutions the cornerstone of a new Islamic financial order. A large-scale diversification of the foreign assets of these countries from the main currency blocs is not possible either. According to the most recent data, western currencies (including the yen) account for over 95 per cent of the official assets of the GCC countries, with the dollar alone accounting for 57 per cent of the official assets. The huge surpluses of the GCC countries will be 'sterilized' in terms of their effect on the distribution of power in the world. They may in fact be put to use to integrate the GCC countries further into the global economic order and to remove any possibility of the GCC acting as the fulcrum of a revitalized Islamic economic bloc. The possibility of oil revenues filtering to the poor of the Islamic world, or providing the wherewithal to revivify Islamic cultural life, is remote indeed.

The third factor is the decisive entry of the US into the affairs of the Islamic world, which has been justified on national security grounds in the wake of the 9/11 attacks. This factor has combined with the other elements to create a powerful momentum towards redefining the Islamic cultural, social, and even religious landscape. The US is now devoting considerable resources to moulding the world of Islam. Its efforts include democracy-building and supporting civil society groups which broadly advocate western values, women's rights movements, the educational reform of the *madrassa* system, and even Sufi movements which are seen as religiously ecumenical. There is a spate of programmes specifically for the Arab world, which include the promotion of private universities modelled after American liberal arts colleges: the so-called 'American University' move-ment. A number of these are now operating in the GCC, and a new univer-sity has been founded in Iraq. All these have clearly developed as an alternative to the dysfunctional and overcrowded state universities, and they aim to graduate students steeped in the verities of a secular and liberal democracy; they will provide the new governing and commercial elites. These universities cannot be compared to the historical American University of Beirut (AUB) and the American University in Cairo (AUC), which were founded in the nineteenth and early twentieth centuries by Protestant missionaries. Although these two universities were pioneers in bringing liberal arts education to the Middle East, they were not part of any overt plan to secularize the Middle East or to give its graduates any political or cultural orientation. In fact, a number of their graduates, especially those of the AUB, were luminaries in the national and radical movements of the area.

Sinister Cities

All of these currents can best be seen in the progress of the hyper-modern cities of the Gulf, which have become aspirational models and destination targets for the thrusting middle classes of the area. Rampant commercialism, brand worship, gigantism, strict class segregation and a calendar of 'festivals' and 'events' designed by marketers have conspired to develop a nightmarish vision of the city, a vision which is entirely antithetical to the ideals of the Islamic city. It is, as the urban critic Mike Davis has termed it, a place where 'Speer meets Disney on the shores of Araby'.[22] These fantasy cities are not some blips on Islam's radar screens – as they most certainly were a few decades ago. In the middle of the twentieth century, the coastal cities of the Gulf were, at best, minor fishing and pearl-diving villages, with a few smugglers' coves interspersed in between. Some countries such as Oman, of course, had an illustrious history and presided over large maritime empires, which encompassed parts of East Africa. But by that time they were well away from Islam's heartlands. However, with the advent of massive oil revenues, the newly sovereign countries of the Gulf became a clean slate upon which a new Islamic urban order, unconstrained by inadequate financial resources, could be built. Post-oil rulers of the first generation were cautious and deliberate in their decisions, mindful of the traditions of their people and the legacy of Islam. But, by the 1990s, the modest and measured rule which marked these countries gave way to the abandonment of their past and the extraordinary embrace of an extreme, even outlandish, form of edgy and frantic capitalism. It is in this respect that the example of the Gulf's cities is likely to be instructive to the rest of the Islamic world. For, behind the sanitized and formalistic protestations of loyalty to Islam, a new challenge is arising that pits the advantages of embracing 'globalization' – even in this weird form – against a historically determined, or traditional, form of Islamic civilization. And the challenge is being championed by the most powerful concentrations of wealth anywhere in the Muslim world.

The reality of the matter is that this model of garish opulence and the flaunting of wealth, status and privilege seem to attract a significant part of the Muslim world's aspiring classes. Dubai in particular has become a magnet for hundreds of thousands of Iranians, Arabs and Pakistanis seeking the good life and hoping to emulate this pattern in their own native countries. The Dubai 'brand' is now an exportable commodity, with large numbers of cities such as Islamabad, Karachi, Cairo, Casablanca and beyond giving way to the gated communities and expensive high rise apartment blocks which are a feature of the 'Dubai experience'.

In fact some of the larger developers in the Gulf countries, for instance the Emaar Group, are now international in their scope and have a special focus on the Islamic world. Their mission is to bring the patterns of Dubai's development to the teeming countries of the Muslim world, where, in spite of the endemic poverty of the masses, they are deemed to have sufficient support from the ambitious middle classes to warrant these expensive developments. A new cycle is beginning in these cities of the Muslim world. Here it is not the foreigners and colonizers who seek to distance themselves from the life of the city, but rather the newly rich and aspiring natives. In and of itself, it is not reprehensible to want to escape the poverty, filth and misery of the decrepit neighbourhoods of Islam's cities. Rather, the issue is what type of future this escape is leading to, and what it portends for the civilization as a whole.

The omens are certainly not good. The branded developments in which the new Muslim urban elites dwell bear no relationship to the ideals of the Islamic city. They are conceived on the basis of exclusion, isolation and fear. The ridiculous names of these developments ('The Lagoons'; 'Fortuna Towers and Residences'; 'The Villas at Bay Village') are nearly all drawn from American real-estate marketing manuals. They play at inventing a sense of community, but in reality are nothing of the sort. The odd mosque which is plonked in the middle of these arid developments is neither welcoming nor in use – except possibly by the army of servants and domestics who keep these fantasies going. There is no community, because people have chosen, or have been persuaded, to huddle together as a class or as a status group. Invariably, access to these developments is severely restricted through sophisticated passes, surveillance methods and 24-hour patrols and security. A 'Southern California' lifestyle is touted as the answer to the anxieties and fears of the middle classes, eager as they are to escape the crowds and clamour of the city.

The combination of gated communities, giant shopping malls and physically isolated workplaces creates an environment which has eroded the forms and function of the Islamic city even further. More importantly, these features will eliminate the possibility of an alternative way of life as people become literally imprisoned in a process which has its own dynamics. This dynamic is not so much about the acceptance of the inevitability of a homogenized and globalized world as the complete failure of imagination on the part of Muslims to construct a future which might address their living concerns while remaining loyal to their legacy. Few middle-class Muslims appreciate the fact that the choices they make will inevitably impact on their values and create new realities for subsequent generations.

The irony is that this oppressive modernity is wholeheartedly embraced by many fundamentalists who fancy themselves as technologically sophisticated or, in their own parlance, 'scientific'. Fundamentalists frequently use the epithet 'scientific' to attribute a gloss of rationalist finality to their argument. Not a few of the fundamentalist *ulemas* in the Gulf and elsewhere have acted as handmaidens to power. Sitting in their giant air- conditioned mega-mosques, with the full panoply of up-to-date audio-visuals and a constant coverage by the satellite channels, they fulminate against modern ways. The preservation of what is traditional and authentic in Islamic art and architecture has fallen to a small band of pioneering architects and town planners who have risen to the challenge of criticizing the effects of modern technology and globalization on the patterns of living in Islamic cities.

The Egyptian Hassan Fathy, whose productive period spanned the decades between the 1960s and 1980s, was one of the first architects of the modern era to use traditional building materials, methods and concepts in his residential designs and plans for new villages.[23] His main concern was to ensure that the functions and forms of his buildings conformed to the demands of an Islamic society: privacy and protection for the family home; the use of courtyards and reception areas; the dependence on natural ventilation and traditional building materials. The principles that Fathy laid down for the revival of architecture and town planning in the Islamic world became a leitmotif for the generation that followed in his wake. In many ways, his concerns predated a great deal of the present preoccupation with environmental issues, a human scale for building, appropriate technology and building techniques, an orientation towards the community and its needs, and the essential value and role of tradition. To Fathy, tradition was not a mechanical repetition or replication of the past; it was a cyclical renewal of life and an ongoing evolution. It also connected the present with a past which had been disrupted both by the intrusion of alien forms and by the advent of the industrial age. His followers, including Abd el-Wahid al-Wakil, have continued and advanced Fathy's work, but have not been able to dent significantly the headlong rush into the post-modern wildernesses of the new urban realities.

The revival of traditional Islamic arts and building methods has been a spotty affair. In fact, until very recently, the only institution of note to teach and train in the traditional Islamic arts was one which had been founded by the Prince of Wales, in London, as part of the prince's School of Traditional Arts. No university in the Islamic world provides a specific degree in traditional Islamic architecture, so complete has been the domination of western concepts of design and building. A small reaction to the virtual disappearance of teaching the traditional skills and crafts does appear to be in the works, but it is clearly insufficient to overturn the years of willful neglect and marginalization of traditional Islamic arts and architecture.

Muslims have distanced themselves to such an extent from their own civilizational roots that it becomes ever more difficult to recreate the bases of their former unique world. In science, technology, and even in the arts, the overlay of decades – and now centuries – of modern norms has drastically curtailed the element of continuity with the past. When Muslims talk about Islamic science, they have in mind the medieval al-Khawarizmi or Ibn al-Haytham, and not some contemporary figure with whom they can identify. In technology, they marvel at some ingenious contraption of long ago, but their world is dominated by the manufactured goods of the modern industrial age. The mighty buildings of the great Ottoman architect Mimar Sinan stand in contrast to the mediocre and unpleasant structures which have so much degraded the environment of Islamic cities. Crafts die, markets sink into decrepitude and the Muslim home is no longer defined by the needs of the extended family. The physical world is rearranged so as to accommodate the motorcar, and, if western cities turn part of their historical centres over to pedestrians, Muslim cities will still elect to drive huge boulevards into their historical centres. If tradition is of any interest to the avant-garde of the Muslim world, this is simply in terms of its commercial value. The rehabilitation of some of the old structures of Islamic cities has more to do with their potential as restaurants or night clubs than with the genuine desire to revive their former usages.

The idea that Islamic civilization is based not only on outer forms but on an inner reality that has spiritual, metaphysical and even cosmological aspects to it is lost to many. A huge collective effort is now needed simply to stop the destruction of the vestiges of Islamic civilization, but it is unclear whether this will be forthcoming. In the final analysis, Muslims must understand that the revival of their civilization is not simply about the rediscovery of an outer piety or conduct and behaviour. Science and technology are not value-free. Neither is a world built around their demands. One cannot revive traditional building methods if there are powerful commercial interests invested in the cement industry. Neither can one construct cities and neighbourhoods conducive to the community spirit if the cityscape is dominated by modern towers of Babel which aggressively flaunt their disdain or disregard for Islamic norms of life.

CHAPTER 11

The Last Crisis

For centuries, the civilization of Islam has been buffeted by powerful adverse currents which have succeeded in draining its vitality and have gradually whittled it down to a shadow of its former self. The most disturbing, far-reaching, and possibly fatal of these currents have been the panoply of disruptive forces associated with the imperial expansion of the West into Muslim lands and with the blast of modernity that accompanied it. A third giant wave, that of globalization, different in form from the mainly political and military challenges of the past, is now cresting over the world of Islam. The global reach of impersonal forces has not spared Muslims or Muslim countries. These forces have rendered ambiguous the traditional boundaries between cultures and civilizations. The information explosion, global economic integration and the spread of mass media are all examples of powerful currents which ignore or circumvent civilizational frontiers. The demand for a continuous improvement in the economic lot of people is now almost universal. Technological prowess, economic vitality and increasing standards of living are what mostly determine the rankings of nations and peoples, to which might be added the culture of democracy and rights. Muslims and the civilization they created have been hurled into these turbulent and unfamiliar waters. Islam as a religion and Islamic civilization as the world which Muslims have created and in which they have lived have been tested for their validity, adaptability and ability to hold on to the loyalty of Muslims.

The ferment in the Islamic world over the past two hundred years has been symptomatic of the deep-seated anxieties which have accompanied these disruptive forces. The three broad cycles which have marked this period – the shock of modernity, the effective break with the past, and the counter-revolution which these have inspired – have led to profound changes in the way Muslims understand and even practice their faith. However, while the faith has proved resilient in its ability to confront and resolve the challenges coming its way, the fate of the civilization itself gives far less cause for optimism. Though religion is the defining feature of Islamic civilization and its main drive, it is not its entirety. It is the other props of the civilization that have atrophied and died. Islamic civilization is now nearly bereft of most of the vital elements that had previously given it coherence and meaning. Whatever has remained is now undergoing its last crisis. Islamic civilization will either suffer the fate of previous world civilizations, which have disappeared as living entities, or will find within itself the capability to redefine the meaning of civilized life and to metamorphose in ways now not entirely evident.

The Last Crisis

No one can dismiss the fervour and commitment with which Muslims at large have tried to grapple with the myriad issues their civilization had to contend with in the recent past. Equally striking, however, is the absence of any continuity or depth to the various reforms and modernizing schemes that have marked Islam's response to the waves of change engulfing it. The short-lived period when traditionalists were still in control ended with the total defeat of these champions of Islam and in their banishment or death. The likes of Abd el-Qadir, the Sanussiya of Libya and Imam Shamil disappeared into memory. Their hopeless *jihads* may have kindled a romantic yearning for epic deeds unsullied by modern ways, but it was their very traditionalism that was held to be responsible for their ultimate defeat. Modernists such as Afghani, Abduh and Ridha neither upgraded the capacity of Islam to respond to the encroachments of the West nor succeeded in harmonizing their version of Islam with the precepts of the modern order. In the end, some of them such as Ridha would turn against the ideals of a 'reformed' Islam and opt for the purer, Salafi variety as the only way to revive the world of Islam. Secularists who had the run over the lands of Islam for nearly fifty years were equally unable to refashion their societies in the European secular mould. Religion did not vanish from their societies in spite of the often draconian measures to eliminate its presence.

Neither has the effort of the last two or three decades to create the bases of a new Islamic civilization been any more successful. The constant degrading of the main tenets of Islamic civilization has continued apace, in spite of the heroic and often solitary attempts to fashion a new understanding of the wellsprings of Islamic civilization and to create the circumstances and opportunities for its regeneration. Bennabi's critique of Islamic civilization left little in the form of a determined programme to reverse the pernicious effects of centuries of stasis of the vitality and creativity of Muslims. The Islamization-of-knowledge movement, which was pioneered by al-Attas, al-Faruqi and others, has sputtered on with a few ambitious publications on 'Islamizing' social sciences. Their effects have been marginal. Liberal reformers of the religion have basically conceded the argument that Muslims are best served if they assume the democratic and liberal verities of the West as their own. Islamic science has gone the way of Islamic architecture, Islamic city planning, Islamic medicine and Islamic economics. It is either spoken of in the past tense or it stumbles along with a few adherents and with little or no vitality.

As each aspect of Islamic civilization has withered away, the remaining few necessarily assume greater significance and increasingly become its defining features. The cultures of Islam continue. They are increasingly parochial and national, linked to racial or ethnic identities and loyalties rather than manifestations of a universal civilization. The formerly universal Islamic civilization is now reduced to two elements that still retain a real vitality and can cross the frontiers of nations and peoples: the religious world of the faithful and pious and the political world of power and government. For many people these become the only extant routes through which Islamic civilization may yet be recreated.

The spiritual or the inner lives of Muslims have shrunk in favour of an Islam based on rules and rituals. Both political Islam and the various fundamentalist orthodoxies privilege the outer forms of piety and observance as a confirmation of the existence of an Islamic basis to society. So do the various autocracies and pseudo-democracies that rule in the Muslim world. It is easy to burnish one's Islamic credentials by building giant mosques and by ostentatiously celebrating the various festivals of Islam. The spread of Quranic channels and religious programmes is another aspect of the concern with the outer manifestations of Islamism. They are improbable platforms for the rediscovery of the inner ethics from which a new civilizational impulse can originate. Secularists in the Muslim world tend to be frightened by these outer forms of Islamic observance, seeing in them the thin edge of the wedge for the imposition of full-blown Sharia law, if Islamists were to come to power. Sharia law merely compounds secularists' anxieties about the dangers inherent in a creeping 'Islamization' of society. Secularists see both as merely way stations to the dismantling of the modern social and cultural mores adopted by many Muslims. Sharia law is seen to restrict radically the possibility of a modern lifestyle. But conformity to a supposedly Islamic outer norm – such as that manifested in forcing or cajoling women to wear headscarves in public – cannot be the way to reconstruct a civilization, although many would combine the two, and see one as a precondition for the other.

There are few signs that the outer aspects of Islamic observance are under threat. There is no crisis of religious belief in Islam comparable to the one that has affected, say, Christianity in western Europe. Mosques are not closing down because of a lack of custom; neither has religion been effectively banned from the public space. Allegiance to Islam has not only survived the modern period but has in fact strengthened. But this is a long way from asserting that the seeds for a rebirth of Islamic civilization are there simply because most Muslims continue to exhibit an extraordinary commitment to their religion. The last crisis of Islamic civilization – the one that will put a definitive end to the civilizational cycle which began with the establishment of Islam as a distinct cultural, political and religious community – will not come from the mass abandonment of religious faith. The fortunes of Islamic civilization are linked more to the success or demise of political Islam.

The politicization of Islam and its turning into an ideology for achieving power is an undoubted pivotal change that has influenced the course of Muslim life and civilization in modern times. However, when Islamists proclaim that Islam 'is a total way of life', what they really mean is that Islamic forms should shroud the modern world. There is no serious questioning about the underlying conceptual framework of this world. The high ground of implicitly acknowledging the authority of the modern framework has already been conceded. The introduction of Sharia, for example, becomes a mechanism by which outer Islamic forms are sustained and sanctioned. In fact Islamists proclaim their belief in a 'scientific' and progressive Islam as a badge of honour, implicitly adopting the world view of science and the merits of unrestricted technological change.

They frequently use their 'rationalist' credentials to advance their claim that they can manage state and society more effectively than others.

In power, it is unlikely that Islamists will generate a new dynamic in Islamic civilization. The claim to see the outer world in an entirely different light rings hollow if one has accepted the underlying assumptions of the modern world. The evolution of modernity owes virtually nothing to Islam, and Islamists have proved utterly indifferent to alternative forms of modernity which are being explored by many groups in the world. It is relatively simple to ban the consumption of alcohol or to change the penal codes in the name of the Sharia; it is an entirely different matter to conceive of an alternative way of ordering people's lives, or of radically changing people's sense of values. The success of political Islam may, paradoxically, prove to be the last crisis of Islamic civilization. For it will remove, once and for all, the possibility that the political route could ever be the basis for rejuvenating or refashioning the elements of a new form of Islamic civilization.

The turn to violence and terror by a small part of the Islamist movement, especially its signature mass murders of innocent civilians, is another decisive break with Islam's civilizational legacy. Islam's detractors make the claim that there is a linear connection between the two best known terrorist phenomena in Islamic history – the Khawarij and the medieval sect of 'Assassins' – and their modern day equivalent. This is to stretch the connection to a breaking point. One, the Khawarij, reaches to the early years of Islam's foundation, to the wars between Ali and Muawiya for control over the caliphate. The other connection, with the Assassins, is superficially more justifiable. They were possibly the first such movement to use terror in a systematic way to achieve political ends. As for their modern counterparts, they have relied on angry and disaffected individuals to forge a violent and disciplined organization, driven by a messianic ideology. But the Assassins were defeated when their final strongholds were overwhelmed in the thirteenth century, and the traces of organized terrorism vanished from the world of Islam until very recent times. The latter-day terrorists of al-Qaeda and other *jihadi* organizations can as easily be connected to the nihilist and terrorist movements of Tsarist Russia, or to the post-war groups that blurred the boundaries between legitimate national and social liberation struggles and terrorism, whether in Indo-China, Sri Lanka, Palestine, Peru, Algeria or Southern Africa.

The turn to violence from extreme Islamist groups is also symptomatic of an inability to address the problems of the Islamic world in the context of the traditional legacy of Islam. When all of Islamdom is seen to have surrendered to the ways of the modern world, the only open route to effect change becomes the political. When, for whatever reason, this is blocked, the recourse to violence becomes almost inevitable. But this is self-contradictory. The *tabula rasa* that extreme Islamists expect to find after their 'victory' is based on the denial of the existence of any vital aspects to Islam's legacy at present. In many ways, therefore, the recourse to terrorism in the name of a grand civilization confirms the disappearance of that civilization from the consciousness of the terrorists and their supporters. The last crisis of Islamic civilization are upon us.

Private Faith: Public Religiosity

Terrorists who use Islam as a political ideology and as a cover for their activities will probably be defeated in the near future. The combination of US military power and the national security and military apparatus of a range of countries will prevail over the threats posed by the likes of al-Qaeda and its *jihadi* offshoots. The political course of Islam will then revolve around two possible outcomes. The first are the on/off attempts to shrink Islam and relegate it to the private sphere and to resist or reject its spread, even in symbolic matters, into the political domain. In nations of the Muslim world where secularism has put down deep roots, whether Turkey or the former Soviet Central Asian republics, the public domain will not easily be given over to Islam. The electoral success of the Muslim democratic AK Party in Turkey has been met by a powerful counter-response from the secular establishment entrenched in the state bureaucracy and in the judiciary. The fracas over the wearing of headscarves by women students inside university campuses is an example of this. The AK Party used its huge parliamentary majority to reverse the ban on the wearing of head-scarves, only to see the state prosecutor counter with a lawsuit which demanded the dissolution of the party and the banning of its leaders – including the country's president and prime minister. Similarly, the fierce response by the leaders of Azerbaijan, Uzbekistan and Turkmenistan to any overt public manifestation of anything but a sanitized Islam is a reminder that decades of Soviet rule and Tsarist tutelage have created a powerful political class determined to keep Islam at bay.

In many of the democracies of western Europe a strong current is building up to reverse the multiculturalism which was the hallmark of post-war policies geared towards Muslim and other minorities. These policies by and large allowed the expression of Islamic sentiment and allegiance at the public level. Starting with the French ban on wearing head-scarves by Muslim schoolchildren, the new current has now extended to a variety of other aspects of public life for which exceptions were made or special privileges were allowed for the benefit of Muslims. Even in Britain, which still clings to a frayed version of multiculturalism, there are now serious doubts about the wisdom of allowing for Muslim 'exceptionalism' in social policies. For example, public outrage met the Archbishop of Canterbury's thoughtful comments about the possibility of adjusting family law for British Muslims so as to accommodate the Sharia's rulings on these matters. At the same time, there are now serious efforts, both in western Europe and in Turkey, to encourage a new reading of the Sharia, designed specifically to generate a 'moderate' version of the faith.

The ultimate purpose of the secularization of Islam would be to reduce its domain to the private sphere, as an individual faith, or at best a community faith. It might inform an individual's actions and decisions, but Islam will not form the basis of any ordering of society or politics. This will bring Islam to the same condition that other, non-established religions have in the modern world. In time, the singularity of Islam will disappear, and with it any possibility of its outer expression having any serious impact on the world at large. Islam would then lose whatever claim it might have to be the incubator of a unique form of a future civilization. Individual Muslims would then participate in a world which would carry no imprint of their religion. They might still claim the historical civilization of Islam as their patrimony, but Islam as such would not feature in the structuring of the outer world they dwell in. The world would have moved on, being driven by other forces, with which Islam has only a distant and tangential relation. Islam might influence individuals either as a moral guide or as a source of inspiration – for example, in specific art forms such as calligraphy or building decoration – but it will no longer define the Muslims' universe. A secularized Islam destroys the essential balance, inherent to Islam, between the individual and the collective.

The Islamization of public life in a large number of Muslim countries provides an opposite set of problems for the prospects for Islam as a civilization. The identification of the state with increased religiosity in the Muslim world has led to the adoption of official policies to promote the role of Islam in public life. However, this has been restricted to outer aspects such as religious observance and the encouragement of widespread conformity to an officially sanctioned form of Islam. The status of *ulemas* is enhanced; the patterns of the workplace are changed to accommodate the times of prayer; subtle pressures are applied to enforce a dress code on women; religious terms and invocations are included in all official functions. All these combine to create a powerful image of a society in which Islam is not only honoured but privileged. But these are, at best, incidental to the issue at hand; and, at worse, they produce a false appreciation of the significance of the Islamization of public life. Ostentatiously loud calls to prayer in the middle of a glittering shopping mall or supermarket cannot disguise the real fact that the markets people visit daily now follow models drawn from outside of Islam. Most banks in the Muslim world now have a special room for offering prayers. The irony is lost on most people that the very existence of interest-based financial institutions is deeply problematic in Islam. Adding a prayer room may be a sop to the religious sensibilities of the employees, but it does not eliminate the obvious contradiction. Encouraging women to wear the head-scarf as a sign of modesty and religious observance is completely negated by the spread of the designer *hijab* as a fashion statement. These conflicts and contradictions abound, but they only help to disguise the almost universal acknowledgement – albeit implicit – that the sources and models of change and development in these societies are now almost entirely based on standards that are incidental to Islam.

It is also unclear how the adoption of Sharia law will advance the cause of recreating the foundations of a new Islamic civilization. Sharia might allow Muslims to order their outer affairs and transactions according to a system that still commands a powerful legitimacy and has many adherents – possibly most of the world's Muslims. Many see it as the best chance for Muslim countries to eliminate despotic power and live under a legitimate rule of law. Recent surveys indicate that a good majority in countries as diverse as Egypt, Pakistan, and Jordan want Sharia as their only source of legislation.[1] Notwithstanding the immense problems in establishing the full gamut of Sharia law in countries and societies which have lived for decades outside of it, the issue of Sharia law affects only one aspect of Islamic civilization: the institutional framework of law-making, justice, politics and government. These issues are immensely significant, no doubt, but they are not the entire story of Islamic civilization. Sharia rule in Muslim countries might remould the forms in which some aspects of modern life is conducted, but it will not necessarily produce a new Islamic civilizational force.

Islam and an Alternative Modernity

All this would seem to indicate that Muslims may have abandoned the creative role Islam can play in mapping out a path for the future in all its manifestations. In many ways this would be a betrayal of Muslims' legacy and a terrible failure of imagination. All the great religious traditions are experiencing a reinvigorated engagement with the modern world – not so much to come to terms with it, but rather to address the huge range of problems that have arisen precisely because of it. In this field, Islam is noted for its absence. Muslims are, at best, bystanders in the great crises of the modern era – from the environmental risks the planet is running to the problems of overpopulation, impoverishment and mass migration. The leadership in tackling these issues is left to others, while Muslims remain mostly mute and ineffectual. There are extraordinary social reformers and visionaries in the Muslim world, for instance Abd el-Sattar Edhi and his emergency medical services in Pakistan, or Muhammad Yunus, the founder of Bangladesh's microfinance institution the Grameen Bank. However, these remain the exception rather than the rule.

But it is in these very areas that Islam can make a great impact on mankind as a whole and confirm its continuing relevance in the modern period. The fact that Islam did not participate in the evolution of modernity does not imply that it cannot participate, or even lead, in the resolution of the crises which are plaguing the world by positing an alternative vision for the future. This vision would be drawn from Islam's own essence as a religion, as a spiritualized world view and as a metaphysics which emphasizes the element of balance in the ordering of the lives and relationships of human beings. This aspect of Islam has been seriously overlooked in the modern period, as the Muslims have focused excessively on the issue of powerlessness and on the threats to the integrity of their religion. A great number of the social, economic and environmental ills that affect the world are related to the imbalances which have become intrinsic to the prevailing order. The dire predictions of the past – from the Malthusian nightmare of an overpopulation facing finite resources to the 1970s Club of Rome prognostications about the collapse of oil reserves – have so far proved to be baseless. Technological innovations and improvements in processes, techniques and management have played a crucial part in eliminating these risks, it is true, and technology may once again come to the rescue of mankind's excesses. But this time round the crisis is likely to be more dreadful.

There is growing recognition that over-reliance on technological advancement to resolve the outer manifestations of imbalances, without tackling their fundamental causes, may have run its course. It is inconceivable, for example, that the entire world can attain the present standards of consumption of the developed countries without a dramatic effect on the balance of resources, global warming and the distribution of wealth and income. If the entire population of China and India were to attain American standards of car ownership and energy consumption, the world's present reserves of oil, coal and iron ore would probably disappear very shortly thereafter. The planet would gradually become uninhabitable as the world's economic powers scramble to control its finite resources and demand the right to over-consume and over-exploit them. The economic growth that many developing countries have experienced over the past decade is at risk of being entirely wiped out by the sudden rise in commodity, raw material and fuel prices, and by the tsunami that has engulfed the global financial system. This augurs an increasing fragility and instability in the world economy. The situation cannot be rectified simply by assuming that market forces, by signalling the presence of scarcities and by directing resources to areas where these might represent a potential profit, will induce the requisite technological response to expand supply. The expectations of limitless material growth must be tempered by the imperative of managing the world's resources in a fair way and providing reasonable opportunity for the world's impoverished peoples to rise out of their unacceptable condition. The need to alter the perceptions and convictions of people about what constitutes the 'good life' therefore becomes almost a prerequisite to navigating through the crises the world is facing and to reaching a sustainable resolution for them.[2]

The stirrings of an alternative modernity are already evident. They go beyond the espousal by celebrities of fashionable global causes or the empty slogans which reduce the real distress of millions of people to the sound bites of marketers. The interconnectedness of things is becoming clearer as the world is knitted ever closer by the forces of globalization. Demand for fuel by very rapidly growing economies leads to sky-high oil prices; these prompt the developed world to push for bio-fuel subsidies; this in turn drives up worldwide grain prices; these cause food riots in poor countries; while oil-producers with scant populations pile up huge cash hordes for which they have no earthly use. (Their native populations already enjoy huge personal incomes, guaranteed emplyoment, free education and healthcare, and subsidized housing, all financed by a fraction of the oil revenues.)

The economic growth which has accompanied globalization begins to lose its lustre if the benefits are disproportionately distributed. In a 2005 report, the UN estimated that the income of the fifty richest people on earth is greater than that of the 400 million poorest. The examples can be multiplied. The mass rejection, from the modern mind-set, of the cardinal virtues, not least wisdom and moderation, seems to be complete. But the world cannot any more sustain the cult of the rampant individual, except at its peril. There are too many 'externalities' and costs for which other individuals, communities and countries have to pay the price. The model of the Promethean man, heroically challenging the gods and brooking no limits to his desires and their fulfilment, has to come to an end. The rugged, autonomous individual so beloved by liberal philosophers and by Hollywood movies simply cannot exist outside the virtuous community. And Islam would add that neither the individual nor the society can be whole if they are not infused with the sense of the transcendent. The wheel returns full-circle.

The Nature of Islam's Mystical Knowledge

The sense of the transcendent in Islam was always nurtured by the acknowledgement of the realities of mystical knowledge. The modern mind is sceptical and unable to grasp the structures of mystical knowledge. The same scepticism, if not downright hostility, towards Islam's legacy of mystical thought embraces modern-day Muslims, and this includes liberal, reformist or fundamentalist Muslims. Some formal lip-service may be paid to mystical knowledge, for no other reason than it belongs in the panoply of Islamic thought; it is in fact central to the understanding of Islam. The decline in the practice of Sufism and the distancing of the rationalizing Shia *mujtahids* from the esoteric aspects of Islam have pushed this knowledge to the outer periphery of Islamic consciousness. And it has remained there while Muslim intellectuals and scholars have tried reforming the Sharia or rationalizing Islamic consciousness as future pathways for Muslims.

There is, of course, a great deal of superstition, mythologizing and absurdities in the mystical currents in Islam, but these occur when tradition decays and loses its interpretative vitality. In a system of beliefs which rests ultimately on the human understanding of a divine text and on the revelatory experience, inspiration is an authentic source of interpretation and validation. The unseen cannot be approached solely by reason and authoritative textual interpretations. The fact that this current, which recognizes the transcendent, has been degraded over time does not alter this truth. Islam needs a new understanding of religion based on intuitive reasoning, precisely because the relevance of the religion will founder without it.

So a spiritualized language for Islam is essential if the creative potential is to be regained. For all its eclecticism, Iqbal's treatment of the dynamic self as seeking its freedom so as to perfect God's attributes offers an example of the type of spiritualized terminology that can draw nearer two different and hitherto incompatible understandings of human freedom. Such terminology can combine the heroic with the ethical in the same individual. But the quest for a spiritualized language for Islam must leap across centuries, since Islamic reformers and thinkers have almost ignored the possibility of reviving the mystical side of Islam. Unlike the voluminous writings on reforming the Sharia or rationalizing Islam, a lexicon of modern Islamic gnosis simply does not exist. It needs to be almost reinvented, as its categories, terms, concepts and meanings have languished except in very narrow philosophical circles and amongst a few of the cognoscenti who have a taste for this type of knowledge. It has not helped, either, that metaphysical Sufism, which is encompassed by this knowledge, has had a chequered history and is subject to periodic attacks from the clerical classes and the Wahhabi/Salafi community. But metaphysical Sufism can provide genuine insights into the nature of reality by cultivating a spirituality of the imagination.

The western tradition has left the mystical tradition behind in its attempt to dominate nature, but the 'imaginary' continues to exert a powerful attraction on the West, and not only through consciousness-raising methods such as meditation (or other self-awareness or self-realization techniques). The western experience has detached self-awareness from knowledge of God, partly because of the general hostility, suspicion and indifference to religious structures of thought. Self-knowledge movements have succeeded in attracting huge followings mainly because they do not claim to offer anything beyond the individual's own self-improvement through the adoption and practice of certain techniques. They have no serious social or collective effect.

The revival of the inner dimensions of Islam cannot be restricted to being simply a matter of method and technique, or the elaboration of an ideology of metaphysical spirituality. Knowledge of God is at the heart of the Islamic Sufi tradition, and its 'modernization' must acknowledge the prior existence of a visionary realm, where God's reality is also manifested. Access to, and understanding of, this realm has its own unique conceptual and linguistic tools and is essential for the evolution of this most ignored aspect of Islam.

The definition of Man in Islam's mystical tradition starts with the recognition that human beings combine in their persons opposing characteristics.

Humans are spiritual as well as corporeal; luminous and dense; subtle and gross; creative and destructive. Which aspect prevails is directly related to the goals and choices that human beings assign for themselves as they progress through life. They start in a condition of ignorance, but can realize a potential for knowledge; they may be despicable and mean, but have the capability of being generous and magnanimous. Their beginning and end is determined by the inevitability of certain death, but also by the choices they make between their caprices and desires on the one hand and the attainment of God's attributes on the other. On the one hand, a human being is no different from an animal; on the other, he or she can aspire to the highest forms of knowledge. The range of options is infinite, as are the possible outcomes; but the true seeker knows that, in the end, perfecting the qualities of God within oneself is the sole purpose of existence.

These qualities or attributes are built in, as it were, into human primordial nature, a type of spiritual DNA. It is only by actualizing these qualities in an arc of spiritual ascent during one's lifetime that human beings can partake in the fullness of existence. Achieving such states, or doing good, becomes a fundamental part of realizing the potentially divine within the human being. This is the definition of what constitutes a full human being (rather than solely the sentient and rational being of the humanists or the philosophers). These traits cannot be acquired, since they are already there, inside. Virtues are not immutable ethical principles that co-exist alongside human beings. They represent the essence of the encounter between Man and God, and they are the bridge that connects the human with the divine. But, while they are imprinted into the fabric of a human being, they stay latent until they are activated by the individual's striving to realize and perfect them. Ethical action, therefore, is not divinely ordained; rather, the divine reality is reached through ethical action. If one seeks to reach God, then one must act ethically.

The ethics of spiritualized Islam are based on a foundation of courtesy and modesty; courtesy towards the names and attributes of God, modesty in terms of the individual's affirmation that these traits are God's alone. A person can aspire to perfect them, but their full measure will always belong to God alone. Some of God's attributes cannot be reproduced in the human – for instance, His oneness or His everlastingness. Others are, such as mercy, compassion, gentleness and beauty. Courtesy regarding God's attributes also implies recognition of their hierarchical nature: mercy precedes wrath; knowledge precedes action, and so on. The significance of courtesy lies in its being not only a guide to human action but also in its scaling of justice where fairness, clemency and punishment must be balanced appropriately.

Nevertheless, the moral drive which generates the actions of the ethical human being cannot be left unregulated and entirely answerable to reason or whim. The Sharia – in the broadest sense of the word – becomes the means to effect a true and lasting guidance for the ethical individual. The word 'Sharia' is derived from the Arabic root word *shar'*, which means road or path; so the Sharia is, etymologically, the pathway to guidance and felicity. For the spiritualized Muslim, the Sharia is not limited to formal rules and strictures. It is the path of prophets, messengers and friends of God. They have mapped the right roads to follow and the wrong roads to avoid. In fact, the search for the correct path to follow is an inner, primordial impulse that exists alongside the latent noble character traits of God in the human being. It must also emerge as part of the full spiritual flowering of a human being. Man seeks justice to perfect God's trait of being the All-Just, but must also seek the correct course through the minefields of the outer world. Human beings can easily be overwhelmed and surrender to the turmoil in the outer world, where conflict, doubt, uncertainty and ambiguity seem to prevail.

The Decay of Islamic Spirituality

The erosion of ethical consciousness in Muslims is due to the weakening of systems which nurtured and protected this consciousness. Apart from the bedrock of the Muslim family, which always acted as the upholder and transmitter of ethical traditions, the social organizations of Muslims at work and worship were also instrumental in providing the scaffolding for their ethical universe. These organizations were not entirely Sufi in form, but most had incorporated the significance of perfecting moral characteristics, though in a vague and unsystematic manner. The remnants of the natural courtesy, generosity and concern for others that are still evident in certain urban classes in the Muslim world are a faint echo of that widespread condition well into recent times. The disorientation resulting from an opposition between the requirements for success (or just survival) in the modern world and the need to maintain an inner moral balance demanded by the religion of Islam has not been successfully mediated. The outer rules of the Sharia – whether modernized or not – or the acceptance of modern norms and values by a rationalizing Islam do not provide the moral compass which can keep Muslims on an even keel. The imbalance frequently leads to despair and violence, or to a lingering sense of personal betrayal of one's traditions and values. Nihilism, reactionary thinking and rigid conservatism are born out of this anxious state of being.

The conservatives, modernists and rationalists in Islam have always looked askance at the spiritual quest of individual Muslims. When seen through the prism of the rationalists, mysticisim is a false system of thought based on superstition, hallucinations, mythologizing and unsubstantiated states and experiences which border on the insane. Modernists see in the aspects of folk Islam the worse kind of primitiveness, mass indoctrination and reasons for a severe embarrassment to their claims of Islam's compatibility with the modern world. Political Islamists follow in the queue of their virulent anti-Sufi predecessors and see in the traditional orders vestiges of antique systems which often follow hereditary leaders and stand in the way of their own totalizing ideologies. Conservatives are fearful of the claim to an inner authority, which supersedes the Sharia and may lead to lax religious practices and dissoluteness. The role of the guiding sheikh in the life of the Sufi orders also creates a parallel religious authority structure to the traditional *ulema* classes.

There was no doubt that the Sufi orders, with a few exceptions, atrophied and sank far below their ideal, and there was an element of truth in all these critiques. Together they have seriously undermined the legitimacy and pertinence of the traditional Sufi orders – though not of Sufism as a reflector of the inner dimensions of Islam. Although the traditional Sufi orders may be well past their prime as a vehicle for spiritualizing the masses, the deeper yearning which they had earlier addressed still remains. In fact it may well have increased, as ex-Islamists join lapsed Muslims fleeing to avoid the ravages of modern hyper-competitive life and look for a home in the spiritual universe. The loss of an outer spiritual reality has not yet fully erased its inner consciousness.

However, the present age cannot easily admit to the validity of this type of knowledge and requires a confirmation that goes beyond the assertion of its traditional tenets. This applies to human beings generally and to modern Muslims in particular. The collapse of totalitarian systems has been equated with the victory of reason over irrationalism – what the social philosopher Karl Popper called 'the most important intellectual, and perhaps even moral, issue of our time': whether reason takes precedence over emotions and passions as the mainsprings of human action. The type of knowledge embodied in intuition, inspiration and guidance is firmly of the non-rational kind, one that cannot be subject to the empirical tests of scientific inquiry or to the rationalizing logic of the intellect. In consequence, it has been relegated to the outer circles of mystical pseudo-knowledge and denied legitimacy as a tool for understanding the world and humans' place in it. The prejudice runs deep and crosses cultures and civilizations.

Knowledge of the unseen in Islam is not a revolt against reason in the same manner, for example, like racist or nationalist philosophies. It never claims to have the total truth but only one aspect of it, whose mastery is necessary in order to complete the human potential to understand the divine. The mysticism which the rationalists scoff at aims to establish the validity of this form of knowledge. It is placed in the same category as, for example, Platonic idealism, and is dismissed as an escapist fantasy with no bearing on humanity's condition or travails. Islamic spirituality is not an exclusivist matter, in spite of the claims of some savants and mystics that it is indeed a superior form of knowledge. No true master of the path would make such a claim. It is a knowledge for which certain people have a profound taste, but their commitment to it does not necessarily lead to their denial of other forms of knowledge.

The western bias against irrational thinking, into which mystical knowledge is lumped, is based on the latter's emotive and passionate content. Once again, Islamic inner spirituality has little to do with emotion and passion, but a lot to do with the systematic striving for an understanding of the attributes of God and the imperative of moral conduct that such seeking generates. The outer forms of the ecstatic states of the Sufis may reflect an inner 'drunkenness', a spiritual intoxication, but this is not the path towards knowledge of God. It may lead to the experience of the unseen, but this is a uniquely individual act, of little or no social consequence. True spiritual knowledge presupposes that individual self-realization is only a transit station to social action.

The Tripod of Islam

The three fields of knowledge in Islam – the knowledge of the inner way, the knowledge of outer realities and the knowledge that connects the two – meld into each other but maintain their distinctness. None can claim an exclusivity or priority over the other, and none by itself is capable of rendering or understanding the truth. The subtlety of this relationship is embedded in Islam, and, according to Islam, in all the great religious traditions of mankind. All three balls have to be kept up in the air all the time. The comprehending, balanced and ethical human being realizes this in his or her knowledge, conduct and actions. The system of argumentation which is critical of rational thinking may be valid for, or within, one aspect of the tripod of knowledge, but it dissolves the connecting thread between the three fields if it is given absolute precedence. This phenomenon is akin to the process of observation in quantum mechanical systems. The very act of observation or measurement changes the initial conditions of the system and renders the results incomplete or indeterminate. Isolating one of the tripods for critical investigation may yield results for that particular field of knowledge but not for the whole, unless knowledge of the whole infuses the process. Keeping one's eye on one ball while being aware of the relative position of all three balls to each other keeps the system afloat.

The unifying tendencies of Islam are not the same as the grand totalizing schemes of philosophers or political theorists. Islam is not an 'idea' that can be put alongside others, such as the Platonic Ideals or the Hegelian Spirit or the Nation. Neither is it a rationalist perspective on man and society which might be compared and contrasted to other empirical or rationalist theories. Society has a reality in Islam, for example, and is not a set of interpersonal relationships based solely on the fact of individuals dealing with each other. The absurd statement of Margaret Thatcher, Britain's prime minister in the 1980s, that ' . . . there is no such thing as society. There are individual men and women, and there are families', has no echo in Islam because, while partially true – all groups are composed of individuals – it destroys that truth by conflating an aspect of it with the whole. Similarly, a collective or idealist definition of truth is necessarily incomplete, and can be often tyrannical. It destroys the possibility of an individual's autonomy for freedom of action.

Islam's would-be reformers have fallen into the very same trap when they focus on an aspect of Islam and claim that its overhaul, re-reading or reinterpretation will create the conditions for the elevation of Muslims. That does not invalidate the critical examination of Islam's legacies but it limits its interpretative potential. Once this limited methodology for assessing Islam's legacy becomes the norm, it will hold no brief for its better understanding or practice. Islam will cease to be *the* reality for Muslims and become yet another system of belief or reasoning. A knowledge, or at least an awareness, of the comprehensive nature of Islamic knowledge should be a precondition for the investigation of the nature of Islam. Al-Ghazzali understood this and tried to reflect it in his synthesis. Of course, the scope and scale of knowledge is vastly greater now than it was in the medieval Islamic period, but this does not vitiate the need to be aware of the present state of knowledge. In fact it makes it even more vital.

However, the starting point for reinventing Islamic civilization must be the independent existence of a uniquely Islamic interpretation of the world, with an ethics rooted in the religion of Islam at the base of the rebirth of Islamic civilization. The nature of knowledge becomes not just a scholarly or philosophical subject but one that goes to the heart of the matter. A literalist faith almost automatically denies the validity of knowledge which emanates from traditions that do not acknowledge the same foundations. Islamic culture then becomes almost parasitic, unable to contribute to the betterment of humankind, yet a consumer of the products and services of others while it smugly asserts its 'superiority'.

This is not far from the vision – and reality – of the Salafist literalists and their *jihadi* fringe. A 'liberal' Islam, on the other hand, is a curious amalgam of western norms and values with their ever-changing composition and a private spirituality which follows, selectively, esoteric aspects of Islam. This kind of Islam is in reality a part of the western tradition – a religion that is not much different from the 'westernization' of other world faiths (for instance, Buddhism in the West). It is unfortunate that such an Islam is frequently conflated with Sufism, which, in the West at least, has become an almost separate religion or cult, as its Sharia aspects are allowed to atrophy.

The Recovery of the Transcendent

Traditional Islam spoke of the three dimensions of the religion: *Islam, Iman, Ihsan*, that is, 'good works', 'faith' and the 'perfection of qualities'. They are based on the *Hadith* of the Prophet's encounter with Gabriel, from which also emerged the classic formulation of the 'five pillars' of Islam: prayer, fasting, *zakat*, hajj, and enjoining the good and prohibiting evil. Essentially, these pillars gave the Muslim's world an outer, institutional and legal, framework; a doctrinal and theological basis for religious belief; and, finally, an inner spiritual journey where the virtues were cultivated and direct experience of the transcendent was sought. The inner dimensions of Islam are in reality little different from those of other great religious traditions, especially the Abrahamaic faiths. The world view and practices of a Christian monastic would not differ, in substance, from those of his or her Muslim counterpart. But in Islam these elements of the religion must be aspects of a single whole and not compartmentalized and separated as secular modernity would demand.

The effects of the tumultuous changes which have engulfed the Muslim world in recent times may not have sundered the interconnectedness of these aspects of Islam, but they have certainly muddled and weakened them. Most Muslims would fiercely affirm their faith – an open assertion of atheism or even agnosticism in the Muslim world is still extremely rare. At the same time, the majority of Muslims – at least those that have been exposed to a secular education and a modern lifestyle – do not make an easy connection between the sacred and the world around them. The Islamists are no better in this regard than the arch-modernists. Both are embarrassed by, or overlook, the significance of the unseen in Muslim consciousness and in the construction of Islam's world view. In fact the entire Quranic revelation is addressed to 'those who believe in the Unseen'.[3] If one does not believe in the unseen, it is difficult to see how one can claim to reconstruct an Islamic civilization.

Most people automatically equate the sense of the transcendent with the type of overtly religious societies which have been rejected in the West. This experience, whether in Europe of America, has not been a generally happy one. The examples of an overbearing priesthood, a prim and hypocritical public piety, rigid conformity in personal and social behaviour, conjure up all that is antithetical to the free human spirit. Very few people in the West have any hankering for the Puritan world of seventeenth-century Massachusetts, the priggish bourgeois life of mid-Victorian England, or the stifling official religiosity of Franco's Spain. But the experience of the transcendent in Islamic society, at least up to the modern period, is in no way comparable to that of the West since the Renaissance. Islamic society was not structured along officially religious lines in the conventional sense of the word. The closest approximations to such a society in the western experience were probably the traditional societies of medieval Europe, where the sacred was fused into the ordinary lives of people.

Modernity did not affect Islam just by separating state from religion, but also by reducing the natural sense of the sacred in people's daily lives. The secular elites in the Muslim world behave no differently from their western counterparts in their ambivalence or hostility to increasing the role of religion in society. Even the terms of disdain and opprobrium used to describe such a possibility draw from the western experience. 'Fundamentalism', 'a return to the Dark Ages', and other such terms and phrases, are liberally used to describe the increased religiosity of Muslim society, even when they have no referents in the Islamic tradition. Nevertheless, these categories have stuck and basically define the debate, as Muslims have become increasingly distant from experiencing the transcendent in their world.

The recovery of the sacred, which is integral to any hope for the recovery of Islamic civilization, revolves around the notion of *ihsan*, the third essential dimension of Islam. In the sensibility of the times, this might veer towards tedious or sanctimonious moralizing, but *ihsan* has nothing to do with controlling or moulding outer forms of behaviour. It is a conscious pursuit on the part of the individual to perfect virtuous qualities which are associated with the inner spiritual journey. This pursuit was undertaken in the past through affiliation to the various Sufi *tariqas*, which had millions of adherents and adepts, or, in the Shia lands, through the more individualist and even solitary path of *irfan*, the metaphysical form of Sufism, which was acceptable to the Shia consciousness. The *tariqas* cannot be compared to the monastic orders of Christianity, if only because of their scale and ubiquity in Islamic public life. The modernist and Islamist assault on the spiritual paths of Islam destroyed a crucial form of organization which had encouraged the inculcation of moral qualities in the mass of the population as well as in the elites. It was not replaced with anything better than just an alternative: of either a dry 'rationalist' or scholastic Islam, or the doubts and moral ambiguities which are a feature of secular life. The *ihsan* aspect of Islam was degraded over time and, with it, nearly all the features of Islamic life that were marked by charitable works, communal solidarity and social concern.

The social action wings of Islamist parties subordinate their work to the overall political imperative of their parties, which ultimately revolve around power and the establishment of some form of an Islamic state. However, there are two notable examples of socially-oriented Islamic movements which have overtly eschewed politics but have nevertheless been very successful over the past decades in developing a mass following. Both aim to rebuild the bases of Islamic moral action, but from entirely different, if not antithetical, perspectives. The first is the Tablighi Jamaat, a movement first launched in North India in 1925 by the cleric Maulana Muhammad Ilyas. Its original intent was to strengthen the Islamic identity of lapsed Indian Muslims and to counter the syncretic tendencies in Indian Islam. In 1946 it began to expand internationally under the guidance of Ilyas's son, Maulana Muhammad Yusuf, targeting the growing South Asian Muslim diasporas in Europe, the Middle East and North America.[4]

The Tablighi Jamaat's main purpose has been to inculcate in its followers a commitment to living a life that is as closely patterned on the early Muslims as possible. Through their dress, their grooming, their strict devotion to the rituals of Islamic piety and an ascetic moral and family code, they seek to inspire in their adherents an absolute commitment to Islam as a way of life. The organization works through loose networks of various sized groups, who undertake proselytizing missions to spread the message of Islam in neighbourhoods, towns and entire countries, in South Asia, South Africa, and the Middle East and, increasingly, in the West. The movement's main international headquarters is now in Britain. Those who in one way or another have been influenced by the Tablighi Jamaat and its 'six principles' now number millions – mainly from the better-educated members of society. The group itself has not escaped its share of controversy, particularly in the post 9/11 environment. Some critics have gone so far as to see in the Tablighi Jamaat a source of radicalization, even a preparatory school for *jihadists*. Others, including Graham Fuller, a former CIA analyst and RAND scholar, consider the organization to be a 'peaceful and apolitical preaching-to-the-people movement'.

The other purportedly non-political group that has achieved a huge following, especially in Turkey and the Turkic-speaking world, is the educational and social reform movement associated with Fethullah Gülen.[5] Gülen, a follower in his youth of Said Nursi, was a former functionary in the state religious bureaucracy. He left it to develop his philosophy of Islamic activism, based on the three mobilizing concepts of *hizmet* (service to country and society); *ikhlas* (sincerity in action) and *himmet* (sensitivity and concern in thought and action). In many ways this movement stands in diametric contrast to the Tablighi Jamaat in its indifference to traditionalism and open missionary work for Islam. The Gülen movement, which had started as a youth-oriented moral regeneration and religious activist movement in the 1960s, began to focus on establishing a stronghold in the educational system of Turkey. This was opened up to the private sector in the early 1980s. Gülen's emphasis has been on tolerance and the openness of Islam to modernity, liberal capitalism and technological progress. His message has resonated with the religiously minded middle classes that are seeking an alternative to both the Islam of the traditional scholars and the aggressive secularism of the state and the country's commercial and cultural elite. Backed by the considerable resources of pious, newly wealthy entrepreneurs and businessmen from Turkey's interior, the Gülen movement has influenced Turkey's media and secondary education. The movement has also been instrumental in organizing powerful business and commercial networks that often stand in opposition to Turkey's western-oriented business groups.

Organizations such as the Tablighi Jamaat and the Gülen movement can provide a moral re-anchoring for Muslims and act as bridges to, or ramparts against, the modern world. But no modern mass movement in Islam has been able to fill the void left by the decay of the classic Sufi and Futuwwa orders that seamlessly integrated the sacred with the profane in the quotidian experience of a huge number of people.[6] While a patchy revitalization of some Sufi orders appears to be taking place, they still have to contend with a weighty historical legacy that limits their adaptability and appeal. The Futuwwa orders, however, have virtually disappeared as a factor in the lives of working Muslims. Their replacement by a modern equivalent would probably be an essential prerequisite for the weaving of Islamic norms back into the meaning and purpose of work. A reaction of sorts has settled in over the past two decades, but the landscape of most Muslim countries is dominated by a shocking disregard for the public good and by chaotic individualism.

What do Muslims want?

In a 2005 poll conducted by the Pew Research Centre on 'Islamic extremism', large majorities of Muslims in countries as diverse as Pakistan (79 per cent), Morocco (70 per cent) and Jordan (63 per cent) viewed themselves as Muslims rather than citizens of their nation–states. Even in countries such as Turkey with its long secular history as a nation–state, 43 per cent viewed themselves as Muslims in the first place, although 29 per cent saw themselves as citizens of the nation–state. Large majorities also welcomed the increasing role of Islam in their societies as well as in politics. Various surveys have also confirmed that the angst Muslims feel is related more to the loss of authenticity in their lives, a sense that 'immorality' is increasing and a concern about western influence in their societies rather than to a desire simply to turn to Islam because of political oppression or autocratic rule.

The majority of Muslims continue to resist a wholesale capitulation to the standards and values of modern western societies, but without knowing precisely what their resistance actually implies. The conflicts emerging from an inner ambiguity directed towards the norms of the modern world and an outer life which is inescapably dominated by these norms have not been either easily or successfully resolved. Nearly everything conspires to make the process of adjustment and adaptation difficult and strewn with problems. The certainty of Islam becomes the only lasting element that is seen to be reliable and consistent. It is still embedded in the collective unconscious of all Muslims. In this lies a vital contradiction. Islam offers an inner certainty to Muslims, but its outer expression as a civilization has been severely curtailed or abandoned. The inherent equilibrium demanded by Islam between the Muslim's inner and outer lives has been disrupted.

So the entire argument as to whether Islam is in conflict with modernity or vice versa is false. The issue is whether Muslims want to create and dwell in a civilizational space which grows out of their own beliefs without disrupting the world of others. This alternative world may be entirely different from that which exists in terms of its structures, demands, values and expectations, or it may be similar to it in parts. Muslims can continue to rail against the excesses of the modern condition, but their objections are useless if their daily lives and aspirations are only a minor variant of the global standard. Given enough time, the ways of the modern world will indeed prevail, notwithstanding the two centuries of rearguard actions on the part of Muslims. The revolt of Islam is doomed to fail if it does not find an outer expression of the faith at all the levels of civilization.

The axiomatic rule is that the gross will prevail over the subtle. The quest for continuous material improvement, a rising standard of living, and an almost fetishistic belief in the power of science and technology is now a nearly universal condition. It underlines the actions of individuals, societies and states. The effects of these factors on religious belief were understood a long time ago. John Wesley, the great eighteenth-century Christian reformer, wrote of 'the continual decay of pure religion ... Wherever riches have increased, the essence of religion has decreased in the same proportion. For religion must necessarily produce both industry and frugality, and these cannot but produce riches. But as riches increase, so will pride, anger and love of the world in all its branches.'[7] The cardinal virtues cease to be social virtues in practice and are reduced to a personal ethics. The response in the West has been to accept the process of secularization as an inevitable consequence of the general increase in wealth and power. The same recipe is now being offered to Islam. Reformers, both in the Muslim world and outside, are, in effect, calling for a 'Christianization' of Islam, a final break between the sacred and the profane in the world of Islam.

The reformers are at least honest in that they forthrightly call for the wholesale adoption of the institutions and processes of modern technological societies. Nevertheless, their vision of Islamic civilization is an empty one – a vague spirituality wafting over a society with a deceptive cultural distinctiveness, one which has effectively merged with the dominant order. Radical Islamists, and even the rank-and-file of 'rationalist' Muslims, suffer from a different conceit, namely that, by picking and choosing from the menu of change, a happy compromise between Islam and what is acceptable from modernity can be fashioned. Change will be run through the filter of Sharia and what is acceptable will be embraced, while what is not will be rejected. This approach, which has been entertained for over a century, has neither produced satisfactory material progress nor strengthened the foundations of Islamic civilization in any way. The fundamental conundrum for all such rationalists and radicals is that the change they are facing is a product of a different and ascendant civilizational order. It can only be internalized successfully if it is refashioned, and then transcended, in a uniquely Islamic framework. The absorption of the legacies of the Byzantines and Persians and their transformation in their encounter with Islam could not have taken place within the world of the Abbasids, were Islam in a subordinate or inferior position to these civilizations.

If Muslims want the very things that modern technological civilization promises and in some cases has delivered, they have to acknowledge the roots of this civilization in order to become an active and creative part of it. Otherwise they will simply be a parasitic attachment to it. It is difficult to see how Islam can contribute to this civilization while rejecting or questioning its premises. If it accepts its premises, then the best that Muslims can do is to 'package' the final products of their civilization in ways which may be culturally or politically acceptable to their own societies. They can even participate in the dominant civilizational order and accept the risks that it might fatally undermine whatever is left of Muslims' basic identity and autonomy. This appears to be the path that the richer societies of the Muslim world have chosen for themselves. The Gulf countries' exuberant embrace of a frantic hyper-modernity only scantily garbed in Islamic idioms is the best example of this. The same path also appeals to the westernized professional classes, who view their Islam as an inoffensive but distinguishing cultural ornament.

However, if Muslims want to live an outer life which is an expression of their innermost faith, they have to reclaim those parts of their public spaces which have been conceded to other world views over the past centuries. A new Islamic civilization can only be carved out from a harsh reality of years of inactivity, lassitude and indifference. And, if it is to be achieved, this will be only after overcoming conditions of great imbalance and adversity. The creative impulses of civilization are now all in the domain of another world order. The challenges are not insurmountable, but they will test to limit Muslims' commitment to Islam as a complete way of life.

If Muslims do not muster the inner resources of their faith to fashion a civilizing outer presence, then Islam as a civilization may indeed disappear. The future may be marked with scattered rebellions of disaffected Muslims, but these will weaken in their intensity and scope. In time, the adjustments, compromises, and expediencies which have marked each Muslim generation's encounter with a world dominated first by the West and now, increasingly, by impersonal technological and market forces will chip away at the possibility of regenerating an Islamic civilization. Islam will simply be another motif in a consumer-driven, self-obsessed, short attention-span global culture; another 'player' in the marketplace for ideas and religions. The retreat of Islam into the private, individual sphere will be complete. The much heralded Islamic 'awakening' of recent times will not be a prelude to the rebirth of an Islamic civilization; it will be another episode in its decline. The revolt of Islam becomes instead the final act of the end of a civilization.

Notes

Prologue: The Axes of Islamic Civilization

1. The report entitled 'Inequality in Asia' can be accessed from the Asian Development Bank website, www.adb.org.
2. Quoted in Pankaj Mishra, *Temptation of the West: How to be Modern in India, Pakistan and Beyond* (Picador: London, 2006), p. 111. Mishra gives a brilliant analysis of the rise of extreme Hindu nationalism (pp. 107–51). He provides a vivid description of the events leading to the frightful massacres in the wake of the destruction of the Babri mosque in Ayodhya in December 1992 and the more targeted pogroms against Muslims in Gujarat in 2002, in which thousands were killed. Edward Luce's book, *In Spite of the Gods: The Strange Rise of Modern India* (Abacus: London, 2006) also covers in detail the profound anti-Muslim strain in modern Hindu nationalism. Luce was the South Asia bureau chief of the London *Financial Times* between 2001 and 2005.
3. Quoted in Denis Judd, *Empire: The British Imperial Experience From 1765 to the Present* (HarperCollins: London, 1996), p. 97.
4. From Ibn Hazm's *Al-Akhlaq*, quoted in Muhammad Abu Laylah *In Pursuit of Virtue: The Moral Theology and Psychology of Ibn Hazm al-Andalusi* (TaHa Publishers: London, 1990).
5. The French philosopher Bertrand de Jouvenel (1903–87) was a profound critic of the modern concept of the autonomous individual, beholden neither to a higher moral law nor to a spiritual legacy. His most famous work was *Du pouvoir*, written in 1945. Bertrand de Jouvenel, *On Power: The Natural History of Its Growth*, Translated by J. F. Huntington (Liberty Fund: Indianapolis, 1993).
6. Muhammad Iqbal, *Shikwa and Jawab-i-Shikwa*, translated by K. Singh (Oxford University Press, Oxford India Paper book: Delhi, 1981), p. 34.

Chapter 1: Tearing the Fabric

1. The collapse of the Mayas has intrigued many people, captivated as they were by images of huge temples swallowed up by the jungle. The most recent evidence suggests that Maya civilization succumbed to environmental degradation and overpopulation. See David L. Webster, *The Fall of the Ancient Maya: Solving the Mystery of the Maya Collapse* (Thames and Hudson: London, 2002).

2. 'Carthage must be destroyed.' Although Carthage was utterly ruined, it has not been erased from western consciousness; it features in historical novels, in operas and in a number of Turner's paintings.

3. 'Islamicate' is a term coined by the historian Marshall Hodgson in his monumental three-volume work *Venture of Islam*, first published in the 1970s.

4. See Bernard Lewis, 'The Roots of Muslim Rage', *Atlantic Monthly*, September 1990.

5. See Martin van Bruinessen, 'The Tariqa Khalwatiyya in South Celebes', in H. A. Poeze and P. Schoorl (eds), *Excursies in Celebes. Ein Gundel Gijdraqen bij het ofschied van J. Noorduyn* (KITLV: Leiden, 1991).

6. The expulsion of the Muslims from Spain took place in stages, over a century after the fall of Granada in 1492, and culminated in an edict of 1609 expelling the last remaining 'secret' Muslims (or *Moriscos*) to North Africa. The Jews fared worse. They were given four months to leave Spain after the fall of Granada. The total number of Muslims expelled over the period amounted to some two million. The number of Jews expelled was around 100,000.

7. The ethnic cleansing of former Ottoman lands is a greatly under-reported tragedy. The historian Justin McCarthy has exposed the scale of the disasters that befell Muslims after the loss of Ottoman territory in the Balkans and in the Caucasus. By his reckoning, nearly five million Muslims died in these events and another five million were expelled to Turkey. See Justin McCarthy, *Death and Exile: The Ethnic Cleansing of Ottoman Muslims 1821–1922* (Darwin Press: Princeton, NJ, 1995).

8. See Nikki R. Keddie: *Sayyid Jamal ad-Din 'al-Afghani': A Political Biography* (University of California Press: Berkeley, California, 1972), p. 107.

9. The wars of Abd el-Qadir against the French are well researched and documented, especially by Algerian and French scholars and writers. One of the best works in English on the life of Abd el-Qadir was written by a contemporary, Charles Henry Churchill, who had met Abd el-Qadir during the latter's exile in Syria. The book, *The Life of Abdel Kader, Ex-Sultan of the Arabs of Algeria* (Chapman and Hall: London, 1867), is now out of print. A more recent work is that of Raphael Danziger, *Abd al-Qadir and the Algerians – Resistance to the French and Internal Consolidation* (Holmes & Meier Publications Inc.: New York, 1977).

10. Quoted in Churchill, *Life of Abdel Kader* (above, n. 9).

11. The spiritual life of Abd el-Qadir is frequently and deliberately overlooked by political Islamists, especially as it was profoundly affected by the metaphysical Sufism of Ibn al'Arabi. Islamists generally abhor Ibn al'Arabi and are deeply suspicious of Sufism. The French academic Michel Chodkiewicz has compiled some of Abd el-Qadir's spiritual commentaries in his book *The Spiritual Writings of Amir 'Abd al-Kader* (SUNY Press: Albany, New York, 1995). Dr Reza Shah-Kazemi, an academic and research associate at the Institute of Ismaili Studies has written a remarkable essay on the relationship between true *Jihad* and the spiritual masters of Islam, with a special emphasis on Abd el-Qadir. The essay can be found in Joseph E. B. Lumbard, ed., *Islam, Fundamentalism and the Betrayal of Tradition* (World Wisdom, Bloomington: Indiana, 2004), ch. 4, pp. 121–43. See also www.sacredweb.com.

12. Quoted in Michel Chodkiewicz, *Spiritual Writings* (above, n. 11), pp. 2–4.

13. See Leila Tarazi Fawaz, *An Occasion for War: Civil Conflict in Lebanon and Damascus in 1860* (University of California Press: Berkeley, California, 1994), especially chapters 4–6.

14. From Ibn al-Arabi's *The Tarjuman al-Ashwaq: A Collection of Mystical Odes*, translated by Reynold A. Nicholson in 1911 (Theosophical Publishing House: London, reprinted by Beshara Publications) in 1977.

15. Churchill, *Life of Abdel Kader* (above, n. 9).

16. Paradoxically, the ire of modernist Algerian scholars was targeted at the Sufi order associated with the Sheikh Ahmad bin Alawi. The latter was a prime influence on a number of prominent European converts to Islam such as the British Museum manuscripts curator, the late Martin Lings.

17. A comprehensive history of Egypt in the first half of the nineteenth century is the study by Afaf Lutfi al-Sayyid Marsot, *Egypt in the Reign of Muhammad Ali* (Cambridge University Press: Cambridge, 1984).

18. An excellent economic history of Japan during this period is that of William W. Lockwood, *The Economic Development of Japan: Growth and Structural Change 1868–1938* (Princeton University Press: Princeton, New Jersey, 1954). A more recent general study is that of W. J. Macpherson, *The Economic Development of Japan, 1868–1941* (Cambridge University Press: Cambridge, 1987).

19. Nikki R. Keddie, *Sayyid Jamal ad-Din 'al-Afghani'* (above, n. 8), p. 193.

20. The Abduh *fatwa* has gained considerable notoriety. Although it came in response to a specific question regarding the permissibility of paying interest on deposits in the government-owned post office system, it was interpreted by commercial interests as authorizing the formation of modern commercial banks.

21. A good general history of the course of Islam in West Africa is that of J. Spenser Trimingham, *A History of Islam in West Africa* (Oxford University Press: New York, 1962).

22. See Francis Robinson, *Atlas of the Islamic World since 1500* (Phaidon Press: Oxford, 1982), pp. 110–30.

23. Hanbalism is one of the four orthodox schools of Sunni Islam, and also the smallest in terms of numbers of adherents.

24. The difficulties inherent in trying to be both 'Islamic' and 'modern' can be seen in the evolution of the Aligarh Muslim University. See David Lelyveld, *Aligarh's First Generation: Muslim Solidarity in British India* (Oxford University Press: Delhi, 1996). Lelyveld tellingly concludes: 'By oversimplifying the compatibility of [Muslim identity] with the institutions of a large scale, plural society, the founders and alumni of the college failed to discover the basis of a new social order or the full inspiration of an ancient ideal.'

Chapter 2: The Break with the Past

1. *Disorienting Encounters: Travels of A Moroccan Scholar in France in 1845–1846. The Voyage of Muhammad as-Saffar*, translated and edited by Susan Gilson Miller (University of California Press: Berkeley, California, 1992), pp. 193–4.

2. See, for example, Marshall G. S. Hodgson, *Rethinking World History: Essays on Europe, Islam and World History* (Cambridge University Press: Cambridge, 1993), especially ch. 7, 'The role of Islam in world history'. Also Fernand Braudel, *The Wheels of Commerce: Civilization and Capitalism: 15th–18th Century, Vol. 2* (HarperCollins: London 1982) and *The Mediterranenan and the Mediterranean World in the Age of Philip II*, Vols 1–2 (Fontana/Collins: London, 1972). For the later stages of Islamic mercantile history, see Bruce Masters, *The Origins of Western Economic Dominance in the Middle East: Mercantilism and the Islamic Economy in Aleppo, 1600–1750* (NYU Press: New York, 1988). An excellent general economic history of the modern Middle East is Roger Owen, *The Middle East in the World Economy 1800–1914* (I. B. Tauris: London, 1993).

3. See Francis Robinson, *Separatism among Indian Muslims: The Politics of the United Provinces' Muslims 1860–1923* (Oxford University Press: Delhi, 1993) on the Muslim landlords of North India (especially ch. 1).

4. See the entry on '*Futuwwa*' in the monumental *Encyclopaedia of Islam*, Vol. II, C–G (Brill: Leiden, 1991). The institution of the Zurkhana ('House of Strength'), for example, which combined callisthenics with devotional exercises, was widespread in the central Islamic lands, from Iraq to the Indian sub-continent. It has practically disappeared in the Muslim world, except in Iran, where it still survives in some fashion.

5. An excellent English-language biography of Ernst Renan is that of David C. J. Lee, *Ernest Renan: In the Shadow of Faith* (Duckworth: London, 1996).

6. Ernst Renan, 'What is a Nation?', in Geoff Eley and Ronald Grigor Suny, eds, *Becoming National: A Reader* (Oxford University Press: Oxford, 1996), pp. 41–55. See especially pp. 52–54.

7. In many instances nationalism has fused with religious identity, but this does not deny Ernest Gellner's assertion that the age of nationalism is also the age of secularism, at least in Europe: Ernest Gellner, *Nationalism* (Phoenix: London, 1977).

8. The Quran insists that there can be no primal loyalty above loyalty to God. 'O Mankind, We have created you from a male and female and have made you peoples and tribes that you may get to know one other. Indeed the most noble in the sight of God, are those with the most piety' (49: 13).

9. See Hamilton A. R. Gibb, *Studies on the Civilization of Islam* (Princeton University Press: Princeton, 1982), especially ch. 4, 'The social significance of the Shuubiya'.

10. Sat'i al-Husri (1879–1967), the ideologue of Arab nationalism, drew freely from the German Romantic philosopher Johann Gottlieb Fichte (1762–1814). Michel 'Aflaq, the founder of the Arab nationalist Baath Party, was a devotee of the French philosopher Henri Bergson (1859–1941) and of his theory of the creative *élan vital* underlying peoples and nations.

11. See, for example, Asher Kaufman, *Reviving Phoenicia: The Search for Identity in Lebanon* (I. B. Tauris: London, 2004).

12. See Martin Kramer, *Islam Assembled: The Advent of the Muslim Congresses* (Columbia University Press: New York, 1986).

13. A good English-language translation of the autobiography is Taha Hussein, *The Days* (American University of Cairo Press: Cairo, 1997), translated by E. H. Paxton, Hilary Wayment and Kenneth Cragg.

14. *Mustaqbal al-Thaqafa fi Misr ('The Future of Culture in Egypt')*, in Taha Hussein, *Al'amal al-Kamila (The Complete Works)* (Dar-ul Kitab al-Labnani: Beirut, 1982).

15. ibid.

16. On the intellectual influence on Iqbal, see Khurram Ali Shafique, *Iqbal* (Iqbal Acedemy Pakistan: Lahore, 2006), pp. 42–5.

17. This was translated into English by the Cambridge scholar Reynold A. Nicholson in 1920. It is now available as *The Secrets of the Self* (Ashraf Publishers: Lahore 1983).

18. From *The Secrets of the Self* (above, n.17), p. 18, lines 211–14.

19. Ibid., p. 90, lines 1018–21.

20. See Fazlur Rahman, *Islam and Modernity* (University of Chicago Press: Chicago 1982), pp. 132–33.

21. Khuran Ali Shafique, *Iqbal* (above, n. 16) pp. 135–48.

22. Ibid., p. 194.

23. An excellent work on the Indian *Khilafat* movement is Gail Minault, *The Indian Khilafat Movement: Religious Symbolism and Political Mobilization in India* (Oxford University Press: Delhi, 1999).

24. Most of the writings on Nursi are in Turkish. A good collection of essays on his life and thought was produced by Ibrahim M. Abu-Rabi', *Islam at the Crossroads: On the Life and Thought of Bediuzzaman Said Nursi* (SUNY Press: Albany, NY, 2003). An important essay on Nursi was written by Professor Hamid Algar of Berkeley. It was included in a book on the Islamic reformer Mawdudi, *Islamic Perspectives: Studies in honour of Sayyid Abul A'la Mawdudi* (Islamic Foundation: Leicester, 1979), pp. 313–35.

25. Algar, *Islamic Perspectives* (above, n. 23), p. 319.

26. All references to, and quotations from, the *Risale* are from the English-language version translated as Said Nursi, *The Words: Volumes 1 and 2* (Kaynak: Izmir, 1997).

27. A Russian term referring to illegal underground publications, surreptitiously distributed.

28. Quoted in M. Ikram Chaghatai, *Muhammad Asad: Europe's Gift to Islam* (Sang-e-Meel: Lahore, 2006). Asad is one of the most interesting figures in twentieth-century pan-Islamism. Born as Leopold Weiss, in Galicia, he converted to Islam in his twenties,

served in the entourage of King Abd el-Aziz in Saudi Arabia, worked with Iqbal and others in the cause of Islam and the Muslims of India, and was interred in India as an enemy alien by the British during the Second World War. Upon his release Asad stayed in India, but then moved to Pakistan after partition. Asad played an important role in the early days of Pakistan, heading its Middle Eastern Bureau at the Foreign Ministry (1950), and later served as Pakistan's ambassador to the UN (1952). He is best known in the West as the author of *The Road to Mecca*, a spiritual autobiography.

29. Adnan Menderes had campaigned to restore the Islamic call to prayer, the *adhan*, from Turkish back to the ritualistic Arabic.
30. See Albert Hourani, *Arabic Thought in the Liberal Age 1798–1939* (Oxford University Press: Oxford, 1970).
31. The Catholic writer and Liberal MP, Hilaire Belloc (1870–1953), had a far more prescient understanding of Islam than any number of social scientists and historians of the period, including Muslim intellectuals. In his 1936 book, entitled *The Great Heresies*, Belloc wrote: 'Of every dozen Mohammedans [sic] in the world today, eleven are actually or virtually subjects of an Occidental power. It would seem as though the great duel was now decided. But can we be certain it is so decided? I doubt it very much. It has always seemed to me possible, and even probable, that there would be a resurrection of Islam and that our sons or our grandsons would see the renewal of that tremendous struggle between the Christian culture and what has been for more than a thousand years its greatest opponent.' Belloc continued, 'May not Islam arise again? In a sense the question is already answered because Islam has never departed. It still commands the fixed loyalty and unquestioning adhesion of all the millions between the Atlantic and the Indus and further afield throughout scattered communities of further Asia . . . The future always comes as a surprise but political wisdom consists in attempting at least some partial judgment of what that surprise may be. And for my part I cannot but believe that a main unexpected thing of the future is the return of Islam. Since religion is at the root of all political movements and changes and since we have here a very great religion physically paralysed but morally intensely alive, we are in the presence of an unstable equilibrium which cannot remain permanently unstable . . .'

Chapter 3: The Counter-Revolt of Islam

1. In fact this was the title of Daniel Lerner's landmark 1958 work on the Middle East, which had an enormous influence on subsequent social science on Islam and the Middle East: Daniel Lerner, *The Passing of Traditional Societies: Modernizing the Middle East* (The Free Press: New York, 1958).
2. Even an acute historian of civilizations who was not unsympathetic to Islam, the Frenchman Fernand Braudel would affirm as much: 'For at all costs, Islam has to modernize and adopt in large measure the technology of the West, on which the world now so much depends. The future hangs on the acceptance or rejection of this world civilization,' he wrote in *A History of Civilizations* (Penguin: London and New York, 1993), p. 99.
3. Ibid, p. 92.
4. A standard history of the Brotherhood is Richard P. Mitchell's *Society of the Muslim Brothers* (Oxford University Press: Oxford, 1993).
5. For a recent scholarly history of the Jama'at, see Seyyed Vali Reza Nasr, *The Vanguard of the Islamic Revolution: The Jama'at-I Islami of Pakistan* (University of California Press: Berkeley, California, 1994).
6. The early days of the Iranian revolution of 1979 were crowded with committees and organizations which sought to remould entire aspects of society into new, theoretically Islamic, casts. Universities, for example, were closed in order to be purged from

unacceptable ideologies and to have their curricula Islamized. See the interview with the reformist intellectual Abdulkarim Soroush, who in an earlier radical manifestation had served on the Cultural Revolution Committee, which oversaw the purging of the universities. The interview is reproduced on Soroush's website www.drsoroush.com under the title 'One cultural revolution was enough'.

7. Most of Bennabi's major works have been translated into English from the original French by Malaysian publishers. The concept of 'colonizablity' appears in several of his works. See Malek Bennabi *Islam in History and Society* (Berita: Kuala Lumpur, 1987); *The Qur'anic Phenomenon* (Islamic Book Trust: Kuala Lumpur, 1991); *On the Origins of Human Society* (The Open Press: Kuala Lumpur, 1998); *The Question of Culture* (Islamic Book Trust: Kuala Lumpur, 2003); *The Question of Ideas* (Islamic Book Trust: Kuala Lumpur, 2003). Bennabi has also been a subject of several theses and studies, the most notable of which (in English) is Mohamed Tahir El-Mesawi *A Muslim Theory of Human Society: An Investigation into the sociological thought of Malik Bennabi* (Thinker's Library, Kuala Lumpur, 1998).

8. Bennabi, *Islam in History and Society* (above, n. 7), p. 49.

9. Ibid.

10. Edward Gibbon, *The Decline and Fall of the Roman Empire* (Bison Books: London, 1979), p. 9.

11. Bennabi *Islam in History and Society* (above, n. 7), pp. 23–33.

12. A detailed political biography of Shariati is Ali Rahnema's *An Islamic Utopian: A Political Biography of Ali Shari'ati* (I. B. Tauris: London and New York, 2000).

13. Ibid., pp. 266–76.

14. Ayatollah Baqir al-Sadr's writings have been analysed in numerous studies in Arabic. They are also the subject of a monograph in English by Chibli Mallat: *The Renewal of Islamic Law: Muhammad Baqer as-Sadr, Najaf and the Shi'i International* (Cambridge University Press: Cambridge, 2004).

15. The Islamic Foundation in Leicester, UK, which was founded in 1973 and was linked to the Jama'at Islami, was an important centre for the propagation of the ideas of Maududi into the Muslim communities of the West through the medium of English.

16. Qutb's younger brother, for example, Muhammad Qutb – an important Islamist thinker in his own right – left for Saudi Arabia in 1972 after his release from prison in Egypt. He taught at a number of Saudi universities, and among his students there was one Osama Bin Laden. Qutb organized the publishing and distribution of his brother's writings from Saudi Arabia.

17. A fascinating book on the diffusion of the Muslim Brotherhood's ideas and supporters into the Maghreb is Tawfiq Muhammad al-Shawi' memoirs, *Nusf Qarn min al-'Amal al-Islami* (*Half a Century of Islamist Work*), 1945–1995 (Dar Al Sharq: Cairo, 1998); Al-Shawi's career as a jurist and educator spanned both North Africa and Saudi Arabia, where he was appointed by King Faisal in 1965 to the academic board of Riyad University.

18. The White Revolution was a series of wide-ranging economic and social reforms which the shah promulgated in 1963 and which were designed to bring Iran to the status of a developed country. Certain aspects of the reforms, such as those affecting clerically owned or controlled land and changes in family law which displaced traditional Islamic categories, were bitterly opposed by the clergy.

19. Until then, nearly all the interpretations and commentaries on the Quran – for instance, those of al-Razi, Tabari, Ibn al-Kathir or Tabarsi – were from the medieval period of Islam. Although these works were held in the highest esteem for their theological or spiritual insights, they still fell short in terms of their relevance to modern circumstances.

20. This so-called *tafsir al-Manar* drew heavily on the *tafsir* of the medieval scholar Ibn al-Kathir.

21. *The Message of the Qur'an*, Translated and explained by Muhammad Asad (Dar al-Andalus: Gibraltar, 1980).

22. An excellent book on the siege of Mecca and its aftermath is Yaroslav Trofimov's *The Siege of Mecca: The Forgotten Uprising in Islam's Holiest Shrine and the birth of al-Qaeda* (Doubleday: New York, 2007).
23. From an interview given by Yaroslav Trofimov to *Reason Magazine*, 27 September 2007, after the publication of his book.
24. Ibid.

Chapter 4: Disenchanting the World

1. The text of Ayatollah Khomeini's speech can be found on the website of the Secretariat of the Supreme Council of the Islamic Revolution, www.iranculture.org.
2. The tenure of Soroush in the Cultural Committee has been subjected to considerable criticsm, given his later repudiation of much of the committee's work and his opposition to clerical rule. See the interview with Soroush, 'One cultural revolution is enough', on his website, www.drsoroush.com.
3. Zia's Islamization measures are treated in Lawrence Ziring, *Pakistan in the Twentieth Century: A Political History* (Oxford University Press: Karachi, 1999), pp. 423–502, and in Ian Talbot, *Pakistan: A Modern History* (Hurst: London, 1998).
4. Orientalist scholarship predated the nineteenth century but was not connected to the imperial domination of Muslim lands. See Robert Irwin, *For Lust of Knowing: The Orientalists and their Enemies* (Allen Lane: London, 2006). The most famous work on orientalism is Edward Said's classic book *Orientalism: Western Conception of the Orient* (Penguin: London, 2003).
5. A huge number of modern Muslim scholars and educators who later became leading figures in their own countries were trained by orientalists in western universities. The effects of orientalist scholarship on Muslim intellectuals has been immense.
6. See Hamilton A. R. Gibb, *Studies on the Civilization of Islam* (Princeton University Press: Princeton, 1982), and his lecture 'Reaction in the Middle East against western culture' reproduced there, pp. 320–35.
7. Ibid., pp. 245–319.
8. The ideological and political background to the language and script reforms in Turkey are treated in Niyazi Berkes, *The Development of Secularism in Turkey* (Routledge: New York, 1998), pp. 473–78.
9. Quoted in the *Guardian*, 11 October 2001.
10. See the brilliant work by George Makdisi, *The Rise of Humanism in Classical Islam and the Christian West* (Edinburgh University Press: Edinburgh, 1990).
11. In his autobiography *The Days*, Taha Hussein describes how his transfer from al-Azhar to the secular Cairo University was an enormously liberating experience. Nasser restructured the al-Azhar university by introducing secular subjects and engineering studies and by bringing it under greater state control. In the period 1958–63, al-Azhar's rector was Mahmud Shaltut, a religious reformer in his own right and a proponent of Islamic universalism. It was during his tenure that al-Azhar officially recognized the Jaafari school of law, the jurisprudential basis of Shia Islam. See Kate Zebiri, *Mahmud Shaltut and Islamic Modernism* (Clarendon Press: Oxford, 1993).
12. See Mohammed Elihachmi Hamdi, *The Politicization of Islam* (Westview Press: Boulder, 1998), pp. 13–17.
13. All the biographical details on al-Attas come from Wan Mohd Nor Wan Daud, *The Educational Philosophy and Practice of Syed Muhammad Naquib al-Attas: An Exposition of the Original Concept of Islamization* (ISTAC: Kuala Lumpur, 1998).
14. See Wan Daud, *Educational Philosophy and Practice* (above, n. 13), pp. 291–423, and also p. 169. See Syed Muhammad Naquib al-Attas, *Islam, Secularism and the Philosophy of the Future* (Mansell: London, 1985).

15. Al-Attas' collected essays are found in Syed Muhammad Naquib al-Attas, *Prologomena to the Metaphysics of Islam: An Exposition of the Fundamental Elements of the Worldview of Islam* (ISTAC: Kuala Lumpur, 1995).
16. Harvey Cox, *The Secular City: Secularization and Urbanization in Theological Perspective,* (Macmillan: New York 1965) p. 2.
17. As al-Attas wrote in his *Prologomena*: 'The disenchantment of nature and terrestrialisation of man has resulted, in the former case, in the reduction of nature to a mere object of utility having only a functional significance and value for scientific and technical management ... and, in the latter case, in the reduction of man, of his transcendent nature as spirit. [It emphasizes] his humanity and physical being, his deification, and so his reliance upon his own rational efforts of enquiry into his origins and final destiny ... His own knowledge thus acquired he now sets up as the criterion for judging the truth or falsehood of his own assertions.'
18. See Wan Daud, *Educational Philosophy and Practice* (above, n. 13), pp. 169–74.
19. Not all those who came into contact with ISTAC were impressed by its potential. A sceptical critique of ISTAC and of the entire experiment of the Islamization of knowledge was made by the Egyptian scholar Mona Abaza. Her book *Debates on Islam and Knowledge in Malaysia and Egypt: Shifting Worlds* (Curzon: Richmond, 2002) is an unflattering – and unbalanced – dissection of the project (see pp. 88–106). Another writer who has taken issue with al-Attas is Ziauddin Sardar, in his memoir *Desperately Seeking Paradise: Journeys of a Sceptical Muslim* (Granta: London, 2004), pp. 303–4.
20. Al-Faruqi has been the subject of several detailed essays and biographies. Abaza devotes him a chapter in her book (above, n. 19), pp. 77–88. Most people have, erroneously in my opinion, attributed the idea of the Islamization of knowledge to Ismail Farouqi. The actual trajectory of the idea can be traced to Attas' memorandum on the Islamization of knowledge in 1973. But the issue has been conclusively put to rest in Wan Daud's book on the subject (above, n. 13). Although Wan Daud is closely linked to al-Attas, this in no way detracts from his methodical exposition of the origins of the Islamization-of-knowledge movement. He has established beyond refutation that the idea itself originated with al-Attas, even though others subsequently took credit for it.
21. In the post 9/11 environment, IIIT also became linked to Osama bin Laden through an improbable chain which established that an IIIT employee provided batteries to al-Qaeda's satellite phones. IIIT became the target of virulent attacks by right-wing think-tanks, politicians and journalists who saw it as part of a vast underground conspiracy.
22. Al-Attas himself held the title of Al-Ghazzali Chair of Islamic Thought.
23. A redaction of the *Ihya* into acceptable Shia doctrinal terms by the seventeenth-century scholar Kashani became a standard work for Shia scholars.
24. Muhammad Abid al-Jabiri, *Takwin al-'Aql al'Arabi* (*The Formation of the Arab Mind*), (Centre for Arab Unity Studies: Beirut, 2006); *Al-'Aql Al'Syasi al-'Arabi* (*The Arab Political Mind*) (Centre for Arab Unity Studies: Beirut, 2007); *Bunyat al'Aql al-'Arabi* (*The Structure of the Arab Mind*) (Centre for Arab Unity Studies: Beirut, 2007).

Chapter 5: The Reformations of Islam

1. Samuel P. Huntington, 'The Clash of Civilizations?', *Foreign Affairs,* Summer 1993. This was followed by his book *The Clash of Civilizations and the Remaking of the World Order* (Simon and Schuster: New York, 1996).
2. Bernard Lewis, 'The Roots of Muslim Rage', *The Atlantic,* September 1990. Lewis followed this up with several articles about Islam's decline and failure, most notably the ones collected in the volume *What Went Wrong? Western Impact and Middle Eastern Response* (Oxford University Press: New York, 2001).

3. The Runnymede Trust, *Islamophobia: A Challenge for Us All* (1997).
4. The Bush White House made a point of emphasizing that its measures were not directed against Islam and Muslims. The California-based, Mauritania-trained Sheikh Hamza Yusuf was an example of the type of Muslim scholars who were being courted by the media for their moderate views. He appeared with Bush at his address to Congress on 20 September 2001, after the 9/11 attacks. A number of such figures became fixtures on the international conference scene and received valued invitations to globalization events such as the World Economic Forum at Davos.
5. There were literally dozens of such articles, essays and later books. A lot of them were authored by academics and experts who had little or no knowledge of the Muslim world. See, for example, James Q. Wilson, 'The Reform Islam Needs', *City Journal*, Autumn 2002. Wilson was a former professor of government at Harvard who had specialized in urban affairs.
6. The funds allocated by the US Government for the Islam 'problem' run literally into billions. They go far beyond the obvious programmes of the US-funded satellite media channels aimed at the Muslim world. They include the work of advocacy and support for democracy of the congressionally funded National Endowment for Democracy, of the United States Institute of Peace, of the International Republican Institute, of the National Democratic Institute, as well as of the direct State Department and USAID cultural and educational programmes focused on the Muslim world.
7. Sir William Muir, whose 1877 *Life of Mahomet* was the standard reference on the Prophet for a generation, perpetrated the earlier claims regarding the truth of the Prophet's experiences and the veracity of Islam. The biography was 'rediscovered' by the Christian right in the post-9/11 world and continues to be used in polemics against Islam.
8. This line of argument found its most fulsome development in Max Weber's famous work *The Protestant Ethic and the Spirit of Capitalism*.
9. It is interesting to note that Muhammad Iqbal, as well as nineteenth-century reformers such as Muhammad Abduh, held a positive view of Luther and the Reformation. But they saw it as a process which made Christianity a more 'pure' religion and brought it closer to Islam. Others, improbably, even saw the Reformation as having been inspired by Islam.
10. This was the main vehicle through which the US secretly funded and supported European intellectuals and writers who were socialists or social democrats but firmly anti-communists. No evidence has materialized to link the US with movements such as the Muslim Brotherhood in the 1950s and 1960s.
11. This was a position adopted by grand ayatollahs such as Abul Qasim al-Khoei in the 1970s and 1980s.
12. Al-Dhahabi, one of Ibn Taymiyya's students, addressed a famous letter to his former teacher where he reprimanded him for his bigotry and baseless accusations. The letter is known by the title *al-Nasihah al-Dhahabiyaah ila ibn Taymiyya* (*The Golden Advice to ibn Taymiyya*).
13. In particular, the 1,000-year old institution of al-Azhar was remarkably resistant to change and only seriously began to re-examine its legacy with the advent of two reforming Sheiks, Mustafa al-Maraghi and especially Mahmud Shaltut in the mid-twentieth century. See Kate Zebiri, *Mahmud Shaltut and Islamic Modernism* (Clarendon Press: Oxford, 1993), pp. 18–20 on al-Maraghi and the reform of the Azhar curriculum.
14. Khaled Abou El Fadl, *Speaking in God's Name: Islamic Law, Authority and Women* (Oneworld Publications: Oxford, 2001).
15. According to the Saudi Sheikh ibn Jibreen, women can only wear brassieres for health or medical reasons. Otherwise this is forbidden, as it could falsely create the impression that a woman is younger and more appealing than she really is. See Abou El Fadl (above, n. 15), pp. 177–81.
16. There were frequent riots and disturbances between the Shia and the Sunni throughout Islamic history, but they never deteriorated into prolonged warfare. Violence accompanied the state's imposition of one sect over the other, but this

happened infrequently in Islam. The exceptions were the imposition of official Sunnism in Egypt after the overthrow of the Shia Fatimid dynasty in the twelfth century and the adoption by Iran of Shiism as the national religion in the sixteenth century. The latter was accompanied by prolonged violence against the Sunnis for nearly a hundred years before the Shia became the majority in Iran.

17. See Sherman A. Jackson, *On the Boundaries of Theological Tolerance in Islam: Abu Hamid al-Ghazali's Faysal al-Tafriqa* (Oxford University Press: Oxford 2002).

18. The funds which the Saudi state made available for the propagation of Wahhabism have not been made public, but they certainly run into hundreds of millions of dollars per annum. In his testimony to the US Senate Judiciary Sub-Committee on Terrorism, Technology and Homeland Security on 26 June 2003, Alex Alexiev, a senior fellow at the Centre for Security Policy, estimated that the Pakistani Islamic school system, the *madrassah*, alone received $350 million from Wahhabi sources.

19. See Stephen Schwartz, 'Getting to know the Sufis', *Weekly Standard*, 7 February 2005.

20. This body, known as *Jama'at al-Taqrib bayna al-Madhahib* (Society for the Conciliation between the Schools of Law), was founded in 1948 by leading scholars from al-Azhar and by Shia *ulemas* from Iraq and Iran. It became very active under the Rector of al-Azhar, Sheikh Mahmud Shaltut, in the late 1950s and 1960s. Shaltut issued a famous and controversial ruling that following the Shia school of law was legitimate for the practising Muslim. A similar organization was started in Iran after the Islamic Revolution. Jordan, through the official *Ahl ul-Bayt* Foundation (that is, the Foundation of the People of the Prophet's Household) has also been active in this domain.

21. See, for example, the 1998 Bin Laden *fatwa* on the obligation to fight the US military presence in Saudi Arabia and his *fatwas* against 'Jews and crusaders'.

22. The resolution read in part: 'Whosoever is an adherent to one of the four Sunni schools (Mathahib) of Islamic jurisprudence (Hanafi, Maliki, Shafi'i and Hanbali), the two Shi'i schools of Islamic jurisprudence (Ja'fari and Zaydi), the Ibadi school of Islamic jurisprudence and the Thahiri school of Islamic jurisprudence is a Muslim. Declaring that person an apostate is impossible and impermissible . . .' The Resolutions of the Amman Message can be found on its website: www.ammanmessage.com.

23. Amman Message (above, n. 22).

24. See Barry Bearak, 'Over World Protest, Taliban are Destroying Ancient Buddhas', *New York Times*, 4 March 2001.

25. Bahaism grew as an offshoot of a millenarian branch of the Shia Muslim faith. See Abbas Amanat, *Resurrection and Renewal: The Making of the Babi Movement in Iran, 1844–1850* (Cornell University Press: Ithaca, 1989).

26. The doctrinal content of Islam became a subject of great controversy during the period of the *Mihna* – the 'Inquisition', an early ninth-century example of the state acting as an enforcer of a religious doctrine. The *Mihna* trials were instigated by the Caliph al-Mamun, to promote allegiance to the doctrine of the created Quran. After desultory efforts to impose it on a resistant public, the doctrine was abandoned by his later successors.

27. Shias, of course, add another dimension to this tripod, namely the knowledge of the imam, but this does not detract from the essence of the construct.

28. See Robin Wright, 'Scholar Emerges as the Martin Luther of Islam – His Interpretation: Freedom of Thought, Democracy Essential', *Los Angeles Times*, 30 January 1995.

29. Soroush's main works have been translated into a number of languages, including English and Arabic. A good introduction to his works is Mahmoud Sadri and Ahmad Sadri, *Reason, Freedom and Democracy in Islam: Essential Writings of Abdolkarim Soroush* (Oxford University Press: New York, 2000).

30. Ibid., p. 31.

31. Ibid., p. 34.

32. Quoted in John von Heyking, 'Mysticism in Contemporary Islamic Political Thought: Orhan Pamuk and Abdolkarim Soroush', *Humanitas Magazine*, Vol. 19, 22 March 2006.
33. Sadri and Sadri (above, n. 29), p. 37.
34. Taha has been the subject of an important biography by Mohamed A. Mahmoud, *Quest for Divinity: A Critical Examination of the Thought of Mahmud Muhammad Taha* (Syracuse University Press: Syracuse, New York, 2007).
35. Harvey Cox, *The Secular City: Secularization and Urbanization in Theological Perspective* (Macmillan: New York, 1965), p. 4.
36. Ibid., p. 241.
37. Dietrich Bonhoeffer, *A Testament to Freedom: The Essential writings of Dietrich Bonhoeffer*, edited by G. B. Kelly and F. Burton Nelson (HarperCollins: New York, 1995), p. 509.

Chapter 6: Territory and Power

1. Samuel P. Huntington, *The Clash of Civilizations and the Remaking of World Order* (Simon & Shuster: New York, 1998), p. 177.
2. For example, in Egypt under Nasser, in Baathist Syria and Iraq, and in Sukarno's Indonesia. India under Nehru, though technically non-aligned, was also tilting towards the Soviet bloc because of a supposedly shared socialist ethos.
3. See Jacob Landau's excellent history of pan-Islam. *The Politics of Pan-Islam: Ideology and Organization* (Oxford University Press: New York, 1994).
4. See Gail Minault, *The Khilafat Movement: Religious Symbolism and Political Mobilization in India* (Oxford India Paperbacks: New Delhi, 1999).
5. See William L. Cleveland, *Islam Against the West: Shakib Arslan and the Campaign for Islamic Nationalism* (University of Texas Press: Texas Austin, 1985).
6. See Ahmed Rashid, *Jihad: The Rise of Militant Islam in Central Asia* (Yale University Press: New Haven and London, 2002), especially pp. 115–37 on Hizb ut-Tahrir.
7. Bush was addressing the Joint Session of Congress on 20 September 2001 following the 9/11 attacks.
8. This was quoted by the London *Times* in its issue of 22 September 2006, from remarks made by former President Musharraf of Pakistan. Musharraf had just released his memoirs *In The Line of Fire*.
9. Other terrorist movements, such as the Tamil Tigers in Sri Lanka and the FARC of Colombia, received scant international attention after the 9/11 attacks. The western world's military and security apparatuses were all mobilized against Islamic movements.
10. See Edward A. Gargan, 'Hindu Rage Against Muslims Transforming Indian Politics', *New York Times* 17 September 1993. 'Slowly, gradually, but with the relentlessness of floodwaters, a growing Hindu rage toward India's Muslim minority has been spreading among India's solid middle class Hindus – its merchants and accountants, its lawyers and engineers – creating uncertainty about the future ability of adherents of the two religions to get along,' wrote Gargan.
11. Egypt, Morocco, Jordan, and even Baathist Syria have cooperated with the US in interrogating and often torturing terror suspects transferred to their custody by the CIA. A case in point is the 'rendition' of Maher Arar, a Canadian–Syrian national, who was transferred to the custody of Syria's notorious intelligence services in 2002, during a stop-over in New York airport. After nearly two years of interrogation and torture, Arar was released and returned to Canada. No evidence was found linking him to al-Qaeda.
12. See Human Rights Watch, *Crackdown on Burmese Muslims*, July 2002. This report can be accessed from www.hrw.org.

13. In his book *The Malady of Islam* (Basic Books, 2003), the Franco-Tunisian writer Abdelwahab Meddeb has a very poignant treatment of the subject of the 'exclusion' of Islam and Muslims by the west.
14. 'Soft' power does not necessarily come to the rescue of states whose vital interests have been threatened.
15. According to Carl Bernstein writing in *Time* magazine, Reagan had signed a secret order in May 1982, National Security Directive 32, that committed the US to support the Solidarity trade union movement in Poland. Three weeks later Reagan met with the Pope, John Paul II, to coordinate and cooperate in the undermining of communism in eastern Europe. See Carl Bernstein, 'The Holy Alliance', *Time*, 24 February 1992.
16. For example, the G-20 group of countries that acts as an inter-governmental group to discuss key global economic issues does include Saudi Arabia. This was a deliberate concession on the part of the western powers and Japan to include a representative from the Islamic world.
17. The World Social Forum, an annual gathering of anti-globalization movements and NGOs, aspires to counter the effects of the much more powerful World Economic Forum (WEF) of Davos. So far it has proved a counterpoint to the WEF, but its influence still lags far behind.
18. See 'Hugo Chavez Moves into Banking', *Economist*, 10 May 2007.
19. From Mahathir's speech to the 20th Al Baraka Symposium For Islamic Economies, Sheraton Imperial Hotel, Kuala Lumpur, 25 June 2001.
20. The Malaysian government followed this up by sponsoring an international conference on a 'Stable and Just Global Monetary System', where the viability of the Islamic gold dinar was discussed. The proceedings were published in book form by the International Islamic University of Malaysia.
21. The Asian financial crisis of 1997 was a turning point in the world economy. The free market policies of the 'Washington Consensus' were held responsible for the dramatic devaluations and economic collapse which affected a large number of Asian countries.

Chapter 7: Where Next for the Islamic State?

1. *Asabiya* – kinship and tribal solidarity – is a key concept in ibn Khaldun's notion of power. See Muhsin Mahdi, *Ibn Khaldun's Philosophy of History* (Chicago: Phoenix edition, 1964), pp. 193–209.
2. Roger Scruton, 'The Political Problem of Islam', *Intercollegiate Review*, Fall 2002.
3. Ibid.
4. Anthony Black's exposition on Islamic political thought puts an end to the absurd idea that Islam has not produced a coherent political theory. See Anthony Black, *The History of Islamic Political Thought: From the Prophet to the Present* (Routledge: New York 2001).
5. See, for example, Bernard Lewis, *What Went Wrong? Western Impact and Middle Eastern Response* (Oxford University Press: Oxford, 2001).
6. See, for example, Abd al-Aziz Sachedina, *The Just Ruler in Shi'ite Islam* (Oxford University Press: New York, 1998) and Fouad Ibrahim, *Al-Faqih wa al-Dawla: Al-Fikr al-Siyasi al-Shi'i* (*The Jurisprudent and the State: Shia Political Thought*) (Dar-ul-Kunooz al-Adabiya: Beirut, 1998) for Shia political thought. For the Sunni world, the most famous treatise on politics is that of the medieval scholar al-Mawardi, *Al-Ahkam al-Sultaniya* (*The Rules of Government*). Hamid Enayat's *Modern Islamic Political Thought* (Islamic Book Trust: Kuala Lumpur, 2001) is still unsurpassed as a general survey of the modern period.
7. See Muhsin Mahdi, *Alfarabi and the Foundations of Islamic Political Philosophy* (Oxford University Press: Karachi, 2001).
8. See Karl Popper, *The Open Society and its Enemies*, Vols 1–2 (Princeton University Press: Princeton, 2002).

9. See, for example, Martin Kramer, *Islam Assembled: The Advent of the Muslim Congresses* (Columbia University Press: New York, 1986), pp. 80–123.

10. Quoted in the global security website, www.globalsecurity.org.

11. Speech by George W. Bush on 5 September 2006 to the Military Officers Association of America.

12. Such a rule need not be 'Islamist' in the conventional sense. Part of the aura of the king of Morocco derives from his title of Amir al-Mumineen 'the Leader of the believers'. The late King Hassan II of Morocco was well versed in Islamic law and theology and presided over religious lectures given during the month of Ramadan. The tradition is continued by his successor, the present King Muhammad V.

13. Quoted in Homa Katouzian, *State and Society in Iran: The Eclipse of the Qajars and the Emergence of the Pahlavis* (I.B. Tauris: London and New York, 2000), pp. 44–5.

14. Quran, 42: 38.

15. 'Do not solicit an office of authority, for if it is given to you for the asking, you will be left therein to your own resources, while if it is given to you without asking, you will be aided [by God] therein.' From the compendia of prophetic sayings (*Hadith*) of Muslim and al-Bukhari. The translation is from Muhammad Asad, *The Principles of State and Government in Islam* (Islamic Book Trust: Kuala Lumpur, ND), p. 46.

16. From the sayings and discourses of Imam Ali, *Nahjul Balagha – The Paths of Erudition* (European Islamic Cultural Centre: Rome, 1984).

17. Bernard Lewis, 'Islam and Liberal Democracy', *Atlantic Monthly*, February 1993.

18. This quotation can be accessed from the White House website at http://www.white-house.gov/news/releases/2001/09/20010920-8.html.

19. See Norman Podhoretz, *World War IV: The Long Struggle against Islamofascism* (Doubleday: New York, 2007).

20. For many critics in the West, Islamic values have been absurdly reduced to women in *purdah*, child brides, honour killings, polygamy, segregated sports and the like.

21. See, for example, Patricia Risso, *Merchants and Faith: Muslim Commerce and Culture in the Indian Ocean* (Westview Press: Boulder, 1995).

22. The rate at which indigenous peoples converted to Islam was relatively slow. For example, in Spain, nearly half the population was still non-Muslim even after 250 years of Muslim rule. It was only after a certain inflection point was reached that the rate of conversion accelerated. In the case of Spain, 90 per cent of the population of Muslim-ruled Spain had become Muslim by about the middle of the twelfth century, 400 years after the Muslim conquest. See Richard Fletcher, *Moorish Spain* (Phoenix Books: London, 1994), especially pp. 35–50, 'The curve of conversion'.

23. A good introductory survey, in English, of the jurisprudence of migration in Islam is 'The Islamic Conception of Migration: Past, Present and Future', by Sami A. Aldeeb Abu Sahlieh, *International Migration Review*, March 1996, pp. 35–57.

24. The two most important scholars who have opined on the migration of Muslims and on their presence in the West are the Egyptian-born cleric Sheikh Yusuf al-Qaradawi and the Lebanese Grand Ayatollah Muhammad Hussein Fadlallah. See the latter's work *Tahaduyat al-Muhajir, bayna al-asala wal mu'asara* (*The Challenges to the Migrant Caught between Authenticity and Modernity*) (Beirut: Dar al-Malak, 2000). Qaradawi works through the Dublin-based foundation the European Council on Fatwa and Research, of which he is the president. The council represents the four orthodox schools of Sunni Islam and groups together a number of scholars based in Europe, mostly with a mildly Salafist bent. Qaradawi himself lives in Qatar.

25. The details of this story were provided by a person who was involved in the preparations for this migration on the side of the UAE. He prefers to remain anonymous.

26. See 'Muslims in the European Union: Discrimination and Islamophobia', *European Monitoring Centre on Racism and Xenophobia*, 2006.

27. Ibid., pp. 30–1.

28. Ibid., pp. 44–50.

29. See Molly Moore, 'In France, Prisons Filled with Muslims', *Washington Post*, 29 April 2008.
30. *Islamophobia: Issues, Challenges and Action*, Commission on British Muslims and Islamophobia, ed. Robin Richardson (Trentham Books: Stoke-on-Trent, 2004).
31. 'Muslims in the European Union' (above, n. 26), pp. 60–84.
32. The role of London in the global network of jihadists has been meticulously analyzed by the Norwegian professor, Brynjar Lia. See Brynjar Lia, *Architect of Global Jihad: The Life of Al-Qaida Strategist Abu Mus'ab al-Suri* (Columbia University Press: New York, 2008). There is no doubt that London was central to the operations of a number of radical Islamist parties and terrorist organizations, especially in the 1990s. However, the oft-made assertion that such terrorists could only function in an environment where they could count on widespread support from within alienated Muslim minorities is not borne out by facts. That did not stop bilious opinion leaders from in fact making such a link between the general Muslim population and terrorism, if only by association.
33. See, for example, Matt Carr, 'You are now entering Eurabia', *Race & Class Magazine*, 48 (1), 2006, pp. 1–22. for the parallels between Islamophobia and anti-Semitism.
34. See Niall Ferguson, 'The Way we Live Now: Eurabia?', *New York Times*, 4 April 2004.
35. See European Stability Initiative, *Islamic Calvinists: Change and Conservatism in Central Anatolia* (Berlin, 2005); Also Metin Heper, 'The Justice and Development Party: Towards a Reconciliation of Islam and Democracy?' Annual Georges A. Kaller Lecture, Tel Aviv University, 16 March 2003.

Chapter 8: Human Rights and Human Duties

1. This quote is from Fallaci's now famous diatribe against Islam 'Rage and Pride', which appeared in the Italian newspaper *Il Corriere dela Sera*, 29 September 2001. Fallaci was not the only writer who vented her spleen against Islam after the 9/11 attacks. Others were the British journalist Melanie Phillips and the writer Polly Toynbee.
2. From Charles Malik, 'God and Man in Contemporary Islamic Thought', 13 September 1971. The article is still kept tellingly, on the website of the Lebanese Forces, a militant Christian right-wing party.
3. Charles Malik's work at the UN on the Universal Declaration is treated in the collection of essays in his honour edited by his son Habib Malik, *The Challenge of Human Rights: Charles Malik and the Universal Declaration* (Centre for Lebanese Studies: Oxford, 2000).
4. The full text of Article 18 reads: 'Everyone has the right to freedom of thought, conscience and religion; this right includes freedom to change his religion or belief, and freedom, either alone or in the community, with others and in public or private, to manifest his religion or belief in teaching, practice, worship and observance.'
5. The Cairo document of 1990 was pre-dated by another attempt at formulating an Islamic perspective on human rights, almost a decade earlier: the Universal Islamic Declaration of Human Rights, issued by the Islamic Council of Europe in 1981 to little effect. That was a document promoted by prominent individuals, including Algeria's former leader Ahmed Ben Bella, but was ignored after a polite reception at UNESCO where it was first presented. Neither the Western world – still preoccupied with the Soviet threat – nor the Muslim world were then at loggerheads on the issue of human rights.
6. An example of these east European movements is the Charter 77 group, founded by Vaclav Havel in Czechoslovakia.
7. To give credibility to their reports, Muslim human rights advocates cite Amnesty International or Human Rights Watch rather than any Islamic human rights group.
8. Iran in particular has been vociferous in its demands for reviewing the Universal Declaration. See, for example, the paper 'Islamic Contribution to Enriching the

Universal Declaration of Human Rights', by Iran's Deputy Foreign Minister M. Javad Zarif. The paper was presented at an October 1988 seminar in Geneva on the issue of Islam and human rights. The paper can be accessed at www.zarif.net.

9. Thus black, Asian or Jewish Britons had legal redress under the anti-racism and anti-Semitism laws.

10. Mohammad Hashim Kamali, *Freedom of Expression in Islam* (Ilmiah Publishers: Kuala Lumpur, 1998).

11. Quoted in R. A. Nicholson, *Literary History of the Arabs* (Curzon Press: London, 1993), pp. 314–24.

12. Ibid., p. 323.

13. Kamali (above, n. 9), pp. 212–50.

14. C. V. Wedgewood, in her classic book *The Thirty Years War* (Anchor Books: New York, 1961), states that the population of the German Empire probably numbered 21 million in 1618. By 1648, at the end of the great wars of religion, the population had dwindled to 13 million. In one incident alone, the Massacre of St Bartholomew's Day in 1572, nearly 5,000 Huguenots were killed in an orgy of sectarian violence in Paris. See Diarmaid MacCulloch, *Reformation: Europe's House Divided 1490–1700* (Penguin: London, 2004), pp. 337–40.

15. The famous 1954 Supreme Court decision on *Brown v Board of Education* which banned segregated public schools drew on this principle.

Chapter 9: Wealth and Poverty

1. Fernand Braudel, *Civilization and Capitalism 15th–18th Century: The Wheels of Commerce* (Collins: London, 1982), p. 556.

2. ibid., p. 558.

3. See David S. Landes, *The Wealth and Poverty of Nations: Why Some Are So Rich and Some So Poor* (Norton: New York and London, 1999), p. 402.

4. See Organisation of the Islamic Conference (OIC), Statistical Economic and Social Research and Training Centre for Islamic Countries (formerly SESRTCIC now known as SESTRIC), Annual Report 2007.

5. See, for example, the paper by Marcus Noland (Senior Fellow, Institute for International Economics), 'Religion, Culture and Economic Performance', Petersen Institute for International Economics, Washington, 2003. Noland concludes emphatically: 'Islam does not appear to be a drag on growth or an anchor of development as alleged. If anything, the opposite appears to be true.'

6. See, for example, Daniel Cohen, *Globalization and its Enemies* (MIT Press: Cambridge, Massachusetts, 2006), pp. 86–91.

7. Charles Tripp, *Islam and the Moral Economy: The Challenge of Capitalism* (Cambridge University Press: Cambridge, 2006). This is a profoundly significant work on the Islamic economy.

8. See, for example, R. B. Serjeant, *The Islamic City* (UNESCO: Paris, 1980) and the essays on 'Markets' by Pedro Chalmeta (pp. 104–14) and 'Economic institutions' by Yusuf Ibish (pp. 114–26).

9. See Roger Owen, *The Middle East in the World Economy 1800–1914* (I. B. Tauris: London and New York, 1993) pp. 100–22 on the Ottoman bankruptcy and pp. 122–53 on Egypt's bankruptcy. Also David S. Landes, *Bankers and Pashas: International Finance and Economic Imperialism in Egypt* (Harper & Row: New York, 1969).

10. Sudan and Nigeria are examples of countries which squandered their patrimony in the post-independence period.

11. The fourteenth-century philosopher ibn Khaldun, was emphatic about the religious obligation of Muslims to use gold as the basis of their currency. 'It should be known since the beginning of Islam and the time of the men around Muhammad and the men

of the second generation, the legal dirham is by general consensus the one, ten of which are equal to seven *mithqal* of gold, and an ounce of gold is forty dirhams,' he wrote in his *Muqaddimah*. See Ibn Khaldun, trans. by Franz Rosenthal, *The Muqaddimah – An Introduction to History* (Routledge and Kegan Paul: London, 1958), Vol 2, p.58.

12. Quran 3: 92.
13. Bruce Ackerman and Anne Alstott, *The Stakeholder Society* (Yale University Press: London and New Haven, 1999).
14. The nationalizations of the pious foundations were started by 'reforming' regimes such as those of Nasser in Egypt and Bourguiba in Tunisia in the 1950s. In Egypt private trusts were also taken over by the state and alienated from their original purpose.
15. See Tripp (above, n7), pp. 127–33.
16. See the article by Tarek el Diwany, 'Islamic banking isn't Islamic', in *The Banker Middle East*, November 2002.
17. ibid.
18. Tripp (above, n. 7), p. 141.
19. See European Central Bank, 'The Impact of Sovereign Wealth Funds on Global Financial Markets', Occasional Paper, No 91, July 2008.
20. OIC, SESTRIC Annual Report 2007 (above, n. 4).
21. ibid.
22. The list can be accessed from the World bank website, www.worldbank.org.
23. OIC SESTRIC (above, n. 4).
24. There has been a number of initiatives to increase agricultural investments from the GCC countries into countries with a good agricultural potential such as Pakistan and parts of East Africa. Such initiatives in the past, especially in the 1970s, have proved unsuccessful. Then the oil exporting Arab countries focused their investment in agriculture on the Sudan, through the inter-governmental Arab Agricultural Development Authority, with very poor results. See, for example, Edmund Sanders, 'Foreigners Farm for Themselves in a Hungry Africa', *Los Angeles Times*, 28 September 2008.
25. Data on the Muslim private sector are derived from the web journal Dinar Standard Ranking of the top 100 companies of the Muslim World (www.dinarstandard.com).
26. Several Dubai-based property developers are branching out on the international scene using the Dubai urban development experience as their 'unique selling point'.
27. See Kito de Boer, Chris Figee, Saeeda Jaffar and Daan Streumer, *Perspectives on the Middle East, North Africa and South Asia* (MENASA) region (McKinsey and Co. Dubai 2008), pp. 113–23.
28. The Sovereign Wealth Funds of the GCC countries are likely to be around $3 trillion by the end of 2009. See Rachel Ziemba, 'What Are GCC Funds Buying? A Look at Their Investment Strategies', RGE Monitor, June 2008.

Chapter 10: The Decline of Creativity

1. Nasr is the only Muslim philosopher whose works have been included in the Library of Living Philosophers; See L. E. Hahn, R. E. Auxier, L. Stone Jr (eds), *The Philosophy of Seyyed Hossein Nasr* (Open Court: Chicago and La Salle, Illinois, 2001). The compendium included twenty-nine critical essays, as well as a fascinating 'Intellectual biography' written by Nasr himself.
2. The 'Traditionalists' have been the subject of a probing study by Mark Sedgwick, *Against the Modern World: Traditionalism and the Secret Intellectual History of the Modern World* (Oxford University Press: Oxford, 2004). Most Muslim intellectuals have taken a hostile or critical attitude towards the 'Traditionalists', and in particular

towards Schuon's theory of the perennial philosophy and the transcendent unity of religions. Opponents of Traditionalist thought have included Syed Naquib al-Attas and Ziauddin Sardar.

3. Guénon is one of the most intriguing figures of the Traditionalist movement. His 1927 book, *The Crisis of the Modern World*, has been undergoing a recent revival.

4. Nearly all the early European proponents of the perennial philosophy had been greatly affected by their encounter with Sheikh Ahmad ibn 'Alawi of Algeria, a Sufi sheikh who was in the line of ibn 'Arabi. Ibn 'Alawi's centre in Algeria received many European visitors in the 1920s and 1930s. Ibn 'Alawi was particularly disliked by Islamic modernists in Algeria such as the great reformist leader Abd el-Hamid ibn Badis, both for his mysticism and for his supposed pliancy towards the colonial French.

5. Nasr edited Schuon's major essays; see Seyyed Hossein Nasr (ed.), *The Essential Writings of Frithjof Schuon* (Element Books: Dorset and Rockbury, Massachmsetts, 1986).

6. See, for example, Seyyed Hossein Nasr, *Traditional Islam in the Modern World* (Kegan Paul International: London and New York, 1987); *Islamic Life and Thought* (SUNY Press: Albany, 1981); *Man and Nature: The Spiritual Crisis in Modern Man* (ABC International Group: Chicago, 1997). An early work which achieved international renown was *An Introduction to Islamic Cosmological Doctrines* (Thames and Hudson: London, 1978).

7. See Seyyed Hossein Nasr, *Islamic Science – An Illustrated Study* (World of Islam Festival Trust: London, 1976) p. 9.

8. From an interview with Nasr published in *Islam and Science*, 302, 2005.

9. See Pervez Hoodbhoy, 'Science and the Islamic World – The Quest for Rapprochement', *Physics Today*, Vol. 60, issue 8, August 2007.

10. Ibid.

11. Maurice Bucaille, *The Bible, the Quran and Science* (Islamic Book Service: India, 2001).

12. *Umm-ul-Qura* means 'Mother of towns', and refers to Mecca.

13. See, Abdel Aziz Duri, 'Governmental Institutions', in R. J. Serjeant (ed.), *The Islamic City*, (UNESCO: Paris, 1980), pp. 52–66.

14. Ibid., pp. 66–90.

15. Ibid., pp. 114–26. Also Bernard Lewis, 'The Islamic Guilds', *Economic History Review*, VIII, November 1937, pp. 20–37.

16. See Titus Burckhardt, *Fez: City of Islam* (The Islamic Texts Society: Cambridge, 1992), p. 76.

17. Marshall Hubert Lyautey, the French governor of Morocco between 1912 and 1925, was mainly responsible for the new urban centres there.

18. See Part III of PBS's 2002 series of reports on Saudi Arabia, *Inside the Kingdom*, for a full interview with Angawi. The interview can be seen on PBS's website: www.pbs.org. The Public Broadcasting System (PBS) is the US publicly supported channel.

19. See Daniel Howden, 'The Destruction of Mecca: Saudi Hardliners are Wiping Out their Own Heritage', *Independent*, London, 6 August 2005.

20. The new plans for the shrines of Imam Hussein and al-Abbas in Karbala, Iraq, show the same disregard for the heritage of the city – reflected, for instance, in the urge to build giant marble piazzas in place of the markets and *souks* of the old town.

21. See Morgan Stanley Global Research, *How Big Could Sovereign Wealth Funds Be by 2015?*, 2007 May 3. This report was compiled *before* the ramp-up in oil prices in 2008.

22. Mike Davis and Daniel Bertrand Monk, *Evil Paradises: Dreams of neo-Liberalism* (The New Press: New York, 2007), pp. 48–69.

23. See Hassan Fathy, *Architecture for the Poor* (University of Chicago Press: Chicago, 1976). Hassan Fathy's life and works were also the subject of a biography; see James Steele *An Architecture for People: The Complete Work of Hassan Fathy* (Whitney Library of Design: New York, 1997).

Chapter 11: The Last Crisis

1. See, for example, Pew Global Attitudes Project, 'Islamic extremism: Common concern for Muslims and western publics', July, 2005.

2. One of the first figures to write about the need to retain a balance between the imperatives of economic growth based on the capitalist model and wider spiritual realization is H. Johannes Witteveen (b. 1921), a Dutch finance minister and later managing director of the International Monetary Fund (1973–1978). See, for example, his paper, 'Economic Globalization in a Broader, Long-Term Perspective: Some Serious Concerns', reproduced in *The Policy Challenges of Global Financial Integration*, FONDAD, The Hague, 1998, www.fondad.org. Witteveen guided the international economy through one of its most turbulent periods, the quadrupling of oil prices in 1973 and the great stagflation of the 1970s. *Time* magazine called him 'the most enigmatic international civil servant since the days of Dag Hammarskjold', and he is a life-long mystic. He is also known as Murshid Karimbaksh. Witteveen is the executive supervisor of the International Sufi Movement, a non-denominational spiritual order founded by the wandering Indian mystic and musician Inayat Khan (1882–1927).

3. Quran 2: 3.

4. There are very few studies on the *Tablighi Jamaat*. The researcher Eva Borreguer, a visiting scholar at Georgetown University, presented a detailed and balanced exposition of the *Tablighi Jamaat* in her lecture at the US Institute of Peace (USIP) on August 8, 2006. The lecture can be accessed at www.usip.org/events/2006/0808_islamist_network.html.

5. Unlike the *Tablighi Jammat*, the Gülen movement has been widely analysed by scholars in universities and think tanks, and its activities have been covered by the Turkish and international media. A good description of the movement's history, scope and purposes can be found in M. Hakan Yavuz, *Islamic Political Identity in Turkey* (Oxford University Press: Oxford and New York, 2003), pp. 179–205. The movement's apparent modernity has not stopped Turkey's secular establishment and its acolytes in seeing the movement as a cleverly disguised Islamist attempt to infiltrate Turkey's secular institutions and society. At the same time, several Islamic organizations have challenged the authenticity of the movement's message. Gülen himself was indicted for anti-state activity and left Turkey. He now resides in the United States.

6. The *Futuwwa* orders have been described in several classical works including Ibn al-Mi'mar, *Kitab al-Futuwwa* [*The Book of Futuwwa*] (Shafiq Press: Baghdad, 1958); and Ibn al-Husain al-Sulami, *Kitab al-Futuwwa*, trans. by Toscun Byrak al-Jarrahi as *The Way of Sufi Chivalry* (Inner Traditions: Rochester, Vermont, 1991). The entry on *Futuwwa in the Encyclopaedia of Islam* Volume II (E. J. Brill, Leiden, 1960–2005) is the best summary on the subject.

7. Quoted in Reinhard Bendix, *Max Weber: An Intellectual Biography* (Anchor Books: New York, 1962), pp. 65–6. A fuller treatment of John Wesley, asceticism and the capitalist ethos is given in Max Weber, *The Protestant Ethic and the Spirit of Capitalism* (Routledge: London and New York, 1992), especially Chapters IV and V, pp. 95–185.

Index

THE
VIOLINIST'S
THUMB

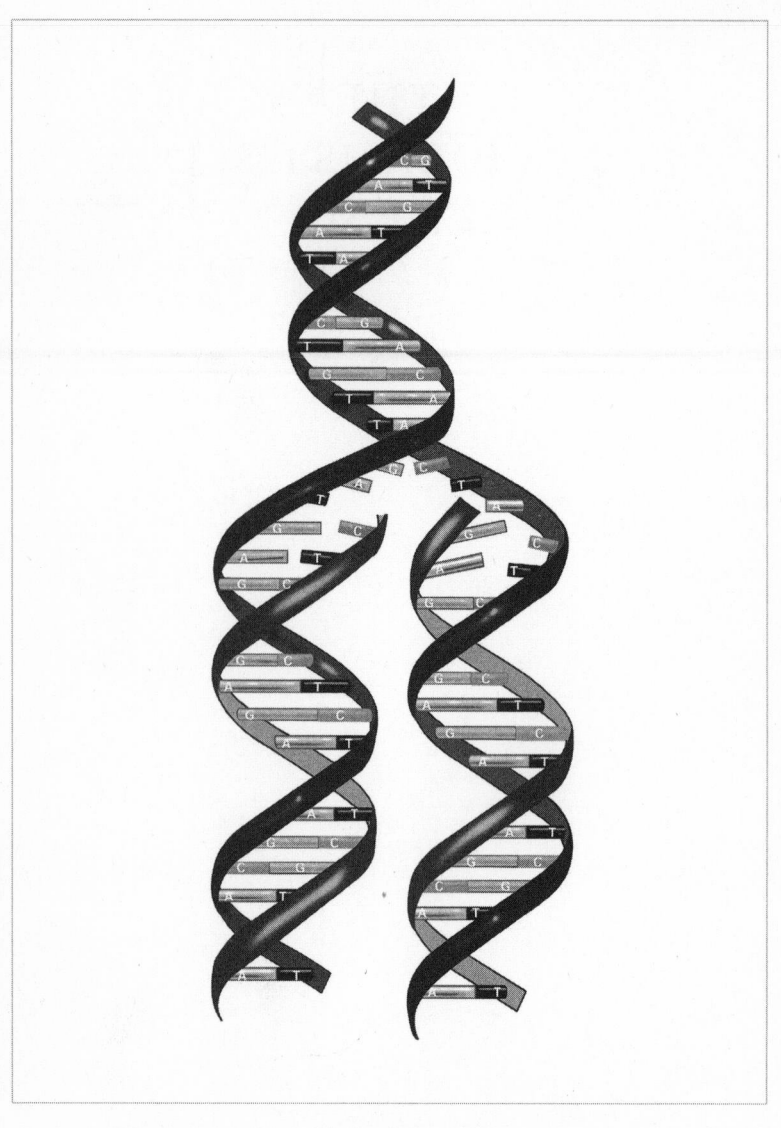

Life, therefore, may be considered a DNA chain reaction.

— Maxim D. Frank-Kamenetskii,
Unraveling DNA

THE
VIOLINIST'S
THUMB

AND OTHER LOST TALES OF LOVE,
WAR, AND GENIUS,
AS WRITTEN BY OUR GENETIC CODE

SAM KEAN

LITTLE, BROWN AND COMPANY
New York   Boston   London

ALSO BY SAM KEAN

The Disappearing Spoon

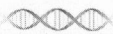

Little, Brown and Company
Hachette Book Group
237 Park Avenue, New York, NY 10017
www.hachettebookgroup.com

First Edition: July 2012

Little, Brown and Company is a division of Hachette Book Group, Inc., and is celebrating its 175th anniversary in 2012. The Little, Brown name and logo are trademarks of Hachette Book Group, Inc.

The publisher is not responsible for websites (or their content) that are not owned by the publisher.

The Hachette Speakers Bureau provides a wide range of authors for speaking events. To find out more, go to www.hachettespeakersbureau.com or call (866) 376-6591.

Frontispiece illustration by Mariana Ruiz and László Németh.

Library of Congress Cataloging-in-Publication Data

Kean, Sam.
 The violinist's thumb : and other lost tales of love, war, and genius, as written by our genetic code / Sam Kean.
    p. cm.
  Includes bibliographical references and index.
  ISBN 978-0-316-18231-7 (hc) / 978-0-316-21267-0 (international)
 1. Genetics—Miscellanea. I. Title.
 QH437.K43 2012
 572.8—dc23   2012007029

10 9 8 7 6 5 4 3 2 1

RRD-C

Printed in the United States of America

Acrostic: n., *an incognito message formed by stringing together the initial letters of lines or paragraphs or other units of composition in a work.*

N.B.: I've hidden a DNA-related acrostic in *The Violinist's Thumb* — a genetic "Easter egg," if you will. If you decode this message, e-mail me through my website (http://samkean.com /contact). Or if you can't figure it out, e-mail me anyway and I'll reveal the answer.

CONTENTS

Part III
Genes and Geniuses:
How Humans Became All Too Human

Part IV
The Oracle of DNA:
Genetics in the Past, Present, and Future

THE
VIOLINIST'S
THUMB

Introduction

his might as well come out up front, first paragraph. This is a book about DNA—about digging up stories buried in your DNA for thousands, even millions of years, and using DNA to solve mysteries about human beings whose solutions once seemed lost forever. And yes, I'm writing this book despite the fact that my father's name is Gene. As is my mother's name. Gene and Jean. Gene and Jean Kean. Beyond being singsong absurd, my parents' names led to a lot of playground jabs over the years: my every fault and foible was traced to "my genes," and when I did something idiotic, people smirked that "my genes made me do it." That my parents' passing on their genes necessarily involved sex didn't help. The taunts were doubly barbed, utterly unanswerable.

Bottom line is, I dreaded learning about DNA and genes in science classes growing up because I knew some witticism would be coming within about two seconds of the teacher turning her back. And if it wasn't coming, some wiseacre was *thinking* it. Some of that Pavlovian trepidation always stayed with me, even when (or especially when) I began to grasp how potent a substance DNA is. I got over the gibes by high school, but the word *gene* still evoked a lot of simultaneous responses, some agreeable, some not.

On the one hand, DNA excites me. There's no bolder topic in science than genetics, no field that promises to push science forward to the same degree. I don't mean just the common (and commonly overblown) promises of medical cures, either. DNA has revitalized every field in biology and remade the very study of human beings. At the same time, whenever someone starts digging into our basic human biology, we resist the intrusion — we don't want to be reduced to mere DNA. And when someone talks about tinkering with that basic biology, it can be downright frightening.

More ambiguously, DNA offers a powerful tool for rooting through our past: biology has become history by other means. Even in the past decade or so, genetics has opened up a whole Bible's worth of stories whose plotlines we assumed had vanished — either too much time had lapsed, or too little fossil or anthropological evidence remained to piece together a coherent narrative. It turns out we were carrying those stories with us the entire time, trillions of faithfully recorded texts that the little monks in our cells transcribed every hour of every day of our DNA dark age, waiting for us to get up to speed on the language. These stories include the grand sagas of where we came from and how we evolved from primordial muck into the most dominant species the planet has known. But the stories come home in surprisingly individual ways, too.

If I could have had one mulligan in school (besides a chance to make up safer names for my parents), I'd have picked a different instrument to play in band. It wasn't because I was the only boy clarinetist in the fourth, fifth, sixth, seventh, eighth, and ninth grades (or not only because of that). It was more because I felt so clumsy working all the valves and levers and blowholes on the clarinet. Nothing to do with a lack of practice, surely. I blamed the deficit on my double-jointed fingers and splayed hitchhiker thumbs. Playing the clarinet wound my fingers into such awkward braids that I constantly felt a need to crack my knuckles, and they'd throb a little. Every blue moon one thumb would even get stuck in place, frozen in extension, and I had to work the joint free with my other hand. My fingers just didn't do what the better girl clarinetists' could. My problems were inherited, I told myself, a legacy of my parents' gene stock.

After quitting band, I had no reason to reflect on my theory about manual dexterity and musical ability until a decade later, when I learned the story of violinist Niccolò Paganini, a man so gifted he had to shake off rumors his whole life that he'd sold his soul to Satan for his talent. (His hometown church even refused to bury his body for decades after his death.) It turns out Paganini had made a pact with a subtler master, his DNA. Paganini almost certainly had a genetic disorder that gave him freakishly flexible fingers. His connective tissues were so rubbery that he could pull his pinky out sideways to form a right angle to the rest of his hand. (Try this.) He could also stretch his hands abnormally wide, an incomparable advantage when playing the violin. My simple hypothesis about people "being born" to play (or not play) certain instruments seemed justified. I should have quit when ahead. I kept investigating and found out that Paganini's syndrome probably caused serious health problems, as joint pain, poor vision, weakness of breath, and fatigue dogged the violinist his whole life. I whimpered about stiff knuckles during early a.m. marching-band practice, but Paganini frequently had to cancel shows at the height of his career and couldn't perform in public during the last years of his life. In Paganini, a passion for music had united with a body perfectly tuned to take advantage of its flaws, possibly the greatest fate a human could hope for. Those flaws then hastened his death. Paganini may not have chosen his pact with his genes, but he was in one, like all of us, and the pact both made and unmade him.

DNA wasn't done telling its stories to me. Some scientists have retroactively diagnosed Charles Darwin, Abraham Lincoln, and Egyptian pharaohs with genetic disorders. Other scientists have plumbed DNA itself to articulate its deep linguistic properties and surprising mathematical beauty. In fact, just as I had crisscrossed from band to biology to history to math to social studies in high school, so stories about DNA began popping up in all sorts of contexts, linking all sorts of disparate subjects. DNA informed stories about people surviving nuclear bombs, and stories about the untimely ends of explorers in the Arctic. Stories about the near extinction of the human species, or pregnant mothers giving cancer to their unborn children. Stories where, as with Paganini, science illuminates art, and even stories where—as with scholars tracing genetic defects through portraiture—art illuminates science.

One fact you learn in biology class but don't appreciate at first is the sheer length of the DNA molecule. Despite being packed into a tiny closet in our already tiny cells, DNA can unravel to extraordinary distances. There's enough DNA in some plant cells to stretch three hundred feet; enough DNA in one human body to stretch roughly from Pluto to the sun and back; enough DNA on earth to stretch across the known universe many, many times. And the further I pursued the stories of DNA, the more I saw that its quality of stretching on and on— of unspooling farther and farther out, and even back, back through time—was intrinsic to DNA. Every human activity leaves a forensic trace in our DNA, and whether that DNA records stories about music or sports or Machiavellian microbes, those tales tell, collectively, a larger and more intricate tale of the rise of human beings on Earth: why we're one of nature's most absurd creatures, as well as its crowning glory.

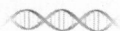

Underlying my excitement, though, is the other side of genes: the trepidation. While researching this book, I submitted my DNA to a genetic testing service, and despite the price tag

($414), I did so in a frivolous state of mind. I knew personal genomic testing has serious shortcomings, and even when the science is solid, it's often not that helpful. I might learn from my DNA that I have green eyes, but then again I do own a mirror. I might learn I don't metabolize caffeine well, but I've had plenty of jittery nights after a late Coke. Besides, it was hard to take the DNA-submission process seriously. A plastic vial with a candy-corn orange lid arrived in the mail, and the instructions told me to massage my cheeks with my knuckles to work some cells loose inside my mouth. I then hocked into the tube repeatedly until I filled it two-thirds full of saliva. That took ten minutes, since the instructions said in all seriousness that it couldn't be just any saliva. It had to be the good, thick, syrupy stuff; as with a draft beer, there shouldn't be much foam. The next day I mailed the genetic spittoon off, hoping for a nice surprise about my ancestry. I didn't engage in any sober reflection until I went to register my test online and read the instructions about redacting sensitive or scary information. If your family has a history of breast cancer or Alzheimer's or other diseases — or if the mere thought of having them frightens you — the testing service lets you block that information. You can tick a box and keep it secret from even yourself. What caught me short was the box for Parkinson's disease. One of the earliest memories I have, and easily the worst of those early memories, is wandering down the hallway of my grandma's house and poking my head into the room where my grandpa, laid low by Parkinson's, lived out his days.

When he was growing up, people always told my father how much he looked like my grandpa — and I got similar comments about looking like my old man. So when I wandered into that room off the hallway and saw a white-haired version of my father propped in a bed with a metal safety rail, I saw myself by extension. I remember lots of white — the walls, the carpet, the sheets, the open-backed smock he wore. I remember him pitched forward to the point of almost tipping over, his smock loose and a fringe of white hair hanging straight down.

I'm not sure whether he saw me, but when I hesitated on the threshold, he moaned and began trembling, which made his voice quake. My grandpa was lucky in some ways; my grandma, a nurse, took care of him at home, and his children visited regularly. But he'd regressed mentally and physically. I remember most of all the thick, syrupy string of saliva pendulous on his chin, full of DNA. I was five or so, too young to understand. I'm still ashamed that I ran.

Now, strangers—and worse, my own self—could peek at whether the string of self-replicating molecules that might have triggered Parkinson's in my grandfather was lurking in my cells, too. There was a good chance not. My grandpa's genes had been diluted by my grandma's genes in Gene, whose genes had in turn been diluted in me by Jean's. But the chance was certainly real. I could face any of the cancers or other degenerative diseases I might be susceptible to. Not Parkinson's. I blacked the data out.

Personal stories like that are as much a part of genetics as all the exciting history—perhaps more so, since all of us have at least one of these stories buried inside us. That's why this book, beyond relating all the historical tales, builds on those tales and links them to work being done on DNA today, and work likely to be done tomorrow. This genetics research and the changes it will bring have been compared to a shifting ocean tide, huge and inevitable. But its consequences will arrive at the shore where we're standing not as a tsunami but as tiny waves. It's the individual waves we'll feel, one by one, as the tide crawls up the shore, no matter how far back we think we can stand.

Still, we can prepare ourselves for their arrival. As some scientists recognize, the story of DNA has effectively replaced the old college Western Civ class as the grand narrative of human existence. Understanding DNA can help us understand where we come from and how our bodies and minds work, and understanding the limits of DNA also helps us understand how our bodies and minds don't work. To a similar degree, we'll have to prepare ourselves for whatever DNA says (and doesn't say) about intractable social problems like gender and race relations, or whether traits like aggression and intelligence are fixed or flexible. We'll also have to decide whether to trust eager thinkers who, while acknowledging that we don't understand completely how DNA works, already talk about the opportunity, even the obligation, to improve on four billion years of biology. To this point of view, the most remarkable story about DNA is that our species survived long enough to (potentially) master it.

The history in this book is still being constructed, and I structured *The Violinist's Thumb* so that each chapter provides the answer to a single question. The overarching narrative starts in the remote microbial past, moves on to our animal ancestries, lingers over primates and hominid competitors like Neanderthals, and culminates with the emergence of modern, cultured human beings with flowery language and hypertrophied brains. But as the book advances toward the final section, the questions have not been fully resolved. Things remain uncertain—especially the question of how this grand human experiment of uprooting everything there is to know about our DNA will turn out.

PART I

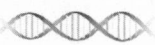

A, C, G, T, and You

How to Read a Genetic Score

1

Genes, Freaks, DNA

How Do Living Things Pass Down Traits to Their Children?

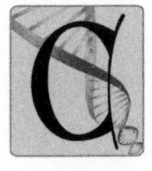hills and flames, frost and inferno, fire and ice. The two scientists who made the first great discoveries in genetics had a lot in common—not least the fact that both died obscure, mostly unmourned and happily forgotten by many. But whereas one's legacy perished in fire, the other's succumbed to ice.

The blaze came during the winter of 1884, at a monastery in what's now the Czech Republic. The friars spent a January day emptying out the office of their deceased abbot, Gregor Mendel, ruthlessly purging his files, consigning everything to a bonfire in the courtyard. Though a warm and capable man, late in life Mendel had become something of an embarrassment to the monastery, the cause for government inquiries, newspaper gossip, even a showdown with a local sheriff. (Mendel won.) No relatives came by to pick up Mendel's things, and the monks burned his papers for the same reason you'd cauterize a wound—to sterilize, and stanch embarrassment. No record survives of what they looked like, but among those documents were sheaves of papers, or perhaps a lab notebook with a plain cover, probably coated in dust from disuse. The yellowed pages would have been full of sketches of pea plants and tables of numbers (Mendel adored numbers), and they probably didn't kick up any more smoke and ash than other papers when incinerated. But the burning of those papers—burned on the exact spot where Mendel had kept his greenhouse years before—destroyed the only original record of the discovery of the gene.

The chills came during that same winter of 1884—as they had for many winters before, and would for too few winters after. Johannes Friedrich Miescher, a middling professor of physiology in Switzerland, was studying salmon, and among his other projects he was indulging a long-standing obsession with a substance—a cottony gray paste—he'd extracted from salmon sperm years before. To keep the delicate sperm from perishing in the open air, Miescher had to throw the windows open to the cold and refrigerate his lab the old-fashioned way, exposing himself day in and day out to the Swiss winter. Getting any work done required superhuman focus, and that was the one asset even people who thought little of Miescher would admit he had. (Earlier in his career, friends had to drag him from his lab bench one afternoon to attend his wedding; the ceremony had slipped his mind.) Despite being so driven, Miescher had pathetically little to show for it—his lifetime scientific output was meager. Still, he kept the windows open and kept shivering year after year, though he knew it was slowly killing him. And he still never got to the bottom of that milky gray substance, DNA.

DNA and genes, genes and DNA. Nowadays the words have become synonymous. The mind rushes to link them, like Gilbert and Sullivan or Watson and Crick. So it seems fitting that Miescher and Mendel discovered DNA and genes almost simultaneously in the 1860s, two monastic men just four hundred miles apart in the German-speaking span of middle Europe. It seems more than fitting; it seems fated.

But to understand what DNA and genes really are, we have to decouple the two words. They're not identical and never have been. DNA is a *thing*—a chemical that sticks to your fingers. Genes have a physical nature, too; in fact, they're made of long stretches of DNA. But in some ways genes are better viewed as conceptual, not material. A gene is really information—more like a story, with DNA as the language the story is written in. DNA and genes combine to form larger structures called chromosomes, DNA-rich volumes that house most of the genes in living things. Chromosomes in turn reside in the cell nucleus, a library with instructions that run our entire bodies.

All these structures play important roles in genetics and heredity, but despite the near-simultaneous discovery of each in the 1800s, no one connected DNA and genes for almost a century, and both discoverers died uncelebrated. How biologists finally yoked genes and DNA together is the first epic story in the science of inheritance, and even today, efforts to refine the relationship between genes and DNA drive genetics forward.

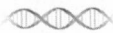

Mendel and Miescher began their work at a time when folk theories—some uproarious or bizarre, some quite ingenious, in their way—dominated most people's thinking about heredity, and for centuries these folk theories had colored their views about why we inherit different traits.

Everyone knew on some level of course that children resemble parents. Red hair, baldness, lunacy, receding chins, even extra thumbs, could all be traced up and down a genealogical tree. And fairy tales—those codifiers of the collective unconscious—often turned on some wretch being a "true" prince(ss) with a royal bloodline, a biological core that neither rags nor an amphibian frame could sully.

That's mostly common sense. But the mechanism of heredity—how exactly traits got passed from generation to generation—baffled even the most intelligent thinkers, and the vagaries of this process led to many of the wilder theories that circulated before and even during the 1800s. One ubiquitous folk theory, "maternal impressions," held that if a pregnant woman saw something ghoulish or suffered intense emotions, the experience would scar her child. One woman who never satisfied an intense prenatal craving for strawberries gave birth to a baby covered with red, strawberry-shaped splotches. The same could happen with bacon. Another woman bashed her head on a sack of coal, and her child had half, but only half, a head of black hair. More direly, doctors in the 1600s reported that a woman in Naples, after being startled by sea monsters, bore a son covered in scales, who ate fish exclusively and gave off fishy odors. Bishops told cautionary tales of a woman who seduced her actor husband backstage in full costume. He was playing Mephistopheles; they had a child with hooves and horns. A beggar with one arm spooked a woman into having a one-armed child. Pregnant women who pulled off crowded streets to pee in churchyards invariably produced bed wetters. Carrying fireplace logs about in your apron, next to the bulging tummy, would produce a grotesquely well-hung lad. About the only recorded happy case of maternal impressions involved a patriotic woman in Paris in the 1790s whose son had a birthmark on his chest shaped like a Phrygian cap—those elfish hats with a flop of material on top. Phrygian caps were symbols of freedom to the new French republic, and the delighted government awarded her a lifetime pension.

Much of this folklore intersected with religious belief, and people naturally interpreted serious birth defects—cyclopean eyes, external hearts, full coats of body hair—as back-of-the-Bible warnings about sin, wrath, and divine justice. One example from the 1680s involved a cruel bailiff in Scotland named Bell, who arrested two female religious dissenters, lashed them to poles near the shore, and let the tide swallow them. Bell added insult by taunting the women, then drowned the younger, more stubborn one with his own hands. Later, when asked about the murders, Bell always laughed, joking that the women must be having a high time now, scuttling around among the crabs. The joke was on Bell: after he married, his children were born with a severe defect that twisted their forearms into two awful pincers. These crab claws proved highly heritable to their children and grandchildren, too. It didn't take a biblical scholar to see that the iniquity of the father had been visited upon the children, unto the third and fourth generations. (And beyond: cases popped up in Scotland as late as 1900.)

If maternal impressions stressed environmental influences, other theories of inheritance had strong congenital flavors. One, preformationism, grew out of the medieval alchemists' quest to create a homunculus, a miniature, even microscopic, human being. Homunculi were the biological philosopher's stone, and creating one showed that an alchemist possessed the power of gods. (The process of creation was somewhat less dignified. One recipe called for fermenting sperm, horse dung, and urine in a pumpkin for six weeks.) By the late 1600s, some protoscientists had stolen the idea of the homunculus and were arguing that one must live inside each female egg cell. This neatly did away with the question of how living embryos arose from seemingly dead blobs of matter. Under preformationist theory, such spontaneous generation wasn't necessary: homuncular babies were indeed preformed and merely needed a trigger, like sperm, to grow. This idea had only one problem: as critics pointed out, it introduced an infinite regress, since a woman necessarily had to have all her future children, as well as their children, and *their* children, stuffed inside her, like Russian *matryoshka* nesting dolls. Indeed, adherents of "ovism" could only deduce that God had crammed the entire human race into Eve's ovaries on day one. (Or rather, day six of Genesis.) "Spermists" had it even worse— Adam must have had humanity entire sardined into his even tinier sperms. Yet after the first microscopes appeared, a few spermists tricked themselves into seeing tiny humans bobbing around in puddles of semen. Both ovism and spermism gained credence in part because they explained original sin: we all resided inside Adam or Eve during their banishment from Eden and therefore all share the taint. But spermism also introduced theological quandaries—for what happened to the endless number of unbaptized souls that perished every time a man ejaculated?

However poetic or deliciously bawdy these theories were, biologists in Miescher's day scoffed at them as old wives' tales. These men wanted to banish wild anecdotes and vague "life forces" from science and ground all heredity and development in chemistry instead.

Miescher hadn't originally planned to join this movement to demystify life. As a young man he had trained to practice the family trade, medicine, in his native Switzerland. But a boyhood typhoid infection had left him hard of hearing and unable to use a stethoscope or hear an invalid's bedside bellyaching. Miescher's father, a prominent gynecologist, suggested a career in research instead. So in 1868 the young Miescher moved into a lab run by the biochemist Felix Hoppe-Seyler, in Tübingen, Germany. Though headquartered in an impressive medieval castle, Hoppe-Seyler's lab occupied the royal laundry room in the basement; he found Miescher space next door, in the old kitchen.

Hoppe-Seyler wanted to catalog the chemicals present in human blood cells. He had already investigated red blood cells, so he assigned white ones to Miescher—a fortuitous decision

Friedrich Miescher (*inset*) discovered DNA in this laboratory, a renovated kitchen in the basement of a castle in Tübingen, Germany. (University of Tübingen library)

for his new assistant, since white blood cells (unlike red ones) contain a tiny internal capsule called a nucleus. At the time, most scientists ignored the nucleus—it had no known function—and quite reasonably concentrated on the cytoplasm instead, the slurry that makes up most of a cell's volume. But the chance to analyze something unknown appealed to Miescher.

To study the nucleus, Miescher needed a steady supply of white blood cells, so he approached a local hospital. According to legend, the hospital catered to veterans who'd endured gruesome battlefield amputations and other mishaps. Regardless, the clinic did house many chronic patients, and each day a hospital orderly collected pus-soaked bandages and delivered the yellowed rags to Miescher. The pus often degraded into slime in the open air, and Miescher had to smell each suppurated-on cloth and throw out the putrid ones (most of them). But the remaining "fresh" pus was swimming with white blood cells.

Eager to impress—and, in truth, doubtful of his own talents—Miescher threw himself into studying the nucleus, as if sheer labor would make up for any shortcomings. A colleague later described him as "driven by a demon," and Miescher exposed himself daily to all manner of chemicals in his work. But without this focus, he probably wouldn't have discovered what he did, since the key substance inside the nucleus proved elusive. Miescher first washed his pus in warm alcohol, then acid extract from a pig's stomach, to dissolve away the cell membranes. This allowed him to isolate a gray paste. Assuming it was protein, he ran tests to identify it. But the paste resisted protein digestion and, unlike any known protein, wouldn't dissolve in salt water, boiling vinegar, or dilute hydrochloric acid. So he tried elementary analysis, charring it until it decomposed. He got the expected elements, carbon, hydrogen, oxygen, and nitrogen, but also discovered 3 percent phosphorus, an element proteins lack. Convinced he'd found something unique, he named the substance "nuclein"—what later scientists called deoxyribonucleic acid, or DNA.

Miescher polished off the work in a year, and in autumn 1869 stopped by the royal laundry to show Hoppe-Seyler. Far from rejoicing, the older scientist screwed up his brow and expressed his doubts that the nucleus contained any sort of special, non-proteinaceous substance. Miescher had made a mistake, surely. Miescher protested, but Hoppe-Seyler insisted on repeating the young man's experiments—step by step, bandage by bandage—

before allowing him to publish. Hoppe-Seyler's condescension couldn't have helped Miescher's confidence (he never worked so quickly again). And even after two years of labor vindicated Miescher, Hoppe-Seyler insisted on writing a patronizing editorial to accompany Miescher's paper, in which he backhandedly praised Miescher for "enhanc[ing] our understanding...of pus." Nevertheless Miescher did get credit, in 1871, for discovering DNA.

Some parallel discoveries quickly illuminated more about Miescher's molecule. Most important, a German protégé of Hoppe-Seyler's determined that nuclein contained multiple types of smaller constituent molecules. These included phosphates and sugars (the eponymous "deoxyribose" sugars), as well as four ringed chemicals now called nucleic "bases"—adenine, cytosine, guanine, and thymine. Still, no one knew how these parts fit together, and this jumble made DNA seem strangely heterogeneous and incomprehensible.

(Scientists now know how all these parts contribute to DNA. The molecule forms a double helix, which looks like a ladder twisted into a corkscrew. The supports of the ladder are strands made of alternating phosphates and sugars. The ladder's rungs—the most important part—are each made of two nucleic bases, and these bases pair up in specific ways: adenine, A, always bonds with thymine, T; cytosine, C, always bonds with guanine, G. [To remember this, notice that the curvaceous letters C and G pair-bond, as do angular A and T.])

Meanwhile DNA's reputation was bolstered by other discoveries. Scientists in the later 1800s determined that whenever cells divide in two, they carefully divvy up their chromosomes. This hinted that chromosomes were important for something, because otherwise cells wouldn't bother. Another group of scientists determined that chromosomes are passed whole and intact from parent to child. Yet another German chemist then discovered that chromosomes were mostly made up of none other than DNA. From this constellation of findings—it took a little imagination to sketch in the lines and see a bigger picture—a small number of scientists realized that DNA might play a direct role in heredity. Nuclein was intriguing people.

Miescher lucked out, frankly, when nuclein became a respectable object of inquiry; his career had stalled otherwise. After his stint in Tübingen, he moved home to Basel, but his new institute refused him his own lab—he got one corner in a common room and had to carry out chemical analyses in an old hallway. (The castle kitchen was looking pretty good suddenly.) His new job also required teaching. Miescher had an aloof, even frosty demeanor—he was someone never at ease around people—and although he labored over lectures, he proved a pedagogical disaster: students remember him as "insecure, restless...myopic... difficult to understand, [and] fidgety." We like to think of scientific heroes as electric personalities, but Miescher lacked even rudimentary charisma.

Given his atrocious teaching, which further eroded his self-esteem, Miescher rededicated himself to research. Upholding what one observer called his "fetish of examining objectionable fluids," Miescher transferred his DNA allegiance from pus to semen. The sperm in semen were basically nuclein-tipped missiles and provided loads of DNA without much extraneous cytoplasm. Miescher also had a convenient source of sperm in the hordes of salmon that clogged the river Rhine near his university every autumn and winter. During spawning season, salmon testes grow like tumors, swelling twenty times larger than normal and often topping a pound each. To collect salmon, Miescher could practically dangle a fishing line from his office window, and by squeezing their "ripe" testes through cheesecloth, he isolated millions of bewildered little swimmers. The downside was that salmon sperm deteriorates at anything close to comfortable temperatures. So Miescher had to arrive at his bench in the chilly early hours before dawn, prop the windows open, and drop the temperature to around 35°F before working. And because of a stingy budget, when his laboratory glassware broke, he sometimes had to pilfer his ever-loving wife's fine china to finish experiments.

From this work, as well as his colleagues' work with other cells, Miescher concluded that all cell nuclei contain DNA. In fact he proposed redefining cell nuclei—which come in a variety of sizes and shapes—strictly as containers for DNA. Though he wasn't greedy about his reputation, this might have been a last stab at glory for Miescher. DNA might still have turned out to be relatively unimportant, and in that case, he would have at least figured out what the mysterious nucleus did. But it wasn't to be. Though we now know Miescher was largely right in defining the nucleus, other scientists balked at his admittedly premature suggestion; there just wasn't enough proof. And even if they bought that, they wouldn't grant Miescher's next, more self-serving claim: that DNA influenced heredity. It didn't help that Miescher had no idea how DNA did so. Like many scientists then, he doubted that sperm injected anything into eggs, partly because he assumed (echoes of the homunculus here) that eggs already contained the full complement of parts needed for life. Rather, he imagined that sperm nuclein acted as a sort of chemical defibrillator and jump-started eggs. Unfortunately Miescher had little time to explore or defend such ideas. He still had to lecture, and the Swiss government piled "thankless and tedious" tasks onto him, like preparing reports on nutrition in prisons and elementary schools. The years of working through Swiss winters with the windows open also did a number on his health, and he contracted tuberculosis. He ended up giving up DNA work altogether.

Meanwhile other scientists' doubts about DNA began to

solidify, in their minds, into hard opposition. Most damning, scientists discovered that there was more to chromosomes than phosphate-sugar backbones and A-C-G-T bases. Chromosomes also contained protein nuggets, which seemed more likely candidates to explain chemical heredity. That's because proteins were composed of twenty different subunits (called amino acids). Each of these subunits could serve as one "letter" for writing chemical instructions, and there seemed to be enough variety among these letters to explain the dazzling diversity of life itself. The A, C, G, and T of DNA seemed dull and simplistic in comparison, a four-letter pidgin alphabet with limited expressive power. As a result, most scientists decided that DNA stored phosphorus for cells, nothing more.

Sadly, even Miescher came to doubt that DNA contained enough alphabetical variety. He too began tinkering with protein inheritance, and developed a theory where proteins encoded information by sticking out molecular arms and branches at different angles—a kind of chemical semaphore. It still wasn't clear how sperm passed this information to eggs, though, and Miescher's confusion deepened. He turned back to DNA late in life and argued that it might assist with heredity still. But progress proved slow, partly because he had to spend more and more time in tuberculosis sanitariums in the Alps. Before he got to the bottom of anything, he contracted pneumonia in 1895, and succumbed soon after.

Later work continued to undermine Miescher by reinforcing the belief that even if chromosomes control inheritance, the proteins in chromosomes, not the DNA, contained the actual information. After Miescher's death, his uncle, a fellow scientist, gathered Miescher's correspondence and papers into a "collected works," like some belle-lettrist. The uncle prefaced the book by claiming that "Miescher and his work will not diminish; on the contrary, it will grow and his discoveries and thoughts will be seeds for a fruitful future." Kind words, but it must have seemed a fond hope: Miescher's obituaries barely mentioned his work on nuclein; and DNA, like Miescher himself, seemed decidedly minor.

At least Miescher died known, where he was known, for science. Gregor Mendel made a name for himself during his lifetime only through scandal.

By his own admission, Mendel became an Augustinian friar not because of any pious impulse but because his order would pay his bills, including college tuition. The son of peasants, Mendel had been able to afford his elementary school only because his uncle had founded it; he attended high school only after his sister sacrificed part of her dowry. But with the church footing the bill, Mendel attended the University of Vienna and studied science, learning experimental design from Christian Doppler himself, of the eponymous effect. (Though only after Doppler rejected Mendel's initial application, perhaps because of Mendel's habit of having nervous breakdowns during tests.)

The abbot at St. Thomas, Mendel's monastery, encouraged Mendel's interest in science and statistics, partly for mercenary reasons: the abbot thought scientific farming could produce better sheep, fruit trees, and grapevines and help the monastery crawl out of debt. But Mendel had time to explore other interests, too, and over the years he charted sunspots, tracked tornadoes, kept an apiary buzzing with bees (although one strain he bred was so nasty-tempered and vindictive it had to be destroyed), and cofounded the Austrian Meteorological Society.

In the early 1860s, just before Miescher moved from medical school into research, Mendel began some deceptively simple experiments on pea plants in the St. Thomas nursery. Beyond enjoying their taste and wanting a ready supply, he chose peas because they simplified experiments. Neither bees nor wind could pollinate his pea blossoms, so he could control which plants mated with which. He appreciated the binary, either/or nature of pea plants, too: plants had tall or short stalks, green or yellow pods, wrinkled or smooth peas, nothing in between. In fact, Mendel's first important conclusion from his work was that some binary traits "dominated" others. For example, crossing purebred green-pead plants with purebred yellow-pead plants produced only yellow-pead offspring: yellow dominated. Importantly, however, the green trait hadn't disappeared. When Mendel mated those second-generation yellow-pead plants with each other, a few furtive green peas popped up—one latent, "recessive" green for every three dominant yellows. The 3:1 ratio* held for other traits, too.

Equally important, Mendel concluded that having one dominant or recessive trait didn't affect whether another, separate trait was dominant or recessive—each trait was independent. For example, even though tall dominated short, a recessive-short plant could still have dominant-yellow peas. Or a tall plant could have recessive-green peas. In fact, every one of the seven traits he studied—like smooth peas (dominant) versus wrinkled peas (recessive), or purple blossoms (dominant) versus white blossoms (recessive)—was inherited independently of the other traits.

This focus on separate, independent traits allowed Mendel to succeed where other heredity-minded horticulturists had failed. Had Mendel tried to describe, all at once, the overall resemblance of a plant to its parents, he would have had too many traits to consider. The plants would have seemed a confusing collage of Mom and Dad. (Charles Darwin, who also grew

---

* This and all upcoming asterisks refer to the Notes and Errata section, which begins on p. 363 and goes into more detail on various interesting points.

and experimented with pea plants, failed to understand their heredity partly for this reason.) But by narrowing his scope to one trait at a time, Mendel could see that each trait must be controlled by a separate factor. Mendel never used the word, but he identified the discrete, inheritable factors we call genes today. Mendel's peas were the Newton's apple of biology.

Beyond his qualitative discoveries, Mendel put genetics on solid quantitative footing. He adored the statistical manipulations of meteorology, the translating of daily barometer and thermometer readings into aggregate climate data. He approached breeding the same way, abstracting from individual plants into general laws of inheritance. In fact, rumors have persisted for almost a century now that Mendel got carried away here, letting his love of perfect data tempt him into fraud.

If you flip a dime a thousand times, you'll get approximately five hundred FDRs and five hundred torches; but you're unlikely to get exactly five hundred of either, because each flip is independent and random. Similarly, because of random deviations, experimental data always stray a tad higher or lower than theory predicts. Mendel should therefore have gotten only approximately a 3:1 ratio of tall to short plants (or whatever other trait he measured). Mendel, however, claimed some almost platonically perfect 3:1s among his thousands of pea plants, a claim that has raised suspicions among modern geneticists. One latter-day fact checker calculated the odds at less than one in ten thousand that Mendel—otherwise a pedant for numerical accuracy in ledgers and meteorological experiments—came by his results honestly. Many historians have defended Mendel over the years or argued that he manipulated his data only unconsciously, since standards for recording data differed back then. (One sympathizer even invented, based on no evidence, an overzealous gardening assistant who knew what numbers Mendel wanted and furtively discarded plants to please his master.) Mendel's original lab notes were burned after his death, so we can't check if he cooked the books. Honestly, though, if Mendel did cheat, it's almost more remarkable: it means he intuited the correct answer—the golden 3:1 ratio of genetics—before having any real proof. The purportedly fraudulent data may simply have been the monk's way of tidying up the vagaries of real-world experiments, to make his data more convincing, so that others could see what he somehow knew by revelation.

Regardless, no one in Mendel's lifetime suspected he'd pulled a fast one—partly because no one was paying attention. He read a paper on pea heredity at a conference in 1865, and as one historian noted, "his audience dealt with him in the way that all audiences do when presented with more mathematics than they have a taste for: there was no discussion, and no questions were asked." He almost shouldn't have bothered, but Mendel published his results in 1866. Again, silence.

Mendel kept working for a few years, but his chance to burnish his scientific reputation largely evaporated in 1868, when his monastery elected him abbot. Never having governed anything before, Mendel had a lot to learn, and the day-to-day headaches of running St. Thomas cut into his free time for horticulture. Moreover, the perks of being in charge, like rich foods and cigars (Mendel smoked up to twenty cigars per day and grew so stout that his resting pulse sometimes topped 120), slowed him down, limiting his enjoyment of the gardens and greenhouses. One later visitor did remember Abbot Mendel taking him on a stroll through the gardens and pointing out with delight the blossoms and ripe pears; but at the first mention of his own experiments in the garden, Mendel changed the subject, almost embarrassed. (Asked how he managed to grow nothing but tall pea plants, Mendel demurred: "It is just a little trick, but there is a long story connected with it, which would take too long to tell.")

Mendel's scientific career also atrophied because he wasted

an increasing number of hours squabbling about political issues, especially separation of church and state. (Although it's not obvious from his scientific work, Mendel could be fiery—a contrast to the chill of Miescher.) Almost alone among his fellow Catholic abbots, Mendel supported liberal politics, but the liberals ruling Austria in 1874 double-crossed him and revoked the tax-exempt status of monasteries. The government demanded seventy-three hundred gulden per year from St. Thomas in payment, 10 percent of the monastery's assessed value, and although Mendel, outraged and betrayed, paid some of the sum, he refused to pony up the rest. In response, the government seized property from St. Thomas's farms. It even dispatched a sheriff to seize assets from inside St. Thomas itself. Mendel met his adversary in full clerical habit outside the front gate, where he stared him down and dared him to extract the key from his pocket. The sheriff left empty-handed.

Overall, though, Mendel made little headway getting the new law repealed. He even turned into something of a crank, demanding interest for lost income and writing long letters to legislators on arcane points of ecclesiastical taxation. One lawyer sighed that Mendel was "full of suspicion, [seeing] himself surrounded by nothing but enemies, traitors, and intriguers." The "Mendel affair" did make the erstwhile scientist famous, or notorious, in Vienna. It also convinced his successor at St. Thomas that Mendel's papers should be burned when he died, to end the dispute and save face for the monastery. The notes describing the pea experiments would become collateral casualties.

Mendel died in 1884, not long after the church-state imbroglio; his nurse found him stiff and upright on his sofa, his heart and kidneys having failed. We know this because Mendel feared being buried alive and had demanded a precautionary autopsy. But in one sense, Mendel's fretting over a premature burial proved prophetic. Just eleven scientists cited his now-classic paper on inheritance in the thirty-five years after his death. And those that did (mostly agricultural scientists) saw his experiments as mildly interesting lessons for breeding peas, not universal statements on heredity. Scientists had indeed buried Mendel's theories too soon.

But all the while, biologists were discovering things about cells that, if they'd only known, supported Mendel's ideas. Most important, they found distinct ratios of traits among offspring, and determined that chromosomes passed hereditary information around in discrete chunks, like the discrete traits Mendel identified. So when three biologists hunting through footnotes around 1900 all came across the pea paper independently and realized how closely it mirrored their own work, they grew determined to resurrect the monk.

Mendel allegedly once vowed to a colleague, "My time will come," and boy, did it. After 1900 "Mendelism" expanded so quickly, with so much ideological fervor pumping it up, that it began to rival Charles Darwin's natural selection as the preeminent theory in biology. Many geneticists in fact saw Darwinism and Mendelism as flatly incompatible — and a few even relished the prospect of banishing Darwin to the same historical obscurity that Friedrich Miescher knew so well.

2

The Near Death of Darwin

Why Did Geneticists Try to Kill Natural Selection?

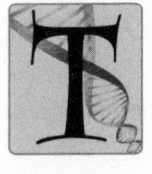his was not how a Nobel laureate should have to spend his time. In late 1933, shortly after winning science's highest honor, Thomas Hunt Morgan got a message from his longtime assistant Calvin Bridges, whose libido had landed him in hot water. Again.

A "confidence woman" from Harlem had met Bridges on a cross-country train a few weeks before. She quickly convinced him not only that she was a regal princess from India, but that her fabulously wealthy maharaja of a father just happened to have opened—coincidence of all coincidences—a science institute on the subcontinent in the very field that Bridges (and Morgan) worked in, fruit fly genetics. Since her father needed a man to head the institute, she offered Bridges the job. Bridges, a real Casanova, would likely have shacked up with the woman anyway, and the job prospect made her irresistible. He was so smitten he began offering his colleagues jobs in India and didn't seem to notice Her Highness's habit of running up extraordinary bills whenever they went carousing. In fact, when out of earshot, the supposed princess claimed to be Mrs. Bridges and charged everything she could to him. When the truth emerged, she tried to extort more cash by threatening to sue him "for transporting her across state lines for immoral purposes." Panicked and distraught—despite his adult activities, Bridges was quite childlike—he turned to Morgan.

Morgan no doubt consulted with his other trusted assistant, Alfred Sturtevant. Like Bridges, Sturtevant had worked with Morgan for decades, and the trio had shared in some of the most important discoveries in genetics history. Sturtevant and Morgan both scowled in private over Bridges's dalliances and escapades, but their loyalty trumped any other consideration here. They decided that Morgan should throw his weight around. In short order, he threatened to expose the woman to the police, and kept up the pressure until Miss Princess disappeared on the next train. Morgan then hid Bridges away until the situation blew over.*

When he'd hired Bridges as a factotum years before, Morgan could never have expected he'd someday be acting as a goodfella for him. Then again, Morgan could never have expected how most everything in his life had turned out. After laboring away in anonymity, he had now become a grand panjandrum of genetics. After working in comically cramped quarters in Manhattan, he now oversaw a spacious lab in California. After lavishing so much attention and affection on his "fly boys" over the years, he was now fending off charges from former assistants that he'd stolen credit for others' ideas. And after fighting so hard for so long against the overreach of ambitious scientific theories, he'd now surrendered to, and even helped expand, the two most ambitious theories in all biology.

Morgan's younger self might well have despised his older self for this last thing. Morgan had begun his career at a curious time in science history, around 1900, when a most uncivil civil war broke out between Mendel's genetics and Darwin's natural selection: things got so nasty, most biologists felt that one theory or the other would have to be exterminated. In this war Morgan had tried to stay Switzerland, refusing at first to accept either theory. Both relied too much on speculation, he felt, and Morgan had an almost reactionary distrust of speculation. If he couldn't see proof for a theory in front of his corneas, he wanted to banish it from science. Indeed, if scientific advances often require a brilliant theorist to emerge and explain his vision with perfect clarity, the opposite was true for Morgan, who was cussedly stubborn and notoriously muddled in his reasoning—anything but literally visible proof bemused him.

And yet that very confusion makes him the perfect guide to follow along behind during the War of the Roses interlude when Darwinists and Mendelists despised each other. Morgan mistrusted genetics and natural selection equally at first, but his patient experiments on fruit flies teased out the half-truths of each. He eventually succeeded—or rather, he and his talented team of assistants succeeded—in weaving genetics and evolution together into the grand tapestry of modern biology.

The decline of Darwinism, now known as the "eclipse" of Darwinism, began in the late 1800s and began for quite rational reasons. Above all, while biologists gave Darwin credit for proving that evolution happened, they disparaged his mechanism for evolution—natural selection, the survival of the fittest—as woefully inadequate for bringing about the changes he claimed.

Critics harped especially on their belief that natural selection merely executed the unfit; it seemed to illuminate nothing about where new or advantageous traits come from. As one wit said, natural selection accounted for the survival, but not the *arrival*, of the fittest. Darwin had compounded the problem by insisting that natural selection worked excruciatingly slowly, on tiny differences among individuals. No one else believed that such minute variations could have any practical long-term difference—they believed in evolution by jerks and jumps. Even Darwin's bulldog Thomas Henry Huxley recalled trying, "much to Mr. Darwin's disgust," to convince Darwin that species sometimes advanced by jumps. Darwin wouldn't budge—he accepted only infinitesimal steps.

Additional arguments against natural selection gathered strength after Darwin died in 1882. As statisticians had demonstrated, most traits for species formed a bell curve: ⌒. Most people stood an average height, for example, and the number of tall or short people dropped smoothly to small numbers on both sides. Traits in animals like speed (or strength or smarts) also formed bell curves, with a large number of average creatures. Obviously natural selection would weed out the slowpokes and idiots when predators snatched them. For evolution to occur, though, most scientists argued that the average had to shift; your average creature had to become faster or stronger or smarter. Otherwise the species largely remained the same. But killing off the slowest creatures wouldn't suddenly make those that escaped any faster—and the escapees would continue having mediocre children as a result. What's more, most scientists assumed that the speed of any rare fast creature would be diluted when it bred with slower ones, producing more mediocrities. According to this logic, species got stuck in ruts of average traits, and the nudge of natural selection couldn't improve them. True evolution, then—men from monkeys—had to proceed by jumps.*

Beyond its apparent statistical problems, Darwinism had something else working against it: emotion. People loathed natural selection. Pitiless death seemed paramount, with superior types always crushing the weak. Intellectuals like playwright George Bernard Shaw even felt betrayed by Darwin. Shaw had adored Darwin at first for smiting religious dogmas. But the more Shaw heard, the less he liked natural selection. And "when its whole significance dawns on you," Shaw later lamented, "your heart sinks into a heap of sand within you. There is a hideous fatalism about it, a ghastly and damnable reduction of beauty and intelligence." Nature governed by such rules, he said, would be "a universal struggle for hogwash."

The triplicate rediscovery of Mendel in 1900 further galvanized the anti-Darwinists by providing a scientific alternative—and soon an outright rival. Mendel's work emphasized not murder and starvation but growth and generation. Moreover, Mendel's peas showed signs of jerkiness—tall or short stalks, yellow or green peas, nothing in between. Already by 1902 the English biologist William Bateson had helped a doctor identify the first known gene in humans (for an alarming but largely benign disorder, alkaptonuria, which can turn children's urine black). Bateson soon rebranded Mendelism "genetics" and became Mendel's bulldog in Europe, tirelessly championing the monk's work, even taking up chess and cigars simply because Mendel loved both. Others supported Bateson's creepy zealotry, however, because Darwinism violated the progressive ethos of the young century. Already by 1904, German scientist Eberhard Dennert could cackle, "We are standing at the death-bed of Darwinism, and making ready to send the friends of the patient a little money, to ensure a decent burial." (A sentiment fit for a creationist today.) To be sure, a minority of biologists defended Darwin's vision of gradual evolution against the Dennerts and Batesons of the world, and defended it fiercely—one historian commented on both sides' "remarkable degree of bitchiness." But these stubborn few could not prevent the eclipse of Darwinism from growing ever darker.

Still, while Mendel's work galvanized the anti-Darwinists, it never quite united them. By the early 1900s, scientists had discovered various important facts about genes and chromosomes, facts that still undergird genetics today. They determined that all creatures have genes; that genes can change, or mutate; that all chromosomes in cells come in pairs; and that all creatures inherit equal numbers of chromosomes from Mom and Dad. But there was no overarching sense of how these discoveries meshed; the individual pixels never resolved into a coherent picture. Instead a baffling array of half theories emerged, like "chromosome theory," "mutation theory," "gene theory," and so on. Each championed one narrow aspect of heredity, and each drew distinctions that seem merely confusing today: some scientists believed (wrongly) that genes didn't reside on chromosomes; others that each chromosome harbored just one gene; still others that chromosomes played no role in heredity at all. It's whiggishly unfair to say, but reading these overlapping theories can be downright frustrating today. You want to scream at the scientists, like a dimwit on *Wheel of Fortune* or something, "Think! It's all right there!" But each fiefdom discounted discoveries by rivals, and they squabbled against each other almost as much as against Darwinism.

As these revolutionaries and counterrevolutionaries bitched it out in Europe, the scientist who eventually ended the Darwin-genetics row was working in anonymity in America. Though he mistrusted both Darwinists and geneticists—too much bloviating about theory all around—Thomas Hunt Morgan had developed an interest in heredity after visiting a botanist in Holland in 1900. Hugo de Vries had been one of the trio who rediscovered Mendel that year, and de Vries's fame in Europe rivaled Darwin's, partly because de Vries had developed a rival theory for the origin of species. De Vriesian "mutation theory" argued that species went through rare but intense mutation periods, during which the parents produced "sports," offspring with markedly different traits. De Vries developed mutation theory after spotting some anomalous evening primroses in an abandoned potato field near Amsterdam. Some of these sport primroses sported smoother leaves, longer stems, or bigger yellow flowers with more petals. And crucially, primrose sports wouldn't mate with the old, normal primroses; they seemed to have jumped past them and become a new species. Darwin had rejected evolutionary jumps because he believed that if one sport emerged, it would have to breed with normal individuals, diluting its good qualities. De Vries's mutation period removed this objection at a stroke: many sports emerged at once, and they could breed only with each other.

The primrose results scored themselves into Morgan's brain. That de Vries had no clue how or why mutations appeared mattered not a lick. At last Morgan saw proof of new species emerging, not speculation. After landing a post at Columbia University in New York, Morgan decided to study mutation periods in animals. He began experiments on mice, guinea pigs, and pigeons, but when he discovered how slowly they bred, he took a colleague's suggestion and tried *Drosophila*, fruit flies.

Like many New Yorkers then, fruit flies had recently immigrated, in their case arriving on boats with the first banana crops in the 1870s. These exotic yellow fruits, usually wrapped in foil, had sold for ten cents per, and guards in New York stood watch over banana trees to prevent eager mobs from stealing the fruit. But by 1907 bananas and flies were common enough in New York that Morgan's assistant could catch a whole horde for research simply by slicing up a banana and leaving it on a windowsill to rot.

Fruit flies proved perfect for Morgan's work. They bred quickly—one generation every twelve days—and survived on food cheaper than peanuts. They also tolerated claustrophobic Manhattan real estate. Morgan's lab—the "fly room," 613 Schermerhorn Hall at Columbia—measured sixteen feet by

Thomas Hunt Morgan's cluttered, squalid fly room at Columbia University. Hundreds of fruit flies swarmed around inside each bottle, surviving on rotten bananas. (The American Philosophical Society)

twenty-three feet and had to accommodate eight desks. But a thousand fruit flies lived happily in a one-quart milk bottle, and Morgan's shelves were soon lined with the dozens of bottles that (legend has it) his assistants "borrowed" from the student cafeteria and local stoops.

Morgan set himself up at the fly room's central desk. Cockroaches scuttled through his drawers, nibbling rotten fruit, and the room was a cacophony of buzzing, but Morgan stood unperturbed in the middle of all, peering through a jeweler's loupe, scrutinizing bottle after bottle for de Vries's mutants. When a bottle produced no interesting specimens, Morgan might squash them with his thumb and smear their guts wherever, often in lab notebooks. Unfortunately for general sanitation, Morgan had many, many flies to smush: although the *Drosophila* bred and bred and bred, he found no sign of sports.

Meanwhile Morgan got lucky in a different arena. In autumn 1909, he filled in for a colleague on sabbatical and taught the only introductory course of his Columbia career. And during that semester he made, one observer noted, "his greatest discovery," two brilliant assistants. Alfred Sturtevant heard about Morgan's class through a brother who taught Latin and Greek at Columbia, and although just a sophomore, Sturtevant impressed Morgan by writing an independent research paper on horses and the inheritance of coat color. (Morgan hailed from Kentucky, and his father and uncle had been famous horse thieves behind Union lines during the Civil War, leading a band known as Morgan's Raiders. Morgan scorned his Confederate past, but he knew his horses.) From that moment on, Sturtevant was Morgan's golden boy and eventually earned a coveted desk in the fly room. Sturtevant cultivated a cultured air, reading widely in literature and doing trickier British crossword puzzles—although, amid the fly room's squalor, someone also once discovered a mummified mouse in his desk. Sturtevant did have one deficiency as a scientist, red-green color blindness. He'd tended horses on the family fruit farm in Alabama largely because he proved useless during harvest, struggling to spot red strawberries on green bushes.

The other undergrad, Calvin Bridges, made up for Sturtevant's poor eyesight, and his stuffiness. At first Morgan merely took pity on Bridges, an orphan, by giving him a job washing filth from milk bottles. But Bridges eavesdropped on Morgan's discussions of his work, and when Bridges began spotting interesting flies with his bare eyes (even through the dirty glass bottles), Morgan hired him as a researcher. It was basically the only job Bridges ever had. A sensuous and handsome man with bouffant hair, Bridges practiced free love *avant la lettre*. He eventually abandoned his wife and children, got a vasectomy, and started brewing moonshine in his new bachelor lair in Manhattan.

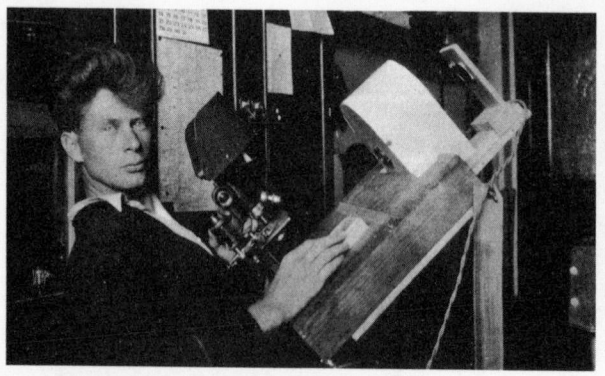

Playboy Calvin Bridges (*left*) and a rare photo of Thomas Hunt Morgan (*right*). Morgan so detested having his picture taken that an assistant who once wanted one had to hide a camera in a bureau in the fly lab and snap the photo remotely by tugging a string. (Courtesy of the National Library of Medicine)

He proceeded to hit on — or flat-out proposition — anything in a skirt, including colleagues' wives. His naive charm seduced many, but even after the fly room became legendary, no other university would blacken its reputation by employing Bridges as anything but a measly assistant.

Meeting Bridges and Sturtevant must have cheered Morgan, because his experiments had all but flopped until then. Unable to find any natural mutants, he'd exposed flies to excess heat and cold and injected acids, salts, bases, and other potential mutagens into their genitals (not easy to find). Still nothing. On the verge of giving up, in January 1910 he finally spotted a fly with a strange trident shape tattooed on its thorax. Not exactly a de Vriesian über-fly, but something. In March two more mutants appeared, one with ragged moles near its wings that made it appear to have "hairy armpits," another with an olive (instead of the normal amber) body color. In May 1910 the most dramatic mutant yet appeared, a fly with white (instead of red) eyes.

Anxious for a breakthrough—perhaps this was a mutation period—Morgan tediously isolated white-eyes. He uncapped the milk bottle, balanced another one upside down on top of it like mating ketchup bottles, and shined a light through the top to coax white-eyes upward. Of course, hundreds of other flies joined white-eyes in the top bottle, so Morgan had to quickly cap both, get a new milk bottle, and repeat the process over and over, slowly dwindling the number with each step, praying to God white-eyes didn't escape meantime. When he finally, finally segregated the bug, he mated it with red-eyed females. Then he bred the descendants with each other in various ways. The results were complex, but one result especially excited Morgan: after crossing some red-eyed descendants with each other, he discovered among the offspring a 3:1 ratio of red to white eyes.

The year before, in 1909, Morgan had heard the Danish botanist Wilhelm Johannsen lecture about Mendelian ratios at Columbia. Johannsen used the occasion to promote his newly minted word, *gene*, a proposed unit of inheritance. Johannsen and others freely admitted that genes were convenient fictions, linguistic placeholders for, well, something. But they insisted that their ignorance about the biochemical details of genes shouldn't invalidate the usefulness of the gene concept for studying inheritance (similar to how psychologists today can study euphoria or depression without understanding the brain in detail). Morgan found the lecture too speculative, but his experimental results—3:1—promptly lowered his prejudice to Mendel.

This was quite a volte-face for Morgan, but it was just the start. The eye-color ratios convinced him that gene theory wasn't bunk. But where were genes actually located? Perhaps on chromosomes, but fruit flies had hundreds of inheritable traits and only four chromosomes. Assuming one trait per chromosome, as many scientists did, there weren't enough to go around. Morgan didn't want to get dragged into debates on so-called chromosome theory, but a subsequent discovery left him no choice: because when he scrutinized his white-eyed flies, he discovered that every last mutant was male. Scientists already knew that one chromosome determined the gender of flies. (As in mammals, female flies have two X chromosomes, males one.) Now the white-eye gene was linked to that chromosome as well—putting two traits on it. Soon the fly boys found other genes—stubby wings, yellow bodies—also linked exclusively to males. The conclusion was inescapable: they'd proved that multiple genes rode around together on one chromosome.* That Morgan had proved this practically against his own will mattered little; he began to champion chromosome theory anyway.

Overthrowing old beliefs like this became a habit with Morgan, simultaneously his most admirable and most maddening trait. Although he encouraged theoretical discussions in the fly room, Morgan considered new theories cheap and facile—worth little until cross-examined in the lab. He didn't seem to grasp that scientists need theories as guides, to decide what's relevant and what's not, to frame their results and prevent muddled thinking. Even undergraduates like Bridges and Sturtevant—and especially a student who joined the fly room later, the abrasively brilliant and brilliantly abrasive Hermann Muller—grew hair-rippingly frustrated with Morgan in the many quarrels they had over genes and heredity. And then, just as exasperating, when someone did wrestle Morgan into a headlock and convince him he was wrong, Morgan would ditch his old ideas and with no embarrassment whatsoever absorb the new ones as obvious.

To Morgan, this quasi plagiarism was no big deal. Everyone was working toward the same goal (*right*, fellas?), and only experiments mattered anyway. And to his credit, his about-faces proved that Morgan listened to his assistants, a contrast to the condescending relationship most European scientists had with their help. For this reason Bridges and Sturtevant always publicly professed their loyalty to Morgan. But visitors sometimes picked up on sibling rivalries among the assistants, and secret smoldering. Morgan didn't mean to connive or manipulate; credit for ideas just meant that little to him.

Nevertheless ideas kept ambushing Morgan, ideas he hated. Because not long after the unified gene-chromosome theory emerged, it nearly unraveled, and only a radical idea could salvage it. Again, Morgan had determined that multiple genes clustered together on one chromosome. And he knew from other scientists' work that parents pass whole chromosomes on to their children. All the genetic traits on each chromosome should therefore always be inherited together—they should always be linked. To take a hypothetical example, if one chromosome's set of genes call for green bristles and sawtooth wings and fat antennae, any fly with one trait should exhibit all three. Such clusters of traits do exist in flies, but to their dismay, Morgan's team discovered that certain linked traits could sometimes become unlinked—green bristles and sawtooth wings, which should always appear together, would somehow show up separately, in different flies. Unlinkings weren't common—linked traits might separate 2 percent of the time, or 4 percent—but they were so persistent they might have undone the entire theory, if Morgan hadn't indulged in a rare flight of fancy.

He remembered reading a paper by a Belgian biologist-priest who had used a microscope to study how sperm and eggs form. One key fact of biology—it comes up over and over—is that all chromosomes come in pairs, pairs of nearly identical twins. (Humans have forty-six chromosomes, arranged in twenty-three pairs.) When sperm and eggs form, these near-twin chromosomes all line up in the middle of the parent cell. During division one twin gets pulled one way, the other the other way, and two separate cells are born.

However, the priest-biologist noticed that, just before the

divvying up, twin chromosomes sometimes interacted, coiling their tips around each other. He didn't know why. Morgan suggested that perhaps the tips broke off during this crossing over and swapped places. This explained why linked traits sometimes separated: the chromosome had broken somewhere between the two genes, dislocating them. What's more, Morgan speculated—he was on a roll—that traits separating 4 percent of the time probably sat farther apart on chromosomes than those separating 2 percent of the time, since the extra distance between the first pair would make breaking along that stretch more likely.

Morgan's shrewd guess turned out correct, and with Sturtevant and Bridges adding their own insights over the next few years, the fly boys began to sketch out a new model of heredity—the model that made Morgan's team so historically important. It said that all traits were controlled by genes, and that these genes resided on chromosomes in fixed spots, strung along like pearls on a necklace. Because creatures inherit one copy of each chromosome from each parent, chromosomes therefore pass genetic traits from parent to child. Crossing over (and mutation) changes chromosomes a little, which helps make each creature unique. Nevertheless chromosomes (and genes) stay mostly intact, which explains why traits run in families. Voilà: the first overarching sense of how heredity works.

In truth, little of this theory originated in Morgan's lab, as biologists worldwide had discovered various pieces. But Morgan's team finally linked these vaguely connected ideas, and fruit flies provided overwhelming experimental proof. No one could deny that sex chromosome linkage occurred, for instance, when Morgan had ten thousand mutants buzzing on a shelf, nary a female among them.

Of course, while Morgan won acclaim for uniting these theories, he'd done nothing to reconcile them with Darwinian natural selection. That reconciliation also arose from work inside the fly room, but once again Morgan ended up "borrowing" the idea from assistants, including one who didn't accept this as docilely as Bridges and Sturtevant did.

Hermann Muller began poking around the fly room in 1910, though only occasionally. Because he supported his elderly mother, Muller lived a haphazard life, working as a factotum in hotels and banks, tutoring immigrants in English at night, bolting down sandwiches on the subway between jobs. Somehow Muller found time to befriend writer Theodore Dreiser in Greenwich Village, immerse himself in socialist politics, and commute two hundred miles to Cornell University to finish a master's degree. But no matter how frazzled he got, Muller used his one free day, Thursday, to drop in on Morgan and the fly boys and bandy about ideas on genetics. Intellectually nimble, Muller starred in these bull sessions, and Morgan granted him a desk in the fly room after he graduated from Cornell in 1912. The problem was, Morgan declined to pay Muller, so Muller's schedule didn't let up. He soon had a mental breakdown.

From then on, and for decades afterward, Muller seethed over his status in the fly room. He seethed that Morgan openly favored the bourgeois Sturtevant and shunted menial tasks like preparing bananas onto the blue-collar, proletariat Bridges. He seethed that both Bridges and Sturtevant got paid to experiment on his, Muller's, ideas, while he scrambled around the five boroughs for pocket change. He seethed that Morgan treated the fly room like a clubhouse and sometimes made Muller's friends work down the hall. Muller seethed above all that Morgan was oblivious to his contributions. This was partly because Muller proved slow in doing the thing Morgan most valued — actually carrying out the clever experiments he (Muller) dreamed up. Indeed, Muller probably couldn't have found a worse mentor than Morgan. For all his socialist leanings, Muller got pretty attached to his own intellectual property, and felt the free and communal nature of the fly room both exploited and ignored his talent. Nor was Muller exactly up for Mr. Congeniality. He harped on Morgan, Bridges, and Sturtevant with tactless criticism, and got almost personally offended by anything but pristine logic. Morgan's breezy dismissal of evolution by natural selection especially irked Muller, who considered it the foundation of biology.

Despite the personality clashes he caused, Muller pushed the fly group to greater work. In fact, while Morgan contributed little to the emerging theory of inheritance after 1911, Muller, Bridges, and Sturtevant kept making fundamental discoveries. Unfortunately, it's hard to sort out nowadays who discovered what, and not just because of the constant idea swapping. Morgan and Muller often scribbled thoughts down on unorganized scraps, and Morgan purged his file cabinet every five years, perhaps out of necessity in his cramped lab. Muller hoarded documents, but many years later, yet another colleague he'd managed to alienate threw out Muller's files while Muller was working abroad. Morgan also (like Mendel's fellow friars) destroyed Bridges's files when the free lover died of heart problems in 1938. Turns out Bridges was a bedpost notcher, and when Morgan found a detailed catalog of fornication, he thought it prudent to burn all the papers and protect everyone in genetics.

But historians can assign credit for some things. All the fly boys helped determine which clusters of traits got inherited together. More important, they discovered that four distinct clusters existed in flies—exactly the number of chromosome pairs. This was a huge boost for chromosome theory because it showed that every chromosome harbored multiple genes.

Sturtevant built on this notion of gene and chromosome linkage. Morgan had guessed that genes separating 2 percent of the time must sit closer together on chromosomes than genes separating 4 percent of the time. Ruminating one evening, Sturtevant realized he could translate those percentages into actual distances. Specifically, genes separating 2 percent of the time must sit twice as close together as the other pair; similar logic held for other percent linkages. Sturtevant blew off his undergraduate homework that night, and by dawn this nineteen-year-old had sketched the first map of a chromosome. When Muller saw the map, he "literally jumped with excitement"—then pointed out ways to improve it.

Bridges discovered "nondisjunction"—the occasional failure of chromosomes to separate cleanly after crossing over and twisting arms. (The excess of genetic material that results can cause problems like Down syndrome.) And beyond individual discoveries, Bridges, a born tinkerer, industrialized the fly room. Instead of tediously separating flies by turning bottle after bottle upside down, Bridges invented an atomizer to puff wee doses of ether over flies and stun them. He also replaced loupes with binocular microscopes; handed out white porcelain plates and fine-tipped paintbrushes so that people could see and manipulate flies more easily; eliminated rotting bananas for a nutritious slurry of molasses and cornmeal; and built climate-controlled cabinets so that flies, which become sluggish in cold, could breed summer and winter. He even built a fly morgue to dispose of corpses with dignity. Morgan didn't always appreciate these contributions—he continued to squish flies wherever they landed, despite the morgue. But Bridges knew that mutants popped up so rarely, and when they did, his biological factory allowed each one to thrive and produce millions of descendants.*

Muller contributed insights and ideas, dissolving apparent contradictions and undergirding lean-to theories with firm logic. And although he had to argue with Morgan until his tongue bled, he finally made the senior scientist see how genes, mutations, and natural selection work together. As Muller (among others) outlined it: Genes give creatures traits, so mutations to genes change traits, making creatures different in color, height, speed, or whatever. But contra de Vries—who saw mutations as large things, producing sports and instant species—most mutations simply tweak creatures. Natural selection then allows the better-adapted of these creatures to survive and reproduce more often. Crossing over comes into play because it shuffles genes around between chromosomes and therefore puts new versions of genes together, giving natural selection still more variety to work on. (Crossing over is so important that some scientists today think that sperm and eggs refuse to form unless chromosomes cross a minimum number of times.)

Muller also helped expand scientists' very ideas about what genes could do. Most significantly, he argued that traits like the ones Mendel had studied—binary traits, controlled by one gene—weren't the only story. Many important traits are controlled by multiple genes, even dozens of genes. These traits will therefore show gradations, depending on which exact genes a creature inherits. Certain genes can also turn the volume up or down on other genes, crescendos and decrescendos that produce still finer gradations. Crucially, however, because genes are discrete and particulate, a beneficial mutation will *not* be diluted between generations. The gene stays whole and intact, so superior parents can breed with inferior types and still pass the gene along.

To Muller, Darwinism and Mendelism reinforced each other beautifully. And when Muller finally convinced Morgan of this, Morgan became a Darwinian. It's easy to chuckle over this—yet another Morgan conversion—and in later writings, Morgan still emphasizes genetics as more important than natural selection. However, Morgan's endorsement was important in a larger sense. Grandiloquent theories (including Darwin's) dominated biology at the time, and Morgan had helped keep the field grounded, always demanding hard evidence. So other biologists knew that if some theory convinced even Thomas Hunt Morgan, it had something going for it. What's more, even Muller recognized Morgan's personal influence. "We should not forget," Muller once admitted, "the guiding personality of Morgan, who infected all the others by his own example—his indefatigable activity, his deliberation, his jolliness, and courage." In the end, Morgan's bonhomie did what Muller's brilliant sniping couldn't: convinced geneticists to reexamine their prejudice against Darwin, and take the proposed synthesis of Darwin and Mendel, natural selection and genetics, seriously.

Many other scientists did indeed take up the work of Morgan's team in the 1920s, spreading the unassuming fruit fly to labs around the world. It soon became the standard animal in genetics, allowing scientists everywhere to compare discoveries on equal terms. Building on such work, a generation of mathematically minded biologists in the 1930s and 1940s began investigating how mutations spread in natural populations, outside the lab. They demonstrated that if a gene gave some creatures even a small survival advantage, that boost could, if compounded long enough, push species in new directions. What's more, most changes would take place in tiny steps, exactly as Darwin had insisted. If the fly boys' work finally showed how to link Mendel with Darwin, these later biologists made the case as rigorous as a Euclidean proof. Darwin had once moaned how "repugnant" math was to him, how he struggled with most anything beyond taking simple measurements. In truth, mathematics buttressed Darwin's theory and ensured his reputation would never lapse again.* And in this way the so-called eclipse of Darwinism in the early 1900s proved exactly that: a period of darkness and confusion, but a period that ultimately passed.

Beyond the scientific gains, the diffusion of fruit flies around the world inspired another legacy, a direct outgrowth of Morgan's "jolliness." Throughout genetics, the names of most genes are ugly abbreviations, and they stand for monstrous freak words that maybe six people worldwide understand. So when discussing, say, the *alox12b* gene, there's often no point in spelling out its name (arachidonate 12-lipoxygenase, 12R type), since doing so confuses rather than clarifies, methinks. (To save everyone a migraine, from now on I'll just state gene acronyms and pretend they stand for nothing.) In contrast, whereas gene names are intimidatingly complex, chromosome names are stupefyingly banal. Planets are named after gods, chemical elements after myths, heroes, and great cities. Chromosomes were named with all the creativity of shoe sizes. Chromosome one is the longest, chromosome two the second longest, and (yawn) so on. Human chromosome twenty-one is actually shorter than chromosome twenty-two, but by the time scientists figured this out, chromosome twenty-one was famous, since having an extra number twenty-one causes Down syndrome. And really, with such boring names, there was no point in fighting over them and bothering to change.

Fruit fly scientists, God bless 'em, are the big exception. Morgan's team always picked sensibly descriptive names for mutant genes like *speck*, *beaded*, *rudimentary*, *white*, and *abnormal*. And this tradition continues today, as the names of most fruit fly genes eschew jargon and even shade whimsical. Different fruit fly genes include *groucho*, *smurf*, *fear of intimacy*, *lost in space*, *smellblind*, *faint sausage*, *tribble* (the multiplying fuzzballs on *Star Trek*), and *tiggywinkle* (after Mrs. Tiggy-winkle, a character from Beatrix Potter). The *armadillo* gene, when mutated, gives fruit flies a plated exoskeleton. The *turnip* gene makes flies stupid. *Tudor* leaves males (as with Henry VIII) childless. *Cleopatra* can kill flies when it interacts with another gene, *asp*. *Cheap date* leaves flies exceptionally tipsy after a sip of alcohol. Fruit fly sex especially seems to inspire clever names. *Ken and barbie* mutants have no genitalia. Male *coitus interruptus* mutants spend just ten minutes having sex (the norm is twenty), while *stuck* mutants cannot physically disengage after coitus. As for females, *dissatisfaction* mutants never have sex at all—they spend all their energy shooing suitors away by snapping their wings. And thankfully, this whimsy with names has inspired the occasional zinger in other areas of genetics. A gene that gives mammals extra nipples earned the name *scaramanga*, after the James Bond villain with too many. A gene that removes blood cells from circulation in fish became the tasteful *vlad tepes*, after Vlad the Impaler, the historical inspiration for Dracula. The backronym for the "POK erythroid myeloid ontogenic" gene in mice—*pokemon*—nearly provoked a lawsuit, since the *pokemon* gene (now known, sigh, as *zbtb7*) contributes to the spread of cancer, and the lawyers for the Pokémon media empire didn't want their cute little pocket monsters confused with tumors. But my winner for the best, and freakiest, gene name goes to the flour beetle's *medea*, after the ancient Greek mother who committed infanticide. *Medea* encodes a protein with the curious property that it's both a poison and its own antidote. So if a mother has this gene but doesn't pass it to an embryo, her body exterminates the fetus—nothing she can do about it. If the fetus has the gene, s/he creates the antidote and lives. (*Medea* is a "selfish genetic element," a gene that demands its own propagation above all, even to the detriment of a creature as a whole.) If you can get beyond the horror, it's a name worthy of the Columbia fruit fly tradition, and it's fitting that the most important clinical work on *medea*—which could lead to very smart insecticides—came after scientists introduced it into *Drosophila* for further study.

But long before these cute names emerged, and even before fruit flies had colonized genetics labs worldwide, the original fly group at Columbia had disbanded. Morgan moved to the California Institute of Technology in 1928 and took Bridges and Sturtevant with him to his new digs in sunny Pasadena. Five years later Morgan became the first geneticist to win the Nobel Prize, "for establishing," one historian noted, "the very principles of genetics he had set out to refute." The Nobel committee has an arbitrary rule that three people at most can share a Nobel, so the committee awarded it to Morgan alone, rather than—as it should have—splitting it between him, Bridges, Sturtevant, and Muller. Some historians argue that Sturtevant did work important enough to win his own Nobel but that his devotion to Morgan and willingness to relinquish credit for ideas diminished his chances. Perhaps in tacit acknowledgment of this, Morgan shared his prize money from the Nobel with Sturtevant and Bridges, setting up college funds for their children. He shared nothing with Muller.

Muller had fled Columbia for Texas by then. He started in 1915 as a professor at Rice University (whose biology department was chaired by Julian Huxley, grandson of Darwin's bulldog) and eventually landed at the University of Texas. Although Morgan's warm recommendation had gotten him the Rice job, Muller actively promoted a rivalry between his Lone Star and Morgan's Empire State groups, and whenever the Texas group made a significant advance, which they trumpeted as a "home run," they preened. In one breakthrough, biologist Theophilus Painter discovered the first chromosomes—inside fruit fly spit glands*—that were large enough to inspect visually, allowing scientists to study the physical basis of genes. But as important as Painter's work was, Muller hit the grand slam in 1927 when he discovered that pulsing flies with radiation would increase their mutation rate by 150 times. Not only did this have health implications, but scientists no longer had to sit around and wait for mutations to pop up. They could mass-produce them. The discovery gave Muller the scientific standing he deserved—and knew he deserved.

Inevitably, though, Muller got into spats with Painter and

other colleagues, then outright brawls, and he soured on Texas. Texas soured on him, too. Local newspapers outed him as a political subversive, and the precursor to the FBI put him under surveillance. Just for fun, his marriage crumbled, and one evening in 1932 his wife reported him missing. A posse of colleagues later found him muddied and disheveled in the woods, soaked by a night of rain, his head still foggy from the barbiturates he'd swallowed to kill himself.

Burned out, humiliated, Muller abandoned Texas for Europe. There he did a bit of a Forrest Gump tour of totalitarian states. He studied genetics in Germany until Nazi goons vandalized his institute. He fled to the Soviet Union, where he lectured Joseph Stalin himself on eugenics, the quest to breed superior human beings through science. Stalin was not impressed, and Muller scurried to leave. To avoid being branded a "bourgeois reactionary deserter," Muller enlisted on the communist side in the Spanish Civil War, working at a blood bank. His side lost, and fascism descended.

Disillusioned yet again, Muller crawled back to the United States, to Indiana, in 1940. His interest in eugenics grew; he later helped establish what became the Repository for Germinal Choice, a "genius sperm bank" in California. And as the capstone to his career, Muller won his own unshared Nobel Prize in 1946 for the discovery that radiation causes genetic mutations. The award committee no doubt wanted to make up for shutting Muller out in 1933. But he also won because the atomic bomb attacks on Hiroshima and Nagasaki in 1945—which rained nuclear radiation on Japan—made his work sickeningly relevant. If the fly boys' work at Columbia had proved that genes existed, scientists now had to figure out how genes worked and how, in the deadly light of the bomb, they too often failed.

3

Them's the DNA Breaks

How Does Nature Read — and Misread — DNA?

August 6, 1945, started off pretty lucky for perhaps the most unlucky man of the twentieth century. Tsutomu Yamaguchi had stepped off his bus near Mitsubishi headquarters in Hiroshima when he realized he'd forgotten his *inkan*, the seal that Japanese salary-men dip in red ink and use to stamp documents. The lapse annoyed him — he faced a long ride back to his boardinghouse — but nothing could really dampen his mood that day. He'd finished designing a five-thousand-ton tanker ship for Mitsubishi, and the company would finally, the next day, send him back home to his wife and infant son in southwest Japan. The war had disrupted his life, but on August 7 things would return to normal.

As Yamaguchi removed his shoes at his boardinghouse door, the elderly proprietors ambushed him and asked him to tea. He could hardly refuse these lonely folk, and the unexpected engagement further delayed him. Shod again, *inkan* in hand, he hurried off, caught a streetcar, disembarked near work, and was walking along near a potato field when he heard a gnat of an enemy bomber high above. He could just make out a speck descending from its belly. It was 8:15 a.m.

Many survivors remember the curious delay. Instead of a normal bomb's simultaneous flash-bang, this bomb flashed and swelled silently, and got hotter and hotter silently. Yamaguchi was close enough to the epicenter that he didn't wait long. Drilled in air-raid tactics, he dived to the ground, covered his eyes, and plugged his ears with his thumbs. After a half-second light bath came a roar, and with it came a shock wave. A moment later Yamaguchi felt a gale somehow *beneath* him, raking his stomach. He'd been tossed upward, and after a short flight he hit the ground, unconscious.

He awoke, perhaps seconds later, perhaps an hour, to a darkened city. The mushroom cloud had sucked up tons of dirt and ash, and small rings of fire smoked on wilted potato leaves nearby. His skin felt aflame, too. He'd rolled up his shirtsleeves after his cup of tea, and his forearms felt severely sunburned. He rose and staggered through the potato field, stopping every few feet to rest, shuffling past other burned and bleeding and torn-open victims. Strangely compelled, he reported to Mitsubishi. He found a pile of rubble speckled with small fires, and many dead coworkers—he'd been lucky to be late. He wandered onward; hours slipped by. He drank water from broken pipes, and at an emergency aid station, he nibbled a biscuit and vomited. He slept that night beneath an overturned boat on a beach. His left arm, fully exposed to the great white flash, had turned black.

All the while, beneath his incinerated skin, Yamaguchi's DNA was nursing even graver injuries. The nuclear bomb at Hiroshima released (among other radioactivity) loads of super-charged x-rays called gamma rays. Like most radioactivity, these rays single out and selectively damage DNA, punching DNA and nearby water molecules and making electrons fly out like uppercut teeth. The sudden loss of electrons forms free radicals, highly reactive atoms that chew on chemical bonds. A chain reaction begins that cleaves DNA and sometimes snaps chromosomes into pieces.

By the mid-1940s, scientists were starting to grasp why the shattering or disruption of DNA could wreak such ruin inside cells. First, scientists based in New York produced strong evidence that genes were made of DNA. This upended the persistent belief in protein inheritance. But as a second study revealed, DNA and proteins still shared a special relationship: DNA *made* proteins, with each DNA gene storing the recipe for one protein. Making proteins, in other words, was what genes did—that's how genes created traits in the body.

In conjunction, these two ideas explained the harm of radioactivity. Fracturing DNA disrupts genes; disrupting genes halts protein production; halting protein production kills cells. Scientists didn't work this out instantly—the crucial "one gene/one protein" paper appeared just days before Hiroshima—but they knew enough to cringe at the thought of nuclear weapons. When Hermann Muller won his Nobel Prize in 1946, he prophesied to the *New York Times* that if atomic bomb survivors "could foresee the results 1,000 years from now...they might consider themselves more fortunate if the bomb had killed them."

Despite Muller's pessimism, Yamaguchi did want to survive, badly, for his family. He'd had complicated feelings about the war—opposing it at first, supporting it once under way, then shading back toward opposition when Japan began to stumble, because he feared the island being overrun by enemies who might harm his wife and son. (If so, he'd contemplated giving them an overdose of sleeping pills to spare them.) In the hours after Hiroshima, he yearned to get back to them, so when he heard rumors about trains leaving the city, he sucked up his strength and resolved to find one.

Hiroshima is a collection of islands, and Yamaguchi had to

cross a river to reach the train station. All the bridges had collapsed or burned, so he steeled himself and began crossing an apocalyptic "bridge of corpses" clogging the river, crawling across melted legs and faces. But an uncrossable gap in the bridge forced him to turn back. Farther upstream, he found a railroad trestle with one steel beam intact, spanning fifty yards. He clambered up, crossed the iron tightrope, and descended. He pushed through the mob at the station and slumped into a train seat. Miraculously the train pulled out soon afterward—he was saved. The train would run all night, but he was finally headed home, to Nagasaki.

A physicist stationed in Hiroshima might have pointed out that the gamma rays finished working over Yamaguchi's DNA in a millionth of a billionth of a second. To a chemist, the most interesting part—how the free radicals gnawed through DNA—would have ceased after a millisecond. A cell biologist would have needed to wait maybe a few hours to study how cells patch up torn DNA. A doctor could have diagnosed radiation sickness—headaches, vomiting, internal bleeding, peeling skin, anemic blood—within a week. Geneticists needed the most patience. The genetic damage to the survivors didn't surface for years, even decades. And in an eerie coincidence, scientists began to piece together how exactly genes function, and fail, during those very decades—as if providing a protracted running commentary on DNA devastation.

However definitive in retrospect, experiments on DNA and proteins in the 1940s convinced only some scientists that DNA was the genetic medium. Better proof came in 1952, from virologists Alfred Hershey and Martha Chase. Viruses, they knew, hijacked cells by injecting genetic material. And because the viruses they studied consisted of only DNA and proteins, genes had to be one or the other. The duo determined which by tagging viruses with both radioactive sulfur and radioactive phosphorus, then turning them loose on cells. Proteins contain sulfur but no phosphorus, so if genes were proteins, radioactive sulfur should be present in cells postinfection. But when Hershey and Chase filtered out infected cells, only radioactive phosphorus remained: only DNA had been injected.

Hershey and Chase published these results in April 1952, and they ended their paper by urging caution: "Further chemical inferences should not be drawn from the experiments presented." Yeah, right. Every scientist in the world still working on protein heredity dumped his research down the sink and took up DNA. A furious race began to understand the structure of DNA, and just one year later, in April 1953, two gawky scientists at Cambridge University in England, Francis Crick and James Watson (a former student of Hermann Muller), made the term "double helix" legendary.

Watson and Crick's double helix was two loooooooong DNA strands wrapped around each other in a right-handed spiral. (Point your right thumb toward the ceiling; DNA twists upward along the counterclockwise curl of your fingers.) Each strand consisted of two backbones, and the backbones were held together by paired bases that fit together like puzzle pieces—angular A with T, curvaceous C with G. Watson and Crick's big insight was that because of this complementary A-T and C-G base pairing, one strand of DNA can serve as a template for copying the other. So if one side reads CCGAGT, the other side must read GGCTCA. It's such an easy system that cells can copy hundreds of DNA bases per second.

However well hyped, though, the double helix revealed zero about how DNA genes actually made proteins—which is, after all, the important part. To understand this process, scientists had to scrutinize DNA's chemical cousin, RNA. Though similar to DNA, RNA is single-stranded, and it substitutes the letter U (uracil) for T in its strands. Biochemists focused on RNA because its concentration would spike tantalizingly whenever cells started making proteins. But when they chased the RNA around the cell, it proved as elusive as an endangered bird; they caught only glimpses before it vanished. It took years of patient experiments to determine exactly what was going on here—exactly how cells transform strings of DNA letters into RNA instructions and RNA instructions into proteins.

Cells first "transcribe" DNA into RNA. This process resembles the copying of DNA, in that one strand of DNA serves as a template. So the DNA string CCGAGT would become the RNA string GGCUCA (with U replacing T). Once constructed, this RNA string leaves the confines of the nucleus and chugs out to special protein-building apparatuses called ribosomes. Because it carries the message from one site to another, it's called messenger RNA.

The protein building, or translation, begins at the ribosomes. Once the messenger RNA arrives, the ribosome grabs it near the end and exposes just three letters of the string, a triplet. In our example, GGC would be exposed. At this point a second type of RNA, called transfer RNA, approaches. Each transfer RNA has two key parts: an amino acid trailing behind it (its cargo to transfer), and an RNA triplet sticking off its prow like a masthead. Various transfer RNAs might try to dock with the messenger RNA's exposed triplet, but only one with complementary bases will stick. So with the triplet GGC, only a transfer RNA with CCG will stick. And when it does stick, the ribosome unloads its amino acid cargo.

At this point the transfer RNA leaves, the messenger RNA shifts down three spots, and the process repeats. A different triplet is exposed, and a different transfer RNA with a different amino acid docks. This puts amino acid number two in place.

Eventually, after many iterations, this process creates a string of amino acids—a protein. And because each RNA triplet leads to one and only one amino acid being added, information should (should) get translated perfectly from DNA to RNA to protein. This same process runs every living thing on earth. Inject the same DNA into guinea pigs, frogs, tulips, slime molds, yeast, U.S. congressmen, whatever, and you get identical amino acid chains. No wonder that in 1958 Francis Crick elevated the DNA → RNA → protein process into the "Central Dogma" of molecular biology.*

Still, Crick's dogma doesn't explain everything about protein construction. For one thing, notice that, with four DNA letters, sixty-four different triplets are possible ($4 \times 4 \times 4 = 64$). Yet all those triplets code for just twenty amino acids in our bodies. Why?

A physicist named George Gamow founded the RNA Tie Club in 1954 in part to figure out this question. A physicist moonlighting in biology might sound odd—Gamow studied radioactivity and Big Bang theory by day—but other carpetbagging physicists like Richard Feynman joined the club as well. Not only did RNA offer an intellectual challenge, but many physicists felt appalled by their role in creating nuclear bombs. Physics seemed life destroying, biology life restoring. Overall, twenty-four physicists and biologists joined the Tie Club's roster— one for each amino acid, plus four honorary inductees, for each DNA base. Watson and Crick joined (Watson as official club "Optimist," Crick as "Pessimist"), and each member sported a four-dollar bespoke green wool tie with an RNA strand embroidered in gold silk, made by a haberdasher in Los Angeles. Club stationery read, "Do or die, or don't try."

Despite its collective intellectual horsepower, in one way the club ended up looking a little silly historically. Problems of perverse complexity often attract physicists, and certain physics-happy club members (including Crick, a physics Ph.D.) threw

RNA Tie Club members sporting green wool ties with gold silk RNA embroidery. From left, Francis Crick, Alexander Rich, Leslie E. Orgel, James Watson. (Courtesy of Alexander Rich)

themselves into work on DNA and RNA before anyone realized how simple the DNA → RNA → proteins process was. They concentrated especially on how DNA stores its instructions, and for whatever reason they decided early on that DNA must conceal its instructions in an intricate code—a biological cryptogram. Nothing excites a boys' club as much as coded messages, and like ten-year-olds with Cracker Jack decoder rings, Gamow, Crick, and others set out to break this cipher. They were soon scribbling away with pencil and paper at their desks, page after page piling up, their imaginations happily unfettered by doing experiments. They devised solutions clever enough to make Will Shortz smile—"diamond codes" and "triangle codes" and "comma codes" and many forgotten others. These were NSA-ready codes, codes with reversible messages, codes with error-correction mechanisms built in, codes that maximized storage density by using overlapping triplets. The RNA boys especially loved codes that used equivalent anagrams (so CAG = ACG = GCA, etc.). The approach was popular because when they eliminated all the combinatorial redundancies, the number of unique triplets was exactly twenty. In other words, they'd seemingly found a link between twenty and sixty-four—a reason nature just *had to* use twenty amino acids.

In truth, this was so much numerology. Hard biochemical facts soon deflated the code breakers and proved there's no profound reason DNA codes for twenty amino acids and not nineteen or twenty-one. Nor was there any profound reason (as some hoped) that a given triplet called for a given amino acid. The entire system was accidental, something frozen into cells billions of years ago and now too ingrained to replace—the QWERTY keyboard of biology. Moreover, RNA employs no fancy anagrams or error-correcting algorithms, and it doesn't strive to maximize storage space, either. Our code is actually choking on wasteful redundancy: two, four, even six RNA triplets can represent the same amino acid.* A few biocryptographers later admitted feeling annoyed when they compared nature's code to the best of the Tie Club's codes. Evolution didn't seem nearly as clever.

Any disappointment soon faded, however. Solving the DNA/RNA code finally allowed scientists to integrate two separate realms of genetics, gene-as-information and gene-as-chemical, marrying Miescher with Mendel for the first time. And it actually turned out better in some ways that our DNA code is kludgy. Fancy codes have nice features, but the fancier a code gets, the more likely it will break down or sputter. And however crude, our code does one thing well: it keeps life going by minimizing the damage of mutations. It's exactly that talent that Tsutoma Yamaguchi and so many others had to count on in August 1945.

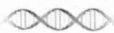

Ill and swooning, Yamaguchi arrived in Nagasaki early on August 8 and staggered home. (His family had assumed him lost; he convinced his wife he wasn't a ghost by showing her his feet, since Japanese ghosts traditionally have none.) Yamaguchi rested that day, swimming in and out of consciousness, but obeyed an order the next day to report to Mitsubishi headquarters in Nagasaki.

He arrived shortly before 11 a.m. Arms and face bandaged, he struggled to relate the magnitude of atomic warfare to his coworkers. But his boss, skeptical, interrupted to browbeat him, dismissing his story as a fable. "You're an engineer," he barked. "Calculate it. How could one bomb…destroy a whole city?" Famous last words. Just as this Nostradamus wrapped up, a white light swelled inside the room. Heat prickled Yamaguchi's skin, and he hit the deck of the ship-engineering office.

"I thought," he later recalled, "the mushroom cloud followed me from Hiroshima."

Eighty thousand people died in Hiroshima, seventy thousand more in Nagasaki. Of the hundreds of thousands of surviving victims, evidence suggests that roughly 150 got caught near both cities on both days, and that a handful got caught within both blast zones, a circle of intense radiation around 1.5 miles wide. Some of these *nijyuu hibakusha*, double-exposure survivors, had stories to make stones weep. (One had burrowed into his wrecked home in Hiroshima, clawed out his wife's blackened bones, and stacked them in a washbasin to return them to her parents in Nagasaki. He was trudging up the street to the parents' house, washbasin under his arm, when the morning air again fell quiet and the sky was once again bleached white.) But of all the reported double victims, the Japanese government has recognized only one official *nijyuu hibakusha*, Tsutomu Yamaguchi.

Shortly after the Nagasaki explosion, Yamaguchi left his shaken boss and office mates and climbed a watchtower on a nearby hill. Beneath another pall of dirty clouds, he watched his cratered-out hometown smolder, including his own house. A tarry radioactive rain began falling, and he struggled down the hill, fearing the worst. But he found his wife, Hisako, and young son, Katsutoshi, safe in an air-raid shelter.

After the exhilaration of seeing them wore off, Yamaguchi felt even more ill than before. In fact, over the next week he did little but lie in the shelter and suffer like Job. His hair fell out. Boils erupted. He vomited incessantly. His face swelled. He lost hearing in one ear. His reburned skin flaked off, and beneath it his flesh glowed raw red "like whale meat" and pierced him with pain. And as badly as Yamaguchi and others suffered during those months, geneticists feared the long-term agony would be equally bad, as mutations slowly began surfacing.

Scientists had known about mutations for a half century by then, but only work on the DNA → RNA → protein process by the Tie Club and others revealed exactly what these mutations consisted of. Most mutations involve typos, the random substitution of a wrong letter during DNA replication: CAG might become CCG, for instance. In "silent" mutations, no harm is done because of the DNA code's redundancy: the before and after triplets call for the same amino acid, so the net effect is like mistyping *grey* for *gray*. But if CAG and CCG lead to different amino acids—a "missense" mutation—the mistake can change a protein's shape and disable it.

Even worse are "nonsense" mutations. When making proteins, cells will continue to translate RNA into amino acids until they encounter one of three "stop" triplets (e.g., UGA), which terminate the process. A nonsense mutation accidentally turns a normal triplet into one of these stop signs, which truncates the protein early and usually disfigures it. (Mutations can also undo stop signs, and the protein runs on and on.) The black mamba of mutations, the "frameshift" mutation, doesn't involve typos. Instead a base disappears, or an extra base squeezes in. Because cells read RNA in consecutive groups of three, an insertion or deletion screws up not only that triplet but every triplet down the line, a cascading catastrophe.

Cells usually correct simple typos right away, but if something goes wrong (and it will), the flub can become permanently fixed in DNA. Every human being alive today was in fact born with dozens of mutations his parents lacked, and a few of those mutations would likely be lethal if we didn't have two copies of every gene, one from each parent, so one can pick up the slack if the other malfunctions. Nevertheless all living organisms continue to accumulate mutations as they age. Smaller creatures that live at high temperatures are especially hard hit: heat on a molecular level is vigorous motion, and the more molecular motion, the more likely something will bump DNA's elbow as it's copying. Mammals are relatively hefty and maintain a constant body temperature, thankfully, but we do fall victim to other mutations. Wherever two T's appear in a row in DNA, ultraviolet sunlight can fuse them together at an odd angle, which kinks DNA. These accidents can kill cells outright or simply irritate them. Virtually all animals (and plants) have special handyman enzymes to fix T-T kinks, but mammals lost them during evolution—which is why mammals sunburn.

Besides spontaneous mutations, outside agents called mutagens can also injure DNA, and few mutagens do more damage than radioactivity. Again, radioactive gamma rays cause free radicals to form, which cleave the phosphate-sugar backbone of DNA. Scientists now know that if just one strand of the double helix snaps, cells can repair the damage easily, often within an hour. Cells have molecular scissors to snip out mangled DNA, and can run enzymes down the track of the undamaged strand

and add the complementary A, C, G, or T at each point. The repair process is quick, simple, and accurate.

Double-strand breaks, though rarer, cause direr problems. Many double breaks resemble hastily amputated limbs, with tattered flaps of single-stranded DNA hanging off both ends. Cells do have two near-twin copies of every chromosome, and if one has a double-strand break, cells can compare its ragged strands to the (hopefully undamaged) other chromosome and perform repairs. But this process is laborious, and if cells sense widespread damage that needs quick repairs, they'll often just slap two hanging flaps together wherever a few bases line up (even if the rest don't), and hastily fill in the missing letters. Wrong guesses here can introduce a dreaded frameshift mutation — and there are plenty of wrong guesses. Cells repairing double-strand breaks get things wrong roughly three thousand times more often than cells simply copying DNA.

Even worse, radioactivity can delete chunks of DNA. Higher creatures have to pack their many coils of DNA into tiny nuclei; in humans, six linear feet cram into a space less than a thousandth of an inch wide. This intense scrunching often leaves DNA looking like a gnarly telephone cord, with the strand crossing itself or folding back over itself many times. If gamma rays happen to streak through and snip the DNA near one of these crossing points, there will be multiple loose ends in close proximity. Cells don't "know" how the original strands lined up (they don't have memories), and in their haste to fix this catastrophe, they sometimes solder together what should be separate strands. This cuts out and effectively deletes the DNA in between.

So what happens after these mutations? Cells overwhelmed with DNA damage can sense trouble and will kill themselves rather than live with malfunctions. This self-sacrifice can spare the body trouble in small doses, but if too many cells die at once, whole organ systems might shut down. Combined with intense burns, these shutdowns led to many deaths in Japan, and some of the victims who didn't die immediately probably wished they had. Survivors remember seeing people's fingernails fall off whole, dropping from their fists like dried shell pasta. They remember human-sized "dolls of charcoal" slumped in alleys. Someone recalled a man struggling along on two stumps, holding a charred baby upside down. Another recalled a shirtless woman whose breasts had burst "like pomegranates."

During his torment in the air-raid shelter in Nagasaki, Yamaguchi—bald, boily, feverish, half deaf—nearly joined this list of casualties. Only dedicated nursing by his family pulled him through. Some of his wounds still required bandages and would for years. But overall he traded Job's life for something like Samson's: his sores mostly healed, his strength returned, his hair grew back. He began working again, first at Mitsubishi, later as a teacher.

Far from escaping unscathed, however, Yamaguchi now faced a more insidious, more patient threat, because if radioactivity doesn't kill cells outright, it can induce mutations that lead to cancer. That link might seem counterintuitive, since mutations generally harm cells, and tumor cells are thriving if anything, growing and dividing at alarming rates. In truth all healthy cells have genes that act like governors on engines, slowing down their rpm's and keeping their metabolisms in check. If a mutation happens to disable a governor, the cell might not sense enough damage to kill itself, but eventually—especially if other genes, like those that control how often a cell divides, also sustain damage—it can start gobbling up resources and choking off neighbors.

Many survivors of Hiroshima and Nagasaki absorbed doses of radiation a hundred times higher—and in one gulp—than the background radiation a normal person absorbs in a year. And the closer survivors got caught to the epicenter, the more deletions and mutations appeared in their DNA. Predictably, cells that divide rapidly spread their DNA damage more quickly, and Japan saw an immediate spike in leukemia, a cancer of prolific white blood cells. The leukemia epidemic started to fade within a decade, but other cancers gained momentum in the meantime — stomach, colon, ovary, lung, bladder, thyroid, breast.

As bad as things were for adults, fetuses proved more vulnerable: any mutation or deletion in utero multiplied over and over in their cells. Many fetuses younger than four weeks spontaneously aborted, and among those that lived, a rash of birth defects, including tiny heads and malformed brains, appeared in late 1945 and early 1946. (The highest measured IQ among the handicapped ones was 68.) And on top of everything else, by the late 1940s, many of the quarter-million *hibakusha* in Japan began to have new children and pass on their exposed DNA.

Experts on radiation could offer little advice on the wisdom of *hibakusha* having children. Despite the high rates of liver or breast or blood cancer, none of the parents' cancerous DNA would get passed to their children, since children inherit only the DNA in sperm and eggs. Sperm or egg DNA could still mutate, of course, perhaps hideously. But no one had actually measured the damage of Hiroshima-like radiation on humans. So scientists had to work on assumptions. Iconoclastic physicist Edward Teller, father of the H-bomb (and RNA Tie Club member), went around suggesting that small pulses of radiation might even benefit humanity — that for all we knew, mutations goosed our genomes. Even among less reckless scientists, not everyone predicted fairy-tale monstrosities and babes with two heads. Hermann Muller had prophesied in the *New York Times* about future generations of Japanese misfortune, but his ideological opposition to Teller and others may have colored his commentary. (In 2011 a toxicologist, after perusing some now-declassified letters between Muller and another colleague, accused them both of lying to the government about the threat that low doses of radioactivity posed for DNA, then manipulating data and later research to cover themselves. Other historians dispute this interpretation.) Even with high doses of radioactivity, Muller ended up backing away from and qualifying his dire early predictions. Most mutations, he reasoned, however harmful, would prove recessive. And the odds of both parents having flaws in the same gene were remote. So at least among the children of survivors, Mom's healthy genes would probably mask any flaws lurking in Dad's, and vice versa.

But again, no one knew anything for certain, and a sword hung over every birth in Hiroshima and Nagasaki for decades, compounding all the normal anxieties of being a parent. This must have been doubly true for Yamaguchi and his wife, Hisako. Both had regained enough vigor by the early 1950s to want more children, no matter the long-term prognosis. And the birth of their first daughter, Naoko, initially supported Muller's reasoning, as she had no visible defects or deformities. Another daughter followed, Toshiko, and she too proved healthy. However bouncing they were at birth, though, both Yamaguchi daughters endured sickly adolescences and adulthoods. They suspect they inherited a genetically compromised immune system from their twice-bombed father and once-bombed mother.

And yet in Japan generally, the long-feared epidemic of cancers and birth defects among children of *hibakusha* never materialized. In fact no large-scale studies have ever found significant evidence that these children had higher rates of any disease, or even higher rates of mutations. Naoko and Toshiko may well have inherited genetic flaws; it's impossible to rule out, and it sure sounds true, intuitively and emotionally. But at least in the vast majority of cases, genetic fallout didn't settle onto the succeeding generation.*

Even many of the people directly exposed to atomic radiation proved more resilient than scientists expected. Yamaguchi's young son Katsutoshi survived for fifty-plus years after Nagasaki before dying of cancer at fifty-eight. Hisako lasted even longer, dying in 2008 of liver and kidney cancer at eighty-eight. The Nagasaki plutonium bomb probably caused both cancers, yes; but at those ages, it's conceivable that either one would have gotten cancer anyway, for unrelated reasons. As for Yamaguchi himself, despite his double exposure at Hiroshima and Nagasaki in 1945, he lived all the way until 2010, sixty-five extra years, finally dying of stomach cancer at ninety-three.

No one can say definitively what set Yamaguchi apart—why he lived so long after being exposed, twice, while others died from a comparative sprinkling of radioactivity. Yamaguchi never underwent genetic testing (at least not extensive testing), and even if he had, medical science might not have known enough to decide. Still, we can hazard educated guesses. First, his cells clearly did a hell of a job repairing DNA, both single-strand breaks and deadly doubles. It's possible he even had slightly superior repair proteins that worked faster or more efficiently, or certain combinations of repair genes that worked especially well together. We can also surmise that although he could hardly have avoided some mutations, they didn't disable key circuits in his cells. Perhaps the mutations fell along stretches of DNA that don't code for proteins. Or perhaps his were mostly "silent" mutations, where the DNA triplet changes but the amino acid, because of redundancy, doesn't. (If that's the case, the kludgy DNA/RNA code that frustrated the Tie Club actually saved him.) Finally, Yamaguchi apparently avoided until late in life any serious damage to the genetic governors in DNA that keep would-be tumors in check. Any or perhaps all of these factors could have spared him.

Or perhaps—and this seems equally likely—he wasn't all that special biologically. Perhaps many others would have survived just as long. And there is, dare I say it, some small hope in that. Even the most deadly weapons ever deployed, weapons that killed tens of thousands at once, that attacked and scrambled people's biological essences, their DNA, didn't wipe out a nation. Nor did they poison the next generation: thousands of children of A-bomb survivors remain alive today, alive and healthy. After more than three billion years of being exposed to cosmic rays and solar radiation and enduring DNA damage in various forms, nature has its safeguards, its methods of mending and preserving the integrity of DNA. And not just the dogmatic DNA whose messages get transcribed into RNA and translated into proteins—but all DNA, including DNA whose subtler linguistic and mathematical patterns scientists are just beginning to explore.*

4

The Musical Score of DNA

What Kinds of Information Does DNA Store?

 lthough inadvertent, a certain pun in *Alice's Adventures in Wonderland* has, in recent years, developed a curious resonance with DNA. In real life, *Alice's* author, Lewis Carroll, taught mathematics at Oxford University as Charles Lutwidge Dodgson, and one famous line in *Alice* (famous among geeks, at least) has the Mock Turtle moaning about "different branches of arithmetic—ambition, distraction, uglification, and derision." Just before that eye roller, though, the Mock Turtle says something peculiar. He maintains that during his school days, he studied not reading and writing but "reeling and writhing." It's probably just another groaner, but that last term, *writhing*, has piqued the interest of some mathematically savvy DNA scientists.

Scientists have known for decades that DNA, a long and active molecule, can tangle itself into some horrific snarls. What scientists didn't grasp was why these snarls don't choke our cells. In recent years, biologists have turned to an obscure twig of mathematics called knot theory for answers. Sailors and seamstresses

Lewis Carroll's Mock Turtle cried over memories of studying "reeling and writhing" in school, a complaint that resonates with modern DNA research into knots and tangles. (John Tenniel)

mastered the practical side of knots many millennia ago, and religious traditions as distant as Celtic and Buddhist hold certain knots sacred, but the systematic study of knots began only in the later nineteenth century, in Carroll/Dodgson's Victorian Britain. At that time the polymath William Thomson, Lord Kelvin, proposed that the elements on the periodic table were really microscopic knots of different shapes. For precision's sake, Kelvin defined his atomic knots as closed loops. (Knots with loose ends, somewhat like shoelaces, are "tangles.") And he defined a "unique" knot as a unique pattern of strands crossing over and under each other. So if you can slide the loops around on one knot and jimmy its over-under crossings to make it look like another, they're really the same knot. Kelvin suggested that the unique shape of each knot gave rise to the unique properties of each chemical element. Atomic physicists soon proved this clever theory false, but Kelvin did inspire Scottish physicist P. G. Tait to make a chart of unique knots, and knot theory developed independently from there.

Much of early knot theory involved playing cat's cradle and tallying the results. Somewhat pedantically, knot theorists defined the most trivial knot — O, what laymen call a circle — as the "unknot." They classified other unique knots by the number of over-under crossings and by July 2003 could identify 6,217,553,258 distinct knots with up to twenty-two over-under do-si-dos — roughly one knot per person on earth. Meanwhile other knot theorists had moved beyond taking simple censuses, and devised ways to transform one knot into another. This usually involved snipping the string at an under-over crossing, passing the top strand below, and fusing the snipped ends — which sometimes made knots more complicated but often simplified them. Although studied by legitimate mathematicians, knot theory retained a sense of play throughout. And America's Cup aspirants aside, no one dreamed of applications for knot theory until scientists discovered knotted DNA in 1976.

Knots and tangles form in DNA for a few reasons: its length, its constant activity, and its confinement. Scientists have effectively run simulations of DNA inside a busy nucleus by putting a long, thin rope in a box and jostling it. The rope ends proved quite adept at snaking their way through the rope's coils, and surprisingly complicated knots, with up to eleven crossings, formed in just seconds. (You probably could have guessed this if you've ever dropped earphones into a bag and tried to pull them out later.) Snarls like this can be lethal because the cellular machinery that copies and transcribes DNA needs a smooth track to run on; knots derail it. Unfortunately, the very processes of copying and transcribing DNA can create deadly knots and tangles. Copying DNA requires separating its two strands, but two interlaced helix strands cannot simply be pulled apart, any more than plaits of tightly braided hair can. What's more, when cells do start copying DNA, the long, sticky strings dangling behind sometimes get tangled together. If the strings won't disentangle after a good tug, cells commit suicide—it's that devastating.

Beyond knots per se, DNA can find itself in all sorts of other topological predicaments. Strands can get welded around each other like interlocking links in a chain. They can get twisted excruciatingly tight, like someone wringing out a rag or giving a snake burn on the forearm. They can get wound up into coils tenser than any rattlesnake. And it's this last configuration, the coils, that loops back to Lewis Carroll and his Mock Turtle. Rather imaginatively, knot theorists refer to such coils as "writhes" and refer to the act of coiling as "writhing," as if ropes or DNA were bunched that way in agony. So could the Mock Turtle, per a few recent rumors, have slyly been referring to knot theory with his "reeling and writhing"?

On the one hand, Carroll was working at a prestigious university when Kelvin and Tait began studying knot theory. He might easily have come across their work, and this sort of play math would have appealed to him. Plus, Carroll did write another book called *A Tangled Tale* in which each section—called not chapters but "knots"—consisted of a puzzle to solve. So he certainly incorporated knotty themes into his writing. Still, to be a party pooper, there's good reason to think the Mock Turtle knew nothing about knot theory. Carroll published *Alice* in 1865, some two years before Kelvin broached the idea of knots on the periodic table, at least publicly. What's more, while the term *writhing* might well have been used informally in knot theory before, it first appeared as a technical term in the 1970s. So it seems likely the Mock Turtle didn't progress much past ambition, distraction, uglification, and derision after all.

Nevertheless, even if the punniness of the line postdates Carroll, that doesn't mean we can't enjoy it today. Great literature remains great when it says new things to new generations, and the loops of a knot quite nicely parallel the contours and convolutions of Carroll's plot anyway. What's more, he probably would have delighted at how this whimsical branch of math invaded the real world and became crucial to understanding our biology.

Different combinations of twists and writhes and knots ensure that DNA can form an almost unlimited number of snarls, and what saves our DNA from this torture are mathematically savvy proteins called topoisomerases. Each of these proteins grasps one or two theorems of knot theory and uses them to relieve tension in DNA. Some topoisomerases unlink DNA chains. Other types nick one strand of DNA and rotate it around the other to eliminate twists and writhes. Still others snip DNA wherever it crosses itself, pass the upper strand beneath the lower, and re-fuse them, undoing a knot. Each topoisomerase saves our DNA from a Torquemada-style doom countless time each year, and we couldn't survive without these math nerds. If knot theory sprang from Lord Kelvin's twisted atoms and then went off on its own, it has now circled back to its billions-of-years-old molecular roots in DNA.

Knot theory hasn't been the only unexpected math to pop up during DNA research. Scientists have used Venn diagrams to study DNA, and the Heisenberg uncertainty principle. The architecture of DNA shows traces of the "golden ratio" of length to width found in classical edifices like the Parthenon. Geometry enthusiasts have twisted DNA into Möbius strips and constructed the five Platonic solids. Cell biologists now realize that, to even fit inside the nucleus, long, stringy DNA must fold and refold itself into a fractal pattern of loops within loops within loops, a pattern where it becomes nearly impossible to tell what scale—nano-, micro-, or millimeter—you're looking at. Perhaps most unlikely, in 2011 Japanese scientists used a Tie Club–like code to assign combinations of A, C, G, and T to numbers and letters, then inserted the code for "$E = mc^2$ 1905!" in the DNA of common soil bacteria.

DNA has especially intimate ties to an oddball piece of math called Zipf's law, a phenomenon first discovered by a linguist. George Kingsley Zipf came from solid German stock—his family had run breweries in Germany—and he eventually became a professor of German at Harvard University. Despite his love of language, Zipf didn't believe in owning books, and unlike his colleagues, he lived outside Boston on a seven-acre farm with a vineyard and pigs and chickens, where he chopped down the Zipf family Christmas tree each December. Temperamentally, though, Zipf did not make much of a farmer; he slept through most dawns because he stayed awake most nights studying (from library books) the statistical properties of languages.

A colleague once described Zipf as someone "who would take roses apart to count their petals," and Zipf treated literature no differently. As a young scholar Zipf tackled James Joyce's *Ulysses*, and the main thing he got out of it was that it contained 29,899 different words, and 260,430 words total. From there Zipf dissected *Beowulf*, Homer, Chinese texts, and the oeuvre of the Roman playwright Plautus. By counting the words in each work, he discovered Zipf's law. It says that the most common word in a language appears roughly twice as often as the second most common word, roughly three times as often as the third most common, a hundred times as often as the hundredth most common, and so on. In English, *the* accounts for 7 percent of words, *of* about half that, *and* a third of that, all way down to obscurities like *grawlix* or *boustrophedon*. These distributions hold just as true for Sanskrit, Etruscan, or hieroglyphics as for modern Hindi, Spanish, or Russian. (Zipf also found them in the prices in Sears Roebuck mail-order catalogs.) Even when people make up languages, something like Zipf's law emerges.

After Zipf died in 1950, scholars found evidence of his law in an astonishing variety of other places—in music (more on this later), city population ranks, income distributions, mass extinctions, earthquake magnitudes, the ratios of different colors in paintings and cartoons, and more. Every time, the biggest or most common item in each class was twice as big or common as the second item, three times as big or common as the third, and so on. Probably inevitably, the theory's sudden popularity led to a backlash, especially among linguists, who questioned what Zipf's law even meant, if anything.* Still, many scientists defend Zipf's law because it feels correct—the frequency of words doesn't seem random—and, empirically, it does describe languages in uncannily accurate ways. Even the "language" of DNA.

Of course, it's not apparent at first that DNA is Zipfian, especially to speakers of Western languages. Unlike most languages DNA doesn't have obvious spaces to distinguish each word. It's more like those ancient texts with no breaks or pauses or punctuation of any kind, just relentless strings of letters. You might think that the A-C-G-T triplets that code for amino acids could function as "words," but their individual frequencies don't look Zipfian. To find Zipf, scientists had to look at groups of triplets instead, and a few turned to an unlikely source for help: Chinese search engines. The Chinese language creates compound words by linking adjacent symbols. So if a Chinese text reads ABCD, search engines might examine a sliding "window" to find meaningful chunks, first AB, BC, and CD, then ABC and BCD. Using a sliding window proved a good strategy for finding meaningful chunks in DNA, too. It turns out that, by some measures, DNA looks most Zipfian, most like a language, in groups of around twelve bases. Overall, then, the most meaningful unit for DNA might not be a triplet, but four triplets working together—a dodecahedron motif.

The *expression* of DNA, the translation into proteins, also obeys Zipf's law. Like common words, a few genes in every cell get expressed time and time again, while most genes hardly ever come up in conversion. Over the ages cells have learned to rely on these common proteins more and more, and the most common one generally appears twice and thrice and quatrice as often as the next-most-common proteins. To be sure, many scientists harrumph that these Zipfian figures don't mean anything; but others say it's time to appreciate that DNA isn't just analogous to but really functions like a language.

And not just a language: DNA has Zipfian musical properties, too. Given the key of a piece of music, like C major, certain notes appear more often than others. In fact Zipf once investigated the prevalence of notes in Mozart, Chopin, Irving Berlin, and Jerome Kern—and lo and behold, he found a Zipfian distribution. Later researchers confirmed this finding in other genres, from Rossini to the Ramones, and discovered Zipfian distributions in the timbre, volume, and duration of notes as well.

So if DNA shows Zipfian tendencies, too, is DNA arranged into a musical score of sorts? Musicians have in fact translated the A-C-G-T sequence of serotonin, a brain chemical, into little ditties by assigning the four DNA letters to the notes A, C, G, and, well, E. Other musicians have composed DNA melodies by assigning harmonious notes to the amino acids that popped up most often, and found that this produced more complex and euphonious sounds. This second method reinforces the idea that, much like music, DNA is only partly a strict sequence of "notes." It's also defined by motifs and themes, by how often certain sequences occur and how well they work together. One biologist has even argued that music is a natural medium for studying how genetic bits combine, since humans have a keen ear for how phrases "chunk together" in music.

Something even more interesting happened when two scientists, instead of turning DNA into music, inverted the process and translated the notes from a Chopin nocturne into DNA. They discovered a sequence "strikingly similar" to part of the gene for RNA polymerase. This polymerase, a protein universal throughout life, is what builds RNA from DNA. Which means, if you look closer, that the nocturne actually encodes an entire life cycle. Consider: Polymerase uses DNA to build RNA. RNA in turn builds complicated proteins. These proteins in turn build cells, which in turn build people, like Chopin. He in turn composed harmonious music—which completed the cycle by encoding the DNA to build polymerase. (Musicology recapitulates ontology.)

So was this discovery a fluke? Not entirely. Some scientists argue that when genes first appeared in DNA, they didn't arise randomly, along any old stretch of chromosome. They began instead as repetitive phrases, a dozen or two dozen DNA bases duplicated over and over. These stretches function like a basic musical theme that a composer tweaks and tunes (i.e., mutates) to create pleasing variations on the original. In this sense, then, genes had melody built into them from the start.

Humans have long wanted to link music to deeper, grander themes in nature. Most notably astronomers from ancient Greece right through to Kepler believed that, as the planets ran their course through the heavens, they created an achingly beautiful *musica universalis*, a hymn in praise of Creation. It turns out that universal music does exist, only it's closer than we ever imagined, in our DNA.

Genetics and linguistics have deeper ties beyond Zipf's law. Mendel himself dabbled in linguistics in his older, fatter days, including an attempt to derive a precise mathematical law for how the suffixes of German surnames (like *-mann* and *-bauer*) hybridized with other names and reproduced themselves each generation. (Sounds familiar.) And heck, nowadays, geneticists couldn't even talk about their work without all the terms they've lifted from the study of languages. DNA has synonyms, translations, punctuation, prefixes, and suffixes. Missense mutations (substituting amino acids) and nonsense mutations (interfering with stop codons) are basically typos, while frameshift mutations (screwing up how triplets get read) are old-fashioned typesetting mistakes. Genetics even has grammar and syntax—rules for combining amino acid "words" and clauses into protein "sentences" that cells can read.

More specifically, genetic grammar and syntax outline the rules for how a cell should fold a chain of amino acids into a working protein. (Proteins must be folded into compact shapes before they'll work, and they generally don't work if their shape is wrong.) Proper syntactical and grammatical folding is a crucial part of communicating in the DNA language. However, communication does require more than proper syntax and grammar; a protein sentence has to *mean* something to a cell, too. And, strangely, protein sentences can be syntactically and grammatically perfect, yet have no biological meaning. To understand what on earth that means, it helps to look at something linguist Noam Chomsky once said. He was trying to demonstrate the independence of syntax and meaning in human speech.

His example was "Colorless green ideas sleep furiously." Whatever you think of Chomsky, that sentence has to be one of the most remarkable things ever uttered. It makes no literal sense. Yet because it contains real words, and its syntax and grammar are fine, we can sort of follow along. It's not quite devoid of meaning.

In the same way, DNA mutations can introduce random amino acid words or phrases, and cells will automatically fold the resulting chain together in perfectly syntactical ways based on physics and chemistry. But any wording changes can change the sentence's whole shape and meaning, and whether the result still makes sense depends. Sometimes the new protein sentence contains a mere tweak, minor poetic license that the cell can, with work, parse. Sometimes a change (like a frameshift mutation) garbles a sentence until it reads like grawlix—the #$%^&@! swear words of comics characters. The cell suffers and dies. Every so often, though, the cell reads a protein sentence littered with missense or nonsense... and yet, upon reflection, it somehow does make sense. Something wonderful like Lewis Carroll's "mimsy borogoves" or Edward Lear's "runcible spoon" emerges, wholly unexpectedly. It's a rare beneficial mutation, and at these lucky moments, evolution creeps forward.*

Because of the parallels between DNA and language, scientists can even analyze literary texts and genomic "texts" with the same tools. These tools seem especially promising for analyzing disputed texts, whose authorship or biological origin remains doubtful. With literary disputes, experts traditionally compared a piece to others of known provenance and judged whether its tone and style seemed similar. Scholars also sometimes cataloged and counted what words a text used. Neither approach is wholly satisfactory—the first too subjective, the second too sterile. With DNA, comparing disputed genomes often involves matching up a few dozen key genes and searching for small differences. But

this technique fails with wildly different species because the differences are so extensive, and it's not clear which differences are
important. By focusing exclusively on genes, this technique also
ignores the swaths of regulatory DNA that fall outside genes.

To circumvent these problems, scientists at the University of
California at Berkeley invented software in 2009 that again
slides "windows" along a string of letters in a text and searches
for similarities and patterns. As a test, the scientists analyzed the
genomes of mammals and the texts of dozens of books like *Peter
Pan*, the Book of Mormon, and Plato's *Republic*. They discovered
that the same software could, in one trial run, classify DNA into
different genera of mammals, and could also, in another trial
run, classify books into different genres of literature with perfect accuracy. In turning to disputed texts, the scientists delved
into the contentious world of Shakespeare scholarship, and their
software concluded that the Bard did write *The Two Noble
Kinsmen*—a play lingering on the margins of acceptance—but
didn't write *Pericles*, another doubtful work. The Berkeley team
then studied the genomes of viruses and archaebacteria, the oldest and (to us) most alien life-forms. Their analysis revealed new
links between these and other microbes and offered new suggestions for classifying them. Because of the sheer amount of data
involved, the analysis of genomes can get intensive; the virus-
archaebacteria scan monopolized 320 computers for a year. But
genome analysis allows scientists to move beyond simple
point-by-point comparisons of a few genes and read the full natural history of a species.

Reading a full genomic history, however, requires more dexterity than reading other texts. Reading DNA requires both
left-to-right and right-to-left reading—boustrophedon reading.

Otherwise scientists miss crucial palindromes and semordnilaps, phrases that read the same forward and backward (and vice versa).

One of the world's oldest known palindromes is an amazing up-down-and-sideways square carved into walls at Pompeii and other places:

S-A-T-O-R
A-R-E-P-O
T-E-N-E-T
O-P-E-R-A
R-O-T-A-S

At just two millennia old, however, *sator...rotas** falls orders of magnitude short of the age of the truly ancient palindromes in DNA. DNA has even invented two kinds of palindromes. There's the traditional, sex-at-noon-taxes type—GATTA-CATTAG. But because of A-T and C-G base pairing, DNA sports another, subtler type that reads forward down one strand and backward across the other. Consider the string CTAGC-TAG, then imagine what bases must appear on the other strand, GATCGATC. They're perfect palindromes.

Harmless as it seems, this second type of palindrome would send frissons of fear through any microbe. Long ago, many microbes evolved special proteins (called "restriction enzymes") that can snip clean through DNA, like wire cutters. And for what-ever reason, these enzymes can cut DNA only along stretches that are highly symmetrical, like palindromes. Cutting DNA has some useful purposes, like clearing out bases damaged by radiation or relieving tension in knotted DNA. But naughty microbes mostly used these proteins to play Hatfields versus McCoys and shred each other's genetic material. As a result microbes have learned the hard way to avoid even modest palindromes.

Not that we higher creatures tolerate many palindromes,

either. Consider CTAGCTAG and GATCGATC again. Notice that the beginning half of either palindromic segment could base-pair with the second half of itself: the first letter with the last (C...G), the second with the penult (T...A), and so on. But for these internal bonds to form, the DNA strand on one side would have to disengage from the other and buckle upward, leaving a bump. This structure, called a "hairpin," can form along any DNA palindrome of decent length because of its inherent symmetry. As you might expect, hairpins can destroy DNA as surely as knots, and for the same reason—they derail cellular machinery.

Palindromes can arise in DNA in two ways. The shortish DNA palindromes that cause hairpins arose randomly, when A's, C's, G's, and T's just happened to arrange themselves symmetrically. Longer palindromes litter our chromosomes as well, and many of those—especially those that wreak havoc on the runt Y chromosome—probably arose through a specific two-step process. For various reasons, chromosomes sometimes accidentally duplicate chunks of DNA, then paste the second copy somewhere down the line. Chromosomes can also (sometimes after double-strand breaks) flip a chunk of DNA by 180 degrees and reattach it ass-backwards. In tandem, a duplication and inversion create a palindrome.

Most chromosomes, though, discourage long palindromes or at least discourage the inversions that create them. Inversions can break up or disable genes, leaving the chromosome ineffective. Inversions can also hurt a chromosome's chances of crossing over—a huge loss. Crossing over (when twin chromosomes cross arms and exchange segments) allows chromosomes to swap genes and acquire better versions, or versions that work better together and make the chromosome more fit. Equally important, chromosomes take advantage of crossing over to perform quality-control checks: they can line up side by side, eyeball each other up and down, and overwrite mutated genes with nonmutated genes. But a chromosome will cross over only with a partner that looks similar. If the partner looks suspiciously different, the chromosome fears picking up malignant DNA and refuses to swap. Inversions look dang suspicious, and in these circumstances, chromosomes with palindromes get shunned.

Y once displayed this intolerance for palindromes. Way back when, before mammals split from reptiles, X and Y were twin chromosomes and crossed over frequently. Then, 300 million years ago, a gene on Y mutated and became a master switch that causes testes to develop. (Before this, sex was probably determined by the temperature at which Mom incubated her eggs, the same nongenetic system that determines pink or blue in turtles and crocodiles.) Because of this change, Y became the "male" chromosome and, through various processes, accumulated other manly genes, mostly for sperm production. As a consequence, X and Y began to look dissimilar and shied away from crossing over. Y didn't want to risk its genes being overwritten by shrewish X, while X didn't want to acquire Y's meathead genes, which might harm XX females.

After crossing over slowed down, Y grew more tolerant about inversions, small and large. In fact Y has undergone four massive inversions in its history, truly huge flips of DNA. Each one created many cool palindromes — one spans three million letters — but each one made crossing over with X progressively harder. This wouldn't be a huge deal except, again, crossing over allows chromosomes to overwrite malignant mutations. Xs could keep doing this in XX females, but when Y lost its partner, malignant mutations started to accumulate. And every time one appeared, cells had no choice but to chop Y down and excise the mutated DNA. The results were not pretty. Once a large chromosome, Y has lost all but two dozen of its original fourteen hundred genes.

At that rate, biologists once assumed that Ys were goners. They seem destined to keep picking up dysfunctional mutations and getting shorter and shorter, until evolution did away with Ys entirely—and perhaps did away with males to boot.

Palindromes, however, may have pardoned Y. Hairpins in a DNA strand are bad, but if Y folds *itself* into a giant hairpin, it can bring any two of its palindromes—which are the same genes, one running forward, one backward—into contact. This allows Y to check for mutations and overwrite them. It's like writing down "A man, a plan, a cat, a ham, a yak, a yam, a hat, a canal: Panama!" on a piece of paper, folding the paper over, and correcting any discrepancies letter by letter—something that happens six hundred times in every newborn male. Folding over also allows Ys to make up for their lack of a sex-chromosome partner and "recombine" with themselves, swapping genes at one point along their lengths for genes at another.

This palindromic fix is ingenious. Too clever, in fact, by half. The system Y uses to compare palindromes regrettably doesn't "know" which palindrome has mutated and which hasn't; it just knows there's a difference. So not infrequently, Y overwrites a good gene with a bad one. The self-recombination also tends to—whoops—accidentally delete the DNA between the palindromes. These mistakes rarely kill a man, but can render his sperm impotent. Overall the Y chromosome would disappear if it couldn't correct mutations like this; but the very thing that allows it to, its palindromes, can unman it.

Both the linguistic and mathematical properties of DNA contribute to its ultimate purpose: managing data. Cells store, call up, and transmit messages through DNA and RNA, and scientists routinely speak of nucleic acids encoding and processing information, as if genetics were a branch of cryptography or computer science.

As a matter of fact, modern cryptography has some roots in genetics. After studying at Cornell University, a young geneticist named William Friedman joined an eccentric scientific think tank in rural Illinois in 1915. (It boasted a Dutch windmill, a pet bear named Hamlet, and a lighthouse, despite being 750 miles from the coast.) As Friedman's first assignment, his boss asked him to study the effects of moonlight on wheat genes. But Friedman's statistical background soon got him drawn into another of his boss's lunatic projects*—proving that Francis Bacon not only wrote Shakespeare's plays but left clues throughout the First Folio that trumpeted his authorship. (The clues involved changing the shapes of certain letters.) Although enthused—he'd loved code breaking ever since he'd read Edgar Allan Poe's "The Gold-Bug" as a child—Friedman determined the supposed references to Bacon were bunkum. Someone could use the same deciphering schemes, he noted, to "prove" that Teddy Roosevelt wrote *Julius Caesar*. Nevertheless Friedman had envisioned genetics as biological code breaking, and after his taste of real code breaking, he took a job in cryptography with the U.S. government. Building on the statistical expertise he'd gained in genetics, he soon cracked the secret telegrams that broke the Teapot Dome bribery scandal open in 1923. In the early 1940s he began deciphering Japanese diplomatic codes, including a dozen infamous cables, intercepted on December 6, 1941, from Japan to its embassy in Washington, D.C., that foreshadowed imminent threat.

Friedman had abandoned genetics because genetics in the first decades of the century (at least on farms) involved too much sitting around and waiting for dumb beasts to breed; it was more animal husbandry than data analysis. Had he been born a generation or two later, Friedman would have seen things differently. By the 1950s biologists regularly referred to A-C-G-T base pairs as biological "bits" and to genetics as a "code" to crack. Genetics *became* data analysis, and continued to develop along those lines thanks in part to the work of a younger contemporary of Friedman, an engineer whose work encompassed both cryptography and genetics, Claude Shannon.

Scientists routinely cite Shannon's thesis at MIT, written in 1937 when he was twenty-one years old, as the most important master's thesis ever. In it Shannon outlined a method to combine electronic circuits and elementary logic to do mathematical operations. As a result, he could now design circuits to perform complex calculations—the basis of all digital circuitry. A decade later, Shannon wrote a paper on using digital circuits to encode messages and transmit them more efficiently. It's only barely hyperbole to say that these two discoveries created modern digital communications from scratch.

Amid these seminal discoveries, Shannon indulged his other interests. At the office he loved juggling, and riding unicycles, and juggling while riding unicycles down the hall. At home he tinkered endlessly with junk in his basement; his lifetime inventions include rocket-powered Frisbees, motorized pogo sticks, machines to solve Rubik's Cubes, a mechanical mouse (named Theseus) to solve mazes, a program (named THROBAC) to calculate in Roman numerals, and a cigarette pack–sized "wearable computer" to rip off casinos at roulette.*

Shannon also pursued genetics in his Ph.D. thesis in 1940. At the time, biologists were firming up the connection between genes and natural selection, but the heavy statistics involved frightened many. Though he later admitted he knew squat about genetics, Shannon dived right in and tried to do for genetics what he'd done for electronic circuits: reduce the complexities into simple algebra, so that, given any input (genes in a population), anyone could quickly calculate the output (what genes would thrive or disappear). Shannon spent all of a few months on the paper and, after earning his Ph.D., was seduced by electronics and never got back around to genetics. It didn't matter. His new work became the basis of information theory, a field so widely applicable that it wound its way back to genetics without him.

With information theory, Shannon determined how to transmit messages with as few mistakes as possible—a goal biologists have since realized is equivalent to designing the best genetic code for minimizing mistakes in a cell. Biologists also adopted Shannon's work on efficiency and redundancy in languages. English, Shannon once calculated, was at least 50 percent redundant. (A pulp novel he investigated, by Raymond Chandler, approached 75 percent.) Biologists studied efficiency too because, per natural selection, efficient creatures should be fitter creatures. The less redundancy in DNA, they reasoned, the more information cells could store, and the faster they could process it, a big advantage. But as the Tie Club knew, DNA is sub-suboptimal in this regard. Up to six A-C-G-T triplets code for just one amino acid: totally superfluous redundancy. If cells economized and used fewer triplets per amino acid, they could incorporate more than just the canonical twenty, which would open up new realms of molecular evolution. Scientists have in fact shown that, if coached, cells in the lab can use fifty amino acids.

But if redundancy has costs, it also, as Shannon pointed out, has benefits. A little redundancy in language ensures that we can follow a conversation even if some syllables or words get garbled. Mst ppl hv lttl trbl rdng sntncs wth lttrs mssng. In other words, while too much redundancy wastes time and energy, a little hedges against mistakes. Applied to DNA, we can now see the point of redundancy: it makes a mutation less likely to introduce a wrong amino acid. Furthermore, biologists have calculated that even if a mutation does substitute the wrong amino acid, Mother Nature has rigged things so that, no matter the change, the odds are good that the new amino acid will have similar chemical and physical traits and will therefore get folded properly. It's an amino acid synonym, so cells can still make out the sentence's meaning.

(Redundancy might have uses outside of genes, too. Noncoding DNA—the long expanses of DNA between genes—contains some tediously redundant stretches of letters, places where it looks like someone held his fingers down on nature's keyboard. While these and other stretches look like junk, scientists don't know if they really are expendable. As one scientist mused, "Is the genome a trash novel, from which you can remove a hundred pages and it doesn't matter, or is it more like a Hemingway, where if you remove a page, the story line is lost?" But studies that have applied Shannon's theorems to junk DNA have found that its redundancy looks a lot like the redundancy in languages—which may mean that noncoding DNA has still-undiscovered linguistic properties.)

All of this would have wowed Shannon and Friedman. But perhaps the most fascinating aspect is that, beyond its other clever features, DNA also scooped us on our most powerful information-processing tools. In the 1920s the influential mathematician David Hilbert was trying to determine if there existed any mechanical, turn-the-crank process (an algorithm) that could solve theorems automatically, almost without thought. Hilbert envisioned humans going through this process with pencils and paper. But in 1936 mathematician (and amateur knotologist) Alan Turing sketched out a machine to do the work instead. Turing's machine looked simplistic—just a long recording tape, and a device to move the tape and mark it—but in principle could compute the answer to any solvable problem, no matter how complex, by breaking it down into small, logical steps. The Turing machine inspired many thinkers, Shannon among them. Engineers soon built working models—we call them computers—with long magnetic tapes and recording heads, much as Turing envisioned.

Biologists know, however, that Turing machines resemble nothing so much as the machinery that cells use to copy, mark, and read long strands of DNA and RNA. These Turing biomachines run every living cell, solving all sorts of intricate problems every second. In fact, DNA goes one better than Turing machines: computer hardware still needs software to run; DNA acts as both hardware and software, both storing information and executing commands. It even contains instructions to make more of itself.

And that's not all. If DNA could do only the things we've seen so far—copy itself perfectly over and over, spin out RNA and proteins, withstand the damage of nuclear bombs, encode words and phrases, even whistle a few choice tunes—it would still stand out as an amazing molecule, one of the finest. But what sets DNA apart is its ability to build things billions of times larger than itself—and set them in motion across the globe. DNA has even kept travelogues of everything its creations have seen and done in all that time, and a few lucky creatures can now, finally, after mastering the basics of how DNA works, read these tales for themselves.

PART II

Our Animal Past

*Making Things That Crawl and
Frolic and Kill*

5

DNA Vindication

Why Did Life Evolve So Slowly —
Then Explode in Complexity?

lmost immediately upon reading the paper, Sister Miriam Michael Stimson must have known that a decade of labor, her life's work, had collapsed. Throughout the 1940s, this Dominican nun — she wore a black-and-white habit (complete with hood) at all times — had carved out a productive, even thriving research career for herself. At small religious colleges in Michigan and Ohio, she had experimented on wound-healing hormones and even helped create a noted hemorrhoid cream (Preparation H) before finding her avocation in studying the shapes of DNA bases.

She progressed quickly in the field and published evidence that DNA bases were changelings — shape-shifters — that could look quite different one moment to the next. The idea was pleasingly simple but had profound consequences for how DNA worked. In 1951, however, two rival scientists obliterated her theory in a single paper, dismissing her work as "slight" and misguided. It was a mortifying moment. As a woman scientist, Sister Miriam carried a heavy burden; she often had to endure patronizing lectures from male colleagues even on her own research topics. And with such a public dismissal, her hard-won reputation was unraveling as quickly and thoroughly as two strands of DNA.

It couldn't have been much consolation to realize, over the next few years, that her repudiation was actually a necessary step in making the most important biological discovery of the century, Watson and Crick's double helix. James Watson and Francis Crick were unusual biologists for their time in that they merely synthesized other people's work and rarely bothered doing experiments. (Even the über-theorist Darwin had run an experimental nursery and trained himself as an expert in barnacles, including barnacle sex.) This habit of "borrowing" got Watson and Crick in trouble sometimes, most notably with Rosalind Franklin, who took the crucial x-rays that illuminated the double helix. But Watson and Crick built on the foundational work of dozens of other, lesser-known scientists as well, Sister Miriam among them. Admittedly, her work wasn't the most important in the field. In fact, her mistakes perpetuated much of the early confusion about DNA. But as with Thomas Hunt Morgan, following along to see how someone faced her errors has its value. And unlike many vanquished scientists, Sister Miriam had the humility, or gumption, to drag herself back into the lab and contribute something to the double helix story in the end.

In many ways biologists in the mid–twentieth century were struggling with the same basic problem—what did DNA look like?—as in Friedrich Miescher's day, when they'd first uncovered its anomalous mix of sugars, phosphates, and ringed bases. Most vexing of all, no one could figure out how the long strands of DNA could possibly mesh and snuggle up together. Today we know that DNA strands mesh automatically because A fits with T, and C with G, but no one knew that in 1950. Everyone assumed letter pairing was random. So scientists had to accommodate every ungainly combination of letters inside their models of DNA: bulky A and G had to fit together sometimes, as did slender C and T. Scientists quickly realized that no matter how these ill-fitting pairs of bases were rotated or jammed together, they would produce dents and bulges, not the sleek DNA shape they expected. At one point Watson and Crick even said to hell with this biomolecular Tetris and wasted months tinkering with an inside-out (and triple-stranded*) DNA model, with the bases facing outward just to get them out of the way.

Sister Miriam tackled an important subproblem of DNA's structure, the precise shapes of the bases. A nun working in a technical field like this might seem strange today, but Miriam recalled later that most women scientists she encountered at conferences and meetings were fellow sisters. Women at the time usually had to relinquish their careers upon marrying, while unmarried women (like Franklin) provoked suspicion or derision and sometimes earned such low pay they couldn't make ends meet. Catholic sisters, meanwhile, respectably unmarried and living in church-run convents, had the financial support and independence to pursue science.

Not that being a sister didn't complicate things, professionally and personally. Like Mendel—born Johann, but Gregor at his monastery—Miriam Stimson and her fellow novices received new names upon entering their convent in Michigan in 1934. Miriam selected Mary, but during the christening ceremony, their archbishop and his assistant skipped an entry on the list, so most women in line were blessed with the wrong handle. No one spoke up, and because no names remained for Miriam, last in line, the clever archbishop used the first name that popped into his head, a man's. The sisterhood was considered a marriage to Christ, and because what God (or archbishops) join together mere humans cannot put asunder, the wrong names became permanent.

These demands for obedience grew more onerous as Sister Miriam started working, and crimped her scientific career. Instead of a full laboratory, her superiors at her small Catholic college spared only a converted bathroom to run experiments in. Not that she had much time to run them: she had to serve as a "wing-nun," responsible for a student dorm, and she had full teaching loads to boot. She also had to wear a habit with an enormous cobra hood even in the lab, which couldn't have made running complicated experiments easy. (She couldn't drive either because the hood obscured her peripheral vision.) Nevertheless Miriam was sincerely clever—friends nicknamed her "M^2"—and as with Mendel, M^2's order promoted and encouraged her love of sci-

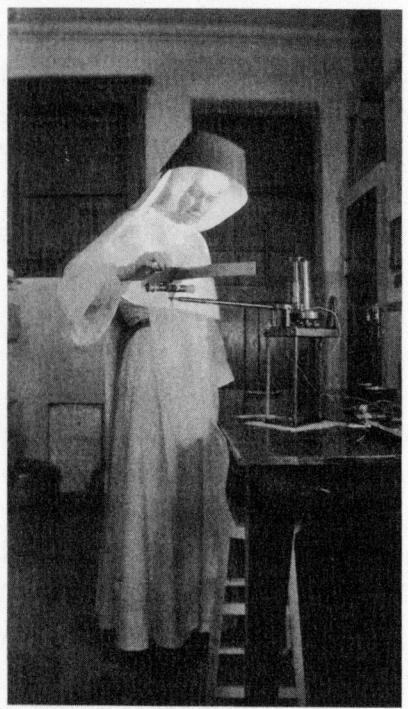

Sister Miriam Michael Stimson, a DNA pioneer, wore her enormous hooded habit even in the laboratory. (Archives: Siena Heights University)

ence. Admittedly, they did so partly to combat godless commies in Asia, but partly also to understand God's creation and care for his creatures. Indeed, Miriam and her colleagues contributed to many areas of medicinal chemistry (hence the Preparation H study). The DNA work was a natural extension of this, and she seemed to be making headway in the late 1940s on the shape of DNA bases, by studying their constituent parts.

Carbon, nitrogen, and oxygen atoms make up the core of A, C, G, and T, but the bases also contain hydrogen, which complicates things. Hydrogen hangs out on the periphery of molecules, and as the lightest and most easily peer-pressured element, hydrogen atoms can get yanked around to different positions, giving the bases slightly different shapes. These shifts aren't a big deal—each is pretty much the same molecule before and after—except the position of hydrogen is critical for holding double-stranded DNA together.

Hydrogen atoms consist of one electron circling one proton. But hydrogen usually shares that negative electron with the inner, ringed part of the DNA base. That leaves its positively charged proton derriere exposed. DNA strands bond together by aligning positive hydrogen patches on one strand's bases with negative patches on the other strand's bases. (Negative patches usually center on oxygen and nitrogen, which hoard electrons.) These hydrogen bonds aren't as strong as normal chemical bonds, but that's actually perfect, because cells can unzip DNA when need be.

Though common in nature, hydrogen bonding seemed impossible in DNA in the early 1950s. Hydrogen bonding requires the positive and negative patches to align perfectly—as they do in A and T, and C and G. But again, no one knew that certain letters paired up—and in other letter combinations the charges don't line up so smartly. Research by Sister M^2 and others further fouled up this picture. Her work involved dissolving

DNA bases in solutions with high or low acidity. (High acidity raises the population of hydrogen ions in a solution; low acidity depresses it.) Miriam knew that the dissolved bases and the hydrogen were interacting somehow in her solution: when she shined ultraviolet light through it, the bases absorbed the light differently, a common sign of something changing shape. But she assumed (always risky) that the change involved hydrogens shifting around, and she suggested that this happens naturally in all DNA. If that was true, DNA scientists now had to contemplate hydrogen bonds not only for mismatched bases, but for multiple forms of each mismatched base. Watson and Crick later recalled with exasperation that even textbooks of the time showed bases with hydrogen atoms in different positions, depending on the author's whims and prejudices. This made building models nearly impossible.

As Sister Miriam published papers on this changeling theory of DNA in the late 1940s, she watched her scientific status climb. Pride goeth before the fall. In 1951 two scientists in London determined that acidic and nonacidic solutions did not shift hydrogens around on DNA bases. Instead those solutions either clamped *extra* hydrogens onto them in odd spots or stripped vulnerable hydrogen off. In other words, Miriam's experiments created artificial, nonnatural bases. Her work was useless for determining anything about DNA, and the shape of DNA bases therefore remained enigmatic.

However faulty Miriam's conclusions, though, some experimental techniques she had introduced with this research proved devilishly useful. In 1949 the DNA biologist Erwin Chargaff adapted a method of ultraviolet analysis that Miriam had pioneered. With this technique, Chargaff determined that DNA contains equal amounts of A and T and of C and G. Chargaff never capitalized on the clue, but did blab about it to every scientist he could corner. Chargaff tried to relay this finding to Linus

Pauling—Watson and Crick's main rival—while on a cruise, but Pauling, annoyed at having his holiday interrupted, blew Chargaff off. The cagier Watson and Crick heeded Chargaff (even though he thought them young fools), and from his insight they determined, finally, that A pairs with T, C with G. It was the last clue they needed, and a few degrees of separation from Sister Miriam, the double helix was born.

Except—what about those hydrogen bonds? It's been lost after a half century of hosannas, but Watson and Crick's model rested on an unwarranted, even shaky, assumption. Their bases fit snugly inside the double helix—and fit with proper hydrogen bonds—only if each base had one specific shape, not another. But after Miriam's work was upended, no one knew what shapes the bases had inside living beings.

Determined to help this time, Sister Miriam returned to the lab bench. After the acid-ultraviolet fiasco, she explored DNA with light from the opposite side of the spectrum, the infrared. The standard way to probe a substance with infrared light involved blending it with liquid, but DNA bases wouldn't always mix properly. So Miriam invented a way to mix DNA with a white powder, potassium bromide. To make samples thin enough to study, Miriam's lab team had to borrow a mold from the nearby Chrysler corporation that would shape the powder into "pills" the diameter of an aspirin, then travel to a local machine shop to stamp the pills, with an industrial press, into discs one millimeter thick. The sight of a cab full of nuns in habit descending on a filthy machine shop tickled the grease monkeys on duty, but Miriam remembered them treating her with gentlemanly politeness. And eventually the air force donated a press to her lab so that she could stamp out discs herself. (She had to hold the press down, students remember, long enough to say two Hail Marys.) Because thin layers of potassium bromide were invisible to infrared, the light tickled only the A's, C's, G's, and T's as it streamed through. And over the next decade, infrared studies with the discs (along with other work) proved Watson and Crick right: DNA bases had only one natural shape, the one that produced perfect hydrogen bonds. At this point, and only at this point, could scientists say they grasped DNA's structure.

Of course, understanding its structure wasn't the final goal; scientists had more research ahead. But although M² continued to do outstanding work—in 1953 she lectured at the Sorbonne, the first woman scientist to do so since Madame Curie—and although she lived until 2002, reaching the age of eighty-nine, her scientific ambitions petered out along the way. In the swinging 1960s, she doffed her hooded habit for the last time (and learned how to drive), but despite this minor disobedience, she devoted herself to her order during her last decades and stopped experimenting. She let other scientists, including two other women pioneers, unravel how DNA actually builds complex and beautiful life.*

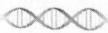

The history of science teems with duplicate discoveries. Natural selection, oxygen, Neptune, sunspots—two, three, even four scientists discovered each independently. Historians continue to bicker about why this happens: perhaps each case was a gigantic coincidence; perhaps one presumed discoverer stole ideas; perhaps the discoveries were impossible before circumstances favored them, and inevitable once they did. But no matter what you believe, scientific simultaneity is a fact. Multiple teams almost sussed out the double helix, and in 1963 two teams did discover another important aspect of DNA. One group was using microscopes to map mitochondria, bean-shaped organs that supply energy inside cells. The other group was pureeing mitochondria and sifting through the guts. Both turned up evidence that mitochondria have their own DNA. In trying to burnish his reputation at the end of the 1800s, Friedrich Miescher had defined the nucleus as the exclusive home for DNA; history once again crossed Friedrich Miescher.

If historical circumstances favor some discoveries, though, science also needs mavericks, those counterclockwise types who see what circumstances blind the rest of us to. Sometimes we even need obnoxious mavericks—because if they're not pugnacious, their theories never penetrate our attention. Such was the case with Lynn Margulis. Most scientists in the mid-1960s explained the origin of mitochondrial DNA rather dully, arguing that cells must have loaned a bit of DNA out once and never gotten it back. But for two decades, beginning in her Ph.D. thesis in 1965, Margulis pushed the idea that mitochondrial DNA was no mere curiosity. She saw it instead as proof of something bigger, proof that life has more ways of mixing and evolving than conventional biologists ever dreamed.

Margulis's theory, endosymbiosis, went like this. We all descended long ago from the first microbes on earth, and all living organisms today share certain genes, on the order of one hundred, as part of that legacy. Soon enough, though, these early microbes began to diverge. Some grew into mammoth blobs, others shrank into specks, and the size difference created opportunities. Most important, some microbes began swallowing and digesting others, while others infected and killed the large and unwary. For either reason, Margulis argued, a large microbe ingested a bug one afternoon long, long ago, and something strange happened: nothing. Either the little Jonah fought off being digested, or his host staved off an internal coup. A standoff followed, and although each one kept fighting, neither could polish the other off. And after untold generations, this initially hostile encounter thawed into a cooperative venture. Gradually the little guy became really good at synthesizing high-octane fuel from oxygen; gradually the whale cell lost its power-producing abilities and specialized instead in providing raw nutrients and shelter. As Adam Smith might have predicted, this division of biolabor benefited each party, and soon neither side could abandon the other without dying. We call the microscopic bugs our mitochondria.

A nice theory overall—but just that. And unfortunately, when Margulis proposed it, scientists didn't respond so nicely. Fifteen journals rejected Margulis's first paper on endosymbiosis, and worse, many scientists outright attacked its speculations. Every time they did, though, she marshaled more evidence and became more pugnacious in emphasizing the independent behavior of mitochondria—that they backstroke about inside cells, that they reproduce on their own schedule, that they have their own cell-like membranes. And their vestigial DNA clinched the case: cells seldom let DNA escape the nucleus to the cellular exurbs, and DNA rarely survives if it tries. We also inherit this DNA differently than chromosome DNA—exclusively from our mothers, since a mother supplies her children with all their mitochondria. Margulis concluded that so-called mtDNA could only have come from once-sovereign cells.

Her opponents countered (correctly) that mitochondria don't work alone; they need chromosomal genes to function, so they're hardly independent. Margulis parried, saying that after three billion years it's not surprising if many of the genes necessary for independent life have faded, until just the Cheshire Cat grin of the old mitochondrial genome remains today. Her opponents didn't buy that—absence of evidence and all—but unlike, say, Miescher, who lacked much backbone for defending himself, Margulis kept swinging back. She lectured and wrote widely on her theory and delighted in rattling audiences. (She once opened a talk by asking, "Any real biologists here? Like molecular biologists?" She counted the raised hands and laughed. "Good. You're going to hate this.")

Biologists did hate endosymbiosis, and the spat dragged on and on until new scanning technology in the 1980s revealed that mitochondria store their DNA not in long, linear chromosomes (as animals and plants do) but in hoops, as bacteria do. The thirty-seven tightly packed genes on the hoop built bacteria-like proteins as well, and the A-C-G-T sequence itself looked remarkably bacterial. Working from this evidence, scientists even identified living relatives of mitochondria, such as typhoid bacteria. Similar work established that chloroplasts—greenish specks that manage photosynthesis inside plants—also contain looped DNA. As with mitochondria, Margulis had surmised that chloroplasts evolved when large ancestor microbes swallowed photosynthesizing pond scum, and Stockholm syndrome ensued. Two cases of endosymbiosis were too much for opponents to explain away. Margulis was vindicated, and she crowed.

In addition to explaining mitochondria, Margulis's theory has since helped solve a profound mystery of life on earth: why evolution damn near stalled after such a promising beginning. Without the kick start of mitochondria, primitive life might never have developed into higher life, much less intelligent human beings.

To see how profound the stall was, consider how easily the universe manufactures life. The first organic molecules on earth probably appeared spontaneously near volcanic vents on the ocean floor. Heat energy there could fuse simple carbon-rich molecules into complex amino acids and even vesicles to serve as crude membranes. Earth also likely imported organics from space. Astronomers have discovered naked amino acids floating in interstellar dust clouds, and chemists have calculated that DNA bases like adenine might form in space, too, since adenine is nothing but five simple HCN molecules (cyanide, of all things) squished into a double ring. Or icy comets might have incubated DNA bases. As ice forms, it gets quite xenophobic and squeezes any organic impurities inside it into concentrated bubbles, pressure-cooking the gook and making the formation of complicated molecules more likely. Scientists already suspect that comets filled our seas with water as they bombarded the early earth, and they might well have seeded our oceans with bio-bits.

From this simmering organic broth, autonomous microorganisms with sophisticated membranes and replaceable moving parts emerged in just a billion years. (Pretty speedy, if you think about it.) And from this common beginning, many distinct species popped up in short order, species with distinct livelihoods and clever ways of carving out a living. After this miracle, however, evolution flatlined: we had many types of truly living creatures, but these microbes didn't evolve much more for well over a billion years—and might never have.

What doomed them was energy consumption. Primitive microbes expend 2 percent of their total energy copying and maintaining DNA, but 75 percent of their energy making proteins from DNA. So even if a microbe develops the DNA for an advantageous and evolutionarily advanced trait—like an enclosed nucleus, or a "belly" to digest other microbes, or an apparatus to communicate with peers—actually building the advanced feature pretty much depletes it. Adding two is out of the question. In these circumstances, evolution idles; cells can get only so sophisticated. Cheap mitochondrial power lifted those restrictions. Mitochondria store as much energy per unit size as lightning bolts, and their mobility allowed our ancestors to add many fancy features at once, and grow into multifaceted organisms. In fact, mitochondria allowed cells to expand their DNA repertoire 200,000 times, allowing them not only to invent new genes but to add tons of regulatory DNA, making them far more flexible when using genes. This could never have happened without mitochondria, and we might never have illuminated this evolutionary dark age without Margulis's theory.

MtDNA opened up whole new realms of science as well, like

genetic archaeology. Because mitochondria reproduce on their own, mtDNA genes are abundant in cells, much more so than chromosome genes. So when scientists go digging around in cavemen or mummies or whatever, they're often rooting out and examining mtDNA. Scientists can also use mtDNA to trace genealogies with unprecedented accuracy. Sperm carry little more than a nuclear DNA payload, so children inherit all their mitochondria from their mothers' much roomier eggs. MtDNA therefore gets passed down largely unchanged through female lines for generation after generation, making it ideal to trace maternal ancestry. What's more, because scientists know how quickly any rare changes do accumulate in a mitochondrial line—one mutation every 3,500 years—they can use mtDNA as a clock: they compare two people's mtDNA, and the more mutations they find, the more years that have passed since the two people shared a maternal ancestor. In fact, this clock tells us that all seven billion people alive today can trace their maternal lineage to one woman who lived in Africa 170,000 years ago, dubbed "Mitochondrial Eve." Eve wasn't the only woman alive then, mind you. She's simply the oldest matrilineal ancestor* of everyone living today.

After mitochondria proved so vital to science, Margulis used her momentum and sudden prestige to advance other offbeat ideas. She began arguing that microbes also donated various locomotor devices to animals, like the tails on sperm, even though those structures lack DNA. And beyond cells merely picking up spare parts, she outlined a grander theory in which endosymbiosis drives all evolution, relegating mutations and natural selection to minor roles. According to this theory, mutations alter creatures only modestly. Real change occurs when genes leap from species to species, or when whole genomes merge, fusing wildly different creatures together. Only after these "horizontal" DNA transfers does natural selection begin, merely to edit out any hopeless monsters that emerge. Meanwhile the hopeful monsters, the beneficiaries of mergers, flourish.

Though Margulis called it revolutionary, in some ways her merger theory just extends a classic debate between biologists who favor (for whatever reasons you want to psychoanalyze) bold leaps and instant species, and biologists who favor conservative adjustments and gradual speciation. The arch-gradualist Darwin saw modest change and common descent as nature's law, and favored a slow-growing tree of life with no overlapping branches. Margulis fell into the radical camp. She argued that mergers can create honest-to-goodness chimeras—blends of creatures technically no different than mermaids, sphinxes, or centaurs. From this point of view, Darwin's quaint tree of life must give way to a quick-spun web of life, with interlocking lines and radials.

However far she strayed into radical ideas, Margulis earned her right to dissent. It's even a little two-faced to praise someone for holding fast to unconventional scientific ideas sometimes and chastise her for not conforming elsewhere; you can't necessarily just switch off the iconoclastic part of the mind when convenient. As renowned biologist John Maynard Smith once admitted, "I think [Margulis is] often wrong, but most of the people I know think it's important to have her around, because she's wrong in such fruitful ways." And lest we forget, Margulis was right in her first big idea, stunningly so. Above all, her work reminds us that pretty plants and things with backbones haven't dominated life's history. Microbes have, and they're the evolutionary fodder from which we multicellular creatures rose.

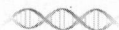

If Lynn Margulis relished conflict, her older contemporary Barbara McClintock shunned it. McClintock preferred quiet rumination over public confrontation, and her peculiar ideas sprang not from any contrarian streak but from pure flakiness. It's fitting, then, that McClintock dedicated her life to navigating the oddball genetics of plants like maize. By embracing the eccentricity of maize, McClintock expanded our notions of what DNA can do, and provided vital clues for understanding a second great mystery of our evolutionary past: how DNA builds multicellular creatures from Margulis's complex but solo cells.

McClintock's bio divides into two eras: the fulfilled, pre-1951 scientist, and the bitter, post-1951 hermit. Not that things were all daffodils before 1951. From a very young age McClintock squabbled intensely with her mother, a pianist, mostly because Barbara showed more stubborn interest in science and sports like ice skating than the girlish pastimes her mother always said would improve her dating prospects. Her mother even vetoed Barbara's dream to (like Hermann Muller and William Friedman before her) study genetics at Cornell, because nice boys didn't marry brainy gals. Thankfully for science, Barbara's father, a physician, intervened before the fall 1919 semester and packed his daughter off to upstate New York by train.

At Cornell, McClintock flourished, becoming the freshmen women's class president and starring in science classes. Still, her science classmates didn't always appreciate her sharp tongue, especially her lashings over their microscopy work. In that era, preparing microscope samples—slicing cells like deli ham and mounting their gelatinous guts on multiple glass slides without spilling—was intricate and demanding work. Actually using scopes was tricky, too: identifying what specks were what inside a cell could flummox even a good scientist. But McClintock mastered microscopy early, becoming legitimately world-class by graduation. As a graduate student at Cornell, she then honed a technique—"the squash"—that allowed her to flatten whole cells with her thumb and keep them intact on one slide, making them easier to study. Using the squash, she became the first scientist to identify all ten maize chromosomes. (Which, as anyone who's ever gone cross-eyed squinting at the spaghetti mess of chromosomes inside real cells knows, ain't easy.)

Cornell asked McClintock to become a full-time researcher and instructor in 1927, and she began studying how chromosomes interact, with assistance from her best student, Harriet Creighton. Both of these tomboys wore their hair short and often dressed mannishly, in knickers and high socks. People mixed up anecdotes about them, too—like which was it exactly who'd shinnied up a drainpipe one morning after forgetting the keys to her second-story office. Creighton was more outgoing; the reserved McClintock would never have bought a jalopy, as Creighton did, to celebrate the end of World War II and cruise to Mexico. Nonetheless they made a wonderful team, and soon made a seminal discovery. Morgan's fruit fly boys had demonstrated years before that chromosomes probably crossed arms and swapped tips. But their arguments remained statistical, based on abstract patterns. And while many a microscopist had seen chromosomes entangling, no one could tell if they actually exchanged material. But McClintock and Creighton knew every corn chromosome's every knob and carbuncle by sight, and they determined that chromosomes did physically exchange segments. They even linked these exchanges to changes in how genes worked, a crucial confirmation. McClintock dawdled in writing up these results, but when Morgan got wind of them, he insisted she publish, posthaste. She did in 1931. Morgan won his Nobel Prize two years later.

Although pleased with the work—it earned her and Creighton bios in, well, *American Men of Science*—McClintock wanted more. She wanted to study not only chromosomes themselves but how chromosomes changed and mutated, and how those changes built complex organisms with different roots and colors and leaves. Unfortunately, as she tried to set up a lab, social circumstances conspired against her. Like the priesthood, universities at the time offered full professorships only to men (except in home ec), and Cornell had no intention of excepting McClintock. She left reluctantly in 1936 and bounced about, working with Morgan out in California for a spell, then taking research positions in Missouri and Germany. She hated both places.

Truth be told, McClintock had other troubles beyond being the wrong gender. Not exactly the bubbly sort, she'd earned a reputation as sour and uncollegial—she'd once scooped a colleague by tackling his research problem behind his back and publishing her results before he finished. Equally problematic, McClintock worked on corn.

Yes, there was money in corn genetics, since corn was a food crop. (One leading American geneticist, Henry Wallace—future vice president to FDR—made his fortune running a seed company.) Corn also had a scientific pedigree, as Darwin and Mendel had both studied it. Ag scientists even showed an interest in corn mutations: when the United States began exploding nukes at Bikini Atoll in 1946, government scientists placed corn seed beneath the airbursts to study how nuclear fallout affected maize.

McClintock, though, pooh-poohed the traditional ends of corn research, like bigger yields and sweeter kernels. Corn was a means to her, a vehicle to study general inheritance and development. Unfortunately, corn had serious disadvantages for such work. It grew achingly slowly, and its capricious chromosomes often snapped, or grew bulges, or fused, or randomly doubled. McClintock savored the complexity, but most geneticists wanted to avoid these headaches. They trusted McClintock's work—no one matched her on a microscope—but her devotion to corn stranded her between pragmatic scientists helping Iowans grow more bushels and pure geneticists who refused to fuss with unruly corn DNA.

At last, McClintock secured a job in 1941 at rustic Cold

Spring Harbor Laboratory, thirty miles east of Manhattan. Unlike before, she had no students to distract her, and she employed just one assistant—who got a shotgun, and instructions to keep the damn crows off her corn. And although isolated out there with her maize, she was happily isolated. Her few friends always described her as a scientific mystic, constantly chasing the insight that would dissolve the complexity of genetics into unity. "She believed in the great inner lightbulb," one friend remarked. At Cold Spring she had time and space to meditate, and settled into the most productive decade of her career, right through 1951.

Her research actually culminated in March 1950, when a colleague received a letter from McClintock. It ran ten single-spaced pages, but whole paragraphs were scribbled out and scribbled over—not to mention other fervid annotations, connected by arrows and climbing like kudzu up and down the margins. It's the kind of letter you'd think about getting tested for anthrax nowadays, and it described a theory that sounded nutty, too. Morgan had established genes as stationary pearls on a chromosomal necklace. McClintock insisted she'd seen the pearls move—jumping from chromosome to chromosome and burrowing in.

Moreover, these jumping genes somehow affected the color of kernels. McClintock worked with Indian corn, the kind speckled with red and blue and found on harvest floats in parades. She'd seen the jumping genes attack the arms of chromosomes inside these kernels, snapping them and leaving the ends dangling like a compound fracture. Whenever this happened, the kernels stopped producing pigment. Later, though, when the jumping gene got restless and randomly leaped somewhere else, the broken arm healed, and pigment production started up again. Amid her scribbling, McClintock suggested that the break had disrupted the gene for making the pigments.

Indeed, this off/on pattern seemed to explain the randomly colored stripes and swirls of her kernels.

In other words, jumping genes controlled pigment production; McClintock actually called them "controlling elements." (Today they're called transposons or, more generally, mobile DNA.) And like Margulis, McClintock parlayed her fascinating find into a more ambitious theory. Perhaps the knottiest biological question of the 1940s was why cells didn't all look alike: skin and liver and brain cells contain the same DNA, after all, so why didn't they act the same? Previous biologists argued that something in the cell's cytoplasm regulated genes, something external to the nucleus. McClintock had won evidence that chromosomes regulated themselves from within the nucleus—and that this control involved turning genes on or off at the right moments.

In fact, (as McClintock suspected) the ability to turn genes off and on was a crucial step in life's history. After Margulis's complex cells emerged, life once again stalled for over a billion years. Then, around 550 million years ago, huge numbers of multicellular creatures burst into existence. The first beings probably were multicellular by mistake, sticky cells that couldn't free themselves. But over time, by precisely controlling which genes functioned at which moments in which stuck-together cells, the cells could begin to specialize—the hallmark of higher life. Now McClintock thought she had insight into how this profound change came about.

McClintock organized her manic letter into a proper talk, which she delivered at Cold Spring in June 1951. Buoyed by hope, she spoke for over two hours that day, reading thirty-five single-spaced pages. She might have forgiven audience members for nodding off, but to her dismay, she found them merely baffled. It wasn't so much her facts. Scientists knew her reputation, so when she insisted she'd seen genes jump about like fleas, most accepted she had. It was her theory about genetic control that bothered them. Basically, the insertions and jumps seemed too random. This randomness might well explain blue versus red kernels, they granted, but how could jumping genes control all development in multicellular creatures? You can't build a baby or a beanstalk with genes flickering on and off haphazardly. McClintock didn't have good answers, and as the hard questions continued, consensus hardened against her. Her revolutionary idea about controlling elements got downgraded* into another queer property of maize.

Barbara McClintock discovered "jumping genes," but when other scientists questioned her conclusions about them, she became a scientific hermit, crushed and crestfallen. *Inset:* McClintock's beloved maize and microscope. (National Institutes of Health, and Smithsonian Institution, National Museum of American History)

This demotion hurt McClintock badly. Decades after the talk, she still smoldered about colleagues supposedly sniggering at her, or firing off accusations—*You dare question the stationary-gene dogma?* There's little evidence people actually laughed or boiled in rage; again, most accepted jumping genes, just not her theory of control. But McClintock warped the memory into a conspiracy against her. Jumping genes and genetic control had become so interwoven in her heart and mind that attacking one meant attacking both, and attacking her. Crushed, and lacking a brawling disposition, she withdrew from science.*

So began the hermit phase. For three decades, McClintock continued studying maize, often dozing on a cot in her office at night. But she stopped attending conferences and cut off communication with fellow scientists. After finishing experiments, she usually typed up her results as if to submit them to a journal, then filed the paper away without sending it. If her peers dismissed her, she would hurt them back by ignoring them. And in her (now-depressive) solitude, her mystic side emerged fully. She indulged in speculation about ESP, UFOs, and poltergeists, and studied methods of psychically controlling her reflexes. (When visiting the dentist, she told him not to bother with Novocain, as she could lock out pain with her mind.) All the while, she grew maize and squashed slides and wrote up papers that went as unread as Emily Dickinson's poems in her day. She was her own sad scientific community.

Meanwhile something funny was afoot in the larger scientific community, a change almost too subtle to notice at first. The molecular biologists whom McClintock was ignoring began spotting mobile DNA in microbes in the late 1960s. And far from this DNA being a mere novelty, the jumping genes dictated things like whether microbes developed drug resistance. Scientists also found evidence that infectious viruses could (just like mobile DNA) insert genetic material into chromosomes and lurk there permanently. Both were huge medical concerns. Mobile DNA has become vital, too, in tracking evolutionary relationships among species. That's because if you compare a few species, and just two of them have the same transposon burrowed into their DNA at the same point among billions of bases, then those two species almost certainly shared an ancestor recently. More to the point, they shared that ancestor more recently than either shared an ancestor with a third species that lacks the transposon; far too many bases exist for that insertion to have happened twice independently. What look like DNA marginalia, then, actually reveal life's hidden recorded history, and for this and other reasons, McClintock's work suddenly seemed less cute, more profound. As a result her reputation stopped sinking, then rose, year by year. Around 1980 something tipped, and a popular biography of the now-wrinkled McClintock, *A Feeling for the Organism*, appeared in July 1983, making her a minor celebrity. The momentum bucked out of control after that, and unthinkably, just as her own work had done for Morgan a half century before, the adulation propelled McClintock to a Nobel Prize that October.

The hermit had been fairy-tale transformed. She became a latter-day Gregor Mendel, a genius discarded and forgotten—only McClintock lived long enough to see her vindication. Her life soon became a rallying point for feminists and fodder for didactic children's books on never compromising your dreams. That McClintock hated the publicity from the Nobel—it interrupted her research and set reporters prowling about her door—mattered little to fans. And even scientifically, winning the Nobel panged her. The committee had honored her "*discovery* of mobile genetic elements," which was true enough. But in 1951 McClintock had imagined she'd unlocked how genes control other genes and control development in multicellular creatures. Instead scientists honored her, essentially, for her microscope skills—for spotting minnows of DNA darting around. For these reasons, McClintock grew increasingly weary of life post-Nobel, even a little morbid: in her late eighties, she started telling friends she'd surely die at age ninety. Months after her ninetieth birthday party, at James Watson's home, in June 1992, she did indeed pass, cementing her reputation as someone who envisioned things others couldn't.

In the end, McClintock's life's work remained unfulfilled. She did discover jumping genes and vastly expanded our understanding of corn genetics. (One jumping gene, *hopscotch*, seems in fact to have transformed the scrawny wild ancestor of corn into a lush, domesticatable crop in the first place.) More generally McClintock helped establish that chromosomes regulate themselves internally and that on/off patterns of DNA determine a cell's fate. Both ideas remain crucial tenets of genetics. But despite her fondest hopes, jumping genes don't control development or turn genes on and off to the extent she imagined; cells do these things in other ways. In fact it took other scientists many years to explain how DNA accomplishes those tasks—to explain how powerful but isolated cells pulled themselves together long ago and started building truly complex creatures, even creatures as complex as Miriam Michael Stimson, Lynn Margulis, and Barbara McClintock.

6

The Survivors, the Livers

What's Our Most Ancient and Important DNA?

enerations of schoolchildren have learned all about the ruinous amounts of money that European merchants and monarchs spent during colonial days searching for the Northwest Passage—a sailing route to cut horizontally through North America to the spices, porcelain, and tea of Indonesia, India, and Cathay (China). It's less well known that earlier generations of explorers had hunted just as hard for, and believed with no less delusional determination in, a north*east* passage that looped over the frosty top of Russia.

One explorer seeking the northeast passage—Dutchman Willem Barentsz, a navigator and cartographer from the coastal lowlands who was known in English annals as Barents, Barentz, Barentson, and Barentzoon—made his first voyage in 1594 into what's known today as the Barents Sea above Norway. While undertaken for mercenary reasons, voyages like Barentsz's also benefited scientists. Scientific naturalists, while alarmed by the occasional monster that turned up in some savage land, could begin to chart how flora and fauna differ across the globe—work that was a kind of forerunner of our common-descent, common-DNA biology today. Geographers also got much-needed help. Many geographers at the time believed that because of the constant summer sun at high latitudes, polar ice caps melted above a certain point, rendering the North Pole a sunny paradise. And nearly all maps portrayed the pole itself as a monolith of black magnetic rock, which explained why the pole tugged on compasses. In his sally into the Barents Sea, Barentsz aimed to discover if Novaya Zemlya, land north of Siberia, was a promontory of yet another undiscovered continent or merely an island that could be sailed around. He outfitted three ships, *Mercury*, *Swan*, and another *Mercury*, and set out in June 1594.

A few months later, Barentsz and his *Mercury* crew broke with the other ships and began exploring the coast of Novaya Zemlya. In doing so, they made one of the more daring runs in exploration history. For weeks, *Mercury* dodged and ducked a veritable Spanish armada of ice floes, foiling disaster for 1,500 miles. At last Barentsz's men grew frazzled enough to beg to turn back. Barentsz relented, having proved he could navigate the Arctic Sea, and he returned to Holland certain he'd discovered an easy passage to Asia.

Easy, if he avoided monsters. The discovery of the New World and the continued exploration of Africa and Asia had turned up thousands upon thousands of never-dreamed-of plants and animals—and provoked just as many wild tales about beasts that sailors swore they'd seen. For their part, cartographers channeled their inner Hieronymus Bosch and spiced up empty seas and steppes on their maps with wild scenes: blood-red krakens splintering ships, giant otters cannibalizing each other, dragons chewing greedily on rats, trees braining bears with macelike branches, not to mention the ever-popular topless mermaid. One important chart of the era, from 1544, shows a rather contemplative

Monsters of all stripes proved wildly popular on early maps and filled in blank expanses of land and sea for centuries. (Detail from the 1539 *Carta Marina*, a map of Scandinavia, by Olaus Magnus)

Cyclops sitting on the western crook of Africa. Its cartographer, Sebastian Münster, later released an influential compendium of maps interleaved with essays on griffins and avaricious ants that mined gold. Münster also held forth on humanoid-looking beasts around the globe, including the Blemmyae, humans whose faces appeared in their chests; the Cynocephali, people with canine faces; and the Sciopods, grotesque land mermaids with one gargantuan foot, which they used to shade themselves on sunny days by lying down and raising it over their heads. Some of these brutes merely personified (or animalified) ancient fears and superstitions. But amid the farrago of plausible myth and fantastical facts, naturalists could barely keep up.

Even the most scientific naturalist during the age of exploration, Carl von Linné, d.b.a. Linnaeus, speculated on monsters. Linnaeus's *Systema Naturae* set forth the binomial system for naming species that we still use today, inspiring the likes of *Homo sapiens* and *Tyrannosaurus rex*. The book also defined a class of animals called "paradoxa," which included dragons, phoenixes, satyrs, unicorns, geese that sprouted from trees, Heracles's nemesis the Hydra, and remarkable tadpoles that not only got smaller as they aged, but metamorphosed into fish. We might laugh today, but in the last case at least, the joke's on us: shrinking tadpoles do exist, although *Pseudis paradoxa* shrink into regular old frogs, not fish. What's more, modern genetic research reveals a legitimate basis for some of Linnaeus's and Münster's legends.

A few key genes in every embryo play cartographer for other genes and map out our bodies with GPS precision, front to back, left to right, and top to bottom. Insects, fish, mammals, reptiles, and all other animals share many of these genes, especially a subset called *hox* genes. The ubiquity of *hox* in the animal kingdom explains why animals worldwide have the same basic body plan: a cylindrical trunk with a head at one end, an anus at the other, and various appendages sprouting in between. (The Blemmyae, with faces low enough to lick their navels, would be unlikely for this reason alone.)

Unusually for genes, *hox* remain tightly linked after hundreds of millions of years of evolution, almost always appearing together along continuous stretches of DNA. (Invertebrates have one stretch of around ten genes, vertebrates four stretches of basically the same ones.) Even more unusually, each *hox*'s position along that stretch corresponds closely to its assignment in the body. The first *hox* designs the top of the head. The next *hox* designs something slightly lower down. The third *hox* something slightly lower, and so on, until the final *hox* designs our nether regions. Why nature requires this top-to-bottom spatial mapping in *hox* genes isn't known, but again, all animals exhibit this trait.

Scientists refer to DNA that appears in the same basic form

in many, many species as highly "conserved" because creatures remain very careful, very conservative, about changing it. (Some *hox* and *hox*-like genes are so conserved that scientists can rip them out of chickens, mice, and flies and swap them between species, and the genes more or less function the same.) As you might suspect, being highly conserved correlates strongly with the importance of the DNA in question. And it's easy to see, literally see, why creatures don't mess with their highly conserved *hox* genes all that often. Delete one of these genes, and animals can develop multiple jaws. Mutate others and wings disappear, or extra sets of eyes appear in awful places, bulging out on the legs or staring from the ends of antennae. Still other mutations cause genitals or legs to sprout on the head, or cause jaws or antennae to grow in the crotchal region. And these are the lucky mutants; most creatures that gamble with *hox* and related genes don't live to speak of it.

Genes like *hox* don't build animals as much as they instruct other genes on how to build animals: each one regulates dozens of underlings. However important, though, these genes can't control every aspect of development. In particular, they depend on nutrients like vitamin A.

Despite the singular name, vitamin A is actually a few related molecules that we non-biochemists lump together for convenience. These various vitamins A are among the most widespread nutrients in nature. Plants store vitamin A as beta carotene, which gives carrots their distinct color. Animals store vitamin A in our livers, and our bodies convert freely between various forms, which we use in a byzantine array of biochemical processes — to keep eyesight sharp and sperm potent, to boost mitochondria production and euthanize old cells. For these reasons, a lack of vitamin A in the diet is a major health concern worldwide. One of the first genetically enhanced foods created by scientists was so-called golden rice, a cheap source of vitamin A with grains tinted by beta carotene.

Vitamin A interacts with *hox* and related genes to build the fetal brain, lungs, eyes, heart, limbs, and just about every other organ. In fact, vitamin A is so important that cells build special drawbridges in their membranes to let vitamin A, and only vitamin A, through. Once inside a cell, vitamin A binds to special helper molecules, and the resulting complex binds directly to the double helix of DNA, turning *hox* and other genes on. While most signaling chemicals get repulsed at the cell wall and have to shout their instructions through small keyholes, vitamin A gets special treatment, and the *hox* build very little in a baby without a nod from this master nutrient.

But be warned: before you dash to the health store for mega-doses of vitamin A for a special pregnant someone, you should know that too much vitamin A can cause substantial birth defects. In fact the body tightly caps its vitamin A concentration, and even has a few genes (like the awkwardly initialed *tgif* gene) that exist largely to degrade vitamin A if its concentration creeps too high. That's partly because high levels of vitamin A in embryos can interfere with the vital, but even more ridiculously named, *sonic hedgehog* gene.

(Yes, it's named for the video game character. A graduate student—one of those wacky fruit fly guys—discovered it in the early 1990s and classified it within a group of genes that, when mutated, cause *Drosophila* to grow spiky quills all over, like hedgehogs. Scientists had already discovered multiple "hedge-hog" genes and named them after real hedgehog species, like the Indian hedgehog, moonrat hedgehog, and desert hedgehog. Robert Riddle thought naming his gene after the speedy Sega hero would be funny. By happenstance, *sonic* proved one of the most important genes in the animal repertoire, and the frivolity has not worn well. Flaws can lead to lethal cancers or heartbreaking birth defects, and scientists cringe when they have to explain to some poor family that *sonic hedgehog* will kill a loved one. As one biologist told the *New York Times* about such names, "It's a cute name when you have stupid flies and you call [a gene] *turnip*. When it's linked to development in humans, it's not so cute anymore.")

Just as *hox* genes control our body's top-to-bottom pattern, *shh*—as scientists who detest the name refer to *sonic hedgehog*—helps control the body's left-right symmetry. *Shh* does so by setting up a GPS gradient. When we're still a ball of protoplasm, the incipient spinal column that forms our midline starts to secrete the protein *sonic* produces. Nearby cells absorb lots of it, faraway cells much less. Based on how much protein they absorb, cells "know" exactly where they are in relation to the midline, and therefore know what type of cell they should become.

But if there's too much vitamin A around (or if *shh* fails for a different reason), the gradient doesn't get set up properly. Cells can't figure out their longitude in relation to the midline, and organs start to grow in abnormal, even monstrous ways. In severe cases, the brain doesn't divide into right and left halves; it ends up as one big, undifferentiated blob. The same can happen with the lower limbs: if exposed to too much vitamin A, they fuse together, leading to sirenomelia, or mermaid syndrome. Both fused brains and fused legs are fatal (in the latter case because holes for the anus and bladder don't develop). But the most distressing violations of symmetry appear on the face. Chickens with too much *sonic* have faces with extra-wide midlines, sometimes so wide that two beaks form. (Other animals get two noses.) Too little *sonic* can produce noses with a single giant nostril, or prevent noses from growing at all. In some severe cases, noses appear in the wrong spot, like on the forehead. Perhaps most distressing of all, with too little *sonic*, the two eyes don't start growing where they should, an inch or so to the left and right of the facial midline. Both eyes end up *on* the midline, producing the very Cyclops* that cartographers seemed so silly for including on their maps.

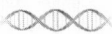

Linnaeus never included Cyclops in his classification scheme, largely because he came to doubt the existence of monsters. He dropped the category of paradoxa from later editions of *Systema Naturae*. But in one case Linnaeus might have been too cynical in dismissing the stories he heard. Linnaeus named the genus that bears reside in, *Ursus,* and he personally named the brown bear *Ursus arctos,* so he knew bears could live in extreme northern climates. Yet he never discussed the existence of polar bears, perhaps because the anecdotes that would have trickled in to him seemed dubious. Who could credit, after all, barroom tales about a ghost-white bear that stalked men across the ice and tore their heads off for sport? Especially when—and people swore this happened, too—if they killed and ate the white bear, it would extract beyond-the-grave revenge by causing their skin to peel off? But such things did happen to Barentsz's men, a horror story that winds its way back and around to the same vitamin A that can produce Cyclopes and mermaids.

Spurred on by the "most exaggerated hopes" of Maurice of Nassau,* a prince of Holland, lords in four Dutch cities filled seven ships with linens, cloths, and tapestries and sent Barentsz back out for Asia in 1595. Haggling delayed the departure until midsummer, and once asea, the captains of the vessels overruled Barentsz (who was merely the navigator) and took a more southerly course than he wished. They did so partly because Barentsz's northerly route seemed mad, and partly because, beyond reaching China, the Dutch seamen were fired by rumors of a remote island whose shores were studded with diamonds. Sure enough, the crew found the island and landed straightaway.

Sailors had been stuffing their pockets with the transparent gems for a number of minutes when, as an olde English account had it, "a great leane white beare came sodainly stealing out" and wrapped his paw around one sailor's neck. Thinking a hirsute sailor had him in a half nelson, he cried out, "Who is that pulles me so by the necke?" His companions, eyes glued to the ground for gems, looked up and just about messed themselves. The polar bear, "falling upon the man, bit his head in sunder, and suckt out his blood."

This encounter opened a centuries-long war between explorers and this "cruell, fierce, and rauenous beast." Polar bears certainly deserved their reputations as mean SOBs. They picked off and devoured any stragglers wherever sailors landed, and they withstood staggering amounts of punishment. Sailors could bury an ax in a bear's back or pump six bullets into its flank— and often, in its rampage, this just made the bear madder. Then again, polar bears had plenty of grievances, too. As one historian notes, "Early explorers seemed to regard it as their duty to kill polar bears," and they piled up carcasses like buffalo hunters later would on the Great Plains. Some explorers deliberately maimed bears to keep as pets and paraded them around in rope nooses. One such bear, hauled aboard a small ship, snapped free from its restraints and, after slapping the sailors about, mutinied and took over the ship. In the bear's fury, though, its noose got tangled in the rudder, and it exhausted itself trying to get free. The brave men retook the ship and butchered the bear.

During the encounter with Barentsz's crew, the bear managed to murder a second sailor, and probably would have kept hunting had reinforcements not arrived from the main ship. A sharpshooter put a bullet clean between the bear's eyes, but the bear shook it off and refused to stop snacking. Other men charged and attacked with swords, but their blades snapped on its head and hide. Finally someone clubbed the beast in the snout and stunned it, enabling another person to slit its throat ear to ear. By this time both sailors had expired, of course, and the rescue squad could do nothing but skin the bear and abandon the corpses.

The rest of the voyage didn't turn out much better for Barentsz's crew. The ships had left too late in the season, and huge floating mines of ice began to threaten their hulls from all sides. The threat swelled each day, and by September, some sailors felt desperate enough to mutiny. Five were hanged. Eventually even Barentsz wilted, fearing the clumsy merchant ships would be stranded in ice. All seven ships returned to port with nothing more than the cargo they'd set out with, and everyone involved lost his frilly shirt. Even the supposed diamonds turned out to be worthless, crumbling glass.

The voyage would have crippled the confidence of a humble man. All Barentsz learned was not to trust superiors. He'd wanted to sail farther north the whole time, so in 1596 he scraped together funds for two more ships and reembarked. Things started smoothly, but once again, Barentsz's ship parted ways with its more prudent companion, helmed by one Captain Rijp. And this time Barentsz pushed too far. He reached the northern tip of Novaya Zemlya and rounded it at last, but as soon as he did so, an unseasonable freeze swept down from the Arctic. The cold stalked his ship southward along the coastline, and each day it became harder to shoulder out room between the floes. Pretty soon Barentsz found himself checkmated, marooned on a continent of ice.

Abandoning their floating coffin—the men could no doubt hear the ice expanding and splintering the ship beneath their feet—the crew staggered ashore to a peninsula on Novaya Zemlya to seek shelter. In their one piece of good luck, they discovered on this treeless island a cache of bleached-white driftwood logs. Naturally the ship's carpenter up and died immediately, but with that wood and a few timbers salvaged from their ship, the dozen crewmen built a log cabin, about eight yards by twelve yards, complete with pine shingles, a porch, and front stairs. With more hope than irony, they called it Het Behouden Huys, the Saved House, and settled down to a grim winter.

Cold was the omnipresent danger, but the Arctic had plenty of other minions to harass the men. In November the sun disappeared for three months, and they grew stir-crazy in their dark, fetid cabin. Perversely, fires threatened them too: the crew almost suffocated from carbon monoxide poisoning one night because of poor ventilation. They managed to shoot some white foxes for fur and meat, but the critters constantly nipped at their food supplies. Even laundry became a black comedy. The men had to stick their clothes almost into their fires to get enough heat to dry them. But the garments could be singed and smoking on one side, and the far side would still be brittle with ice.

For sheer day-to-day terror, however, nothing matched the run-ins with polar bears. One of Barentsz's men, Garrit de Veer, recorded in his diary of the voyage that the bears practically laid siege to Het Behouden Huys, raiding with military precision the barrels of beef, bacon, ham, and fish stacked outside. One bear, smelling a meal on the hearth one night, crept up with such stealth that it had padded up the back stairs and crossed the back door's threshold before anyone noticed. Only a lucky musket shot (which passed through the bear and startled it) prevented a massacre in the tiny quarters.

Fed up, half insane, lusty for revenge, the sailors charged outdoors and followed the blood in the snow until they tracked down and killed the invader. When two more bears attacked over the next two days, the sailors again cut them down. Suddenly in high spirits and hungry for fresh meat, the men decided to feast on the bears, stuffing themselves with anything edible. They gnawed the cartilage off bones and sucked the marrow

Scenes from Barentsz's doomed voyage over the frosty top of Russia. Clockwise from top left: encounters with polar bears; the ship crushed in ice; the hut where the crew endured a grim winter in the 1590s. (Gerrit de Veer, *The Three Voyages of William Barents to the Arctic Regions*)

out, and cooked up all the fleshy victuals—the heart, kidneys, brain, and, most succulent of all, the liver. And with that meal, in a godforsaken cabin at eighty degrees north latitude, European explorers first learned a hard lesson about genetics—a lesson other stubborn Arctic explorers would have to keep learning over and over, a lesson scientists would not understand fully for centuries. Because while polar bear liver may look the same purplish red as any mammal's liver and smell of the same raw ripeness and jiggle the same way on the tines of a fork, there's one big difference: on the molecular level, polar bear liver is supersaturated with vitamin A.

Understanding why that's so awful requires taking a closer look at certain genes, genes that help immature cells in our bodies transform into specialized skin or liver or brain cells or whatever. This was part of the process Barbara McClintock longed to comprehend, but the scientific debate actually predated her by decades.

In the late 1800s, two camps emerged to explain cell specialization, one led by German biologist August Weismann.* Weismann studied zygotes, the fused product of a sperm and egg that formed an animal's first cell. He argued that this first cell obviously contained a complete set of molecular instructions, but that each time the zygote and its daughter cells divided, the cells lost half of those instructions. When cells lost the instructions for all but one type of cell, that's what they became. In contrast, other scientists maintained that cells kept the full set of instructions after each division, but ignored most of the instructions after a certain age. German biologist Hans Spemann decided the issue in 1902 with a salamander zygote. He centered one of these large, soft zygotes in his microscopic crosshairs, waited until it divided into two, then looped a blond strand of his infant daughter Margrette's hair around the boundary between them. (Why Spemann used his daughter's hair isn't clear, since he wasn't bald. Probably the baby's hair was finer.) When he tightened this noose, the two cells split, and Spemann pulled them into different dishes, to develop separately. Weismann would have predicted two deformed half salamanders. But both of Spemann's cells grew into full, healthy adults. In fact, they were genetically identical, which means Spemann had effectively cloned them—in 1902. Scientists had rediscovered Mendel not long before, and Spemann's work implied that cells must retain instructions but turn genes on and off.

Still, neither Spemann nor McClintock nor anyone else could explain how cells turned genes off, the mechanism. That took decades' more work. And it turns out that although cells don't lose genetic information per se, cells do lose access to this information, which amounts to the same thing. We've already seen that DNA must perform incredible acrobatics to fit its entire serpentine length into a tiny cell nucleus. To avoid forming knots during this process, DNA generally wraps itself like a yo-yo string around spools of protein called histones, which then get stacked together and buried inside the nucleus. (Histones were some of the proteins that scientists detected in chromosomes early on, and assumed controlled heredity instead of DNA.) In addition to keeping DNA tangle free, histone spooling prevents cellular machinery from getting at DNA to make RNA, effectively shutting the DNA off. Cells control spooling with chemicals called acetyls. Tacking an acetyl ($COCH_3$) onto a histone unwinds DNA; removing the acetyl flicks the wrist and coils DNA back up.

Cells also bar access to DNA by altering DNA itself, with molecular pushpins called methyl groups (CH_3). Methyls stick best to cytosine, the C in the genetic alphabet, and while methyls don't take up much space—carbon is small, and hydrogen is the smallest element on the periodic table—even that small bump can prevent other molecules from locking onto DNA and turning a gene on. In other words, adding methyl groups mutes genes.

Each of the two hundred types of cells in our bodies has a unique pattern of coiled and methylated DNA, patterns established during our embryonic days. Cells destined to become skin cells must turn off all the genes that produce liver enzymes or neurotransmitters, and something reciprocal happens for everything else. These cells not only remember their pattern for the rest of their lives, they pass on the pattern each time they divide as adult cells. Whenever you hear scientists talking about turning genes on or off, methyls and acetyls are often the culprit. Methyl groups in particular are so important that some scientists have proposed adding a fifth official letter to the DNAlphabet*—A, C, G, T, and now mC, for methylated cytosine.

But for additional and sometimes finer control of DNA, cells turn to "transcription factors" like vitamin A. Vitamin A and other transcription factors bind to DNA and recruit other molecules to start transcribing it. Most important for our purposes, vitamin A stimulates growth and helps convert immature cells into full-fledged bone or muscle or whatever at a fast clip. Vitamin A is especially potent in the various layers of skin. In adults, for instance, vitamin A forces certain skin cells to crawl upward from inside the body to the surface, where they die and become the protective outer layer of skin. High doses of vitamin A can also damage skin through "programmed cell death." This genetic program, a sort of forced suicide, helps the body eliminate sickly cells, so it's not always bad. But for unknown reasons, vitamin A also seems to hijack the system in certain skin cells—as Barentsz's men discovered the hard way.

After the crew tucked into their polar bear stew, rich with burgundy liver chunks, they became more ill than they ever had in their lives. It was a sweaty, fervid, dizzying, bowels-in-a-vice sickness, a real biblical bitch of a plague. In his delirium, the diarist Garrit de Veer remembered the female bear he'd helped butcher, and moaned, "Her death did vs more hurt than her life." Even more distressing, a few days later de Veer realized that many men's skin had begun to peel near their lips or mouths, whatever body parts had touched the liver. De Veer noted with panic that three men fell especially "sicke," and "we verily thought that we should haue lost them, for all their skin came of[f] from the foote to the head."

Only in the mid–twentieth century did scientists determine why polar bear livers contain such astronomical amounts of vitamin A. Polar bears survive mostly by preying on ringed and bearded seals, and these seals raise their young in about the most demanding environment possible, with the 35°F Arctic seas wicking away their body heat relentlessly. Vitamin A enables the seals to survive in this cold: it works like a growth hormone, stimulating cells and allowing seal pups to add thick layers of skin and blubber, and do so quickly. To this end, seal mothers store up whole crates of vitamin A in their livers and draw on this store the whole time they're nursing, to make sure pups ingest enough.

Polar bears also need lots of vitamin A to pack on blubber. But even more important, their bodies tolerate toxic levels of vitamin A because they couldn't eat seals—about the only food source in the Arctic—otherwise. One law of ecology says that poisons accumulate as you move up a food chain, and carnivores at the top ingest the most concentrated doses. This is true of any toxin or any nutrient that becomes toxic at high levels. But unlike many other nutrients, vitamin A doesn't dissolve in water, so when a king predator overdoses, it can't expel the excess through urine. Polar bears either have to deal with all the vitamin A they swallow, or starve. Polar bears adapted by turning their livers into high-tech biohazard containment facilities, to filter vitamin A and keep it away from the rest of the body. (And even with those livers, polar bears have to be careful about intake. They can dine on animals lower on the food chain, with lesser concentrations. But some biologists have wryly noted that if polar bears cannibalized their own livers, they would almost certainly croak.)

Polar bears began evolving their impressive vitamin A–fighting capabilities around 150,000 years ago, when small groups of Alaskan brown bears split off and migrated north to the ice caps. But scientists always suspected that the important genetic changes that made polar bears *polar bears* happened almost right away, instead of gradually over that span. Their reasoning was this. After any two groups of animals split geographically, they begin to acquire different DNA mutations. As the mutations accumulate, the groups develop into different species with different bodies, metabolisms, and behaviors. But not all DNA changes at the same rate in a population. Highly conserved genes like *hox* change grudgingly slowly, at geological paces. Changes in other genes can spread quickly, especially if creatures face environmental stress. For instance, when those brown bears wandered onto the bleak ice sheets atop the Arctic Circle, any beneficial mutations to fight the cold—say, the ability to digest vitamin A–rich seals—would have given some of those bears a substantial boost, and allowed them to have more cubs and take better care of them. And the greater the environmental pressure, the faster such genes can and will spread through a population.

Another way to put this is that DNA clocks—which look at the number and rate of mutations in DNA—tick at different speeds in different parts of the genome. So scientists have to be careful when comparing two species' DNA and dating how long ago they split. If scientists don't take conserved genes or accelerated changes into account, their estimates can be wildly off. With these caveats in mind, scientists determined in 2010 that polar bears had armed themselves with enough cold-weather defenses to become a separate species in as few as twenty thousand years after wandering away from ancestral brown bears— an evolutionary wink.

As we'll see later, humans are Johnny-come-latelies to the meat-eating scene, so it's not surprising that we lack the polar bear's defenses—or that when we cheat up the food chain and eat polar bear livers, we suffer. Different people have different genetic susceptibility to vitamin A poisoning (called hypervitaminosis A), but as little as one ounce of polar bear liver can kill an adult human, and in a ghastly way.

Our bodies metabolize vitamin A to produce retinol, which special enzymes should then break down further. (These enzymes also break down the most common poison we humans ingest, the alcohol in beers, rums, wines, whiskeys, and other booze.)

But polar bear livers overwhelm our poor enzymes with vitamin A, and before they can break it all down, free retinol begins circulating in the blood. That's bad. Cells are surrounded by oil-based membranes, and retinol acts as a detergent and breaks the membranes down. The guts of cells start leaking out incontinently, and inside the skull, this translates to a buildup of fluids that causes headaches, fogginess, and irritability. Retinol damages other tissues as well (it can even crimp straight hair, turning it kinky), but again the skin really suffers. Vitamin A already flips tons of genetic switches in skin cells, causing some to commit suicide, pushing others to the surface prematurely. The burn of more vitamin A kills whole additional swaths, and pretty soon the skin starts coming off in sheets.

We hominids have been learning (and relearning) this same hard lesson about eating carnivore livers for an awfully long time. In the 1980s, anthropologists discovered a 1.6-million-year-old *Homo erectus* skeleton with lesions on his bones characteristic of vitamin A poisoning, from eating that era's top carnivores. After polar bears arose—and after untold centuries of casualties among their people—Eskimos, Siberians, and other northern tribes (not to mention scavenging birds) learned to shun polar bear livers, but European explorers had no such wisdom when they stormed into the Arctic. Many in fact regarded the prohibition on eating livers as "vulgar prejudice," a superstition about on par with worshipping trees. As late as 1900 the English explorer Reginald Koettlitz relished the prospect of digging into polar bear liver, but he quickly discovered that there's sometimes wisdom in taboos. Over a few hours, Koettlitz felt pressure building up inside his skull, until his whole head felt crushed from the inside. Vertigo overtook him, and he vomited repeatedly. Most cruelly, he couldn't sleep it off; lying down made things worse. Another explorer around that time, Dr. Jens Lindhard, fed polar bear liver to nineteen men under his care as an experiment. All became wretchedly ill, so much so that some showed signs of insanity. Meanwhile other starved explorers learned that not just polar bears and seals have toxically elevated levels of vitamin A: the livers of reindeer, sharks, swordfish, foxes, and Arctic huskies* can make excellent last meals as well.

For their part, after being blasted by polar bear liver in 1597, Barentsz's men got wise. As the diarist de Veer had it, after their meal, "there hung a pot still ouer the fire with some of the liuer in it. But the master tooke it and cast it out of the dore, for we had enough of the sawce thereof."

The men soon recovered their strength, but their cabin, clothes, and morale continued to disintegrate in the cold. At last, in June, the ice started melting, and they salvaged rowboats from their ship and headed to sea. They could only dart between small icebergs at first, and they took heavy flak from pursuing polar bears. But on June 20, 1597, the polar ice broke, making real sailing possible. Alas, June 20 also marked the last day on earth of the long-ailing Willem Barentsz, who died at age fifty. The loss of their navigator sapped the courage of the remaining twelve crew members, who still had to cross hundreds of miles of ocean in open boats. But they managed to reach northern Russia, where the locals pitied them with food. A month later they washed ashore on the coast of Lapland, where they ran into, of all people, Captain Jan Corneliszoon Rijp, commander of the very ship that Barentsz had ditched the winter before. Overjoyed—he'd assumed them dead—Rijp carried the men home to the Netherlands* in his ship, where they arrived in threadbare clothes and stunning white fox fur hats.

Their expected heroes' welcome never materialized. That same day another Dutch convoy returned home as well, laden with spices and delicacies from a voyage to Cathay around the southern horn of Africa. Their journey proved that merchant ships could make that long voyage, and while tales of starvation and survival were thrilling, tales of treasure truly stirred the Dutch people's hearts. The Dutch crown granted the Dutch East India Company a monopoly on traveling to Asia via Africa, and an epic trade route was born, a mariner's Silk Road. Barentsz and crew were forgotten.

Perversely, the monopoly on the African route to Asia meant that other maritime entrepreneurs could seek their fortunes only via the northeast passage, so forays into the 500,000-square-mile Barents Sea continued. Finally, salivating over a possible double monopoly, the Dutch East India Company sent its own crew—captained by an Englishman, Henry Hudson—north in 1609. Once again, things got fouled up. Hudson and his ship, the *Half Moon*, crawled north past the tip of Norway as scheduled. But his crew of forty, half of them Dutch, had no doubt heard tales of starvation, exposure, and, God help them, skin peeling off people's bodies head to toe—and mutinied. They forced Hudson to turn west.

If that's what they wanted, Hudson gave it to them, sailing all the way west to North America. He skimmed Nova Scotia and put in at a few places lower down on the Atlantic coast, including a trip up a then-unnamed river, past a skinny swamp island. While disappointed that Hudson had not circled Russia, the Dutch made lemonade by founding a trading colony called New Amsterdam on that isle, Manhattan, within a few years. It's sometimes said of human beings that our passion for exploration is in our genes. With the founding of New York, this was almost literally the case.

7

The Machiavelli Microbe

How Much Human DNA Is Actually Human?

A farmer from Long Island arrived with trepidation at the Rockefeller Institute in Manhattan in 1909, a sick chicken tucked under his arm. A seeming plague of cancer had been wiping out chicken coops across the United States that decade, and the farmer's Plymouth Rock hen had developed a suspicious tumor in its right breast. Nervous about losing his stocks, the farmer turned the hen over to Rockefeller scientist Francis P. Rous, known as Peyton, for a diagnosis. To the farmer's horror, instead of trying to cure the chicken, Rous slaughtered it to get a look at the tumor and run some experiments. Science, though, will be forever grateful for the pollocide.

After extracting the tumor, Rous mashed up a few tenths of an ounce, creating a wet paste. He then filtered it through very small porcelain pores, which removed tumor cells from circulation and left behind mostly just the fluid that exists between cells. Among other things, this fluid helps pass nutrients around, but it can also harbor microbes. Rous injected the fluid into another Plymouth Rock's breast. Soon enough, the second chicken developed a tumor. Rous repeated the experiment with other breeds, like Leghorn fowls, and within six months they developed cancerous masses, about an inch by an inch, too. What was notable, and baffling, about the setup was the filtering step. Since Rous had removed any tumor cells before making the injections, the new tumors couldn't have sprung from old tumor cells reattaching themselves in new birds. The cancer had to have come from the fluid.

Though annoyed, the farmer couldn't have sacrificed his hen to a better candidate to puzzle out the chicken pandemic. Rous, a medical doctor and pathologist, had a strong background with domesticated animals. Rous's father had fled Virginia just before the Civil War and settled in Texas, where he met Peyton's mother. The whole family eventually moved back east to Baltimore, and after high school, Rous enrolled at the Johns Hopkins University, where he supported himself in part by writing, for five dollars a pop, a column called "Wild Flowers of the Month" for the *Baltimore Sun,* about flora in Charm City. Rous gave up the column after entering Johns Hopkins medical school but soon had to suspend his studies. He cut his hand on a tubercular cadaver bone while performing an autopsy, and when he developed tuberculosis himself, school officials ordered a rest cure. But instead of a European-style cure—an actually restful stint in a mountain sanitarium—Rous took a good ol' American cure and worked as a ranch hand in Texas. Though small and slender, Rous loved ranching and developed a keen interest in farm animals. After recovering, he decided to specialize in microbial biology instead of bedside medicine.

All the training on the ranch and in his labs, and all the evidence of the chicken case, pointed Rous to one conclusion. The chickens had a virus, and the virus was spreading cancer. But all his training also told Rous the idea was ridiculous—and his colleagues seconded that. *Contagious cancer, Dr. Rous? How on earth could a virus cause cancer?* Some argued that Rous had misdiagnosed the tumors; perhaps the injections caused an inflammation peculiar to chickens. Rous himself later admitted, "I used to quake in the night for fear that I had made an error." He did publish his results, but even by the circuitous standards of scientific prose, he barely admitted what he believed at some points: "It is perhaps not too much to say that [the discovery] points to the existence of a new group of entities which cause in chickens neoplasms [tumors] of diverse character." But Rous was cagey to be circumspect. A contemporary remembered that his papers on the chicken cancers "were met with reactions ranging from indifference to skepticism and outright hostility."

Most scientists quietly forgot about Rous's work over the next few decades, and for good reason. Because even though a few discoveries from that time linked viruses and cancers biologically, other findings kept pushing them apart. Scientists had determined by the 1950s that cancer cells go haywire in part because their genes malfunction. Scientists had also determined that viruses have small caches of their own genetic material. (Some used DNA; others, like Rous's, used RNA.) Though not technically alive, viruses used that genetic material to hijack cells and make copies of themselves. So viruses and cancer both reproduced uncontrollably, and both used DNA and RNA as common currency—intriguing clues. Meanwhile, however, Francis Crick had published his Central Dogma in 1958, that DNA generates RNA, which generates proteins, in that order. According to this popular understanding of the dogma, RNA viruses like Rous's couldn't possibly disrupt or rewrite the DNA of cells: this would run the dogma backward, which wasn't allowed. So despite the biological overlap, there seemed no way for viral RNA to interface with cancer-causing DNA.

The matter stood at an impasse—data versus dogma—until

a few young scientists in the late 1960s and early 1970s discovered that nature cares little for dogmas. It turns out that certain viruses (HIV is the best-known example) manipulate DNA in heretical ways. Specifically, the viruses can coax an infected cell into reverse-transcribing viral RNA into DNA. Even scarier, they then trick the cell into splicing the newly minted viral DNA back into the cell's genome. In short, these viruses fuse with a cell. They show no respect for the Maginot Line we'd prefer to draw between "their" DNA and "our" DNA.

This strategy for infecting cells might seem convoluted: why would an RNA virus like HIV bother converting itself into DNA, especially when the cell has to transcribe that DNA back into RNA later anyway? It seems even more baffling when you consider how resourceful and nimble RNA is compared to DNA. Lone RNA can build rudimentary proteins, whereas lone DNA sort of just sits there. RNA can also build copies of itself *by itself*, like that M. C. Escher drawing of two hands sketching themselves into existence. For these reasons, most scientists believe that RNA probably predated DNA in the history of life, since early life would have lacked the fancy innards-copying equipment cells have nowadays. (This is called the "RNA world" theory.*)

Nevertheless, early Earth was rough-and-tumble, and RNA is pretty flimsy compared to DNA. Because it's merely single-stranded, RNA letters are constantly exposed to assaults. RNA also has an extra oxygen atom on its ringed sugars, which stupidly cannibalizes its own vertebrae and shreds RNA if it grows too long. So to build anything lasting, anything capable of exploring, swimming, growing, fighting, mating—truly living— fragile RNA had to yield to DNA. This transition to a less corruptible medium a few billion years ago was arguably the most important step in life's history. In a way it resembled the transition in human cultures away from, say, Homer's oral poetry to mute written work: with a stolid DNA text, you miss the RNA-like versatility, the nuances of voice and gesture; but we wouldn't even have the *Iliad* and the *Odyssey* today without papyrus and ink. DNA lasts.

And that's why some viruses convert RNA into DNA after infecting cells: DNA is sturdier, more enduring. Once these *retro*viruses—so named because they run the DNA → RNA → protein dogma backward—weave themselves into a cell's DNA, the cell will faithfully copy the virus genes so long as they both shall live.

The discovery of viral DNA manipulation explained Rous's poor chickens. After the injection, the viruses found their way through the intercellular fluid into the muscle cells. They then ingratiated themselves with the chicken DNA and turned the machinery of each infected muscle cell toward making as many copies of themselves as possible. And it turns out—here's the key—one great strategy for the viruses to spread like mad was to convince the cells harboring viral DNA to spread like mad, too. The viruses did this by disrupting the genetic governors that prevent cells from dividing rapidly. A runaway tumor (and a lot of dead birds) was the result. Transmissible cancers like this are atypical—most cancers have other genetic causes—but for many animals, virus-borne cancers are significant hazards.

This new theory of genetic intrusions was certainly unorthodox. (Even Rous doubted aspects of it.) But if anything, scientists of the time actually underestimated the ability of viruses and other microbes to invade DNA. You can't really attach degrees to the word *ubiquitous*; like being unique, something either is or isn't ubiquitous. But indulge me for a moment in marveling over the complete, total, and utter ubiquity of microbes on a microscopic scale. The little buggers have colonized every known living thing—humans have ten times more microorganisms feasting inside us than we do cells—and saturated every possible ecological niche. There's even a class of viruses that infect only other parasites,* which are scarcely larger than the viruses themselves. For reasons of stability, many of these microbes invade DNA, and they're often nimble enough about changing or masking their DNA to evade and outflank our bodies' defenses. (One biologist calculated that HIV alone has swapped more A's, C's, G's, and T's into and out of its genes in the past few decades than primates have in fifty million years.)

Not until the completion of the Human Genome Project around 2000 did biologists grasp how extensively microbes can infiltrate even higher animals. The name *Human* Genome Project even became something of a misnomer, because it turned out that 8 percent of our genome isn't human at all: a quarter billion of our base pairs are old virus genes. Human genes actually make up less than 2 percent of our total DNA, so by this measure, we're four times more virus than human. One pioneer in studying viral DNA, Robin Weiss, put this evolutionary relationship in stark terms: "If Charles Darwin reappeared today," Weiss mused, "he might be surprised to learn that humans are descended from viruses as well as from apes."

How could this happen? From a virus's point of view, colonizing animal DNA makes sense. For all their deviousness and duplicity, retroviruses that cause cancer or diseases like AIDS are pretty stupid in one respect: they kill their hosts too quickly and die with them. But not all viruses rip through their hosts like microscopic locusts. Less ambitious viruses learn to not disrupt too much, and by showing some restraint they can trick a cell into quietly making copies of themselves for decades. Even better, if viruses infiltrate sperm or egg cells, they can trick their host into passing on viral genes to a new generation, allowing a virus to "live" indefinitely in the host's descendants. (This is happening right now in koalas, as scientists have caught retroviral DNA spreading through koala sperm.) That these viruses have adulterated so much DNA in so many animals hints that this infiltration happens all the time, on scales a little frightening to think about.

Of all the extinct retrovirus genes loaded into human DNA, the vast majority have accumulated a few fatal mutations and no longer function. But otherwise these genes sit intact in our cells and provide enough detail to study the original virus. In fact, in 2006 a virologist in France named Thierry Heidmann used human DNA to resurrect an extinct virus—*Jurassic Park* in a petri dish. It proved startlingly easy. Strings of some ancient viruses appear multiple times in the human genome (the number of copies ranges from dozens to tens of thousands). But the fatal mutations appear, by chance, at different points in each copy. So by comparing many strings, Heidmann could deduce what the original, healthy string must have been simply by counting which DNA letter was most common at each spot. The virus was benign, Heidmann says, but when he reconstituted it and injected it into various mammalian cells—cat, hamster, human—it infected them all.

Rather than wring his hands over this technology (not all ancient viruses are benign) or prophesy doom about it falling into the wrong hands, Heidmann celebrated the resurrection as a scientific triumph, naming his virus *Phoenix* after the mythological bird that rose from its own ashes. Other scientists have replicated Heidmann's work with other viruses, and together they founded a new discipline called paleovirology. Soft, tiny viruses don't leave behind rocky fossils, like the ones paleontologists dig up, but the paleovirologists have something just as informative in fossil DNA.

Close examination of this "wet" fossil record suggests that our genome might be even more than 8 percent virus. In 2009, scientists discovered in humans four stretches of DNA from something called the bornavirus, which has infected hoofed animals since time immemorial. (It's named after a particularly nasty outbreak among horses in 1885, in a cavalry unit near Borna, Germany. Some of the army horses went stark mad and smashed their own skulls in.) About forty million years ago, a few stray bornaviruses jumped into our monkey ancestors and took refuge in their DNA. It had lurked undetected and unsuspected since then because bornavirus is not a retrovirus, so scientists didn't think it had the molecular machinery to convert RNA to DNA and insert itself somewhere. But lab tests prove that bornavirus can indeed somehow weave itself into human DNA in as few as thirty days. And unlike the mute DNA we inherited from retroviruses, two of the four stretches of borna DNA work like bona fide genes.

Scientists haven't pinned down what those genes do, but they might well make proteins we all need to live, perhaps by boosting our immune systems. Allowing a nonlethal virus to invade our DNA probably inhibits other, potentially worse viruses from doing the same. More important, cells can use benign virus proteins to fight off other infections. It's a simple strategy, really: casinos hire card counters, computer security agencies hire hackers, and no one knows how to combat and neutralize viruses better than a reformed germ. Surveys of our genomes suggest that viruses gave us important regulatory DNA as well. For instance, we've long had enzymes in our digestive tracts to break down starches into simpler sugars. But viruses gave us switches to run those same enzymes in our saliva, too. As a result starchy foods taste sweet inside our mouths. We certainly wouldn't have such a starch-tooth for breads, pastas, and grains without these switches.

These cases may be only the beginning. Almost half of human DNA consists of (à la Barbara McClintock) mobile elements and jumping genes. One transposon alone, the 300-base-long *alu*, appears a million times in human chromosomes and forms fully 10 percent of our genome. The ability of this DNA to detach itself from one chromosome, crawl to another, and burrow into it like a tick looks awfully viruslike. You're not supposed to interject feelings into science, but part of the reason it's so fascinating that we're 8 percent (or more) fossilized virus is that it's so creepy that we're 8 percent (or more) fossilized virus. We have an inborn repugnance for disease and impurity, and we see invading germs as something to shun or drive out, not as intimate parts of ourselves—but viruses and viruslike particles have been tinkering with animal DNA since forever. As one scientist who tracked down the human bornavirus genes said, highlighting the singular, "Our whole notion of ourselves as a species is slightly misconceived."

It gets worse. Because of their ubiquity, microbes of all kinds—not just viruses but bacteria and protozoa—can't help but steer animal evolution. Obviously microbes shape a population by killing some creatures through disease, but that's only part of their power. Viruses, bacteria, and protozoa bequeath new genes to animals on occasion, genes that can alter how our bodies work. They can manipulate animal minds as well. One Machiavellian microbe has not only colonized huge numbers of animals without detection, it has stolen animal DNA—and might even use that DNA to brainwash our minds for its own ends.

Sometimes you acquire wisdom the hard way. "You can visualize a hundred cats," Jack Wright once said. "Beyond that, you can't. Two hundred, five hundred, it all looks the same." This wasn't just speculation. Jack learned this because he and his wife, Donna, once owned a Guinness-certified world record 689 housecats.

It started with Midnight. Wright, a housepainter in Ontario, fell in love with a waitress named Donna Belwa around 1970, and they moved in together with Donna's black, long-haired cat. Midnight committed a peccadillo in the yard one night and became pregnant, and the Wrights didn't have the heart to break up her litter. Having more cats around actually brightened the home, and soon after, they felt moved to adopt strays from the local shelter to save them from being put down. Their house became known locally as Cat Crossing, and people began dropping off more strays, two here, five there. When the *National Enquirer* held a contest in the 1980s to determine who had the most cats in one house, the Wrights won with 145. They soon appeared on *The Phil Donahue Show*, and after that, the "donations" really got bad. One person tied kittens to the Wrights' picnic table and drove off; another shipped a cat via courier on a plane—and made the Wrights pay. But the Wrights turned no feline away, even as their brood swelled toward seven hundred.

Bills reportedly ran to $111,000 per year, including individually wrapped Christmas toys. Donna (who began working at home, managing Jack's painting career) rose daily at 5:30 a.m. and spent the next fifteen hours washing soiled cat beds, emptying litter boxes, forcing pills down cats' throats, and adding ice to kitty bowls (the friction of so many cats' tongues made the water too warm to drink otherwise). But above all she spent her days feeding, feeding, feeding. The Wrights popped open 180 tins of cat food each day and bought three extra freezers to fill with pork, ham, and sirloin for the more finicky felines. They eventually took out a second mortgage, and to keep their heavily leveraged bungalow clean, they tacked linoleum to the walls.

Jack and Donna eventually put their four feet down and by the late 1990s had reduced the population of Cat Crossing to just 359. Almost immediately it crept back up, because they couldn't bear to go lower. In fact, if you read between the lines here, the Wrights seemed almost addicted to having cats around— addiction being that curious state of getting acute pleasure and acute anxiety from the same thing. Clearly they loved the cats. Jack defended his cat "family" to the newspapers and gave each cat an individual name,* even the few that refused to leave his closet. At the same time, Donna couldn't hide the torment of being enslaved to cats. "I'll tell you what's hard to eat in here," she once complained, "Kentucky Fried Chicken. Every time I eat it, I have to walk around the house with the plate under my chin." (Partly to keep cats away, partly to deflect cat hair from her sticky drumsticks.) More poignantly, Donna once admitted, "I get a little depressed sometimes. Sometimes I just say, 'Jack, give me a few bucks,' and I go out and have a beer or two. I sit there for a few hours and it's great. It's peaceful—no cats anywhere." Despite these moments of clarity, and despite their mounting distress,* she and Jack couldn't embrace the obvious solution: ditch the damn cats.

To give the Wrights credit, Donna's constant cleaning made their home seem rather livable, especially compared to the prehistoric filth of some hoarders' homes. Animal welfare inspectors not infrequently find decaying cat corpses on the worst premises, even inside a home's walls, where cats presumably burrow to escape. Nor is it uncommon for the floors and walls to rot and suffer structural damage from saturation with cat urine. Most striking of all, many hoarders deny that things are out of control—a classic sign of addiction.

Scientists have only recently begun laying out the chemical and genetic basis of addiction, but growing evidence suggests that cat hoarders cling to their herds at least partly because they're hooked on a parasite, *Toxoplasma gondii*. Toxo is a one-celled protozoan, kin to algae and amoebas; it has eight thousand genes. And though originally a feline pathogen, Toxo has diversified its portfolio and can now infect monkeys, bats, whales, elephants, aardvarks, anteaters, sloths, armadillos, and marsupials, as well as chickens.

Wild bats or aardvarks or whatever ingest Toxo through infected prey or feces, and domesticated animals absorb it indirectly through the feces found in fertilizers. Humans can also absorb Toxo through their diet, and cat owners can contract it through their skin when they handle kitty litter. Overall it infects one-third of people worldwide. When Toxo invades mammals, it usually swims straight for the brain, where it forms tiny cysts, especially in the amygdala, an almond-shaped region in the mammal brain that guides the processing of emotions, including pleasure and anxiety. Scientists don't know why, but the amygdala cysts can slow down reaction times and induce jealous or aggressive behavior in people. Toxo can alter people's sense of smell, too. Some cat hoarders (those most vulnerable to Toxo) become immune to the pungent urine of cats—they stop smelling it. A few hoarders, usually to their great shame, reportedly even crave the odor.

Toxo does even stranger things to rodents, a common meal for cats. Rodents that have been raised in labs for hundreds of generations and have never seen a predator in their whole lives will still quake in fear and scamper to whatever cranny they can find if exposed to cat urine; it's an instinctual, totally hardwired fear. Rats exposed to Toxo have the opposite reaction. They still fear other predators' scents, and they otherwise sleep, mate, navigate mazes, nibble fine cheese, and do everything else normally. But these rats adore cat urine, especially male rats. In fact they more than adore it. At the first whiff of cat urine, their amygdalae throb, as if meeting females in heat, and their testicles swell. Cat urine gets them off.

Toxo toys with mouse desire like this to enrich its own sex life. When living inside the rodent brain, Toxo can split in two and clone itself, the same method by which most microbes reproduce. It reproduces this way in sloths, humans, and other species, too. Unlike most microbes, though, Toxo can also have sex (don't ask) and reproduce sexually—but only in the intestines of cats. It's a weirdly specific fetish, but there it is. Like most organisms, Toxo craves sex, so no matter how many times it has passed its genes on through cloning, it's always scheming to get back inside those erotic cat guts. Urine is its opportunity. By making mice attracted to cat urine, Toxo can lure them toward cats. Cats happily play along, of course, and pounce, and the morsel of mouse ends up exactly where Toxo wanted to be all along, in the cat digestive tract. Scientists suspect that Toxo learned to work its mojo in other potential mammal meals for a similar reason, to ensure that felines of all sizes, from tabbies to tigers, would keep ingesting it.

This might sound like a just-so story so far—a tale that sounds clever but lacks real evidence. Except for one thing. Scientists have discovered that two of Toxo's eight thousand genes help make a chemical called dopamine. And if you know anything about brain chemistry, you're probably sitting up in your chair about now. Dopamine helps activate the brain's reward circuits, flooding us with good feelings, natural highs. Cocaine, Ecstasy, and other drugs also play with dopamine levels, inducing artificial highs. Toxo has the gene for this potent, habit-forming chemical in its repertoire—twice—and whenever an infected brain senses cat urine, consciously or not, Toxo starts pumping it out. As a result, Toxo gains influence over mammalian behavior, and the dopamine hook might provide a plausible biological basis for hoarding cats.*

Toxo isn't the only parasite that can manipulate animals. Much like Toxo, a certain microscopic worm prefers paddling around in the guts of birds but often gets ejected, forcefully, in bird droppings. So the ejected worm wriggles into ants, turns them cherry red, puffs them up like Violet Beauregarde, and convinces other birds they're delicious berries. Carpenter ants also fall victim to a rain-forest fungus that turns them into mindless zombies. First the fungus hijacks an ant's brain, then pilots it toward moist locations, like the undersides of leaves. Upon arriving, the zombified ant bites down, and its jaws lock into place. The fungus turns the ant's guts into a sugary, nutritious goo, shoots a stalk out of its brain, and sends out spores to infect more ants. There's also the so-called Herod bug—the *Wolbachia* bacteria, which infects wasps, mosquitoes, moths, flies, and beetles. *Wolbachia* can reproduce only inside female insects' eggs, so like Herod in the Bible, it often slaughters infant males wholesale, by releasing genetically produced toxins. (In certain lucky insects, *Wolbachia* has mercy and merely fiddles with the genes that determine sex in insects, converting male grubs into females ones—in which case a better nickname might be the Tiresias bug.) Beyond creepy-crawlies, a lab-tweaked version of one virus can turn polygamous male voles—rodents who normally have, as one scientist put it, a "country song... love 'em and leave 'em" attitude toward vole women—into utterly faithful stay-at-home husbands, simply by injecting some repetitive DNA "stutters" into a gene that adjusts brain chemistry. Exposure to the virus arguably even made the voles smarter. Instead of blindly having sex with whatever female wandered near, the males began associating sex with one individual, a trait called "associative learning" that was previously beyond them.

The vole and Toxo cases edge over into uncomfortable territory for a species like us that prizes autonomy and smarts. It's one thing to find broken leftover virus genes in our DNA, quite another to admit that microbes might manipulate our emotions and inner mental life. But Toxo can. Somehow in its long coevolution with mammals, Toxo stole the gene for dopamine production, and the gene has proved pretty successful in influencing animal behavior ever since—both by ramping up pleasure around cats and by damping any natural fear of cats. There's also anecdotal evidence that Toxo can alter other fear signals in the brain, ones unrelated to cats, and convert those impulses into ecstatic pleasure as well. Some emergency room doctors report that motorcycle crash victims often have unusually high numbers of Toxo cysts in their brains. These are the hotshots flying along highways and cutting the S-turns as sharp as possible—the people who get off on risking their lives. And it just so happens that their brains are riddled with Toxo.

It's hard to argue with Toxo scientists who—while thrilled about what Toxo has uncovered about the biology of emotions and the interconnections between fear, attraction, and addiction— also feel creeped out by what their work implies. One Stanford University neuroscientist who studies Toxo says, "It's slightly frightening in some ways. We take fear to be basic and natural. But something can not only eliminate it but turn it into this esteemed thing, attraction. Attraction can be manipulated so as to make us attracted to our worst enemy." That's why Toxo deserves the title of the Machiavellian microbe. Not only can it manipulate us, it can make what's evil seem good.

Peyton Rous's life had a happy if complicated ending. During World War I, he helped establish some of the first blood banks by developing a method to store red blood cells with gelatin and sugar—a sort of blood Jell-O. Rous also bolstered his early work on chickens by studying another obscure but contagious tumor, the giant papilloma warts that once plagued cottontail rabbits in the United States. Rous even had the honor, as editor of a scientific journal, of publishing the first work to firmly link genes and DNA.

Nevertheless, despite this and other work, Rous grew suspicious that geneticists were getting ahead of themselves, and he refused to connect the dots that other scientists were eagerly connecting. For example, before he would publish the paper linking genes and DNA, he made the head scientist strike out a sentence suggesting that DNA was as important to cells as amino acids. Indeed, Rous came to reject the very idea that viruses cause cancer by injecting genetic material, as well as the idea that DNA mutations cause cancer at all. Rous believed viruses promoted cancer in other ways, possibly by releasing toxins; and although no one knows why, he struggled to accept that microbes could influence animal genetics quite as much as his work implied.

Still, Rous never wavered in his conviction that viruses cause tumors somehow, and as his peers unraveled the complicated details of his contagious chicken cancer, they began to appreciate the clarity of his early work all the more. Respect was still grudging in some quarters, and Rous had to endure his much younger son-in-law winning a Nobel Prize for medicine in 1963. But in 1966 the Nobel committee finally vindicated Francis Peyton Rous with a prize of his own. The gap between Rous's important papers and his Nobel, fifty-five years, is one of the longer in prize history. But the win no doubt proved one of the most satisfying, even if he had just four years to enjoy it before dying in 1970. And after his death, it ceased to matter what Rous himself had believed or rejected; young microbiologists, eager to explore how microbes reprogram life, held him up as an idol, and textbooks today cite his work as a classic case of an idea condemned in its own time and later exonerated by DNA evidence.

The story of Cat Crossing also ended in a complicated fashion. As the bills piled higher, creditors nearly seized the Wrights' house. Only donations from cat lovers saved them. Around this time, newspapers also began digging into Jack's past, and reported that, far from being an innocent animal lover, he'd once been convicted of manslaughter for strangling a stripper. (Her body was found on a roof.) Even after these crises passed, the daily hassles continued for Jack and Donna. One visitor reported that "neither had any vacation, any new clothes, any furniture, or draperies." If they rose in the night to go to the bathroom, the dozens of cats on their bed would expand like amoebas to fill the warm hollow, leaving no room to crawl back beneath the covers. "Sometimes you think it'll make you crazy," Donna once confessed. "We can't get away...I cry just about every day in the summertime." Unable to stand the little indignities anymore, Donna eventually moved out. Yet she got drawn back in, unable to walk away from her cats. She returned every dawn to help Jack cope.*

Despite the near certainty of Toxo exposure and infection, no one knows to what extent (if any) Toxo turned Jack and Donna's life inside out. But even if they were infected—and even if neurologists could prove that Toxo manipulated them profoundly—it's hard to censure someone for caring so much for animals. And in a (much, much) larger perspective, the behavior of hoarders might be doing some greater evolutionary good, in the Lynn Margulis sense of mixing up our DNA. Interactions with Toxo and other microbes have certainly influenced our evolution at multiple stages, perhaps profoundly. Retroviruses colonized our genome in waves, and a few scientists argue that it's not a coincidence that these waves appeared just before mammals began to flourish and just before hominid primates emerged. This finding dovetails with another recent theory that microbes may explain Darwin's age-old quandary of the origin of new species. One traditional line of demarcation between species is sexual reproduction: if two populations can't breed and produce viable children, they're separate species. Usually the reproductive barriers are mechanical (animals don't "fit") or biochemical (no viable embryos result). But in one experiment with *Wolbachia* (the Herod-Tiresias bug), scientists took two populations of infected wasps that couldn't produce healthy embryos in the wild and gave them antibiotics. This killed the *Wolbachia*— and suddenly allowed the wasps to reproduce. *Wolbachia* alone had driven them apart.

Along these lines, a few scientists have speculated that if HIV ever reached truly epidemic levels and wiped out most people on earth, then the small percentage of people immune to HIV (and they do exist) could evolve into a new human species. Again, it comes down to sexual barriers. These people couldn't have sex with the nonimmune population (most of us) without killing us off. Any children from the union would have a good chance of dying of HIV, too. And once erected, these sexual and reproductive barriers would slowly but inevitably drive the two populations apart. Even more wildly, HIV, as a retrovirus, could someday insert its DNA into these new humans in a permanent way, joining the genome just as other viruses have. HIV genes would then be copied forever in our descendants, who might have no inkling of the destruction it once wrought.

Of course, saying that microbes infiltrate our DNA may be nothing but a species-centric bias. Viruses have a haiku-like quality about them, some scientists note, a concentration of genetic material that their hosts lack. Some scientists also credit viruses with creating DNA in the first place (from RNA) billions of years ago, and they argue that viruses still invent most new genes today. In fact the scientists who discovered bornavirus DNA in humans think that, far from the bornavirus forcing this DNA into us primates, our chromosomes *stole* this DNA instead. Whenever our mobile DNA starts swimming about, it often grabs other scraps of DNA and drags them along to wherever it's going. Bornavirus replicates only in the nucleus of cells, where our DNA resides, and there's a good chance that mobile DNA mugged the bornavirus long ago, kidnapped its DNA, and kept it around when it proved useful. Along these lines, I've accused Toxo of stealing the dopamine gene from its more sophisticated mammalian hosts. And historical evidence suggests it did. But Toxo also hangs out primarily in the cell nucleus, and there's no theoretical reason we couldn't have stolen this gene from it instead.

It's hard to decide what's less flattering: that microbes outsmarted our defenses and inserted, wholly by accident, the fancy genetic tools that mammals needed to make certain evolutionary advances; or that mammals had to shake down little germs and steal their genes instead. And in some cases these truly were advances, leaps that helped make us human. Viruses probably created the mammalian placenta, the interface between mother and child that allows us to give birth to live young and enables us to nurture our young. What's more, in addition to producing dopamine, Toxo can ramp up or ramp down the activity of hundreds of genes inside human neurons, altering how the brain works. The bornavirus also lives and works between the ears, and some scientists argue that it could be an important source for adding variety to the DNA that forms and runs the brain. This variety is the raw material of evolution, and passing around microbes like the bornavirus from human to human, probably via sex, might well have increased the chances of someone getting beneficial DNA. In fact, most microbes responsible for such boosts likely got passed around via sex. Which means that, if microbes were as important in pushing evolution forward as some scientists suggest, STDs could be responsible in some way for human genius. Descended from apes indeed.

As the virologist Luis Villarreal has noted (and his thoughts apply to other microbes), "It is our inability to perceive viruses, especially the silent virus, that has limited our understanding of the role they play in all life. Only now, in the era of genomics, can we more clearly see ubiquitous footprints in the genomes of all life." So perhaps we can finally see too that people who hoard cats aren't crazy, or at least not merely crazy. They're part of the fascinating and still-unfolding story of what happens when you mix animal and microbe DNA.

8

Love and Atavisms

What Genes Make Mammals Mammals?

iven the thousands upon thousands of babies born in and around Tokyo each year, most don't attract much attention, and in December 2005, after forty weeks and five days of pregnancy, a woman named Mayumi quietly gave birth to a baby girl named Emiko. (I've changed the names of family members for privacy's sake.) Mayumi was twenty-eight, and her blood work and sonograms seemed normal throughout her pregnancy. The delivery and its aftermath were also routine—except that for the couple involved, of course, a first child is never routine. Mayumi and her husband, Hideo, who worked at a petrol station, no doubt felt all the normal fluttering anxieties as the ob-gyn cleared the mucus from Emiko's mouth and coaxed her into her first cry. The nurses drew blood from Emiko for routine testing, and again, everything came back normal. They clamped and cut Emiko's umbilical cord, her lifeline to her mother's placenta, and it dried out eventually, and the little stub blackened and fell off in the normal fashion, leaving her with a belly button. A few

days later, Hideo and Mayumi left the hospital in Chiba, a suburb across the bay from Tokyo, with Emiko in their arms. All perfectly normal.

Thirty-six days after giving birth, Mayumi began bleeding from her vagina. Many women experience vaginal hemorrhages after birth, but three days later, Mayumi also developed a robust fever. With the newborn Emiko to take care of, the couple toughed out Mayumi's spell at home for a few days. But within a week, the bleeding had become uncontrollable, and the family returned to the hospital. Because the wound would not clot, doctors suspected something was wrong with Mayumi's blood. They ordered a round of blood work and waited.

The news was not good. Mayumi tested positive for a grim blood cancer called ALL (acute lymphoblastic leukemia). While most cancers stem from faulty DNA—a cell deletes or miscopies an A, C, G, or T and then turns against the body—Mayumi's cancer had a more complicated origin. Her DNA had undergone what's called a Philadelphia translocation (named after the city in which it was discovered in 1960). A translocation takes place when two *non-twin* chromosomes mistakenly cross over and swap DNA. And unlike a mutational typo, which can occur in any species, this blunder tends to target higher animals with specific genetic features.

Protein-producing DNA—genes—actually makes up very little of the total DNA in higher animals, as little as 1 percent. Morgan's fly boys had assumed that genes almost bumped up against each other on chromosomes, strung along tightly like Alaska's Aleutian Islands. In reality genes are precious rare, scattered Micronesian islands in vast chromosomal Pacifics.

So what does all that extra DNA do? Scientists long assumed it did nothing, and snubbed it as "junk DNA." The name has haunted them as an embarrassment ever since. So-called junk DNA actually contains thousands of critical stretches that turn genes on and off or otherwise regulate them—the "junk" manages genes. To take one example, chimpanzees and other primates have short, fingernail-hard bumps (called spines) studding their penises. Humans lack the little prick pricks because sometime in the past few million years, we lost sixty thousand letters of regulatory junk DNA—DNA that would otherwise coax certain genes (which we still have) into making the spines. Besides sparing vaginas, this loss decreases male sensation during sex and thereby prolongs copulation, which scientists suspect helps humans pair-bond and stay monogamous. Other junk DNA fights cancer, or keeps us alive moment to moment.

To their amazement, scientists even found junk DNA—or, as they say now, "noncoding DNA"—cluttering genes themselves. Cells turn DNA into RNA by rote, skipping no letters. But with the full RNA manuscript in hand, cells narrow their eyes, lick a red pencil, and start slashing—think Gordon Lish hacking down Raymond Carver. This editing consists mostly of chopping out unneeded RNA and stitching the remaining bits together to make the actual messenger RNA. (Confusingly, the excised parts are called "introns," the included parts "exons." Leave it to scientists...) For example, raw RNA with both exons (capital letters) and introns (lowercase) might read: abcdefGHijklmnOpqrSTuvwxyz. Edited down to exons, it says GHOST.

Lower animals like insects, worms, and their ick ilk contain only a few short introns; otherwise, if introns run on for too long or grow too numerous, their cells get confused and can no longer string something coherent together. The cells of mammals show more aptitude here; we can sift through pages and pages of needless introns and never lose the thread of what the exons are saying. But this talent does have disadvantages. For one, the RNA-editing equipment in mammals must work long, thankless hours: the average human gene contains eight introns, each an average of 3,500 letters long—thirty times longer than the exons they surround. The gene for the largest human protein, *titin*, contains 178 fragments, totaling 80,000 bases, all of which must be stitched together precisely. An even more ridiculously sprawling gene—*dystrophin*, the Jacksonville of human DNA— contains 14,000 bases of coding DNA among 2.2 million bases of intron cruft. Transcription alone takes sixteen hours. Overall this constant splicing wastes incredible energy, and any slipups can ruin important proteins. In one genetic disorder, improper splicing in human skin cells wipes out the grooves and whorls of fingerprints, rendering the fingertips completely bald. (Scientists have nicknamed this condition "immigration delay disease," since these mutants get a lot of guff at border crossings.) Other splicing disruptions are more serious; mistakes in *dystrophin* cause muscular dystrophy.

Animals put up with this waste and danger because introns give our cells versatility. Certain cells can skip exons now and then, or leave part of an intron in place, or otherwise edit the same RNA differently. Having introns and exons therefore gives cells the freedom to experiment: they can produce different RNA at different times or customize proteins for different environments in the body.* For this reason alone, mammals especially have learned to tolerate vast numbers of long introns.

But as Mayumi discovered, tolerance can backfire. Long introns provide places for non-twin chromosomes to get tangled up, since there are no exons to worry about disrupting. The Philadelphia swap takes places along two introns—one on chromosome nine, one on chromosome twenty-two—that are exceptionally long, which raises the odds of these stretches coming into contact. At first our tolerant cells see this swap as no big deal, since it's fiddling "only" with soon-to-be-edited introns. It is a big deal. Mayumi's cells fused two genes that should never be fused—genes that formed, in tandem, a monstrous hybrid protein that couldn't do the job of either individual gene properly. The result was leukemia.

Doctors started Mayumi on chemotherapy at the hospital, but they had caught the cancer late, and she remained quite ill. Worse, as Mayumi deteriorated, their minds started spinning: what about Emiko? ALL is a swift cancer, but not that swift. Mayumi almost certainly had it when pregnant with Emiko. So could the little girl have "caught" the cancer from her mother? Cancer among expectant women is not uncommon, happening once every thousand pregnancies. But none of the doctors had ever seen a fetus catch cancer: the placenta, the organ that connects mother to child, should thwart any such invasion, because in addition to bringing nutrients to the baby and removing waste, the placenta acts as part of the baby's immune system, blocking microbes and rogue cells.

Still, a placenta isn't foolproof—doctors advise pregnant women not to handle kitty litter because Toxo can occasionally slip through the placenta and ravage the fetal brain. And after doing some research and consulting some specialists, the doctors realized that on rare occasions—a few dozen times since the first known instance, in the 1860s—mothers and fetuses came down with cancer simultaneously. No one had ever *proved* anything about the transmission of these cancers, however, because mother, fetus, and placenta are so tightly bound up that questions of cause and effect get tangled up, too. Perhaps the fetus gave the cancer to the mother in these cases. Perhaps they'd both been exposed to unknown carcinogens. Perhaps it was just a sickening coincidence—two strong genetic predispositions for cancer going off at once. But the Chiba doctors, working in 2006, had a tool no previous generation did: genetic sequencing. And as the Mayumi-Emiko case progressed, these doctors used genetic sequencing to pin down, for the first time, whether or not it's possible for a mother to give cancer to her fetus. What's more, their detective work highlighted some functions and mechanisms of DNA unique to mammals, traits that can serve as a springboard for exploring how mammals are genetically special.

Of course, the Chiba doctors weren't imagining their work would take them so far afield. Their immediate concern was treating Mayumi and monitoring Emiko. To their relief, Emiko looked fine. True, she had no idea why her mother had been taken from her, and any breast-feeding—so important to mammalian mothers and children—ceased during chemotherapy. So she certainly felt distress. But otherwise Emiko hit all her growth and development milestones and passed every medical examination. Everything about her seemed, again, normal.

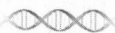

Saying so might creep expectant mothers out, but you can make a good case that fetuses are parasites. After conception, the tiny embryo infiltrates its host (Mom) and implants itself. It proceeds to manipulate her hormones to divert food to itself. It makes Mom ill and cloaks itself from her immune system, which would otherwise destroy it. All well-established games that parasites play. And we haven't even talked about the placenta.

In the animal kingdom, placentas are practically a defining trait of mammals.* Some oddball mammals that split with our lineage long ago (like duck-billed platypi) do lay eggs, just as fish, reptiles, birds, insects, and virtually every other creature do. But of the roughly 2,150 types of mammals, 2,000 have a placenta, including the most widespread and successful mammals, like bats, rodents, and humans. That placental mammals have expanded from modest beginnings into the sea and sky and every other niche from the tropics to the poles suggests that placentas gave them—gave us—a big survival boost.

As probably its biggest benefit, the placenta allows a mammal mother to carry her living, growing children within her. As a result she can keep her children warm inside the womb and run away from danger with them, advantages that spawning-into-water and squatting-on-nest creatures lack. Live fetuses also have longer to gestate and develop energy-intensive organs like the brain; the placenta's ability to pump bodily waste away helps the brain develop, too, since fetuses aren't stewing in toxins. What's more, because she invests so much energy in her developing fetus — not to mention the literal and intimate connection she feels because of the placenta — a mammal mom feels incentive to nurture and watch over her children, sometimes for years. (Or at least feels the need to nag them for years.) The length of this investment is rare among animals, and mammal children reciprocate by forming unusually strong bonds to their mothers. In one sense, then, the placenta, by enabling all this, made us mammals caring creatures.

That makes it all the more creepy that the placenta, in all likelihood, evolved from our old friends the retroviruses. But from a biological standpoint, the connection makes sense. Clamping on to cells happens to be a talent of viruses: they fuse their "envelopes" (their outer skin) to a cell before injecting their genetic material into it. When a ball of embryonic cells swims into the uterus and anchors itself there, the embryo also fuses part of itself with the uterine cells, by using special fusion proteins. And the DNA that primates, mice, and other mammals use to make the fusion proteins appears to be plagiarized from genes that retroviruses use to attach and meld their envelopes. What's more, the uterus of placental mammals draws heavily on other viruslike DNA to do its job, using a special jumping gene called *mer20* to flick 1,500 genes on and off in uterine cells. With both organs, it seems we once again borrowed some handy genetic material from a parasite and adapted it to our own ends. As a bonus, the viral genes in the placenta even provide extra immunity, since the presence of retrovirus proteins (either by warning them off, or outcompeting them) discourages other microbes from circling the placenta.

As another part of its immune function, the placenta filters out any cells that might try to invade the fetus, including cancer cells. Unfortunately, other aspects of the placenta make it down-right attractive to cancer. The placenta produces growth hormones to promote the vigorous division of fetal cells, and some cancers thrive on these growth hormones, too. Furthermore, the placenta soaks up enormous amounts of blood and siphons off nutrients for the fetus. That means that blood cancers like leukemia can lurk inside the placenta and flourish. Cancers genetically programmed to metastasize, like the skin cancer melanoma, take to the blood as they slither around inside the body, and they find the placenta quite hospitable as well.

In fact, melanoma is the most common cancer that mothers and fetuses get simultaneously. The first recorded simultaneous cancer, in 1866, in Germany, involved a roaming melanoma that randomly took root in the mother's liver and the child's knee. Both died within nine days. Another horrifying case claimed a twenty-eight-year-old Philadelphia woman, referred to only as "R. McC" by her doctors. It all started when Ms. McC got a brutal sunburn in April 1960. Shortly afterward a half-inch-long mole sprung up between her shoulder blades. It bled whenever she touched it. Doctors removed the mole, and no one thought about it again until May 1963, when she was a few weeks pregnant. During a checkup, doctors noticed a nodule beneath the skin on her stomach. By August the nodule had widened even faster than her belly, and other, painful nodules had sprung up. By January, lesions had spread to her limbs and face, and her doctors opened her up for a cesarean section. The boy inside appeared fine—a full seven pounds, thirteen ounces. But his mother's abdomen was spotted with dozens of tumors, some of them black. Not surprisingly, the birth finished off what little strength she had. Within an hour, her pulse dropped to thirty-six beats per minute, and though her doctors resuscitated her, she died within weeks.

And the McC boy? There was hope at first. Despite the widespread cancer, doctors saw no tumors in Ms. McC's uterus or placenta—her points of contact with her son. And although he was sickly, a careful scan of every crevice and dimple revealed no suspicious-looking moles. But they couldn't check inside him. Eleven days later tiny, dark blue spots began breaking out on the newborn's skin. Things deteriorated quickly after that. The tumors expanded and multiplied, and killed him within seven weeks.

Mayumi had leukemia, not melanoma, but otherwise her family in Chiba reprised the McC drama four decades later. In the hospital, Mayumi's condition deteriorated day by day, her immune system weakened by three weeks of chemotherapy. She finally contracted a bacterial infection and came down with encephalitis, inflammation of the brain. Her body began to convulse and seize—a result of her brain panicking and misfiring—and her heart and lungs faltered, too. Despite intensive care, she died two days after contracting the infection.

Even worse, in October 2006, nine months after burying his wife, Hideo had to return to the hospital with Emiko. The once-bouncing girl had fluid in her lungs and, more troublesome, a raw, fever-red mass disfiguring her right cheek and chin. On an MRI, this premature jowl looked enormous—as large as tiny Emiko's brain. (Try expanding your cheek as far as it will go with air, and its size still wouldn't be close.) Based on its location within the cheek, the Chiba doctors diagnosed sarcoma, cancer of the connective tissue. But with Mayumi in the back of their minds, they consulted experts in Tokyo and England and decided to screen the tumor's DNA to see what they could find.

They found a Philadelphia swap. And not just any Philadelphia swap. Again, this crossover takes place along two tremendously long introns, 68,000 letters long on one chromosome, 200,000 letters long on the other. (This chapter runs about 30,000 letters.) The two arms of the chromosomes could have crossed over at any one of thousands of different points. But the DNA in both Mayumi's and Emiko's cancer had crossed over at the same spot, down the same letter. This wasn't chance. Despite lodging in Emiko's cheek, the cancer basically was the same.

But who gave cancer to whom? Scientists had never solved this mystery before; even the McC case was ambiguous, since the fatal tumors appeared only after the pregnancy started. Doctors pulled out the blood-spot card taken from Emiko at birth and determined that the cancer had been present even then. Further genetic testing revealed that Emiko's normal (non-tumor) cells did *not* show a Philadelphia swap. So Emiko had not inherited any predisposition to this cancer—it had sprung up sometime between conception and the delivery forty weeks later. What's more, Emiko's normal cells also showed, as expected, DNA from both her mother and father. But her cheek tumor cells contained no DNA from Hideo; they were pure Mayumi. This proved, indisputably, that Mayumi had given cancer to Emiko, not vice versa.

Whatever sense of triumph the scientists might have felt, though, was muted. As so often happens in medical research, the most interesting cases spring from the most awful suffering. And in virtually every other historical case where a fetus and mother had cancer simultaneously, both had succumbed to it quickly, normally within a year. Mayumi was already gone, and as the doctors started the eleven-month-old Emiko on chemotherapy, they surely felt these dismal odds weighing on them.

The geneticists on the case felt something different nagging them. The spread of the cancer here was essentially a transplant of cells from one person to another. If Emiko had gotten an organ from her mother or had tissue grafted onto her cheek, her body would have rejected it as foreign. Yet cancer, of all things, had taken root without triggering the placenta's alarms or drawing the wrath of Emiko's immune system. How? Scientists ultimately found the answer in a stretch of DNA far removed from the Philadelphia swap, an area called the MHC.

Biologists back to Linnaeus's time have found it a fascinating exercise to list all the traits that make mammals *mammals*. One place to start—it's the origin of the term, from the Latin for breast, *mamma*—is nursing. In addition to providing nutrition, breast milk activates dozens of genes in suckling infants, mostly in the intestines, but also possibly in spots like the brain. Not to throw any more panic into expectant mothers, but it seems that artificial formula, however similar in carbs, fats, proteins, vitamins, and for all I know taste, just can't goose a baby's DNA the same way.

Other notable traits of mammals include our hair (even whales and dolphins have a comb-over), our unique inner ear and jaw structure, and our odd habit of chewing food before swallowing (reptiles have no such manners). But on a microscopic level, one place to hunt for the origin of mammals is the MHC, the major histocompatibility complex. Nearly all vertebrates have an MHC, a set of genes that helps the immune system. But the MHC is particularly dear to mammals. It's among the most gene-rich stretches of DNA we have, over one hundred genes packed into a small area. And similar to our intron/exon editing equipment, we have more sophisticated and more extensive MHCs than other creatures.* Some of those hundred genes have over a thousand different varieties in humans, offering a virtually unlimited number of combinations to inherit. Even close relatives can differ substantially in their MHC, and the differences among random people are a hundred times higher than those along most other stretches of DNA. Scientists sometimes say that humans are over 99 percent genetically identical. Not along their MHCs they aren't.

MHC proteins basically do two things. First, some of them grab a random sampling of molecules from inside a cell and put them on display on the cellular surface. This display lets other cells, especially "executioner" immune cells, know what's going on inside the cell. If the executioner sees the MHC mounting nothing but normal molecules, it ignores the cell. If it sees abnormal material—fragments of bacteria, cancer proteins, other signs of malfeasance—it can attack. The diversity of the MHC helps mammals here because different MHC proteins fasten on to and raise the alarm against different dangers, so the more diversity in the mammalian MHC, the more things a creature can combat. And crucially, unlike with other traits, MHC genes don't interfere with each other. Mendel identified the first dominant traits, cases where some versions of genes "win out" over others. With the MHC, all the genes work independently, and no one gene masks another. They cooperate; they codominate.

As for its second, more philosophical function, the MHC allows our bodies to distinguish between self and nonself. While mounting protein fragments, MHC genes cause little beard hairs to sprout on the surface of every cell; and because each creature has a unique combination of MHC genes, this cellular beard hair will have a unique arrangement of colors and curls. Any nonself interlopers in the body (like cells from animals or other people) of course have their own MHC genes sprouting their own unique beards. Our immune system is so precise that it will recognize those beards as different, and—even if those cells betray no signs of diseases or parasites—marshal troops to kill the invaders.

Destroying invaders is normally good. But one side effect of the MHC's vigilance is that our bodies reject transplanted organs unless the recipients take drugs to suppress their immune systems. Sometimes even that doesn't work. Transplanting organs from animals could help alleviate the world's chronic shortage of organ donors, but animals have such bizarre (to us) MHCs that our bodies reject them instantly. We even destroy tissues and blood vessels *around* implanted animal organs, like retreating soldiers burning crops so that the enemy can't use them for nourishment either. By absolutely paralyzing the immune system, doctors have kept people alive on baboon hearts and livers for a few weeks, but so far the MHC always wins out.

For similar reasons, the MHC made things difficult for mammal evolution. By all rights, a mammal mother should attack the fetus inside her as a foreign growth, since half its DNA, MHC and otherwise, isn't hers. Thankfully, the placenta mediates this conflict by restricting access to the fetus. Blood pools in the placenta, but no blood actually crosses through to the fetus, just nutrients. As a result, a baby like Emiko should remain perfectly, parasitically invisible to Mayumi's immune cells, and Mayumi's cells should never cross over into Emiko. Even if a few do slip through the placental gate, Emiko's own immune system should recognize the foreign MHC and destroy them.

But when scientists scrutinized the MHC of Mayumi's cancerous blood cells, they discovered something that would be almost admirable in its cleverness, if it weren't so sinister. In humans, the MHC is located on the shorter arm of chromosome six. The scientists noticed that this short arm in Mayumi's cancer cells was even shorter than it should be—because the cells had deleted their MHC. Some unknown mutation had simply wiped it from their genes. This left them functionally invisible on the outside, so neither the placenta nor Emiko's immune cells could classify or recognize them. She had no way to scrutinize them for evidence that they were foreign, much less that they harbored cancer.

Overall, then, scientists could trace the invasion of Mayumi's cancer to two causes: the Philadelphia swap that made them malignant, and the MHC mutation that made them invisible and allowed them to trespass and burrow into Emiko's cheek. The odds of either thing happening were low; the odds of them happening in the same cells, at the same time, in a woman who happened to be pregnant, were astronomically low. But not zero. In fact, scientists now suspect that in most historical cases where mothers gave cancer to their fetuses, something similar disabled or compromised the MHC.

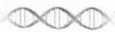

If we follow the thread far enough, the MHC can help illuminate one more aspect of Hideo and Mayumi and Emiko's story, a thread that runs back to our earliest days as mammals. A developing fetus has to conduct a whole orchestra of genes inside every cell, encouraging some DNA to play louder and hushing other sections up. Early on in the pregnancy, the most active genes are the ones that mammals inherited from our egg-laying, lizardlike ancestors. It's a humbling experience to flip through a biology textbook and see how uncannily similar bird, lizard, fish, human, and other embryos appear during their early lives. We humans even have rudimentary gill slits and tails—honest-to-god atavisms from our animal past.

After a few weeks, the fetus mutes the reptilian genes and turns on a coterie of genes unique to mammals, and pretty soon the fetus starts to resemble something you could imagine naming after your grandmother. Even at this stage, though, if the right genes are silenced or tweaked, atavisms (i.e., genetic throwbacks) can appear. Some people are born with the same extra nipples that barnyard sows have.* Most of these extra nipples poke through the "milk line" running vertically down the torso, but they can appear as far away as the sole of the foot. Other atavistic genes leave people with coats of hair sprouting all over their bodies, including their cheeks and foreheads. Scientists can even distinguish (if you'll forgive the pejoratives) between "dog-faced" and "monkey-faced" coats, depending on the coarseness, color, and other qualities of the hair. Infants missing a snippet at the end of chromosome five develop *cri-du-chat*, or "cry of the cat" syndrome, so named for their caterwauling chirps and howls. Some children are also born with tails. These tails— usually centered above their buttocks—contain muscles and nerves and run to five inches long and an inch thick. Sometimes tails appear as side effects of recessive genetic disorders that

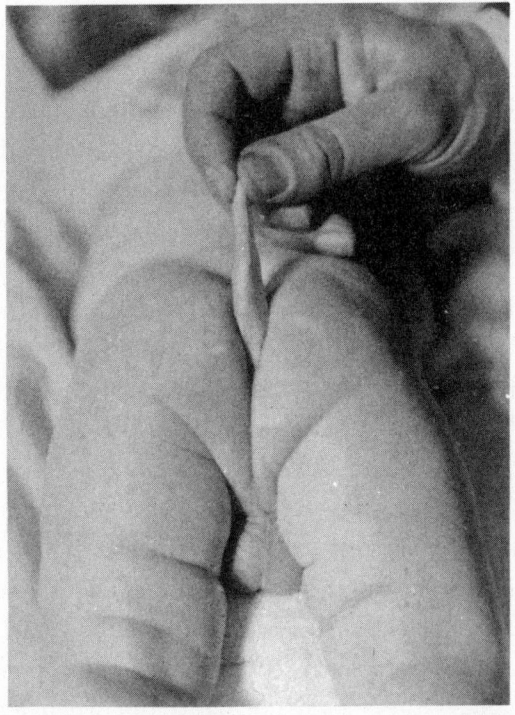

A hale and healthy baby boy born with a tail—a genetic throwback from our primate past. (Jan Bondeson, *A Cabinet of Medical Curiosities*, reproduced by permission)

cause widespread anatomical problems, but tails can appear idio-syncratically as well, in otherwise normal children. Pediatricians have reported that these boys and girls can curl their tails up like an elephant's trunk, and that the tails contract involuntarily when children cough or sneeze.* Again, all fetuses have tails at six weeks old, but they usually retract after eight weeks as tail cells die and the body absorbs the excess tissue. Tails that persist probably arise from spontaneous mutations, but some children with tails do have betailed relatives. Most get the harmless appendage removed just after birth, but some don't bother until adulthood.

All of us have other atavisms dormant within us as well, just waiting for the right genetic signals to awaken them. In fact, there's one genetic atavism that none of us escapes. About forty days after conception, inside the nasal cavity, humans develop a tube about 0.01 inches long, with a slit on either side. This incip-ient structure, the vomeronasal organ, is common among mam-mals, who use it to help map the world around them. It acts like an auxiliary nose, except that instead of smelling things that any sentient creature can sniff out (smoke, rotten food), the vomero-nasal organ detects pheromones. Pheromones are veiled scents vaguely similar to hormones; but whereas hormones give our bod-ies internal instructions, pheromones give instructions (or at least winks and significant glances) to other members of our species.

Because pheromones help guide social interactions, espe-cially intimate encounters, shutting off the VNO in certain mammals can have awkward consequences. In 2007, scientists at Harvard University genetically rewired some female mice to disable their VNOs. When the mice were by themselves, not much changed—they acted normally. But when let loose on regular females, the altered mice treated them like the Romans did the Sabine women. They stormed and mounted the maidens, and despite lacking the right equipment, they began thrusting their hips back and forth. The bizarro females even groaned like men, emitting ultrasonic squeals that, until then, were heard only from male mice at climax.

Humans rely less on scent than other mammals do; throughout our evolution we've lost or turned off six hundred common mammalian genes for smell. But that makes it all the more striking that our genes still build a VNO. Scientists have even detected nerves running from the fetal VNO to the brain, and have seen these nerves send signals back and forth. Yet for unknown reasons, despite going through the trouble of creating the organ and wiring it up, our bodies neglect this sixth sense, and after sixteen weeks it starts shriveling. By adulthood, it has retracted to the point that most scientists dispute whether humans even have a VNO, much less a functional one.

The debate about the human VNO fits into a larger and less-than-venerable historical debate over the supposed links between scent, sexuality, and behavior. One of Sigmund Freud's nuttier friends, Dr. Wilhelm Fliess, classified the nose as the body's most potent sex organ in the late 1800s. His "nasal reflux neurosis theory" was an unscientific hash of numerology, anecdotes about masturbation and menstruation, maps of hypothetical "genital spots" inside the nose, and experiments that involved dabbing cocaine on people's mucus membranes and monitoring their libidos. His failure to actually explain anything about human sexuality didn't lower Fliess's standing; to the contrary, his work influenced Freud, and Freud allowed Fliess to treat his patients (and, some have speculated, Freud himself) for indulging in masturbation. Fliess's ideas eventually died out, but pseudoscientific sexology never has. In recent decades, hucksters have sold perfumes and colognes enriched with pheromones, which supposedly make the scentee a sexual magnet. (Don't hold your breath.) And in 1994 a U.S. military scientist requested $7.5 million from the air force to develop a pheromone-based "gay bomb." His application described the weapon as a "distasteful but completely non-lethal" form of warfare. The pheromones would be sprayed over the (mostly male) enemy troops, and the smell would somehow—the details were tellingly sketchy, at least outside the scientist's fantasies—whip them into such a froth of randiness that they'd drop their weapons and make whoopee instead of war. Our soldiers, wearing gas masks, would simply have to round them up.*

Perfumes and gay bombs aside, some legitimate scientific work has revealed that pheromones can influence human behavior. Forty years ago, scientists determined that pheromones cause the menstrual cycles of women who live together to converge toward the same date. (That's no urban legend.) And while we may resist reducing human love to the interaction of chemicals, evidence shows that raw human lust—or more demurely, attraction—has a strong olfactory component. Old anthropology books, not to mention Charles Darwin himself, used to marvel that in societies that never developed the custom of kissing, potential lovers often sniffed each other instead of smooching. More recently, Swedish doctors ran some experiments that echo the dramatic Harvard study with mice. The doctors exposed straight women, straight men, and homosexual men to a pheromone in male sweat. During this exposure, the brain scans of straight women and gay men—but not straight men—showed signs of mild arousal. The obvious follow-up experiment revealed that pheromones in female urine can arouse straight men and gay women, but not straight women. It seems the brains of people with different sexual orientations respond differently to odors from either sex. This doesn't prove that humans have a functioning VNO, but it does suggest we've retained some of its pheromone-detecting ability, perhaps by genetically shifting its responsibilities to our regular nose.

Probably the most straightforward evidence that smells can influence human arousal comes from—and we've finally circled back to it—the MHC. Like it or not, your body advertises your MHC every time you lift your arm. Humans have a high concentration of sweat glands in the armpit, and mixed in with the excreted water, salt, and oil are pheromones that spell out exactly what MHC genes people have to protect them from disease. These MHC ads drift into your nose, where nasal cells can work out how much the MHC of another person differs from your own. That's helpful in judging a mate because you can estimate the probable health of any children you'd have together. Remember that MHC genes don't interfere with each other—they codominate. So if Mom and Dad have different MHCs, baby will inherit their combined disease resistance. The more genetic disease resistance, the better off baby will be.

This information trickles into our brains unconsciously but can make itself known when we suddenly find a stranger unaccountably sexy. It's impossible to say for sure without testing, but when this happens, the odds are decent that his or her MHC is notably different from your own. In various studies, when women sniffed a T-shirt worn to bed by men they never saw or met, the women rated the men with wild MHCs (compared to their own) as the sexiest in the batch. To be sure, other studies indicate that, in places already high in genetic diversity, like parts of Africa, having a wildly different MHC doesn't increase attraction. But the MHC-attraction link does seem to hold in more genetically homogeneous places, as studies in Utah have shown. This finding might also help explain why—because they have more similar MHCs than average—we find the thought of sex with our siblings repugnant.

Again, there's no sense in reducing human love to chemicals; it's waaaay more complex than that. But we're not as far removed from our fellow mammals as we might imagine. Chemicals do prime and propel love, and some of the most potent chemicals out there are the pheromones that advertise the MHC. If two people from a genetically homogeneous locale—take Hideo and Mayumi—came together, fell in love, and decided to have a child, then as far as we can ever explain these things biologically, their MHCs likely had something to do with it. Which makes it all the more poignant that the disappearance of that same MHC empowered the cancer that almost destroyed Emiko.

Almost. The survival rate for both mothers and infants with simultaneous cancer has remained abysmally low, despite great advances in medicine since 1866. But unlike her mother, Emiko responded to treatment well, partly because her doctors could tailor her chemotherapy to her tumor's DNA. Emiko didn't even need the excruciating bone-marrow transplants that most children with her type of cancer require. And as of today (touch wood) Emiko is alive, almost seven years old and living in Chiba.

We don't think of cancer as a transmissible disease. Twins can nevertheless pass cancer to each other in the womb; transplanted organs can pass cancer to the organ recipient; and mothers can indeed pass cancer to their unborn children, despite the defenses of the placenta. Still, Emiko proves that catching an advanced cancer, even as a fetus, doesn't have to be fatal. And cases like hers have expanded our view of the MHC's role in cancer, and demonstrated that the placenta is more permeable than most scientists imagined. "I'm inclined to think that maybe cells get by [the placenta] in modest numbers all the time," says a geneticist who worked with Emiko's family. "You can learn a lot from very odd cases in medicine."

In fact, other scientists have painstakingly determined that most if not all of us harbor thousands of clandestine cells from our mothers, stowaways from our fetal days that burrowed into our vital organs. Every mother has almost certainly secreted away a few memento cells from each of her children inside her, too. Such discoveries are opening up fascinating new facets of our biology; as one scientist wondered, "What constitutes our psychological self if our brains are not entirely our own?" More personally, these findings show that even after the death of a mother or child, cells from one can live on in the other. It's another facet of the mother-child connection that makes mammals special.

9

Humanzees and Other Near Misses

When Did Humans Break Away from Monkeys, and Why?

God knows the evolution of human beings didn't stop with fur, mammary glands, and placentas. We're also primates—although that was hardly something to brag about sixty million years ago. The first rudimentary primates probably didn't crack one pound or live beyond six years. They probably lived in trees, hopped about instead of striding, hunted nothing bigger than insects, and crept out of their hovels only at night. But these milquetoast midnight bug-biters got lucky and kept evolving. Tens of millions of years later, some clever, opposable-thumbed, chest-beating primates arose in Africa, and members of one of those lines of primates literally rose onto two feet and began marching across the savannas. Scientists have studied this progression intensely, picking it apart for clues about the essence of humanity. And looking back on the whole picture—that *National Geographic* sequence of humans getting up off our knuckles, shedding our body hair, and renouncing our prognathous jaws—we can't help but think about our emergence a little triumphantly.

Still, while the rise of human beings was indeed precious, our DNA—like the slave in Roman times who followed a triumphant general around—whispers in our ears, *Remember, thou art mortal.* In reality the transition from apelike ancestor to modern human being was more fraught than we appreciate. Evidence tattooed into our genes suggests that the human line almost went extinct, multiple times; nature almost wiped us out like so many mastodons and dodos, with nary a care for our big plans. And it's doubly humbling to see how closely our DNA sequence still resembles that of so-called lower primates, a likeness that conflicts with our inborn feeling of preordainment— that we somehow sit superior to other creatures.

One strong piece of evidence for that inborn feeling is the revulsion we feel over the very idea of mixing human tissues with tissues from another creature. But serious scientists throughout history have attempted to make human-animal chimeras, most recently by adulterating our DNA. Probably the all-time five-alarmer in this realm took place in the 1920s, when a Russian biologist named Ilya Ivanovich Ivanov tried to unite human genes with chimpanzee genes in some hair-raising experiments that won the approval of Joseph Stalin himself.

Ivanov started his scientific career around 1900, and worked with physiologist Ivan Pavlov (he of the drooling dogs) before branching out to become the world's expert in barnyard insemination, especially with horses. Ivanov crafted his own instruments for the work, a special sponge to sop up semen and rubber catheters to deliver it deep inside the mares. For a decade, he worked with the Department for State Stud-Farming, an official bureau that supplied the ruling Romanov government with pretty horses. Given those political priorities, it's not hard to imagine why the Romanovs were overthrown in 1917, and when the Bolsheviks took over and founded the Soviet Union, Ivanov found himself unemployed.

It didn't help Ivanov's prospects that most people at the time considered artificial insemination shameful, a corruption of natural copulation. Even those who championed the technique went to ridiculous lengths to preserve an aura of organic sex. One prominent doctor would wait outside a barren couple's room, listening at the keyhole while they went at it, then rush in with a baster of sperm, practically push the husband aside, and spurt it into the woman—all to trick her egg cells into thinking that insemination had happened during the course of inter-course. The Vatican banned artificial insemination for Catho-lics in 1897, and Russia's Greek Orthodox Church similarly condemned anyone, like Ivanov, who practiced it.

But the religious snit eventually helped Ivanov's career. Even while mired in the barnyard, Ivanov had always seen his work in grander terms—not just a way to produce better cows and goats, but a way to probe Darwin's and Mendel's fundamental theories of biology, by mixing embryos from different species. After all, his sponges and catheters removed the main barrier to such work, coaxing random animals to conjugate. Ivanov had been chewing over the ultimate test of Darwinian evolution, human-zees, since 1910, and he finally (after consulting with Hermann Muller, the Soviet-loving *Drosophila* scientist) screwed up the courage to request a research grant in the early 1920s.

Ivanov applied to the people's commissar of enlightenment, the official who controlled Soviet scientific funding. The com-missar, a theater and art expert in his former life, let the proposal languish, but other top Bolsheviks saw something promising in Ivanov's idea: a chance to insult religion, the Soviet Union's avowed enemy. These farsighted men argued that breeding humanzees would be vital "in our propaganda and in our strug-gle for the liberation of the working people from the power of the Church." Ostensibly for this reason, in September 1925— just months after the Scopes trial in the United States—the

Soviet government granted Ivanov $10,000 ($130,000 today) to get started.

Ivanov had good scientific reasons to think the work could succeed. Scientists knew at the time that human and primate blood showed a remarkable degree of similarity. Even more exciting, a Russian-born colleague, Serge Voronoff, was wrapping up a series of sensational and supposedly successful experiments to restore the virility of elderly men by transplanting primate glands and testicles into them. (Rumors spread that Irish poet William Butler Yeats had undergone this procedure. He hadn't, but the fact that people didn't dismiss the rumor as rubbish says a lot about Yeats.) Voronoff's transplants seemed to show that, at least physiologically, little separated lower primates and humans.

Ivanov also knew that quite distinct species can reproduce together. He himself had blended antelopes with cows, guinea pigs with rabbits, and zebras with donkeys. Besides amusing the tsar and his minions (very important), this work proved that animals whose lines had diverged even millions of years ago could still have children, and later experiments by other scientists provided further proof. Pretty much any fantasy you've got—lions with tigers, sheep with goats, dolphins with killer whales— scientists have fulfilled it somewhere. True, some of these hybrids were and are sterile, genetic dead ends. But only some: biologists find many bizarre couplings in the wild, and of the more than three hundred mammalian species that "outbreed" naturally, fully one-third produce fertile children. Ivanov fervently believed in crossbreeding, and after he sprinkled some good old Marxist materialism into his calculations—which denied human beings anything as gauche as a soul that might not condescend to commingle with chimps—then his humanzee experiments seemed, well, doable.

Scientists don't know even today whether humanzees, however icky and unlikely, are at least possible. Human sperm can

A modern zonkey—a zebra-donkey mix. Ilya Ivanov created zonkeys (which he called "zeedonks") and many other genetic hybrids before pursuing human-zees. (Tracy N. Brandon)

pierce the outer layer of some primate eggs in the lab, the first step in fertilization, and human and chimpanzee chromosomes look much the same on a macro scale. Heck, human DNA and chimp DNA even enjoy each other's company. If you prepare a solution with both DNAs and heat it up until the double strands unwind, human DNA has no problem embracing chimp DNA and zipping back up with it when things cool down. They're that similar.*

What's more, a few primate geneticists think that our ancestors resorted to breeding with chimps long *after* we'd split away to become a separate species. And according to their controversial but persistent theory, we copulated with chimps far longer than most of us are comfortable thinking about, for a million years. If true, our eventual divergence from the chimp line was a complicated and messy breakup, but not inevitable. Had things gone another way, our sexual proclivities might well have rubbed the human line right out of existence.

The theory goes like this. Seven million years ago some unknown event (maybe an earthquake opened a rift; maybe half the group got lost looking for food one afternoon; maybe a bitter butter battle broke out) split a small population of primates. And with every generation they remained apart, these two separate groups of chimp-human ancestors would have accumulated mutations that gave them unique characteristics. So far, this is standard biology. More unusually, though, imagine that the two groups reunited some time later. Again, the reason is impossible to guess; maybe an ice age wiped out most of their habitats and squeezed them together into small woodland refugia. Regardless, we don't need to propose any outlandish, Marquis de Sade motivations for what happened next. If lonely or low in numbers, the protohumans might eagerly—despite having forsworn the comforts of protochimps for a million years—have welcomed them back into their beds (so to speak) when the groups reunited. A million years may seem like forever, but the two protos would have been less distinct genetically than many interbreeding species today. So while this interbreeding might have produced some primate "mules," it might have produced fertile hybrids as well.

Therein lay the danger for protohumans. Scientists know of at least one case in primate history, with macaques, when two long-separate species began mating again and melded back into one, eliminating any special differences between them. Our interbreeding with chimps was no weekend fling or dalliance; it was long and involved. And if our ancestors had said what the hell and settled down with protochimpanzees permanently, our unique genes could have drowned in the general gene pool in the same way. Not to sound all eugenicky, but we would have humped ourselves right out of existence.

Of course, this all assumes that chimps and humans did revert to sleeping together after an initial split. So what's the evidence for this charge? Most of it lies on our (wait for it) sex chromosomes, especially the X. But it's a subtle case.

When female hybrids have fertility trouble, the flaw usually traces back to their having one X from one species, one X from another. For whatever reason, reproduction just doesn't go as smoothly with a mismatch. Mismatched sex chromosomes hit males even harder: an X and a Y from different species almost always leave them shooting blanks. But infertility among women is a bigger threat to group survival. A few fertile males can still impregnate loads of females, but no gang of fertile males can make up for low female fecundity, because females can have children only so quickly.

Nature's solution here is genocide. That is, gene-o-cide: nature will eliminate any potential mismatches among the inter-breeders by eradicating the X chromosome of one species. It doesn't matter which, but one has to go. It's a war of attrition, really. Depending on the messy details of how many proto-chimps and protohumans interbred, and then whom exactly the first generation of hybrids reproduced with, and then their differential birthrates and mortality—depending on all that, one species' X chromosomes probably appeared in higher numbers initially in the gene pool. And in the subsequent generations, the X with the numbers advantage would slowly strangle the other one, because anyone with similar Xs would outbreed the half-breeds.

Notice there's no comparable pressure to eliminate nonsex chromosomes. Those chromosomes don't mind being paired with chromosomes from the other species. (Or if they do mind, their quarrel likely won't interfere with making babies, which is what counts to DNA.) As a result, the hybrids and their descendants could have been full of mismatched nonsex chromosomes and survived just fine.

Scientists realized in 2006 that this difference between sex and nonsex chromosomes might explain a funny characteristic of human DNA. After the initial split between their lines, protochimps and protohumans should have started down different paths and accumulated different mutations on each chromosome. And they did, mostly. But when scientists look at chimps and humans today, their Xs look more uniform than other chromosomes. The DNA clock on X got reset, it seems; it retained its girlish looks.

We hear the statistic sometimes that we have 99 percent of our DNA coding region in common with chimps, but that's an average, overall measure. It obscures the fact that human and chimp Xs, a crucial chromosome for Ivanov's work, look even more identical up and down the line. One parsimonious way to explain this similarity is interbreeding and the war of attrition that would probably have eliminated one type of X. In fact, that's why scientists developed the theory about protohuman and protochimp mating in the first place. Even they admit it sounds a little batty, but they couldn't puzzle out another way to explain why human and chimp X chromosomes have less variety than other chromosomes.

Fittingly, however (given the battle of the sexes), research related to Y chromosomes may contradict the X-rated evidence for human-chimp interbreeding. Again, scientists once believed that Y—which has undergone massive shrinkage over the past 300 million years, down to a chromosomal stub today—would one day disappear as it continued to shed genes. It was considered an evolutionary vestige. But in truth Y has evolved rapidly even in the few million years since humans swore off chimpanzees (or vice versa). Y houses the genes to make sperm, and sperm production is an area of fierce competition in wanton species. Many different protogents would have had sex with each protolady, so one gent's sperm constantly had to wrestle with another gent's inside her vagina. (Not appetizing, but true.) One evolutionary strategy to secure an advantage here is to produce loads and loads of sperm each time you ejaculate. Doing so of course requires copying and pasting lots of DNA, because each sperm needs its own genetic payload. And the more copying that takes place, the more mutations that occur. It's a numbers game.

However, these inevitable copying mistakes plague the X chromosome less than any other chromosome because of our reproductive biology. Just like making sperm, making an egg requires copying and pasting lots of DNA. A female has equal numbers of every chromosome: two chromosome ones, two chromosome twos, and so on, as well as two Xs. So during the production of eggs, each chromosome, including the Xs, gets copied equally often. Males also have two copies of chromosomes one through twenty-two. But instead of two Xs, they have one X and one Y. During the production of sperm, then, the X gets copied less often compared to other chromosomes. And because it gets copied less often, it picks up fewer mutations. That mutation gap between X and other chromosomes widens even more when—because of Y chromosome–fueled sperm competition—males begin churning out loads of sperm. Therefore, some biologists argue, the seeming lack of mutations on X when comparing chimps and humans might not involve an elaborate and illicit sexual history. It might result from our basic biology, since X should always have fewer mutations.*

Regardless of who's right, work along these lines has undermined the old view of the Y as a misfit of the mammal genome; it's quite sophisticated in its narrow way. But for humans, it's hard to say if the revisionary history is for the better. The pressure to develop virile sperm is much higher in chimps than humans because male chimps have more sex with different partners. In response, evolution has remade the chimp Y thoroughly top to bottom. So thoroughly, in fact, that—contrary to what most men probably want to believe—chimps have pretty much left us guys in the dust evolutionarily. Chimps simply have tougher, smarter swimmers with a better sense of direction, and the human Y looks obsolete in comparison.

But that's DNA for you—humbling. As one Y-chromosome specialist comments, "When we sequenced the chimp genome, people thought we'd understand why we have language and write poetry. But one of the most dramatic differences turns out to be sperm production."

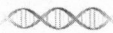

Talking about Ivanov's experiments in terms of DNA is a little anachronistic. But scientists in his day did know that chromosomes shuttled genetic information down through the generations and that chromosomes from mothers and fathers had to be compatible, especially in numbers. And based on the preponderance of evidence, Ivanov decided that chimps and humans had similar enough biologies to push forward.

After securing funds, Ivanov arranged through a colleague in Paris to work at a primate research station in colonial French Guinea (modern Guinea). The conditions at the station were deplorable: the chimps lived in cages exposed to the weather, and half of the seven hundred chimps that local poachers had netted and dragged back had died of disease or neglect. Nevertheless Ivanov enlisted his son (another triple *i*: Ilya Ilich Ivanov) and began chugging thousands of nautical miles back and forth between Russia, Africa, and Paris. The Ivanovs eventually arrived in sultry Guinea, ready to begin experiments, in November 1926.

Because the captives were sexually immature, too young to conceive, Ivanov wasted months furtively checking their pubic fur each day for menstrual blood. Meanwhile fresh inmates kept piling in, right up until Valentine's Day 1927. Ivanov had to keep his work secret to avoid angry questions from the Guineans, who had strong taboos against humans mating with primates, based on local myths about hybrid monsters. But finally, on February 28, two chimps named Babette and Syvette had their periods. At eight o'clock the next morning, after visiting an anonymous local donor, Ivanov and son approached their cages armed with a syringe of sperm. They were also armed with two Browning pistols: Ivanov Jr. had been bitten and hospitalized a few days before. The Ivanovs didn't end up needing the Brownings, but only because they more or less raped the chimps, binding Babette and Syvette in nets. The virgin chimps thrashed about anyway, and Ivanov managed to jam the syringe only into their vaginas, not into their uteruses, the preferred spot for deposits. Not surprisingly, this experiment failed, and Babette and Syvette got their periods again weeks later. Many juvenile chimps died of dysentery in the following months, and Ivanov managed to inseminate just one more female that spring (she was drugged). This attempt also failed, meaning Ivanov had no living human-zees to haul back to the Soviet Union to win more funding.

Perhaps wary that the commissar of enlightenment might not give him a second chance, Ivanov began pursuing new projects and new avenues of research, some in secret. Before leaving for Africa, he'd helped break ground on the first Soviet primate station, in Sukhumi, in modern-day Georgia, one of the few semitropical areas in the Soviet empire, and conveniently located in the homeland of the new Soviet leader, Joseph Stalin. Ivanov also courted a wealthy but flaky Cuban socialite named Rosalià Abreu, who operated a private primate sanctuary on her estate in Havana—partly because she believed that chimpanzees had psychic powers and deserved protection. Abreu initially agreed to house Ivanov's experiments but withdrew her offer because she feared newspapers would get hold of the story. She was right to worry. The *New York Times* caught wind of the story anyway after some of Ivanov's American supporters appealed to the publicity-hungry American Association for the Advancement of Atheism for funding and it began trumpeting the idea. The *Times* story* prompted the Ku Klux Klan to send out letters warning Ivanov about doing his devil's work on their side of the Atlantic, as it was "abominable to the Creator."

Meanwhile Ivanov was finding it expensive and annoying to keep a large chimp harem healthy and safe, so he devised a plan to turn his experimental protocol inside out. Females in primate societies can have children only so quickly, while one virile male can spread his seed widely at little cost. So instead of keeping multiple female chimps around to impregnate with human sperm, Ivanov decided to secure one male chimp and impregnate human women. Simple as that.

To this end, Ivanov made secret contact with a colonial doctor in the Congo and asked the doctor to let him inseminate patients. When the doctor asked why on earth his patients would consent, Ivanov explained that they wouldn't tell them. This satisfied the doctor, and Ivanov beat cheeks from French Guinea down to the Congo, where everything seemed ready to go. At the last second, however, the local governor intervened and informed Ivanov that he could not perform the experiment in the hospital: he had to do it outdoors. Offended at the interference, Ivanov refused; the unsanitary conditions would compromise his work and the safety of his patients, he said. But the governor held firm. Ivanov called the debacle a "terrible blow" in his diary.

Until his last day in Africa, Ivanov kept hunting down leads for other women to inseminate, but nothing came of them. So when he finally left French Guinea in July 1927, he decided no more fooling around in far-flung places. He would shift his operations to the newly opened Soviet primate station at Sukhumi. He would also sidestep the hassles of female chimp harems by finding one reliable male stud and coaxing Soviet women to reproduce with him.

As feared, Ivanov had trouble finding funding for his revised experiments, but the Society of Materialist Biologists took up Ivanov's work as a proper Bolshevik cause and ponied up. Before he could get started, however, most of the Sukhumi primates fell sick and died that winter. (Though balmy by Soviet standards, Sukhumi was pretty far north for African primates.) Luckily, the one primate to pull through was male—Tarzan, a twenty-six-year-old orangutan. All Ivanov needed now were human recruits. Officials, though, informed Ivanov he could not offer the recruits money for being surrogates. They had to volunteer, out of ideological amour for the Soviet state, a less tangible reward than a bounty. This further delayed things, but nevertheless, by spring 1928, Ivanov had his mark.

Her name comes down to us only as "G." Whether she was slender or stout, freckled or fair, a madame or a charwoman, we have no idea. All we have is a heartrending and elliptical letter she wrote to Ivanov: "Dear Professor[:] With my private life in ruins, I don't see any sense in my further existence.... But when I think that I could do a service for science, I feel enough courage to contact you. I beg you, don't refuse me."

Ivanov assured her he wouldn't. But as he made arrangements to bring G to Sukhumi and inseminate her, Tarzan died of a brain hemorrhage. No one had had time to milk him for sperm, either. Once again the experiment stalled.

This time, permanently. Before he could round up another ape, the Soviet secret police arrested Ivanov in 1930 for obscure reasons and exiled him to Kazakhstan. (The official charge was that old standby, "counterrevolutionary activities.") Already past sixty, Ivanov took to prison about as well as his primates had, and

Soviet biologist Ilya Ivanovich Ivanov went further than any scientist ever has in trying to breed primates with humans. (Institute of the History of Natural Sciences and Technology, Russian Academy of Sciences)

his health grew fragile. He was cleared of the bogus charges in 1932, but the day before he was to leave prison, he, like Tarzan, had a brain hemorrhage. Within a few days, he joined Tarzan in that giant primate research station in the sky.

After Ivanov died, his scientific agenda disintegrated. Few other scientists had the skill to inseminate primates, and just as important, no scientifically advanced country was as willing as the Soviet Union to trash every ethical guideline out there and fund such work. (Although to be fair, even hardened Politburo officials threw up in their mouths when Ivanov revealed his clandestine attempt to impregnate hospitalized women in the Congo with chimp sperm.) As a result, since the 1920s scientists have done virtually no research on human-primate hybrids. Which means that Ivanov's most pressing question remains open: could G and a beast like Tarzan have produced a child?

In one way, maybe. In 1997 a biologist in New York applied for a patent on a process to mix embryonic cells from humans and chimps and gestate them in a surrogate mother. The biologist considered the project technically feasible, even if he himself never intended to make a humanzee chimera; he merely wanted to prevent some nefarious person from obtaining a patent first. (The patent office turned the claim down in 2005 because, among other things, patenting a half human could violate the Thirteenth Amendment's prohibition against slavery and owning another human.) However, the process would have required no actual hybridization—no actual mixing of the two species' DNA. That's because the chimp and human embryonic cells would have come into contact only after fertilization; so each individual cell in the body would retain its wholly chimp or wholly human nature. The creature would have been a mosaic, not a hybrid.

Nowadays scientists could easily splice bits of human DNA into chimp embryos (or vice versa), but this would be little more than a tweak biologically. True hybridization requires the old-fashioned fifty-fifty mingling of sperm and eggs, and almost all respectable scientists today would lay money on human-chimp fertilization being impossible. For one, the molecules that form a zygote and start it dividing are specific to each species. And even if a viable humanzee zygote did form, humans and chimps regulate DNA very differently. So the job of getting all that DNA to cooperate and turn genes off and on in sync and make proper skin and liver and especially brain cells would be daunting.

Another reason to doubt that humans and chimps could produce children is the different chromosome count in the two species, a fact that emerged only after Ivanov's time. Getting an accurate chromosome count was surprisingly tricky for most of the twentieth century. DNA remains quite tangled inside the nucleus except for the few moments right before a cell divides, when compact chromosomes form. Chromosomes also have a bad habit of melting together after cells die, which makes counting harder still. Counting is therefore easiest in recently living samples of cells that divide often—like the sperm-making cells inside male gonads. Finding fresh monkey testes wasn't too onerous even in the early 1900s (Lord knows they killed enough monkeys then), and biologists determined that close primate relatives like chimps, orangutans, and gorillas all had forty-eight chromosomes. But lingering taboos made obtaining human testes more difficult. People didn't donate their bodies to science back then, and some desperate biologists—much like those anatomists in the Renaissance who robbed graves—took to lurking near the town gallows to harvest the testicles of condemned criminals. There was simply no other way to get fresh samples.

Given the difficult circumstances, work on human chromosome number remained sketchy; guesses ranged from sixteen to fifty-some. And despite the constant counts in other species, some European scientists beholden to racial theories proclaimed that Asian, black, and white people clearly had different numbers of chromosomes. (No points for guessing who they thought had most.) A Texas biologist named Theophilus Painter—who later discovered the gigantic salivary chromosomes in fruit flies—finally killed the theory of varying chromosome number with a definitive study in 1923. (Rather than depend on the criminal-justice system for raw material, Painter counted his blessings that a former student worked at a lunatic asylum and had access to freshly castrated inmates.) But even Painter's best slides showed human cells with either forty-six or forty-eight chromosomes, and after going round and round and counting and recounting them from every which angle, Painter still couldn't decide. Perhaps worried his paper would be rejected if he didn't at least pretend to know, Painter acknowledged the confusion, took a breath, and guessed—wrongly. He said that humans have forty-eight, and that became the standard figure.

After three decades and the invention of far better microscopes (not to mention an easing of restrictions on human tissues), scientists had rectified the boner, and by 1955 they knew that humans had forty-six chromosomes. But as so often happens, deposing one mystery just inaugurated another, because now scientists had to figure out how humans ended up two chromosomes down anyway.

Surprisingly, they determined that the process started with something like a Philadelphia swap. Around a million years ago, in some fateful man or woman, what were the twelfth and thirteenth human chromosomes (and still are the twelfth and thirteenth chromosomes in many primates) entwined their arms at the very tip, to try and swap material. But instead of separating cleanly, twelve and thirteen got stuck. They fused together at their ends, like one belt buckled onto another. This amalgam eventually became human chromosome number two.

Fusions like this are actually not uncommon—they occur once every thousand births—and most tip-to-tip fusions go unnoticed because they don't upset anyone's health. (The ends of chromosomes often contain no genes, so nothing gets disrupted.) However, notice that a fusion by itself can't explain the drop from forty-eight to forty-six. A fusion leaves a person with forty-seven chromosomes, not forty-six, and the odds of two identical fusions in the same cell are pretty remote. And even after the drop to forty-seven, the person still has to pass his genes on, a serious barrier.

Scientists did eventually puzzle out what must have happened. Let's go back a million years, when most protohumans had forty-eight chromosomes, and follow a hypothetical Guy, who has forty-seven. Again, a chromosome fused at the tips won't affect Guy's day-to-day health. But having an odd number of chromosomes will cripple the viability of his sperm, for a simple reason. (If you prefer to think of a female, the same arguments apply to her eggs.) Say the fusion left Guy with one normal chromosome 12, one normal 13, and a 12-13 hybrid. During sperm production, his body has to divide those three chromosomes into two cells at one point, and if you do the math, there are only a few possible ways to divvy them up. There's {12} and {13, 12-13}, or {13} and {12, 12-13}, or {12, 13} and {12-13}. The first four sperm either are missing a chromosome or have a duplicate, practically a cyanide capsule for an embryo. The last two cases have the proper amount of DNA for a normal child. But only in the sixth case does Guy pass the fusion on. Overall, then, because of the odd number, two-thirds of Guy's children die in the womb, and just one-sixth inherit the fusion. But any Junior with the fusion would then face the same terrible odds trying to reproduce. Not a good recipe for spreading the fusion—and again, that's still only forty-seven chromosomes, not forty-six.

What Guy needs is a Doll with the same two fused chromosomes. Now, the odds of two people with the same fusion meeting and having children might seem infinitesimal. And they would be—except in inbred families. Relatives share enough genes that, given one person with a fusion, the chances of finding a cousin or half sibling with the same fusion don't round down to zero so easily. What's more, while the odds of Guy and Doll having a healthy child remain low, every thirty-sixth spin of the genetic roulette wheel (because $1/6 \times 1/6 = 1/36$), the child would inherit *both* fused chromosomes, giving him forty-six total. And here's the payoff: Junior and his forty-six chromosomes would have a much easier time having children. Remember that the fusion itself doesn't disable or ruin a chromosome's

DNA; lots of healthy people worldwide have fusions. It's only reproduction that gets tricky, since fusions can lead to an excess or deficit of DNA in embryos. But because he has an even number of chromosomes, little Junior wouldn't have any unbalanced sperm cells: each would have exactly the right amount of DNA to run a human, just packaged differently. As a result, all his children would be healthy. And if his children start having their own children—especially with other relatives who have forty-six or forty-seven chromosomes—the fusion could start to spread.

Scientists know this scenario isn't just hypothetical, either. In 2010 a doctor in rural China discovered a family with a history of consanguineous (similar-blood) marriages. And among the various overlapping branches of the family tree, he discovered a male who had forty-four chromosomes. In this family's case, the fourteenth and fifteenth chromosomes had fused, and consistent with the example of Guy and Doll, they had a brutal record of miscarriages and spontaneous abortions in their past. But from that wreckage, a perfectly healthy man with two fewer chromosomes emerged—the first known stable reduction since our ancestors started down the path to forty-six chromosomes a million years ago.*

In one sense, then, Theophilus Painter was right: for most of our primate history, the human line did have the same number of chromosomes as many primates. And until that transition, the hybrids that Ivanov coveted were far more possible. Having a different number of chromosomes won't always prevent breeding; horses have sixty-four chromosomes, and donkeys sixty-two. But again, molecular gears and cogs don't turn nearly as smoothly when chromosomes don't correspond. Indeed, it's telling that Painter published his study in 1923, just before Ivanov started his experiments. Had Painter guessed forty-six instead of forty-eight, that might have been a serious blow to Ivanov's hopes.

And perhaps not just Ivanov's. The issue remains disputed,

and most historians dismiss the story as legend, if not outright legerdemain. But according to documents that a Russian historian of science unearthed in Soviet archives, Joseph Stalin himself approved the funding for Ivanov's work. This is strange, since Stalin abhorred genetics: he later allowed his scientific hatchet man Trofim Lysenko to outlaw Mendelian genetics in the Soviet Union, and, poisoned by Lysenko's influence, angrily rejected Hermann Muller's eugenics program to breed better Soviet citizens. (Muller fled in response, and colleagues he left behind were shot as "enemies of the people.") And that discrepancy—supporting Ivanov's indecent proposals, yet rejecting Muller's so vehemently—has led a few Russian historians to suggest (and here's the dubious bit) that Stalin dreamed of using Ivanov's humanzees as slaves. The legend really took off in 2005 when, through a series of convoluted attributions, the *Scotsman* newspaper in Great Britain quoted unnamed Moscow newspapers quoting still more recovered documents that themselves supposedly quoted Stalin as saying: "I want a new invincible human being, insensitive to pain, resistant and indifferent about the quality of food they eat." On the same day, the *Sun* tabloid also quoted Stalin as saying he thought it best if humanzees have "immense strength but...an underdeveloped brain," presumably so they wouldn't revolt or be miserable enough to kill themselves. Apparently Stalin coveted the beasts to build his Trans-Siberian Railway through Gulag-land, one of history's all-time biggest boondoggles, but his primary goal was repopulating the Red Army, which in World War I (as in most Russian wars) had suffered massive losses.

It's a fact that Stalin approved funding for Ivanov. But not much, and he approved funding for hundreds of other scientists as well. And I've seen no firm evidence—or any evidence, really—that Stalin lusted after a humanzee army. (Nor that he planned, as some suggest, to seek immortality by harvesting humanzee glands

and transplanting them into himself and other top Kremlin officials.) Still, I have to admit it's a hell of a lot of fun to speculate
about this. If Stalin did take a creepy interest in Ivanov's work,
that might explain why Ivanov got funding just as Stalin consolidated his power and decided to rebuild the military. Or why Ivanov established the primate station in Georgia, Stalin's
homeland. Or why the secret police arrested Ivanov after his
failures, and why Ivanov couldn't pay surrogate mothers but had
to find volunteers who would reproduce for the love of Mother
Russia—because after nursing, they would turn their "sons"
and "daughters" over to Papa Stalin anyway. The international
counterfactuals are even more fascinating. Would Stalin have
sent monkey battalions over the North Pole, to invade North
America? Would Hitler still have signed the nonaggression pact
if he'd known Stalin was polluting the Caucasian race like this?

Still, assuming Ivanov could even create humanzees, Papa's
purported military plans would probably have come to naught.
If nothing else—and I'm ignoring the difficulty of training half
chimps to drive tanks or shoot Kalashnikovs—the Soviet Union's
climate alone would probably have annihilated them. Ivanov's
primates suffered from being too far north on the palm-treed
coast of Georgia, so it seems doubtful that even a hybrid would
have survived Siberia or months of trench warfare.*

What Stalin really needed weren't humanzees but
Neanderthals—big, bad, hairy hominids adapted to icy weather.
But of course Neanderthals had gone extinct tens of thousands
of years before, for reasons that remain blurry. Some scientists
once believed that we actively drove Neanderthals into extinction through war or genocide. That theory has fallen out of
favor, and theories about competition over food or climate
change have come to the fore. But in all likelihood, there was
nothing inevitable about our survival and their death. In fact,
for much of our evolution, we humans were probably as dainty

and vulnerable as Ivanov's primates: cold snaps, habitat loss, and natural disasters seem to have crashed our population numbers time and again. And far from this being distant history, we're still dealing with the repercussions. Notice that we've once again explained one mystery of human DNA—how an inbred family might drop two chromosomes—only to raise another—how that new DNA became standard in all humans. It's possible that the ancient twelve-thirteen fusion created fancy new genes, giving the family survival advantages. But probably not. A more plausible explanation is that we suffered a genetic bottleneck—that something wiped out everyone on earth except a few tribes, and that whatever genes those dumb-lucky survivors had spread far and wide. Some species get caught in bottlenecks and never escape—behold Neanderthals. As the scars in our DNA attest, we human beings scraped through some pretty narrow bottlenecks ourselves, and might easily have joined our thick-browed brethren in Darwin's dustbin.

PART III

Genes and Geniuses

How Humans Became All Too Human

10

Scarlet A's, C's, G's, and T's

Why Did Humans Almost Go Extinct?

C risp mice in golden batter. Panther chops. Rhino pie. Trunk of elephant. Crocodile for breakfast. Sliced porpoise head. Horse's tongue. Kangaroo ham.

Yes, domestic life was a trifle off at William Buckland's. Some of his Oxford houseguests best remembered the front hallway, lined like a catacomb with the grinning skulls of fossilized monsters. Others remembered the live monkeys swinging around, or the pet bear dressed in a mortarboard cap and academic robes, or the guinea pig nibbling on people's toes beneath the dinner table (at least until the family hyena crushed it one afternoon). Fellow naturalists from the 1800s remembered Buckland's bawdy lectures on reptile sex (though not always fondly; the young Charles Darwin thought him a buffoon, and the *London Times* sniffed that Buckland needed to watch himself "in the presence of ladies"). And no Oxonian ever forgot the performance art stunt he pulled one spring when he wrote "G-U-A-N-O" on the lawn with bat feces, to advertise it as fertilizer. The word did indeed blaze green all summer.

But most people remembered William Buckland for his diet.

William Buckland ate his way through most of the animal
kingdom. (Antoine Claudet)

A biblical geologist, Buckland held the story of Noah's ark dear,
and he ate his way through most of Noah's litter, a habit he called
"zoophagy." Any flesh or fluid from any beast was eligible for
ingestion, be it blood, skin, gristle, or worse. While touring a
church once, Buckland startled a local vicar—who was showing
off the miraculous "martyr's blood" that dripped from the raf-
ters every night—by dropping to the stone floor and dabbing
the stain with his tongue. Between laps Buckland announced,
"It's bat urine." Overall Buckland found few animals he couldn't
stomach: "The taste of mole was the most repulsive I knew," he
once mused. "Until I tasted a bluebottle [fly]."*

Buckland may have hit upon zoophagy while collecting fossils in some remote pocket of Europe with limited dining options.

It may have been a harebrained scheme to get inside the minds of the extinct animals whose bones he dug up. Mostly, though, he just liked barbecuing, and he kept up his hyper-carnivorous activities well into old age. But in one sense, the most amazing thing about Buckland's diet wasn't the variety. It was that Buckland's intestines, arteries, and heart could digest so much flesh, period, and not harden over the decades into a nineteenth-century Body Worlds exhibit. Our primate cousins could never survive the same diet, not even close.

Monkeys and apes have molars and stomachs adapted to pulping plant matter, and eat mostly vegan diets in the wild. A few primates, like chimpanzees, do eat a few ounces of termites or other animals each day on average, and boy do they love tucking into small, defenseless mammals now and then. But for most monkeys and apes, a high-fat, high-cholesterol diet trashes their insides, and they deteriorate at sickening speeds compared to modern humans. Captive primates with regular access to meat (and dairy) often end up wheezing around inside their cages, their cholesterol pushing 300 and their arteries paved with lard. Our protohuman ancestors certainly also ate meat: they left too many stone cleavers lying next to piles of megamammal bones for it all to be coincidence. But for eons early humans probably suffered no less than monkeys for their love of flesh — Paleolithic Elvises wandering the savanna.

So what changed between then and now, between Grunk in ancient Africa and William Buckland at Oxford? Our DNA. Twice since we split off from chimps, the human *apoE* gene has mutated, giving us distinct versions. Overall it's the strongest candidate around (though not the only candidate) for a human "meat-eating gene." The first mutation boosted the performance of killer blood cells that attack microbes, like the deadly microbes lingering in mouthfuls of raw flesh. It also protected against chronic inflammation, the collateral tissue damage that occurs when microbial infections never quite clear up. Unfortunately this *apoE* probably mortgaged our long-term health for short-term gain: we could eat more meat, but it left our arteries looking like the insides of Crisco cans. Lucky for us, a second mutation appeared 220,000 years ago, which helped break nasty fats and cholesterol down and spared us from premature decrepitude. What's more, by sweeping dietary toxins from the body, it kept cells fitter and made bones denser and tougher to break in middle age, further insurance against early death. So even though early humans ate a veritable Roman-orgy diet compared to their fruitarian cousins, *apoE* and other genes helped them live twice as long.

Before we congratulate ourselves, though, about getting our hands on better *apoE*s than monkeys, a few points. For starters, bones with hack marks and other archaeological evidence indicate that we started dining on meat eons before the cholesterol-fighting *apoE* appeared, at least 2.5 million years ago. So for millions of years we were either too dim to link eating meat and early retirement, too pathetic to get enough calories without meat, or too brutishly indulgent to stop sucking down food we knew would kill us. Even less flattering is what the germicidal properties of the earlier *apoE* mutation imply. Archaeologists have found sharpened wooden spears from 400,000 years ago, so some caveman studs were bringing home bacon by then. But what about before that? The lack of proper weapons, and the fact that *apoE* combats microbes—which thrive in shall we say less-than-fresh cuts of carrion—hint that protohumans scavenged carcasses and ate putrid leftovers. At best, we waited for other animals to fell game, then scared them off and stole it, hardly a gallant enterprise. (At least we're in good company here. Scientists have been having the same debate for some time about *Tyrannosaurus rex*: Cretaceous alpha-killer, or loathsome poacher?)

Once again DNA humbles and muddies our view of ourselves. And *apoE* is just one of many cases where DNA research has transformed our knowledge of our ancient selves: filling in forgotten details in some narratives, overthrowing long-held beliefs in others, but always, always revealing how fraught hominid history has been.

To appreciate how much DNA can supplement, annotate, or plain rewrite ancient history, it helps to look back to the days when scholars first started digging up human remains and studying them — the beginnings of archaeology and paleontology. These scientists started off with confidence about human origins, were thrown into confusion by unsettling finds, and only recently flowed back toward (if not all the way to) clarity, thanks largely to genetics.

Except in unnatural cases, like Dutch sailors massacring dodos, virtually no scientist before 1800 believed that species went extinct. They had been created as is, and that was that. But a French naturalist named Jean-Léopold-Nicolas-Frédéric Cuvier upended this notion in 1796. Cuvier was a formidable man, half Darwin, half Machiavelli. He later latched onto Napoleon and rode the little dictator's blue coattails to the pinnacle of European scientific power; by life's end, he was Baron Cuvier. But along the way the baron proved himself one of the great naturalists ever (his power wasn't undeserved), and he built an authoritative case that species could in fact vanish. The first clue came when he recognized that an ancient pachyderm, unearthed in a quarry near Paris, had no living descendants. Even more spectacularly, Cuvier disproved old legends about the so-called *Homo diluvii testis* skeleton. These bones, unearthed years before in Europe, resembled a deformed man with stunted limbs. Folklore had identified "him" as one of the lecherous and corrupted folk that God had expunged with Noah's flood. The less credulous

Cuvier correctly identified the skeleton as, of all things, a titanic salamander that had long ago disappeared from the earth.

Still, not everyone believed Cuvier about the impermanence of species. The keen amateur naturalist (and U.S. president) Thomas Jefferson instructed Lewis and Clark to keep their eyes peeled inside the Louisiana Territory for giant sloths and mastodons. Fossils of both creatures had previously turned up in North America, drawing huge crowds to dig sites. (Charles Willson Peale's painting *The Exhumation of the Mastodon* captures the scene elegantly.) Jefferson wanted to track down living examples of these beasts for patriotic reasons: he was fed up with

The Exhumation of the Mastodon, by Charles Willson Peale, showing the discovery of mastodon bones in New York in 1801. U.S. president Thomas Jefferson argued that mastodons must still be lumbering across North America, and ordered Lewis and Clark to keep their eyes peeled. (MA5911, courtesy of the Maryland Historical Society)

European naturalists who, without ever coming within an ocean of America, dismissed the fauna here as sickly, weak, and stunted, a snobby theory called "American degeneracy." Jefferson wanted to prove American wildlife was as big and hairy and virile as European beasts, and underlying his hope that mastodons and giant sloths still roamed (or inched across) the Great Plains was the belief that species cannot go extinct.

Although William Buckland came down more with the sober extinctionists than the excitable nonextinctionists, he contributed to the debate in his characteristically flamboyant way. For his honeymoon, Buckland dragged his wife specimen hunting across Europe; and even while hiking to remote outcroppings and pickaxing rocks for fossils, he insisted on wearing black academic robes and often a top hat. In addition to bones, Buckland grew obsessed with fossilized hunks of animal shit, called coprolites, which he generously donated to museums. But Buckland made discoveries exciting enough to be forgiven his eccentricities. In one case he excavated an ancient underground predators' lair in Yorkshire, with plenty of snarly teeth and gnawed-on skulls to wow the public. But the work had great scientific merit and bolstered the extinctionist case: the predators were cave hyenas, and since those hyenas no longer lived in England, they must have gone extinct. More profoundly—and fitting, given his proclivity for meat—Buckland identified some vast bones exhumed from an English quarry as a new species of giant reptile, the first example of the most terrifying carnivores ever, dinosaurs. He named it *Megalosaurus.**

However confident he was with extinct animals, Buckland wavered, even equivocated, on the more loaded question of whether ancient human lineages ever existed. Although an ordained minister, Buckland didn't believe in the aleph-by-aleph accuracy of the Old Testament. He speculated that geological eras had existed before "In the Beginning," eras populated with the likes of *Megalosaurus*. Nevertheless, like virtually all scientists, Buckland hesitated to contradict Genesis regarding human origins and our special, recent creation. In 1823, when Buckland unearthed the alluring Red Lady of Paviland—a skeleton covered with seashell jewelry and dusted with red ocher makeup—he ignored plenty of contextual evidence and identified her as a witch or prostitute from no earlier than Roman times. The lady was actually thirty thousand years old (and a man). Buckland also dismissed clear evidence at another site of chipped-flint tools appearing in the same soil layer as pre-Genesis beasts like mammoths and saber-toothed tigers.

Even less forgivable, Buckland pretty much dropped a steaming coprolite on one of the most spectacular archaeological discoveries ever. In 1829 Philippe-Charles Schmerling unearthed, among some ancient animal remains, a few uncanny, human-but-not-quite-human bones in Belgium. Basing his conclusions especially on skull fragments from a child, he suggested they belonged to an extinct hominid species. Buckland examined the bones in 1835 at a scientific meeting but never removed his biblical blinders. He rejected Schmerling's theory and, instead of saying so quietly, proceeded to humiliate him. Buckland often claimed that because of various chemical changes, fossilized bones naturally stick to the tongue, whereas fresher bones don't. During a lecture at the meeting, Buckland placed onto his tongue one of the animal bones (a bear's) that Schmerling had found mixed in with the hominid remains. The bear bone stuck fast, and Buckland continued to lecture, the bone flopping about hilariously. He then challenged Schmerling to stick his "extinct human" bones to his own tongue. They fell off. Ergo they weren't ancient.

Though hardly definitive proof, the dismissal lingered in the minds of paleontologists. So when more uncanny skulls turned up in Gibraltar in 1848, prudent scientists ignored them. Eight years later—and just months after the death of Buckland, the last great Deluge scientist—miners worked loose still more of the odd bones from a limestone quarry in Germany's Neander Valley. One scholar, channeling Buckland, identified them as belonging to a deformed Cossack who had been injured by Napoleon's army and crawled into a cliff-side cave to die. But this time two other scientists reasserted that the remains belonged to a distinct line of hominids, a race more outcast than the biblical Ishmaelites. Perhaps it helped that, among the various bones, the duo had located an adult skullcap down to the eye sockets, which emphasized the thick, glowering brow we still associate with Neanderthals.*

With their eyes opened—and with the publication in 1859 of a little book by Charles Darwin—paleontologists began to find Neanderthals and related hominids across Africa, the Middle East, and Europe. The existence of ancient humans became a scientific fact. But just as predictably, the new evidence provoked new confusion. Skeletons can shift in the ground as rock formations buckle, fouling up attempts to date or interpret them. Bones also scatter and get crushed into smithereens, forcing scientists to rebuild entire creatures from a few stray molars or metatarsals—a subjective process open to dissension and differing interpretations. There's no guarantee either that scientists will find representative samples: if scientists in AD 1,000,000 discovered what remains of Wilt Chamberlain, Tom Thumb, and Joseph Merrick, would they even classify them as the same species? For these reasons, every new discovery of *Homo* this and *Homo* that in the 1800s and 1900s incited further and often nasty debate. And decade after decade passed without the ultimate questions (Were all archaic humanoids our ancestors? If not, how many twigs of humanity existed?) becoming clearer. As the old joke went, put twenty paleontologists into a room, and you'd get twenty-one different schemes for human evolution. One world expert in archaic human genetics, Svante Pääbo, has noted, "I'm often rather surprised about how much scientists fight in paleontology....I suppose the reason is that paleontology is a rather data-poor science. There are probably more paleontologists than there are important fossils in the world."

Such was the general state of things when genetics invaded paleontology and archaeology beginning in the 1960s—and *invaded* is the apt word. Despite their quarrels, U-turns, and antiquated tools, paleontologists and archaeologists had figured out a lot about human origins. They didn't need a savior, thanks. So many of them resented the intrusion of biologists with their DNA clocks and molecular-based family trees, hotshots intent on overturning decades of research with a single paper. (One anthropologist scoffed at the strictly molecular approach as "no muss, no fuss, no dishpan hands. Just throw some proteins into a laboratory apparatus, shake them up, and bingo!—we have an answer to questions that have puzzled us for three generations.") And really, the older scientists' skepticism was warranted: paleogenetics turned out to be beastly hard, and despite their promising ideas, paleogeneticists had to spend years proving their worth.

One problem with paleogenetics is that DNA is thermodynamically unstable. Over time, C chemically degrades into T, and G degrades into A, so paleogeneticists can't always believe what they read in ancient samples. What's more, even in the coldest climates, DNA breaks down into gibberish after 100,000 years; samples older than that harbor virtually no intact DNA. Even in relatively fresh samples, scientists might find themselves piecing together a billion-base-pair genome from fragments just fifty letters long—proportionally equivalent to reconstructing your typical hardcover from strokes, loops, serifs, and other fragments smaller than the tittle on an *i*.

Oh, and most of those fragments are junk. No matter where a corpse falls—the coldest polar ice cap, the driest Saharan dune—bacteria and fungi will worm inside and smear their own DNA around. Some ancient bones contain more than 99 percent foreign DNA, all of which must be laboriously extracted. And that's the easy kind of contamination to deal with. DNA spreads so easily from human contact (even touching or breathing on a sample can pollute it), and ancient hominid DNA so closely mirrors our own, that ruling out human contamination in samples is almost impossible.

These obstacles (plus a few embarrassing retractions over the years) have pushed paleogeneticists into near paranoia about contamination, and they demand controls and safeguards that seem a better fit for a biological warfare lab. Paleogeneticists prefer samples no human has ever handled—ideally, ones still dirty from remote dig sites, where workers use surgical masks and gloves and drop everything into sterile bags. Hair is the best material, since it absorbs fewer contaminants and can be bleached clean, but paleogeneticists will settle for less fragile bone. (And given the paucity of uncontaminated sites, they often settle for bones in museum storage lockers, especially bones so boring no one ever bothered studying them before.)

The sample selected, scientists bring it into a "clean room" maintained at higher-than-normal air pressure, so that air currents—and more to the point, the floating scraps of DNA that can ride around on air currents—cannot flow inward when the door opens. Anyone allowed inside the room dresses toe to top in sterile scrubs with face masks and booties and two pairs of gloves, and they get pretty used to the odor of the bleach swabbed over most surfaces. (One lab bragged that its technicians, presumably while in their suits, are given sponge baths in bleach.) If the sample is bone, scientists use dentist drills or picks to shave off a few grams of powder. They might even doctor the drill so it rotates only at 100 rpm, since the heat of a standard, 1,000-rpm drill can fry DNA. They then dissolve the nib of powder with chemicals, which liberates the DNA. At this point paleogeneticists often add tags—snippets of artificial DNA—to every fragment. That way they can tell if extraneous DNA, which lacks the tag,* ever infiltrates the sample after it leaves the clean room. Scientists might also note the racial backgrounds of technicians and other scientists (and probably even janitors) at the lab, so that if unexpected ethnic sequences show up, they can judge whether their sample was compromised.

After all this preparation, the actual DNA sequencing begins. We'll talk about this process in detail later, but basically scientists determine the A-C-G-T sequence of each individual DNA fragment, then use sophisticated software to piece the many, many fragments together. Paleogeneticists have successfully applied this technique to stuffed quaggas, cave bear skulls, woolly mammoth tufts, bees in amber, mummy skin, even Buckland's beloved coprolites. But the most spectacular work along these lines comes from Neanderthal DNA. After the discovery of Neanderthals, many scientists classified them as archaic humans—the first (before the metaphor became tired) missing link. Others put Neanderthals on their own terminal branch of evolution, while some European scientists considered Neanderthals the ancestors of some human races but not others. (Again, *sigh*, you can guess which races they singled out, Africans and Aborigines.) Regardless of the exact taxonomy, scientists considered Neanderthals thick-witted and lowbrow, and it didn't surprise anyone that they'd died out. Eventually some dissenters began arguing that Neanderthals showed more smarts than they got credit for: they used stone tools, mastered fire, buried their dead (sometimes with wildflowers), cared for the weak and lame, and possibly wore jewelry and played bone flutes. But the scientists couldn't prove that Neanderthals hadn't watched humans do these things first and aped them, which hardly takes supreme intelligence.

DNA, though, permanently changed our view of Neanderthals. As early as 1987, mitochondrial DNA showed that Neanderthals weren't direct human ancestors. At the same time, when the complete Neanderthal genome appeared in 2010, it turned out that the butt of so many *Far Side* cartoons was pretty darn human anyway; we share well north of 99 percent of our genome with them. In some cases this overlap was homely: Neanderthals likely had reddish hair and pale skin; they had the most common blood type worldwide, O; and like most humans, they couldn't digest milk as adults. Other findings were more profound. Neanderthals had similar MHC immunity genes, and also shared a gene, *foxp2*, associated with language skills, which means they may have been articulate.

It's not clear yet whether Neanderthals had alternative versions of *apoE*, but they got more of their protein from flesh than we did and so probably had some genetic adaptations to metabolize cholesterol and fight infections. Indeed, archaeological evidence suggests that Neanderthals didn't hesitate to eat even their own dead—perhaps as part of primitive shamanic rituals, perhaps for darker reasons. At a cave in northern Spain, scientists have discovered the fifty-thousand-year-old remains of twelve murdered Neanderthal adults and children, many of them related. After the deed, their probably starving assailants butchered them with stone tools and cracked their bones to suck the marrow, cannibalizing every edible ounce. A gruesome scene, but it was from this surfeit of 1,700 bones that scientists extracted much of their early knowledge of Neanderthal DNA.

Like it or not, similar evidence exists for human cannibalism. Each hundred-pound adult, after all, could provide starving comrades with forty pounds of precious muscle protein, plus edible fat, gristle, liver, and blood. More uncomfortably, archaeological evidence has long suggested that humans tucked into each other even when not famished. But for years questions persisted about whether most nonstarvation cannibalism was religiously motivated and selective or culinary and routine. DNA suggests routine. Every known ethnic group worldwide has one of two genetic signatures that help our bodies fight off certain diseases that cannibals catch, especially mad-cow-like diseases that come from eating each other's brains. This defensive DNA almost certainly wouldn't have become fixed worldwide if it hadn't once been all too necessary.

As the cannibalism DNA shows, scientists don't rely entirely on ancient artifacts for information about our past. Modern human DNA holds clues as well. And about the first thing scientists noticed when they began surveying modern human DNA is its lack of variety. Roughly 150,000 chimps and around the same number of gorillas are living today, compared to some seven billion humans. Yet humans have less genetic diversity than these monkeys, significantly less. This suggests that the worldwide population of humans has dipped far below the population of chimps and gorillas recently, perhaps multiple times. Had the Endangered Species Act existed way back when, *Homo sapiens* might have been the Paleolithic equivalent of pandas and condors.

Scientists disagree on why our population decreased so much, but the origins of the debate trace back to two different theories— or really, two different weltanschauungs—first articulated in William Buckland's day. Virtually every scientist before then upheld a catastrophist view of history—that floods, earthquakes, and other cataclysms had sculpted the planet quickly, throwing up mountains over a long weekend and wiping out species overnight. A younger generation—especially Buckland's student Charles Lyell, a geologist—pushed gradualism, the idea that winds, tides, erosion, and other gentle forces shaped the earth and its inhabitants achingly slowly. For various reasons (including some posthumous smear campaigns), gradualism became associated with proper science, catastrophism with lazy reasoning and theatrical biblical miracles, and by the early 1900s catastrophism itself had been (and this puts it mildly) annihilated in science. Eventually the pendulum swung back, and catastrophism became respectable again after 1979, when geologists discovered that a city-sized asteroid or comet helped eradicate the dinosaurs. Since then, scientists have accepted that they can uphold a proper gradualist view for most of history and still allow that some pretty apocalyptic events have taken place. But this acceptance makes it all the more curious that one ancient calamity, the first traces of which were discovered within a year of the dino impact, has received far less attention. Especially considering that some scientists argue that the Toba supervolcano almost eliminated a species far more dear to us than dinosaurs: *Homo sapiens.*

Getting a grasp on Toba takes some imagination. Toba is— or was, before the top 650 cubic miles blew off—a mountain in Indonesia that erupted seventy-odd thousand years ago. But because no witnesses survived, we can best appreciate its terror by comparing it (however faintly) to the second-largest known eruption in that archipelago, the Tambora eruption of 1815.

In early April 1815, three pillars of fire straight out of Exodus blasted out of Tambora's top. Tens of thousands died as psychedelic orange lava surfed down the mountainside, and a tsunami five feet high and traveling at 150 miles per hour battered nearby islands. People fifteen hundred miles away (roughly from New York to mid–South Dakota) heard the initial blast, and the world went black for hundreds of miles around as a smoke plume climbed ten miles into the sky. That smoke carried with it enormous amounts of sulfurous chemicals. At first, these aerosols seemed harmless, even pleasant: in England, they intensified the pinks, oranges, and bloody reds of the sunsets that summer, a celestial drama that probably influenced the land- and sunscapes of painter J. M. W. Turner. Later effects were less cute. By 1816—popularly known as The Year Without a Summer—the sulfurous ejecta had mixed homogeneously into the upper atmosphere and began reflecting sunlight back into space. This loss of heat caused freak July and August snowstorms in the fledgling United States, and crops failed widely (including Thomas Jefferson's corn at Monticello). In Europe Lord Byron wrote a dire poem in July 1816 called "Darkness," which opens, "I had a dream, which was not all a dream. / The bright sun was extinguish'd ... / Morn came and went—and came, and brought no day, / And men ... / Were chill'd into a selfish prayer for light." A few writers happened to holiday with Byron that summer near Lake Geneva, but they found the days so dreary that they mostly sulked indoors. Channeling their mood, some took to telling ghost stories for entertainment—one of which, by young Mary Shelley, became *Frankenstein*.

Now, with all that in mind about Tambora, consider that Toba spewed for five times longer and ejected a dozen times more material—millions of tons of vaporized rock per second* at its peak. And being so much bigger, Toba's enormous black basilisk of a plume could do proportionately more damage. Because of prevailing winds, most of the plume drifted westward. And some scientists think that a DNA bottleneck began when the smoke, after sweeping across south Asia, scythed into the very grasslands in Africa where humans lived. According to this theory, the destruction happened in two phases. In the short term, Toba dimmed the sun for six years, disrupted seasonal rains, choked off streams, and scattered whole cubic miles of hot ash (imagine wading through a giant ashtray) across acres and acres of plants, a major food source. It's not hard to imagine the human population plummeting. Other primates might have suffered less at first because humans camped on the eastern edge of Africa, in Toba's path, whereas most primates lived inland, sheltered somewhat behind mountains. But even if Toba spared other animals initially, no one escaped the second phase. Earth was already mired in an Ice Age in 70,000 BC, and the persistent reflection of sunlight into space might well have exacerbated it. We have evidence that the average temperature dropped twenty-plus degrees in some spots, after which the African savannas— our ancient homes—probably contracted like puddles in August heat. Overall, then, the Toba-bottleneck theory argues that the initial eruption led to widespread starvation, but the deepening Ice Age is what really pinned the human population down.

Macaque, orangutan, tiger, gorilla, and chimpanzee DNA also show some signs of bottlenecking right around Toba, but humans really suffered. One study suggested that the human population, worldwide, might have dropped to forty adults. (The world record for fitting people in a phone booth is twenty-five.) That's an outlandishly pessimistic guess even among disaster scientists, but it's common to find estimates of a few thousand adults, below what some minor-league baseball teams draw. Given that these humans might not have been united in one place either, but scattered in small, isolated pockets around Africa, things look even shakier for our future. If the Toba-bottleneck theory is true, then the lack of diversity in human DNA has a simple explanation. We damn near went extinct.

Not surprisingly—more infighting—many archaeologists find that explanation for low genetic diversity way too pat, and the theory remains contentious. It's not the existence of a bottleneck per se that rankles. It's well established that the protohuman breeding population (roughly equivalent to the number of fertile adults) dropped alarmingly at times in the past million years. (Which, among other things, probably allowed a freakish trait like forty-six chromosomes to spread.) And many scientists see strong evidence in our DNA for at least one major bottleneck after anatomically modern humans arose 200,000 years ago.

What rankles scientists is linking any bottleneck to Toba; suspicion of the old, bad catastrophism looms.

Some geologists contest that Toba wasn't as powerful as their colleagues claim. Others doubt Toba could have decimated populations thousands of miles away, or that one puny mountain could throw up enough sulfurous spume to intensify a global ice age. Some archaeologists have also found evidence (disputed, inevitably) of stone tools right above and below some six-inch-thick Toba ash layers, which implies not extinction but continuity right where Toba should have done the most damage. We have genetic reasons to question a Toba bottleneck as well. Most important, geneticists simply cannot distinguish, retroactively, between the lack of diversity induced by a short but severe bottleneck and the lack of diversity induced by a longer but milder bottleneck. In other words, there's ambiguity: if Toba did crush us down to a few dozen adults, we'd see certain patterns in our DNA; but if a population was held down to a few thousand, as long as it was held down consistently, those people's DNA would show *the same* signatures after maybe a thousand years. And the wider the time frame, the less likely Toba had anything to do with the bottleneck.

William Buckland and others would have recognized this debate instantly: whether small but persistent pressures could have held our clever species down for so long, or whether it took a cataclysm. But it's a measure of progress that, unlike the rout of catastrophism in Buckland's day and the century of scorn that followed, modern scientific catastrophists can make their case heard. And who knows? The Toba supervolcano may yet join the dinosaur-killing space rock as one of the world's premier disasters.

So what does all this DNA archaeology add up to? As the field has come into its own, scientists have pulled together an overarching summary of how modern humans emerged and spread across the globe.

Perhaps most important, DNA confirmed our African origins. A few archaeological holdouts had always maintained that humankind arose in India or Asia, but a species generally shows the highest genetic diversity near its origin, where it's had the longest time to develop. That's exactly what scientists see in Africa. As one example, African peoples have twenty-two versions of a particular stretch of DNA linked to the all-important insulin gene—only three of which, total, appear in the rest of the world. For ages anthropologists lumped all African peoples into one "race," but the genetic truth is that the larger world's diversity is more or less a subset of African diversity.

DNA can also embellish the story of human origins with details about how we behaved long ago and even what we looked like. Around 220,000 years ago, the *apoE* meat-eating gene emerged and began to spread, introducing the possibility of productive old age. Just twenty thousand years later, another mutation allowed the hair on our heads to (unlike monkey hair or body hair) grow indefinitely long—a "haircut gene." Then, thirty thousand years later, we began wearing skins as clothes, a fact scientists determined by comparing the DNA clocks of head lice (which live only on scalps) and of related but distinct body lice (which live only in clothes) and figuring out when they diverged. In ways large and small, these changes transformed societies.

Suitably attired and perfectly coiffed, humans seem to have started making inroads from Africa into the Middle East maybe 130,000 years ago (our first imperial impulse). But something— cold weather, homesickness, predators, a Neanderthal NO TRESPASSING sign—halted their sprawl and drove them back to Africa. The human population bottlenecked over the next few tens of thousands of years, perhaps because of Toba. Regardless, humans scraped through and eventually recovered. But this time, instead of cowering and waiting for the next extinction threat, small clans of humans, as few as a few thousand people total, began establishing settlements beyond Africa, in waves beginning about sixty thousand years ago. These clans probably crossed the Red Sea at low tide, Moses style, through a southern point called Bab el Mandeb, the Gate of Grief. Because bottlenecks had isolated these clans for millennia, they'd developed unique genetic traits. So as they spread into new lands and their population doubled and redoubled, these traits blossomed into the unique features of European and Asian populations today. (In a touch Buckland would have appreciated, this multipronged dispersal from Africa is sometimes called the Weak Garden of Eden theory. But this tale is actually better than the biblical version; we didn't lose Eden but learned to make other Edens across the world.)

As we expanded beyond Africa, DNA kept a marvelous travelogue. In Asia, genetic analysis has revealed two distinct waves of human colonization: an earlier wave sixty-five thousand years ago that skirted India and led to the settlement of Australia, making the Aborigines the first real explorers in history; and a later wave that produced modern Asians and led to humanity's first population boom, forty thousand years ago, when 60 percent of humankind lived on the Indian, Malay, and Thai peninsulas. In North America, a survey of different genetic pools suggests that the first Americans paused for perhaps ten thousand years on the Bering land bridge between Siberia and Alaska, as if trembling to break away from Asia and enter the New World. In South America, scientists have discovered MHC genes from Amerindians in native Easter Islanders, and the thorough blending of those genes in the islanders' otherwise Asian chromosomes indicates that someone was making *Kon-Tiki*–like sea voyages back and forth to the Americas in the early 1000s, back when Columbus was mere specks of DNA spread among his great-great-great-(...)-great-grandparents' gonads. (Genetic analysis of sweet potatoes, bottle gourds, and chicken bones also indicates pre-Columbian contact.) In Oceania, scientists have tied the diffusion and winnowing of people's DNA to the diffusion and winnowing of their languages. It turns out that people in southern Africa, the cradle of humanity, not only have richer DNA than anyone else but richer languages, with up to one hundred distinct sounds, including the famous *tchk-tchk* clicks. Languages from intermediately diverse lands have fewer sounds (English has forty-some). Languages at the far end of our ancient migration, like Hawaiian, use around a dozen sounds, and Hawaiian people show correspondingly uniform DNA. It all adds up.

Looking beyond our species a tad, DNA can also illuminate one of the biggest mysteries of archaeology: what happened to Neanderthals? After Neanderthals had thrived in Europe for ages, something slowly strangled them into smaller and smaller territories, and the last ones expired about thirty-five thousand years ago in southern Europe. The profusion of theories to explain what doomed them—climate change, catching diseases from humans, competition for food, homicide (by *Homo sapiens*), "mad Neanderthal" disease from eating too many brains—is an unmistakable sign that nobody has the faintest. But with the decoding of the Neanderthal genome, we know at last that Neanderthals didn't disappear, not entirely. We carried their seed inside us across the globe.

After emerging from Africa around sixty thousand years ago, clans of humans eventually wandered into Neanderthal lands in the Levantine. Boys eyed girls, tyrannical hormones took over, and pretty soon little humanderthals were running around—a replay of when archaic humanoids bedded proto-chimpanzees (*plus ça change*). What happened next is hazy, but the groups divorced and did so asymmetrically. Perhaps some outraged human elders stormed off, taking their despoiled children and humanderthal grandchildren with them. Perhaps only Neanderthal men bagged human women, who then left with their clan. Perhaps the groups parted amicably, but all the half-breeds left in Neanderthal care died when the humans pushed on and colonized the planet at large. Anyhow, when these Paleolithic Lewises and Clarks parted from their Neanderthal lovers, they carried some Neanderthal DNA in their gene pool. Enough, in fact, that we all still have a few percent's worth inside us today—equivalent to the amount you inherited from each great-great-great-grandparent. It's not yet clear what all this DNA does, but some of it was MHC immunity DNA—which means that Neanderthals may have unwittingly helped destroy themselves by giving humans the DNA to fight new diseases in the new lands we took from Neanderthals. Oddly, however, there seems to have been no reciprocity: no uniquely human DNA, disease-fighting or otherwise, has shown up in any Neanderthals so far. No one knows why.

And actually only some of us absorbed Neanderthal DNA. All the amour took place on the pivot between Asia and Europe, not in Africa proper. Which means that the people who carried Neanderthal DNA forward weren't ancient Africans (who, insofar as scientists can tell, never hooked up with Neanderthals) but the early Asians and Europeans, whose descendants populated the rest of the world. The irony is too rich not to point out. When arranging the different human races in tiers, from just below the angels to just above the brutes, smug racialist scientists of the 1800s always equated black skin with "subhuman" beasts like Neanderthals. But facts is facts: pure Nordic Europeans carry far more Neanderthal DNA than any modern African. One more time, DNA debases.

Just to frustrate archaeologists, however, evidence turned up in 2011 that Africans had their own extra-species liaisons. Certain tribes who stayed at home in central Africa and never saw a Neanderthal in their lives seem to have acquired chunks of noncoding DNA from other, unnamed, and now-extinct archaic humans, and did so well after the early Asians and Europeans had left. As scientists continue to catalog human diversity around the world, DNA memories of other assignations will no doubt surface in other groups, and we'll have to ascribe more and more "human" DNA to other creatures.

Really, though, tallying whether this or that ethnic group has less archaic DNA than another misses the point. The emerging and vital truth isn't who is more Neanderthal than whom. It's that all peoples, everywhere, enjoyed archaic human lovers whenever they could. These DNA memories are buried deeper inside us than even our ids, and they remind us that the grand saga of how humans spread across the globe will need some personal, private, all-too-human amendments and annotations—rendezvous here, elopements there, and the commingling of genes most everywhere. At least we can say that all humans are united in sharing this shame (if shame it is) and in sharing these scarlet A's, C's, G's, and T's.

11

Size Matters

How Did Humans Get Such Grotesquely Large Brains?

The expansion of our ancestors across the globe required more than luck and persistence. To dodge extinction after extinction, we also needed us some brains. There's clearly a biological basis for human intelligence; it's too universal not to be inscribed in our DNA, and (unlike most cells) brain cells use almost all the DNA we have. But despite centuries of inquiry, by everyone from phrenologists to NASA engineers, on subjects from Albert Einstein to idiot savants, no one quite knows where our smarts come from.

Early attempts to find the biological basis of intelligence played off the idea that bigger was better: more brain mass meant more thinking power, just like more muscles meant more lifting power. Although intuitive, this theory has its shortcomings; whales and their twenty-pound brains don't dominate the globe. So Baron Cuvier, the half Darwin, half Machiavelli from Napoleonic France, suggested that scientists also examine a creature's brain-body ratio, to measure its relative brain weight as well.

Nonetheless scientists in Cuvier's day maintained that bigger brains did mean finer minds, especially *within* a species. The best evidence here was Cuvier himself, a man renowned (indeed, practically stared at) for the veritable pumpkin atop his shoulders. Still, no one could say anything definitive about Cuvier's brain until 7 a.m. on Tuesday, May 15, 1832, when the greatest and most shameless doctors in Paris gathered to conduct Cuvier's autopsy. They sliced open his torso, sluiced through his viscera, and established that he had normal organs. This duty dispatched, they eagerly sawed through his skull and extracted a whale of a specimen, sixty-five ounces, over 10 percent larger than any brain measured before. The smartest scientist these men had ever known had the biggest brain they'd ever seen. Pretty convincing.

By the 1860s, though, the tidy size-smarts theory had started unraveling. For one, some scientists questioned the accuracy of the Cuvier measurement—it just seemed too outré. No one had bothered to pickle and preserve Cuvier's brain, unfortunately, so these later scientists grasped at whatever evidence they could find. Someone eventually dug up Cuvier's hat, which was indeed commodious; it fell over the eyes of most everyone who donned it. But those wise in the ways of milliners pointed out that the hat's felt might have stretched over the years, leading to overestimates. Tonsorial types suggested instead that Cuvier's bushy hairdo had made his head merely appear enormous, biasing his doctors to expect (and, because expecting, find) a vast brain. Still others built a case that Cuvier suffered from juvenile hydrocephaly, a feverish swelling of the brain and skull when young. In that case, Cuvier's big head might be accidental, unrelated to his genius.*

Arguing about Cuvier wasn't going to solve anything, so to get more data on more people, cranial anatomists developed methods to gauge the volumes of skulls. Basically, they plugged every hole and filled the skulls (depending on their preference)

Baron Cuvier—a half-Darwin, half-Machiavelli biologist
who lorded over French science during and after Napoleon—had one of the largest human brains ever recorded.
(James Thomson)

with a known amount of peas, beans, rice, millet, white pepper-
corn, mustard seed, water, mercury, or lead buckshot. Imagine
rows of skulls on a table, funnels protruding from each one, an
assistant humping around buckets of quicksilver or burlap bags
of grain from the market. Whole monographs were published
on these experiments, but they produced still more baffling
results. Were Eskimos, who had the largest brainpans, really the
smartest people on earth? What's more, the skulls of the newly
discovered Neanderthal species were actually roomier than human
skulls by an average of six cubic inches.

As it turns out, that's just the start of the confusion. Again, without correlating strictly, a bigger brain does generally make a species smarter. And because monkeys, apes, and humans are all pretty sharp, scientists assumed that intense pressure must have come to bear on primate DNA to boost brain size. It was basically an arms race: big-brain primates win the most food and survive crises better, and the only way to beat them is to get smarter yourself. But nature can be stingy, too. Based on genetic and fossil evidence, scientists can now track how most primate lineages have evolved over many millions of years. It turns out that certain species' bodies, and not infrequently their brains, shrank over time—they became cranial runts. Brains consume a lot of energy (around 20 percent of human calories), and in times with chronic food shortages, the DNA that won out in primates was the miserly DNA that scrimped on building up brains.

The best-known runt today is probably the "hobbit" skeleton from the Indonesian island of Flores. When it was discovered in 2003, many scientists declared it a stunted or microcephalic (tiny-headed) human; no way evolution was irresponsible enough to let the brains of a hominid dwindle that much, brains being about all we hominids have going. But nowadays most scientists accept that the brains of hobbits (officially, *Homo floresiensis*) did shrink. Some of this diminution might relate to so-called island dwarfism: islands, being severely finite, have less food, so if an animal can tune down some of the hundreds of genes that control its height and size, it can get by with fewer calories. Island dwarfism has shrunk mammoths, hippos, and other stranded species to pygmy sizes, and there's no reason to think this pressure wouldn't squash a hominid, even if the cost is a punier brain.*

By some measures, modern humans are runts, too. We've probably all gone to a museum and snickered over the wee suit of armor that a king of England or some other big swinging dick from history wore—what a shrimp! But our ancestors would giggle at our clothes just the same. Since about 30,000 BC, our DNA has diminished the average human body size by 10 percent (roughly five inches). The vaunted human brain dwindled by at least 10 percent over that span, too, and a few scientists argue it has shrunk even more.

Scientists filling skulls with buckshot or millet in the early 1900s didn't know about DNA, of course, but even with their crude tools, they could tell the brain size–intelligence theory didn't add up. One famous study of geniuses—it got a two-page spread in the *New York Times* in 1912—did find some truly capacious organs. Russian writer Ivan Turgenev's brain topped seventy ounces, compared to a human average of fifty. At the same time, the brains of statesman Daniel Webster and mathematician Charles Babbage, who dreamed up the first programmable computer, were merely average. And poor Walt Whitman had to sound his barbaric yawp over the rooftops with a command center of just forty-four ounces. Even worse was Franz Joseph Gall. Though an intelligent scientist—he proposed for the first time that different brain regions have different functions—Gall also founded phrenology, the analysis of head lumps. To his followers' eternal shame, he weighed in at a measly forty-two ounces.

To be fair, a technician dropped Whitman's brain before measuring it. It crumbled into pieces like a dried-out cake, and it's not clear whether they found all of them, so maybe Walt could have made a better showing. (No such mishap with Gall.) Regardless, by the 1950s the size-smarts theory had received some fatal wounds, and any lingering association between brain heft and braininess died for good a few hours after Albert Einstein himself died in 1955.

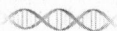

After suffering an aortic aneurysm on April 13, 1955, Einstein found himself the subject of an international death watch. He finally succumbed to internal hemorrhaging at 1:15 a.m. on April 18. His body arrived shortly thereafter at a local hospital in Princeton, New Jersey, for a routine autopsy. At this point the pathologist on duty, Thomas Harvey, faced a stark choice.

Any one of us might have been tempted the same way—who wouldn't want to know what made Einstein *Einstein?* Einstein himself expressed interest in having his brain studied after he died, and even sat for brain scans. He decided against preserving the best part of himself only because he loathed the thought of people venerating it, the twentieth-century equivalent of a medieval Catholic relic. But as Harvey arranged the scalpels in his autopsy room that night, he knew humankind had just one chance to salvage the gray matter of the greatest scientific thinker in centuries. And while it may be too strong to say *stole*, by 8 a.m. the next morning—without next-of-kin permission, and against Einstein's notarized wish for cremation—Harvey had shall we say *liberated* the physicist's brain and released the body to the family without it.

The disappointment started immediately. Einstein's brain weighed forty-three ounces, at the low end of normal. And before Harvey could measure anything more, word of the relic spread, just as Einstein had feared. During a discussion in school the next day about the loss of Einstein, Harvey's son, normally a laconic lad, blurted out, "My dad's got his brain!" A day later, newspapers across the country mentioned Harvey's plans in their front-page obits. Harvey did eventually convince the remaining Einsteins, who were sure peeved, to grant permission for further study. So after measuring its dimensions with calipers and photographing it for posterity with his 35 mm black-and-white camera, Harvey sawed the brain into 240 taffy-sized hunks and lacquered each one in celloidin. Harvey was soon mailing the blobs in mayo jars to neurologists, confident that the forthcoming scientific insights would justify his peccadillo.

Fragments of Einstein's brain, shellacked in hard celloidin after the physicist's death in 1955. (Getty Images)

This certainly wasn't the first autopsy of a famous person to take a lurid turn. Doctors set aside Beethoven's ear bones in 1827 to study his deafness, but a medical orderly nicked them. The Soviet Union founded an entire institute in part to study Lenin's brain and determine what makes a revolutionary a revolutionary. (The brains of Stalin and Tchaikovsky also merited preservation.) Similarly, and despite the body being mutilated by mobs, Americans helped themselves to half of Mussolini's brain after World War II, to determine what made a dictator a dictator. That same year the U.S. military seized four thousand pieces of human flesh from Japanese coroners to study nuclear radiation damage. The spoils included hearts, slabs of liver and brain, even disembodied eyeballs, all of which doctors stored in jars in radiation-proof vaults in Washington, D.C., at a cost to taxpayers of $60,000 per year. (The U.S. repatriated the remains in 1973.)

Even more grotesquely, William Buckland—in a story that's possibly apocryphal, but that his contemporaries believed—topped his career as a gourmand when a friend opened a silver snuffbox to show off a desiccated morsel of Louis XIV's heart. "I have eaten many strange things, but have never eaten the heart of a king," Buckland mused. Before anyone thought to stop him, Buckland wolfed it down. One of the all-time raciest stolen body parts was the most private part of Cuvier's patron, Napoleon. A spiteful doctor lopped off L'Empereur's penis during the autopsy in 1821, and a crooked priest smuggled it to Europe. A century later, in 1927, the unit went on sale in New York, where one observer compared it to a "maltreated strip of buckskin shoelace." It had shriveled to one and one-half inches, but a urologist in New Jersey bought it anyway for $2,900. And we can't wrap up this creepy catalog without noting that yet another New Jersey doctor disgracefully whisked away Einstein's eyeballs in 1955. The doctor later refused Michael Jackson's offer to pay millions for them—partly because the doc had grown fond of gazing into them. As for the rest of Einstein's body, take heart (sorry). It was cremated, and no one knows where in Princeton his family scattered the ashes.*

Perhaps the most disheartening thing about the whole Einstein fiasco is the paltry knowledge scientists gained. Neurologists ended up publishing only three papers on Einstein's brain in forty years, because most found nothing extraordinary there. Harvey kept soliciting scientists to take another look, but after the initial null results came back, the brain chunks mostly just sat around. Harvey kept each section wrapped in cheesecloth and piled them into two wide-mouthed glass cookie jars full of formaldehyde broth. The jars themselves sat in a cardboard box labeled "Costa Cider" in Harvey's office, tucked behind a red beer cooler. When Harvey lost his job later and took off for greener pastures in Kansas (where he moved in next door to author and junkie William S. Burroughs), the brain rode shotgun in his car.

In the past fifteen years, though, Harvey's persistence has been justified, a little. A few cautious papers have highlighted some atypical aspects of Einstein's brain, on both microscopic and macroscopic levels. Coupled with loads of research into the genetics of brain growth, these findings may yet provide some insight into what separates a human brain from an animal brain, and what pushes an Einstein a few standard deviations beyond that.

First, the obsession with overall brain size has given way to obsessing over the size of certain brain parts. Primates have particularly beefy neuron shafts (called axons) compared to other animals and can therefore send information through each neuron more quickly. Even more important is the thickness of the cortex, the outermost brain layer, which promotes thinking and dreaming and other flowery pursuits. Scientists know that certain genes are crucial for growing a thick cortex, partly because it's so sadly obvious when these genes fail: people end up with primitively tiny brains. One such gene is *aspm*. Primates have extra stretches of DNA in *aspm* compared to other mammals, and this DNA codes for extra strings of amino acids that bulk up the cortex. (These strings usually start with the amino acids isoleucine and glutamine. In the alphabetic abbreviations that biochemists use for amino acids, glutamine is usually shortened to Q [G was taken] and isoleucine to plain I—which means we probably got an intelligence boost from a string of DNA referred to, coincidentally, as the "IQ domain.")

In tandem with increasing cortex size, *aspm* helps direct a process that increases the density of neurons in the cortex, another trait that correlates strongly with intelligence. This increase in density happens during our earliest days, when we have loads of stem cells, undeclared cells that can choose any path and become any type of cell. When stem cells begin dividing in the incipient brain, they can either produce more stem cells, or they can settle down, get a job, and become mature neurons. Neurons are good, obviously, but each time a neuron forms, the production of new stem cells (which can make additional neurons in the future) stops. So getting a big brain requires building up the base population of stem cells first. And the key to doing that is making sure that stem cells divide evenly: if the cellular guts get divided equally between both daughter cells, each one becomes another stem cell. If the split is unequal, neurons form prematurely.

To facilitate an even split, *aspm* guides the "spindles" that attach to chromosomes and pull them apart in a nice, clean, symmetrical way. If *aspm* fails, the split is uneven, neurons form too soon, and the child is cheated of a normal brain. To be sure, *aspm* isn't *the* gene responsible for big brains: cell division requires intricate coordination among many genes, with master regulator genes conducting everything from above, too. But *aspm* can certainly pack the cortex with neurons* when it's firing right— or sabotage neuron production if it misfires.

Einstein's cortex had a few unusual features. One study found that, compared to normal elderly men, his had the same number of neurons and the same average neuron size. However, part of Einstein's cortex, the prefrontal cortex, was thinner, which gave him a greater density of neurons. Closely packed neurons may help the brain process information more quickly—a tantalizing find considering that the prefrontal cortex orchestrates thoughts throughout the brain and helps solve multistep problems.

Further studies examined certain folds and grooves in Einstein's cortex. As with brain size, it's a myth that simply having more folds automatically makes a brain more potent. But folding does generally indicate higher functioning. Smaller and dumber monkeys, for instance, have fewer corrugations in their cortexes. As, interestingly, do newborn humans. Which means that as we mature from infants to young adults, and as genes that wrinkle our brains start kicking on, every one of us relives millions of years of human evolution. Scientists also know that a lack of brain folds is devastating. The genetic disorder "smooth brain" leaves babies severely retarded, if they even survive to term. Instead of being succulently furrowed, a smooth brain looks eerily polished, and cross sections of it, instead of showing scrunched-up brain fabric, look like slabs of liver.

Einstein had unusual wrinkles and ridges in the cortex of his parietal lobe, a region that aids in mathematical reasoning and image processing. This comports with Einstein's famous declaration that he thought about physics mostly through pictures: he formulated relativity theory, for instance, in part by imagining what would happen if he rode around bareback on light rays. The parietal lobe also integrates sound, sight, and other sensory input into the rest of the brain's thinking. Einstein once declared that abstract concepts achieved meaning in his mind "only through their connection with sense-experiences," and his family remembers him practicing his violin whenever he got stuck with a physics problem. An hour later, he'd often declare, "I've got it!" and return to work. Auditory input seemed to jog his thinking. Perhaps most telling, the parietal wrinkles and ridges in Einstein's lobes were steroid thick, 15 percent bigger than normal. And whereas most of us mental weaklings have skinny right parietal lobes and even skinnier left parietal lobes, Einstein's were equally buff.

Finally, Einstein appeared to be missing part of his middle brain, the parietal operculum; at the least, it didn't develop fully. This part of the brain helps produce language, and its lack might explain why Einstein didn't speak until age two and why until age seven he had to rehearse every sentence he spoke aloud under his breath. But there might have been compensations. This region normally contains a fissure, or small gap, and our thoughts get routed the long way around. The lack of a gap might have meant that Einstein could process certain information more speedily, by bringing two separate parts of his brain into unusually direct contact.

All of which is exciting. But is it exciting bunkum? Einstein feared his brain becoming a relic, but have we done something equally silly and reverted to phrenology? Einstein's brain has deteriorated into chopped liver by now (it's even the same color), which forces scientists to work mostly from old photographs, a less precise method. And not to put too fine a point on it, but Thomas Harvey coauthored half of the various studies on the "extraordinary" features of Einstein's brain, and he certainly had an interest in science learning something from the organ he purloined. Plus, as with Cuvier's swollen brain, maybe Einstein's features are idiosyncratic and had nothing to do with genius; it's hard to tell with a sample size of one. Even trickier, we can't sort out if unusual neurofeatures (like thickened folds) caused Einstein's genius, or if his genius allowed him to "exercise" and build up those parts of his brain. Some skeptical neuroscientists note that playing the violin from an early age (and Einstein started lessons at six) can cause the same brain alterations observed in Einstein.

And if you had hopes of dipping into Harvey's brain slices and extracting DNA, forget it. In 1998, Harvey, his jars, and a writer took a road trip in a rented Buick to visit Einstein's granddaughter in California. Although weirded out by Grandpa's brain, Evelyn Einstein accepted the visitors for one reason. She was poor, reputedly dim, and had trouble holding down a job — not exactly an Einstein. In fact Evelyn was always told she'd been adopted by Einstein's son, Hans. But Evelyn could do a little math, and when she started hearing rumors that Einstein had canoodled with various lady friends after his wife died, Evelyn realized she might be Einstein's bastard child. The "adoption" might have been a ruse. Evelyn wanted to do a genetic paternity test to settle things, but it turned out that the embalming process had denatured the brain's DNA. Other sources of his DNA might still be floating around—strands in mustache brushes, spittle on pipes, sweated-on violins—but for now we know more about the genes of Neanderthals who died fifty thousand years ago than the genes of a man who died in 1955.

But if Einstein's genius remains enigmatic, scientists have sussed out a lot about the everyday genius of humans compared to that of other primates. Some of the DNA that enhances human intelligence does so in roundabout ways. A two-letter frameshift mutation in humans a few million years ago deactivated a gene that bulked up our jaw muscles. This probably allowed us to get by with thinner, more gracile skulls, which in turn freed up precious cc's of skull for the brain to expand into. Another surprise was that *apoE*, the meat-eating gene, helped a lot, by helping the brain manage cholesterol. To function properly, the brain needs to sheathe its axons in myelin, which acts like rubber insulation on wires and prevents signals from short-circuiting or misfiring. Cholesterol is a major component of myelin, and certain forms of *apoE* do a better job distributing brain cholesterol where it's needed. *ApoE* also seems to promote brain plasticity.

Some genes lead to direct structural changes in the brain. The *lrrtm1* gene helps determine which exact patches of neurons control speech, emotion, and other mental qualities, which in turn helps the human brain establish its unusual asymmetry and left-right specialization. Some versions of *lrrtm1* even reverse parts of the left and right brain—and increase your chances of being left-handed to boot, the only known genetic association for that trait. Other DNA alters the brain's architecture in almost comical ways: certain inheritable mutations can cross-wire the sneeze reflex with other ancient reflexes, leaving people achooing uncontrollably—up to forty-three times in a row in one case—after looking into the sun, eating too much, or having an orgasm. Scientists have also recently detected 3,181 base pairs of brain "junk DNA" in chimpanzees that got deleted in humans. This region helps stop out-of-control neuron growth, which can lead to big brains, obviously, but also brain tumors. Humans gambled in deleting this DNA, but the risk apparently paid off, and our brains ballooned. The discovery shows that it's not always what we gained with DNA, but sometimes what we lost, that makes us human. (Or at least makes us nonmonkey: Neanderthals didn't have this DNA either.)

How and how quickly DNA spreads through a population can reveal which genes contribute to intelligence. In 2005 scientists reported that two mutated brain genes seem to have swept torrentially through our ancestors, *microcephalin* doing so 37,000 years ago, *aspm* just 6,000 years ago. Scientists clocked this spread by using techniques first developed in the Columbia fruit fly room. Thomas Hunt Morgan discovered that certain versions of genes get inherited in clusters, simply because they reside near each other on chromosomes. As an example, the A, B, and D versions of three genes might normally appear together; or (lowercase) a, b, and d might appear together. Over time, though, chromosomal crossing-over and recrossing will mix the groups, giving combos like a, B, and D; or A, b, and D. After enough generations, every combination will appear.

But say that B mutates to B_0 at some point, and that B_0 gives people a hell of a brain tune-up. At that point it could sweep through a population, since B_0 people can outthink everyone else. (That spread will be especially easy if the population drops very low, since the novel gene has less competition. Bottlenecks aren't always bad!) And notice that as B_0 sweeps through a population, the versions of A/a and D/d that happen to be sitting next to B_0 in the first person with the mutation will *also* sweep through the population, simply because crossing over won't have time to break the trio apart. In other words, these genes will ride along with the advantageous gene, a process called genetic hitchhiking. Scientists see especially strong signs of hitchhiking with *aspm* and *microcephalin*, which means they spread especially quickly and probably provided an especially strong advantage.

Beyond any specific brain-boosting genes, DNA regulation might explain a lot about our gray matter. One flagrant difference between human and monkey DNA is that our brain cells splice DNA far more often, chopping and editing the same string of letters for many different effects. Neurons mix it up so much, in fact, that some scientists think they've upended one central dogma of biology—that all cells in your body have the same DNA. For whatever reason, our neurons allow much more free play among mobile DNA bits, the "jumping genes" that wedge themselves randomly into chromosomes. This changes the DNA patterns in neurons, which can change how they work. As one neuroscientist observes, "Given that changing the firing patterns of single neurons can have marked effects on behavior...it is likely that some [mobile DNA], in some cells, in some humans, will have significant, if not profound, effects on the final structure and function of the human brain." Once again viruslike particles may prove important to our humanity.

If you're skeptical that we can explain something as ineffable as genius by studying something as reductive as DNA, a lot of scientists are right there with you. And every so often a case like that of savant Kim Peek pops up—a case that so mocks our understanding of how DNA and brain architecture influence intelligence that even the most enthusiastic neuroscientist seeks the consolation of a stiff bourbon and starts to think seriously about going into administration.

Peek, a Salt Lake City native, was actually a megasavant, a souped-up version of what's impolitely but accurately known as an idiot savant. Instead of being limited to poignantly empty skills like drawing perfect circles or listing all the Holy Roman Emperors in order, Peek had encyclopedic knowledge of geography, opera, American history, Shakespeare, classical music, the Bible—basically all of Western Civ. Even more intimidating, Peek had Google-like recall of any sentence in the nine thousand books he'd memorized, starting at eighteen months old. (When finished with a book, he returned it to his shelf with the spine upside down to indicate he'd knocked it off.) If it makes you less insecure, Peek did know loads of useless crap, too, like the complete U.S. zip code system. He also memorized *Rain Man*, a movie he inspired, and knew Mormon theology in lobotomizing detail.*

Trying to get some, any, sort of measure on Peek's talents, doctors in Utah began scanning his brain in 1988. In 2005, NASA got involved for whatever reason and took complete MRI and tomography scans of Peek's mental plumbing. The scans revealed that Peek lacked the tissue that connects the brain's right hemisphere to the left. (Peek's father remembered, in fact, that Peek could move each eye independently of the other as an infant, probably because of that disconnect between the right and left halves.) The left hemisphere, which focuses on big-picture ideas, also seemed misshaped—more lumpen and squished than normal brains. But beyond these details, scientists learned little. In the end, then, even NASA-level technology could reveal only abnormal features, *problems* with Peek's brain. If you wanted to know why Peek couldn't button his own clothes or why he could never remember where to find the silverware, despite living at his father's house for decades, there you go. As to the basis of his talents, NASA shrugged.

But doctors also knew Peek had a rare genetic disorder, FG syndrome. In FG syndrome, a single malfunctioning gene can't flick the on switch for a stretch of DNA that neurons need to develop properly. (They're very picky, neurons.) And as with most savants, the fallout from these problems clustered in Peek's left brain, possibly because the big-picture-oriented left hemisphere takes longer to develop in utero. A malfunctioning gene therefore has more time to inflict injury there. But in a strange twist, injuring the normally dominant left hemisphere can actually coax out the talents of the detail-conscious right brain. Indeed, the talents of most savants—artistic mimicry, perfect musical regurgitation, feats of calendary calculation—all cluster in the brain's less-vulnerable right half. Sadly, then, it may be true that those suppressed right-brained talents can never surface unless the domineering left hemisphere suffers damage.

Geneticists have made similar discoveries using the Neanderthal genome. Scientists are currently mining Neanderthal and human DNA for evidence of hitchhiking, trying to identify DNA that swept through humankind after the Neanderthal-human split and therefore helped distinguish us from Neanderthals. They've found about two hundred regions so far, most of which contain at least a few genes. Some of these human-Neanderthal differences are real yawners about bone development or metabolism. But scientists have also identified a handful of genes related to cognition. Paradoxically, though, having certain variants of these genes—far from being linked to Nobel Prizes or MacArthur grants—increases the risk of Down syndrome, autism, schizophrenia, and other mental disorders. It seems that a more complicated mind is a more fragile mind; if these genes did uplift our intelligence, taking them on also introduced risk.

And yet for all that frailty, a brain with faulty DNA can be miraculously resilient in other circumstances. In the 1980s, a neurologist in England scanned the freakishly large head of a young man referred to him for a checkup. He found little inside the skull case but cerebrospinal fluid (mostly salt water). The young man's cortex was basically a water balloon, a sac one millimeter thick surrounding a sloshing inner cavity. The scientist guessed the brain weighed perhaps five ounces. The young man also had an IQ of 126 and was an honors mathematics student at his university. Neurologists don't even pretend to know how these so-called high-functioning hydrocephalics (literally "waterheads") manage to live normal lives, but a doctor who studied another famous hydrocephalic, a civil servant in France with two children, suspects that if the brain atrophies slowly over time, it's plastic enough to reallocate important functions before it loses them completely.

Peek—who had a Cuvier-sized noggin himself—had an IQ of 87. It was probably so low because he reveled in minutiae and couldn't really process intangible ideas. For instance, scientists noticed he couldn't grasp common proverbs—the leap to the metaphorical was too far. Or when Peek's father told him to lower his voice once in a restaurant, Peek slid down in his chair, bringing his larynx closer to the ground. (He did seem to grasp that puns are theoretically funny, possibly because they involve a more mathematical substitution of meanings and words. He once responded to a query about Lincoln's Gettysburg Address by answering, "Will's house, 227 NW Front St. But he stayed there only one night—he gave the speech the next day.") Peek struggled with other abstractions as well and was basically helpless domestically, as reliant as a child on his father's care. But given his other talents, that 87 seems almost criminally unfair and certainly doesn't capture him.*

Peek died of a heart attack around Christmas in 2009, and

his body was buried. So there will be no Einstein-like afterlife for his remarkable brain. His brain scans still exist, but for now they mostly just taunt us, pointing out gaps in what we know about the sculpting of the human mind—what separated Peek from Einstein, or even what separates everyday human smarts from simian intelligence. Any deep appreciation of human intellect will require understanding the DNA that builds and designs the web of neurons that think our thoughts and capture each "Aha!" But it will also require understanding environmental influences that, like Einstein's violin lessons, goose our DNA and allow our big brains to fulfill their potential. Einstein was Einstein because of his genes, but not only because of them.

The environment that nurtured Einstein and the rest of us everyday geniuses didn't arise by accident. Unlike other animals, humans craft and design our immediate environments: we have culture. And while brain-boosting DNA was necessary for creating culture, it didn't suffice. We had big brains during our scavenger-gatherer days (perhaps bigger brains than now), but achieving sophisticated culture also required the spread of genes to digest cooked food and handle a more sedentary lifestyle. Perhaps above all we needed behavior-related genes: genes to help us tolerate strangers and live docilely under rulers and tolerate monogamous sex, genes that increased our discipline and allowed us to delay gratification and build things on generational time-scales. Overall, then, genes shaped what culture we would have, but culture bent back and shaped our DNA, too. And understanding the greatest achievements of culture—art, science, politics—requires understanding how DNA and culture intersect and evolve together.

12

The Art of the Gene

How Deep in Our DNA Is Artistic Genius?

rt, music, poetry, painting—there are no finer expressions of neural brilliance, and just like Einstein's or Peek's genius, genetics can illuminate some unexpected aspects of the fine arts. Genetics and visual art even trace a few parallel tracks across the past 150 years. Paul Cézanne and Henri Matisse couldn't have developed their arrestingly colorful styles if European chemists hadn't invented vibrant new dyes and pigments in the 1800s. Those dyes and pigments simultaneously allowed scientists to study chromosomes for the first time, because they could finally stain chromosomes a color different from the uniform blah of the rest of the cell. Chromosomes in fact take their name from the Greek for color, *chrōma*, and some techniques to tint chromosomes—like turning them "Congo red" on shimmering green backgrounds—would have turned Cézanne and Matisse a certain shade with envy. Meanwhile silver staining—a by-product of the new photographic arts—provided the first clean pictures of other cell structures, and photography itself allowed scientists to

study time lapses of dividing cells and see how chromosomes got passed around.

Movements like cubism and Dadaism—not to mention competition from photography—led many artists to abandon realism and experiment with new kinds of art in the early twentieth century. And piggybacking on the insights gained from staining cells, photographer Edward Steichen introduced "bio-art" in the 1930s, with an early foray into genetic engineering. An avid gardener, Steichen began (for obscure reasons) soaking delphinium seeds in his gout medication one spring. This doubled the chromosome number in these purple flowers, and although some seeds produced "stunted, febrile rejects," others produced Jurassic-sized flora with eight-foot stalks. In 1936 Steichen exhibited five hundred delphiniums at the Museum of Modern Art in New York City and earned mostly rapturous reviews from newspapers in seventeen states: "Giant spikes... brilliant dark blues," one reviewer wrote, "a plum color never before seen... startlingly black eyes." The plums and blues may have startled, but Steichen—a nature-worshipping pantheist—echoed Barbara McClintock in insisting that the real art lay in controlling the development of the delphiniums. These views on art alienated some critics, but Steichen insisted, "A thing is beautiful if it fulfills its purpose—if it functions."

By the 1950s, a preoccupation with form and function eventually pushed artists into abstractionism. Studies of DNA coincidentally tagged along. Watson and Crick spent as many hours as any sculptor ever did creating physical models for their work, crafting various mock-ups of DNA from tin or cardboard. The duo settled on the double helix model partly because its austere beauty bewitched them. Watson once recalled that every time he saw a spiral staircase, he grew more convinced that DNA must look equally elegant. Crick turned to his wife, Odile, an artist, to draw the chic double helix that wound up and down the margin of their famous first paper on DNA. And later, Crick recalled a drunken Watson ogling their slender, curvy model one night and muttering, "It's so beautiful, you see, so beautiful." Crick added: "Of course, it was."

But like their guesses about the shapes of A, C, G, and T, Watson and Crick's guess about the overall shape of DNA rested on a somewhat shaky foundation. Based on how fast cells divide, biologists in the 1950s calculated that the double helix would have to unravel at 150 turns per second to keep up, a furious pace. More worrisome, a few mathematicians drew on knot theory to argue that separating the strands of helical DNA—the first step for copying them—was topologically impossible. That's because two unzipped helix strands cannot be pulled apart laterally—they're too intertwined, too entangled. So in 1976 a few scientists began promoting a rival "warped-zipper" structure for DNA. Here, instead of one long smooth right-handed helix, right- and left-handed half helixes alternated up and down the length of DNA, which would allow it to pull apart cleanly. To answer the criticisms of double helixes, Watson and Crick occasionally discussed alternative forms of DNA, but they (especially Crick) would almost immediately dismiss them. Crick often gave sound technical reasons for his doubts, but added once, tellingly, "Moreover, the models were ugly." In the end, the mathematicians proved right: cells cannot simply unwind double helixes. Instead they use special proteins to snip DNA, shake its windings loose, and solder it back together later. However elegant itself, a double helix leads to an awfully awkward method of replication.*

By the 1980s scientists had developed advanced genetic engineering tools, and artists began approaching scientists about collaborating on "genetic art." Honestly, your tolerance for bullroar has to be pretty high to take some claims for genetic art seriously: pace bioartist George Gessert, do "ornamental plants, pets, sporting animals, and consciousness-altering drug plants" really constitute "a vast, unacknowledged genetic folk art"? And some perversities—like an albino bunny reconfigured with jelly-fish genes that made it glow green—were created, the artist admitted, largely to goad people. But for all the glibness, some genetic art plays the provocateur effectively; like the best science fiction, it confronts our assumptions about science. One famous piece consisted solely of one man's sperm DNA in a steel frame, a "portrait" that the artist claimed was "the most realist portrait in [London's National] Portrait Gallery"—because, after all, it revealed the donor's naked DNA. That might seem harshly reductive; but then again, the portrait's "subject" had headed the British arm of arguably the most reductionist biological project ever, the Human Genome Project. Artists have also encoded quotes from Genesis about man's dominion over nature into the A-C-G-T sequence of common bacteria—words that, if the bacteria copy their DNA with high fidelity, could survive millions of years longer than the Bible will. From the ancient Greeks onward, the Pygmalion impulse—the desire to fashion "living" works of art—has driven artists and will only grow stronger as biotechnology advances.

Scientists themselves have even succumbed to the temptation to turn DNA into art. To study how chromosomes wriggle about in three dimensions, scientists have developed ways to "paint" them with fluorescent dyes. And karyotypes—the familiar pictures of twenty-three chromosomes paired up like paper dolls—have been transformed from dull dichromatic images into pictures so flamboyantly incandescent that a fauvist would blush. Scientists have also used DNA itself to build bridges, snowflakes, "nano-flasks," kitschy smiley faces, Rock 'Em Sock 'Em Robot look-alikes, and Mercator maps of every continent. There are mobile DNA "walkers" that cartwheel along like a Slinky down the stairs, as well as DNA boxes with lids that open, turned by a DNA "key." Scientist-artists call these fanciful constructions "DNA origami."

To create a piece of DNA origami, practitioners might start with a virtual block on a computer screen. But instead of the block being solid, like marble, it consists of tubes stacked together, like a rectangular bundle of drinking straws. To "carve" something—say, a bust of Beethoven—they first digitally chisel at the surface, removing small segments of tubes, until the leftover tubes and tube fragments have the right shape. Next they thread one long strand of *single*-stranded DNA through every tube. (This threading happens virtually, but the computer uses a DNA strand from a real virus.) Eventually the strand weaves back and forth enough to connect every contour of Beethoven's face and hair. At this point, the sciartists digitally dissolve away the tubes to reveal pure, folded-up DNA, the blueprint for the bust.

To actually build the bust, the sciartists inspect the folded DNA strand. Specifically, they look for short sequences that reside far apart on the unfolded, linear DNA string, but lie close together in the folded configuration. Let's say they find the sequences AAAA and CCCC right near each other. The key step comes now, when they build a separate snippet of real DNA, TTTTGGGG, whose first half complements one of those four-letter sequences and whose second half complements the other. They build this complement base by base using commercial equipment and chemicals, and mix it with the long, unwound viral DNA. At some point the TTTT of the snippet bumps into the AAAA of the long strand, and they lock together. Amid the molecular jostling, the snippet's GGGG will eventually meet and lock onto the CCCC, too, "stapling" the long DNA strand together there. If a unique staple exists for every other joint, too, the sculpture basically assembles itself, since each staple will yank faraway parts of the viral DNA into place. In all, it takes a week to design a sculpture and prepare the DNA. Sciartists then mix the staples and viral DNA, incubate things at 140°F for an hour, and cool it to room temperature over another week. The result: a billion microbusts of Ludwig van.

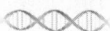

Beyond the fact that you can spin DNA itself into art, the two intersect on more profound levels. The most miserable societies in human history still found time to carve and color and croon, which strongly implies that evolution wired these impulses into our genes. Even animals show artistic urges. If introduced to painting, chimpanzees often skip feedings to keep smearing canvases and sometimes throw tantrums if scientists take their brushes and palettes away. (Cross, sunburst, and circle motifs dominate their work, and chimps favor bold, Miró-esque lines.) Some monkeys also have musical biases as ruthless as any hipster's,* as do birds. And birds and other creatures are far more discriminating connoisseurs of dance than your average *Homo sapiens*, since many species dance to communicate or court lovers.

Still, it's not clear how to fix such impulses in a molecule. Does "artistic DNA" produce musical RNA? Poetic proteins? What's more, humans have developed art qualitatively different from animal art. For monkeys, an eye for strong lines and symmetry probably helps them craft better tools in the wild, nothing more. But humans infuse art with deeper, symbolic meanings. Those elks painted on cave walls aren't just elks, they're *elks we will hunt tomorrow* or *elk gods*. For this reason, many scientists suspect that symbolic art springs from language, since language teaches us to associate abstract symbols (like pictures and words) with real objects. And given that language has genetic roots, perhaps untangling the DNA of language skills can illuminate the origins of art.

Perhaps. As with art, many animals have hardwired proto-language skills, with their warbles and screeches. And studies of human twins show that around half of the variability in our normal, everyday aptitude with syntax, vocabulary, spelling, listening comprehension—pretty much everything—traces back to DNA. (Linguistic disorders show even stronger genetic correlation.) The problem is, attempts to link linguistic skills or deficits to DNA always run into thickets of genes. Dyslexia, for instance, links to at least six genes, each of which contributes unknown amounts. Even more confusing, similar genetic mutations can produce different effects in different people. So scientists find themselves in the same position as Thomas Hunt Morgan in the fruit fly room. They know that genes and regulatory DNA "for" language exist; but how exactly that DNA enhances our eloquence—increasing neuron counts? sheathing brain cells more efficiently? fiddling with neurotransmitter levels?—no one knows.

Given this disarray, it's easy to understand the excitement, even hype, that attended the recent discovery of a purported master gene for language. In 1990 linguists inferred the gene's existence after studying three generations of a London family known only (for privacy) as the KEs. In a simple pattern of single-gene dominance, half the KEs suffer from a strange suite of language malfunctions. They have trouble coordinating their lips, jaws, and tongues, and stumble over most words, becoming especially incomprehensible on the phone. They also struggle when asked to ape a sequence of simple facial expressions, like opening their mouths, sticking out their tongues, and uttering an *uuuuaaaahh* sound. But some scientists argue that the KEs' problems extend beyond motor skills to grammar. Most of them know the plural of *book* is *books*, but seemingly because they've memorized that fact. Give them made-up words like *zoop* or *wug*, and they cannot figure out the plural; they see no connection between *book/books* and *zoop/zoops*, even after years of language therapy. They also fail fill-in-the-blank tests about the past tense, using words like "bringed." The IQs of affected KEs sink pretty low—86 on average, versus 104 for nonaffected KEs. But the language hiccups probably aren't a simple cognitive deficit: a few afflicted KEs have nonverbal IQ scores above average, and they can spot logical fallacies in arguments when tested. Plus, some scientists found that they understand reflexives just fine (e.g., "he washed him" versus "he washed himself"), as well as passive versus active voice and possessives.

It baffled scientists that one gene could cause such disparate symptoms, so in 1996 they set out to find and decode it. They narrowed its locus down to fifty genes on chromosome seven and were tediously working through each one when they caught a break. Another victim turned up, CS, from an unrelated family. The boy presented with the same mental and mandibular problems, and doctors spotted a translocation in his genes: a Philadelphia-like swap between the arms of two chromosomes, which interrupted the *foxp2* gene on chromosome seven.

Like vitamin A, the protein produced by *foxp2* clamps onto other genes and switches them on. Also like vitamin A, *foxp2* has a long reach, interacting with hundreds of genes and steering fetal development in the jaw, gut, lungs, heart, and especially the brain. All mammals have *foxp2*, and despite billions of years of collective evolution, all versions look pretty much the same; humans have accumulated just three amino acid differences compared to mice. (This gene looks strikingly similar in songbirds as well, and is especially active when they're learning new songs.) Intriguingly, humans picked up two of our amino-acid changes after splitting from chimps, and these changes allow *foxp2* to interact with many new genes. Even more intriguingly, when scientists created mutant mice with the human *foxp2*, the mice had different neuron architecture in a brain region that (in us) processes language, and they conversed with fellow mice in lower-pitched, baritone squeaks.

Conversely, in the affected KEs' brains, the regions that help produce language are stunted and have low densities of neurons. Scientists have traced these deficits back to a single A-for-G mutation. This substitution altered just one of *foxp2*'s 715 amino acids, but it's enough to prevent the protein from binding to DNA. Unfortunately, this mutation occurs in a different part of the gene than the human-chimp mutations, so it can't explain much about the evolution and original acquisition of language. And regardless, scientists still face a cause-and-effect tangle with the KEs: did the neurological deficits cause their facial clumsiness, or did their facial clumsiness lead to brain atrophy by discouraging them from practicing language? *Foxp2* can't be the only language gene anyway, since even the most afflicted in the KE clan aren't devoid of language; they're orders of magnitude more eloquent than any simian. (And sometimes they seemed more creative than the scientists testing them. When presented with the puzzler "Every day he walks eight miles. Yesterday he _____ ," instead of answering, "*walked* eight miles," one afflicted KE muttered, "had a rest.") Overall, then, while *foxp2* reveals something about the genetic basis of language and symbolic thought, the gene has proved frustratingly inarticulate so far.

Even the one thing scientists had all agreed on with *foxp2* — its unique form in humans — proved wrong. *Homo sapiens* split from other *Homo* species hundreds of thousands of years ago, but paleogeneticists recently discovered the human version of *foxp2* in Neanderthals. This might mean nothing. But it might mean that Neanderthals also had the fine motor skills for language, or the cognitive wherewithal. Perhaps both: finer motor skills might have allowed them to use language more, and when they used it more, maybe they found they had more to say.

All that's certain is that the *foxp2* discovery makes another debate about Neanderthals, over Neanderthal art, more urgent. In caves occupied by Neanderthals, archaeologists have discovered flutes made from bear femurs, as well as oyster shells stained red and yellow and perforated for stringing on necklaces. But good luck figuring out what these trinkets meant to Neanderthals. Again, perhaps Neanderthals just aped humans and attached no symbolic meaning to their toys. Or perhaps humans, who often colonized Neanderthal sites after Neanderthals died, simply tossed their worn-out flutes and shells in with Neanderthal rubbish, scrambling the chronology. The truth is, no one has any idea how articulate or artsy-fartsy Neanderthals were.

So until scientists catch another break—find another KE family with different DNA flaws, or root out more unexpected genes in Neanderthals—the genetic origins of language and symbolic art will remain murky. In the meantime we'll have to content ourselves with tracing how DNA can augment, or make a mess of, the work of modern artists.

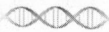

No different than with athletes, tiny bits of DNA can determine whether budding musicians fulfill their talents and ambitions. A few studies have found that one key musical trait, perfect pitch, gets inherited with the same dominant pattern as the KE language deficit, since people with perfect pitch passed it to half their children. Other studies found smaller and subtler genetic contributions for perfect pitch instead, and found that this DNA must act in concert with environmental cues (like music lessons) to bestow the gift. Beyond the ear, physical attributes can enhance or doom a musician as well. Sergei Rachmaninoff's gigantic hands—probably the result of Marfan syndrome, a genetic disorder—could span twelve inches, an octave and a half on the piano, which allowed him to compose and play music that would tear the ligaments of lesser-endowed pianists. On the other mitt, Robert Schumann's career as a concert pianist collapsed because of focal dystonia—a loss of muscle that caused his right middle finger to curl or jerk involuntarily. Many people with this condition have a genetic susceptibility, and Schumann compensated by writing at least one piece that avoided that finger entirely. But he never let up on his grinding practice schedule, and a jerry-built mechanical rack he designed to stretch the finger may have exacerbated his symptoms.

Still, in the long, gloried history of ailing and invalid musicians, no DNA proved a more ambivalent friend and ambiguous foe than the DNA of nineteenth-century musician Niccolò Paganini, the violin virtuoso's violin virtuoso. The opera composer (and noted epicurean) Gioacchino Rossini didn't like acknowledging that he ever wept, but one of the three times he owned up to crying* was when he heard Paganini perform. Rossini bawled then, and he wasn't the only one bewitched by the ungainly Italian. Paganini wore his dark hair long and performed his concerts in black frock coats with black trousers, leaving his pale, sweaty face hovering spectrally onstage. He also cocked his hips at bizarre angles while performing, and sometimes crossed his elbows at impossible angles in a rush of furious bowing. Some connoisseurs found his concerts histrionic, and accused him of fraying his violin strings before shows so they'd snap dramatically midperformance. But no one ever denied his showmanship: Pope Leo XII named him a Knight of the Golden Spur, and royal mints struck coins with his likeness. Many critics hailed him as the greatest violinist ever, and he has proved almost a singular exception to the rule in classical music that only composers gain immortality.

Paganini rarely if ever played the old masters during his concerts, preferring his own compositions, which highlighted his finger-blurring dexterity. (Ever a crowd-pleaser, he also included lowbrow passages where he mimicked donkeys and roosters on his violin.) Since his teenage years, in the 1790s, Paganini had labored over his music; but he also understood human psychology and so encouraged various legends about the supernatural origins of his gifts. Word got around that an angel had appeared at Paganini's birth and pronounced that no man would ever play the violin so sweetly. Six years later, divine favor seemingly resurrected him from a Lazarus-like doom. After he fell into a cataleptic coma, his parents gave him up for dead—they wrapped him in a burial shroud and everything—when, suddenly, something made him twitch beneath the cloth, saving him by a whisker from premature burial. Despite these miracles, people more often attributed Paganini's talents to necromancy, insisting he'd signed a pact with Satan and exchanged his immortal soul for shameless musical talent. (Paganini fanned these rumors by holding concerts in cemeteries at twilight and giving his compositions names like "Devil's Laughter" and "Witches' Dance," as if he had firsthand experience.) Others argued that he'd acquired his skills in dungeons, where he'd supposedly been incarcerated for eight years for stabbing a friend and had nothing better to do than practice violin. More sober types scoffed at these stories of witchcraft and iniquity. They patiently explained that Paganini had hired a crooked surgeon to snip the motion-limiting ligaments in his hands. Simple as that.

However ludicrous, that last explanation hits closest to the mark. Because beyond Paganini's passion, charisma, and capacity for hard work, he did have unusually supple hands. He could unfurl and stretch his fingers impossibly far, his skin seemingly about to rip apart. His finger joints themselves were also freakishly flexible: he could wrench his thumb across the back of his hand to touch his pinky (try this), and he could wriggle his midfinger joints *laterally*, like tiny metronomes. As a result, Paganini could dash off intricate riffs and arpeggios that other violinists didn't dare, hitting many more high and low notes in swift succession—up to a thousand notes per minute, some claim. He could double- or triple-stop (play multiple notes at once) with ease, and he perfected unusual techniques, like left-handed pizzicato, a plucking technique, that took advantage of his plasticity. Normally the right hand (the bow hand) does pizzicato, forcing the violinist to chose between bowing or plucking during each passage. With left-handed pizzicato, Paganini didn't have to choose. His nimble fingers could bow one note and pluck the next, as if two violins were playing at once.

Beyond being flexible, his fingers were deceptively strong, especially the thumbs. Paganini's great rival Karol Lipiński watched him in concert one evening in Padua, then retired to Paganini's room for a late dinner and some chitchat with Paganini and friends. At the table, Lipiński found a disappointingly scanty spread for someone of Paganini's stature, mostly eggs and bread. (Paganini could not even be bothered to eat that and contented himself with fruit.) But after some wine and some jam sessions on the guitar and trumpet, Lipiński found himself staring at Paganini's hands. He even embraced the master's "small bony fingers," turning them over. "How is it possible," Lipiński marveled, "for these thin small fingers to achieve things acquiring extraordinary strength?" Paganini answered, "Oh, my fingers are stronger than you think." At this he picked up a saucer of thick crystal and suspended it over the table, fingers below, thumb on top. Friends gathered around to laugh—they'd seen the trick before. While Lipiński stared, bemused, Paganini flexed his thumb almost imperceptibly and—*crack!*—snapped the saucer into two shards. Not to be outdone, Lipiński grabbed a plate and tried to shatter it with his own thumb, but couldn't come close. Nor could Paganini's friends. "The saucers remained just as they were before," Lipiński recalled, "while Paganini laughed maliciously" at their futility. It seemed almost unfair, this combination of power and agility, and those who knew Paganini best, like his personal physician, Francesco Bennati, explicitly credited his success to his wonderfully tarantular hands.

Of course, as with Einstein's violin training, sorting out cause and effect gets tricky here. Paganini had been a frail child, sickly and prone to coughs and respiratory infections, but he nevertheless began intensive violin lessons at age seven. So perhaps he'd simply loosened up his fingers through practice. However, other symptoms indicate that Paganini had a genetic condition called Ehlers-Danlos syndrome. People with EDS cannot make much collagen, a fiber that gives ligaments and tendons some rigidity and toughens up bone. The benefit of having less collagen is circus flexibility. Like many people with EDS, Paganini could bend all his joints alarmingly far backward (hence his contortions onstage). But collagen does more than

Widely considered the greatest violinist ever, Niccolò Paganini owed much of his gift to a genetic disorder that made his hands freakishly flexible. Notice the grotesquely splayed thumb. (Courtesy of the Library of Congress)

prevent most of us from touching our toes: a chronic lack can lead to muscle fatigue, weak lungs, irritable bowels, poor eyesight, and translucent, easily damaged skin. Modern studies have shown that musicians have high rates of EDS and other hypermobility syndromes (as do dancers), and while this gives them a big advantage at first, they tend to develop debilitating knee and back pain later, especially if, like Paganini, they stand while performing.

Constant touring wore Paganini down after 1810, and although he'd just entered his thirties, his body began giving out on him. Despite his growing fortune, a landlord in Naples evicted him in 1818, convinced that anyone as skinny and sickly as Paganini must have tuberculosis. He began canceling engagements, unable to perform his art, and by the 1820s he had to sit out whole years of tours to recuperate. Paganini couldn't have known that EDS underlay his general misery; no doctor described the syndrome formally until 1901. But ignorance only heightened his desperation, and he sought out quack apothecaries and doctors. After diagnosing syphilis and tuberculosis and who knows what else, the docs prescribed him harsh, mercury-based purgative pills, which ravaged his already fragile insides. His persistent cough worsened, and eventually his voice died completely, silencing him. He had to wear blue-tinted shades to shield his sore retinas, and at one point his left testicle swelled, he sobbed, to the size of "a little pumpkin." Because of chronic mercury damage to his gums, he had to bind his wobbly teeth with twine to eat.

Sorting out why Paganini finally died, in 1840, is like asking what knocked off the Roman Empire—take your pick. Abusing mercury drugs probably did the most intense damage, but Dr. Bennati, who knew Paganini before his pill-popping days and was the only doctor Paganini never dismissed in a rage for fleecing him, traced the real problem further back. After examining Paganini, Bennati dismissed the diagnoses of tuberculosis and syphilis as spurious. He noted instead, "Nearly all [Paganini's] later ailments can be traced to the extreme sensitivity of his skin." Bennati felt that Paganini's papery EDS skin left him vulnerable to chills, sweats, and fevers and aggravated his frail constitution. Bennati also described the membranes of Paganini's throat, lungs, and colon—all areas affected by EDS—as highly susceptible to irritation. We have to be cautious about reading too much into a diagnosis from the 1830s, but Bennati clearly traced Paganini's vulnerability to something inborn. And in the light of modern knowledge, it seems likely Paganini's physical talents and physical tortures had the same genetic source.

Paganini's afterlife was no less doomed. On his deathbed in Nice, he refused communion and confession, believing they would hasten his demise. He died anyway, and because he'd skipped the sacraments, during Eastertide no less, the Catholic Church refused him proper burial. (As a result his family had to schlep his body around ignominiously for months. It first lay for sixty days in a friend's bed, before health officials stepped in. His corpse was next transferred to an abandoned leper's hospital, where a crooked caretaker charged tourists money to gawk at it, then to a cement tub in an olive oil processing plant. Family finally smuggled his bones back into Genoa in secret and interred him in a private garden, where he lay for thirty-six years, until the church finally forgave him and permitted burial.*)

Paganini's ex post facto excommunication fueled speculation that church elders had it in for Paganini. He did cut the church out of his ample will, and the Faustian stories of selling his soul couldn't have helped. But the church had plenty of nonfictional reasons to spurn the violinist. Paganini gambled flagrantly, even betting his violin once before a show. (He lost.) Worse, he caroused with maidens, charwomen, and blue-blooded dames all across Europe, betraying a truly capacious appetite for fornication. In his most ballsy conquests, he allegedly seduced two of

Napoleon's sisters, then discarded them. "I am ugly as sin, yet all I have to do," he once bragged, "is play my violin and women fall at my feet." The church was not impressed.

Nevertheless Paganini's hypersexual activity brings up a salient point about genetics and fine arts. Given their ubiquity, DNA probably encodes some sort of artistic impulses—but why? Why should we respond so strongly to the arts? One theory is that our brains crave social interaction and affirmation, and shared stories, songs, and images help people bond. Art, in this view, fosters societal cohesion. Then again, our cravings for art could be an accident. Our brain circuits evolved to favor certain sights, sounds, and emotions in our ancient environment, and the fine arts might simply exploit those circuits and deliver sights, sounds, and emotions in concentrated doses. In this view, art and music manipulate our brains in roughly the same way that chocolate manipulates our tongues.

Many scientists, though, explain our lust for art through a process called sexual selection, a cousin of natural selection. In sexual selection, the creatures that mate the most often and pass on their DNA don't necessarily do so because they have survival advantages; they're simply prettier, sexier. Sexy in most creatures means brawny, well-proportioned, or lavishly decorated— think bucks' antlers and peacocks' tails. But singing or dancing can also draw attention to someone's robust physical health. And painting and witty poetry highlight someone's mental prowess and agility—talents crucial for navigating the alliances and hierarchies of primate society. Art, in other words, betrays a sexy mental fitness.

Now, if talents on par with Matisse or Mozart seem a trifle elaborate for getting laid, you're right; but immodest overabundance is a trademark of sexual selection. Imagine how peacock tails evolved. Shimmering feathers made some peacocks more attractive long ago. But big, bright tails soon became normal, since genes for those traits spread in the next generations. So only males with even bigger and brighter feathers won attention. But again, as the generations passed, everyone caught up. So winning attention required even more ostentation—until things got out of hand. In the same way, turning out a perfect sonnet or carving a perfect likeness from marble (or DNA) might be we thinking apes' equivalent of four-foot plumage, fourteen-point antlers, and throbbing-red baboon derrieres.*

Of course, while Paganini's talents raised him to the apex of European society, his DNA hardly made him worthy stud material: he was a mental and physical wreck. It just goes to show that people's sexual desires can all too easily get misaligned from the utilitarian urge to pass on good genes. Sexual attraction has its own potency and power, and culture can override our deepest sexual instincts and aversions, making even genetic taboos like incest seem attractive. So attractive, in fact, that in certain circumstances, those very perversions have informed and influenced our greatest art.

With Henri Toulouse-Lautrec, painter and chronicler of the Moulin Rouge, his art and his genetic lineage seem as tightly entwined as the strands of a double helix. Toulouse-Lautrec's family traced its line back to Charlemagne, and the various counts of Toulouse ruled southern France as de facto kings for centuries. Though proud enough to challenge the power of popes—who excommunicated the Toulouse-Lautrecs ten separate times—the lineage also produced pious Raymond IV, who for God's glory led a hundred thousand men during the first Crusade to pillage Constantinople and Jerusalem. By 1864, when Henri was born, the family had lost political power but still ruled vast estates, and their lives had settled into a baronial fugue of endless shooting, fishing, and boozing.

Scheming to keep the family lands intact, the various Toulouse-Lautrecs usually married each other. But these consanguineous marriages gave harmful recessive mutations a chance to crawl out from their caves. Every human alive carries a few malignant mutations, and we survive only because we possess two copies of every gene, allowing the good copy to offset the bum one. (With most genes the body gets along just fine at 50 percent of full manufacturing capacity, or even less. *Foxp2*'s protein is an exception.) The odds of two random people both having a deleterious mutation in the same gene sink pretty low, but relatives with similar DNA can easily pass two copies of a flaw to their children. Henri's parents were first cousins; his grandmothers, sisters.

At six months, Henri weighed just ten pounds, and the soft spots on his head reportedly hadn't closed at age four. His skull seemed swollen, too, and his stubby arms and legs attached at odd angles. Even as a teenager he walked with a cane sometimes, but it didn't prevent him from falling, twice, and fracturing both femurs, neither of which healed soundly. Modern doctors can't agree on the diagnosis, but all agree Toulouse-Lautrec suffered from a recessive genetic disorder that, among other pains, left his bones brittle and stunted his lower limbs. (Though he was usually listed as four eleven, estimates of his adult height ranged as low as four foot six—a man's torso propped top-heavy onto child-size legs.) Nor was he the family's only victim. Toulouse-Lautrec's brother died in infancy, and his runtish cousins, also products of consanguineous marriages, had both bone deformities and seizure disorders.*

And honestly, the Toulouse-Lautrecs escaped unscathed compared to other inbred aristocrats in Europe, like the hapless Hapsburg dynasty in seventeenth-century Spain. Like sovereigns throughout history, the Hapsburgs equated incest with bloodline "purity," and they bedded only other Hapsburgs whose pedigrees they knew intimately. (As the saying goes: with nobility, familiarity breeds.) The Hapsburgs sat on many thrones throughout Europe, but the Iberian branch seemed especially intent on cousin lovin'—four of every five Spanish Hapsburgs married family members. In the most backward Spanish villages at the time, 20 percent of peasant babies usually died. That number rose to 30 percent among these Hapsburgs, whose mausoleums were positively stuffed with miscarriages and stillborns, and another 20 percent of their children died before age ten. The unlucky survivors often suffered—as seen in royal portraits—from the "Hapsburg lip," a malformed and prognathous jaw that left them looking rather apish.* And the cursed lip grew worse every generation, culminating in the last Spanish Hapsburg king, pitiful Charles II.

Charles's mother was his father's niece, and his aunt doubled as his grandmother. The incest in his past was so determined and sustained that Charles was slightly *more* inbred than a brother-sister love child would be. The results were ugly in every sense. His jaw was so misshapen he could barely chew, his tongue so bloated he could barely speak. The feebleminded monarch didn't walk until age eight, and although he died just shy of forty, he had an honest-to-goodness dotage, full of hallucinations and convulsive episodes. Not learning their lesson, Hapsburg advisers had imported yet another cousin to marry Charles and bear him children. Mercifully, Charles often ejaculated prematurely and later fell impotent, so no heir was forthcoming, and the dynasty ceased. Charles and other Hapsburg kings had employed some of the world's great artists to document their reigns, and not even Titian, Rubens, and Velázquez could mask that notorious lip, nor the general Hapsburg decline across Europe. Still, in an era of dubious medical records, their beautiful portraits of ugliness remain an invaluable tool to track genetic decadence and degeneracy.

Despite his own genetic burden, Toulouse-Lautrec escaped the mental wreckage of the Hapsburgs. His wit even won him popularity among his peers—mindful of his bowed legs and limp, boyhood friends often carried him from spot to spot so he could keep playing. (Later his parents bought him an oversized tricycle.) But the boy's father never forgave his son's handicaps. More than anyone else, the strapping, handsome, bipolar Alphonse Toulouse-Lautrec romanticized his family's past. He often dressed up in chain mail like Ray IV, and once lamented to an archbishop, "Ah, Monseigneur! The days are gone when the Counts of Toulouse could sodomize a monk and hang him afterwards if it pleased them." Alphonse bothered having children only because he wanted hunting companions, and after it became clear that Henri would never tramp through a countryside with a gun, Alphonse wrote the boy out of his will.

Instead of hunting, Toulouse-Lautrec took up another family tradition, art. Various uncles had painted with distinction as amateurs, but Henri's interest coursed deeper. From infancy onward he was always doodling and sketching. At a funeral at age three, unable to sign his name yet, he offered to ink an ox into the guest registry instead. And when laid up with broken legs as a teenager, he began drawing and painting seriously. At age fifteen, he and his mother (also estranged from Count Alphonse) moved to Paris so Toulouse-Lautrec could earn a baccalaureate degree. But when the budding man-child found himself in the continent's art capital, he blew off studying and fell in with a crowd of absinthe-drinking bohemian painters. His parents had encouraged his artistic ambitions before, but now their indulgence soured into disapproval over his new, dissolute life. Other family members were outraged. One reactionary uncle dug out Toulouse-Lautrec's juvenilia left behind at the family estate and held a Savonarola-style bonfire of the vanities.

Painter Henri Toulouse-Lautrec, the offspring of first cousins, had a genetic disorder that stunted his growth and subtly shaped his art. He often sketched or painted from unusual points of view. (Henri Toulouse-Lautrec)

But Toulouse-Lautrec had immersed himself in the Paris art scene, and it was then, in the 1880s, that his DNA began to shape his art. His genetic disorder had left him frankly unattractive, bodily and facially—rotting his teeth, swelling his nose, and causing his lips to flop open and drool. To make himself more appealing to women, he masked his face somewhat with a stylish beard and also, like Paganini, encouraged certain rumors. (He allegedly earned the nickname "Tripod" for his stumpy legs and long, you know.) Still, the funny-looking "dwarf" despaired of ever winning a mistress, so he began cruising for women in the slummy Paris bars and bordellos, sometimes disappearing into them for days. And in all of noble Paris, that's where this aristocrat found his inspiration. He encountered scores of tarts and lowlifes, but despite their low status Toulouse-Lautrec took the time to draw and paint them, and his work, even when shading comic or erotic, lent them dignity. He found something human, even noble, in dilapidated bedrooms and back rooms, and unlike his impressionist predecessors, Toulouse-Lautrec renounced sunsets, ponds, sylvan woods, all outdoor scenes. "Nature has betrayed me," he explained, and he forswore nature in return, preferring to have cocktails at hand and women of ill repute posing in front of him.

His DNA likely influenced the type of art he did as well. With his stubby arms, and with hands he mocked as *grosses pattes* (fat paws), manipulating brushes and painting for long stretches couldn't have been easy. This may have contributed to his decision to devote so much time to posters and prints, less awkward mediums. He also sketched extensively. The Tripod wasn't always extended in the brothels, and during his downtime, Henri whipped up thousands of fresh drawings of women in intimate or contemplative moments. What's more, in both these sketches and his more formal portraits of the Moulin Rouge, he often took unusual points of view—drawing figures from below (a "nostril view"), or cutting their legs out of the frame (he loathed dwelling on others' legs, given his own shortcomings), or raking scenes at upward angles, angles that someone of greater physical but lesser artistic stature might never have perceived. One model once remarked to him, "You are a genius of deformity." He responded, "Of course I am."

Unfortunately, the temptations of the Moulin Rouge—casual sex, late nights, and especially "strangling the parakeet," Toulouse-Lautrec's euphemism for drinking himself stupid—depleted his delicate body in the 1890s. His mother tried to dry him out and had him institutionalized, but the cures never took. (Partly because Toulouse-Lautrec had a custom hollowed-out cane made, to fill with absinthe and drink from surreptitiously.) After relapsing again in 1901, Toulouse-Lautrec had a brain-blowing stroke and died from kidney failure just days later, at thirty-six. Given the painters in his glorious family line, he probably had some genes for artistic talent etched inside him; the counts of Toulouse had also bequeathed him his stunted skeleton, and given their equally notable history of dipsomania, they probably gave him genes that contributed to his alcoholism as well. As with Paganini, if Toulouse-Lautrec's DNA made him an artist in one sense, it undid him at last.

PART IV

The Oracle of DNA

Genetics in the Past, Present, and Future

13

The Past Is Prologue — Sometimes

What Can (and Can't) Genes Teach Us About Historical Heroes?

ll of them are past helping, so it's not clear why we bother. But whether it's Chopin (cystic fibrosis?), Dostoyevsky (epilepsy?), Poe (rabies?), Jane Austen (adult chicken pox?), Vlad the Impaler (porphyria?), or Vincent van Gogh (half the *DSM*), we're incorrigible about trying to diagnose the famous dead. We persist in guessing despite a rather dubious record, in fact. Even fictional characters sometimes receive unwarranted medical advice. Doctors have confidently diagnosed Ebenezer Scrooge with OCD, Sherlock Holmes with autism, and Darth Vader with borderline personality disorder.

A gawking fascination with our heroes certainly explains some of this impulse, and it's inspiring to hear how they overcame grave threats. There's an undercurrent of smugness, too: *we* solved a mystery previous generations couldn't. Above all, as one doctor remarked in the *Journal of the American Medical Association* in 2010, "The most enjoyable aspect of retrospective diagnoses [is that] there is always room for debate and, in the face of no definitive evidence, room for new theories and claims." Those claims often take the form of extrapolations—counterfactual sweeps that use mystery illnesses to explain the origins of masterpieces or wars. Did hemophilia bring down tsarist Russia? Did gout provoke the American Revolution? Did bug bites midwife Charles Darwin's theories? But while our amplified knowledge of genetics makes trawling through ancient evidence all the more tempting, in practice genetics often adds to the medical and moral confusion.

For various reasons—a fascination with the culture, a ready supply of mummies, a host of murky deaths—medical historians have pried especially into ancient Egypt and into pharaohs like Amenhotep IV. Amenhotep has been called Moses, Oedipus, and Jesus Christ rolled into one, and while his religious heresies eventually destroyed his dynasty, they also ensured its immortality, in a roundabout way. In the fourth year of his reign in the mid-1300s BC, Amenhotep changed his name to Akhenaten ("spirit of the sun god Aten"). This was his first step in rejecting the rich polytheism of his forefathers for a starker, more monotheistic worship. Akhenaten soon constructed a new "sun-city" to venerate Aten, and shifted Egypt's normally nocturnal religious services to Aten's prime afternoon hours. Akhenaten also announced the convenient discovery that he was Aten's long-lost son. When hoi polloi began grumbling about these changes, he ordered his praetorian thugs to destroy any pictures of deities besides his supposed father, whether on public monuments or some poor family's crockery. Akhenaten even became a grammar nazi, purging all traces of the plural hieroglyphic *gods* in public discourse.

Akhenaten's seventeen-year reign witnessed equally heretical changes in art. In murals and reliefs from Akhenaten's era, the birds, fish, game, and flowers start to look realistic for the first time. Akhenaten's harem of artists also portrayed his royal family—including Nefertiti, his most favored wife, and Tutankhamen, his heir apparent—in shockingly mundane domestic scenes, eating meals or caressing and smooching. Yet despite the care to get most details right, the bodies themselves of the royal family members appear grotesque, even deformed. It's all the more mysterious because servants and other less-exalted humans in these portraits still look, well, human. Pharaohs in the past had had themselves portrayed as North African Adonises, with square shoulders and dancers' physiques. Not Akhenaten; amid the otherwise overwhelming naturalism, he, Tut, Nefertiti, and other blue bloods look downright alien.

Archaeologists describing this royal art sound like carnival barkers. One promises you'll "recoil from this epitome of physical repulsiveness." Another calls Akhenaten a "humanoid praying mantis." The catalog of freakish traits could run for pages: almond-shaped heads, squat torsos, spidery arms, chicken legs (complete with knees bending backward), Hottentot buttocks, Botox lips, concave chests, pendulous potbellies, and so on. In many pictures Akhenaten has breasts, and the only known nude statue of him has an androgynous, Ken-doll crotch. In short, these works are the anti-*David*, the anti–*Venus de Milo*, of art history.

As with the Hapsburg portraits, some Egyptologists see the pictures as evidence of hereditary deformities in the pharaonic line. Other evidence dovetails with this idea, too. Akhenaten's older brother died in childhood of a mysterious ailment, and a few scholars believe Akhenaten was excluded from court ceremonies when young because of physical handicaps. And in his son Tut's tomb, amid the plunder, archaeologists discovered 130 walking canes, many showing signs of wear. Unable to resist, doctors have retroactively diagnosed these pharaohs with all sorts of ailments, like Marfan syndrome and elephantiasis. But however suggestive, each diagnosis suffered from a crippling lack of hard evidence.

The Egyptian pharaoh Akhenaten (*seated left*) had his court artists depict him and his family as bizarre, almost alien figures, leading many modern doctors to retrodiagnose Akhenaten with genetic ailments. (Andreas Praefcke)

Enter genetics. The Egyptian government had long hesitated to let geneticists have at their most precious mummies. Boring into tissues or bones inevitably destroys small bits of them, and paleogenetics was pretty iffy at first, plagued by contamination and inconclusive results. Only in 2007 did Egypt relent, allowing scientists to withdraw DNA from five generations of mummies, including Tut and Akhenaten. When combined with meticulous CT scans of the corpses, this genetic work helped resolve some enigmas about the era's art and politics.

First, the study turned up no major defects in Akhenaten or his family, which hints that the Egyptian royals looked like normal people. That means the portraits of Akhenaten—which sure don't look normal—probably didn't strive for verisimilitude. They were propaganda. Akhenaten apparently decided that his status as the sun god's immortal son lifted him so far above the normal human rabble that he had to inhabit a new type of body in public portraiture. Some of Akhenaten's strange features in the pictures (distended bellies, porcine haunches) call to mind fertility deities, so perhaps he wanted to portray himself as the womb of Egypt's well-being as well.

All that said, the mummies did show subtler deformities, like clubbed feet and cleft palates. And each succeeding generation had more to endure. Tut, of the fourth generation, inherited both clubfoot and a cleft palate. He also broke his femur when young, like Toulouse-Lautrec, and bones in his foot died because of poor congenital blood supply. Scientists realized why Tut suffered so when they examined his genes. Certain DNA "stutters" (repetitive stretches of bases) get passed intact from parent to child, so they offer a way to trace lineages. Unfortunately for Tut, both his parents had the same stutters—because his mom and dad had the same parents. Nefertiti may have been Akhenaten's most celebrated wife, but for the crucial business of producing an heir, Akhenaten turned to a sister.

This incest likely compromised Tut's immune system and did the dynasty in. Akhenaten had, one historian noted, "a pathological lack of interest" in anything beyond Egypt, and Egypt's foreign enemies gleefully raided the kingdom's outer edges, imperiling state security. The problem lingered after Akhenaten died, and a few years after the nine-year-old Tut assumed the throne, the boy renounced his father's heresies and restored the ancient gods, hoping for better fortune. It didn't come. While working on Tut's mummy, scientists found scads of malarial DNA deep inside his bones. Malaria wasn't uncommon then; similar tests reveal that both of Tut's grandparents had it, at least twice, and they both lived until their fifties. However, Tut's malarial infection, the scientists argued, "added one strain too many to a body that"—because of incestuous genes—"could no longer carry the load." He succumbed at age nineteen. Indeed, some strange brown splotches on the walls inside Tut's tomb provide clues about just how sudden his decline was. DNA and chemical analysis has revealed these splotches as biological in origin: Tut's death came so quickly that the decorative paint on the tomb's inner walls hadn't dried, and it attracted mold after his retinue sealed him up. Worst of all, Tut compounded his genetic defects for the next generation by taking a half sister as his own wife. Their only known children died at five months and seven months and ended up as sorry swaddled mummies in Tut's tomb, macabre additions to his gold mask and walking sticks.

Powerful forces in Egypt never forgot the family's sins, and when Tut died heirless, an army general seized the throne. He in turn died childless, but another commander, Ramses, took over. Ramses and his successors expunged most traces of Akhenaten, Tut, and Nefertiti in the annals of the pharaohs, erasing them with the same determination Akhenaten had shown in erasing other gods. As a final insult, Ramses and his heirs erected buildings over Tut's tomb to conceal it. In fact, they concealed it so well that even looters struggled to find it. As a result, Tut's treasures survived mostly intact over the centuries—treasures that, in time, would grant him and his heretical, incestuous family something like immortality again.

To be sure, for every well-reasoned retrodiagnosis—Tut, Toulouse-Lautrec, Paganini, Goliath (gigantism, definitely)—there are some doozies. Probably the most egregious retrodiagnosis began in 1962, when a doctor published a paper on porphyria, a group of red-blood-cell disorders.

Porphyria leads to a buildup of toxic by-products that can (depending on the type) disfigure the skin, sprout unwanted body hair, or short-circuit the nerves and induce psychosis. The doctor thought this sounded a lot like werewolves, and he floated the idea that widespread fables about wolf-people might have a medical basis. In 1982 a Canadian biochemist went one better. He noted other symptoms of porphyria—blistering in sunlight, protruding teeth, bloody red urine—and started giving talks suggesting that the disease seemed more likely to inspire tales about vampires. When pressed to explain, he declined to write up a scientific paper, and followed up instead (not a good sign) by appearing on a national U.S. talk show. On Halloween. Viewers heard him explain that "vampire" porphyrics had roamed about at night because of the blistering, and had probably found relief from their symptoms by drinking blood, to replace missing blood components. And what of the famously infectious vampire bite? Porphyric genes run in families, he argued, but it often takes stress or shock to trigger an outbreak. A brother or sister nipping at you and sucking your blood surely qualifies as stressful.

The show drew lots of attention and soon had worried-sick porphyrics asking their physicians if they would mutate into blood-lusting vampires. (A few years later, a deranged Virginia man even stabbed and dismembered his porphyric buddy to protect himself.) These incidents were all the more unfortunate because the theory is hogwash. If nothing else, the traits we consider classically vampiric, like a nocturnal nature, weren't common in folklore vampires. (Most of what we know today are late-nineteenth-century tropes that Bram Stoker invented.) Nor do the supposed scientific facts tally. Drinking blood would bring no relief, since the blood components that cure porphyria don't survive digestion. And genetically, while many porphyrics do suffer from sunburns, the really horrific, blistering burns that might evoke thoughts of supernatural evil are limited to one rare type of porphyria mutation. Just a few hundred cases of it have been documented, ever, far too few to explain the widespread vampire hysteria of centuries past. (Some villages in eastern Europe were tilling their graveyards once per week to search for vampires.) Overall, then, the porphyria fiasco explains more about modern credulity—how willingly people believe things with a scientific veneer—than the origins of folklore monsters.

A more plausible (but still hotly disputed) case of history pivoting around porphyria took place during the reign of Great Britain's King George III. George didn't burn in sunlight but did urinate what looked like rosé wine, among other signs of porphyria, such as constipation and yellowed eyes. He also had rambling fits of insanity. He once solemnly shook hands with an oak branch, convinced he'd finally had the pleasure with the King of Prussia; and in an admittedly vampiric twist, he complained he couldn't see himself in mirrors. At his shrieking worst, ministers confined George to a straitjacket. True, George's symptoms didn't fit porphyria perfectly, and his mental fits were unusually intense for porphyrics. But his genes might have carried complicating factors: hereditary madness was endemic among European royalty between about 1500 and 1900, and most were George's relatives. Regardless of the cause, George suffered his first fit in early 1765, which frightened Parliament enough to pass an act clarifying who should assume power if the king went stark mad. The king, offended, sacked the prime minister. But amid the chaos that spring, the Stamp Act had passed, which began to poison the American colonies' relationship with George. And after a new prime minister took over, the scorned former prime minister decided to focus his remaining power on punishing the colonies, a favorite hobby. Another influential statesman, William Pitt, who wanted to keep America in the empire, might conceivably have blunted that vengeance. But Pitt suffered from another highly heritable disease, gout (possibly triggered by a rich diet or by drinking cheap, lead-tainted Portuguese wines). Laid up, Pitt missed some crucial policy debates in 1765 and afterward, and mad King George's government eventually pushed the American colonists too far.

The new United States rid itself of dynastic lines and bypassed the hereditary insanity that demented European rulers. Of course, U.S. presidents have had their own share of ailments. John F. Kennedy was congenitally sickly—he missed two-thirds of kindergarten owing to illness—and was (incorrectly) diagnosed with hepatitis and leukemia in prep school. When he reached adulthood, doctors sliced open his thigh every two months to insert hormonal pellets, and the family reportedly kept emergency medicine in safety-deposit boxes around the country. Good thing. Kennedy collapsed regularly and received last rites multiple times before becoming president. Historians now know Kennedy had Addison's disease, which ruins the adrenal glands and depletes the body of cortisol. One common side effect of Addison's, bronze skin, might well have supplied Kennedy with his vivacious and telegenic tan.

But it was a serious disease overall, and although his rivals for the presidency in 1960—first Lyndon Johnson, then Richard Nixon—didn't know exactly what ailed JFK, they didn't shy away from spreading rumors that he would (cringe) die during his first term. In response, Kennedy's handlers misled the public through cleverly worded statements. Doctors discovered Addison's in the 1800s as a side effect of tuberculosis; this became known as "classic" Addison's. So Kennedy's people could say with a straight face that he "does not now nor has he ever had an ailment classically described as Addison's disease, which is a tuberculose destruction of the adrenal gland." In truth most cases of Addison's are innate; they're autoimmune attacks coordinated by MHC genes. Moreover, Kennedy probably had at least a genetic susceptibility to Addison's, since his sister Eunice also suffered from it. But short of disinterring Kennedy, the exact genetic contribution (if any) will remain obscure.

With Abraham Lincoln's genetics, doctors have an even trickier case, since they don't know for certain if he suffered from a disease. The first hint that he might have came in 1959 when a physician diagnosed a seven-year-old with Marfan syndrome. After tracking the disease through the boy's family tree, the doctor discovered, eight generations back, one Mordecai Lincoln Jr., the great-great-grandfather of Abe. Although this was suggestive—Lincoln's gaunt physique and spidery limbs look classically Marfan, and it's a dominant genetic mutation, so it runs in families—the discovery proved nothing, since the boy might have inherited the Marfan mutation from any of his ancestors.

The mutated Marfan gene creates a defective version of fibrillin, a protein that provides structural support for soft tissues. Fibrillin helps form the eyes, for instance, so Marfan victims often have poor eyesight. (This explains why some modern doctors diagnosed Akhenaten as Marfanoid; he might naturally have preferred his kingdom's sun god to Egypt's squinting nocturnal deities.) More important, fibrillin girds blood vessels: Marfan victims often die young after their aortas wear out and rupture. In fact, examining blood vessels and other soft tissue was the only sure way to diagnose Marfan for a century. So without Lincoln's soft tissues, doctors in 1959 and after could only pore over photos and medical records and argue about ambiguous secondary symptoms.

The idea of testing Lincoln's DNA emerged around 1990. Lincoln's violent death had produced plenty of skull bits and bloody pillowcases and shirt cuffs to extract DNA from. Even the pistol ball recovered from Lincoln's skull might have traces of DNA. So in 1991 nine experts convened to debate the feasibility, and ethics, of running such tests. Right away a congressman from Illinois (natch) jumped into the fray and demanded that the experts determine, among other things, whether Lincoln would have endorsed the project. This proved difficult. Not only did Lincoln die before Friedrich Miescher even discovered DNA, but Lincoln left no statement (why would he?) of his views on privacy in posthumous medical research. What's more, genetic testing requires pulping small bits of priceless artifacts—and scientists still might not get a solid answer. As a matter of fact, the Lincoln committee realized disturbingly late in the process how complicated getting a diagnosis would be. Emerging work showed that Marfan syndrome could arise from many different fibrillin mutations, so geneticists would have to search through long swaths of DNA to diagnose it—a much harder prospect than searching for a single-point mutation. And if they found nothing, Lincoln still might have Marfan's, through an unknown mutation. Plus, other diseases can mimic Marfan's by garbling other genes, adding to the complications. A serious scientific venture suddenly looked shaky, and it didn't bolster anyone's confidence when garish rumors emerged that a Nobel laureate wanted to clone and hawk "authentic Lincoln DNA" embedded in amber jewelry. The committee eventually scrapped the whole idea, and it remains on hold today.

Though ultimately futile, the attempt to study Lincoln's DNA did provide some guidelines for judging the worth of other retrogenetics projects. The most important scientific consideration is the quality of current technology and whether (despite the frustration of waiting) scientists should hold off and let future generations do the work. Moreover, while it seems obvious that scientists need to prove they can reliably diagnose a genetic disease in living people first, in Lincoln's case they started rushing forward without this assurance. Nor could the technology in 1991 have skirted the inevitable DNA contamination of well-handled artifacts like bloody cuffs and pillowcases. (For this reason, one expert suggested practicing first on the anonymous bones of Civil War amputees piled up in national museums.)

As far as ethical concerns, some scientists argued that historians already invade people's diaries and medical records, and retrogenetics simply extends this license. But the analogy doesn't quite hold, because genetics can reveal flaws even the person in question didn't know about. That's not so terrible if they're safely dead, but any living descendants might not appreciate being outed. And if invading someone's privacy is unavoidable, the work should at least attempt to answer weighty or otherwise unanswerable questions. Geneticists could easily run tests to determine if Lincoln had wet or dry earwax, but that doesn't exactly illuminate Lincoln the man. A diagnosis of Marfan syndrome arguably would. Most Marfan victims die young from a ruptured aorta; so perhaps Lincoln, fifty-six when assassinated,* was doomed to never finish his second term anyway. Or if tests ruled out Marfan, they might point toward something else. Lincoln deteriorated visibly during his last months in office; the *Chicago Tribune* ran an editorial in March 1865 urging him, war or no war, to take time off and rest before stress and overwork killed him. But perhaps it wasn't stress. He might have been afflicted with another Marfan-like disease. And because some of these diseases cause significant pain and even cancer, Lincoln might conceivably have *known* he'd die in office (as FDR later did). This would put Lincoln's change of vice presidents in 1864 and his plans for postwar leniency toward the Confederacy in new light. Genetic tests could also reveal whether the brooding Lincoln had a genetic predilection for depression, a popular but largely circumstantial theory nowadays.

Similar questions apply to other presidents. Given Kennedy's Addison's, perhaps Camelot would have expired prematurely no matter what. (Conversely, Kennedy might not have pushed himself and risen so quickly in politics if he hadn't sensed the

Reaper.) And the genetics of Thomas Jefferson's family brings up fascinating contradictions about his views on slavery.

In 1802 several scurrilous newspapers began suggesting that Jefferson had fathered children with a slave "concubine." Sally Hemings had caught Jefferson's eye in Paris when she served him during his stint as American minister there. (She was probably his late wife's half sister; Jefferson's father-in-law had a slave mistress.) Sometime after returning home to Monticello, Jefferson allegedly took Sally as his lover. Jefferson's newspaper enemies jeered her as the "African Venus," and the Massachusetts legislature publicly debated Jefferson's morals, including the Hemings affair, in 1805. But even friendly eyewitnesses recall that Sally's sons in particular were cocoa-colored doppelgängers of Jefferson. A guest once caught one Hemings boy in tableau behind Jefferson's shoulder during a dinner party, and the resemblance flabbergasted him. Through diaries and other documents, historians later determined that Jefferson was in residence at Monticello nine months before the birth of each of Sally's children. And Jefferson emancipated each of those children at age twenty-one, a privilege he did not extend to other slaves. After moving away from Virginia, one of those freed slaves, Madison, bragged to newspapers that he knew Jefferson was his father, and another, Eston, changed his surname to Jefferson partly because of his resemblance to statues of TJ in Washington, D.C.

Jefferson always denied fathering any slave children, however, and many contemporaries didn't believe the charges either; some blamed nearby cousins instead, or other Jefferson relatives. So in the late 1990s scientists effectively hooked Jefferson up to a genetic polygraph. Because the Y chromosome cannot cross over and recombine with other chromosomes, males pass down the full, unchanged Y to each son. Jefferson had no recognized sons, but other male relatives with the same Jefferson Y, like his uncle, Field Jefferson, did have sons. Field Jefferson's sons had their own sons in turn, and they their own sons, and the Jefferson Y eventually got passed down to a few males living today. Luckily, Eston Hemings's line had also produced males every generation, and geneticists tracked members of both families down in 1999. Their Ys were perfect matches. Of course, the test proved only that *a* Jefferson had fathered Sally Hemings's children, not which specific Jefferson. But given the additional historical evidence, a case against Jefferson for child support looks strong.

Again, it's undeniably titillating to speculate about Jefferson's private life—love blossoming in Paris, his pining for Sally while stuck in sultry D.C.—but *l'affaire* also illuminates Jefferson's character. He would have fathered Eston Hemings in 1808, six years after the first allegations appeared—which reveals either enormous hubris or sincere devotion to Sally. And yet like many of the English monarchs he despised, Jefferson disavowed his bastard children, to salvage his reputation. Even more uncomfortably, Jefferson publicly opposed, and authored legislation to make illegal, marriages between blacks and whites, pandering to fears of miscegenation and racial impurity. It seems a damning account of hypocrisy in perhaps our most philosophical president.

Since the Jefferson revelations, Y-chromosome testing has become an increasingly crucial tool in historical genetics. This does have one downside, in that the patrilineal Y defines someone rather narrowly: you can learn about only one of his many, many ancestors in any generation. (Similar limitations arise with matrilineal mtDNA.) Despite this caveat Y can reveal a surprising amount. For example, Y testing reveals that the biggest biological stud in history probably wasn't Casanova or King Solomon but Genghis Khan, the ancestor of sixteen million men today: one in two hundred males on earth carries his testes-determining chromosome. When the Mongols conquered a territory, they fathered as many children as possible with local women, to tie them to their new overlords. ("It's pretty clear what they were doing when they weren't fighting," one historian commented.) Genghis apparently took on much of this burden himself, and central Asia is littered with his litters today.

Archaeologists have studied the Y and other chromosomes to untangle Jewish history as well. The Old Testament chronicles how Jews once divided themselves into the kingdoms of Judea and Israel, independent states that probably developed distinct genetic markers, since people tended to marry within their extended family. After many millennia of Jewish exiles and diasporas, many historians had given up hope of tracing exactly where the remnants of each kingdom had ended up. But the prevalence of unique genetic signatures (including diseases) among modern Ashkenazi Jews, and other unique genetic signatures among Sephardic and Oriental Jews, has allowed geneticists to trace ancient lineages, and determine that the original biblical divisions have largely persisted through time. Scholars have also traced the genetic origins of Jewish priestly castes. In Judaism, the Cohanim, who all supposedly descended from Aaron, brother of Moses, have special ceremonial roles in temple rites. This honor passes from Cohanim father to Cohanim son, exactly like the Y. And it turns out that Cohanim across the world do indeed have very similar Ys, indicating a single patriarchal line. Further study shows that this "Y-chromosomal Aaron" lived, roughly, in Moses's time, confirming the truth of Jewish tradition. (At least in this case. Levites, a related but distinct Jewish group, also pass down religious privileges in a patrilineal way. But Levites around the world rarely share the same Y, so either Jewish tradition bungled this story,* or Levite wives slept around behind their husbands' backs.)

What's more, studying Jewish DNA has helped confirm a once scarcely credible legend among the Lemba tribesmen in Africa. The Lemba had always maintained that they had Jewish roots—that ages and ages ago, a man named Buba led them out of Israel to southern Africa, where they continue today to spurn pork, circumcise boys, wear yarmulke-like hats, and decorate their homes with emblems of elephants surrounded by six-sided Stars of David. The Buba tale sounded awfully tall to archaeologists, who explained these "Black Hebrews" as a case of cultural transmission, not human emigration. But Lemba DNA ratifies their Jewish roots: 10 percent of Lemba men overall, and half the males in the oldest, most revered families—the priestly caste—have none other than the signature Cohanim Y.

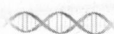

While studying DNA can be helpful in answering some questions, you can't always tell if a famous someone suffered from a genetic disorder just by testing his or her descendants. That's because even if scientists find a clean genetic signal for a syndrome, there's no guarantee the descendants acquired the defective DNA from their celebrated great-great-whatever. That fact, along with the reluctance of most caretakers to disinter ancient bones for testing, leaves many medical historians doing old-fashioned genetic analysis—charting diseases in family trees and piecing together diagnoses from a constellation of symptoms. Perhaps the most intriguing and vexing patient undergoing analysis today is Charles Darwin, because of both the elusive nature of his illness and the possibility that he passed it to his children by marrying a close relative—a potentially heartbreaking example of natural selection in action.

After enrolling in medical school in Edinburgh at age sixteen, Darwin dropped out two years later, when surgery lessons began. In his autobiography Darwin tersely recounted the scenes he endured, but he did describe watching an operation on a sick boy, and you can just imagine the thrashing and screaming in those days before anesthesia. The moment both changed and presaged Darwin's life. Changed, because it convinced him to drop out and do something else for a living. Presaged, because the surgery roiled Darwin's stomach, a premonition of the ill health that dogged him ever after.

His health started to fall apart aboard HMS *Beagle*. Darwin had skipped a prevoyage physical in 1831, convinced he would fail it, and once asea he proved an inveterate landlubber, constantly laid low by seasickness. His stomach could handle only raisins for many meals, and he wrote woeful letters seeking advice from his father, a physician. Darwin did prove himself fit during the *Beagle*'s layovers, taking thirty-mile hikes in South America and collecting loads of samples. But after returning to England in 1836 and marrying, he deteriorated into a honest-to-gosh invalid, a wheezing wreck who often disgusted even himself.

It would take the genius of Akhenaten's greatest court caricaturist to capture how cramped and queasy and out-of-sorts Darwin usually felt. He suffered from boils, fainting fits, heart flutters, numb fingers, insomnia, migraines, dizziness, eczema, and "fiery spokes and dark clouds" that hovered before his eyes. The strangest symptom was a ringing in his ears, after which — as thunder follows lightning — he'd always pass horrendous gas. But above all, Darwin barfed. He barfed after breakfast, after lunch, after dinner, brunch, teatime — whenever — and kept going until he was dry heaving. In peak form he vomited twenty times an hour, and once vomited twenty-seven days running. Mental exertion invariably made his stomach worse, and even Darwin, the most intellectually fecund biologist ever, could make no sense of this. "What thought has to do with digesting roast beef," he once sighed, "I cannot say."

The illness upended Darwin's whole existence. For healthier air, he retreated to Down House, sixteen miles from London, and his intestinal distress kept him from visiting other people's homes, for fear of fouling up their privies. He then invented rambling, unconvincing excuses to forbid friends from calling on him in turn: "I suffer from ill-health of a very peculiar kind," he wrote to one, "which prevents me from all mental excitement, which is always followed by spasmodic sickness, and I do not think I could stand conversation with you, which to me would be so full of enjoyment." Not that isolation cured him. Darwin never wrote for more than twenty minutes without stabbing pain somewhere, and he cumulatively missed years of work with various aches. He eventually had a makeshift privy installed behind a half-wall, half-screen in his study, for privacy's sake — and even grew out his famous beard largely to soothe the eczema always scratching at his face.

That said, Darwin's sickness did have its advantages. He never had to lecture or teach, and he could let T. H. Huxley, his bulldog, do the dirty work of sparring with Bishop Wilberforce and other opponents while he lay about the house and refined his work. Uninterrupted months at home also let Darwin keep up his correspondence, through which he gathered invaluable evidence of evolution. He dispatched many an unwary naturalist on some ridiculous errand to, say, count pigeon tail feathers, or search for greyhounds with tan spots near their eyes. These requests seem strangely particular, but they revealed intermediate evolutionary forms, and in sum they reassured Darwin that natural selection took place. In one sense, then, being an invalid might have been as important to *On the Origin of Species* as visiting the Galápagos.

Darwin understandably had a harder time seeing the benefits of migraines and dry heaving, and he spent years searching for relief. He swallowed much of the periodic table in various medicinal forms. He dabbled in opium, sucked lemons, and took "prescriptions" of ale. He tried early electroshock therapy—a battery-charged "galvanization belt" that zapped his abdomen.

The most eccentric cure was the "water cure," administered by a former classmate from medical school. Dr. James Manby Gully had had no serious plans to practice medicine while in school, but the family's coffee plantation in Jamaica went bust after Jamaican slaves gained their freedom in 1834, and Gully had no choice but to see patients full-time. He opened a resort in Malvern in western England in the 1840s, and it quickly became a trendy Victorian spa; Charles Dickens, Alfred, Lord Tennyson, and Florence Nightingale all took cures there. Darwin decamped to Malvern in 1849 with his family and servants.

The water cure basically consisted of keeping patients as moist as possible at all times. After a 5 a.m. cock-a-doodle-doo, servants wrapped Darwin in wet sheets, then doused him with buckets of cold water. This was followed by a group hike that included plenty of hydration breaks at various wells and mineral springs. Back at their cottages, patients ate biscuits and drank more water, and the completion of breakfast opened up the day to Malvern's main activity, bathing. Bathing supposedly drew blood away from the inflamed inner organs and toward the skin, providing relief. Between baths, patients might have a refreshing cold water enema, or strap themselves into a wet abdominal compress called a "Neptune Girdle." Baths often lasted until dinner, which invariably consisted of boiled mutton, fish, and, obviously, some sparkling local H_2O. The long day ended with Darwin crashing asleep into a (dry) bed.

Would that it worked. After four months at this hydrosanitarium, Darwin felt bully, better than at any time since the *Beagle*, able to hike seven miles a day. Back at Down House he continued the cure in a relaxed form, constructing a sweat lodge for use every morning, followed by a polar-bear plunge into a huge cistern (640 gallons) filled with water as cold as 40°F. But as work piled up on Darwin again, the stress got to him, and the

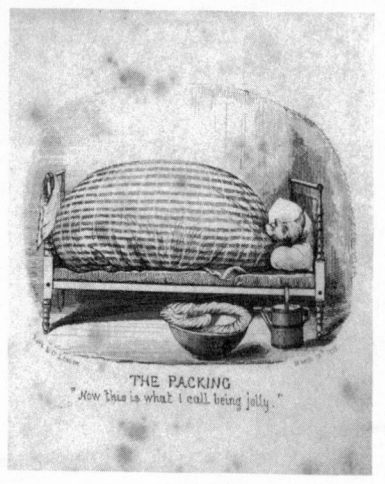

THE PACKING
"Now this is what I call being jolly."

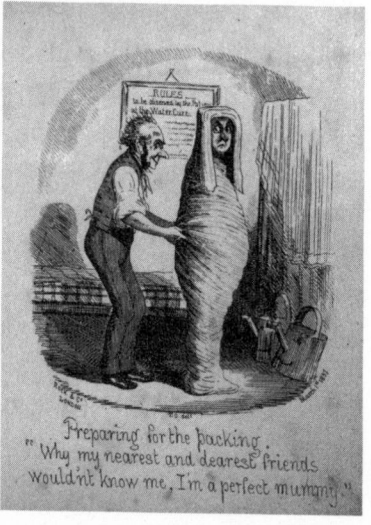

Preparing for the packing.
"Why my nearest and dearest friends
wouldn't know me, I'm a perfect mummy."

The Douche.
Oh! Oh! Oh! Oh!!!!!!!

Scenes from the popular "water cure" in Victorian times, for patients with stubborn ailments. Charles Darwin underwent a similar regime to cure his own mystery illness, which dogged him most of his adult life. (Courtesy of the National Library of Medicine) water cure lost its power. He relapsed, and despaired of ever knowing the cause of his frailty.

Modern doctors have scarcely done better. A list of more or less probable retrodiagnoses includes middle-ear damage, pigeon allergies, "smoldering hepatitis," lupus, narcolepsy, agoraphobia, chronic fatigue syndrome, and an adrenal-gland tumor. (That last one might explain Darwin's Kennedy-esque bronze glow late in life, despite being a hitherto pasty Englishman who spent most hours indoors.) One reasonably convincing diagnosis is Chagas' disease, which causes flu-like symptoms. Darwin might have picked it up from the South American "kissing bug," since he kept a kissing bug as a pet on the *Beagle*. (He delighted at how it sucked blood from his finger, puffing up like a tick.) But Chagas' disease doesn't fit all Darwin's symptoms. And it's possible that Chagas merely crippled Darwin's digestive tract and left him vulnerable to deeper, dormant genetic flaws. Indeed, other semiplausible diagnoses, like "cyclical vomiting syndrome" and severe lactose intolerance,* have strong genetic components. In addition, much of Darwin's family was sickly growing up, and his mother, Susannah, died of undetermined abdominal trouble when Darwin was eight.

These genetic concerns become all the more poignant because of what happened to Darwin's children. Roughly 10 percent of leisure-class Victorians married blood relatives, and Darwin did his part by marrying Emma Wedgwood, his first cousin. (They shared a grandfather in Josiah Wedgwood, the crockery maven.) Of the ten Darwin children, most were sickly. Three proved infertile as adults, and three died young, roughly double the child mortality rate in England. One, Charles Waring, survived nineteen months; Mary Eleanor lived twenty-three days. When his favorite child, Anne Elizabeth, fell ill, Darwin took her to Dr. Gully for the water cure. When she died anyway, at age ten, it snuffed the last lingering remnant of Darwin's religious faith.

Despite any bitterness toward God, Darwin mostly blamed himself for his children's infirmity. While most children born to first cousins are healthy (well north of 90 percent), they do have higher risks for birth defects and medical problems, and the numbers can creep higher still in unlucky families. Darwin stood uneasily ahead of his time in suspecting this danger. He tested the effects of inbreeding in plants, for instance, not only to shore up his theories of heredity and natural selection but also to see if he could shed light on his own family's ailments. Darwin meanwhile petitioned Parliament to include a question about consanguineous marriages and health in the 1871 census. When the petition failed, the idea continued to fester, and Darwin's surviving children inherited his anxieties. One son, George, argued for outlawing cousin marriages in England, and his (childless) son Leonard presided over the First International Congress of Eugenics in 1912, a congress devoted, ironically enough, to breeding fitter human beings.

Scientists could possibly identify Darwin's ailment with a DNA sample. But unlike Lincoln, Darwin died meekly of a heart attack, leaving no bloody pillowcases. And so far Westminster Abbey refuses to allow DNA sampling of Darwin's bones, partly because doctors and geneticists can't agree what to test for. Complicating things, some doctors conclude that Darwin's illness had a serious hypochondriac edge, too, or sprung from other causes that we can't pin down so easily. Indeed, our focus on Darwin's DNA might even be misplaced, a product of our times. It should serve as a warning that when Freudianism was ascendant, many scientists saw Darwin's illness as the consequence of an Oedipal struggle: the claim was that, unable to overthrow his biological father (an imposing man), Darwin instead "slew the Heavenly Father in the realm of natural history," as one doctor gushed. To such thinking, Darwin's suffering "obviously" derived from repressed guilt for this patricide.

Perhaps our groping about in DNA sequences for the roots of illnesses like Darwin's will look equally quaint someday. And regardless, this groping about misses a deeper point about Darwin and others—that they persevered, despite their illnesses. We tend to treat DNA as a secular soul, our chemical essence. But even a full rendering of someone's DNA reveals only so much.

14

Three Billion Little Pieces

Why Don't Humans Have More Genes Than Other Species?

Considering its scale, its scope, its ambition, the Human Genome Project—a multidecade, multibillion-dollar effort to sequence all human DNA—was rightly called the Manhattan Project of biology. But few anticipated at the outset that the HGP would be beset with just as many moral ambiguities as the venture in Los Alamos. Ask your biologist friends for a précis of the project, in fact, and you'll get a pretty good handle on their values. Do they admire the project's government scientists as selfless and steadfast or dismiss them as stumbling bureaucrats? Do they praise the private-sector challenge to the government as heroic rebellion or condemn it as greedy self-aggrandizement? Do they think the project succeeded or harp on its disappointments? Like any complex epic, the sequencing of the human genome can support virtually any reading.

The HGP traces its pedigree to the 1970s, when British biologist Frederick Sanger, already a Nobel laureate, invented a method to sequence DNA—to record the order of the A's, C's,

G's, and T's and thereby (hopefully) determine what the DNA does. In brief, Sanger's method involved three basic steps: heating the DNA in question until its two strands separated; breaking those strands into fragments; and using individual A's, C's, G's, and T's to build new complementary strands based on the fragments. Cleverly, though, Sanger sprinkled in special radioactive versions of each base, which got incorporated into the complements. Because Sanger could distinguish whether A, C, G, or T was producing radioactivity at any point along the complement, he could also deduce which base resided there, and tally the sequence.*

Sanger had to read these bases one by one, an excruciatingly tedious process. Nevertheless it allowed him to sequence the first genome, the fifty-four hundred bases and eleven genes of the virus φ-X174. (This work won Sanger a second Nobel in 1980—not bad for someone who once confessed he could never have attended Cambridge University "if my parents had not been fairly rich.") In 1986 two biologists in California automated Sanger's method. And instead of using radioactive bases, they substituted fluorescent versions of A, C, G, and T, each of which produced a different color when strummed by a laser—DNA in Technicolor. This machine, run by a computer, suddenly made large-scale sequencing projects seem feasible.

Strangely, though, the U.S. government agency that funded most biology research, the National Institutes of Health, showed zero interest in DNA sequencing. *Who*, the NIH wondered, *wanted to wade through three billion letters of formless data?* Other departments weren't so dismissive. The Department of Energy considered sequencing a natural extension of its work on how radioactivity damages DNA, and it appreciated the transformative potential of the work. So in April 1987, the DoE opened the world's first human genome project, a seven-year, $1-billion effort centered in Los Alamos, across town from the site of the

Manhattan Project. Funnily enough, as soon as NIH bureaucrats heard the B-word, *billion*, they decided sequencing made
sense after all. So in September 1988 the NIH set up a rival
sequencing institute to scoop up its share of the budgetary pie. In
a scientific coup, it secured James Watson as the institute's chief.

By the 1980s, Watson had developed a reputation as the
"Caligula of biology," someone who, as one science historian put
it, "was given license to say anything that came to his mind and
expect to be taken seriously. And unfortunately he did so, with a
casual and brutal offhandedness." Still, however much he repulsed
some of them personally, Watson retained the intellectual respect
of his colleagues, which proved crucial for his new job, since few
big-name biologists shared his enthusiasm for sequencing. Some
biologists disliked the reductionist approach of the HGP, which
threatened to demote human beings to dribbles of data. Others
feared the project would swallow up all available research funds
but not yield usable results for decades, a classic boondoggle.
Still others simply found the work unbearably monotonous, even
with machines helping. (One scientist cracked that only incarcerated felons should have to sequence—"twenty megabases
[each]," he suggested, "with time off for accuracy.") Most of all,
scientists feared losing autonomy. A project so extensive would
have to be coordinated centrally, and biologists resented the idea
of becoming "indentured servants" who took orders on what
research to pursue. "Many people in the American scientific
community," one early HGP supporter moaned, "will support
small mediocrity before they can even consider the possibility
that there can be some large excellence."

For all his crassness, Watson assuaged his colleagues' fears
and helped the NIH wrest control of the project from the DoE.
He canvassed the country, giving a stump speech about the
urgency of sequencing, and emphasized that the HGP would
sequence not only human DNA but mouse and fruit fly DNA, so

all geneticists would benefit. He also suggested mapping human chromosomes first thing, by locating every gene on them (similar to what Charles Sturtevant did in 1911 with fruit flies). With the map, Watson argued, any scientist could find her pet gene and make progress studying it without waiting fifteen years, the NIH's timeline for sequencing. With this last argument, Watson also had his eye on Congress, whose fickle, know-nothing members might yank funding if they didn't see results last week. To further persuade Congress, some HGP boosters all but promised that as long as Congress ponied up, the HGP would liberate humans from the misery of most diseases. (And not just diseases; some hinted that hunger, poverty, and crime might cease.) Watson brought in scientists from other nations, too, to give sequencing international prestige, and soon the HGP had lumbered to life.

Then Watson, being Watson, stepped in it. In his third year as HGP director, he found out that the NIH planned to patent some genes that one of its neuroscientists had discovered. The idea of patenting genes nauseated most scientists, who argued that patent restrictions would interfere with basic research. To compound the problem, the NIH admitted it had only located the genes it wanted to patent; it had no idea what the genes did. Even scientists who supported DNA patents (like biotech executives) blanched at this revelation. They feared that the NIH was setting a terrible precedent, one that would promote the rapid discovery of genes above everything else. They foresaw a "genome grab," where businesses would sequence and hurriedly patent any gene they found, then charge "tolls" anytime anyone used them for any purpose.

Watson, who claimed that no one had consulted him on all this, went apoplectic, and he had a point: patenting genes could undermine the public-good arguments for the HGP, and it would certainly renew scientists' suspicions. But instead of laying out his concerns calmly and professionally, Caligula lit into his boss at the NIH, and behind her back he told reporters the policy was moronic and destructive. A power struggle ensued, and Watson's supervisor proved the better bureaucratic warrior: she raised a stink behind the scenes, Watson alleges, about conflicts of interest in biotech stock he owned, and continued her attempts to muzzle him. "She created conditions by which there was no way I could stay," Watson fumed. He soon resigned.

But not before causing more trouble. The NIH neuroscientist who'd found the genes had discovered them with an automated process that involved computers and robots and little human contribution. Watson didn't approve of the procedure because it could identify only 90 percent of human genes, not the full set. Moreover—always a sucker for elegance—he sneered that the process lacked style and craft. In a hearing before the U.S. Senate about the patents, Watson dismissed the operation as something that "could be run by monkeys." This didn't exactly charm the NIH "monkey" in question, one J. Craig Venter. In fact, partly because of Watson, Venter soon became (in)famous, an international scientific villain. Yet Venter found himself quite suited to the role. And when Watson departed, the door suddenly opened for Venter, perhaps the only scientist alive who was even more polarizing, and who could dredge up even nastier feelings.

Craig Venter started raising hell in childhood, when he'd sneak his bicycle onto airport runways to race planes (there were no fences) and then ditch the cops that chased him. In junior high, near San Francisco, he began boycotting spelling tests, and in high school, his girlfriend's father once held a gun to Venter's head because of the lad's overactive Y chromosome. Later Venter shut down his high school with two days of sit-ins and marches to protest the firing of his favorite teacher—who happened to be giving Venter an F.*

Despite a GPA well below the Mendoza Line, Venter hypnotized himself into believing he would achieve something magnificent in life, but he lacked much purpose beyond that delusion. At twenty-one, in August 1967, Venter joined a M*A*S*H-like hospital in Vietnam as a medic. Over the next year he watched hundreds of men his own age die, sometimes with his hands on them, trying to resuscitate them. The waste of lives disgusted him, and with nothing specific to live for, Venter decided to commit suicide by swimming out into the shimmering-green South China Sea until he drowned. A mile out, sea snakes surfaced around him. A shark also began thumping him with its skull, testing him as prey. As if suddenly waking up, Venter remembered thinking, *What the fuck am I doing?* He turned and scrambled back to shore.

Vietnam stirred in Venter an interest in medical research, and a few years after earning a Ph.D. in physiology in 1975, he landed at the NIH. Among other research, he wanted to identify all the genes our brain cells use, but he despaired over the tedium of finding genes by hand. Salvation came when he heard about a colleague's method of quickly identifying the messenger RNA that cells use to make proteins. Venter realized this information could reveal the underlying gene sequences, because he could reverse-transcribe the RNA into DNA. By automating the technique, he soon cut down the price for detecting each gene from $50,000 to $20, and within a few years he'd discovered a whopping 2,700 new genes.

These were the genes the NIH tried to patent, and the brouhaha established a pattern for Venter's career. He'd get itchy to do something grand, get irritated over slow progress, and find shortcuts. Other scientists would then denounce the work as cheating; one person compared his process for discovering genes to Sir Edmund Hillary taking a helicopter partway up Mount Everest. Whereafter Venter would strongly encourage his detractors to get bent. But his arrogance and gruffness often ended up alienating his allies, too. For these reasons, Venter's reputation grew increasingly ugly in the 1990s: one Nobel laureate jokingly introduced himself by looking Venter up and down and saying, "I thought you were supposed to have horns." Venter had become a sort of Paganini of genetics.

Devil or no, Venter got results. And frustrated by the bureaucracy at the NIH, he quit in 1992 and joined an unusual hybrid organization. It had a nonprofit arm, TIGR (the Institute for Genomic Research), dedicated to pure science. It also had—an ominous sign to scientists—a very-much-for-profit arm backed by a health-care corporation and dedicated to capitalizing on that research by patenting genes. The company made Venter rich by loading him with stock, then loaded TIGR with scientific talent by raiding thirty staff members from the NIH. And true to its rebellious demeanor, once the TIGR team settled in, it spent the next few years refining "whole-genome shotgun sequencing," a radicalized version of Sanger's old-fashioned sequencing methods.

The NIH consortium planned to spend its first few years and its first billion dollars constructing meticulous maps of each chromosome. That completed, scientists would divide each chromosome into segments and send each segment to different labs. Each lab would make copies of the segment and then "shotgun" them—use intense sound waves or another method to blast them into tiny, overlapping bits roughly a thousand bases long. Scientists would next sequence every bit, study how they overlapped, and piece them together into a coherent overall sequence. As observers have noted, the process was analogous to dividing a novel into chapters, then each chapter into sentences. They'd photocopy each sentence and shotgun all the copies into random phrases—"Happy families are all," "are all alike; every unhappy," "every unhappy family is unhappy," and "unhappy in its own way." They would then reconstruct each sentence based on the overlaps. Finally, the chromosome maps, like a book's index, would tell them where their passage was situated overall.

Venter's team loved the shotgun but decided to skip the slow mapping step. Instead of dividing the chromosome into chapters and sentences, they wanted to blast the whole book into overlapping smithereens right away. They'd then whirlwind everything together at once by using banks of computers. The consortium had considered this whole-genome shotgun approach but had dismissed it as slapdash, prone to leaving gaps and putting segments in the wrong place. Venter, however, proclaimed that speed should trump precision in the short term; scientists needed some, any data now, he argued, more than they needed perfect data in fifteen years. And Venter had the fortune to start working in the 1990s, when computer technology exploded and made impatience almost a virtue.

Almost—other scientists weren't so thrilled. A few patient geneticists had been working since the 1980s to sequence the first genome of a fully living creature, a bacterium. (Sanger sequenced only viruses, which aren't fully alive; bacteria have vastly bigger genomes.) These scientists were creeping, tortoise-like, toward finishing their genome, when in 1994 Venter's team began scorching through the two million bases of *Haemophilus influenzae*, another bacterium. Partway through the process, Venter applied for NIH funds to support the work; months later, he received a pink rejection notice, denying him money because of the "impossible" technique he proposed using. Venter laughed; his genome was 90 percent done. And soon afterward the hare won the race: TIGR blew by its poky rivals and published its genome just one year after starting. TIGR completed another full bacterium sequence, of *Mycoplasma genitalium*, just months later. Ever cocky,

Venter not only gloated about finishing both first—and without a red cent from the NIH—he also printed up T-shirts for the second triumph that read I ♥ MY GENITALIUM.

However begrudgingly impressed, HGP scientists had doubts, sensible doubts, that what worked for bacterial DNA would work for the far more complicated human genome. The government consortium wanted to piece together a "composite" genome—a mishmash of multiple men's and women's DNA that would average out their differences and define a Platonic ideal for each chromosome. The consortium felt that only a cautious, sentence-by-sentence approach could sort through all the distracting repeats, palindromes, and inversions in human DNA and achieve that ideal. But microprocessors and sequencers kept getting speedier, and Venter gambled that if his team gathered enough data and let the computers churn, it could beat the consortium. To give due credit, Venter didn't invent shotgunning or write the crucial computer algorithms that pieced sequences together. But he had the hubris (or chutzpah—pick your word) to ignore his distinguished detractors and plunge forward.

And boy did he. In May 1998, Venter announced that he'd cofounded a new company to more or less destroy the international consortium. Specifically, he planned to sequence the human genome in three years—four years before the consortium would finish—and for one-tenth of its $3 billion budget. (Venter's team threw the plans together so quickly the new company had no name; it became Celera.) To get going, Celera's parent corporation would supply it with hundreds of $300,000, state-of-the-science sequencers, machines that (although monkeys could probably run them) gave Venter more sequencing power than the rest of the world combined. Celera would also build the world's largest nonmilitary supercomputer to process data. As a last gibe, even though his work threatened to make them superfluous, Venter suggested to consortium leaders that they could still find valuable work to do. Like sequencing mice.

Venter's challenge demoralized the public consortium. Watson compared Venter to Hitler invading Poland, and most HGP scientists feared they'd fare about as well. Despite their head start, it didn't seem implausible that Venter could catch and pass them. To appease its scientists' demands for independence, the consortium had farmed its sequencing out to multiple U.S. universities and had formed partnerships with labs in Germany, Japan, and Great Britain. With the project so scattered, even some insiders believed the HGP satellites would never finish on time: by 1998, the eighth of the HGP's fifteen years, the groups had collectively sequenced just 4 percent of human DNA. U.S. scientists were especially trembling. Five years earlier, Congress had eighty-sixed the Superconducting Super Collider, a massive particle accelerator in Texas, after delays and overruns had bloated its budget by billions of dollars. The HGP seemed similarly vulnerable.

Key HGP scientists, however, refused to cower. Francis Collins took over the consortium after Watson's resignation, albeit over the objection of some scientists. Collins had done fundamental genetics work at the University of Michigan; he'd found the DNA responsible for cystic fibrosis and Huntington's disease and had consulted on the Lincoln DNA project. He was also fervently Christian, and some regarded him as "ideologically unsound." (After receiving the consortium job offer, Collins spent an afternoon praying in a chapel, seeking Jesus's guidance. Jesus said go for it.) It didn't help matters that, in contrast to the flamboyant Venter, Collins seemed dowdy, once described as having "home-cut hair [and a] Ned Flanders mustache." Collins nevertheless proved politically adept. Right after Venter announced his plans, Collins found himself on a flight with one of Venter's bosses at Celera's money-hungry parent corporation. Thirty thousand feet up, Collins bent the boss's ear, and by the time they landed, Collins had sweet-talked him into supplying the same fancy sequencers to government labs. This pissed Venter off no end. Then, to reassure Congress, Collins announced that the consortium would make the changes necessary to finish the full sequence two years early. It would also release a "rough draft" by 2001. This all sounded grand, but in practical terms, the new timetable forced Collins to eliminate many slower satellite programs, cutting them out of the historic project entirely. (One axed scientist complained of "being treated with K-Y jelly by the NIH" before being you-know-whated guess-where.)

Collins's burly, bearded British counterpart in the consortium was John Sulston, a Cambridge man who'd helped sequence the first animal genome, a worm's. (Sulston was also the sperm donor whose DNA appeared in the supposedly realistic portrait in London.) For most of his career, Sulston had been a lab rat— apolitical, and happiest when holed up indoors and fussing with equipment. But in the mid-1990s, the company that supplied his DNA sequencers began meddling with his experiments, denying Sulston access to raw data files unless he purchased an expensive key, and arguing that it, the company, had the right to analyze Sulston's data, possibly for commercial purposes. In response Sulston hacked the sequencers' software and rewrote their code, cutting the company off. From that moment on, he'd grown wary of business interests and became an absolutist on the need for scientists to exchange DNA data freely. His views became influential when Sulston found himself running one of the consortium's multimillion-dollar labs at the (Fred) Sanger Centre in England. Celera's parent corporation happened to be the same company he'd tangled with before about data, and Sulston viewed Celera itself as Mammon incarnate, certain to hold DNA data hostage and charge researchers exorbitant fees to peruse it. Upon hearing Venter's announcement, Sulston roused his fellow scientists with a veritable St. Crispin's Day speech at a conference. He climaxed by announcing that his institute would double its funding to fight Venter. His troops huzzahed and stomped their feet.

And so it began: Venter versus the consortium. A furious scientific competition, but a peculiar one. Winning was less about insight, reasoning, craft—the traditional criteria of good science—and more about who had the brute horsepower to work faster. Mental stamina was also critical, since the genome competition had, one scientist noted, "all the psychological ingredients of a war." There was an arms race. Each team spent tens of millions to scale up its sequencing power. There was subterfuge. At one point two consortium scientists reviewed for a magazine the fancy new sequencers Celera was using. They gave them a decidedly mixed review—but meanwhile their bosses were secretly negotiating to buy dozens of the machines for themselves. There was intimidation. Some third-party scientists received warnings about their careers being over if they collaborated with Venter, and Venter claims the consortium tried to block publication of his work. There was tension among purported allies. Venter got into innumerable fights with his managers, and a German scientist at one consortium meeting screamed hysterically at Japanese colleagues for making mistakes. There was propaganda. Venter and Celera crowed their every achievement, but whenever they did, Collins would dismiss their "*Mad* magazine" genome, or Sulston would appear on television to argue that Celera had pulled another "con." There was even talk of munitions. After employees received death threats from Luddites, Celera cut down trees near its corporate campus to prevent snipers from nesting in them, and the FBI warned Venter to scan his mail in case a Unabomber wannabe targeted him.

Naturally, the nastiness of the competition titillated the

public and monopolized its attention. But all the while, work of real scientific value was emerging. Under continued criticism, Celera felt it once again had to prove that whole-genome shotgunning worked. So it laid aside its human genome aspirations and in 1999 began sequencing (in collaboration with an NIH-funded team at the University of California, Berkeley) the 120 million bases of the fruit fly genome. To the surprise of many, they produced an absolute beaut: at a meeting just after Celera finished, *Drosophila* scientists gave Venter a standing ovation. And once both teams ramped up their human genome work, the pace was breathtaking. There were still disputes, naturally. When Celera claimed it had surpassed one billion bases, the consortium rejected the claim because Celera (to protect its business interests) didn't release the data for scientists to check. One month later, the consortium itself bragged that it surpassed a billion bases; four months after, it preened over passing two billion. But the harping couldn't diminish the real point: that in just months, scientists had sequenced more DNA, way more, than in the previous two decades combined. Geneticists had excoriated Venter during his NIH days for churning out genetic information without knowing the function. But everyone was playing Venter's game now: blitzkrieg sequencing.

Other valuable insights came when scientists started analyzing all that sequence data, even preliminarily. For one, humans had an awful lot of DNA that looked microbial, a stunning possibility. What's more, we didn't seem to have enough genes. Before the HGP most scientists estimated that, based on the complexity of humans, we had 100,000 genes. In private, Venter remembers a few straying as high as 300,000. But as the consortium and Celera rifled through the genome, that estimate dropped to 90,000, then 70,000, then 50,000—and kept sinking. During the early days of sequencing, 165 scientists had set up a pool with a $1,200 pot for whoever came closest to guessing the correct number of human genes. Usually the entries in a bubble-gum-counting contest like this cluster in a bell curve around the correct answer. Not so with the gene sweepstakes: with every passing day the low guesses looked like the smartest bets.

Thankfully, though, whenever science threatened to become the real HGP story, something juicy happened to distract everyone. For example, in early 2000 President Clinton announced, seemingly out of the clear blue sky, that the human genome belonged to all people worldwide, and he called on all scientists, including ones in the private sector, to share sequence information immediately. There were also whispers of the government eliminating gene patents, and investors with money in sequencing companies stampeded. Celera got trampled, losing $6 billion in stock value — $300 million of it Venter's — in just weeks. As a balm against this and other setbacks, Venter tried around this time to secure a piece of Einstein's brain, to see if someone could sequence its DNA after all,* but the plan came to naught.

Almost touchingly, a few people held out hope that Celera and the consortium could still work together. Sulston had put the kibosh on a cease-fire with Venter in 1999, but shortly thereafter other scientists approached Venter and Collins to broker a truce. They even floated the idea of the consortium and Celera publishing the 90-percent-complete rough draft of the human genome as one joint paper. Negotiations proceeded apace, but government scientists remained chary of Celera's business interests and bristled over its refusal to publish data immediately. Throughout the negotiations, Venter displayed his usual charm; one consortium scientist swore in his face, countless others behind his back. A *New Yorker* profile of Venter from the time opened with a (cowardly anonymous) quote from a senior scientist: "Craig Venter is an asshole." Not surprisingly, plans for a joint publication eventually disintegrated.

Appalled by the bickering, and eyeing an upcoming election,

Bill Clinton finally intervened and convinced Collins and Venter to appear at a press conference at the White House in June 2000. There the two rivals announced that the race to sequence the human genome had ended—in a draw. This truce was arbitrary and, given the lingering resentments, largely bogus. But rather than growling, both Collins and Venter wore genuine smiles that summer day. And why not? It was less than a century after scientists had identified the first human gene, less than fifty years after Watson and Crick had elucidated the double helix. Now, at the millennium, the sequencing of the human genome promised even more. It had even changed the nature of biological science. Nearly three thousand scientists contributed to the two papers that announced the human genome's rough draft. Clinton had famously declared, "The era of big government is over." The era of big biology was beginning.

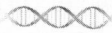

The two papers outlining the rough draft of the human genome appeared in early 2001, and history should be grateful that the joint publication fell apart. A single paper would have forced the two groups into false consensus, whereas the dueling papers highlighted each side's unique approach—and exposed various canards that had become accepted wisdom.

In its paper, Celera acknowledged that it had poached the free consortium data to help build part of its sequence—which sure undermined Venter's rebel street cred. Furthermore, consortium scientists argued that Celera wouldn't even have finished without the consortium maps to guide the assembly of the randomly shotgunned pieces. (Venter's team published angry rebuttals.) Sulston also challenged the Adam Smith–ish idea that the competition increased efficiency and forced both sides to take innovative risks. Instead, he argued, Celera diverted energy away from sequencing and toward silly public posturing—and sped up the release only of the "fake" rough draft anyway.

Of course, scientists loved the draft, however rough, and the consortium would never have pushed itself to publish one so soon had Venter not flipped his gauntlet at their face. And whereas the consortium had always portrayed itself as the adults here—the ones who didn't care about speedy genomic hot-rodding, just accuracy—most scientists who examined the two drafts side by side proclaimed that Celera did a better job. Some said its sequence was twice as good and less riddled with virus contamination. The consortium also (quietly) put the lie to its criticisms of Venter by copying the whole-genome shotgun approach for later sequencing projects, like the mouse genome.

By then, however, Venter wasn't around to bother the public consortium. After various management tussles, Celera all but sacked Venter in January 2002. (For one thing, Venter had refused to patent most genes that his team discovered; behind the scenes, he was a rather indifferent monomaniacal capitalist.) When Venter left, Celera lost its sequencing momentum, and the consortium claimed victory, loudly, when it alone produced a full human genome sequence in early 2003.*

After years of adrenalized competition, however, Venter, like a fading football star, couldn't simply walk away. In mid-2002 he diverted attention from the consortium's ongoing sequencing efforts by revealing that Celera's composite genome had actually been 60 percent Venter sperm DNA; he had been the primary "anonymous" donor. And, undisturbed by the tsk-tsking that followed his revelation—"vainglorious," "egocentric," and "tacky" were some of the nicer judgments—Venter decided he wanted to analyze his pure DNA, unadulterated by other donors. To this end, he founded a new institute, the Center for the Advancement of Genomics (TCAG, har, har), that would spend $100 million over four years to sequence him and him alone.

This was supposed to be the first complete individual genome—the first genome that, unlike the Platonic HGP genome, included both the mother's and father's genetic contributions, as well as every stray mutation that makes a person unique. But because Venter's group spent four whole years polishing his genome, base by base, a group of rival scientists decided to jump into the game and sequence another individual first—none other than Venter's old nemesis, James Watson. Ironically, the second team—dubbed Project Jim—took a cue from Venter and tried to sweep away the prize with new, cheaper, dirtier sequencing methods, ripping through Watson's full genome in four months and for a staggeringly modest sum, around $2 million. Venter, being Venter, refused to concede defeat, though, and this second genome competition ended, probably inevitably, in another draw: the two teams posted their sequences online within days of each other in summer 2007. The speedy machines of Project Jim wowed the world, but Venter's sequence once again proved more accurate and useful for most research.

(The jockeying for status hasn't ended, either. Venter remains active in research, as he's currently trying to determine [by subtracting DNA from microbes, gene by gene] the minimum genome necessary for life. And however tacky the action might have seemed, publishing his individual genome might have put him in the catbird seat for the Nobel Prize—an honor that, according to the scuttlebutt that scientists indulge in over late-night suds, he covets. A Nobel can be split among three people at most, but Venter, Collins, Sulston, Watson, and others could all make legitimate claims for one. The Swedish Nobel committee would have to overlook Venter's lack of decorum, but if it awards him a solo Nobel for his consistently excellent work, Venter can claim he won the genome war after all.*)

So what did all the HGP competition earn us, science-wise? Depends on whom you ask.

Most human geneticists aim to cure diseases, and they felt certain that the HGP would reveal which genes to target for heart disease, diabetes, and other widespread problems. Congress in fact spent $3 billion largely on this implicit promise. But as Venter and others have pointed out, virtually no genetic-based cures have emerged since 2000; virtually none appear imminent, either. Even Collins has swallowed hard and acknowledged, as diplomatically as possible, that the pace of discoveries has frustrated everyone. It turns out that many common diseases have more than a few mutated genes associated with them, and it's nigh impossible to design a drug that targets more than a few genes. Worse, scientists can't always pick out the significant mutations from the harmless ones. And in some cases, scientists can't find mutations to target at all. Based on inheritance patterns, they know that certain common diseases must have significant genetic components—and yet, when scientists scour the genes of victims of those diseases, they find few if any shared genetic flaws. The "culprit DNA" has gone missing.

There are a few possible reasons for these setbacks. Perhaps the real disease culprits lie in noncoding DNA that lies outside of genes, in regions scientists understand only vaguely. Perhaps the same mutation leads to different diseases in different people because of interactions with their other, different genes. Perhaps the odd fact that some people have duplicate copies of some genes is somehow critically important. Perhaps sequencing, which blasts chromosomes into bits, destroys crucial information about chromosome structure and architectural variation that could tell scientists what genes work together and how. Most scary of all—because it highlights our fundamental ignorance—perhaps the idea of a common, singular "disease" is illusory. When doctors see similar symptoms in different people—fluctuating blood sugar, joint pain, high cholesterol—they naturally assume similar causes. But regulating blood sugar or cholesterol requires scores of genes to work together, and a mutation in any one gene in the cascade could disrupt the whole system. In other words, even if the large-scale symptoms are identical, the underlying genetic causes—what doctors need to pinpoint and treat—might be different. (Some scientists misquote Tolstoy to make this point: perhaps all healthy bodies resemble each other, while each unhealthy body is unhealthy in its own way.) For these reasons, some medical scientists have mumbled that the HGP has— kinda, sorta, so far—flopped. If so, maybe the best "big science" comparison isn't the Manhattan Project but the Apollo space program, which got man to the moon but fizzled afterward.

Then again, whatever the shortcomings (so far) in medicine, sequencing the human genome has had trickle-down effects that have reinvigorated, if not reinvented, virtually every other field of biology. Sequencing DNA led to more precise molecular clocks, and revealed that animals harbor huge stretches of viral DNA. Sequencing helped scientists reconstruct the origins and evolution of hundreds of branches of life, including those of our primate relatives. Sequencing helped trace the global migration of humans and showed how close we came to extinction. Sequencing confirmed how few genes humans have (the lowest guess, 25,947, won the gene sweepstakes), and forced scientists to realize that the exceptional qualities of human beings derive not so much from having special DNA as from regulating and splicing DNA in special ways.

Finally, having a full human genome—and especially having the individual genomes of Watson and Venter—emphasized a point that many scientists had lost sight of in the rush to sequence: the difference between reading a genome and understanding it. Both men risked a lot by publishing their genomes. Scientists across the world pored over them letter by letter, looking for flaws or embarrassing revelations, and each man had different attitudes about this risk. The *apoE* gene enhances our ability to eat meat but also (in some versions) multiplies the risk for Alzheimer's disease. Watson's grandmother succumbed to Alzheimer's years ago, and the prospect of losing his own mind was too much to bear, so he requested that scientists not reveal which *apoE* gene he had. (Unfortunately, the scientists he trusted to conceal these results didn't succeed.*) Venter blocked nothing about his genome and even made private medical records available. This way, scientists could correlate his genes with his height and weight and various aspects of his health—information that, in combination, is much more medically useful than genomic data alone. It turns out that Venter has genes that incline him toward alcoholism, blindness, heart disease, and Alzheimer's, among other ailments. (More strangely, Venter also has long stretches of DNA not normally found in humans but common in chimps. No one knows why, but no doubt some of Venter's enemies have suspicions.) In addition, a comparison between Venter's genome and the Platonic HGP genome revealed far more deviations than anyone expected—four million mutations, inversions, insertions, deletions, and other quirks, any of which might have been fatal. Yet Venter, now approaching seventy years old, has skirted these health problems. Similarly, scientists have noted two places in Watson's genome with two copies of devastating recessive mutations—for Usher syndrome (which leaves victims deaf and blind), and for Cockayne syndrome (which stunts growth and prematurely ages people). Yet Watson, well over eighty, has never shown any hint of these problems.

So what gives? Did Watson's and Venter's genomes lie to us? What's wrong with our reading of them? We have no reason to think Watson and Venter are special, either. A naive perusal of anybody's genome would probably sentence him to sicknesses, deformities, and a quick death. Yet most of us escape. It seems that, however powerful, the A-C-G-T sequence can be circumscribed by extragenetic factors—including our epigenetics.

15

Easy Come, Easy Go?

How Come Identical Twins Aren't Identical?

The prefix *epi-* implies something piggybacking on something else. Epiphyte plants grow on other plants. Epitaphs and epigraphs appear on gravestones and in portentous books. Green things like grass happen to reflect light waves at 550 nm (phenomenon), yet our brains register that light as a *color*, something laden with memory and emotion (epiphenomenon). When the Human Genome Project left scientists knowing almost less than before in some ways—how could twenty-two thousand measly genes, fewer than some grapes have, create complex human beings?— geneticists renewed their emphasis on gene regulation and gene-environment interactions, including *epi*genetics.

Like genetics, epigenetics involves passing along certain biological traits. But unlike genetic changes, epigenetic changes don't alter the hardwired A-C-G-T sequence. Instead epigenetic inheritance affects how cells access, read, and use DNA. (You can think about DNA genes as hardware, epigenetics as software.) And while biology often distinguishes between environment (nurture) and genes (nature), epigenetics combines nature with nurture in novel ways. Epigenetics even hints that we can sometimes inherit the nurture part—that is, inherit biological memories of what our mothers and fathers (or grandmothers and grandfathers) ate and breathed and endured.

Frankly, it's tricky to sort out true epigenetics (or "soft inheritance") from other gene-environment interactions. It doesn't help that epigenetics has traditionally been a grab bag of ideas, the place scientists toss every funny inheritance pattern they discover. On top of everything else, epigenetics has a cursed history, littered with starvation, disease, and suicide. But no other field holds such promise for achieving the ultimate goal of human biology: making the leap from HGP molecular minutiae to understanding the quirks and individuality of full-scale human beings.

Though advanced science, epigenetics actually revives an ancient debate in biology, with combatants who predate Darwin—the Frenchman Jean-Baptiste Lamarck and his countryman, our old friend Baron Cuvier.

Just as Darwin made his name studying obscure species (barnacles), Lamarck cut his teeth on *vermes*. *Vermes* translates to "worms" but in those days included jellyfish, leeches, slugs, octopuses, and other slippery things that naturalists didn't stoop to classify. Lamarck, more discriminating and sensitive than his colleagues, rescued these critters from taxonomic obscurity by highlighting their unique traits and separating them into distinct phyla. He soon invented the term *invertebrates* for this miscellanea, and in 1800 went one better and coined the word *biology* for his whole field of study.

Lamarck became a *biologist* through roundabout means. The moment his pushy father died, Lamarck dropped out of seminary school, bought a creaky horse, and, just seventeen years old, galloped away to join the Seven Years' War. His daughter later claimed that Lamarck distinguished himself there, earning a battlefield promotion to officer, though she often exaggerated his achievements. Regardless, Lt. Lamarck's career ended ignominiously when his men, playing some sort of game that involved lifting Lamarck by his head, injured him. The military's loss was biology's gain, and he soon became a renowned botanist and vermologist.

Not content with dissecting worms, Lamarck devised a grandiloquent theory—the first scientific one—about evolution. The theory had two parts. The overarching bit explained why evolution happened period: all creatures, he argued, had

Jean-Baptiste Lamarck devised perhaps the first scientific theory of evolution. Though mistaken, his theory resembles in some ways the modern science of epigenetics. (Louis-Léopold de Boilly)

"inner urges" to "perfect" themselves by becoming more complex, more like mammals. The second half dealt with the mechanics of evolution, how it occurred. And this was the part that overlaps, conceptually at least, with modern epigenetics, because Lamarck said that creatures changed shape or behavior in response to their environment, then passed those acquired traits on.

For instance, Lamarck suggested that wading shorebirds, straining to keep their derrieres dry, stretched their legs microscopically farther each day and eventually acquired longer legs, which baby birds inherited. Similarly, giraffes reaching to the tippity-tops of trees for leaves acquired long necks and passed those on. It supposedly worked in humans, too: blacksmiths, after swinging hammers year after year, passed their impressive musculature down to their children. Note that Lamarck didn't say that creatures *born* with longer appendages or faster feet or whatever had an advantage; instead creatures worked to develop those traits. And the harder they worked, the better the endowment they passed to their children. (Shades of Weber there, and the Protestant work ethic.) Never a modest man, Lamarck announced the "perfecting" of his theory around 1820.

After two decades of exploring these grand metaphysical notions about life in the abstract, Lamarck's actual physical life began unraveling. His academic position had always been precarious, since his theory of acquired traits had never impressed some colleagues. (One strong, if glib, refutation was that Jewish boys still needed circumcising after three millennia of snip-snipping.) He'd also slowly been going blind, and not long after 1820, he had to retire as professor of "insects, worms, and microscopic animals." Lacking both fame and income, he soon became a pauper, wholly reliant on his daughter's care. When he died in 1829, he could only afford a "rented grave"—meaning his *vermes*-eaten remains got just five years' rest before they were dumped in the Paris catacombs to make room for a new client.

But a bigger posthumous insult awaited Lamarck, courtesy of the baron. Cuvier and Lamarck had actually collaborated when they'd first met in postrevolutionary Paris, if not as friends then as friendly colleagues. Temperamentally, though, Cuvier was 179 degrees opposed to Lamarck. Cuvier wanted facts, facts, facts, and distrusted anything that smacked of speculation— basically all of Lamarck's late work. Cuvier also rejected evolution outright. His patron Napoleon had conquered Egypt and lugged back tons of scientific booty, including murals of animals and mummies of cats, crocodiles, monkeys, and other beasts. Cuvier dismissed evolution because these species clearly hadn't changed in thousands of years, which seemed a good fraction of the earth's lifetime back then.

Rather than limit himself to scientific refutations, Cuvier also used his political power to discredit Lamarck. As one of the many hats he wore, Cuvier composed eulogies for the French scientific academy, and he engineered these *éloges* to ever-so-subtly undermine his deceased colleagues. Poisoning with faint praise, he opened Lamarck's obit by lauding his late colleague's dedication to vermin. Still, honesty compelled Cuvier to point out the many, many times his dear friend Jean-Baptiste had strayed into bootless speculation about evolution. Baron Cuvier also turned Lamarck's undeniable gift for analogies against him, and sprinkled the essay with caricatures of elastic giraffes and damp pelican bums, which became indelibly linked to Lamarck's name. "A system resting on such foundations may amuse the imagination of a poet," Cuvier summed up, "but it cannot for a moment bear the examination of anyone who has dissected the hand, the viscera, or even a feather." Overall, the "eulogy" deserves the title of "cruel masterpiece" that science historian Stephen Jay Gould bestowed. But all morality aside, you do have to hand it to the baron here. To most men, writing eulogies would have been little more than a pain in the neck. Cuvier saw that he could parlay this small burden into a great power, and had the savviness to pull it off.

After Cuvier's takedown, a few romantic scientists clung to Lamarckian visions of environmental plasticity, while others, like Mendel, found Lamarck's theories wanting. Many, though, had trouble making up their minds. Darwin acknowledged in print that Lamarck had proposed a theory of evolution first, calling him a "justly celebrated naturalist." And Darwin did believe that some acquired characteristics (including, rarely, circumcised penises) could be passed down to future generations. At the same time, Darwin dismissed Lamarck's theory in letters to friends as "veritable rubbish" and "extremely poor: I got not fact or idea from it."

One of Darwin's beefs was his belief that creatures gained advantages mostly through inherent traits, traits fixed at birth, not Lamarck's acquired traits. Darwin also emphasized the excruciating pace of evolution, how long everything took, because inborn traits could spread only when the creatures with advantages reproduced. In contrast, Lamarck's creatures took control of their evolution, and long limbs or big muscles spread everywhere lickety-split, in one generation. Perhaps worst, to Darwin and everyone else, Lamarck promoted exactly the sort of empty teleology—mystical notions of animals perfecting and fulfilling themselves through evolution—that biologists wanted to banish from their field forever.*

Equally damning to Lamarck, the generation after Darwin discovered that the body draws a strict line of demarcation between normal cells and sperm and egg cells. So even if a blacksmith had the tris, pecs, and delts of Atlas himself, it doesn't mean squat. Sperm are independent of muscle cells, and if the blacksmith's sperms are 98-milligram weaklings DNA-wise, so too might his children be weaklings. In the 1950s, scientists reinforced this idea of independence by proving that body cells can't alter the DNA in sperm or egg cells, the only DNA that matters for inheritance. Lamarck seemed dead forever.

In the past few decades, though, the *vermes* have turned. Scientists now see inheritance as more fluid, and the barriers between genes and the environment as more porous. It's not all about genes anymore; it's about expressing genes, or turning them on and off. Cells commonly turn DNA off by dotting it with small bumps called methyl groups, or turn DNA on by using acetyl groups to uncoil it from protein spools. And scientists now know that cells pass those precise patterns of methyls and acetyls on to daughter cells whenever they divide—a sort of "cellular memory." (Indeed, scientists once thought that the methyls in neurons physically recorded memories in our brains. That's not right, but interfering with methyls and acetyls can interfere with forming memories.) The key point is that these patterns, while mostly stable, are not permanent: certain environmental experiences can add or subtract methyls and acetyls, changing those patterns. In effect this etches a memory of what the organism was doing or experiencing into its cells—a crucial first step for any Lamarck-like inheritance.

Unfortunately, bad experiences can be etched into cells as easily as good experiences. Intense emotional pain can sometimes flood the mammal brain with neurochemicals that tack methyl groups where they shouldn't be. Mice that are (however contradictory this sounds) bullied by other mice when they're pups often have these funny methyl patterns in their brains. As do baby mice (both foster and biological) raised by neglectful mothers, mothers who refuse to lick and cuddle and nurse. These neglected mice fall apart in stressful situations as adults, and their meltdowns can't be the result of poor genes, since biological and foster children end up equally histrionic. Instead the aberrant methyl patterns were imprinted early on, and as neurons kept dividing and the brain kept growing, these patterns perpetuated themselves. The events of September 11, 2001, might have scarred the brains of unborn humans in similar ways. Some pregnant women in Manhattan developed post-traumatic stress disorder, which can epigenetically activate and deactivate at least a dozen genes, including brain genes. These women, especially the ones affected during the third trimester, ended up having children who felt more anxiety and acute distress than other children when confronted with strange stimuli.

Notice that these DNA changes aren't *genetic*, because the A-C-G-T string remains the same throughout. But epigenetic changes are de facto mutations; genes might as well not function. And just like mutations, epigenetic changes live on in cells and their descendants. Indeed, each of us accumulates more and more unique epigenetic changes as we age. This explains why the personalities and even physiognomies of identical twins, despite identical DNA, grow more distinct each year. It also means that that detective-story trope of one twin committing a murder and both getting away with it—because DNA tests can't tell them apart—might not hold up forever. Their epigenomes could condemn them.

Of course, all this evidence proves only that body cells can record environmental cues and pass them on to other body cells, a limited form of inheritance. Normally when sperm and egg unite, embryos erase this epigenetic information—allowing you to become *you*, unencumbered by what your parents did. But other evidence suggests that some epigenetic changes, through mistakes or subterfuge, sometimes get smuggled along to new generations of pups, cubs, chicks, or children—close enough to bona fide Lamarckism to make Cuvier and Darwin grind their molars.

The first time scientists caught this epigenetic smuggling in action was in Överkalix, a farming hamlet in the armpit between

Sweden and Finland. It was a tough place to grow up during the 1800s. Seventy percent of households there had five or more children—a quarter, ten or more—and all those mouths generally had to be fed from two acres of poor soil, which was all most families could scrape together. It didn't help that the weather above sixty-six degrees north latitude laid waste to their corn and other crops every fifth year or so. During some stretches, like the 1830s, the crops died almost every year. The local pastor recorded these facts in the annals of Överkalix with almost lunatic fortitude. "Nothing exceptional to remark," he once observed, "but that the eighth [consecutive] year of crop failure occurred."

Not every year was wretched, naturally. Sporadically, the land blessed people with an abundance of food, and even families of fifteen could gorge themselves and forget the scarce times. But during those darkest winters, when the corn had withered and the dense Scandinavian forests and frozen Baltic Sea prevented emergency supplies from reaching Överkalix, people slit the throats of hogs and cows and just held on.

This history—fairly typical on the frontier—would probably have gone unremarked except for a few modern Swedish scientists. They got interested in Överkalix because they wanted to sort out whether environmental factors, like a dearth of food, can predispose a pregnant woman's child to long-term health problems. The scientists had reason to think so, based on a separate study of 1,800 children born during and just after a famine in German-occupied Holland—the *Hongerwinter* of 1944–45. Harsh winter weather froze the canals for cargo ships that season, and as the last of many favors to Holland, the Nazis destroyed bridges and roads that could have brought relief via land. The daily ration for Dutch adults fell to five hundred calories by early spring 1945. Some farmers and refugees (including Audrey Hepburn and her family, trapped in Holland during the war) took to gnawing tulip bulbs.

After liberation in May 1945, the ration jumped to two thousand calories, and this jump set up a natural experiment: scientists could compare fetuses who gestated during the famine to fetuses who gestated afterward, and see who was healthier. Predictably, the starved fetuses were generally smaller and frailer babies at birth, but in later years they also had higher rates of schizophrenia, obesity, and diabetes. Because the babies came from the same basic gene pool, the differences probably arose from epigenetic programming: a lack of food altered the chemistry of the womb (the baby's environment) and thereby altered the expression of certain genes. Even sixty years later, the epigenomes of those who'd starved prenatally looked markedly different, and victims of other modern famines—the siege of Leningrad, the Biafra crisis in Nigeria, the Great Leap Forward in Mao's China—showed similar long-term effects.

But because famines had happened so often in Överkalix, the Swedish scientists realized they had an opportunity to study something even more intriguing: whether epigenetic effects could persist through multiple generations. Kings of Sweden had long demanded crop records from every parish (to prevent anyone from cheating on fealties), so agricultural data existed for Överkalix from well before 1800. Scientists could then match the data with the meticulous birth, death, and health records the local Lutheran church kept. As a bonus, Överkalix had very little genetic influx or outflow. The risk of frostbite and a garish local accent kept most Swedes and Lapps from moving there, and of the 320 people the scientists traced, just nine abandoned Överkalix for greener pastures, so scientists could follow families for years and years.

Some of what the Swedish team uncovered—like a link between maternal nutrition and a child's future health—made sense. Much of it didn't. Most notably, they discovered a robust link between a child's future health and a *father's* diet. A father obviously doesn't carry babies to term, so any effect must have slipped in through his sperm. Even more strangely, the child got a health boost only if the father faced starvation. If the father gorged himself, his children lived shorter lives with more diseases.

The influence of the fathers turned out to be so strong that scientists could trace it back to the father's father, too—if grandpa Harald starved, baby grandson Olaf would benefit. These weren't subtle effects, either. If Harald binged, Olaf's risk of diabetes increased fourfold. If Harald tightened his belt, Olaf lived (after adjusting for social disparities) an average of thirty years longer. Remarkably, this was a far greater effect than starvation or gluttony had on Grandpa himself: grandpas who starved, grandpas who gorged, and grandpas who ate just right all lived to the same age, seventy years.

This father/grandfather influence didn't make any genetic sense; famine couldn't have changed the parent's or child's DNA sequence, since that was set at birth. The environment wasn't the culprit, either. The men who starved ended up marrying and reproducing in all different years, so their children and grandchildren grew up in different decades in Överkalix, some good, some bad—yet all benefited, as long as Dad or his dad had done without.

But the influence might make epigenetic sense. Again, food is rich in acetyls and methyls that can flick genes on and off, so bingeing or starving can mask or unmask DNA that regulates metabolism. As for how these epigenetic switches got smuggled between generations, scientists found a clue in the timing of the starvation. Starving during puberty, during infancy, during peak fertility years—none of that mattered for the health of a man's child or grandchild. All that mattered was whether he binged or starved during his "slow growth period," a window from about nine to twelve years old, right before puberty. During this phase, males begin setting aside a stock of cells that will become sperm. So if the slow growth period coincided with a feast or famine, the pre-sperm might be imprinted with unusual methyl or acetyl patterns, patterns that would get imprinted on actual sperm in time.

Scientists are still working out the molecular details of what must have happened at Överkalix. But a handful of other studies about soft paternal inheritance in humans supports the idea that sperm epigenetics has profound and inheritable effects. Men who take up smoking before eleven years old will have tubbier children, especially tubbier boys, than men who start smoking later, even if the grade-school smokers snuff the habit sooner. Similarly, the hundreds of millions of men in Asia and Africa who chew the pulp of betel nuts—a cappuccino-strength stimulant—have children with twice the risk of heart disease and metabolic ailments. And while neuroscientists cannot always find anatomical differences between healthy brains and brains addled with psychoses, they have detected different methyl patterns in the brains of schizophrenics and manic-depressives, as well as in their sperm. These results have forced scientists to revise their assumption that a zygote wipes clean all the environmental tarnish of sperm (and egg) cells. It seems that, Yahweh-like, the biological flaws of the fathers can be visited unto their children, and their children's children.

The primacy of sperm in determining a child's long-term health is probably the most curious aspect of the whole soft inheritance business. Folk wisdom held that maternal impressions, like exposure to one-armed men, was devastating; modern science says paternal impressions count as much or more. Still, these parent-specific effects weren't wholly unexpected, since scientists already knew that maternal and paternal DNA don't quite contribute equally to children. If male lions mount female tigers, they produce a liger—a twelve-foot cat twice as heavy as your average king of the jungle. But if a male tiger knocks up a lion, the resulting tiglon isn't nearly as hefty. (Other mammals show similar discrepancies. Which means that Ilya Ivanov's attempts to impregnate female chimpanzees and female humans weren't as symmetrical as he'd hoped.) Sometimes maternal and paternal DNA even engage in outright combat for control of the fetus. Take the *igf* gene (please).

For once, spelling out a gene's name helps make sense of it: *igf* stands for "insulin-like growth factor," and it makes children in the womb hit their size milestones way earlier than normal. But while fathers want both of a child's *igf* genes blazing away, to produce a big, hale baby that will grow up fast and pass its genes on early and often, mothers want to temper the *igf*s so that baby number one doesn't crush her insides or kill her in labor before she has other children. So, like an elderly couple fighting over the thermostat, sperm tend to snap their *igf* into the on position, while eggs snap theirs off.

Hundreds of other "imprinted" genes turn off or on inside us, too, based on which parent bestowed them. In Craig Venter's genome, 40 percent of his genes displayed maternal/paternal differences. And deleting the exact same stretch of DNA can lead to different diseases, depending on whether Mom's or Dad's chromosome is deficient. Some imprinted genes even switch allegiance over time: in mice (and presumably in humans) maternal genes maintain control over brains as children, while paternal genes take over later in life. In fact, we probably can't survive without proper "epigender" imprinting. Scientists can easily engineer mice embryos with two sets of male chromosomes or two sets of female chromosomes, and according to traditional genetics, this shouldn't be a big deal. But these double-gendered embryos expire in the womb. When scientists mixed in a few cells from the opposite sex to help the embryos survive, the males[2] became huge Botero babies (thanks to *igf*) but had puny brains. Females[2] had small bodies but oversized brains. Variations, then, between the brain sizes of Einstein and Cuvier might be nothing but a quirk of their parents' bloodlines, like male pattern baldness.

So-called parent-of-origin effects have also revived interest in one of the most egregious scientific frauds ever perpetrated. Given the subtlety of epigenetics—scientists have barely gotten a handle in the past twenty years—you can imagine that a scientist stumbling across these patterns long ago would have struggled to interpret his results, much less convince his colleagues of them. And Austrian biologist Paul Kammerer did struggle, in science and love and politics and everything else. But a few epigeneticists today see his story as maybe, just maybe, a poignant reminder about the peril of making a discovery ahead of its time.

Paul Kammerer had an alchemist's ambitions to remake nature, coupled with a teenage boy's talent for harassing small animals. Kammerer claimed he could change the colors of salamanders—or give them polka dots or pinstripes—simply by foisting them into landscapes of unusual hues. He forced sun-loving praying mantises to dine in the dark, and amputated the proboscises of sea squirts just to see the effect on their future children. He even claimed he could grow certain amphibians with or without eyes, depending on how much sunlight they got as youngsters.

Kammerer's triumph, and his undoing, were a series of experiments on the midwife toad, a most peculiar species. Most toads mate in water, then let their fertilized eggs float away freely. Midwife toads make love on land, but because tadpole eggs are more vulnerable on land, the male midwife toad ties the bundle of eggs to his back legs like a bunch of grapes and hops along with them until they hatch. Unmoved by this charming habit, Kammerer decided in 1903 to start forcing midwife toads to breed in water, by cranking the heat way, way up in their aquariums. The tactic worked—the toads would have shriveled like dried apricots if they hadn't spent all their time submerged—and those that survived became more waterlike each generation. They had longer gills, produced a slippery jelly coating to water-proof their eggs, and (remember this) developed "nuptial pads"—black, calluslike growths on their forelimbs, to help male toads grip their slippery mates during aqueous coitus. Most intriguing, when Kammerer returned these abused toads to cooler and moister tanks and let them reproduce, the toads' *descendants* (who never experienced the desert conditions) supposedly inherited the water-breeding preferences and passed them along to still more descendants.

Kammerer announced these results around 1910. Over the next decade, he used this and other experiments (and no experiment of his ever failed, it seemed) to argue that animals could be molded to do or be almost anything, given the proper environment. Saying such things at the time had deep Marxist implications, since Marxism held that the only thing keeping the wretched masses down was their terrible environment. But as a committed socialist, Kammerer readily extended his arguments to human society: to his thinking, nurture *was* nature, a unified concept.

Indeed, while biology itself was in serious confusion at the time—Darwinism remained controversial, Lamarckism was all but dead, Mendel's laws hadn't yet triumphed—Kammerer promised he could unite Darwin, Lamarck, and Mendel. For instance, Kammerer preached that the proper environment could actually cause advantageous genes to spring into existence. And far from scoffing, people lapped his theories up; his books became best-sellers, and he lectured to SRO audiences worldwide. (In these "big-show talks" Kammerer also suggested "curing" homosexuals with testicle transplants and enacting American-style Prohibition worldwide, since Prohibition would undoubtedly produce

Paul Kammerer, a tormented Austrian biologist who perpetrated one of the great frauds in science history, may have been an unwitting pioneer in epigenetics. (Courtesy of the Library of Congress)

a generation of American Übermenschen, a race "born without any desire for liquor.")

Unfortunately, the more prominent Kammerer became—he soon anointed himself a "second Darwin"—the shakier his science looked. Most disturbing, Kammerer had withheld crucial details about his amphibian experiments in his scientific reports. Given his ideological posturing, many biologists thought he was blowing smoke, especially William Bateson, Mendel's bulldog in Europe.

A ruthless man, Bateson never shied away from attacking

other scientists. During the eclipse of Darwinism around 1900, he got into an especially nasty row with his former mentor, a Darwin defender named Walter Weldon. Bateson quickly went Oedipal on Weldon by landing himself on the board of a scientific society that allocated biology funding, then cutting Weldon off. Things got so bad later that when Weldon died in 1906, his widow blamed Bateson's rancor for the death, even though Weldon died from a heart attack while cycling. Meanwhile a Weldon ally, Karl Pearson, blocked Bateson's papers from appearing in journals, and also attacked Bateson in his (Pearson's) house organ, a journal called *Biometrika*. When Pearson refused Bateson the courtesy of responding in print, Bateson printed up fake copies of *Biometrika* complete with facsimile covers, inserted his response inside, and distributed them to libraries and universities without any indication they were fraudulent. A limerick at the time summed things up thus: "Karl Pearson is a biometrician / and this, I think, is his position. / Bateson and co. / [I] hope they may go / to monosyllabic perdition."

Now Bateson demanded a chance to examine Kammerer's toads. Kammerer defied him by refusing to supply specimens, and critics continued to roast Kammerer, unimpressed with his excuses. The chaos of World War I temporarily halted the debate, as it left Kammerer's lab in shambles and his animals dead. But as one writer put it, "If World War I did not completely ruin Austria and Kammerer with it, Bateson moved in after the war to finish the job." Under relentless pressure, Kammerer finally, in 1926, let an American ally of Bateson's examine the only midwife toad he'd preserved. This biologist, reptile expert Gladwyn Kingsley Noble, reported in *Nature* that the toad looked entirely normal, except for one thing. The nuptial pads weren't present. However, someone had injected black ink under the toad's skin with a syringe, to make it appear they were. Noble didn't use the word *fraud*, but he didn't have to.

Biology erupted. Kammerer denied any wrongdoing, alluding to sabotage by unnamed political enemies. But the howling of other scientists increased, and Kammerer despaired. Just before the damning *Nature* paper, Kammerer had accepted a post in the Soviet Union, a state favorable to his neo-Lamarckian theories. Six weeks later, Kammerer wrote to Moscow that he couldn't in good conscience accept the job anymore. All the negative attention on him would reflect badly on the great Soviet state.

Then the resignation letter took a dark turn. "I hope I shall gather together enough courage and strength," Kammerer wrote, "to put an end [to] my wrecked life tomorrow." He did, shooting himself in the head on September 23, 1926, on a rocky rural trail outside Vienna. It seemed a sure admission of guilt.

Still, Kammerer always had his defenders, and a few historians have built a not unreasonable case for his innocence. Some experts believe that nuptial pads actually appeared, and that Kammerer (or an overzealous assistant) injected ink merely to "touch up" the evidence. Others believe that political opponents did frame Kammerer. The local national socialist party (precursor of the Nazi party) supposedly wanted to tarnish Kammerer, who was part Jewish, because his theories cast doubt on the inborn genetic superiority of Aryans. What's more, the suicide can't necessarily be pinned on Noble's exposé. Kammerer had chronic money problems and had already become mentally unhinged over one Alma Mahler Gropius Werfel. Werfel worked as Kammerer's unpaid lab assistant for a spell, but she's best known as the tempestuous ex-wife of (among others) composer Gustav Mahler.* She had a fling with the geeky Kammerer, and while it was just another lay to her, Kammerer grew obsessed. He once threatened to blow his brains out all over Mahler's tombstone if she didn't marry him. She laughed.

On the other hand, a prosecutor in any Kammerer case could point out some uncomfortable facts. First, even the unscientific

Werfel, a socialite and dilettante composer of light ditties, recognized that Kammerer was sloppy in the lab, keeping terrible records and constantly (albeit unconsciously, she felt) ignoring results that contradicted his pet theories. Even more damning, scientific journals had caught Kammerer fudging data before. One scientist called him "the father of photographic image manipulation."

Regardless of Kammerer's motive, his suicide ended up smearing Lamarckism by association, since nasty political types in the Soviet Union took up Kammerer's cause. Officials first decided to shoot an agitprop film to defend his honor. *Salamandra* tells the story of a Kammerer-like hero (Professor Zange) undone by the machinations of a reactionary priest (a stand-in for Mendel?). The priest and an accomplice sneak into Zange's lab and inject ink into a salamander one night; the next day, Zange is humiliated when someone dunks the specimen into a bath in front of other scientists and the ink leaks out, clouding the water. After losing his job, Zange ends up begging for food in the streets (accompanied, oddly, by a monkey rescued from an evil lab). But just as he decides to off himself, a woman rescues him and drags him away to the Soviet paradise. As laughable as this sounds, the soon-to-be agricultural czar of the Soviet Union, Trofim Lysenko, basically believed the myth: he considered Kammerer a martyr to socialist biology and began championing Kammerer's theories.

Or at least parts of them. With Kammerer conveniently dead, Lysenko could emphasize only his neo-Lamarckian ideas, which suited Soviet ideology better. And burning with Lamarckian zeal, Lysenko rose to power in the 1930s and began liquidating scores of non-Lamarckian geneticists (including a protégé of Bateson), either having them killed outright or starving them in the Gulag. Unfortunately, the more people he disappeared, the more Soviet biologists had to pay fealty to Lysenko's twisted ideas. A British scientist at the time reported that talking to

Lysenko about genetics "was like trying to explain the differential calculus to a man who did not know his twelve times table. He was...a biological circle-squarer." Not surprisingly, Lysenkoism destroyed Soviet agriculture—millions died in famines—but officials refused to abandon what they saw as the spirit of Kammerer.

However unfair, the association with the Kremlin doomed both Kammerer's reputation and Lamarckism in the following decades, though Kammerer's defenders continued to plead his case. Most notably (and ironically, given his denunciation of communism elsewhere) in 1971 novelist Arthur Koestler wrote a nonfiction book, *The Case of the Midwife Toad*, to exonerate Kammerer. Among other things, Koestler dug up a 1924 paper about the discovery of a wild midwife toad *with nuptial pads*. This doesn't necessarily clear Kammerer but does hint that midwife toads have latent genes for nuptial pads. Perhaps a mutation during Kammerer's experiments had brought them out.

Or perhaps epigenetics had. Some scientists have noted recently that, among other effects, Kammerer's experiments changed the thickness of the gelatinous coat that surrounds midwife toad eggs. Because this jelly is rich in methyls, changing the thickness might switch genes on or off, including atavistic genes for nuptial pads or other traits. Equally intriguing, whenever Kammerer mated toads, he insisted that the father's land/water breeding preference "undisputedly" dominated over the female's preference in the next generations. If Dad liked dry sex, ditto his children and grandchildren, and the same proved true if Dad preferred water sex. Such parent-of-origin effects play an important role in soft inheritance, and these toad trends echo those from Överkalix.

To be sure, even if Kammerer did stumble onto epigenetic effects, he didn't understand them—and he probably still (unless you buy the proto-Nazi conspiracy) committed fraud by injecting ink. But in some ways, that makes Kammerer all the more fascinating. His record of bluster, propaganda, and scandal helps explain why many scientists, even during the chaotic eclipse of Darwinism, refused to consider epigenetic-like theories of soft inheritance. Yet Kammerer might have been both a scoundrel and an unwitting pioneer: someone willing to lie for a greater ideological truth—but someone who may not have been lying after all. Regardless, he grappled with the same issues geneticists still grapple with today—how the environment and genes interact, and which one, if either, dominates in the end. Indeed, it's poignant to wonder how Kammerer might have reacted if only he'd known about, say, Överkalix. He was living and working in Europe just when some of the transgenerational effects were emerging in the Swedish village. Fraud or no fraud, had he seen even traces of his beloved Lamarckism, he might not have felt desperate enough to take his own life.

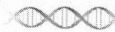

Epigenetics has expanded so rapidly in the past decade that trying to catalog every advance can get pretty overwhelming. Epigenetic mechanisms do things as frivolous as give mice polka-dot tails—or as serious as push people toward suicide (perhaps a final irony in the Kammerer case). Drugs like cocaine and heroin seem to spool and unspool the DNA that regulates neurotransmitters and neurostimulants (which explains why drugs feel good), but if you keep on chasing the dragon, that DNA can become permanently misspooled, leading to addiction. Restoring acetyl groups in brain cells has actually resurrected forgotten memories in mice, and more work emerges every day showing that tumor cells can manipulate methyl groups to shut off the genetic governors that would normally arrest their growth. Some scientists think they can even tease out information about Neanderthal epigenetics someday.

All that said, if you want to make a biologist cranky, start expounding about how epigenetics will rewrite evolution or help us escape our genes, as if they were fetters. Epigenetics does alter how genes function, but doesn't vitiate them. And while epigenetic effects certainly exist in humans, many biologists suspect they're easy come, easy go: methyls and acetyls and other mechanisms might well evaporate within a few generations as environmental triggers change. We simply don't know yet whether epigenetics can *permanently* alter our species. Perhaps the underlying A-C-G-T sequence always reasserts itself, a granite wall that emerges as the methyl-acetyl graffiti wears away.

But really, such pessimism misses the point, and promise, of epigenetics. The low genetic diversity and low gene count of human beings seem unable to explain our complexity and variety. The millions upon millions of different combinations of epigenes just might. And even if soft inheritance evaporates after, say, a half-dozen generations, each one of us lives for two or three generations only—and on those timescales, epigenetics makes a huge difference. It's much easier to rewrite epigenetic software than to rewire genes themselves, and if soft inheritance doesn't lead to true genetic evolution, it does allow us to adapt to a rapidly shifting world. As a matter of fact, thanks to the new knowledge that epigenetics lends us—about cancer, about cloning, about genetic engineering—our world will likely shift even more rapidly in the future.

16

Life as We Do (and Don't) Know It

What the Heck Will Happen Now?

round the end of the 1950s, a DNA biochemist (and RNA Tie Club member) named Paul Doty was strolling through New York, minding his own, when a street vendor's wares caught his eye, and he halted, bewildered. The vendor sold lapel buttons, and among the usual crude assortment, Doty noticed one that read "DNA." Few people worldwide knew more about DNA than Doty, but he assumed the public knew little about his work and cared less. Convinced the initialism stood for something else, Doty asked the vendor what D-N-A might be. The vendor looked the great scientist up and down. "Get with it, bud," he barked in New Yawk brogue. "Dat's da gene!"

Jump forward four decades to the summer of 1999. Knowledge of DNA had mushroomed, and Pennsylvania legislators, stewing over the impending DNA revolution, asked a bioethics expert (and Celera board member) named Arthur Caplan to advise them on how lawmakers might regulate genetics. Caplan obliged, but things got off to a rocky start. To gauge his audience, Caplan opened with a question: "Where are your genes?"

Where are they located in the body? Pennsylvania's best and brightest didn't know. With no shame or irony, one quarter equated their genes with their gonads. Another overconfident quarter decided their genes resided in their brains. Others had seen pictures of helixes or something but weren't sure what that meant. By the late 1950s, the term *DNA* was enough a part of the zeitgeist to grace a street vendor's button. *Dat's da gene.* Since then public understanding had plateaued. Caplan later decided, given their ignorance, "Asking politicians to make regulations and rules about genetics is dangerous." Of course, befuddlement or bewilderment about gene and DNA technology doesn't prevent anyone from having strong opinions.

That shouldn't surprise us. Genetics has fascinated people practically since Mendel tilled his first pea plant. But a parasite of revulsion and confusion feeds on that fascination, and the future of genetics will turn on whether we can resolve that push-pull, gotta-have-it-won't-stand-for-it ambivalence. We seem especially mesmerized/horrified by genetic engineering (including cloning) and by attempts to explain rich, complicated human behavior in terms of "mere" genes—two often misunderstood ideas.

Although humans have been genetically engineering animals and plants since the advent of agriculture ten thousand years ago, the first explicit genetic engineering began in the 1960s. Scientists basically started dunking fruit fly eggs in DNA goo, hoping that the porous eggs would absorb something. Amazingly these crude experiments worked; the flies' wings and eyes changed shape and color, and the changes proved heritable. A decade later, by 1974, a molecular biologist had developed tools to splice DNA from different species together, to form hybrids. Although this Pandora restricted himself to microbes, some biologists saw these chimeras and shivered—who knew what was next? They decided that scientists had gotten ahead of themselves, and called for a moratorium on this recombinant

DNA research. Remarkably, the biology community (including the Pandora) agreed, and voluntarily stopped experimenting to debate safety and rules of conduct, almost a unique event in science history. By 1975 biologists decided they did understand enough to proceed after all, but their prudence reassured the public.

That glow didn't last. Also in 1975, a slightly dyslexic myrmecologist born in evangelical Alabama and working at Harvard published a six-pound, 697-page book called *Sociobiology*. Edward O. Wilson had labored for decades in the dirt over his beloved ants, figuring out how to reduce the byzantine social interactions of serfs, soldiers, and queens into simple behavioral laws, even precise equations. In *Sociobiology* the ambitious Wilson extended his theories to other classes, families, and phyla, ascending the evolutionary ladder rung by rung to fish, birds, small mammals, mammalian carnivores, and primates. Wilson then plowed straight through chimps and gorillas to his notorious twenty-seventh chapter, "Man." In it, he suggested that scientists could ground most if not all human behavior—art, ethics, religion, our ugliest aggressions—in DNA. This implied that human beings were not infinitely malleable but had a fixed nature. Wilson's work also implied that some temperamental and social differences (between, say, men and women) might have genetic roots.

Wilson later admitted he'd been politically idiotic not to anticipate the firestorm, maelstrom, hurricane, and plague of locusts that such suggestions would cause among academics. Sure enough, some Harvard colleagues, including the publicly cuddly Stephen Jay Gould, lambasted *Sociobiology* as an attempt to rationalize racism, sexism, poverty, war, a lack of apple pie, and everything else decent people abhor. They also explicitly linked Wilson with vile eugenics campaigns and Nazi pogroms— then acted surprised when other folks lashed out. In 1978, Wilson was defending his work at a scientific conference when a few half-wit activists stormed onstage. Wilson, in a wheelchair with a broken ankle, couldn't dodge or fight back, and they wrested away his microphone. After charging him with "genocide," they poured ice water over his head, and howled, "You're all wet."

By the 1990s, thanks to its dissemination by other scientists (often in softer forms), the idea that human behavior has firm genetic roots hardly seemed shocking. Similarly, we take for granted today another sociobiological tenet, that our hunter-scavenger-gatherer legacy left us with DNA that still biases our thinking. But just as the sociobiology ember was flickering, scientists in Scotland spurted kerosene on the public's fear of genetics by announcing, in February 1997, the birth of probably the most famous nonhuman animal ever. After transferring adult sheep DNA into four hundred sheep eggs, then zapping them *Frankenstein*-style with electricity, the scientists managed to produce twenty viable embryos—clones of the adult donor. These clones spent six days in test tubes, then 145 in utero, during which time nineteen spontaneously aborted. Dolly lived.

In truth, most of the humans gawking at this little lamb cared nothing about Dolly qua Dolly. The Human Genome Project was rumbling along in the background, promising scientists a blueprint of humanity, and Dolly stoked fears that scientists were ramping up to clone one of our own—and with no moratorium in sight. This frankly scared the bejeezus out of most people, although Arthur Caplan did field one excited phone call about the possibility of cloning Jesus himself. (The callers planned to lift DNA from the Shroud of Turin, natch. Caplan remembered thinking, "You are trying to bring back one of the few people that are supposed to come back anyway.")

Dolly's pen mates accepted her, and didn't seem to care about her ontological status as a clone. Nor did her lovers—she eventually gave birth to six (naturally begotten) lambs, all strapping.

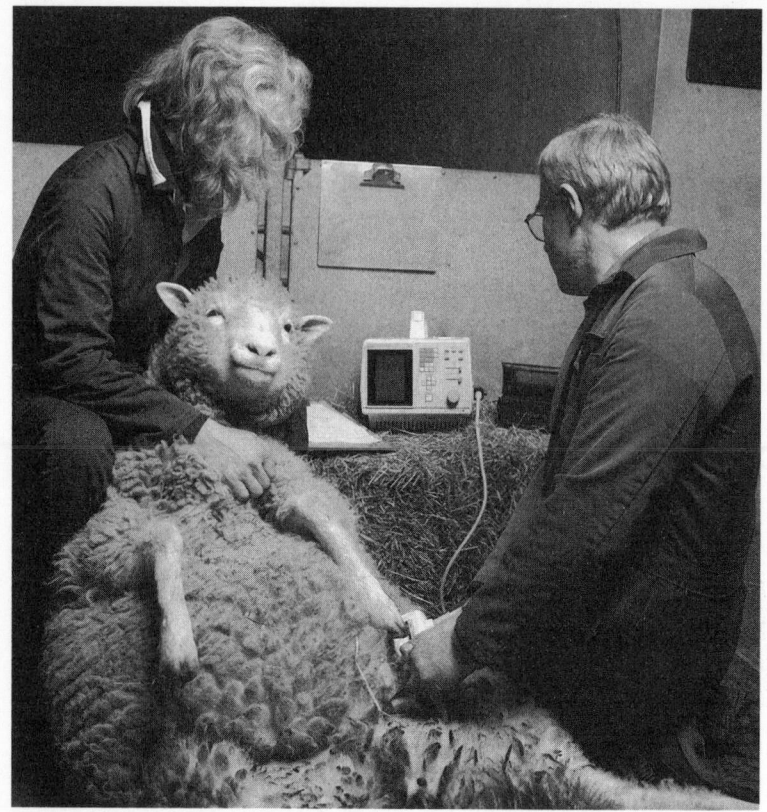

Dolly, the first cloned mammal, undergoes a checkup. (Photo courtesy of the Roslin Institute, University of Edinburgh)

But for whatever reason, human beings fear clones almost instinctively. Post-Dolly, some people hatched sensational supposes about clone armies goose-stepping through foreign capitals, or ranches where people would raise clones to harvest organs. Less outlandishly, some feared that clones would be burdened by disease or deep molecular flaws. Cloning adult DNA requires turning on dormant genes and pushing cells to divide, divide, divide. That sounds a lot like cancer, and clones do seem prone to tumors. Many scientists also concluded (although Dolly's midwives dispute this) that Dolly was born a genetic geriatric, with unnaturally old and decrepit cells. Arthritis did in fact stiffen Dolly's legs at a precocious age, and she died at age six (half her breed's life span) after contracting a virus that, à la Peyton Rous, gave her lung cancer. The adult DNA used to clone Dolly had been—like all adult DNA—pockmarked with epigenetic changes and warped by mutations and poorly patched breaks. Such flaws might have corrupted her genome before she was ever born.*

But if we're toying with playing god here, we might as well play devil's advocate, too. Suppose that scientists overcome all the medical limitations and produce perfectly healthy clones. Many people would still oppose human cloning on principle. Part of their reasoning, however, relies on understandable but thankfully faulty assumptions about genetic determinism, the idea that DNA rigidly dictates our biology and personality. With every new genome that scientists sequence, it becomes clearer that genes deal in probabilities, not certainties. A genetic *influence* is just that, only that. Just as important, epigenetic research shows that the environment changes how genes work and interact, so cloning someone faithfully might require preserving every epigenetic tag from every missed meal and every cigarette. (Good luck.) Most people forget too that it's already too late to avoid exposure to human clones; they live among us even now, monstrosities called identical twins. A clone and its parent would be no more alike than twins are with all their epigenetic differences, and there's reason to believe they'd actually be less alike.

Consider: Greek philosophers debated the idea of a ship whose hull and decks were gradually rotting, plank by plank; eventually, over the decades, every original scrap of wood got replaced. Was it still the same ship at the end? Why or why not? Human beings present a similar stumper. Atoms in our body get recycled many, many times before death, so we don't have the same bodies our whole lives. Nevertheless we feel like the same person. Why? Because unlike a ship, each human has an uninterrupted store of thoughts and remembrances. If the human soul exists, that mental memory cache is it. But a clone would have different memories than his parent—would grow up with different music and heroes, be exposed to different foods and chemicals, have a brain wired differently by new technologies. The sum of these differences would be dissimilar tastes and inclinations—leading to a dissimilar temperament and a distinct soul. Cloning would therefore not produce a doppelgänger in anything but literal superficialities. Our DNA does circumscribe us; but where we fall within our range of possibilities—our statures, what diseases we'll catch, how our brains handle stress or temptation or setbacks—depends on more than DNA.

Make no mistake, I'm not arguing in favor of cloning here. If anything, this argues against—since what would be the point? Bereaved parents might yearn to clone Junior and ease that ache every time they walked by his empty room, or psychologists might want to clone Ted Kaczynski or Jim Jones and learn how to defuse sociopaths. But if cloning won't fulfill those demands—and it almost certainly cannot—why bother?

Cloning not only riles people up over unlikely horrors, it distracts from other controversies about human nature that genetic research can, and has, dredged up. As much as we'd like to close our eyes to these quarrels, they don't seem likely to vanish.

Sexual orientation has some genetic basis. Bees, birds, beetles, crabs, fish, skinks, snakes, toads, and mammals of all stripes (bison, lions, raccoons, dolphins, bears, monkeys) happily get frisky with their own sex, and their coupling often seems hardwired. Scientists have discovered that disabling even a single gene in mice—the suggestively named *fucM* gene—can turn female mice into lesbians. Human sexuality is more nuanced, but gay men (who have been studied more extensively than gay women) have substantially more gay relatives than heterosexual men raised in similar circumstances, and genes seem like one strong differentiator.

This presents a Darwinian conundrum. Being gay decreases the likelihood of having children and passing on any "gay genes," yet homosexuality has persisted in every last corner of the globe throughout all of history, despite often-violent persecution. One theory argues that perhaps gay genes are really "man-loving" genes—androphilic DNA that makes men love men but also makes women who have it lust after men, too, increasing their odds of having children. (Vice versa for gynophilic DNA.) Or perhaps homosexuality arises as a side effect of other genetic interactions. Multiple studies have found higher rates of left-handedness and ambidextrousness among gay men, and gay men frequently have longer ring fingers, too. No one really believes that holding a salad fork in one hand or the other causes homosexuality, but some far-reaching gene might influence both traits, perhaps by fiddling with the brain.

These discoveries are doubled-edged. Finding genetic links would validate being gay as innate and intrinsic, not a deviant "choice." That said, people already tremble about the possibility of screening for and singling out homosexuals, even potential homosexuals, from a young age. What's more, these results can be misrepresented. One strong predictor of homosexuality is the number of older biological brothers someone has; each one increases the odds by 20 to 30 percent. The leading explanation is that a mother's immune system mounts a progressively stronger response to each "foreign" Y chromosome in her uterus, and this immune response somehow induces homosexuality in the fetal brain. Again, this would ground homosexuality in biology—but you can see how a naive, or malicious, observer could twist this immunity link rhetorically and equate homosexuality with a disease to eradicate. It's a fraught picture.

Race also causes a lot of discomfort among geneticists. For one thing, the existence of races makes little sense. Humans have lower genetic diversity than almost any animal, but our colors and proportions and facial features vary as wildly as the finalists each year at Westminster. One theory of race argues that near extinctions isolated pockets of early humans with slight variations, and as these groups migrated beyond Africa and bred with Neanderthals and Denisovans and who knows what else, those variations became exaggerated. Regardless, some DNA must differ between ethnic groups: an aboriginal Australian husband and wife will never themselves produce a freckled, red-haired Seamus, even if they move to the Emerald Isle and breed till doomsday. Color is encoded in DNA.

The sticking point, obviously, isn't Maybelline-like variations in skin tone but other potential differences. Bruce Lahn, a geneticist at the University of Chicago, started his career cataloging palindromes and inversions on Y chromosomes, but around 2005 he began studying the brain genes *microcephalin* and *aspm*, which influence the growth of neurons. Although multiple versions exist in humans, one version of each gene had numerous hitchhikers and seemed to have swept through our ancestors at about Mach 10. This implied a strong survival advantage, and based on their ability to grow neurons, Lahn took a small leap and argued that these genes gave humans a cognitive boost. Intriguingly, he noted that the brain-boosting versions of *microcephalin* and *aspm* started to spread, respectively, around 35,000 BC and 4,000 BC, when, respectively, the first symbolic art and the first cities appeared in history. Hot on the trail, Lahn screened different populations alive today and determined that the brain-boosting versions appeared several times more often among Asians and Caucasians than among native Africans. *Gulp.*

Other scientists denounced the findings as speculative, irresponsible, racist, and wrong. These two genes exercise themselves in many places beyond the brain, so they may have aided ancient Europeans and Asians in other ways. The genes seem to help sperm whip their tails faster, for one thing, and might have outfitted the immune system with new weapons. (They've also been linked to perfect pitch, as well as tonal languages.) Even more damning, follow-up studies determined that people with these genes scored no better on IQ tests than those without them. This pretty much killed the brain-boosting hypothesis, and Lahn—who, for what it's worth, is a Chinese immigrant— soon admitted, "On the scientific level, I am a little bit disap- pointed. But in the context of the social and political controversy, I am a little bit relieved."

He wasn't the only one: race really bifurcates geneticists. Some swear up and down that race doesn't exist. It's "biologi- cally meaningless," they maintain, a social construct. *Race* is indeed a loaded term, and most geneticists prefer to speak some- what euphemistically of "ethnic groups" or "populations," which they confess do exist. But even then some geneticists want to censor investigations into ethnic groups and mental aptitude as inherently wounding—they want a moratorium. Others remain confident that any good study will just prove racial equality, so what the hey, let them continue. (Of course the act of lecturing us about race, even to point out its nonexistence, probably just reinforces the idea. Quick—don't think of green giraffes.)

Meanwhile some otherwise very pious scientists think the "biologically meaningless" bit is baloney. For one thing, some ethnic groups respond poorly—for purely biochemical reasons— to certain medications for hepatitis C and heart disease, among other ailments. Other groups, because of meager conditions in their ancient homelands, have become vulnerable to metabolic disorders in modern times of plenty. One controversial theory argues that descendants of people captured in slave raids in Africa have elevated rates of hypertension today in part because ancestors of theirs whose bodies hoarded nutrients, especially salt, more easily survived the awful oceanic voyages to their new homes. A few ethnic groups even have higher immunity to HIV, but each group, again, for different biochemical reasons. In these and other cases—Crohn's disease, diabetes, breast cancer—doctors and epidemiologists who deny race completely could harm people.

On a broader level, some scientists argue that races exist because each geographic population has, indisputably, distinct versions of some genes. If you examine even a few hundred snippets of someone's DNA, you can segregate him into one of a few broad ancestral groups nearly 100 percent of the time. Like it or not, those groups do generally correspond to people's traditional notion of races—African, Asian, Caucasian (or "swine-pink," as one anthropologist put it), and so on. True, there's always genetic bleed-over between ethnic groups, especially at geographic crossroads like India, a fact that renders the concept of race useless—too imprecise—for many scientific studies. But people's self-identified social race does predict their biological population group pretty well. And because we don't know what every distinct version of every stretch of DNA does, a few polemical and very stubborn scientists who study races/populations/ whatever-you-want-to-call-thems argue that exploring potential differences in intellect is fair game—they resent being censored. Predictably, both those who affirm and those who deny race accuse the other side of letting politics color their science.*

Beyond race and sexuality, genetics has popped up recently in discussions of crime, gender relations, addiction, obesity, and many other things. Over the next few decades, in fact, genetic factors and susceptibilities will probably emerge for almost every human trait or behavior—take the over on that one. But regardless of what geneticists discover about these traits or behaviors, we should keep a few guidelines in mind when applying genetics to social issues. Most important, no matter the biological under-pinnings of a trait, ask yourself if it really makes sense to con-demn or dismiss someone based on how a few microscopic genes behave. Also, remember that most of our genetic predilections for behavior were shaped by the African savanna many thou-sands if not millions of years ago. So while "natural" in some sense, these predilections don't necessarily serve us well today, since we live in a radically different environment. What happens in nature is a poor guide for making decisions anyway. One of the biggest boners in ethical philosophy is the naturalistic fal-lacy, which equates nature with "what's right" and uses "what's natural" to justify or excuse prejudice. We human beings are *humane* in part because we can look beyond our biology.

In any study that touches on social issues, we can at least pause and not draw sensational conclusions without reasonably complete evidence. In the past five years, scientists have consci-entiously sought out and sequenced DNA from more and more ethnic groups worldwide, to expand what remains, even today, an overwhelmingly European pool of genomes available to study. And some early results, especially from the self-explanatory 1,000 Genomes Project, indicate that scientists might have over-estimated the importance of genetic sweeps—the same sweeps that ignited Lahn's race-intelligence firecracker.

By 2010 geneticists had identified two thousand versions of human genes that showed signs of being swept along; specifi-cally, because of low diversity around these genes, it looked as if hitchhiking had taken place. And when scientists looked for what differentiated these swept-along versions from versions not swept along, they found cases where a DNA triplet had mutated and now called for a new amino acid. This made sense: a new amino acid could change the protein, and if that change made someone fitter, natural selection might indeed sweep it through a population. However, when scientists examined other regions, they found the same signs of sweeps in genes with *silent* mutations—mutations that, because of redundancy in the genetic code, didn't change the amino acid. Natural selection cannot have swept these changes along, because the mutation would be invisible and offer no benefits. In other words, many apparent DNA sweeps could be spurious, artifacts of other evolutionary processes.

That doesn't mean that sweeps never happen; scientists still believe that genes for lactose tolerance, hair structure, and a few other traits (including, ironically, skin color) did sweep through various ethnic groups at various points as migrants encountered new environments beyond Africa. But those might represent rare cases. Most human changes spread slowly, and probably no one ethnic group ever "leaped ahead" in a genetic sweepstakes by acquiring blockbuster genes. Any claims to the contrary— especially considering how often supposedly scientific claims about ethnic groups have fallen apart before—should be handled with caution. Because as the old saw says, it's not what we don't know that stirs up trouble, it's what we do know that just ain't so.

Becoming wiser in the ways of genetics will require not only advances in understanding how genes work, but advances in computing power. Moore's Law for computers—which says that microchips get roughly twice as powerful every two years—has held for decades, which explains why some pet collars today could outperform the Apollo mission mainframes. But since 1990 genetic technology has outstripped even Moore's projections. A modern DNA sequencer can generate more data in twenty-four hours than the Human Genome Project did in ten long years, and the technology has become increasingly convenient, spreading to labs and field stations worldwide. (After killing Osama bin Laden in 2011, U.S. military personnel identified him—by matching his DNA to samples collected from relatives—within hours, in the middle of the ocean, in the dead of the a.m.) Simultaneously, the cost of sequencing an entire genome has gone into vacuum free-fall—from $3,000,000,000 to $10,000, from $1 per base pair to around 0.0003¢. If scientists want to study a single gene nowadays, it's often cheaper to sequence the entire genome instead of bothering to isolate the gene first and sequence just that part.

Of course, scientists still need to *analyze* the bajillions of A's, C's, G's, and T's they're gathering. Having been humbled by the HGP, they know they can't just stare at the stream of raw data and expect insights to pop out, *Matrix* style. They need to consider how cells splice DNA and add epigenetic marginalia, much more complicated processes. They need to study how genes work in groups and how DNA packages itself in three dimensions inside the nucleus. Equally important, they need to determine how culture—itself a partial product of DNA—bends back and influences genetic evolution. Indeed, some scientists argue that the feedback loop between DNA and culture has not only influenced but outright dominated human evolution over the past sixty thousand years or so. Getting a handle on all of this will require serious computing horsepower. Craig Venter demanded a supercomputer, but geneticists in the future might need to turn to DNA itself, and develop tools based on its amazing computational powers.

On the software side of things, so-called genetic algorithms can help solve complicated problems by harnessing the power of evolution. In short, genetic algorithms treat the computer commands that programmers string together as individual "genes" strung together to make digital "chromosomes." The programmer might start with a dozen different programs to test. He encodes the gene-commands in each one as binary 0s and 1s and strings them together into one long, chromosome-like sequence (0001010111011101010...). Then comes the fun part. The programmer runs each program, evaluates it, and orders the best programs to "cross over"—to exchange strings of 0s and 1s, just like chromosomes exchange DNA. Next the programmer runs these hybrid programs and evaluates them. At this point the best cross over and exchange more 0s and 1s. The process then repeats, and continues again, and again, allowing the programs to evolve. Occasional "mutations"—flipping 0s to 1s, or vice versa—add more variety. Overall, genetic algorithms combine the best "genes" of many different programs into one near-optimal one. Even if you start with moronic programs, genetic evolution improves them automatically and zooms in on better ones.

On the hardware (or "wetware") side of things, DNA could someday replace or augment silicon transistors and physically perform calculations. In one famous demonstration, a scientist used DNA to solve the classic traveling salesman problem. (In this brainteaser, a salesman has to travel to, say, eight cities scattered all over a map. He must visit each city once, but once he leaves a city he cannot visit it again, even just to pass through on his way somewhere else. Unfortunately, the cities have convoluted roads between them, so it's not obvious in what order to visit.)

To see how DNA could possibly solve this problem, consider a hypothetical example. First thing, you'd make two sets of DNA snippets. All are single-stranded. The first set consists of the eight cities to visit, and these snippets can be random A-C-G-T strings: Sioux Falls might be AGCTACAT, Kalamazoo TCGA-CAAT. For the second set, use the map. Every road between two cities gets a DNA snippet. However—here's the key—instead of making these snippets random, you do something clever. Say Highway 1 starts in Sioux Falls and ends in Kalamazoo. If you make the first half of the highway's snippet the A/T and C/G complement of half of Sioux Falls's letters, and make the second half of the highway's snippet the A/T and C/G complement of half of Kalamazoo's letters, then Highway 1's snippet can physically link the two cities:

(Sioux Falls)   (Kalamazoo)   (Fargo)

A G C T A C A T   T C G A C A A T   G T A G T A A T ...

\ \ \ \   / / / /   \ \ \ \   / / / /

T G T A A G C T   G T T A C A T C ...

(Road 1)   (Road 2)

After encoding every other road and city in a similar way, the calculation begins. You mix a pinch of all these DNA snippets in a test tube, and presto change-o, one good shake computes the answer: somewhere in the vial will be a longer string of (now) double-stranded DNA, with the eight cities along one strand, in the order the salesman should visit, and all the connecting roads on the complementary strand.

Of course, that answer will be written in the biological equivalent of machine code (GCGAGACGTACGAATCC...) and will need deciphering. And while the test tube contains many copies of the correct answer, free-floating DNA is unruly, and the tube also contains trillions of wrong solutions—solutions that skipped cities or looped back and forth endlessly between two cities. Moreover, isolating the answer requires a tedious week of purifying the right DNA string in the lab. So, yeah, DNA computing isn't ready for *Jeopardy*. Still, you can understand the buzz. One gram of DNA can store the equivalent of a trillion CDs, which makes our laptops look like the gymnasium-sized behemoths of yesteryear. Plus, these "DNA transistors" can work on multiple calculations simultaneously much more easily than silicon circuits. Perhaps best of all, DNA transistors can assemble and copy themselves at little cost.

If deoxyribonucleic acid can indeed replace silicon in computers, geneticists would effectively be using DNA to analyze its own habits and history. DNA can already recognize itself; that's how its strands bond together. So DNA computers would give the molecule another modest level of reflexivity and self-awareness. DNA computers could even help DNA refine itself and improve its own function. (Makes you wonder who's in charge...)

And what kinds of DNA improvements might DNA computing bring about? Most obviously, we could eradicate the subtle malfunctions and stutters that lead to many genetic diseases. This controlled evolution would finally allow us to circumvent the grim waste of natural selection, which requires that the many be born with genetic flaws simply so that the few can advance incrementally. We might also improve our daily health, cinching our stomachs in by engineering a gene to burn high-fructose corn syrup (a modern answer to the ancient *apoE* meat-eating gene). More wildly, we could possibly reprogram our fingerprints or hairstyles. If global temperatures climb and climb, we might want to increase our surface area somehow to radiate heat, since squatter bodies retain more heat. (There's a reason Neanderthals in Ice Age Europe had beer keg chests.) Furthermore, some thinkers suggest making DNA adjustments not by tweaking existing genes but by putting updates on an extra pair of chromosomes and inserting them into embryos*—a software patch. This might prevent intergenerational breeding but would bring us back in line with the primate norm of forty-eight.

These changes could make human DNA worldwide even more alike than it is now. If we tinker with our hair and eye color and figures, we might end up looking alike, too. But based on the historical pattern with other technologies, things might well go the other way instead: our DNA could become as diverse as our taste in clothing, music, and food. In that case, DNA could go all postmodern on us, and the very notion of a standard human genome could disappear. The genomic text would become a palimpsest, endlessly overwriteable, and the metaphor of DNA as "the" blueprint or "the" book of life would no longer hold.

Not that it ever really did hold, outside our imaginations. Unlike books and blueprints, both human creations, DNA has no fixed or deliberate meaning. Or rather, it has only the meaning we infuse it with. For this reason we should interpret DNA cautiously, less like prose, more like the complicated and solemn utterances of an oracle.

As with scientists studying DNA, pilgrims to the Delphic oracle in ancient Greece always learned something profound about themselves when they inquired of it—but rarely what they assumed they'd learned at first. The general-king Croesus once asked Delphi if he should engage another emperor in battle. The oracle answered, "You will destroy a great empire." Croesus did—his own. The oracle informed Socrates that "no one is wiser." Socrates doubted this, until he'd canvassed and interrogated all the reputedly wise men around. He then realized that, unlike them, he at least admitted his ignorance and didn't fool himself into "knowing" things he didn't. In both cases, the truth emerged only with time, with reflection, when people had gathered all the facts and could parse the ambiguities. The same with DNA: it all too often tells us what we want to hear, and any dramatist could learn a thing about irony from it.

Unlike Delphi, our oracle still speaks. From so humble a beginning, despite swerves and near extinctions, our DNA (and RNA and other 'NAs) did manage to create us—creatures bright enough to discover and decipher the DNA inside them. But bright enough as well to realize how much that DNA limits them. DNA has revealed a trove of stories about our past that we thought we'd lost forever, and it has endowed us with sufficient brains and curiosity to keep mining that trove for centuries more. And despite that push-pull, gotta-have-it-won't-stand-for-it ambivalence, the more we learn, the more tempting, even desirable, it seems to change that DNA. DNA endowed us with imagination, and we can now imagine freeing ourselves from the hard and heartbreaking shackles it puts on life. We can imagine remaking our very chemical essences; we can imagine remaking life as we know it. This oracular molecule seems to promise that if we just keep pushing, keep exploring and sounding out and tinkering with our genetic material, then life as we know it will cease. And beyond all the intrinsic beauty of genetics and all the sobering insights and all the unexpected laughs that it provides, it's that promise that keeps drawing us back to it, to learn more and more and yet still more about our DNA and our genes, our genes and our DNA.

Epilogue

Genomics Gets Personal

lthough they know better, many people versed in science, even many scientists, still fear their genes on some subliminal level. Because no matter how well you understand things intellectually, and no matter how many counterexamples turn up, it's still hard to accept that having a DNA signature for a disease doesn't condemn you to develop the disease itself. Even when this registers in the brain, the gut resists. This discord explains why memories of his Alzheimer's-ridden grandmother convinced James Watson to suppress his *apoE* status. It also explains, when I plumbed my own genes, why boyhood memories of fleeing from my grandfather convinced me to conceal any hints about Parkinson's disease.

During the writing of this book, however, I discovered that Craig Venter had published everything about his genome, uncensored. Even if releasing it publicly seemed foolhardy, I admired his aplomb in facing down his DNA. His example fortified me, and every day that passed, the discrepancy between what I'd concluded (that people should indeed face down their genes) and how I was behaving (hiding from my Parkinson's status) nagged me more and more. So eventually I sucked it up, logged on to the testing company, and clicked to break the electronic seal on that result.

Admittedly, it took another few seconds before I could look up from my lap to the screen. As soon as I did, I felt a narcotic of relief flood through me. I felt my shoulders and limbs unwind: according to the company, I had no increased risk for Parkinson's after all.

I whooped. I rejoiced—but should I have? There was a definite irony in my happiness. Genes don't deal in certainties; they deal in probabilities. That was my mantra before I peeked, my way of convincing myself that even if I had the risky DNA, it wouldn't *inevitably* ravage my brain. But when things looked less grim suddenly, I happily dispensed with uncertainty, happily ignored the fact that lower-risk DNA doesn't mean I've inevitably escaped anything. Genes deal in probabilities, and some probability still existed. I knew this—and for all that, my relief was no less real. It's the paradox of personal genetics.

Over the next months, I shooed away this inconvenient little cognitive dissonance and concentrated on finishing the book, forgetting that DNA always gets the last word. On the day I dotted the last *i*, the testing company announced some updates to old results, based on new scientific studies. I pulled up my browser and started scrolling. I'd seen previous rounds of updates before, and in each case the new results had merely corroborated what I'd already learned; my risks for things had certainly never changed much. So I barely hesitated when I saw an update for Parkinson's. Fortified and foolhardy, I clicked right through.

Before my mind registered anything, my eyes lit on some green letters in a large font, which reinforced my complacency. (Only red lettering would have meant *watch out*.) So I had to read the accompanying text a few times before I grasped it: "Slightly higher odds of developing Parkinson's disease."

Higher? I looked closer. A new study had scrutinized DNA at a different spot in the genome from the results I'd seen before. Most Caucasian people like me have either CT or TT at the spot in question, on chromosome four. I had (per the fat green letters) CC there. Which meant, said the study, higher odds.

I'd been double-crossed. To expect a genetic condemnation and receive it in due course is one thing. But to expect a condemnation, get pardoned, and find myself condemned again? Infinitely more torture.

Somehow, though, receiving this genetic sentence didn't tighten my throat as it should have. I felt no panic, either, no fight-or-flight jolt of neurotransmitters. Psychologically, this should have been the worst possible thing to endure—and yet my mind hadn't erupted. I wasn't exactly pumped up about the news, but I felt more or less tranquil, untroubled.

So what happened between the first revelation and the second, the setup and the would-be knockdown? Without sounding too pompous, I guess I got an education. I knew now that for a complex disease like Parkinson's—subject to the sway of many genes—any one gene probably contributes little to my risk. I then investigated what a "slightly higher" risk meant, anyway—just 20 percent, it turns out. And that's for a disease that affects (as further digging revealed) only 1.6 percent of men anyway. The new study was also, the company admitted, "preliminary," subject to amendments and perhaps outright reversals. I might still be saddled with Parkinson's as an old man; but somewhere in the generational shuffling of genes, somewhere between Grandpa Kean and Gene and Jean, the dangerous bits might well have been dealt out—and even if they're still lurking, there's no guarantee they'll flare up. There's no reason for the little boy in me to keep fleeing.

It had finally penetrated my skull: probabilities, not certainties. I'm not saying personal genetics is useless. I'm glad to know, for instance (as other studies tell me), that I face higher odds of developing prostate cancer, so I can always make sure the doctor dons a rubber glove to check for that as I age. (Something to look forward to.) But in the clinic, for a patient, genes are just another tool, like blood work or urinalysis or family history. Indeed, the most profound changes that genetic science brings about likely won't be instant diagnoses or medicinal panaceas but mental and spiritual enrichment—a more expansive sense of who we humans are, existentially, and how we fit with other life on earth. I enjoyed having my DNA sequenced and would do it again, but not because I might gain a health advantage. It's more that I'm glad I was here, am here, in the beginning.

ACKNOWLEDGMENTS

First off, a thank-you to my loved ones. To Paula, who once again held my hand and laughed with me (and at me when I deserved it). To my two siblings, two of the finest people around, lucky additions to my life. To all my other friends and family in D.C. and South Dakota and around the country, who helped me keep perspective. And finally to Gene and Jean, whose genes made this book possible. :)

I would furthermore like to thank my agent, Rick Broadhead, for embarking on another great book with me. And thank you as well to my editor at Little, Brown, John Parsley, who helped shape and improve the book immensely. Also invaluable were others at and around Little, Brown who've worked with me on this book and on *Spoon*, including William Boggess, Carolyn O'Keefe, Morgan Moroney, Peggy Freudenthal, Bill Henry, Deborah Jacobs, Katie Gehron, and many others. I offer thanks, too, to the many, many scientists and historians who contributed to individual chapters and passages, either by fleshing out stories, helping me hunt down information, or offering their time to explain something. If I've left anyone off this list, my apologies. I remain thankful, if embarrassed.

NOTES AND ERRATA

Chapter 1: *Genes, Freaks, DNA*

p. 26, The 3:1 ratio: Welcome to the endnotes! Wherever you see an asterisk (*) in the text, you can flip back here to find digressions, discussions, scuttlebutt, and errata about the subject at hand. If you want to flip back immediately for each note, go right ahead; or if you prefer, you can wait and read all the notes after finishing each chapter, as a sort of afterword. This first endnote provides a refresher for Mendelian ratios, so if you're comfortable with that, feel free to move along. But do flip back again. The notes get more salacious. Promise.

The refresher: Mendel worked with dominant traits (like tallness, capital *A*) and recessive traits (like shortness, lowercase *a*). Any plant or animal has two copies of each gene, one from Mom, one from Dad. So when Mendel crossed *AA* plants with *aa* plants (below, left), the progeny were all *Aa* and therefore all tall (since *A* dominates *a*):

	A	A
a	Aa	Aa
a	Aa	Aa

	A	a
A	AA	Aa
a	Aa	aa

When Mendel crossed one *Aa* with another (above, right), things got more interesting. Each *Aa* can pass down *A* or *a*, so there are four possibilities for the offspring: *AA*, *Aa*, *aA*, and *aa*. The first three are again tall, but the last one will be short, though it came from tall parents. Hence a 3:1 ratio. And just to be clear, the ratio holds in plants, animals, whatever; there's nothing special about peas.

The other standard Mendelian ratio comes about when *Aa* mates with *aa*. In this case, half the children will be *aa* and won't show the dominant trait. Half will be *Aa* and will show it.

	A	a
a	Aa	aa
a	Aa	aa

This 1:1 pattern is especially common in family trees when a dominant *A* trait is rare or arises spontaneously through a mutation, since every rare *Aa* would have to mate with the more common *aa*.

Overall the 3:1 and 1:1 ratios pop up again and again in classic genetics. If you're curious, scientists identified the first recessive gene in humans in 1902, for a disorder that turned urine black. Three years later, they pinned down the first dominant human gene, for excessively stubby fingers.

Chapter 2: *The Near Death of Darwin*

p. 32, until the situation blew over: The details about Bridges's private life appear in *Lords of the Fly*, by Robert Kohler.

p. 34, to proceed by jumps: When they were both young, in the 1830s, Darwin convinced his first cousin, Francis Galton, to drop out of medical school and take up mathematics instead. Darwin's later defenders must have rued this advice many, many times, for it was Galton's pioneering statistical work on bell curves—and Galton's relentless arguments, based on that work—that most seriously undermined Darwin's reputation.

As detailed in *A Guinea Pig's History of Biology*, Galton had gathered some of his evidence for bell curves in his typically eccentric way, at the International Health Exhibition in London in 1884. The expo was as much a social affair as a scientific endeavor: as patrons wandered through exhibits about sanitation and sewers, they gulped mint juleps and spiked arrack punch and kumiss (fermented mare's milk produced by horses on-site) and generally had a gay old time. Galton set up a booth at the expo as well and doggedly measured the stature, eyesight, and hearing of nine thousand occasionally intoxicated Englishmen. He also tested their strength with fairground games that involved punching and squeezing various contraptions, a task that proved more difficult than Galton had anticipated: oafs who didn't understand the equipment constantly broke it, and others wanted to show off their strength and impress girls. It was a true fairground atmosphere, but Galton had little fun: he later described "the stupidity and wrong-headedness" of his fellow fairgoers as "so great as to be scarcely credible." But as expected, Galton gathered enough data to confirm that human traits also formed bell curves. The finding further bolstered his confidence that he, not Cousin Charles, understood how evolution proceeded, and that small variations and small changes played no important role.

This wasn't the first time Galton had thwarted Darwin, either. From the day he published *On the Origin of Species*, Darwin was aware that his theory lacked something, badly. Evolution by natural selection requires creatures to inherit favorable traits, but no one (save an obscure monk) had any idea how that worked. So Darwin spent his last years devising a theory, pangenesis, to explain that process.

Pangenesis held that each organ and limb pumped out microscopic spores called gemmules. These circulated inside a creature, carrying information about both its inborn traits (its nature) and also any traits it acquired during its lifetime (its environment, or nurture). These gemmules got filtered out by the body's erogenous zones, and copulation allowed male and female gemmules to mix like two drops of water when males deposited their semen.

Although ultimately mistaken, pangenesis was an elegant theory. So when Galton designed an equally elegant experiment to hunt for gemmules in rabbits, Darwin heartily encouraged the emprise. His hopes were soon dashed. Galton reasoned that if gemmules circulated, they must do so in the blood. So he began transfusing blood among black, white, and silver hares, hoping to produce a few mottled mongrels when they had children. But after years of breeding, the results were pretty black-and-white: not a single multishaded rabbit appeared. Galton published a quickie scientific paper suggesting that gemmules didn't exist, at which point the normally avuncular Darwin went apoplectic. The two men had been warmly exchanging letters for years on scientific and personal topics, often flattering each other's ideas. This time Darwin lit into Galton, fuming that he'd never once mentioned gemmules circulating in blood, so transfusing blood among rabbits didn't prove a damn thing.

On top of being disingenuous—Darwin hadn't said boo about blood not being a good vehicle for gemmules when Galton was doing all the work—Darwin was deceiving himself here. Galton had indeed destroyed pangenesis and gemmules in one blow.

p. 42, together on one chromosome: Sex-linked recessive traits like these show up more often in males than in females for a simple reason. An XX female with a rare white-eye gene on one X would almost certainly have the red-eye gene on the other X. Since red dominates white, she wouldn't have white eyes. But an XY male has no backup if he gets the white-eye gene on his X; he will be white-eyed by default. Geneticists call females with one recessive version "carriers," and they pass the gene to half their male children. In humans hemophilia is one example of a sex-linked trait, Sturtevant's red-green color blindness another.

p. 47, produce millions of descendants: Many different books talk a bit about the fly room, but for the full history, check out *A Guinea Pig's History of Biology*, by Jim Endersby, one of my favorite books ever. Endersby also touches on Darwin's adventures with gemmules, Barbara McClintock (from chapter 5), and other fascinating tales.

p. 49, his reputation would never lapse again: A historian once wisely noted that "in reading Darwin, as in reading Shakespeare or the Bible, it is possible to support almost any viewpoint desirable by focusing on certain isolated passages." So you have to be careful when drawing broad conclusions from Darwin quotes. That said, Darwin's antipathy for math seemed genuine, and some have suggested that even elementary equations frustrated him. In one of history's ironies, Darwin ran his own experiments on plants in the primrose genus, just like de Vries, and came up with clear 3:1 ratios among offspring traits. He obviously wouldn't have linked this to Mendel, but he seems not to have grasped that ratios might be important at all.

p. 52, inside fruit fly spit glands: *Drosophila* go through a pupa stage where they encase themselves in gluey saliva. To get as many saliva-producing genes going as possible, salivary-gland cells repeatedly double their chromosomes, which creates gigantic "puff chromosomes," chromosomes of truly Brobdingnagian stature.

Chapter 3: *Them's the DNA Breaks*

p. 60, the "Central Dogma" of molecular biology: Despite its regal name, the Central Dogma has a mixed legacy. At first, Crick intended the dogma to mean something general like *DNA makes RNA, RNA makes proteins.* Later he reformulated it more precisely, talking about how "information" flowed from DNA to RNA to protein. But not every scientist absorbed the second iteration, and just like old-time religious dogmas, this one ended up shutting down rational thought among some adherents. "Dogma" implies unquestionable truth, and Crick later admitted, roaring with laughter, that he hadn't even known the definition of dogma when he defined his—it just sounded learned. Other scientists paid attention in church, however, and as word of this supposedly inviolable dogma spread, it transmogrified in many people's minds into something less precise, something more like *DNA exists just to make RNA, RNA just to make proteins.* Textbooks sometimes refer to this as the Central Dogma even today. Unfortunately this bastardized dogma seriously skews the truth. It hindered for decades (and still occasionally hinders) the recognition that DNA and especially RNA do much, much more than make proteins.

Indeed, while basic protein production requires messenger RNA (mRNA), transfer RNA (tRNA), and ribosomal RNA (rRNA), dozens of other kinds of regulatory RNA exist. Learning about all the different functions of RNA is like doing a crossword puzzle when you know the last letters of an answer but not the opening, and you run through the alphabet under your breath. I've seen references to aRNA, bRNA, cRNA, dRNA, eRNA, fRNA, and so on, even the scrabbulous qRNA and zRNA. There's also rasiRNA and tasiRNA, piRNA, snoRNA, the Steve Jobs–ish RNAi, and others. Thankfully, mRNA, rRNA, and tRNA cover all the genetics we'll need in this book.

p. 62, can represent the same amino acid: To clarify, each triplet represents only one amino acid. But the inverse is *not* true, because some amino acids are represented by more than one triplet. As an example, GGG can only be glycine. But GGU, GGC, and GGA also code for glycine, and that's where the redundancy comes in, because we really don't need all four.

p. 69, onto the succeeding generation: A few other events in history have exposed masses of people to radioactivity, most notoriously at the Chernobyl nuclear power plant in modern Ukraine. The 1986 Chernobyl meltdown exposed people to different types of radioactivity than the Hiroshima and Nagasaki bombs — fewer gamma rays and more radioactive versions of elements like cesium, strontium, and iodine, which can invade the body and unload on DNA at short range. Soviet officials compounded the problem by allowing crops to be harvested downwind of the accident and allowing cows to graze on exposed grass, then letting people eat and drink the contaminated milk and produce. The Chernobyl region has already reported some seven thousand cases of thyroid cancer, and medical officials expect sixteen thousand extra cancer deaths over the next few decades, an increase of 0.1 percent over background cancer levels.

And in contrast to Hiroshima and Nagasaki, the DNA of children of Chernobyl victims, especially children of men near Chernobyl, does show signs of increased mutations. These results remain disputed, but given the different exposure patterns and dosage levels — Chernobyl released hundreds of times more radioactivity than either atomic bomb — they could be real. Whether those mutations actually translate to long-term health problems among Chernobyl babies remains to be seen. (As an imperfect comparison, some plants and birds born after Chernobyl showed high mutation rates, but most seemed to suffer little for that.)

Sadly, Japan will now have to monitor its citizens once again for the long-term effects of fallout because of the breech of the Fukushima Daiichi nuclear power plant in spring 2011. Early government reports (some of which have been challenged) indicate that the damage was contained to an area one-tenth the size of Chernobyl's exposure footprint, mostly because radioactive elements at Chernobyl escaped into the air, while in Japan the ground and water absorbed them. Japan also intercepted most contaminated food and drink near Fukushima within six days. As a result, medical experts suspect the total number of cancer deaths in Japan will be correspondingly small — around one thousand extra deaths over the next few decades, compared to the twenty thousand who died in the earthquake and tsunami.

p. 71, just beginning to explore: For a full account of Yamaguchi's story—and for eight other equally riveting tales—see *Nine Who Survived Hiroshima and Nagasaki*, by Robert Trumbull. I can't recommend it highly enough.

For more detail on Muller and many other players in early genetics (including Thomas Hunt Morgan), check out the wonderfully comprehensive *Mendel's Legacy*, by Elof Axel Carlson, a former student of Muller's.

For a detailed but readable account of the physics, chemistry, and biology of how radioactive particles batter DNA, see *Radiobiology for the Radiologist*, by Eric J. Hall and Amato J. Giaccia. They also discuss the Hiroshima and Nagasaki bombs specifically.

Finally, for an entertaining rundown of early attempts to decipher the genetic code, I recommend Brian Hayes's "The Invention of the Genetic Code" in the January–February 1998 issue of *American Scientist*.

Chapter 4: *The Musical Score of DNA*

p. 78, even meant, if anything: Zipf himself believed that his law revealed something universal about the human mind: laziness. When speaking, we want to expend as little energy as possible getting our points across, he argued, so we use common words like *bad* because they're short and pop easily to mind. What prevents us from describing every last coward, rogue, scuzzbag, bastard, malcontent, coxcomb, shit-for-brains, and misanthrope as "bad" is other people's laziness, since they don't want to mentally parse every possible meaning of the word. They want precision, pronto. This tug-of-war of slothfulness results in languages where common words do the bulk of the work, but rarer and more descriptive words must appear now and then to appease the damn readers.

That's clever as far as it goes, but many researchers argue that any "deep" explanation of Zipf's law is, to use another common word, crap. They point out that something like a Zipfian distribution can arise in almost any chaotic situation. Even computer programs that spit out random letters and spaces—digital orangutans banging typewriters—can show Zipfian distributions in the resulting "words."

p. 82, evolution creeps forward: The analogy between genetic language and human language seems fuzzy to some, almost too cute to be true. Analogies can always be taken too far, but I think that some of this dismissal stems from our sort-of-selfish tendency to think that language can only be sounds that humans make. Language is wider than just us: it's the rules that govern any communication. And cells as surely as people can take feedback from their environment and adjust what they "say" in response. That they do so with molecules instead of air-pressure waves (i.e., sound) shouldn't prejudice us. Recognizing this, a few recent cellular biology textbooks have included chapters on Chomsky's theories about the underlying structure of languages.

p. 84, *sator...rotas:* The palindrome means something like "The farmer Arepo works with his plow," with *rotas*, literally "wheels," referring to the back-and-forth motion that plows make as they till. This "magic square" has delighted enigmatologists for centuries, but scholars have suggested it might have served another purpose during imperial Roman reigns of terror. An anagram of these twenty-five letters spells out *paternoster*, "Our Father," twice, in an interlocking cross. The four letters left over from the anagram, two *a*'s and two *o*'s, could then refer to the alpha and omega (famous later from the Book of Revelation). The theory is that, by sketching this innocuous palindrome on their doors, Christians could signal each other without arousing Roman suspicion. The magic square also reportedly kept away the devil, who traditionally (so said the church) got confused when he read palindromes.

p. 88, his boss's lunatic projects: Friedman's boss, "Colonel" George Fabyan, had quite a life. Fabyan's father started a cotton company called Bliss Fabyan and groomed Fabyan to take over. But succumbing to wanderlust, the boy ran away to work as a Minnesota lumberjack instead, and his outraged and betrayed father disinherited him. After two years, Fabyan tired of playing Paul Bunyan and decided to get back into the family business — by applying, under an assumed name, to a Bliss Fabyan office in St. Louis. He quickly set all sort of sales records, and his father at corporate HQ in Boston soon summoned this young go-getter to his office to talk about a promotion. In walked his son.

After this Shakespearean reunion, Fabyan thrived in the cotton business and used his wealth to open the think tank. He funded all sorts of research over the years but fixated on Shakespeare codes. He tried to publish a book after he supposedly broke the code, but a filmmaker working on some adaptations of Shakespeare sued to stop publication, arguing that its contents would "shatter" Shakespeare's reputation. For whatever reason, the local judge took the case — centuries of literary criticism apparently fell under his jurisdiction — and, incredibly, sided with Fabyan. His decision concluded, "Francis Bacon is the author of the works so erroneously attributed to William Shakespeare," and he ordered the film producer to pay Fabyan $5,000 in damages.

Most scholars look on arguments against Shakespeare's authorship about as kindly as biologists do on theories of maternal impressions. But several U.S. Supreme Court justices, most recently in 2009, have also voiced opinions that Shakespeare could not have written his plays. The real lesson here is that lawyers apparently have different standards of truth and evidence than scientists and historians.

p. 89, to rip off casinos at roulette: The casino gambit never paid off. The idea started with the engineer Edward Thorp, who in 1960 recruited Shannon to help him. At the roulette table, the two men worked as a team, though they pretended not to know each other. One watched the roulette ball as it spun around the wheel and noted the exact moment it passed certain points. He then used a toe-operated switch in his shoe to send signals to the small computer in his pocket, which in turn transmitted radio signals. The other man, wearing an earpiece, heard these signals as musical notes, and based on the tune, he would know where to toss his money. They painted any extruding wires (like the earpiece's) the color of flesh and pasted the wires to their skin with spirit gum.

Thorp and Shannon calculated an expected yield of 44 percent from their scheme, but Shannon turned chicken on their first test run in a casino and would only place dime bets. They won more often than not, but, perhaps after eyeing some of the heavies manning the casino door, Shannon lost his appetite for the enterprise. (Considering that the two men had ordered a $1,500 roulette wheel from Reno to practice, they probably *lost* money on the venture.) Abandoned by his partner, Thorp published his work, but it apparently took a number of years before casinos banned portable electronics outright.

Chapter 5: *DNA Vindication*

p. 97, an inside-out (and triple-stranded): For an account of the embarrassment and scorn Watson and Crick endured for this odd DNA model, please see my previous book, *The Disappearing Spoon*.

p. 102, complex and beautiful life: For a more detailed account of Miriam's life, I highly recommend *The Soul of DNA*, by Jun Tsuji.

p. 107, the oldest matrilineal ancestor: Using this logic, scientists also know that Mitochondrial Eve had a partner. All males inherit Y chromosomes from their fathers alone, since females lack the Y. So all men can trace strictly paternal lines back to find this Y-chromosomal Adam. The kicker is that, while simple laws of mathematics prove that this Adam and Eve must have existed, the same laws reveal that Eve lived tens of thousands of years earlier than Adam. So the Edenic couple could never have met, even if you take into account the extraordinary life expectancies in the Bible.

By the by, if we relax the strictly patrilineal or strictly matrilineal bit and look for the last ancestor who—through men *or* women—passed at least some DNA to every person alive today, that person lived only about five thousand years ago, long after humans had spread over the entire earth. Humans are strongly tribal, but genes always find a way to spread.

p. 114, got downgraded: Some historians argue that McClintock struggled to communicate her ideas partly because she couldn't draw, or at least didn't. By the 1950s molecular biologists and geneticists had developed highly stylized cartoon flowcharts to describe genetic processes. McClintock, from an older generation, never learned their drawing conventions, a deficit that—combined with the complexity of maize in the first place—might have made her ideas seem too convoluted. Indeed, some students of McClintock recall that they never remember her drawing any diagrams, ever, to explain anything. She was simply a verbal person, rutted in *logos*.

Compare this to Albert Einstein, who always maintained that he thought in pictures, even about the fundamentals of space and time. Charles Darwin was of McClintock's ilk. He included just one picture, of a tree of life, in the hundreds of pages of *On the Origin of Species*, and one historian who studied Darwin's original notebook sketches of plants and animals acknowledged he was a "terrible drawer."

p. 115, she withdrew from science: If you're interested in learning more about the reception of McClintock's work, the scholar most responsible for challenging the canonical version of her life's story is Nathaniel Comfort.

Chapter 6: *The Survivors, the Livers*

p. 125, producing the very Cyclops: Most children born with cyclopia (the medical term) don't live much past delivery. But a girl born with cyclopia in India in 2006 astounded doctors by surviving for at least two weeks, long enough for her parents to take her home. (No further information about her survival was available after the initial news reports.) Given the girl's classic symptoms—an undivided brain, no nose, and a single eye—it was almost certain that *sonic hedgehog* had malfunctioned. And sure enough, news outlets reported that the mother had taken an experimental cancer drug that blocks *sonic*.

p. 125, Maurice of Nassau: Prince Mo belonged to the dynastic House of Orange in the Netherlands, a family with an unusual (and possibly apocryphal) legend attached to its name. Centuries ago, wild carrots were predominantly purple. But right around 1600, Dutch carrot farmers, indulging in old-fashioned genetic engineering, began to breed and cultivate some mutants that happened to have high concentrations of the vitamin A variant beta carotene—and in doing so developed the first orange carrots. Whether farmers did this on their own or (as some historians claim) to honor Maurice's family remains unknown, but they forever changed the texture, flavor, and color of this vegetable.

p. 130, German biologist August Weismann: Although an undisputed brainiac and hall-of-fame biologist, Weismann once claimed— uproariously, given the book's mammoth size—to have read *On the Origin of Species* in one sitting.

p. 131, a fifth official letter to the DNAlphabet: A few scientists have even expanded the alphabet to six, seven, or eight letters, based on chemical variations of methylated cytosine. Those letters are called (if you're into the whole brevity thing) hmC, fC, and caC. It's not clear, though, whether these "letters" function independently or are just intermediate steps in the convoluted process by which cells strip the m from mC.

p. 136, and Arctic huskies: The tale of the husky liver is dramatic, involving a doomed expedition to reach the South Pole. I won't expand on the story here, but I have written something up and posted it online at http://samkean.com/thumb-notes. My website also contains links to tons of pictures (http://samkean.com/thumb-pictures), as well as other notes a little too digressive to include even here. So if you're interested in reading about Darwin's role in musicals, perusing an infamous scientific fraud's suicide note, or seeing painter Henri Toulouse-Lautrec nude on a public beach, take a look-see.

p. 136, carried the men home to the Netherlands: Europeans did not set eyes on the Huys again until 1871, when a party of explorers tracked it down. The white beams were green with lichen, and they found the hut sealed hermetically in ice. The explorers recovered, among other detritus, swords, books, a clock, a coin, utensils, "muskets, a flute, the small shoes of the ship's boy who had died there, and the letter Barents put up the chimney for safekeeping" to justify what some might see as a cowardly decision to abandon his ship on the ice.

Chapter 7: *The Machiavelli Microbe*

p. 141, the "RNA world" theory: Though RNA probably preceded DNA, other nucleic acids—like GNA, PNA, or TNA—might have preceded both of them. DNA builds its backbone from ringed deoxyribose sugars, which are more complicated than the building blocks likely available on the primordial earth. Glycol nucleic acid and peptide nucleic acid look like better candidates because neither uses ringed sugars for its vertebrae. (PNA doesn't use phosphates either.) Threose nucleic acid does use ringed sugars, but again, sugars simpler than DNA's. Scientists suspect those simpler backbones proved more robust as well, giving these 'NAs an advantage over DNA on the sun-scorched, semimolten, and oft-bombarded early earth.

p. 143, viruses that infect only other parasites: This idea of parasites feasting on parasites always puts me in mind of a wonderful bit of doggerel by Jonathan Swift:

> *So nat'ralists observe, a flea*
> *Hath smaller fleas that on him prey,*
> *And these have smaller fleas that bite 'em,*
> *And so proceed ad infinitum.*

For my taste, a mathematician named Augustus De Morgan outdid even Swift on this theme:

Great fleas have little fleas upon their backs to bite 'em,
And little fleas have lesser fleas, and so ad infinitum.
And the great fleas themselves, in turn, have greater fleas to go on,
While these again have greater still, and greater still, and so on.

p. 148, gave each cat an individual name: A sample: Stinky, Blindy, Sam, Pain-in-the-Ass, Fat Fuck, Pinky, Tom, Muffin, Tortoise, Stray, Pumpkin, Yankee, Yappy, Boots the First, Boots the Second, Boots the Third, Tigger, and Whisky.

p. 148, despite their mounting distress: In addition to the $111,000 yearly, there were occasional unexpected costs, like when an animal lib person cut a hole in the fence to spring as many cats as possible. Jack said there were still so many cats around that they didn't notice the dozens that escaped until a nun knocked on their door and asked if the cats climbing onto roofs throughout the neighborhood were theirs. Um, yes.

p. 150, a plausible biological basis for hoarding cats: To be scrupulous: scientists have not yet run controlled studies on the correlation between Toxo levels in the brain and hoarding. So it's possible that the link between Toxo, dopamine, cats, and hoarding could come to naught. Nor can Toxo explain everything about hoarding behavior, since people occasionally hoard dogs, too.

But most animal hoarders do hoard felines, and scientists involved in the Toxo studies find the link plausible and have said so publicly. They've simply seen too much evidence of how Toxo can change the hardwired behavior of rodents and other creatures. And regardless of how strong its influence turns out to be, Toxo still seeps dopamine into your brain.

p. 154, to help Jack cope: Over the years, Jack and Donna have given many interviews about their lives and struggles. A few sources include: *Cats I Have Known and Loved*, by Pierre Berton; "No Room to Swing a Cat!," by Philip Smith, *The People*, June 30, 1996; "Couple's Cat Colony Makes Record Books—and Lots of Work!," by Peter Cheney, *Toronto Star*, January 17, 1992; *Current Science*, August 31, 2001; "Kitty Fund," *Kitchener-Waterloo Record*, January 10, 1994; "$10,000 Averts Ruin for Owners of 633 Cats," by Kellie Hudson, *Toronto Star*, January 16, 1992; and *Scorned and Beloved: Dead of Winter Meetings with Canadian Eccentrics*, by Bill Richardson.

Chapter 8: *Love and Atavisms*

p. 160, customize proteins for different environments in the body: In one extreme example, fruit flies carve up the RNA of the *dscam* gene into 38,016 distinct products—roughly triple the number of genes a fruit fly has. So much for the one gene/one protein theory!

p. 162, practically a defining trait of mammals: Nature loves playing gotcha, and for almost everything you call a "unique" mammalian trait, there's an exception: reptiles with a rudimentary placenta, for instance, or insects that give birth to live young. But in general, these are mammalian traits.

p. 167, more extensive MHCs than other creatures: In humans, the MHC is often called the HLA, but since we're focused on mammals here, I'll use the general term.

p. 170, the same extra nipples that barnyard sows have: Though best known for the telephone, Alexander Graham Bell had a keen interest in genetics and dreamed of breeding fitter humans. To learn more about biology, he bred sheep with extra nipples and studied the inheritance patterns.

p. 172, tails contract involuntarily when children cough or sneeze: For more on human tails, see Jan Bondeson's wonderful *A Cabinet of Medical Curiosities.* The book also has an astounding chapter on maternal impressions (like those in chapter 1), as well as many other gruesome tales from the history of anatomy.

p. 174, simply have to round them up: The scientist did not end up winning funding for his research. And to be fair, he didn't intend to spend all $7.5 million developing the gay bomb. Some of that money would have gone to, among other projects, a separate bomb that would have given the enemy epically bad breath, to the point of inducing nausea. No word on whether the scientist ever realized he could combine the two bombs into the most frustrating weapon in history.

Chapter 9: *Humanzees and Other Near Misses*

p. 182, They're that similar: In fact, this is how scientists first determined that chimps, not gorillas, are our closest living relatives. Scientists performed the first DNA hybridization experiments in the 1980s by mixing chimp, gorilla, and human DNA in a hot, steamy bath. When things cooled down, human DNA stuck to chimp DNA more readily than it did to gorilla DNA. QED.

p. 186, should always have fewer mutations: This isn't the place to even attempt to resolve this debate, but the scientists who first proposed the interbreeding theory have of course tried to counterrefute this supposed refutation. And the original scientists do have a point: in their paper announcing the theory way back in 2006, they actually anticipated this criticism about the X looking more uniform because of sperm production rates. Specifically, they noted that while X chromosomes should indeed look more alike for that reason, the X chromosomes they studied looked even more alike than this scenario could account for.

Naturally, the refuting scientists are busy countering the counterrefutations. It's all very technical and a bit arcane, but exciting, given the stakes...

p. 189, The *Times* story: In addition to its salacious details, the *Times* story also included this bizarre—and bizarrely egalitarian—quote: one scientist was convinced "that if the orang[utan] be hybridized with the yellow race, the gorilla with the black race, and the chimpanzees with the white race, all three hybrids will reproduce themselves." What's striking, especially for the time, is the insistence that all human beings, regardless of color, were kin to brutes.

p. 196, the path to forty-six chromosomes a million years ago: To anticipate a question, yes, chromosomes can split, too, by a process called fission. In the primate line, our current chromosome numbers three and twenty-one were once yoked together into a team, and formed our longest chromosome for millions of years. Numbers fourteen and fifteen also split before the rise of great apes long ago, and both retain a funny, off-center shape today as a legacy. In some ways, then, the fourteen-fifteen fusion in the Chinese man was the ultimate genetic atavism, returning him to the ancestral, pre-ape state!

p. 198, months of trench warfare: For more on Ivanov's life, the most authoritative and least sensationalistic source is a paper by Kirill Rossiianov, in *Science in Context*, from the summer 2002 issue: "Beyond Species: Il'ya Ivanov and his experiments on cross-breeding humans with anthropoid apes."

Chapter 10: *Scarlet A's, C's, G's, and T's*

p. 204, "Until I tasted a bluebottle [fly]": The supply of Buckland anecdotes is pretty much bottomless. One of his friends' favorites was the time he and a stranger sitting across from him on a long train ride both fell asleep in their seats. Buckland woke up to find that some red slugs formerly nestled in his pockets had escaped, and were now sliming their way across his companion's bald pate. Buckland discreetly exited at the next stop. Buckland also inspired his equally eccentric son Frank, who inherited his predilection for zoophagy and actually pioneered some of the more outré dishes the Buckland family ate. Frank had a standing agreement with the London Zoo that he got a shank of whatever animals died there.

Despite insulting Buckland, Darwin also indulged in zoophagy, even joining the Glutton Club at Cambridge, where he and companions dined on hawks, owls, and other beasts. On the *Beagle* voyage, Darwin ate ostrich omelets and armadillo roasted in its case, and after tucking into an agouti, a coffee-colored rodent that weighs twenty pounds, he declared it "the very best meat I ever tasted."

For more details on Buckland's life, work, family, and eccentricities, I highly recommend *The Heyday of Natural History*, by Lynn Barber, and *Bones and Ochre*, by Marianne Sommer.

p. 209, He named it *Megalosaurus*: It later came to light that another scientist had discovered *Megalosaurus* bones in the 1600s, including a tree trunk of a femur. But he'd classified them as the bones of giant humans, a decision that Buckland's work disproved. Strangely, two knobs on the end of that femur apparently traced out with Michelangelo-like verisimilitude the lower half of the human male package, inspiring a less-than-dignified moniker for the purported giants. Arguably, then, based on scientific priority in naming, the first known dinosaur species should be called *Scrotum humanum*. Buckland's more proper name stuck, though.

p. 211, thick, glowering brow we still associate with Neanderthals: The professor who identified the purported Cossack had decided the brow was shaped that way because the victim spent so many days furrowing it in pain. The professor apparently even believed the Cossack had scampered up sixty feet of sheer rock while mortally wounded, disrobed completely, and buried himself two feet deep in clay.

p. 214, which lacks the tag: Lately, some DNA tags (a.k.a. DNA watermarks) have gotten rather elaborate, encoding names, e-mail addresses, or famous quotations—things nature couldn't have inserted by chance. One research team headed by Craig Venter encoded the following quotes in A's, C's, G's, and T's, then wove them into a synthetic genome that they created from scratch and inserted into a bacterium:

> To live, to err, to fall, to triumph, to recreate life out of life.
> — JAMES JOYCE, *A Portrait of the Artist as a Young Man*

> See things not as they are, but as they might be.
> — From *American Prometheus*, a book about Robert Oppenheimer

> What I cannot build, I cannot understand.
> — RICHARD FEYNMAN (the words written on his blackboard at the time of his death)

Unfortunately Venter bungled the last quote. Feynman actually wrote, "What I cannot create, I do not understand." Venter also ran into trouble with the Joyce quote. Joyce's family (which controls his estate) is reputedly stingy about letting anyone (including a bacterium) quote him without express written permission.

p. 218, millions of tons of vaporized rock per second: Compared to Mount Saint Helens, Toba spewed two thousand times more crap into the air. Of volcanoes worldwide, Toba is one of the few rivals to the giga-volcano currently smoldering beneath Wyoming, which will blow Yellowstone and everything around it sky-high someday.

Chapter 11: *Size Matters*

p. 227, accidental, unrelated to his genius: Stephen Jay Gould gives a highly entertaining rendition of the story of Cuvier's autopsy in *The Panda's Thumb*. Gould also wrote a masterly, two-part article about the life of Jean-Baptiste Lamarck—whom we'll meet in chapter 15—in his collection *The Lying Stones of Marrakech*.

p. 229, the cost is a punier brain: Partly to determine how and why hobbits shrank, scientists are currently drilling a hobbit tooth to extract DNA. It's a dicey procedure, since hobbits (unlike Neanderthals) lived in exactly the sort of tropical climate that degrades DNA the quickest. Attempts to extract hobbit DNA have always failed so far.

Studying hobbit DNA should help scientists determine if it really belongs in the genus *Homo*, a contentious point. Until 2010, scientists knew of only two other *Homo* species—Neanderthals, and possibly hobbits— still alive when *Homo sapiens* began overrunning the planet. But scientists recently had to add another to the list, the Denisovans (dun-EE-suh-vinz), named after a cave in cold Siberia where a five-year-old girl died tens of thousands of years ago. Her bones looked Neanderthal when scientists discovered them amid ancient layers of dirt and goat feces in 2010, but DNA extracted from a knucklebone shows enough distinctions to count as a separate line of *Homo*—the first extinct species discovered solely through genetic (not anatomical) evidence.

Traces of Denisovan DNA are found today in Melanesians, the people who originally settled the islands between New Guinea and Fiji. Apparently the Melanesians ran into Denisovans somewhere on the long haul from Africa to the South Seas and, as their ancestors had with Neanderthals, interbred with them. Today Melanesians have up to 8 percent non–*Homo sapiens* DNA. But beyond these clues, the Denisovans remain a mystery.

p. 233, scattered the ashes: Want more? Galileo's finger, Oliver Cromwell's skull, and Jeremy Bentham's entire decapitated head (including its freakishly shrunken skin) all went on posthumous display over the centuries. Thomas Hardy's heart reportedly got eaten by a cat. Phrenologists stole Joseph Haydn's head just before burial, and cemetery workers stole Franz Schubert's "larvae-laden" hair while transferring him to a new grave. Someone even held a jar in front of Thomas Edison's mouth during his death rattle to capture his last breath. The jar immediately went on exhibit in a museum.

I could probably go on for another page listing famous body parts that found new life—Percy Bysshe Shelley's heart, Grover Cleveland's cancerous jaw, supposed bits of Jesus's foreskin (the Divine Prepuce)—but let me wrap up by pointing out that there are no legs to the persistent rumor that the Smithsonian Institution owns John Dillinger's penis.

p. 235, pack the cortex with neurons: The overall genetic algorithm to add bulk and density to the brain might be amazingly simple. The biologist Harry Jerison has proposed the following example. Imagine a stem cell whose DNA programs it to "divide thirty-two times, then stop." If no cells die, you'd end up with 4,294,967,296 neurons. Now imagine tweaking that code to "divide thirty-four times, then stop." This would lead to two more doublings, or 17,179,869,184 neurons.

The difference between 4.3 billion neurons and 17.2 billion neurons, Jerison notes, would be roughly the difference between the chimpanzee cortex population and the human cortex population. "The code may seem overly simple," Jerison says, but "instructions that are significantly more complex may be beyond the capacity of genes to encode information."

p. 241, knew Mormon theology in lobotomizing detail: It's unclear if Peek, a devout Mormon, knew about the rift that genetic archaeology has recently opened within the Church of Latter-Day Saints. Mormons have traditionally believed—ever since Joseph Smith, just fourteen years old, copied down Jehovah's very words in 1820—that both Polynesians and American Indians descended from a doughty Jewish prophet, Lehi, who sailed from Jerusalem to America in 600 BC. Every DNA test ever conducted on these peoples disagrees on this point, however: they're not Middle Eastern in the slightest. And this contradiction not only invalidates the literalness of the Mormon holy books, it upsets the complicated Mormon eschatology about which brown peoples will be saved during end times, and which groups therefore need proselytizing to in the meantime. This finding has caused a lot of soul wringing among some Mormons, especially university scientists. For some, it crushed their faith. Most run-of-the-mill Latter-Day Saints presumably either don't know or have absorbed the contradiction and moved on.

p. 243, certainly doesn't capture him: For an account that does succeed in capturing Peek's talents, see "Inside the Mind of a Savant," by Donald Treffert and Daniel Christensen, in the December 2005 issue of *Scientific American.*

Chapter 12: *The Art of the Gene*

p. 247, awfully awkward method of replication: The warped-zipper model with its alternating left and right helixes actually debuted twice in 1976 (more simultaneous discovery). First a team in New Zealand published the idea. Shortly thereafter, a team working independently in India came forward with two warped-zipper models, one identical to the New Zealanders' and one with some of the A's, C's, G's, and T's flipped upside down. And true to the cliché of intellectual rebels everywhere, almost all the members of both teams were outsiders to molecular biology and had no preconceived notions that DNA had to be a double helix. One New Zealander wasn't a professional scientist, and one Indian contributor had never heard of DNA!

p. 250, musical biases as ruthless as any hipster's: Monkeys either ignore human music or find it irritating, but recent studies with cotton-top tamarins, monkeys in South America, have confirmed that they respond strongly to music tailored for them. David Teie, a cellist based in Maryland, worked with primatologists to compose music based on the calls that tamarins use to convey fear or contentment. Specifically, Teie patterned his work on the rising and falling tones in the calls, as well as their duration, and when he played the various opuses, the cotton-tops showed visible signs of relaxation or anxiety. Showing a good sense of humor, Teie commented to a newspaper, "I may be just a schmo to you. But, man, to monkeys I am Elvis."

p. 255, the three times he owned up to crying: Because you're dying to know, the first time Rossini cried was when his first opera flopped. The bawling with Paganini was the second. The third and final time, Rossini, a bona fide glutton, was boating with friends when—horror of horrors—his picnic lunch, a delectable truffled turkey, fell overboard.

p. 260, the church finally forgave him and permitted burial: Biographies of Paganini are surprisingly scarce in English. One short and lively introduction to his life—with lots of details about his illnesses and postmortem travails—is *Paganini*, by John Sugden.

p. 262, throbbing-red baboon derrieres: For whatever reason, some classic American writers paid close attention to debates in the early 1900s about sexual selection and its role in human society. F. Scott Fitzgerald, Ernest Hemingway, Gertrude Stein, and Sherwood Anderson all addressed the animal aspects of courtship, male passion and jealousy, sexual ornamentation, and so on. In a similar way, genetics itself shook some of these writers. In his fascinating *Evolution and the "Sex Problem,"* Bert Bender writes that "although Mendelian genetics was a welcome discovery for Jack London, who heartily embraced it as a rancher who practiced selective breeding, others, such as Anderson, Stein, and Fitzgerald, were deeply disturbed." Fitzgerald especially seemed obsessed with evolution, eugenics, and heredity. Bender points out that he makes constant references to eggs in his work (West Egg and East Egg are but two examples), and Fitzgerald once wrote about "the cut-in system at dances, which favors the survival of the fittest." Even Gatsby's "old sport," his nickname for Nick Carraway, the narrator of *The Great Gatsby*, probably has its roots in the early habit among geneticists of calling mutants "sports."

p. 263, bone deformities and seizure disorders: Armand Leroi's *Mutants* explores in more detail what specific disease Toulouse-Lautrec might have had, and also the effect on his art. In fact I highly recommend the book overall for its many fascinating tales, like the anecdote about the lobster claw–like birth defects mentioned in chapter 1.

p. 264, looking rather apish: The lip was more obvious in pictures of men, but women didn't escape these genes. Reportedly, Marie Antoinette, part of another branch of the family, had strong traces of the Hapsburg lip.

Chapter 13: *The Past Is Prologue — Sometimes*

p. 282, Lincoln, fifty-six when assassinated: Funnily enough, Lincoln's assassin got caught up in a genetic contretemps of his own in the 1990s. Two historians at the time were peddling a theory that it wasn't John Wilkes Booth but an innocent bystander whom Union soldiers tracked, captured, and killed in Bowling Green, Virginia, in 1865, twelve days after the assassination. Instead, the duo argued, Booth gave the troops the slip, fled west, and lived thirty-eight increasingly wretched years in Enid, Oklahoma, before committing suicide in 1903. The only way to know was to exhume the body in Booth's grave, extract DNA, and test it against his living relatives. The caretakers of the cemetery refused, however, so Booth's family (spurred on by the historians) sued. A judge denied their petition, partly because the technology at the time probably couldn't have resolved the matter; but the case could in theory be reopened now.

For more details on Booth's and Lincoln's DNA see, well, *Abraham Lincoln's DNA and Other Adventures in Genetics*, by Philip R. Reilly, who sat on the original committee that studied the feasibility of testing Lincoln.

p. 285, Jewish tradition bungled this story: Overall, though, Jewish people were acute observers of hereditary phenomena. By AD 200, the Talmud included an exemption to not circumcise a young boy if two older brothers had bled to death after their circumcisions. What's more, Jewish law later exempted half brothers of the deceased as well — but only if they had the same mother. If the half brother shared a father, then the circumcision should proceed. The children of women whose sisters' babies had bled to death also received exemptions, but not the children of men whose brothers' babies had. Clearly Jewish people understood a long time ago that the disease in question — probably hemophilia, an inability of blood to clot — is a sex-linked disease that affects mostly males but gets passed down through the mother.

p. 291, severe lactose intolerance: If the world were just, we would call the condition not "lactose intolerance" but "lactose tolerance," since the ability to digest milk is the oddity and only came about because of a recent mutation. Actually, two recent mutations, one in Europe, one in Africa. In both cases the mutation disabled a region on chromosome two that, in adults, should halt production of the enzyme that digests lactose, a sugar in milk. And while the European one came first historically (about 7,000 BC), one scientist said the African gene spread especially quickly: "It is basically the strongest signal of selection ever observed in any genome, in any study, in any population in the world." Lactose tolerance is also a wonderful example of gene-culture coevolution, since the ability to digest milk would not have benefited anyone before the domestication of cattle and other beasts, which gave a steady supply of milk.

Chapter 14: *Three Billion Little Pieces*

p. 295, tally the sequence: If you like to get your fingernails dirty, you can visit http://samkean.com/thumb-notes for the gritty details of Sanger's work.

p. 299, giving Venter an F: Not a biology teacher but an English teacher inspired this devotion from Venter. And what an English teacher! It was Gordon Lish, later famous as the editor of Raymond Carver.

p. 307, Einstein's brain, to see if someone could sequence its DNA after all: Celera people had a thing about celebrity DNA kitsch. According to James Shreeve's riveting book, *The Genome War*, the lead architect of Celera's ingenious supercomputer program kept on his office bookshelf a "pus-stained Band-Aid" in a test tube—an homage to Friedrich Miescher. By the way, if you're interested in a long insider's account of the HGP, Shreeve's book is the best written and most entertaining I know of.

p. 309, in early 2003: Actually this declaration of being "done" was arbitrary as well. Work on some parts of the human genome—like the hypervariable MHC region—continued for years, and cleanup work continues even today as scientists tidy up small mistakes and sequence segments that, for technical reasons, can't be sequenced by conventional means. (For instance, scientists usually use bacteria for the photocopying step. But some stretches of human DNA happen to poison bacteria, so bacteria delete them instead of copying, and they disappear.) Finally, scientists have not yet tackled telomeres and centromeres, segments that, respectively, make up the ends and central girdles of chromosomes, because those regions are too repetitive for conventional sequencers to make sense of.

So why did scientists declare the work done in 2003? The sequence did meet at that point a sensible definition of done: fewer than one error per 10,000 bases over 95 percent of the DNA regions that contain genes. Just as important, though, PR-wise, early 2003 was the fiftieth anniversary of Watson and Crick's discovery of the double helix.

p. 310, Venter can claim he won the genome war after all: On the other hand, it might actually *bolster* Venter's reputation in a topsy-turvy way if he lost out on the Nobel. The loss would confirm his status as an outsider (which endeared him to many people) and would give historians something to argue about for generations, making Venter the central (and perhaps tragic) figure in the HGP story.

Watson's name doesn't come up often in discussions about the Nobel, but he arguably deserves one for compelling Congress—not to mention the majority of geneticists in the country—to give sequencing a chance. That said, Watson's recent gaffes, especially his disparaging comments about the intelligence of Africans (more on this later), may have killed his chances. It sounds crude for me to say, but the Nobel committee might wait for Watson to croak before giving out any HGP-related prizes.

If either Watson or Sulston won, it would be his second Nobel, matching Sanger as the only double winner in medicine/physiology. (Sulston won his prize for worm work in 2002.) Like Watson, though, Sulston has entangled himself in some controversial politics. When WikiLeaks founder Julian Assange got arrested in 2010—charged with sexual assault in Sweden, the Nobel homeland—Sulston offered many thousands of pounds for bail. It seems Sulston's commitment to the free and unimpeded flow of information doesn't stop at the laboratory door.

p. 313, to conceal these results didn't succeed: An amateur scientist named Mike Cariaso outed Watson's *apoE* status by taking advantage of genetic hitchhiking. Again, because of hitchhiking, each different version of a gene will have, purely by chance, certain versions of other genes associated with it—genes that travel with it down the generations. (Or if there aren't genes nearby, each version of the gene will at least have certain junk DNA associated with it.) So if you wanted to know which version of *apoE* someone had, you could look at *apoE* itself or, just as good, look at the genes flanking it. The scientists in charge of scrubbing this information from Watson's genome of course knew this, and they erased the information near *apoE*. But they didn't erase enough. Cariaso realized this mistake and, simply by looking up Watson's publicly available DNA, figured out his *apoE* status.

As described in *Here Is a Human Being*, by Misha Angrist, Cariaso's revelation was a shock, not least because he was something of an expat bum: "The facts were inescapable: The Nobel Prize–winning [Watson] had asked that of his 20,000+ genes... just one lousy gene—one!—not be made public. This task was left to the molecular brain trust at Baylor University, one of the top genome centers in the world.... But the Baylor team was outfoxed by a thirty-year-old autodidact with a bachelor's degree who preferred to spend most of his time on the Thai-Burmese border distributing laptops and teaching kids how to program and perform searches in Google."

Chapter 15: *Easy Come, Easy Go?*

p. 319, banish from their field forever: History has a funny sense of humor. Darwin's grandfather Erasmus Darwin, a physician, actually published an independent and fairly outlandish theory of evolution (in verse, no less) that resembled Lamarck's. Samuel Taylor Coleridge even coined the word "Darwining" to pooh-pooh such speculation. Erasmus also started the family tradition of raising the hackles of religious folk, as his work appeared on the papal index of banned books.

In another irony, just after Cuvier died, he himself got smeared in the same way he'd smeared Lamarck. Based on his views, Cuvier became indelibly linked to catastrophism and an antievolutionary outlook on natural history. So when Charles Darwin's generation needed a foil to represent stodgy old thinking, the pumpkin-headed Frenchman was perfect, and Cuvier's reputation suffers even today for their lancing. Payback's a bitch.

p. 331, the tempestuous ex-wife of (among others) composer Gustav Mahler: Alma Mahler also had the good taste to marry painter Gustav Klimt and Bauhaus designer Walter Gropius, among others. She became such a notorious jezebel in Vienna that Tom Lehrer wrote a song about her. The refrain goes: "Alma, tell us! / All modern women are jealous. / Which of your magical wands / Got you Gustav and Walter and Franz?" I have a link to the full lyrics on my website.

Chapter 16: *Life as We Do (and Don't) Know It*

p. 341, before she was ever born: Since Dolly, scientists have cloned cats, dogs, water buffalo, camels, horses, and rats, among other mammals. In 2007 scientists created embryonic clones from adult monkey cells and let them develop enough to see different tissues. But the scientists snuffed the embryos before they came to term, so it's unclear whether the monkey clones would have developed normally. Primates are harder to clone than other species because removing the nucleus of the donor egg (to make way for the clone's chromosomes) tears out some of the special apparatus that primate cells need to divide properly. Other species have more copies of this apparatus, called spindle fibers, than primates do. This remains a major technical obstacle to human cloning.

p. 346, letting politics color their science: Psychoanalyze this how you will, but both James Watson and Francis Crick have stuck their size tens into their mouths with impolitic public comments about race, DNA, and intelligence. Crick lent support to research in the 1970s on why some racial groups had—or, more truthfully, were tested to have—higher or lower IQs than others. Crick thought we could form better social policies if we knew that certain groups had lower intellectual ceilings. He also said, more bluntly, "I think it likely that more than half the difference between the average IQ of American whites and Negroes is due to genetic reasons."

Watson's gaffe came in 2007 while on tour to promote his charmingly titled autobiography, *Avoid Stupid People*. At one point he proclaimed, "I'm inherently gloomy about the prospect of Africa," since "social policies are based on the fact that their intelligence is the same as ours. Whereas all the testing says, not really." After the media flagellated him, Watson lost his job (as head of Cold Spring Harbor Laboratory, Barbara McClintock's old lab) and more or less retired in semidisgrace.

It's hard to know how seriously to take Watson here, given his history of saying crude and inflammatory things—about skin color and sex drive, about women ("People say it would be terrible if we made all girls pretty. I think it would be great"), about abortion and sexuality ("If you could find the gene which determines sexuality and a woman decides she doesn't want a homosexual child, well, let her"), about obese people ("Whenever you interview fat people, you feel bad, because you know you're not going to hire them"), et cetera. The Harvard black studies scholar Henry Louis Gates Jr. later probed Watson about the Africa comments in a private meeting and concluded that Watson wasn't so much racist as "racialist"—someone who sees the world in racial terms and believes that genetic gaps may exist between racial groups. Gates also noted, though, that Watson believes that if such gaps do exist, the *group* differences shouldn't bias our views toward talented *individuals*. (It's analogous to saying that black people may be better at basketball, but the occasional Larry Bird can still thrive.) You can read Gates's thoughts at http://www.washingtonpost.com/wp-dyn/content/article/2008/07/10/AR2008071002265.html.

As always, DNA had the last word. Along with his autobiography, Watson released his genome to the public in 2007, and some scientists decided to plumb it for markers of ethnicity. Lo and behold, they discovered that Watson might have, depending on the accuracy of his sequence, up to sixteen times more genes from black Africans than a typical Caucasian has—the genetic equivalent of a black great-grandfather.

p. 352, an extra pair of chromosomes and inserting them into embryos: Among other people, Nicholas Wade makes this suggestion in *Before the Dawn*, a masterly tour of all aspects of human origins—linguistic, genetic, cultural, and otherwise.

SELECTED BIBLIOGRAPHY

Here's a list of books and papers I consulted while writing *The Violinist's Thumb*. Anything marked with an asterisk I recommend especially. I've annotated the ones I recommend especially for further reading.

Chapter 1: *Genes, Freaks, DNA*

Bondeson, Jan. *A Cabinet of Medical Curiosities*. W. W. Norton, 1999.
  *Contains an astounding chapter on maternal impressions, including the fish boy of Naples.
Darwin, Charles. *On the Origin of Species*. Introduction by John Wyon Burrow. Penguin, 1985.
————. *The Variation of Animals and Plants Under Domestication*. J. Murray, 1905.
Henig, Robin Marantz. *The Monk in the Garden*. Houghton Mifflin Harcourt, 2001.
  *A wonderful general biography of Mendel.
Lagerkvist, Ulf. *DNA Pioneers and Their Legacy*. Yale University Press, 1999.
Leroi, Armand Marie. *Mutants: On genetic variety and the human body*. Penguin, 2005.
  *A fascinating account of maternal impressions, including the lobster claw–like birth defects.

Chapter 2: *The Near Death of Darwin*

Carlson, Elof Axel. *Mendel's Legacy*. Cold Spring Harbor Laboratory Press, 2004.
  *Loads of anecdotes about Morgan, Muller, and many other key players in early genetics, by a student of Muller's.
Endersby, Jim. *A Guinea Pig's History of Biology*. Harvard University Press, 2007.

*A marvelous history of the fly room. One of my favorite books ever, in fact. Endersby also touches on Darwin's adventures with gemmules, Barbara McClintock, and other tales.

Gregory, Frederick. *The Darwinian Revolution*. DVDs. Teaching Company, 2008.

Hunter, Graeme K. *Vital Forces*. Academic Press, 2000.

Kohler, Robert E. *Lords of the Fly*. University of Chicago Press, 1994.
*Includes details about Bridges's private life, like the anecdote about his Indian "princess."

Steer, Mark, et al., eds. *Defining Moments in Science*. Cassell Illustrated, 2008.

Chapter 3: *Them's the DNA Breaks*

Hall, Eric J., and Amato J. Giaccia. *Radiobiology for the Radiologist*. Lippincott Williams and Wilkins, 2006.
*A detailed but readable account of how exactly radioactive particles batter DNA.

Hayes, Brian. "The Invention of the Genetic Code." *American Scientist*, January–February 1998.
*An entertaining rundown of early attempts to decipher the genetic code.

Judson, Horace F. *The Eighth Day of Creation*. Cold Spring Harbor Laboratory Press, 2004.
*Includes the story of Crick not knowing what *dogma* meant.

Seachrist Chiu, Lisa. *When a Gene Makes You Smell Like a Fish*. Oxford University Press, 2007.

Trumbull, Robert. *Nine Who Survived Hiroshima and Nagasaki*. Dutton, 1957.
*For a fuller account of Yamaguchi's story—and for eight other equally riveting tales—I can't recommend this book enough.

Chapter 4: *The Musical Score of DNA*

Flapan, Erica. *When Topology Meets Chemistry*. Cambridge University Press, 2000.

Frank-Kamenetskii, Maxim D. *Unraveling DNA*. Basic Books, 1997.

Gleick, James. *The Information*. HarperCollins, 2011.

Grafen, Alan, and Mark Ridley, eds. *Richard Dawkins*. Oxford University Press, 2007.

Zipf, George K. *Human Behavior and the Principle of Least Effort*. Addison-Wesley, 1949.

———. *The Psycho-biology of Language*. Routledge, 1999.

Chapter 5: *DNA Vindication*

Comfort, Nathaniel C. "The Real Point Is Control." *Journal of the History of Biology* 32 (1999): 133–62.

*Comfort is the scholar most responsible for challenging the mythic, fairy-tale version of Barbara McClintock's life and work.

Truji, Jan. *The Soul of DNA*. Llumina Press, 2004.
*For a more detailed account of Sister Miriam, I highly recommend this book, which chronicles her life from its earliest days to the very end.

Watson, James. *The Double Helix*. Penguin, 1969.
*Watson recalls multiple times his frustration over the different shapes of each DNA base.

Chapter 6: *The Survivors, the Livers*

Hacquebord, Louwrens. "In Search of *Het Behouden Huys*." *Arctic* 48 (September 1995): 248–56.

Veer, Gerrit de. *The Three Voyages of William Barents to the Arctic Regions*. N.p., 1596.

Chapter 7: *The Machiavelli Microbe*

Berton, Pierre. *Cats I Have Known and Loved*. Doubleday Canada, 2002.

Dulbecco, Renato. "Francis Peyton Rous." In *Biographical Memoirs*, vol. 48. National Academies Press, 1976.

McCarty, Maclyn. *The Transforming Principle*. W. W. Norton, 1986.

Richardson, Bill. *Scorned and Beloved: Dead of Winter Meetings with Canadian Eccentrics*. Knopf Canada, 1997.

Villarreal, Luis. "Can Viruses Make Us Human?" *Proceedings of the American Philosophical Society* 148 (September 2004): 296–323.

Chapter 8: *Love and Atavisms*

Bondeson, Jan. *A Cabinet of Medical Curiosities*. W. W. Norton, 1999.
*A marvelous section on human tails, from a book chock-full of gruesome tales from the history of anatomy.

Isoda, T., A. Ford, et al. "Immunologically Silent Cancer Clone Transmission from Mother to Offspring." *Proceedings of the National Academy of Sciences of the United States of America* 106, no. 42 (October 20, 2009): 17882–85.

Villarreal, Luis P. *Viruses and the Evolution of Life*. ASM Press, 2005.

Chapter 9: *Humanzees and Other Near Misses*

Rossiianov, Kirill. "Beyond Species." *Science in Context* 15, no. 2 (2002): 277–316.
*For more on Ivanov's life, this is the most authoritative and least sensationalistic source.

Chapter 10: *Scarlet A's, C's, G's, and T's*

Barber, Lynn. *The Heyday of Natural History*. Cape, 1980.
  *A great source for information about the Bucklands, *père* and *fils*.
Carroll, Sean B. *Remarkable Creatures*. Houghton Mifflin Harcourt, 2009.
Finch, Caleb. *The Biology of Human Longevity*. Academic Press, 2007.
Finch, Caleb, and Craig Stanford. "Meat-Adaptive Genes Involving Lipid Metabolism Influenced Human Evolution." *Quarterly Review of Biology* 79, no. 1 (March 2004): 3–50.
Sommer, Marianne. *Bones and Ochre*. Harvard University Press, 2008.
Wade, Nicholas. *Before the Dawn*. Penguin, 2006.
  *A masterly tour of all aspects of human origins.

Chapter 11: *Size Matters*

Gould, Stephen Jay. "Wide Hats and Narrow Minds." In *The Panda's Thumb*. W. W. Norton, 1980.
  *A highly entertaining rendition of the story of Cuvier's autopsy.
Isaacson, Walter. *Einstein: His Life and Universe*. Simon and Schuster, 2007.
Jerison, Harry. "On Theory in Comparative Psychology." In *The Evolution of Intelligence*. Psychology Press, 2001.
Treffert, D., and D. Christensen. "Inside the Mind of a Savant." *Scientific American*, December 2005.
  *A lovely account of Peek by the two scientists who knew him best.

Chapter 12: *The Art of the Gene*

Leroi, Armand Marie. *Mutants: On Genetic Variety and the Human Body*. Penguin, 2005.
  *This marvelous book discusses in more detail what specific disease Toulouse-Lautrec might have had, and also the effect on his art.
Sugden, John. *Paganini*. Omnibus Press, 1986.
  *One of the few biographies of Paganini in English. Short, but well done.

Chapter 13: *The Past Is Prologue — Sometimes*

Reilly, Philip R. *Abraham Lincoln's DNA and Other Adventures in Genetics*. Cold Spring Harbor Laboratory Press, 2000.
  *Reilly sat on the original committee that studied the feasibility of testing Lincoln's DNA. He also delves into the testing of Jewish people's DNA, among other great sections.

Chapter 14: *Three Billion Little Pieces*

Angrist, Misha. *Here Is a Human Being*. HarperCollins, 2010.
  *A lovely and personal rumination on the forthcoming age of genetics.
Shreeve, James. *The Genome War*. Ballantine Books, 2004.

*If you're interested in an insider's account of the Human Genome Project, Shreeve's book is the best written and most entertaining I know of.

Sulston, John, and Georgina Ferry. *The Common Thread*. Joseph Henry Press, 2002.

Venter, J. Craig. *A Life Decoded: My Genome—My Life*. Penguin, 2008.
*The story of Venter's entire life, from Vietnam to the HGP and beyond.

Chapter 15: *Easy Come, Easy Go?*

Gliboff, Sander. "Did Paul Kammerer Discover Epigenetic Inheritance? No and Why Not." *Journal of Experimental Zoology* 314 (December 15, 2010): 616–24.

Gould, Stephen Jay. "A Division of Worms." *Natural History*, February 1999.
*A masterly two-part article about the life of Jean-Baptiste Lamarck.

Koestler, Arthur. *The Case of the Midwife Toad*. Random House, 1972.

Serafini, Anthony. *The Epic History of Biology*. Basic Books, 2002.

Vargas, Alexander O. "Did Paul Kammerer Discover Epigenetic Inheritance?" *Journal of Experimental Zoology* 312 (November 15, 2009): 667–78.

Chapter 16: *Life as We Do (and Don't) Know It*

Caplan, Arthur. "What If Anything Is Wrong with Cloning a Human Being?" *Case Western Reserve Journal of International Law* 35 (Fall 2003): 69–84.

Segerstråle, Ullica. *Defenders of the Truth*. Oxford University Press, 2001.

Wade, Nicholas. *Before the Dawn*. Penguin, 2006.
*Among other people, Nicholas Wade suggested adding the extra pair of chromosomes.

INDEX

Italic page numbers refer to illustrations.